page 338

D A

N e w
B r u n s w i c k

Lawrence
La Pocatiere
St-Pamphile
magny
St-Phamphile

Edmundston
Fort Kent
Madaw
St Leonard
Grand Falls
Dickey
Winterville
Caribou
Plaster Rock
Perth-Andover
Stickney
Doakstown
Ludlow
Boiestown
Ashland
Presque Isle
Machias
Knowles Corner
Woodstock
Fredericton
Newcastle
Mt. Katahdin 5267
Patten
Island Falls
Houlton
Canterbury
Oromocto
Tracy
Hampstead
Allagash Wilderness Waterway
North East Carry
Baxter State Park
Millinocket
East Millinocket
Danforth
McAdam
Westfield Beach
Rockwood
Moosehead Lake
M a i n e
Mattawamkeag
Topsfield
Moosehead
Greenville
Lincoln
Princeton
St Stephen
Calais
Saint John
Bingham
Guilford
Dover-Foxcroft
Milo
Howland
Wesley
Pennfield
ckman
stratton
Kingfield
Phillips
Farmington
Newport
Bangor
Aurora
Deblois
Machias
Machias
Eastport
Lubec
Whiting
Grand Manan Island
Weymouth
Pittsfield
Ellsw
Steuben
Bar Harbour
Jonesport
Waterville
Belfast
Blue Hill
Acadia National Park
Freeport
N o v a
Augusta
Camden
Stonington
Meteghan
S c o t i a
Lewiston
Auburn
Waldoboro
Rockland
Brunswick
Saco
ebunk
New Harbor
Portland
Yarmouth

page 356
page 344

G u l f o f M a i n e

Massachusetts Bay
page 160
cetown
Cape Cod
e Cod Bay
Chatham
Monomoy Island
nls
Nantucket Island
Nantucket

A T L A N T I C

O C E A N

INSIGHT GUIDES

NEW ENGLAND

Discovery
CHANNEL

APA PUBLICATIONS

Part of the Langenscheidt Publishing Group

INSIGHT GUIDE
NEW ENGLAND

Editorial
Editor
Brian Bell
Updating Editors
Kay and Bill Scheller
Principal Photographers
Kindra Clineff, Richard Nowitz, Abraham Nowitz, Daniella Nowitz

Distribution
North America
Langenscheidt Publishers, Inc.
36–36 33rd Street, 4th Floor
Long Island City, New York 11106
Fax: (1) 718 784 0640

UK & Ireland
GeoCenter International Ltd
Meridian House, Churchill Way West
Basingstoke, Hampshire RG21 6YR
Fax: (44) 1256 817988

Australia
Universal Publishers
1 Waterloo Road
Macquarie Park, NSW 2113
Fax: (61) 2 9888 9074

New Zealand
Hema Maps New Zealand Ltd (HNZ)
Unit 2, 10 Cryers Road
East Tamaki, Auckland 2013
Fax: (64) 9 273 6479

Worldwide
**Apa Publications GmbH & Co.
Verlag KG (Singapore branch)**
38 Joo Koon Road, Singapore 628990
Tel: (65) 6865 1600. Fax: (65) 6861 6438

Printing
Insight Print Services (Pte) Ltd
38 Joo Koon Road, Singapore 628990
Tel: (65) 6865 1600. Fax: (65) 6861 6438

©2009 Apa Publications GmbH & Co.
Verlag KG (Singapore branch)
All Rights Reserved
First Edition 1984
Eighth Edition 2009

CONTACTING THE EDITORS
We would appreciate it if readers would alert us to errors or outdated information by writing to:
**Insight Guides, P.O. Box 7910, London SE1 1WE, England.
Fax: (44) 20 7403 0290.
insight@apaguide.co.uk**

www.insightguides.com

ABOUT THIS BOOK

A region with such a rich history and culture as New England lends itself especially well to the approach taken by the award-winning Insight series. The first Insight Guide pioneered the use of creative full-colour photography in travel guides in 1970. Since then, we have expanded our range to cater for our readers' need not only for reliable information about a destination but also for a real understanding of that destination. Now, when the Internet can supply inexhaustible – but not always reliable – facts, our books marry text and pictures to provide that much more elusive quality: knowledge. To achieve this, they rely heavily on the authority of locally based writers and photographers.

How to use this book

The book is carefully structured to convey an understanding of New England and its culture and to guide readers through its sights and attractions:

◆ The Features section, identified by a red colour bar, covers the region's history and culture in lively, authoritative essays written by specialists.

◆ The Places section, with a blue bar, provides full details of all the sights and areas worth seeing. The chief places of interest are coordinated by number with specially drawn maps.

◆ The Travel Tips section, with a yellow bar, at the back of the book, offers a point of reference for information on travel, accommodations, restaurants and other practical aspects of the region. Information may be located quickly using the index printed on the back cover flap, which also serves as a bookmark.

LEFT: fall in New England.
BELOW: a souvenir of Salem.

Maryland, has worked around the world for Insight Guides since the 1980s and his two children are now accomplished photographers in their own right.

The book's editor was **Brian Bell**, a former editorial director of Insight Guides whose exploration of New England over very many years has been guided by his Connecticut-born wife.

This edition builds on earlier ones edited by **Jay Itzkowitz** and **Sue Gordon**. The writers whose text has been adapted from earlier editions are **Mark Bastian, Marcus Brooke, Tom Brosnahan, Kay Cassill, Kimberly Grant, Inez and Jonathan Keller, Molly Kuntz, Tim Locke, Sandy MacDonald, Julie Michaels, Mark Muro, Adam Nossiter, Norman Sibley, Mark Silber, Bryan Simmons** and **Peter Spiro**.

Zoë Goodwin was cartographic editor and **Steven Lawrence** was picture editor. **Elizabeth Cook** compiled the index.

A note on public holidays

The dates when many summer attractions open and close are linked to major public holidays. Visitors from overseas should note that the dates for the principal ones mentioned are: *Memorial Day*, last Monday in May; *Labor Day*, first Monday in September; and *Columbus Day*, second Monday in October. For a full list, see page 418.

The contributors

Nothing stands still, even in such a tradition-saturated region, and for this edition of one of Insight's classic titles the text has been thoroughly overhauled and expanded by **Kay and Bill Scheller**, a Vermont-based husband-and-wife team who have also written new features on literature and education (two areas in which New England excels). In addition, virtually all the photographs in this edition are new.

Much of the eye-catching photography is the work of **Kindra Clineff**, whose work encompasses national magazine shoots and major advertising campaigns, at home and abroad. She cultivates a perennial garden and keeps bees at her historic 17th-century home in Massachusetts.

Many other photographs come from **Richard, Abraham** and **Daniella Nowitz**. Richard, who lives in

Map Legend

— · —	International Boundary
— — —	State Boundary
— · —	National Park/Reserve
— — — —	Ferry Route
🚇	Subway
✈ ✈	Airport: International/Regional
🚌	Bus Station
✉	Post Office
ℹ	Tourist Information
∴	Archaeological Site
🏛 † ✝	Church/Ruins
☾	Mosque
🏰	Castle/Ruins
∩	Cave
🗿	Statue/Monument
★	Place of Interest
⚑	Beach
🗼	Lighthouse

The main places of interest in the Places section are coordinated by number (e.g. ❶) with a full-color map, and a symbol at the top of every right-hand page tells you where to find the map.

Contents

Introduction

America's Attic 19
People of New England 22

History

Decisive Dates 28
Beginnings 32
Birth of a Nation 40
Decline and Revival 48

Features

The Maritime Tradition 57
The Puritan Tradition 62
The Literary Tradition 66
The Education Tradition 72
The Tradition of Good Food......76
The Architectural Tradition 82

Photo Features

Living History 38
The Diner 80
Boston's Freedom Trail 102
Museum of Fine Arts 132
Newport Mansions 232
Wildlife 334

Places

Introduction 95
Boston, MA 101
Cambridge, MA 124
North of Boston 135
West of Boston 146
South of Boston 152
Cape Cod and the Islands 158
Central Massachusetts 186
Pioneer Valley 192
The Berkshires 200
Rhode Island.......................213
Connecticut 237
Vermont 271
New Hampshire 307
Maine 339

Information Panels

The Shakers 47
Sporting Traditions 75
Salem's Witches 143
Nantucket's Stormy Past 178
Whale Watching 180
Active Vacations...................226
The Coming of the Casinos 261
Covered Bridges 294
The Ski Scene 299
The Fall 324

LEFT: Cranes Beach, Ipswich, Massachusetts.
BOTTOM LEFT: statue of Massasoit, protector of the Pilgrims, Plymouth.
BOTTOM RIGHT: lobster weathervane, Boston.

Maps

New England **96–7**
Boston, MA **98–9**
Cambridge, MA **125**
Boston Daytrips **134**
Salem, MA **141**
Lexington & Concord **148–9**
Plymouth, MA **154**
Cape Cod & the Islands, and Provincetown **160**
Central Massachusetts **187**
Worcester, MA **188**
Pioneer Valley **192**
Springfield, MA **193**
The Berkshires **201**
Rhode Island **214**
Providence, RI **217**
Newport, RI **221**
Connecticut **236**
Hartford, CT **240**
Vermont and New Hampshire **266–7**
Burlington, VT **289**
Portsmouth, NH **310**
Manchester, NH **312**
Maine **338**
Portland, ME **344**
Mount Desert Island **356**
Boston Subway **433**

Inside front cover: New England
Inside back cover: Boston

Travel Tips

TRANSPORTATION

Getting There
By Air **370**
By Train **370**
Getting Around
By Air **371**
By Bus and Train **371**
By Car **371**
By Water **372**

ACCOMMODATIONS

Choosing Accommodations **373**
Boston **374**
Cape Cod and the Islands **376**
The rest of Massachusetts **378**
Rhode Island **381**
Connecticut **382**
Vermont **384**
New Hampshire **390**
Maine **393**

ACTIVITIES

Cinema, Classical Music **399**
Ballet, Opera, Theatre **400**
Cabaret, Folk Music, Jazz **402**
Rock and Pop **403**
Gay Venues **404**
Spectator Sports **404**
Biking **404**
Canoeing, Kayaking, Rafting **405**
Fishing **406**
Hiking **406**
Sailing **407**
Sightseeing Cruises **407**
Skiing **408**
Children's Activities **408**

SHOPPING

What to Buy **410**
Outlet Shopping **412–3**

A–Z: PRACTICAL INFORMATION

Accidents, Emergencies **414**
Alcohol **414**
Budgeting for a Trip **414**
Childcare **414**
Climate, Clothing **415**
Customs Regulations **415**
Disabled Access **416**
Discounts **416**
Electricity **416**
Embassies/Consulates **416**
Foliage **416**
Gasoline **416**
Gays and Lesbians **416**
Health and Medical Care **416**
Internet Access **417**
Money Matters **417**
Newspapers, Magazines **417**
Opening Hours **417**
Passports and Immigration **418**
Pets **418**
Postal Services **418**
Public Holidays **418**
Radio Stations **418**
Smoking **418**
Telephones **419**
TV Stations **419**
Tipping **419**
Tourist Information **419**
Websites **419**
Weights and Measures **419**
What to Read **420**

THE BEST OF NEW ENGLAND: TOP ATTRACTIONS

The region's dramatic past is imaginatively re-created, while the land and sea provide a wide range of outdoor recreations

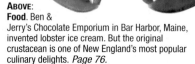

ABOVE:
Food. Ben & Jerry's Chocolate Emporium in Bar Harbor, Maine, invented lobster ice cream. But the original crustacean is one of New England's most popular culinary delights. *Page 76.*

ABOVE: Fall foliage. Leaf-peepers seek out the best spots to marvel at spectacular hues of red, yellow and orange. *Page 324.*
LEFT: Cape Cod National Seashore. More than 40 miles (65km) of secluded beaches, vast stretches of sand dunes, crashing surf, and swimming in the bracing Atlantic. *Page 164*

LEFT: Shelburne Museum, Vermont. Peerless collection of Americana, including the *Ticonderoga. Page 291*

ABOVE: **Newport**, Rhode Island. Extravagant mansions that are monuments to America's Gilded Age. *Pages 232–3.*
LEFT: **Mystic Seaport**, Connecticut. A replica of an old whaling port, with vessels such as the *Charles W. Morgan*. *Page 259.*

ABOVE: **Freedom Trail**, Boston, Massachusetts. Follow the 2½-mile (4-km) red-brick path linking the major Revolutionary War sites. *Pages 102–5.*
RIGHT: **Acadia National Park**. The famed "rock-bound coast of Maine" preserved in a rugged 41,000-acre parkland. *Pages 355–8.*

ABOVE: **Old Sturbridge Village**, Massachusetts. An 1840 New England village re-created, with voluble costumed interpreters. *Page 190.*
RIGHT: **White Mountains**, New Hampshire. A vast tract of rugged peaks, hiking trails and ski slopes – and a unique cog railway. *Pages 322–3.*

THE BEST OF NEW ENGLAND: EDITOR'S CHOICE

Setting priorities, the sights worth seeing, best hiking and skiing, unique attractions... here, at a glance, are our recommendations, plus tips even the locals may not know

THE TOP HISTORIC SITES

- **Freedom Trail, Boston**. Follow the red brick path that links Boston's most important Revolutionary sites, including the Old State House, Paul Revere's Home, the Old North Church, and the 1797 frigate *Constitution*, alias "Old Ironsides." *See pages 102–5.*
- **Lowell National Historical Park, MA**. With many of its massive textile mills still intact, the city's core is now a National Historical Park. Tour downtown by canal boat or trolley, and visit a mill where power looms still turn out cloth. *See pages 146.*
- **Salem Maritime National Historic Site, MA**. In the cradle of America's first mercantile fortunes, an old waterfront quarter contains an 1819 Custom House, the home of a merchant prince, and the replica of a 1797 sailing ship. *See page 140.*
- **Minute Man National Historical Park, MA**. The events of April 18 and 19, 1775, are brought to life on Lexington Green, where Minute Men and British soldiers first exchanged fire, and at Concord's North Bridge, where Revolutionary hostilities began in earnest. *See page 148.*
- **Coolidge State Historic Site, VT**. The preserved birthplace of President Calvin Coolidge

In 1775 the Minute Men were ready to fight the British at a minute's notice.

isn't just a single home, but all of Plymouth Notch village. You can visit the house where Coolidge took the oath of office by kerosene lamp on learning of President Harding's death. *See page 278.*

THE BEST PARKS

- **Baxter State Park, ME**. This wilderness tract deep in Maine's interior is crowned with Mt. Katahdin, the northern terminus of the Appalachian Trail. This is the place to look for moose, black bears... and supreme solitude. *See pages 360.*
- **Acadia National Park, ME**. Nowhere is the famed "rock-bound coast of Maine" better exemplified – and better preserved – than in this rugged parkland. *See pages 355–8.*
- **Boston Harbor Islands**. A short boat ride away from downtown Boston, these varied islands offer old forts, historic lighthouses, wilderness hiking and surf fishing. Some islands have overnight camping facilities. *See page 108.*

LEFT: mercantile memories on Salem's waterfront.

THE FINEST MUSEUMS

● **Museum of Fine Arts, Boston**. One of the world's great museums, whose collections include some of the best Impressionist paintings outside Paris. *See pages 132–3.*

● **Shelburne Museum, VT**. This matchless collection of Americana, folk and fine art, and vernacular

ABOVE: the Museum of Fine Arts in Boston.

New England architecture features the restored 1906 Lake Champlain steamer *Ticonderoga*. *See page 291.*

● **Old Sturbridge Village, MA**. A striking recreation of a New England village circa 1840. Costumed artisans demonstrate their skills. *See page 190.*

● **Isabella Stewart Gardner Museum, Boston**. A Venetian palazzo with fine art, antique furniture, and a flower-filled interior courtyard. *See pages 121–2.*

● **Sterling and Francine Clark Art Institute, MA**. The small but superb Clark houses a fine American collection and first-rate Impressionists from Europe. *See page 206.*

ABOVE: sparks fly at Boston's Museum of Science.

BEST FOR FAMILIES

● **Museum of Science, Boston**. Five stories of science and technology made fun, ranging from natural history to computers, from the human body to space flight. On site are an Omni Theater, planetarium, and laser-light show. *See pages 122–3.*

● **Mount Washington Cog Railway, NH**. An improbable artifact of Victorian technology, the railway climbs right to the roof of New England, the 6,288-ft (1,917-meter) Mount Washington, using steam locomotives that push coaches up a narrow-gauge track laid in 1869. A ride to remember. *See page 329.*

● **Mystic Seaport, CT**. In this re-creation of a

19th-century waterfront community, shops and chandleries line the narrow streets and the *Charles W. Morgan*, the last surviving American whaling vessel to sail under canvas, rests at wharfside. *See page 259.*

● **The "Big E", MA**. There are state and county fairs all over New England, but the biggest is the region-wide Eastern States Exposition in West Springfield. Animal exhibits and judging, amusement rides, and big-name acts fill the 175-acre (71-hectare) grounds for 17 days in September. *See pages 193–4.*

● **Ben & Jerry's Factory Tour, VT**. The tour tells the story of how two unlikely entrepreneurs created the famous ice cream, revealing the alchemy behind flavors such as Cherry Garcia and Phish Food. *See page 282.*

RECOMMENDED HIKES

● **Appalachian Trail**. Linking every state except Rhode Island, the Georgia-to-Maine Appalachian Trail's northernmost portion offers opportunities for day or overnight hiking. *See page 226.*

● **The Long Trail**. Vermont's rugged trail, which partly overlaps the Appalachian, scales the Green Mountain peaks. *See page 283.*

● **Appalachian Mountain Club Huts, NH**. The

RIGHT: hiking along the Appalachian Trail.

staffed huts offer White Mountain ramblers meals and lodging in the heart of the lofty Presidential Range. *See page 323.*

THE TOP COLLEGE TOWNS

● **Cambridge, MA**. Home to Harvard and the Massachusetts Institute of Technology (MIT); both have specialized museums, with Harvard's Fogg Art Museum and Peabody Science museums among the region's finest. Harvard Square bustles with shops, bookstores, restaurants, and clubs; Central Square, near MIT, offers inexpensive eateries and eclectic shops. *See pages 124–7.*

● **Northampton, MA**. This compact city is a hub for five colleges. Right in town is the renowned Smith College Museum of Art; the main street has many galleries, ethnic restaurants, craft shops, book stores, and art cinemas. *See page 195.*

● **Hanover, NH**. Here is one of the region's loveliest town greens, surrounded by the stately buildings of Dartmouth College.

The school's Hood Museum of Art and Baker Memorial Library are cultural highlights. *See page 319.*

● **Burlington, VT**. The architectural treasures of the University of Vermont dominate the hilltop above the state's largest city. Church Street Marketplace is lined with boutiques, bars, and restaurants, and the waterfront sparkles with marinas, a natural history museum, and a bike path. *See pages 289–90.*

● **New Haven, CT**. This is home to some of America's most spectacular collegiate Gothic architecture on the campus of Yale University. Yale's impressive array of museums include a center for British art, a rare book and manuscript library, a museum of natural history, and even a collection of musical instruments. *See pages 254–6.*

ABOVE: Harvard University campus, Cambridge.

THE FINEST HISTORIC HOUSES

● **Gillette Castle, CT**. A medieval stone mansion on a site overlooking the Connecticut River in East Haddam. *See page 249.*

● **Salem, MA**. The homes preserved by the Peabody-Essex Museum and Salem Maritime National Historic Site represent the pinnacle of the austerely beautiful Federal style of architecture. *See pages 140–2.*

● **Longfellow House, Cambridge, MA**. This spacious Georgian mansion was George Washington's HQ early in the Revolution, and was later the home of Henry Wadsworth Longfellow. *See page 127.*

● **Portsmouth, NH**. A treasure trove of Georgian and Federal architecture, including the one-time home of naval hero John Paul Jones. *See pages 308–11.*

● **Newport, RI**. The greatest monuments to America's Gilded Age are the wildly extravagant mansions along Bellevue Avenue. The Breakers, Rosecliff, The Elms, and other monuments to untaxed riches were, amazingly, used for only a few weeks in summer. *See pages 222–4 and 232–3.*

LEFT: Beechwood, the Astors' mansion in Newport.

THE BEST BEACHES

● **Block Island, RI**. It's worth the ferry ride to enjoy these uncrowded strands – remote Mohegan Bluffs, calm State Beach, and Surfers Beach. *See pages 228–9.*

● **Crane Beach, MA**. A beautifully preserved stretch of sand with views reaching from Cape Ann right to the distant shores of New Hampshire and Maine. *See page 137.*

● **Plum Island, MA**. Parking is limited, so there are never towel-to-towel crowds. A bonus: the island is one of the East's premier birding destinations. *See page 136.*

● **Cape Cod National Seashore**. Options for sunning and (brisk) swimming range from easy-to-reach Nauset in the south to the dune-circled Province Lands and Pilgrim Heights beaches in Provincetown and Truro. *See page 164.*

● **Hammonasset State Beach, CT**. The gentle, generally warm waters of Long Island Sound wash this broad, superbly maintained beach that has plenty of parking, and changing facilities. *See page 257.*

ABOVE: snowboarding at Sunday River Ski Resort.

THE TOP SKI AREAS

● **Stowe Mountain Resort, VT**. Some trails, including the famous "Front Four" on Mt. Mansfield, date from the 1930s. The resort boasts spectacular terrain, aerial gondolas, and superb lodging. *See page 283.*

● **Killington, VT**. New England's biggest ski area has 200 trails and nearly three dozen lifts. The resort is a study in superlatives – steepest mogul run, a 3,140-ft (955-meter) vertical drop, and a 10-mile downhill trail. *See page 279.*

● **Jay Peak, VT**. The most reliable snow cover and a variety of trails: harrowing steeps, long cruising runs, and even a slow skiing zone. *See page 287.*

● **Sugarloaf, ME**. Plenty of intermediate runs, but nearly half the trails are black diamonds. Glade action is terrific. *See pages 361–2.*

● **Sunday River, ME**. Offers great grooming, high-speed quad lifts, and a double-diamond mogul run as foil to its more forgiving cruisers. *See page 362.*

ABOVE: part of Cape Cod National Seashore.

PICK OF THE PERFORMING ARTS

● **Boston Symphony Orchestra and Boston Pops** perform at the Symphony Hall and Hatch concert shell, and in Tanglewood's sylvan setting in Lenox. *See pages 123, 204.*

● **Vermont Mozart Festival**. Indoor and out-door summer venues for concerts of works by Mozart and other favorites. *See page 400.*

● **Jacob's Pillow Dance Festival, MA**. Indoor and outdoor theaters showcase classic works in a lovely Berkshires setting. *See page 204.*

● **Goodspeed Opera House, CT**. This 1876 theater by the Connecti-cut River is the venue for professional musical revivals and original pro-ductions. *See page 249.*

● **American Repertory Theater, Cambridge, MA**. Harvard's Loeb Drama Center puts on revivals and original works. *See page 401.*

ABOVE: Berkshires dance.

AMERICA'S ATTIC

Old England traditions blended with New
World values to create six distinctive
states, each with its own character

New England "is a finished place," wrote the Pulitzer Prize-winning author Bernard De Voto in 1936. "Its destiny is that of Florence or Venice, not Milan, while the American empire careens onward towards its unpredicted end... It is the first American section to be finished, to achieve stability in its conditions of life. It is the first old civilization, the first permanent civilization in America."

De Voto was only partly right; in the decades since he wrote, New England has changed and changed again – like the rest of America, it's hardly ever finished. But New England has done more than most places to preserve its most cherished touchstones of memory: Paul Revere's almost medieval house, the battlefields of Lexington and Concord, cobblestone streets that whaling captains trod, the haunts of the Adamses and Kennedys – even the most beloved baseball park in the land. New England never forgets that it was here that the first cries of American Independence were heard, here that the movement to abolish slavery found fertile ground, here that education achieved its fullest flowering, here that American art and literature attained their greatest refinement.

Past and present

This is America's attic, crammed with marvelous antiques of every description. Here are the homes of Hawthorne, Emerson, Dickinson, and Melville; souvenirs of seafaring from centuries past; houses and churches in whose gables and steeples can be read a national architectural history. The countryside abounds with inspiring vistas, enchanted with the bright golds and reds of fall, slumbering beneath winter's heavy snows, bursting with the green rebirth of spring, and joyful in summer's flowering.

The alluring variety embraces Maine's coast, its rocky promontories pointing to adventure; New Hampshire's forest-encircled lakes and gaunt granite

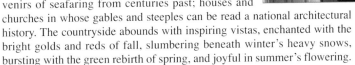

PRECEDING PAGES: the whaling ship *C.W. Morgan* at Mystic Seaport; the Museum of Fine Arts in Boston; the village of Tunbridge in Vermont. **LEFT:** the past on sale at Brimfield Antiques Show, Massachusetts. **ABOVE LEFT:** Hartwell Tavern, Concord, Massachusetts. **ABOVE RIGHT:** exhibit in First Harrison Gray Otis House, Boston.

peaks; Vermont's mountains, rising above a green patchwork quilt of dairy farms and woodlands; the gentle Berkshire Hills; Connecticut's trim colonial towns; Newport's well-preserved luxury; the charming villages and rolling dunes of Cape Cod and the islands; and Boston's vibrant cityscape.

If Boston is a state of mind – a remark variously attributed by the city's contentious academics to Mark Twain, Ralph Waldo Emerson, and Thomas G. Appleton – so is New England, to an even greater degree. And it is a state of mind well worth embracing.

The lay of the land

New England encompasses 66,672 sq. miles (172,680 sq. km), and consists of the states of Massachusetts, Rhode Island, Connecticut, Vermont, New Hampshire, and Maine. It is bounded by Canada to the north, the Atlantic Ocean to the east, Long Island Sound to the south, and New York State to the west. Moving inland from the coastal lowlands in the south and east, the terrain gradually rises to forested hills and culminates in the weather-beaten peaks of the Appalachian system, represented by the White Mountains to the north and the Green and Taconic Mountains and Berkshire Hills to the west.

How was it all formed? Perhaps 2 billion years ago, a vast ocean trough of sediment was convulsed upward by an upheaval of the earth's crust, forming ancestors of the Appalachian mountains. The intense heat generated metamorphosed sandstone and limestone deposits into the schists and marble now found in the southeastern lowlands and Berkshire Hills of Massachusetts and in Vermont's Green Mountains. Later, streaks of intrusive rocks formed, represented by the granite of Rhode Island, New Hampshire, and Maine, and the reddish rocks of the Connecticut River Valley.

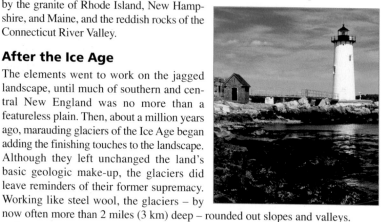

After the Ice Age

The elements went to work on the jagged landscape, until much of southern and central New England was no more than a featureless plain. Then, about a million years ago, marauding glaciers of the Ice Age began adding the finishing touches to the landscape. Although they left unchanged the land's basic geologic make-up, the glaciers did leave reminders of their former supremacy. Working like steel wool, the glaciers – by now often more than 2 miles (3 km) deep – rounded out slopes and valleys.

When the glaciers melted, the oceans claimed many areas that are landlocked today. In parts of Maine, Atlantic waves crashed against shores up to 75 miles (120 km) inland from the present coastline. Evidence of marine activity has been found at more than 500 ft (150 meters) above today's sea level. Hundreds of lakes once thrived where there are none now. The waters gradually receded, and the land, relieved of its burden of ice, rebounded slowly upward. New England assumed its present configuration. ❑

TOP: Cape Cod beach. **ABOVE RIGHT:** lighthouse at Portsmouth, New Hampshire. **RIGHT:** the much painted fisherman's shack Motif #1 at Rockport, Massachusetts.

THE PEOPLE OF NEW ENGLAND

**New England's indomitable Puritan heritage is
complemented by the pioneering spirit shared
by the region's numerous immigrant ethnic groups**

The product of centuries of "plain living and high thinking," New Englanders have long considered themselves the conscience of the nation. New England has contributed more distinguished legislators, writers, teachers, and thinkers to the United States than has any other region. It's true that it had a head start on the rest of America. But even after the other states had caught up in terms of population, the flow of outstanding people produced by this unpromising land never let up.

The Puritan heritage, and the region's harsh landscape and weather, have led New Englanders to view life a bit more seriously than do the residents of more forgiving cultures and climes. Although New Englanders have, as a rule, eschewed frivolity, they're quite in favor of individualism, provided that it enhances self-reliance and does not impinge on others' rights to pursue their own individual vision.

Most would consider this fierce independence to be a carryover from colonial days. However, the genius of the New England style is that it is an amalgam of all the disparate groups that have settled here and forged common bonds and goals: Native Americans, English, African-Americans, Irish, Italians, French Canadians, Latin Americans, Asians... The list continues to grow.

The Algonquins

When the first English settlers arrived in the early 17th century, most of the native inhabitants were concentrated in Rhode Island, Connecticut, and Massachusetts. They were divided into tribes with well-established rivalries and territories. All of Algonquin blood, they were friendly to the first English settlers. The Mohegans and Pequots of Connecticut, the Wampanoags of Massachusetts, and the Narragansetts of Rhode Island imparted

their age-old hunting, fishing, farming, and canoe-making skills to the newcomers.

But this honeymoon was to last only about 15 years. In 1636, the English waged war against the Pequots in revenge for some real or imagined Indian outrage. The Narragansetts took the fatal step of allying themselves with the English, destroying the possibility of a united native front. When the war was over, the Pequots had been obliterated. By 1670, there were 75,000 English settlers in New England and only about 10,000 Indians. The natives had sold much of their land, their settlements having been penetrated everywhere. A sizeable minority had been converted to Christianity and lived in "Praying Towns."

The wars of 1675–76 marked the last desperate

gasp of native resistance. In 1675, an alliance to fight the English – formed by the Wampanoag's chief, Metacomet ("King Philip"), with several smaller tribes – was crushed. Then it was the Narragansetts' turn. By the time the English were through with them in 1676, fewer than 70 were left out of the original 4,000 to 5,000.

The proud Puritans

The world has rarely seen a group of immigrants quite like the New England Puritans of the 17th century. Fleeing religious persecution in England, they were fired by an extraordinary sense of mission. Although most of these first immigrants were

thought of as a distinctive nation-within-a-nation by other Americans at the end of the 18th century. As Yale president Timothy Dwight said in 1798, New Englanders were distinguished by their "love of science and learning," their "love of liberty," their "morality," "piety" and "unusual spirit of enquiry."

The rest of the country was more likely to characterize Yankees, as they became known, as speculators, entrepreneurs, inventors, or investors. (The term *Yankee* today means "northerner" in the American South, "New Englander" in the North, and refers to a descendant of the original English settlers in New England itself.) They were men like early 19th-century Boston textile baron Francis Cabot Lowell,

peasants and artisans, an unusually large number of educated men – ministers, theologians and teachers – were among them. These learned men set a tone for the Puritan community of strict disciplined piety, with religion pervading every aspect of life.

For 200 years, New England's population consisted overwhelmingly of descendants of this tightly knit, homogeneous group and other Englishmen who followed. Having grown from a strictly controlled religious state to a cradle of revolutionary democratic ideas, this community was

LEFT: the Puritan heritage, recreated here in Plimoth Plantation, is a powerful one. **ABOVE:** famous faces through the ages from the Café du Barry mural on Newbury Street in Boston's Back Bay.

NATIVE AMERICANS TODAY

Today there are an estimated 40,000 American Indians in New England. Only a minority live on the region's nine existing reservations, and a new consciousness of tribal identity has taken hold. Since the 1960s, the annual 4th of July powwow of the Mashpee Wampanoag of Cape Cod, previously a modest affair, has grown to include more dances, rituals, and meetings with other tribes.

Several tribes have fought legal battles to regain land taken by the colonists. The most unusual case was of the Mashantucket Pequots in Connecticut, who in 1992 won a Supreme Court ruling to keep open their Foxwoods High Stakes and Bingo (now Foxwoods Resort Casino, the largest casino in the western hemisphere).

who established one of America's first modern factories; or members of the great Boston families that made their fortunes in Far East trade.

Indomitable Yankees

The farther you get from from Boston, the more the Yankee image is likely to be that of a yeoman than an aristocrat. Vermont's first inhabitants, for instance, were hardy trappers, and later farmers; and this has contributed to the independent characteristics of the modern Vermonter. When neighboring states were laying claim to its territory during the Revolution, Vermont declared itself an independent republic. It maintained this status for

14 years, during which time it declared universal suffrage (excepting women, of course) and prohibited slavery. It was the first state to do so.

New Hampshire Yankees are much like their cousins to the west, but are supposedly less tolerant than Vermonters, politically more conservative, and more frugal and stubborn. The Maine Yankee was historically the most isolated inhabitant of the three northern states. Roads connecting Maine to the outside were poor. "Downeasters," as they are called, had to put up with bad weather and unyielding terrain. This may explain why they're commonly characterized as crusty and quirky; they have a reputation for being down to earth and for saying little beyond what counts.

Rhode Island and Connecticut Yankees are perhaps less distinctive than other old New Englanders. The original populations of these states were the products of the first emigrations from Massachusetts, but they have since been influenced considerably – and had their own influence diminished – by their closer proximity to the Middle Atlantic states. Providence is heavily Italian, and Newport became a preserve of New Yorkers.

African-Americans

The first African-Americans in New England came to Boston from the West Indies in 1638 as "perpetual servants." By 1752, Boston's 5,000 African-Americans constituted 10 percent of the population. That percentage declined dramatically during the Revolution, when Tory masters fled the region, removing their entire households. By the end of the 18th century, Massachusetts abolished slavery, and Connecticut soon followed.

In Boston, a thriving black community congre-

WHY BOSTON'S BRAHMINS WERE EXALTED

New Englanders considered themselves the national elite. The self-proclaimed heads of this elite were the Boston Brahmins – rich Boston families such as the Lowells, Cabots, Welds, Lodges, and Saltonstalls, who mostly secured their fortunes in the first half of the 19th century in shipping, and later in the railroad, banking, and textile industries. The name "Brahmin" is that of the priestly caste among the Hindus; it was first cited, if not originally applied, by the doctor, poet, and essayist Oliver Wendell Holmes, Sr., who described the Brahmin caste in 1860 as "the harmless, inoffensive, untitled aristocracy."

The archetypal Brahmin attended Harvard and belonged to one of its exclusive "final clubs" such as the Porcellian or

Fly; he lived on Beacon Hill or in the Back Bay, with a summer place at Beverly Farms or Manchester-by-the-Sea on the North Shore. And he (and she) is by no means extinct, but is merely keeping a seemly low profile.

Few of today's Brahmins descend from the *Mayflower* Pilgrims, 17th-century Puritans, or even rich 18th-century merchants. It was the rise in trade and, eventually, industry that followed American independence that created most of their wealth. Some Brahmin families even have a few economic skeletons in their closets, having gotten rich, according to their their Irish nemesis, the late Boston mayor James Michael Curley, "selling opium to the Chinese, rum to the Indians, or trading in slaves."

gated on the northern slope of Beacon Hill. Though poor, it was organized and ambitious. About 2 percent of the population were doctors, ministers, teachers, or lawyers. Black-owned shops served as informal community centers, and black churches helped bring the community together.

Although blacks in 19th-century Boston rarely lived outside their own quarter, they did mingle freely. Black and white laborers drank together in North End taverns, and after 1855, when schools were desegregated, children of both races studied together. (Boston's tensions of the 1970s were the result of court-ordered busing to achieve racially balanced schools in otherwise homogenous neigh-

household domestics. Even well into the 1950s, few gains were made in improving the lot of this underclass. Although the number of blacks holding white-collar jobs in Boston more than doubled between 1950 and 2000, the vast majority remained poor and resolutely working class. Boston's black community – now representing roughly a quarter of the population – has made considerable strides, and, in 2006, an African-American, Deval Patrick, was elected governor of Massachusetts.

Connecticut and Rhode Island are the only other New England states with long-standing black minorities (respectively 9 and 4.5 percent). Many relocated from the South in the 1870s to work on

borhoods.) Black students attended Harvard before the Civil War. Freemen laborers could be found in every New England industry, especially along the coast. Often half of crews of whaling vessels were African-American, and it was black labor that built much of Providence and New Haven. Massachusetts was unique in allowing blacks to stand for a political party (the Abolitionist Free-Soil Party in 1850) in elections to the state legislature.

The decline suffered by the region after the Civil War was particularly devastating to those struggling to subsist as porters, laborers, janitors and

tobacco farms. Hartford, New Haven, and Bridgeport are the primary black population centers in Connecticut, but even smaller communities such as New London have neighborhoods in which blacks have lived since the 18th century.

Northern New England is overwhelmingly white, reflecting a historic lack of industrial jobs and a virtual absence of slavery among the early settlers. In the 1990s, however, a small number of Africans, particularly Somalis in Portland and Lewiston, Maine, have settled in the region.

Irish power

The Potato Famine of 1845–50 killed at least a million people in Ireland, and drove another million to seek better conditions elsewhere. Many

LEFT: students at Harvard University, Cambridge.
ABOVE: visitors to Applefest, Vermont's biggest apple festival and craft show, held in October at South Hero.

came to Massachusetts. They did not receive a warm welcome, however. Not unlike the British oppressors back home, Yankees showed contempt for Catholicism, and, in turn, the Irish felt little sympathy for the idealism of the reform-minded Yankees. During the Civil War, Irish immigrants in Boston rioted when faced with a draft; the war, they felt, was about the freeing of slaves, a cause in which they had no specific interest.

The Irish community in Massachusetts grew rapidly and they soon went into politics, with great success. The first Irish-born mayor of Boston was elected in 1884, and the first Irish governor took office in 1918. Between the world wars, the Irish

controlled both Boston and state politics. A new economic as well as political clout was typified by Joe Kennedy, the father of the late President John F. Kennedy, who penetrated the Yankee stronghold of finance and banking on Boston's State Street.

Middle-class Irish have long been assimilated into the mainstream of Boston and Massachusetts life. Especially in South Boston and Charlestown, though, blue-collar Irish have fiercely maintained the separateness both of their communities and of their ethnic identity. To this day, many residents identify more with their neighborhoods than with the city as a whole.

French-Canadians

French-Canadians have been emigrating to New England since the 1850s. Although there are more French-Canadians in Massachusetts than in any other New England state, their influence is most evident in New Hampshire, where they make up as much as a quarter of the population; and in Maine, where – especially in the close-knit potato farming communities of far northern Aroostook County – 15 percent of the people are only one or two generations from Canadian birth.

The Canadians came to work in the textile mills, and (in the north) as lumberjacks and farmers. More than any other group in New England, they have clung to their distinctive ethnic identity. They are strongly Catholic, and there are still many who grew up speaking French at home.

The Italian influx

Italians came to the United States in the first decades of the 20th century, most as poor peasants from southern Italy and Sicily. Many settled in Massachusetts and Rhode Island, and a distinctive community of mostly northern Italians brought their stonecutting and carving skills to the granite center of Barre, Vermont. Despite the incursions of gentrification, Italians have managed to preserve a distinctive village subculture in certain areas, such as Boston's North End and East Boston and the Federal Hill neighborhood of Providence.

The Italians quickly climbed the economic ladder, making their money in law, real estate, construction, and a variety of other businesses. Like the Irish, they also found their way into politics.

Jewish settlers

These were among the earliest colonists: a community was established in Newport, Rhode Island, in 1658, with the help of Puritan dissident Roger

WHERE PEOPLE LIVE

New England's population is around 14 million, with the Atlantic coast more urban than western areas. The 10 biggest cities, with estimated current population, are:

- ❶ Boston, Massachusetts: 600,000
- ❷ Worcester, Massachusetts: 175,000
- ❸ Providence, Rhode Island: 173,000
- ❹ Springfield, Massachusetts: 150,000
- ❺ Bridgeport, Connecticut: 138,000
- ❻ Hartford, Connecticut: 125,000
- ❼ New Haven, Connecticut: 124,000
- ❽ Stamford, Connecticut: 119,000
- ❾ Manchester, New Hampshire: 110,000
- ❿ Waterbury, Connecticut: 107,000

Williams. The first families, from Holland, were Sephardics, descendants of exiles expelled from Spain at the end of the 15th century. Nineteen years after arriving in Newport, they organized North America's second congregation (the first was in New York). Free of the restrictions imposed in the Old World, they prospered in Newport.

The Newport community began to dissolve around the beginning of the 19th century as members emigrated to other parts of the country. For 100 years, there was little Jewish presence in New England, mainly because of the intolerance and rigidity of the Protestant Yankees. But by the end of the century, Boston had become a much more

paper mill town of Rumford, Maine, produced one of America's outstanding Polish public figures, the late senator and secretary of state Edmund Muskie.

Other late arrivals

New England has pockets of small ethnic groups which contribute greatly to the region's diversity. As in the rest of America, its new citizens are now drawn heavily from Asia, Latin America, and the Middle East. Every New England city has a sizeable Hispanic community; in Holyoke, Massachusetts, Hispanics make up more than 40 percent of the population.

There has been a Chinese quarter in Boston for

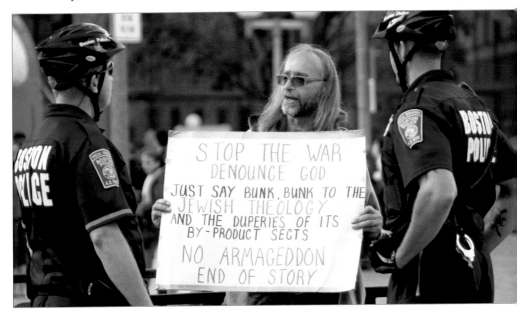

ethnically and religiously diverse place, and so Jews from Eastern Europe began to settle there in large numbers. By 1910, 42,000 East Europeans, mostly Jewish, lived in the Boston area. Ten years later 10 percent of Boston's population was Jewish. Jews have made their mark in New England, notably in education: one-third of the Harvard faculty is Jewish.

Non-Jewish eastern Europeans have also made their mark. Poles have settled throughout the region; in Massachusetts, the Pioneer Valley city of Chicopee has a sizeable Polish population. The

LEFT: dollar bills are pinned to a statue of San Gennaro at Boston's annual Little Italy street festival.
ABOVE: protests have a long pedigree in New England.

much of the past century, but today there are Chinese – and, increasingly, Vietnamese – immigrants in all parts of the region.

There are Syrians and Lebanese in Rhode Island, Armenians in Worcester and Watertown, Massachusetts, and Bosnian and Sudanese immigrants in Burlington, Vermont. Greek-Americans live throughout the area, with particularly strong representation in Lowell, Massachusetts – also home to a vibrant Cambodian community.

Portuguese communities exist along the coast, in such fishing ports as New Bedford and Provincetown. Their founders arrived in the 19th century from the Azores, as whaling hands picked up by American ships. When whaling foundered, they shifted to fishing and into the textile mills. ❑

DECISIVE DATES

ABOVE: Viking longboats arrived from Norway around AD 1000.

9000 BC
Earliest evidence of human activity in New England, at Shawville, Vermont.

AD 1000
The Viking Leif Erikson discovers Vinland the Good, the location of which remains unknown.

14th–15th centuries
The Algonquin Indians arrive.

THE EARLY COLONISTS
1497
John Cabot explores North American coast.

ABOVE: Giovanni da Verrazano.

1524
Giovanni da Verrazano, sailing under the French flag, travels as far north as Narrangansett Bay.

1602–6
Bartholomew Gosnold, Martin Pring, and George Weymouth lead successful expeditions to the region. Weymouth returns with five Indians abducted from the coast of Maine.

1607
One hundred adventurers, funded by the Plymouth Company, build Fort St George on Parker's Island, Maine, and winter there.

1609
Venturing from Quebec via the St Lawrence and Richelieu rivers, Samuel de Champlain is the first European to visit the lake later named for him.

1620
The Plymouth Company finances a group of 66 Puritans to establish a permanent settlement in North America. They leave on the Mayflower, and sight Cape Cod on November 11. In mid-December they found Plymouth Colony.

1630
The Massachusetts Bay Colony is founded by John Winthrop on the Shawmut Peninsula, where the settlement of Boston begins.

1635
The country's first secondary school, the Boston Latin School, is established.

1636
Harvard College is established. Reverend Roger Williams is banished from the Massachusetts Bay Colony and founds Providence, Rhode Island. War erupts with the Pequots.

ABOVE: Roger Williams, preacher and founder of Providence.

1639
The first printing press is set up, in Cambridge.

1675–76
King Philip's War sees Indian society virtually wiped out.

1692
Salem witch trials: 400 stand accused of sorcery and other crimes. Of those found guilty, 20 are executed.

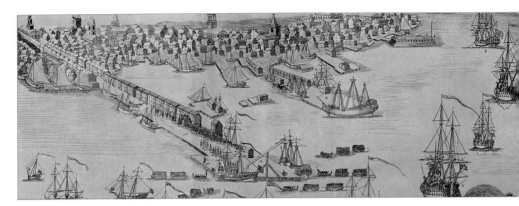

ABOVE: an engraving by Paul Revere shows the British fleet in Boston harbor in 1768.

1701
The Collegiate School (later Yale) is founded.

1712
Captain Christopher Hussey of Nantucket becomes the first New Englander to capture a sperm whale.

THE ROAD TO INDEPENDENCE
1764
The Revenue Act, imposed by Britain, taxes sugar, silk, and some wines. The *Hartford Courant* is first published as the *Connecticut Courant*.

1765
The Stamp Act taxes commercial and legal documents, newspapers, and playing cards. Widespread demonstrations are held.

1767
The Townshend Acts place harsh duties on paper, glass, and tea. Two regiments of British troops land at Boston to impose order.

1770
On March 5, five colonists are killed outside the Custom House by Redcoats in what is known as the "Boston Massacre."

1773
On December 16, in the "Boston Tea Party," 60 men (disguised as Mohawk Indians and blacks) dump tea over the railings of three ships in Boston Harbor in protest against taxes on tea.

1774
Britain retaliates against the Boston Tea Party by imposing the Coercive Acts, including the Boston Port Act which closes Boston Harbor. On September 5 the First Continental Congress convenes at Philadelphia and starts to organize an army.

1775
On the night of April 18, Paul Revere and William Dawes ride from Boston to warn of the impending arrival of 700 British troops sent to destroy an arms depot in Concord. The following day the two sides engage at Lexington in the first battle of the Revolution. On June 17 the British force an American retreat at the Battle of Bunker Hill near Boston (actually fought on Breed's Hill), but only after massive casualties.

1776
In March, George Washington drives the British from Boston. On July 4, the Declaration of Independence is adopted.

BOOM AND BUST
1789
Samuel Slater is engaged by financier Moses Brown to set up a cotton mill at Pawtucket.

1791
Vermont, briefly an independent republic, joins the Union.

1800
Poor conditions at Pawtucket lead workers to strike in the nation's first industrial action.

BELOW: Joseph Warren, physician and patriot, dies at Bunker Hill, 1775.

1820
Maine, formerly part of Massachusetts, is admitted to the Union as a state.

1826
The growing community surrounding the Merrimack Manufacturing Company's showpiece cotton mill is renamed Lowell after its founder.

ABOVE: the perils of whaling.

1831
The Abolitionist William Lloyd Garrison founds the weekly *Liberator* newspaper.

1833
New England's first steam railroad opens between Boston and Lowell, Massachusetts.

1845
Henry David Thoreau pioneers ecological concerns by building a cabin at Walden Pond, near Concord, Massachusetts.

1845–50
More than 1,000 Irish immigrants fleeing from the Potato Famine at home arrive in Boston each month.

1851
Herman Melville's novel *Moby-Dick* is published.

1852
Uncle Tom's Cabin, by Harriet Beecher Stowe, encourages the Abolitionist movement.

1854
The Boston Public Library becomes the world's first free municipal library.

1861
Whaling declines as kerosene replaces whale oil for lighting.

1870
Boston's Museum of Fine Arts is founded; it opens in 1876.

1880s
Irish immigrants start to control Boston politics.

1881
The Boston Symphony Orchestra makes its debut.

1886
Great Barrington, Massachusetts, pioneers the use of street lights.

1891
Basketball is invented in Springfield, Massachusetts.

1920
Italian anarchists Sacco and Vanzetti arrested for payroll rob-

ABOVE: textiles boom in the 1800s.

bery and murder; their execution in 1927 causes major protests.

1923
Vermont's Calvin Coolidge becomes US President when Warren Harding dies in office.

1929
The Wall Street Crash and the resultant Great Depression hit New England hard. Its manufacturing industry, especially textiles and shoes, begins a long decline.

1938
A hurricane in September is New England's worst natural disaster.

BELOW: Boston in 1853 – detail from a John White Allen Scott painting.

1944

A conference at Bretton Woods, New Hampshire, attempts to create the framework for a postwar world monetary system.

1854

The first nuclear submarine, USS *Nautilus*, in launched at Groton, Connecticut.

MODERN TIMES

1960

Masssachusetts Senator John F. Kennedy is elected US President.

ABOVE: Massachusetts senator Jack Kennedy's campaign buttons, 1960.

1960s–1980s

New England's economy is transformed by the arrival of high-technology industries.

1980s–1990s

New England cod fishery collapses as a result of declining stocks.

1982

The first *Cheers*, the hit TV show set in a Boston bar, is screened.

1990

Vermont elects the nation's only Independent congressman, the socialist Bernie Sanders.

1992

The Mashantucket Pequot Indians open the controversial but very profitable Foxwoods Casino in Connecticut. It is soon followed by Mohegan Sun.

1997

Sebastian Junger's best-selling *The Perfect Storm* tells the story of a doomed Gloucester trawler. Hollywood films it in 2000.

2000

Vermont advances gay rights by passing a civil unions bill. Four years later, Massachusetts recognizes gay marriages.

2002

Controversy rages over aesthetics vs. renewable energy as giant windmills for electrical generation are proposed for Vermont ridgetops and Nantucket Sound.

2003

A fire in a Rhode Island nightclub kills 100 after a band's pyrotechnic display ignites soundproofing. In New Hampshire, Gene Robinson is consecrated as the Anglican Church's first gay bishop. New Hampshire's iconic rock formation, the Old Man of the Mountain, collapses.

2004

Boston's Red Sox, based at Fenway Park, take World Series baseball crown for the first time in 86 years. They win again in 2007.

2005

Completion of America's biggest ever public works project, the "Big Dig," which moved Boston's Central Artery underground and added a third harbor tunnel. The playwright Arthur Miller dies in Connecticut, aged 89.

2006

Vermont's Independent congressman Bernie Sanders elected to US Senate. Massachusetts elects its first African-American governor, Deval Patrick.

2008

Edward Kennedy, JFK's only surviving brother, is diagnosed with brain cancer. Film star Paul Newman dies at Westport, Connecticut. In the battle for the White House, Barack Obama wins the Democratic primaries in Connecticut, Maine and Vermont; Hillary Clinton carries Massachusetts, New Hampshire and Rhode Island. Obama wins all six states in the November election.

2009

The cash-strapped *Boston Globe* starts running front-page ads. ❑

BELOW: Boston's Fenway Park.

BEGINNINGS

The first Indians arrived in the region around 12000 BC,
but it was the landing of the Pilgrim Fathers
in 1620 that changed the face of America for ever

lthough, as the name suggests, it was the English who sowed the seeds of New England's fortune, they were not the first to gaze on these northern shores. Anthropologists generally agree that the first pilgrims reached North America overland from Asia via the then-frozen Bering Straits, arriving on the continent between 12,000 and 25,000 years ago.

The oldest fossil finds of human activity in New England, uncovered in Shawville, Vermont, and Wapunucket, Massachusetts, date respectively to 9000 and 4000 BC and include a variety of spear points, knives, pendants, and ancient house floors. These early settlers were to witness the landing of the Vikings in AD 1000, the first documented European visitors to North America. Initially, the Vikings got on well with the natives, cordially trading Viking cloth for local furs. But soon hostilities broke out and the Vikings abandoned the new world.

The Algonquins

The Algonquins seeped into the New England forests probably sometime during the 14th or 15th centuries. They did not come in droves; by 1600, no more than 25,000 Indians populated New England, fewer than one for every 2 sq. miles (5 sq. km). Nor did this population comprise a unified culture: the Algonquins broke down into at least 10 tribal divisions. Tribes included the Narragansetts of present-day Rhode Island, the Abenaki of

In 1848, workers laying railroad tracks in Charlotte, Vermont, more than 150 miles (240 km) from the Atlantic Ocean, unearthed the skeleton of an unexpected prehistoric resident: a whale.

Maine, the Pennacooks of New Hampshire, and the Massachusetts of their namesake, as well as lesser groups such as the Nipmucs, Nausets, Pocumtucks, and Niantics. Some tribes had no more than 200 or 300 members.

Far from being the nomads of later characterizations, the Algonquins were agricultural and semi-sedentary, wandering little more than the fashionable Bostonians who summer on Cape Cod. Tribal communities moved with the seasons, following established routes restricted to particular tribal domains. In the winter they occupied the sheltered valleys of the interior, in the warmer months the fertile coastal areas.

But the Indians had to toil year round to feed and clothe themselves. With an excellent understanding of agricultural techniques, they grew crops such as beans, pumpkins, and tobacco, but relied most heavily on maize, the Indian corn. Meat and fish sufficiently balanced the vegetable fare. Plentiful moose and beaver, turkey and goose, lobsters and clams, salmon and bass, along with other delectables, made for a varied menu.

Path to settlement

The early European explorers were not mere adventurers, but determined fortune hunters seeking an easier passage to the Orient and its treasures – and, incidentally, seeking to save heathen souls. When the Genoese sailor Cristoforo Colombo (latinized

for the Crown, considering that England based its claim to all America east of the Rockies and north of Florida on the extent of Cabot's exploration.

For most of the 16th century, Spanish conquistadors dominated the New World, where they profitably exploited resource-rich Central and South America. After Cabot's venture, the less inviting and accessible north was largely neglected and the Northwest Passage remained a merchant's dream.

The English take over

In the closing decades of the 16th century, Elizabeth I's England eclipsed Spain as master of the seas. Recognizing conquest and colonization as

as Christopher Columbus) was trying to finance his expedition, he spoke of riches and trade. So when he returned with a new continent, but with no gold or spices, he was ridiculed and disgraced.

Columbus's countryman Giovanni Caboto (John Cabot), searching for the Northwest Passage to the East, received slightly better treatment from his patron, Henry VII of England. The first European since the Norse to visit America's northern shores (at Labrador, historians believe), Cabot was blessed with a huge royal pension of £20 a year after his 1497 expedition. It was a good bargain

LEFT: early contacts with the native tribes were generally peaceful. **ABOVE:** *Indians Fishing*, a late 16th-century painting by John White.

HOW ALGONQUIN SOCIETY WORKED

Politics and state affairs were left in the charge of the *sachem*, a hereditary chief who commanded each tribe in much the same way that monarchs ruled medieval Europe. The *powwows*, or medicine men, gained considerable political might as the vicars of Indian religion. They combined healing with religion through mystical rites.

In no sense did the Algonquins comprise a nation in the modern European style. Unlike their Iroquois neighbors to the west, no council, senate, or chief-of-chiefs disciplined the Algonquin tribes toward unified action. Divided into sachemships, New England's Indians were not simply disunited; they were constantly at each other's throats. This lack of unity gave the white settlers an advantage.

a path to power, the late-starting English were to take over from the conquistadors as pioneers of the New World.

In 1583, equipped with a royal charter to discover "remote heathen and barbarious land not actually possessed by any Christian prince or people… and to have, hold, occupy and enjoy" such territories, Sir Humphrey Gilbert was the first Englishman to attempt the settlement of North America. Sailing from Plymouth with his flagship *Delight* and three other vessels, Gilbert intended to establish a trading post at the mouth of the Penobscot River. But after reasserting English control of Newfoundland, he sailed south to disaster: three

out of the four ships sank and Gilbert himself died.

The first years of the 17th century saw a renewed interest in exploration. In 1606, James I granted charters for two new ventures, the Virginia Companies of London and Plymouth, giving the latter rights to found a colony somewhere between North Carolina and Nova Scotia. Loaded with the usual arms and foodstuffs, some livestock, and trinkets to trade with the natives, the first band of 100 adventurers built Fort St George on Parker's Island in Maine. There they wintered but, finding no evidence of precious metals, and the weather "extreme unseasonable and frosty," the group left the following spring.

Recognizing the need to plan more carefully, the Plymouth Company next commissioned the experienced surveyor John Smith to take a critical look at the region's potential for settlement and profit. Smith is credited as the first to give the region its name of "New England."

Answering a higher call

The explorers of the 16th century were driven by the profit motive. Since they discovered neither the coveted Northwest Passage nor gold and diamonds, they couldn't discern the promise of the New World. Decades of work produced no more than a few crude maps and travelogues.

Renaissance Europe did not foster religious tolerance. Dissent was treason, and heretics mounted the same scaffolds as did traitors. To the Puritans, devotees of more extreme Protestant beliefs than their Church of England (Anglican) countrymen, the symbols of papal domination – jeweled miters, elaborate rituals, and power-hungry bishops – were the Devil's work, from which the Anglican establishment had not sufficiently distanced itself. Even more disturbing to the Puritans was the persecution they suffered under James I in his attempts to impose religious conformity.

A group of Puritans from Lincolnshire struck a deal with the Plymouth Company to finance a settlement in the unpopulated north of America. In 1620, 66 of these pilgrims left from Plymouth on the 180-ton *Mayflower*, carrying everything they needed to start and maintain a self-sufficient community. The trip itself was no luxury cruise, and after more than two months at sea the travelers "were not a little joyful" to sight Cape Cod on November 11. Deciding that the sandy cape lacked fresh water and arable land, the group dispatched Captain Miles Standish (nicknamed "Captain Shrimp" because of his height) to find a more fertile site. In mid-December, the Pilgrims disembarked at Plymouth Rock.

> *Among the best-known Algonquin tribes in the New England area were the Mohegan, Pequot, Narragansett, Wampanoag, Massachusett, Nipmuc, Pennacook, and Passamaquoddy. Tribal intermarriage was common.*

The first winter was a miserable ordeal, testing fully the hardened Puritan will. Scurvy, pneumonia, and other infections killed more than half of the settlers, including Governor John Carver. At any one time, no more than six or seven remained in good health. But spring brought better times, notably the signing of a treaty of friendship with the local Indians, one of whom, Squanto, had been temporarily abducted to England by an earlier expedition and now recommended cooperation.

Heavenly aspirations

Acknowledging the native contribution, the Pilgrims hosted a feast of celebration nearing the first anniversary of their arrival. In this first Thanksgiving, both natives and newcomers enjoyed a meal of roasted game (including turkey), eel, fruits, vegetables, and cornbread. A few weeks later, 35 freedom-seekers, well stocked with provisions, joined the *Mayflower*

English inhabitant had been the scholarly hermit William Blaxton, who promptly removed himself to Rhode Island. As Charles I and Archbishop William Laud tightened the screws of persecution back home, the Massachusetts Bay Colony grew quickly despite primitive conditions.

Growth was not limited to the area of the first landings on the Massachusetts shore. The reverends Thomas Hooker and Samuel Stone, along with former Bay governor John Haynes, left Cambridge for Connecticut, where they settled the towns of Hartford, Wethersfield, and Windsor. Two Londoners, Theophilus Eaton and John Davenport, soon after established themselves at New

survivors, and by the spring of 1624, Plymouth was a thriving village of more than 30 cottages.

In 1628 another group of Puritans, led by Thomas Dudley, Thomas Leverett, and John Winthrop, obtained a royal charter as the "Company of the Massachusetts Bay in New England." The next summer, 350 hopefuls arrived at Salem, followed by another 1,500 in 1630. Not only more numerous than the Plymouth Pilgrims but also better financed, the Massachusetts Bay Company founded the town of Boston that year on the Shawmut peninsula – a neck of land whose only prior

LEFT: eight-year-old Anne Pollard, the first white woman to set foot in Boston (1630). **ABOVE:** settlers mingle with natives at Plimoth Plantation.

THE BIRTH OF HARVARD

Some 2,000 immigrants arrived each year between 1630 and 1637, and new communities such as Ipswich, Dorchester, Concord (the first inland village), Dedham, and Watertown sprang up. In 1636, the Puritan clergy established Harvard College to train future ministers. The Great and General Court – to this day the name of the Massachusetts legislature – was formed to manage administrative and judicial affairs, a governor and deputy governor being indirectly chosen by the colony's freeholders. At the town level, landowners convened to discuss problems – a practical arrangement since, even as late as 1700, the average town included no more than 200 or 300 families.

Haven. The Plymouth Colony had been operating a trading post on Maine's Kennebec River since 1627, and New World magnates John Mason and Sir Ferdinando Gorges tried to develop vast property grants in New Hampshire and Maine, but these ambitious ventures were humbled by the region's daunting inhospitality.

Elsewhere, groups of New Englanders helped pave the frontiers outside the region. Puritan communities transplanted to New York, North Carolina, and Georgia maintained ties with their old homes. One such group, from Westmorland, Connecticut, continued to send representatives to the Connecticut Assembly long after moving to Pennsylvania.

> Everyone played a part in running Algonquin communities. While the men hunted, the women sowed and harvested the fields, tended the children, and maintained the portable family wigwams. The Algonquins were dumbfounded by the perceived laziness of English women.

The founding of Providence

In the early years of Massachusetts Bay, the Reverend Roger Williams took it upon himself to condemn the shackles of imposed religion, preaching from his pulpit in Salem that "forced worship stinks in God's nostrils." His compatriots in the General Court banished him from the colony in 1636.

But Williams did not return to England. He turned instead to Canonicus and Miantonomi, the two Narragansett leaders he had befriended in the course of studying the native population. The chieftains saw fit to grant him, *gratis*, a large tract on the Pawtuxet River. Here, Williams founded Providence. Fellow exiles joined him over the next few years – Anne Hutchinson and William Coddington on nearby Rhode Island (so named because someone thought it resembled the Greek island of Rhodes), and Samuel Gorton in Warwick.

Though the new settlement grew slowly – from fewer than 20 families in 1638 to no more than 1,000 individuals three decades later – the Providence and Rhode Island plantations proved an unholy thorn in Massachusetts' underbelly. No kind words here: Hutchinson, with her "very voluble tongue," lambasted her former parish with "Call it whore and strumpet not a Church of Christ;" while back in Massachusetts, the ordinarily restrained Cotton Mather continually insulted the colony as the "fag end of creation," "the sewer of New England," and, ever so cleverly, "Rogue's Island."

But Rhode Island lived up to its intent, and religious freedom was guaranteed by a 1663 royal charter. It welcomed New England's first Jewish émigrés in 1662, along with scores of Quakers and French Huguenots.

Violence breaks out

Missionary zeal alienated many of the natives (*see box on opposite page*), but it was empire-building that led to bloodshed. At first, there was plenty of

PURITAN INTOLERANCE

The 19th-century social satirist Artemus Ward (real name: Charles Farrar Browne) once observed: "The Puritans nobly fled from a land of despotism to a land of freedom, where they could not only enjoy their own religion, but could prevent everybody else from enjoying his." Dictating rules of conduct not just for the church but for all worldly pursuits, the Puritans were far less tolerant of social or theological deviation than their oppressors back in England had been. Indeed, in 1661, the king himself intervened to protect Quakers in the Bay Colony after several were hanged publicly on Boston Common. As has often been the case in American history, injustice belied the slogans of liberty.

LEFT: Roger Williams believed in fair dealings with Native Americans. **RIGHT:** King Philip's War, a vicious conflict in 1675–76, broke the Indians' spirit.

room for the natives and settlers to coexist peacefully. About a third of the Algonquin inhabitants had fallen victim to a great plague in the early 1600s, leaving their lands underpopulated when the *Mayflower* landed. But, as the ambitious English settlements expanded and pushed south, friction between the two peoples was the inevitable result.

In 1636 war erupted with the Pequots (a fearsome tribe whose name means "destroyer" in Algonquian), and battles at Fort Mystic and Fairfield, Connecticut, saw several hundred lives lost on both sides. It was King Philip's War (1675–76), however, that marked the demise of Indian society in most of New England. The Nipmuc, Narragansett, and Wampanoag forces, nominally led by Philip (whose real name was Metacomet), suffered from chronic tribal disunity and were outnumbered by at least five to one. At the "Great Swamp Fight" near present-day South Kingston, Rhode Island, 2,000 Narragansetts were slain (many of them women and children trapped in burning wigwams) in one of the fiercest battles ever fought on New England soil. The Indian will was broken; for them, the war had been a holocaust.

For the settlers, whose initial ascetic zeal had been diluted, politics, not religion, would be the rallying call of a new era. ❏

THE CRUSADE TO CONVERT THE ALGONQUINS

Although the Puritans owed much to the Algonquins for their cooperation in the early days of settlement, and although they professed no racial prejudice against the Indians (one contemporary theory held that they were descended from a lost tribe of Israel), the Puritans soon assumed the task of converting their new-found neighbors from their heathen ways.

The Bible was translated into the Algonquian language. The Reverend John Eliot set up a string of "Praying Towns" of Christian Algonquins. During the 1660s and early 1670s, these communities may have accounted for as many as one-fifth of all New England Indians. But the Puritans were looking for more than religious fellow-travelers; they sought to create nothing less than a breed of neo-Englishmen.

As the historian Alden T. Vaughan concluded, the natives would have had to "forsake their theology, their language, their political and economic structures, their habitations and clothing, their social mores, their customs of work and play" – in short, commit cultural suicide – to please the Puritans sufficiently. Several Algonquins were sent to Harvard to receive ministerial training, but only one, Caleb Cheeshahteaumuck, graduated.

Many natives took to drinking the "strong water" introduced by the English, and were chastised for their supposed indolence, a cardinal Puritan sin. The virtues of the proud Algonquin society were not appreciated.

LIVING HISTORY

Nowhere in the United States is history taken more seriously, and replayed so lovingly, than in New England

There's a well-worn joke about how many New Englanders it takes to change a light bulb. The punch line? "Six. One to change the bulb, and five to wax nostalgic about how nice the old one was." Indeed, visitors to the region might well conclude that New Englanders blur the line between past and present, and refuse to think of the past as "past" at all: the six states do at times resemble a big open-air attic, from which nothing is ever discarded – at least not without a fight.

There is, of course, plenty that's new about New England – just look at the Boston skyline. But the American historic preservation movement was born here, in successful campaigns to save artifacts as diverse as the gaslights on Beacon Hill, the frigate "Old Ironsides," and hundreds of upcountry barns.

Perhaps the most prominent examples of this passion for keeping the past alive are New England's "living history" museums, entire indoor-and-outdoor environments in which the modern world scarcely intrudes. Usually harking back to the region's commonly perceived late 18th- and early 19th-century golden age – a time of self-sufficient farms and villages, and seaports bustling with trade – these institutions range from experiments in period agriculture, such as Woodstock, Vermont's Billings Farm *(page 277)* to old-time religious enclaves like Hancock Shaker Village *(see page 205)* in the Berkshires, to Portsmouth, New Hampshire's Strawbery Banke *(see page 308)*, a neighborhood preserved *in situ*.

ABOVE AND BELOW: At Plimoth Plantation in Plymouth, Massachusetts *(visiting details, page 155)*, re-enactors reach back much farther than Sturbridge or Mystic days. They represent the first white New Englanders the Pilgrims who arrived here in 1620. Their homes are thatched huts, their crops and farmyard animals true to their era, and their accents – like the accents of the "sailors" aboard the *Mayflower II* anchored in Plymouth harbor – have a carefully recreated Jacobean lilt, particular to the part of England the Pilgrims hailed from, that resembles neither a modern British nor American mode of speaking. Most fascinating of all, their answers to visitors' questions reflect only what a man or woman of the early 17th century would know about. Any reference to the modern world – even, naturally, to the American Revolution – is met by Plimoth's settlers with feigned incomprehension, even incredulity.

LEFT: Actors in "living history" museums assume the manners and vocabulary of pioneers.

KEEPING ALIVE OLD SKILLS

At Massachusetts' Old Sturbridge Village, historic structures from around New England were brought together to suggest a tidy and prosperous small town circa 1840. The "town" is "inhabited" by no fewer than 120 costumed time-travelers, including a blacksmith, cooper (barrelmaker), potter, shoemaker, tinsmith, and printer, each in his or her own shop.

"With the rare exception, our artisans have no previous experience in the trades they demonstrate," says Sturbridge's Tom Kelleher. "Often, it's better if a person doesn't bring modern skills to the role." Instead, the village's trade-shop staff receive training in their occupations, beyond the extensive introductory sessions that cover historical background and communication skills. "Some of our people have even gone on to make a living doing what they demonstrated here," says Kelleher, "making pottery, barrels, and ironware, and even hand-setting lead type." *For visiting details, see page 190.*

LEFT: The most ambitious projects involve the re-creation of long-ago communities through meticulous research, relocation of period buildings, and the interpretive efforts of costumed staff playing the parts of townspeople, farmers, and artisans.

BELOW: Hancock Shaker Village, near Pittsfield in Massachusetts, recreates 20 19th-century homes.

ABOVE: The focus of activity at Mystic Seaport *(visiting details, page 259)* is a working preservation shipyard, where the technology of the days of "wooden ships and iron men" is employed to maintain an historic fleet that includes the port's showpiece, the whaler *Charles W. Morgan* (pictured). The emphasis is on the life of seafarers and their support system on shore. Sixty antique structures, most moved to the site, recreate a coastal village of the mid-19th century.

BIRTH OF A NATION

Lexington Green's "shot heard round the world" in 1775 signaled the start of the American Revolution and the fight for independence

Struggles over home rule were not new to New England. But the northern colonies had, for the most part, been left to their own devices from the first landing at Plymouth until the dramatic Stamp Act crisis of 1765. When the mother country attempted to rein in her distant child, the reaction had been quick and biting, a portent of the more drastic rebellion that lay ahead.

Suffering serious political turmoil in the early 17th century, highlighted by the beheading of Charles I, England had little time to attend to the governing of dissident settlers 3,000 miles from London. The Puritans gladly filled the vacuum and took on the responsibilities of *de facto* autonomy.

Puritan values

Even before reaching their destination, the Pilgrims signed the famous Mayflower Compact, creating a government "to enact, constitute, and frame such just and equal Laws, Ordinances, Acts, Constitutions, and offices, from time to time, as shall be thought most meet and convenient for the general good." John Winthrop and his followers carried with them their royal charter when they sailed to Massachusetts, and in

Governor John Winthrop believed strongly in aristocratic rule. He wrote: "A democracy is, among civil nations, accounted the meanest and worst of all firms of government."

1631 the freemen of the new colony gave an oath of fidelity not to the king but to the Bay Company and its officers. The settlers agreed that if England tried to impose its own governor on them, "we ought not to accept him, but defend our lawful possessions."

Fifty-five years later, they were given the chance. In 1686, James II unilaterally revoked the northern colonies' sacred charters and consolidated English holdings from Maine to New Jersey into a vast Dominion of New England in America. The monarch justified his decision as a security measure, a benevolent protection from the French and Indians. The Puritans were not convinced. They scorned the king's first envoy, Joseph Dudley, an avid Anglican, as having "as many virtues as can consist with so great a thirst for honor and power." They branded his succes-

ABOVE: Paul Revere, a key figure in the fight for independence, painted by John Singleton Copley.
RIGHT: the Boston Massacre of March 5, 1770.

sor, Edmund Andros, "the greatest tyrant who ever ruled in this country."

A strong cue from England itself moved New England to action and revolt. At the "Glorious Revolution" of early 1689, William and Mary, in cahoots with Parliament, seized the throne from James II. New England spontaneously erupted; Andros and his cronies were dragged from state house to jail cell. The old powers of self-government were largely restored, along with a certain mutual respect between Crown and colonies.

But a later English king, George III, presided over the loss of Britain's New World empire. Initial attempts by London to raise taxes in New England were successfully resisted *(see box below)*. But in 1767 Britain's prime minister, Charles Townshend, boasted: "I dare tax America." Parliament passed the Townshend Acts, imposing harsh duties on such imports as paper, glass, and tea. Two regiments of British troops landed at Boston to put some muscle behind the waning control of Governor Thomas Hutchinson.

The Boston Massacre

The Redcoats were not well received. On the night of March 5, 1770, a crowd of several hundred rowdy Bostonians gathered to taunt a lone "lobster-back" standing guard outside the customs

WHY THE STAMP ACT WAS HATED

Needing to cover the cost of keeping troops in the colonies, Britain's parliament passed a Revenue Act in 1764 taxing on sugar, silk, and certain wines. Boycotts were proclaimed. The infamous Stamp Act followed a year later, requiring that all commercial and legal documents, newspapers, and playing cards be taxed.

The measure was fiercely assailed. Stamp distributors were hanged in effigy and ridiculed at mock trials. Liberty was buried in symbolic funerals. New Englanders, who had no say in electing British parliamentarians, argued that there should be no taxation without representation. Britain's prime minister, William Pitt, responded by repealing the Stamp Act in March 1766.

house on King Street (present-day State Street). When shouts turned to stones and snowballs, seven Redcoats came to aid the sentry. One fired into the melee without orders, others followed, and, after the smoke had cleared, three colonists lay dead (including a black man named Crispus Attucks) and two were mortally wounded. The American revolt had its first martyrs, and the growing anti-British element in New England had a field day with the nocturnal showdown.

Tempers cooled after the Boston Massacre. In the early 1770s, economic prosperity returned to the colonies. A once-again pragmatic Parliament struck down the Townshend Acts – all except one, that is. To assert the king's authority, and to try to raise at least some revenue, Britain maintained the tax on East Indian tea, a not insignificant gesture given that tea was about as important as bread to the 18th-century diet.

American addicts turned to smuggled Dutch blends or to "Liberty Tea," a nasty brew made from sage, currant, or plantain leaves. The British responded by subsidizing their brand and, in September 1773, flooded the market with about half a million pounds of the "pestiential herb," with shipments to points all along the eastern seaboard. It didn't work.

Boston emerged once again as the focus of resistance. The Massachusetts Committee of Correspondence, an unofficial legislature, and

off the city by naval blockade. The First Continental Congress convened angrily in Philadelphia on September 5, 1774. Revolution was at hand.

A shot heard round the world

An uneasy stalemate prevailed from the fall of 1774 to the spring of 1775. British garrisons controlled only the major towns. The countryside became virtually unpoliceable. New Englanders stockpiled arms and ammunition to prepare for the inevitable conflict.

The rebels didn't have to wait long for war. In early April 1775, London instructed Boston commander General Thomas Gage to quash seditious

the local chapter of the Sons of Liberty, a fast-growing secret society at the forefront of revolutionary activism, barred the piers and demanded that Governor Hutchinson send home the tea-laden *Dartmouth*.

When he refused, the protesters' reaction was swift and calculatedly theatrical. On December 16, 60 men (among them Sam Adams and John Hancock) disguised as Mohawk Indians and blacks descended on the *Dartmouth* and two sister ships. Boston Harbor was turned into a teapot as they dumped 342 crates over the railings. The Boston Tea Party, as it came to be called, was a display of profound disrespect to Parliament and the king. Parliament responded with the so-called Coercive Acts. Most infamously, the Boston Port Act sealed

activities in rural Massachusetts, where a Provincial Congress had assumed de facto governmental control. Late on April 18, Gage dispatched a contingent of 700 soldiers to destroy a makeshift arms depot in Concord, 20 miles (32 km) west of Boston. At Lexington, 70 citizen soldiers, the original Minutemen (who could be summoned for duty at a minute's notice), lay in wait for the British, having been forewarned by the daring early-morning rides from Boston of patriots Paul Revere and William Dawes.

The two forces met on the town common. A musket was fired. Minutes later, eight Americans

ABOVE: *First News of the Battle of Lexington* by William Tylee Ranney (1813–57). **RIGHT:** the Battle of Bunker Hill, painted by Winthrop Chandler (1747–90).

lay dead. The British continued on to Concord, where the colonial militia triggered, in Ralph Waldo Emerson's words, "the shot heard round the world." The Minutemen made up for their lack of numbers by employing unconventional guerrilla tactics, harassing the enemy with crack sniper fire. By nightfall they had killed 273 British soldiers.

Sensational accounts of these skirmishes sent settlers reaching for their rifles. "The devastation committed by the British troops on their retreat," reported one, "is almost beyond description, such as plundering and burning of dwelling houses and other buildings, driving into the street women in child bed, killing old men in their houses

unarmed." Among the dead bodies, the card of compromise lay discarded.

Independence is declared

The war's first year did not go well for Britain *(see box below)* and, on July 4, 1776, the Declaration of Independence was adopted by the Continental Congress. Of the signatories, 14 came from the charter states of Massachusetts, Connecticut, New Hampshire, and Rhode Island. Except for Newport, Rhode Island, not taken from the British until October 1779, New England had achieved its independence.

After the Treaty of Paris ended the Revolutionary War in 1783, the magnates of New England's

THE BATTLE OF BUNKER HILL

The first major engagement of the war, the Battle of Bunker Hill, broke out in June 1775 on the Charlestown peninsula, across the Charles River from Boston. To consolidate control of overland access to the port city, Continental Army General Artemus Ward ordered the fortification of Bunker's Hill (as it was then known), although it was actually on adjoining Breed's Hill that the Americans dug in.

The British could not allow such a build-up if they were to entertain even the faintest hope of holding Boston. On June 17, Redcoats scaled Breed's slopes twice but were rebuffed. In a desperate third attempt they succeeded, but only because the colonial force had

exhausted its supply of ammunition. It was for this reason, and not out of bravery, that Colonel William Prescott issued his famous command: "Don't fire until you see the whites of their eyes, men."

Bunker Hill was a costly victory for the Crown, which suffered more than 1,000 casualties. Optimism, seen in remarks like General John Burgoyne's "We'll soon find elbow room," was reduced to the doubting reflections of another British officer: "This victory has cost us very dear indeed... Nor do I see that we enjoy one solid benefit in return, or are likely to reap from it any one advantage whatever." Less than a year later, under siege by George Washington, Gage evacuated his troops to Halifax.

prosperous cities turned to protect their newly established interests as the 13 independent colonies hammered out an integrated union. Concerned that a centralized federal government would prove as insensitive to local sentiment as had the Crown, revolutionary heroes Sam Adams and John Hancock gave only grudging support to the Constitution. Rhode Island, in more than a dozen votes between 1787 and 1789, voted it down and ratified it only after the Bill of Rights was added.

The industrial age

New England's leaders became increasingly reactionary as they guarded their economic interests.

In Massachusetts, poor hill farmers rose against the state government in Shays' Rebellion of 1786, demonstrating that genuine equality remained a dream. In 1812, fearing the loss of a thriving maritime trade, New England firmly opposed renewed and greater conflict with Great Britain.

But the first two decades of the 19th century showed how vulnerable maritime trade was to the whims of international politics. The Napoleonic Wars, President Thomas Jefferson's Embargo Acts, and the War of 1812 severely hampered New England's chase after an honest, apolitical dollar. Recognizing that it is best not to put all one's commercial eggs in one flimsy basket, its merchants turned to the herald of a new industrial age.

The machine age

In the fall of 1789, a teenage Samuel Slater sailed from England to New York disguised as a common laborer, defying British laws forbidding the emigration of skilled mechanics. For seven years he had apprenticed to Jedediah Strutt, a partner of the famed innovator Richard Arkwright, and knew the specifications of Arkwright's factory-sized, cotton-spinning machine.

In America, the reduction of raw cotton was still being done by laborers working in their own homes on individual looms. An early attempt at consolidating the process, a mill at Beverly, Massachusetts, had been a failure owing to the crudeness of its machinery. Arkwright's device, already proven across the Atlantic, was the answer, so Quaker financier Moses Brown engaged Slater to come to Providence and put his knowledge to use. Together, they built America's first successful cotton mill on the Blackstone River at Pawtucket.

TRADING IN TEA AND RUM, SPICES AND SLAVES

When not calling comrades to religious or political barricades, the colonial New Englander attended to the more practical pursuit of commerce: it was both out of the seas and on the seas that New England's money was made. Codfish provided a lucrative export to Catholic Europe, while whaling provided oil for lighting and lubricants.

New England was at the pivot of the profitable Triangular Trade: in harbors like Newport, a fleet of 350 ships unloaded West Indian molasses and reloaded with rum. From there, the rum was transported to Africa, where it was traded for slaves who were shipped to the West Indies and, in turn, traded for molasses.

New England shipyards gained world fame for crafting swift, easily managed ocean-going vessels, a tradition launched even before Pilgrim settlement with the construction of the Virginia in the short-lived Popham colony in Maine in 1607.

Although disrupted by the Revolution, maritime trade bounced back quickly, mining the riches of China and India so coveted by the early American explorers. In 1792, Boston's Columbia threaded the Straits of Magellan en route to Canton to trade for tea, spices, silk, and opium. The magnates of rival Salem – Elias Hasket Derby, Joseph Peabody, and Billy Gray – preferred to sail east, skirting the southern tip of Africa on frequent and successful ventures to the Orient.

With underpaid workers kept at the grind for 70 hours a week, Pawtucket became the site of the nation's first strike in 1800. It was left to Bostonian Francis Cabot Lowell (from the family that would later produce a Harvard president, a celebrated astronomer, and three poets) to take a more enlightened approach.

During a two-year visit to England, Lowell became an avid industrial tourist and, on his return to Massachusetts, he was determined to duplicate British weaving feats. Putting up $10,000 of his own money, he collected another $90,000 from the so-called "Boston Associates" – the families of Lawrence, Cabot, Eliot, Higginson, and others –

ment. New England's first company town was, in the words of the English novelist Anthony Trollope, "the realization of commercial utopia." Soon the efficient new factory system – if not its early paternalism – would spread up the Merrimack River to Lawrence, Massachusetts, and ultimately to the vast Amoskeag mills at Manchester, New Hampshire, destined to become the greatest producer of cotton cloth on Earth.

Life on the frontier

Not everybody shared in the boom. During the second half of the 18th century, the northern areas of New England had enjoyed a dramatic infusion

to establish a small mill (with a power loom and 1,700 spindles) at Waltham.

A "commercial utopia"

Lowell died in 1817, but his plans were realized by his associates under the aegis of the Merrimack Manufacturing Company. In 1820, the mill was moved to a tract on the Merrimack River, just above the village of Chelmsford.

The Merrimack Company took care of its people. Though grievously overworked by modern standards, "mill girls" enjoyed clean, safe dormitory housing and opportunities for cultural enrich-

of people, as land began to grow scarce in the densely populated coastal areas. More than 100 new towns were established in New Hampshire in the 15 years preceding the Revolution; between 1790 and 1800, the populations of Vermont and Maine nearly doubled.

On the craggy hillsides, the pioneers set up small farms, built their own houses and barns, and raised wheat, corn, pigs, and cattle to fill the dinner table. These rugged families prided themselves on being almost completely self-sufficient; in fact, it used to be said of upcountry farms that all they needed to import were nails and salt. This was a new frontier, New England's frontier.

But this frontier's potential was limited by nature. The climate was inhospitable: in 1816, for

LEFT: the *USS Constitution* takes on the British navy in 1812. **ABOVE:** Boston's Old State House, around 1801.

instance, a June snowfall resulted in total crop failure. Agricultural machinery could not plough the irregular farmland. As for those famous New England stone walls, they were in actuality a practical by-product of what many disillusioned farmers called the region's prime produce: rocks. Property consolidation was difficult, as families jealously guarded original claims; small-scale production could not compete with more efficient new suppliers elsewhere in the United States and around the world. As far as agriculture was concerned, northern New England had seen its zenith by 1850.

After that, a slow, sapping decline attacked upland vitality. By the turn of the century,

population growth had leveled and agricultural production dived. More than half of New Hampshire's farmland lay abandoned. Cheese production in Maine, New Hampshire, and Vermont fell by 95 percent between 1849 and 1919. The California Gold Rush of 1849 drew young men from the farms. The Civil War took away even more, with veterans often heading west to seek their fortunes rather than returning to their fathers' stony acres. And girls went to the Massachusetts mills.

Athenaeums for all

Boston had become established as the center of cultural activities *(see box)*. Elsewhere, Salem's Peabody Essex Museum – founded in part as a repository of curiosities brought home by the city's far-faring merchant captains – now preserves historic homes as well. In Hartford, the Wadsworth Athenaeum was founded as an art museum in 1842 by local businessman Daniel Wadsworth ("athenaeum" was a cultural catch-all title in the 19th century; the Providence Athenaeum, once a haunt of Edgar Allan Poe, is still a private library).

The future of American libraries, though, lay in the public domain. Here, too, New England was a leader: in 1854, the Boston Public Library became the world's first free municipal library.

Cradle of the Revolution, pioneer in commerce and industry, and now America's cultural capital – New England had shown its leadership in one realm after another. But as the 20th century approached, it would have to face a challenge not of invention, but re-invention. ❑

LEFT: one of an outstanding collection of 19th-century figureheads in Salem's Peabody Essex Museum.

HOW BOSTON BECAME THE ATHENS OF AMERICA

Long before the wheels of industry started to turn, New England minds had been establishing a cultural life unparalleled in the New World. In education, the media, the arts, and letters, America now looked to New England for guidance and inspiration. Boston led the way.

Colonial New Englanders had enriched their intellectual life by founding such pioneer colleges as Harvard, Yale, Dartmouth, and Brown. As the 19th century progressed, and with the interest on their old China Trade money compounded tremendously via investment in the new manufacturing technologies, Boston's first families sponsored a new round of institutions that would lend weight to the city's position as "the Athens of America."

The Handel and Haydn Society dates from 1815, the New England Conservatory of Music from 1867, and the Boston Symphony Orchestra – founded and supported for 40 years by the arch-Brahmin Major Henry Lee Higginson – from 1881. The BSO is the parent organization of the less classically-oriented Boston Pops, and makes its summer home at the renowned Tanglewood Music festival in the Berkshires.

Boston's magnificent Museum of Fine Arts (1876) evolved from a collection room in the Boston Athenaeum – itself a great New England Institution, founded in 1807 and still one of America's premier privately-owned libraries (there are only 1,049 proprietary shareholders).

The Shakers

These disciplined people were famous for their unique way of life, their manner of worship, and their influential craftsmanship

ABOVE: history preserved at Hancock Shaker Village.

The founder of the Shakers was Ann Lee, born in 1736 in Manchester, England. An illiterate factory-worker, she was a woman of deep convictions at a time of religious persecution. She became the spritual leader of a group of dissidents from the Anglican Church called the "Shaking Quakers" because of the movements they made as the holy spirit took hold of them and purged their sins.

Persecuted and sent to jail, she had a vision that she had a mission to teach a new way of life, one where men and women were equal, free from lust, greed and violence, with their lives governed by material and spiritual simplicity. She was convinced that only through celibacy could men and women further Christ's kingdom on Earth.

After a second vision, she and eight followers set sail for New York in 1770. It was not until the 1780s, however, that converts were attracted in great numbers. Mother Ann died in 1783, soon after a prosetylizing tour of New England and before the full flowering of Shakerism. At its peak in the 1840s, more than 6,000 members lived in 19 communities.

The Shakers, officially known as the United Society of Believers in Christ's Second Appearing, aimed for perfection in life. Devoted to orderliness and simplicity, they were also dedicated to such progressive notions as sexual equality (facilities for men and women were identical and jobs were shared on a rota), and they welcomed technological advances that might improve the quality of their work. They were inventors (of, for instance, the circular saw and clothes pegs). They ran model farms and, as keen gardeners, were the first to packet and sell seeds; they also marketed medicinal herbs. They sold their meticulously crafted baskets, boxes, chairs and textiles. By blending discipline, business acumen, ingenuity and superb craftsmanship, they achieved prosperity, both spiritual and financial.

Celibacy, a key principle, made it difficult for communities to renew themselves, but their ranks were swelled by converts, and orphans were adopted. Numbers dwindled after the mid-1800s, though, and today just a handful of "Believers" remain, in Sabbathday Lake, Maine. Shaker ideals of simplicity and practicality live on, however, in a legacy of architecture, furniture and crafts.

The villages at Canterbury, NH, and Hancock, Mass., are preserved as museums, where visitors watch craftsmen make baskets, boxes and chairs in the Shaker manner. In the Dwelling Houses they can see the efficient kitchens, the wall pegs on which chairs and utensils were hung, and the built-in cupboards designed so that no dust could accumulate on top or underneath. ❑

RIGHT: the Shaker dance, an integral part of worship and an alternative to the tremblings of early believers.

DECLINE AND REVIVAL

Following the industrial and cultural zenith of the
18th and 19th centuries, New England faced
economic recession and political corruption

By the beginning of the modern era, New
England had come to represent America's
achievements and ideals – or, conversely,
it could be said that America was New England
writ large. But no one looking at the American
social and economic landscape in 1900 could
doubt that the nation's energy and drive now
found their sources in other places – in the
dynamo of New York, in the raw busy cities of
the Midwest, and even in upstart California.

At the national political level, too, New England's influence diminished. Locally, corruption
and social divisions blemished the birthplace of
American democracy and wellspring of the abolitionist and other reform movements.

Much of the trouble began with the vanishing
of the ethnic and religious homogeneity which
had aided the old political consensus. Uprooted
by the Potato Famine of 1845–50, the Irish sailed
to the land of opportunity, arriving in Boston at a
rate of more than 1,000 a month. Immigrants from
Quebec and throughout Europe followed:
Catholics, Jews and Orthodox Christians upset
Protestant homogeneity. The influx touched every
corner of New England; even in backwater New
Hampshire, one out of every five residents had
adopted, not inherited, the American flag.

Electoral corruption

In the wake of this human shock wave, a pre-
dictable anti-immigrant backlash erupted among
the established citizenry, whose forebears had
fought so hard to achieve democracy and equal
rights. The doors of society were shut to even the
most successful of the new arrivals, and their children and grandchildren. In the 1850s, the openly
racist Know-Nothing Party controlled governor-
ships in Massachusetts, Rhode Island, Connecti-

cut, and New Hampshire. Later organizations such
as the American Protective Association and the
Immigrant Restriction League gathered substantial memberships in their efforts to contain the
electoral power of their upstart neighbors.

Their efforts failed. No matter how unfamiliar
the immigrants were with the workings of democracy, they soon learned the power of votes well
orchestrated – particularly the Irish. In 1881, John
Breen of Tipperary became the first Irish-born
politician to take high office as mayor of
Lawrence, Massachusetts. His triumph launched
fellow Irishmen not only to political influence but

ABOVE: Mayor James Curley, a legend in Boston.
RIGHT: a busy Boston wharf in the late 19th century.

"*The political condition of Rhode Island is notorious, acknowledged and it is shameful,*" wrote one influential journalist, Lincoln Steffens. "*Rhode Island is a State for sale and cheap.*"

also to political domination. Hugh O'Brien, a journalist, won the mayoral election in Boston three years later, and Patrick Andrew Collin represented Suffolk County with a congressional seat in Washington. By the turn of the century, all levels of government were being run by what was, after all, the majority of the population.

But with newfound responsibility came insidi-

ous corruption. Rhode Island, once again, was the object of biting criticism as Boss Charles Brayton and the *Providence Journal* ring bought their way to office. Individual votes cost the political machine between $2 and $5 in normal elections, as much as $30 in hotly contested ones.

Many leaders, vividly embodied in the figure of James Michael Curley, abused the privileges of solid ethnic support. Curley displayed enormous political staying-power: he was elected mayor of Boston five times in the first four decades of the 20th century; and governor of the state for one term, 1934–38. The Irish Mussolini, as his detractors tagged him, improved the eco-

"BANNED IN BOSTON"

In Boston, cultural freedoms came under increasingly harsh attack as Irish Catholic activists and the Yankee heirs to the Puritan tradition found common ground. Led by Catholic leader William Cardinal O'Connell and the associated Watch and Ward Society, moralists lobbied successfully for prohibitions on such classics as Theodore Dreiser's *An American Tragedy* and Ernest Hemingway's *The Sun Also Rises*; they also gained control over what could and could not appear on the Boston stage. "Banned in Boston!" became a double-edged term of opprobrium: the moral watchdogs took pride in it, while elsewhere in the land people snapped up the controversial books and packed the theaters.

nomic welfare of his less privileged constituents. His imperious methods, however, were suspect. Curley doled out jobs and money to community leaders who in turn carefully steered their neighborhoods in the appropriate direction each time election day rolled around. There was some justification to the accusation of the critics: "This is a Republic and not a Kingdom." When the mayor went to a ball game at Fenway Park, howitzers trumpeted his arrival.

Jobs and capital migrate

Days of industrial glory passed. In much the same way that international competition now threatens American industrial jobs, other regions of the country challenged and overcame New England

and its once-proud manufacturers. Hourly wages in the northeast averaged 16 to 60 percent higher than those below the Mason-Dixon line. The South also remained relatively free of labor unions, a distinct advantage to employers with bitter memories of the strikes that shut down textile mills in Lawrence, Massachusetts, in 1912 and at the Amoskeag mills in Manchester, New Hampshire, in 1922. The Great Depression made the situation even more bleak, and the manufacturing boost given by World War II provided only a temporary respite *(see box below)*.

Poverty was endemic. In 1930, only 81 out of 5,030 apartments in Boston's North End had refrigerators. Only one in two had bathrooms.

The bulldozers move in

By the 1950s, it was clear that the economic malaise was not confined to factories; New England's cities and towns were also showing their age. One remedy was renovation. Boston led the way by establishing a redevelopment authority. Without sacrificing the charm of its venerable Beacon Hill and Back Bay neighborhoods, the Massachusetts capital set about remaking its downtown into a new landscape of civic structures, office buildings, and modern apartments.

Other cities followed suit, with greater and lesser degrees of success; from Portland, Maine to Rutland, Vermont, noble old train stations came crashing down, with the wrecker's ball tearing all too freely into the downtown streets around them. Often, the result was a bland city center of sterile office plazas and suburban-style malls. The smaller and more economically disadvantaged cities usually came out best in the long run: places like Newburyport in Massachusetts and New London in Connecticut saved their old downtowns by neglecting them until restoration and adaptive re-use had become popular.

Urban renewal would have been simply window dressing without a revival of the regional economy. Salvation would have to come through exploitation of New England's particular resources. But what were they? They certainly weren't oil, gas, or minerals. Just about the only thing of value New England takes out of the

THE GREAT DEPRESSION TAKES ITS TOLL

Industrial production in Massachusetts alone fell by $1 billion during the 1930s. Unemployment in factory towns left idle a quarter of the total labor pool. Even the mighty Amoskeag mills finally closed their doors in 1935.

New England felt the brunt of the Great Depression. In Boston it cramped even upper-class lifestyle, but the worst hardships were suffered in the already squalid working-class quarters. Here, wages halved, and unemployment was almost 40 percent after the 1929 Wall Street crash. By the end of 1935, nearly a quarter of Manchester's families were receiving public welfare.

Like the rest of the country, New England was jerked suddenly from the Depression by World War II. Shipyards hummed in Bath, Maine and Quincy, Massachusetts. In Hartford and Springfield and even Island Pond, Vermont, workers assembled guns for the Allied armies. But peace came to a New England that still hadn't solved its core economic difficulties – the migration of jobs to states where labor was cheaper, the aging of the manufacturing infrastructure, and a location that was at the outer corner of America's transporation network, instead of at its center. New England, to put it simply, was getting old.

ground is granite and marble from the quarries of Vermont. Manufacturing hadn't disappeared altogether; the Bath Iron Works in Maine still builds ships for the Navy, and there are still specialty textile, footwear, and machinery factories scattered throughout the six states. But these are hardly growth industries. When New England searched for the key to future prosperity, it looked to its most protean and dependable resource of all: its people.

More precisely, it looked to people and to education, one of the oldest New England pursuits. When it became clear that the high technology and financial service sectors would become prime drivers of the American economy, New England

on the Democratic ticket for president, boasting of the "Massachusetts Miracle" that had lifted his state to prosperity.

A need for new directions

High-technology schemes, whether promising or hare-brained, gave a boost to the burgeoning financial services industry. Boston became an investment banking capital, and the center of the mutual-fund business. Fidelity, Putnam, and MFS all headquartered here. In Hartford, two dozen insurance companies, dominated by titans such as Aetna, still call the Connecticut capital home.

High technology and finance have been at the

was ready. The concentration of colleges and universities in the Boston area provided a splendid resource at the dawn of the computer age.

This was the era of Wang laboratories and the Digital Equipment Company (now both subsumed into other corporations), of Edwin Land's Polaroid, and of Raytheon's growth in step with a military now dependent on sophisticated technology. By the 1970s, Route 128 – the beltway surrounding Boston and its inner suburbs – was touted on official road signs as "America's Technology Highway." In 1988, Michael Dukakis ran

LEFT: the past revisited in Lowell, Massachusetts.
ABOVE: Boston City Hall, built in the 1960s, was much criticized for its New Brutalism.

core of the boom-and-bust cycle of the past quarter century. Both industries flew high in the mid-1980s and again in the late 1990s, and both caught cold when the economy sneezed in the 2000s. Not all of the ill-fated dot-coms were based in California, and many of the dreams and fortunes that crashed with them belonged to New Englanders. But in most areas, the region's economy has been broad-based enough to prevent the kind of protracted catastrophe that the exodus of the textile industry had created.

Nor has New England suffered as much as other regions of the country from the steep decline in housing values that accompanied the mortgage crisis of 2007 and 2008 – in large part, most analysts believe, because real estate prices in the six states simply hadn't gone along for as wild a ride during the boom that preceded the bust. Chalk it up, some say, to New England's vaunted calm steadiness. A more likely reason, others claim, is that there weren't many places here where developers could overbuild, flooding the market.

Economic stereotypes aside, not everyone in New England designs computer chips or manages a mutual fund, just as the entire working population never ran power looms or shoe-stitching machines. The diversification of the region's economy ranges from the rise of "electronic cottages," in which individuals run publishing, consulting, and other businesses from their homes, to the tra-

ditional pursuits of farming, logging, and fishing.

Life hasn't been easy for people involved in those primary industries. Dairy farmers, mostly centered in Vermont, have seen their ranks dwindle as expenses spiral and milk prices stagnate. The forest products industry struggles against foreign competition and high energy costs; throughout northern New Hampshire and Maine, paper mills – once reliable blue-collar employers – have closed, while the vast tracts of woodlands owned by their parent companies increasingly have been sold, to face the possibility of subdivision and vacation-home development.

Alarmed by this threat to the integrity and wildness of the "Great North Woods" that ranges from northern Maine to New York State, activists have proposed – and, in the northeastern corner of Vermont, have accomplished – government purchase and protection of large swaths of forest. There has even been lobbying for the establishment of a national park that would take in much of the Maine woods, although many local residents are fearful of government intrusion and regulation.

Farther south, along the Atlantic coast, the men and women who sail out of Gloucester and other fishing ports have had nothing but bad news for the past 20 years or more – the cod stocks on Georges Bank have been drastically depleted, and restrictions on fishing mean that many boats no longer leave the harbor. Maine's lobster fishery remains viable, although the stalwarts who brave the Atlantic in their small lobster boats are in thrall to the fluctuating price of fuel.

That same price spiral applies to heating as well as transportation, in a region more heavily dependent on oil for heat than any in the United States.

A STREAK OF POLITICAL INDEPENDENCE

There haven't been any New England presidents since Kennedy in 1961–63, although Massachusetts Senator John F. Kerry performed strongly in the 2004 election. But the New Hampshire presidential primary, always the first of the election season, forces contenders and voters alike to listen to what people are thinking about in this small corner of the nation; in 2008, after all, it was New Hampshire that gave Democrat Hillary Clinton the boost she needed to stay in competition with Barack Obama for five more months.

New England also made national political headlines with the 2001 defection of Republican Senator Jim Jeffords of Vermont, who, by declaring himself an Independent, gave Democrats a temporary upper hand in the US Senate; and

the 2006 election of Vermonter Bernie Sanders to a Senate again controlled by Democrats. Sanders, a Brooklyn-born socialist who previously served as mayor of Burlington and as Vermont's lone member of the US House of Representatives, ran as an independent but votes with the Democratic majority.

"Independent" is the operative political word in New England, regardless of the conventional political labels worn by its leaders. Several Maine governors in recent years have been Independents. So is Connecticut Senator Joseph Lieberman, the 2000 Democratic vice-presidential candidate, who gave up his old party affiliation after losing a primary election to an anti-Iraq War candidate in 2006.

As for the third great consumer of energy, electrical generation, New Englanders are eager to innovate in a "green" direction, but argue as to which technologies to embrace. Controversy swirls around proposals to erect giant windmills in Nantucket Sound, where they would be visible from Cape Cod shores, and on ridgelines in northern Vermont. That might spoil famous views.

> Windpower is environmentally benign, but unspoiled views are a local treasure – and a vital foundation of the tourism economy.

political attention that it hadn't enjoyed since the heyday of the Adamses, two centuries ago.

Deep divisions

This independent streak reveals deep divisions over many issues. New Englanders have long led the way in protecting the environment, but every economic slump makes jobs vs. development regulations an issue in state elections. Education is a time-honored priority, but tempers flare over financing schools via property taxes vs. broad-based levies. New Englanders, who provided leaders for the abolitionist and early feminist movements and sent "Freedom Riders" south dur-

Plenty to argue about

Argument and controversy, of course, have long been bread and butter to New Englanders. And since the days of the earliest settlements, one of the best ways to learn what people in these six states are thinking has been to drop in at a town meeting. Naturally, these are an annual event only in smaller communities; but sometimes it seems as if all New England is one big town meeting. Every four years the debates take on a national dimension and, with the 1960 election of Massachusetts Senator John F. Kennedy as president of the United States, New England regained a place as a focus of national

LEFT: lobsterman at Penobscot Bay, Maine.
ABOVE: Boston's ultra-modern waterfront.

ing the 1960s Civil Rights struggle, now find themselves embroiled in the debate over gay rights. Vermont's 2000 establishment of "civil unions" (a form of virtual marriage) for gays and lesbians now sparks little local comment, but a Massachusetts Supreme Court ruling allowing gay marriage met with considerable protest. And in the prevailing national debate of the early 21st century, the majority of the region's citizens staunchly opposed the Iraq War. At town meetings in 2008, two Vermont municipalities actually voted to indict President George Bush and Vice-President Dick Cheney for war crimes if they set foot within their jurisdictions. Few Vermonters are surprised by the fact that theirs is the only state in the Union that George W. Bush never visited while in office. ❑

THE MARITIME TRADITION

The sea has always been important to New Englanders – first for transport and trade and as a fishing ground, more recently for recreation

The first generation of Europeans in America all had the same "baptism by sea:" a two-month voyage across the stormy North Atlantic. Most of the settlers who came were landlubbers; many had never seen the ocean before. But shipbuilding was one of the first enterprises the early colonists undertook. Ships maintained the connection to the homeland and provided an income from trade. The vast virgin forests of the New World supplied materials for their construction. One hundred years after the Pilgrims stepped on Plymouth Rock, New England's coastal shipyards were launching a ship a day. With labor and lumber costs so much cheaper than those in England, American-made ships dominated the market.

For the early settlers, the sea brought news from home, fresh legions of colonists to do battle with the wilderness, and ships involved in the Trian-

Battered by storms that seemed endless, the tiny yet sturdy barque Mayflower *was driven across Cape Cod Bay in November 1620 and into the mainland at a place the Pilgrims named Plymouth.*

gular Trade (the transport of slaves, molasses, and rum between ports in Africa, the Caribbean, and New England). The vast virgin forests of colonial Maine seemed an inexhaustible storehouse of straight, lofty white pines for the masts of the Royal Navy. The fishing grounds teemed with food for the taking.

One of the first important acts of the Great and

General Court of Massachusetts was to set standards for the regulation and encouragement of the fishing industry. Early on, fishing was seen as a prime source of the region's prosperity. Codfish, high in protein, iodine, and Vitamin A, nourished not just New Englanders, but also colonists in Mid-Atlantic and Southern towns.

The whaling boom

Lamps were fired by vegetable and animal oils; candles were made from animal tallow. The light was dim and the lamps were smoky until someone made the discovery that blubber from a beached whale could be rendered, and the oil extracted would provide a clearer, brighter light.

Whales beached themselves frequently on the

PRECEDING PAGES: decorative buoys in Cape Cod.
LEFT: in the harbor at Stonington, Connecticut.
RIGHT: Boston harbor in the late 19th century.

New England shores, and whaling began as a shore activity. Teams of townsfolk gathered whenever they saw a whale, tethering it to a stake to prevent the tide taking it out to sea. The blubber was cut away, rendered in the kettles of a "try-works" set up on the beach and transformed into a high-quality oil which could be burned in the town's lamps or traded. Soon such business became an industry *(see box)*.

Watery highways

In colonial times, overland routes were expensive to build and maintain, so coastal freighters and passenger boats carried colonists and their wares from Boston to New York and Philadelphia. Dozens of boats out of Salem harbor headed for home with decks full of salt cod. The more enterprising captains headed south, where they unloaded their cod at Philadelphia or Annapolis and took on corn and flour, beans, and barrels of pork, which could be sold at a greater profit at home than could codfish. New England never produced such goods in sufficient quantities; cod it had in great abundance.

Though a boon to New England's maritime economy, the coastal trade, like fishing and whaling, was not an easy way to make a living. Every trip between Boston and ports to the south

HOW THE WHALERS' OIL LIT UP THE CAPITALS OF EUROPE

The demand for whale oil became so great that fishermen, hoping to get rich from its sale, began to pursue whales along the shore, thus initiating New England's whaling industry. The trade took a great leap forward in 1712, when Captain Christopher Hussey of Nantucket was blown off course into deep water and accidentally bagged the first sperm whale. Although it had teeth in lieu of coveted baleen – bony upper jaw slats useful as stays for collars and corsets – the spermaceti oil proved far superior to that of the already endangered "right" whale (so called because it was the right one to pursue). Nantucket whalers came to specialize in the pursuit of this purer, lighter, and more profitable oil.

Whalers out of Nantucket and New Bedford pursued their mammoth quarry for months, even years, as far as the Pacific, until their holds were filled with barrels of the oil that would fire the nation's lamps and illumine the capitals of Europe. The whaling ships themselves served as complete processing plants.

Until 1859, when petroleum was discovered in Pennsylvania and distillers began producing kerosene, the sea was the world's great proven oil reserve. For a closer look at this fascinating chapter in maritime history, see the last surviving whaler, the *Charles W. Morgan*, tied up at Mystic Seaport in Connecticut, or visit the whaling museums in Nantucket or New Bedford.

involved a voyage around Cape Cod, and the weather that had so discouraged the Pilgrims was a constant threat. Ships and men were regularly lost to the ravages of the sea.

Though fishing and the coastal trade helped New England employ its people and pay its bills, the region was not a rich one. Because it always imported more goods than it exported, ways had to be found to reduce the trade deficit.

Merchants and sea captains from New England towns saw themselves as the world's transport agents: if they couldn't produce the goods from their rocky soil and primitive industries, they reasoned, at least they could carry across the oceans

brought home art treasures, luxury goods, and curiosities from exotic destinations. The Peabody-Essex Museum of Salem *(see page 141)* is filled with the wealth that came to New England on returning merchant ships.

Clocks, shoes, and ice

As time went by, the new republic developed industries that produced goods for trade. Connecticut's household utensils, machines, clocks, pistols, and rifles, plus shoes and cloth from Rhode Island and Massachusetts, ultimately made their way around the world.

Perhaps the most ingenious export of all was

the goods produced by others. New England merchant vessels undertook long and arduous voyages to Europe, Africa, and the Orient. And it was not only the cargoes that were put up for sale: the ships themselves were frequently on the auctioning block, bringing added revenue to their builders back home in New England.

Trade was good to the region. While the pioneer towns of inland America were primitive and rough, New England seaports took on the polish of wealth and culture. Fortunes made at sea were translated into fine mansions and patronage of the arts. From the profits of their voyages, captains

LEFT: whalers might pursue their quarry for months.
ABOVE: a mural of Mystic Seaport, Connecticut.

ice. Cut from ponds, rivers, and lakes, ice was packed in sawdust, loaded into fast clipper ships and sent off to Cuba, South America, and beyond. The rulers of the British Raj in India sipped drinks cooled by ice from New England. In exchange for a commodity that was free for the cutting, New Englanders brought back spices, fine porcelain, silks, and other items.

The taming of the sea

The war of 1812 sent New England's maritime commerce into depression, but by the mid-19th century its seaports returned to glory during the brief heyday of the clipper ship. "Never, in these United States, has the brain of man conceived, or the hand of man fashioned, so perfect a thing as the clipper ship," wrote the great Massachusetts historian Samuel Eliot Morison.

But the clippers' days were numbered, as were those of the larger, bulkier schooners carrying up to six masts, built to transport coal and other heavy loads that clippers, with their small holds, could never profitably carry. Neither clipper nor schooner could go anywhere when the wind failed – but the new steamships could travel even in a dead calm, and even keep to schedule. They could work their way around Cape Cod, ignoring the winds that had caused so much trouble since Pilgrim times. Steam also powered the new railroads that linked the Atlantic and

Pacific coasts, putting out of business the ships that had sailed all the way around South America to reach California.

Safer waves

Today, the sea is still a major source of income – and at a much lower price in lives lost to storms. Although yachts, motorboats, and fishing fleets fill the harbors, disasters at sea are a relative rarity. A century ago whole families, even most of a town, might be lost to a single ferocious storm. There are still tragedies at sea – the 1991 foundering of the *Andrea Gail*, as recounted in Sebastian Junger's 1997 book *The Perfect Storm*, was a true story – but radar, radio, and stricter safety precautions help prevent many accidents.

Cruising the coast

Perhaps the clearest indication of the taming of the sea is this: the perilous voyage undertaken by the Pilgrims in 1620 is now done for sport. Transatlantic yacht racing began in 1866 when the *Henrietta* raced the *Vesta* to England. In 1851, the schooner *America* won the Royal Yacht Squadron Cup, and the America's Cup became the great event of yachting with the first race held in Newport in 1870. The beauty and science of yacht design and racing is pursued passionately in Newport and in dozens of other ports along the coast.

New England's waters are particularly suited to yachting: Long Island, off the coast of Connecticut, protects spacious Long Island Sound; and Cape Cod Bay has provided calm sailing ever since the days of the Pilgrims. With the cutting of the Cape Cod Canal and the establish-

HOW THE SEA HAS BEEN TAMED TO SERVICE TOURISM

In previous centuries, a New Englander either went to sea to earn a living, or remained a landlubber. But now New England's seacoast has become a major playground, and the variety of maritime sports seems limitless. As in so many other realms, the world of work has become the world of play, and places once associated solely with danger and hardship are visited just for fun.

A hundred years ago, for example, "wreckers" used to trudge the beaches of New England with a keen eye for the remains of lost ships. Today, the beaches serve a distinctly different purpose. Forty miles (64 km) of Cape Cod's sandy beaches have been set aside as the Cape Cod National Seashore, one of the great tourist attractions of New Eng-

land. The beaches of Connecticut, Rhode Island, New Hampshire, and Maine continue to attract visitors.

Today, reliable ferries carry vacationers to Nantucket, Martha's Vineyard, Block Island, and the outer islands along the Maine coast. Tourists stroll among the handsome sea captains' houses, and explore in museums the world of the seafaring men who built them.

The whalers that sailed out of New Bedford and Nantucket are long gone. Yet boats from a dozen ports still head out each day in search of whales, but now it's tourists' cameras, not harpoons, that are aimed at them. It's strange that the leviathans that once made New England "oil-rich" should still be helping its economy.

ment of the Intra-coastal Waterway, coastal cruising has been made safer and more enjoyable than ever before.

The high point of coastal cruising in New England is a run along the rocky shore of Maine. The jagged coast, cut with bays, inlets, coves, peninsulas, and islands, is some 3,500 miles (5,600 km) long, and blessed with exceptional beauty. One of the most thrilling ways to see it is aboard a windjammer out of Rockport or Camden. Since 1935, these sturdy sailing ships have taken amateur crews out into the cold waters to experience New England's maritime heritage at first hand.

began to show up in restaurants and supermarkets. Others reluctantly sold their boats, and took government subsidies for job retraining.

Regulation has met with some success, although many fear that cod can never be restored to anything like their former abundance. But one thing is certain: the waterfront taverns of Gloucester are no place to praise the work of conservationists or fisheries biologists.

Northern New England's legendary lobster fleet still finds a copious catch, though captains now must venture into deeper waters. Boaters along the coast will often see the colorful bobbing floats that mark the location of the fish-baited traps on

Still a working sea

By the late 1980s it had become clear to lawmakers that the New England fishing industry was on its way to over-fishing itself out of existence. Massachusetts fishermen of New Bedford, Provincetown and Gloucester were forced to go farther and farther out to catch fewer and fewer fish. Although many fishermen – a fiercely independent lot – disagreed, laws were enacted to monitor the once fertile fishing banks. Some fishermen trained their sights on more abundant, less glamorous fish: formerly overlooked species

LEFT: "widow's walks" were built on top of sea-facing houses so that sailors' wives could watch for their husbands' return. **ABOVE:** today's leisure cruising.

the bottom; each captain has his own float design. Captain Linda Greenlaw's 2002 book *The Lobster Chronicles* provides a first-hand account of of the lobster fishery.

Long Island Sound's lobster populations, have crashed, possibly because of warming waters; blue crabs, however, are now filling a niche in the Sound. Mainers have taken to fishing for crabs, too; the species pursued in their colder waters is the Jonah, or Peekytoe. Soft-shell "steamer" clams are dug from coastal mudflats, while dredgers take scallops and hard-shell quahog clams offshore. Even though the codfish has yielded to the computer as the most important element in New England's economic life, the sea still plays a central role. ❑

THE PURITAN TRADITION

The acerbic journalist H. L. Mencken quipped that a Puritan is someone tormented by the fact that somebody, somewhere, is having fun. To what extent does the settlers' austere mind-set influence life in New England today?

The Puritans did more than settle New England; they created it. Yet today people laud the optimism of the Pilgrims, not the values of the Puritans, and employ puritanism as a pejorative term denoting an excess of zeal in pursuing rigid ideas of morality and law. Nor is this a 21st-century judgment: in 1917 the writer H. L. Mencken dismissed puritanism as "all that's unattractive about American culture, compounded over time by evangelism, moralism from political demagogues, and relentless money-grubbing."

Certainly, the creed was not a cozy one. Out of the Calvinistic doctrines regarding humanity's inherent evil and the predestination of the soul grew a society that was stern and uncompromising. At its best, the Puritans' dogma was a hard one, an ultimate faith that required everyone –

The early Puritans' moralism and sense that they were an elect people guided by God can still be sensed in social and environmental campaigners.

from the most prominent minister to the humblest child – to strain toward an ineffable God.

Puritans argued that humans, in their fallen state, could never know God and could thus never truly know the state of their own souls. Salvation came not through human action, but through God's mysterious grace. Abject though we human creatures may be, we must always examine our conscience, always repent our inevitable sin, always attempt to lead a just life.

Spiritual values

The Puritans' difficult faith stood them in good stead: regarding discipline and hard work as spiritual values, these early settlers labored long for

the greater glory of God – and incidentally accumulated considerable wealth and built prosperous communities. At their worst, the Puritans came to identify worldly success with godliness, nonconformity with devil-worship. Their faith found little room for gentleness or pleasure.

In America, as in England, class distinctions were important. But the Puritans, eschewing such worldly signs of status as expensive clothes and fancy carriages, had to devise other more subtle ways of indicating social class. Thus, the title "Master" was reserved exclusively for educated men.

The search for perfection

Education was essential to the Puritans' vision of what their new society in America was to be. Most of the settlers were well educated; four officers of the Massachusetts Bay Colony – John Winthrop, Sir Richard Saltonstall, Isaac Johnson, and John Humphrey – had attended Cambridge University. For them, the journey to the New World was more than an adventure to a new frontier; it was a chance to transport their old society in purified form to a new land. Discontented in a country where they were persecuted for their religious practices, they came to America to build an ideal society, their "city on a hill." These men knew that unless they provided for the education of clergymen, they might quickly lose sight of the New (and perfect) England.

A society in which education established one's

lege in 1636. Harvard was the first of a succession of New England colleges founded upon strong religious foundations but destined to provide a secular education for future generations *(see pages 72, 124).*

The witch hunts

In the mid-1600s, when the fever for witch-killing blew across the North Atlantic from Europe, the colonies of Rhode Island, Connecticut and Massachusetts joined the pack with decrees of death. Connecticut quickly seized and executed nine victims. Bostonians hanged Margaret Jones of Charlestown on a bright June day in 1648, and for

credentials before God and the world was destined to develop an impressive school system. As early as 1635, Boston voted a declaration that "our brother, Mr Philemon Pormont shall be intreated to become scholemaster for teaching and noutering of children with us."

Pormont established Boston Latin School, the country's first secondary school and still one of Boston's finest high schools. And with the goal of educating a native New England ministry still in view, Massachusetts Bay Colony officials chartered the institution that was to become Harvard Col-

LEFT: John Winthrop, the Puritan leader who aimed to build an ideal society. **ABOVE:** the idealized *First Thanksgiving* (1914) by Jennie Augusta Brownscombe.

an encore on Boston Common they hanged the beautiful and cultured Anne Hibbins, widow of the colony's former representative to England.

Against that lunatic background, the fanatical Rev. Cotton Mather sensed a great opportunity for self-promotion and professional success. He was already the colony's most highly acclaimed clergyman. He was learned, brilliant, ambitious, but he yearned for more. He longed to succeed his father, the Rev. Increase Mather, as the president of Harvard. He decided it would boost his reputation and enhance his career if he could identify assorted witches and promote their executions. So he went to work and soon focused on a witch-suspect named Goodwife Glover, the mother of a North End laundress. With Mather's help, poor Mrs Glover quickly wound up in the noose of a Boston Common gallows rope.

The most notorious expression of religious hysteria emerged in the Salem witch trials of 1692 which the playwright Arthur Miller described as "one of the strangest and most awful chapters in human history." The trials grew from the feverish imaginations of adolescent girls who became swept up in tales of voodoo and mysticism as told to them by Tituba, a slavewoman from Barbados. All too eager to discover depravity in someone else, the Puritans sat in eager judgment on the accused. Unrelenting in their desire to purge their world of evil and in their arrogant belief in their own righteousness, they sent 20 innocent people to their death *(see page 143)*.

Arthur Miller's celebrated play The Crucible, *based on the Salem witch trials of 1692, still seemed strangely relevant when first produced in 1953.*

Cradle of reformation

As if to live down the small-mindedness of their predecessors, the New England philosophers and legislators of the 19th century stood in the very vanguard of political reform. Having abolished slavery themselves by the end of the 18th century, high-minded New Englanders dedicated themselves to nationwide abolition. William Lloyd Garrison founded his weekly newspaper the *Liberator* in Boston in 1831 (not all shared his views at that time: he was nearly killed by a Boston mob in 1835) and persisted until 1865, when the 13th amendment was finally passed. Joining him in the struggle were writers such as Harriet Beecher Stowe, who delivered one of the Abolitionist movement's most effective tracts in the form of her best-selling 1852 novel, *Uncle Tom's Cabin*.

After the Civil War, New England's reformists turned their attention to the labor abuses brought on by the Industrial Revolution and to the role of women in society. The first women's college to open in the US was Vassar Female College, founded in Poughkeepsie, New York, in 1861. By 1879, four outstanding colleges for women had been established in Massachusetts: Smith, Wellesley, Mount Holyoke, and Radcliffe.

Despite this growing willingness to entertain

THE TRANSCENDENTALISTS WHO PURSUED UTOPIA

The gradual liberalization of New England's churches and colleges in the 18th century gave way to a true intellectual flowering in the 19th century. Flushed with the success of the Revolutionary War and the founding of a nation that was growing prosperous from the lucrative China trade, the Puritan temperament was ready for an overhaul, perhaps even a transformation.

Many New Englanders were embracing the doctrines of Unitarianism, which taught that God was a single rather than tripartite entity, and rejected such old Calvinist mainstays as predestination and the innate baseness of the human personality. Henry Ware, who founded Harvard's Divinity School in 1819, was a Unitarian, as was the great Boston pastor William Ellery Channing. Unitarianism's liberal cast of thought prepared the ground for the sweet optimism of transcendentalism, a mystical philosophy which argued the existence of an Oversoul unifying all creation, and which preached the primacy of insight over reason and the inherent goodness of humankind.

The movement spawned several experiments in living, the best known being Henry David Thoreau's solitary retreat on Walden Pond, and short-lived communal farms at Brook Farm in Concord and Fruitlands in Harvard, Massachusetts. Led by Ralph Waldo Emerson, the movement attracted some of the brightest minds of the day. Today, at transcendentalists.com, its ideas inhabit the internet.

change – reinforced by decades of stability and prosperity – remnants of the Puritan strain persisted. For the most part, New England remained a deeply moral, and occasionally moralistic, society. At their worst, New Englanders suppressed books they deemed offensive to public taste, and considered theater – and, worse yet, actors – a pernicious influence on impressionable minds. "Banned in Boston" entered the language.

The demon drink

Blue laws, first introduced in Connecticut in 1781 to control public and private conduct, especially on the Sabbath, enjoyed regular revivals in the cold hand of Puritanism in each new dictum about what we should and shouldn't eat. But New England wasn't going to get settled by people out to have fun; the soil and the climate would not have cooperated. On the credit side, Puritan legal principles helped craft the Constitution, with its emphasis on the supremacy of law.

As for the Puritan sense of rectitude and moral improvement, it survives today in activist movements – strong in new England – dedicated to social change and promoting environment-friendly policies. Ironically, the Puritans' conservative zeal lives on in what has become one of the country's most progressive regions.   ❑

19th and 20th centuries and to this day you cannot buy alcohol in the state on Sundays, except in restaurants. In Massachusetts, would-be imbibers must wait till noon to purchase alcohol on Sundays, and large retail stores may not open on Thanksgiving and Christmas. Yet the evils of alcohol were seen in a more nuanced light by Increase Mather, who wrote: "Drink is in itself a good creature of God, and to be received with thankfulness, but the abuse of drink is from Satan."

What, then, is the true Puritan legacy? It's easy to grumble about arcane liquor laws, or to see the

LEFT: the influential Puritan minister and educator, Rev. Increase Mather (1639–1723). **ABOVE:** the witch trials were conducted in an atmosphere of hysteria.

WHERE DEMOCRACY HAS TEETH

Town meetings were central to the social and political structures of the Puritan settlers. A serious attempt was made to introduce a high degree of participation and, although this could produce outbursts of extreme intolerance, the principle is still pursued. Getting agreement for an annual budget can be a nightmare for a town manager in many New England towns as public meetings packed with ferociously articulate local taxpayers take the proposals apart. It is not uncommon for a budget to be rejected twice before the level of spending is sufficiently reduced to placate the cost-conscious citizens. Local issues from liquor licencing to dog fouling in public parks can generate considerable heat at public debates.

THE LITERARY TRADITION

The fascination with the supernatural that inspired
Cotton Mather in the 17th century is echoed
today in the work of Stephen King

The Massachusetts Bay Colony was barely 10 years old when its first printing press turned out a new edition of the Book of Psalms. The 1640 *Bay Psalm Book* represented not only the beginning of American printing, but, as it was a fresh translation, of American literature as well. Along with Scriptures and sermons, 17th-century New England writers favored histories and biographies extolling the Puritan experiment.

The religious strain in early New England writing is nowhere more pronounced than in Nathaniel Ward's *The Simple Cobbler of Agawam* (1647). Ward, a minister at the Massachusetts town of Ipswich (then Agawam), sounded the clarion note of Puritan intolerance with his words: "If the devil have his free option, I believe he would ask nothing else, but liberty to enfranchise all false religions."

The sacred and the secular

Increase Mather was a prolific writer who used historical narrative to elevate – or at least frighten – the New England faithful. In *An Essay for the Recording of Illustrious Providences* (1684) he told of the Devil tormenting Massachusetts villagers, and credited a Connecticut River flood as "an awful intimation of Divine displeasure." His son, Cotton Mather, was author of more than 400 works, and a dogged chronicler of supernatural manifestations. His 1689 *Memorable Providences, Relating to Witchcrafts and Possessions* helped set the stage for the 1692 Salem witch hysteria.

Although the early 18th century in New England is remembered as the age of Reverend Jonathan Edwards and his staunch religious orthodoxy – his famous 1741 sermon "Sinners in

PIONEERING POETS

New England produced two poets of merit in the 17th century. Anne Bradstreet, who arrived with the first settlers of Boston in 1630, collected her early work in *The Tenth Muse Lately Sprung Up in America* (1650). After relying on British models and stock poetic themes laced with religion, she later found inspiration in her own life experiences.

Edward Taylor, a Massachusetts pastor, was the finest 17th-century American poet. His religious meditations have been compared to the English metaphysical poetry of his era; and his observations on commonplace subjects, as in "To a Spider Catching A Fly," reveal a talent for observation and terse description that transcends their purpose as religious metaphor.

the Hands of an Angry God" must have made his congregation's blood run cold – it was also an era in which secular concerns became a part of the colonial life of letters. In Boston, James Franklin (brother of Benjamin) published one of New England's first successful newspapers, the *New England Courant*, beginning in 1721. The *Courant* introduced the urbane essay style of Addison and Steele to the American colonies. Isaiah Thomas began publishing his *Massachusetts Spy* in 1770, airing revolutionary sentiments.

The early Federal period was the age of the "Connecticut Wits," a coterie noted for their Federalist politics and fondness for formal Augustan

William Cullen Bryant was still a New Englander when, in 1811, he wrote the first draft of his poem "Thanatopsis" (published 1817, expanded 1821) at the age of 17. "Thanatopsis" (Greek for "a view of death") is noteworthy not only for reflecting the new romantic feeling in English poetry, but for presaging the influential role that nature would play in the Transcendentalist movement of the coming decades.

The Golden Age

The era which critic Van Wyck Brooks called "the flowering of New England" began with the 1836 publication of an essay called "Nature," by Ralph

poetry. Among them were lawyers John Trumbull and Joel Barlow, and longtime Yale president Timothy Dwight. The best remembered of their works is Barlow's *The Hasty Pudding*, a mock-heroic tribute to the simple cornmeal concoction that still appears on New England menus as "Indian Pudding."

Although he made his fame in New York City as a newspaper editor, Massachusetts-born

LEFT: Cotton Mather, author of more than 400 works. **ABOVE:** an 1875 literary portrait in Boston includes Oliver Wendell Holmes (standing on left), and (left to right, seated) John Greenleaf Whittier, Ralph Waldo Emerson, John Lothrop Motley, Nathaniel Hawthorne, and Henry Wadsworth Longfellow.

Waldo Emerson, a young clergyman from Concord, Massachusetts. Emerson, a Unitarian, found in that denomination's liberal humanism a cornerstone for the philosophy of Transcendentalism. The Transcendental movement emphasized the unity of the individual soul with the rest of creation and with the divine; its principles informed Emerson's poetry and essays such as "Self-Reliance," as well as the work of Bronson Alcott (father of *Little Women* author Louisa May Alcott), Margaret Fuller, and Jones Very.

Emerson owned land just outside Concord, on Walden Pond, and it was here that his friend Henry David Thoreau built a cabin and spent two years living the life of rustic simplicity and contemplation which he chronicled in *Walden* (1854).

Thoreau coupled the Transcendentalists' near-mystical sense of the oneness of man and nature with a naturalist's eye for observation, as in *A Week on the Concord and Merrimack Rivers* and *The Maine Woods*; and with the fierce independence of conscience that blazes in his seminal essay "Civil Disobedience."

Fireside entertainment

Even if no longer strictly Puritan in their theology, New Englanders like Thoreau brought the Puritan's moral rectitude to the greatest national drama of their day, the struggle over slavery. The abolitionist movement had deep roots in New

England, home of William Lloyd Garrison and his uncompromising newspaper *The Liberator*, of *Uncle Tom's Cabin* (1852) author Harriet Beecher Stowe, and of John Greenleaf Whittier, a Quaker poet devoted to the cause. Whittier, though, is today remembered less as an abolitionist than as one of the "fireside poets" of the post-Civil War years. Working in genres such as the pastoral (Whittier's 1866 "Snow-Bound") and historical narrative (Henry Wadsworth Longfellow's "Evangeline" and "The Song of Hiawatha," published respectively in 1847 and 1855), these now largely neglected figures gave their contemporaries a common popular literature, often read aloud at the fireside. Theirs was a genteel tradition sustained by writers such as Oliver Wendell Holmes, Sr., a prolific poet and author of the droll essays collected in *The Autocrat of the Breakfast-Table* (1858).

One of the finest New England poets lived a secluded life in Amherst, Massachusetts, far from literary salons. Emily Dickinson had a gemcutter's way with language, crafting nearly 1,800 short lyric poems in which sharp observation of the material world was a prism for the timeless and universal. She shunned publication, and the first volume of her work didn't appear until 1890 – four years after her death.

The two New England giants of American literature in the mid-19th century defy any association with a school or movement of their day. Nathaniel Hawthorne *(see panel)* had an early

LEFT: statue of Nathaniel Hawthorne in his native Salem. **RIGHT:** the enduring image of *Moby-Dick*, and its author Herman Melville.

NATHANIEL HAWTHORNE

The descendant of Salem Puritans, Hawthorne (1804–64) grew up with a family legend of a Judge Hawthorne who, as a magistrate at the witchcraft trials, was cursed by a woman he convicted. Hawthorne would later use this story in *The House of the Seven Gables*.

In fact, much of Hawthorne's darkly romantic work was drawn from real life. In the 1836 tale, *The Minister's Black Veil*, the protagonist explains: "If I hide my face for sorrow, there is cause enough, and if I cover it for secret sin, what mortal might not do the same." Hawthorne was no doubt familiar with the story of the Rev. Joseph Moody of York, Maine, who, after accidentally shooting and killing a friend on a hunting trip, became morbidly frightened of having his

friend's family and fiancée look upon him, and therefore covered his face with a black handkerchief.

Young Goodman Brown, one of Hawthorne's greatest tales, also draws on his Salem heritage. In what may be a dream, Brown, wandering in the dark forest, comes upon the devil, who leads him to a clearing where villagers are engaged in devil-worship; among the congregation is Faith, Goodman's wife. In this tale, Hawthorne depicts a world sunk in evil: if Goodman Brown's vision is true, the devil rules; if not, and if Goodman has imagined innocent people in Satan's service, he reveals, like the Salem Puritans, the depth of his own corruption.

His birthplace in Salem can be visited *(see page 141)*.

flirtation with Transcendentalism and radical communalism (his *The Blithedale Romance* is based in part on the Brook Farm commune is Massachusetts), but he was far too independent a figure to fit comfortably into the Concord where he spent part of his early career. Hawthorne mined the annals and mores of Puritan New England for the themes of guilt and consequence that inform *The Scarlet Letter* (1850) and *The House of the Seven Gables* (1851). His short stories, many deeply allegorical, are often set in a mythic Puritan past.

Herman Melville *(see panel below)* was born in New York City, but spent much of his working life in New England. His masterpiece, *Moby-Dick*, employs the New England settings of New Bedford and Nantucket, both important whaling ports in the 19th century.

Indian Summer

The post-Civil War "Indian Summer" of New England literature was the era of William Dean Howells, a midwesterner who edited *The Atlantic Monthly* and made Boston the setting of *A Modern Instance* (1882) and *The Rise of Silas Lapham* (1885), both of which deal with men on the make in a city flush with prosperity.

Henry James (1843–1916), who was in his

HERMAN MELVILLE

At the age of 20, Melville set sail on a packet to Liverpool in England, and two years later, in 1841, traveled to the South Seas on the whaler *Acushnet*. Although he later jumped ship to join the US Navy, it was to be a life-changing voyage, for it provided him with his first successful books, *Typee or a Peep at Polynesian Life* (1846) and *Omoo: A Narrative of Adventures in the South Seas* (1847).

He married Elizabeth Shaw, whose father was chief justice of Massachusetts, and they had four children. He continued to write sea stories, mostly because he needed to earn money, but he was inspired by the dark genius of Nathaniel Hawthorne to attempt the epic narrative that became *Moby-Dick, or The Whale* (1851). This masterpiece,

written while he was living in Pittsfield, Massachusetts, draws upon the character of Yankee whalers Melville met during his own time in the "fishery" but the tale of Captain Ahab's relentless pursuit of the whale that had bitten off his leg assumes allegorical overtones as the crew of the *Pequod* are carried to their doom by Ahab's monomania.

Like much of his work, *Moby-Dick* was better received in England than in America. After a breakdown, Melville visited Hawthorne in Liverpool, where Hawthorne was serving as American consul. Later he worked as a customs officer in New York harbor. He died in 1891, his work largely forgotten.

In recent years, some critics have perceived homoerotic overtones in works such as *Pierre* and *Billy Budd*.

mature period as much a British as an American writer, set many of his short stories in Boston's upper-class society, which also provided the milieu for *The Europeans* (1878) and for *The Bostonians* (1886), James's satire on the city's radical and reformist circles.

The late 1800s also saw the rise of the Regional movement in American literature, represented in New England by figures such as Sarah Orne Jewett, a novelist of coastal Maine; and Rowland Robinson, a Vermonter with a sharp ear for the dialect of upcountry Yankees and French-Canadian immigrants.

And it was an age that saw one writer who

New England family but a resident of rural Vermont and New Hampshire for much of his life, created a universal language out of dry, economical Yankee speech.

In the theater, Eugene O'Neill (1888–1953), brought up partly in Connecticut and associated as a young man with the Provincetown Players on Cape Cod, offered the bleak *Desire Under the Elms* and the uncharacteristically comic *Ah, Wilderness,* both with New England settings.

Local fiction in the 20th century ranged from John P. Marquand's skewering appraisal of the Boston Brahmin class run to ground in *The Late George Apley* (1937) to philosopher George San-

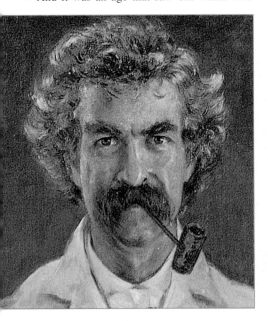

belonged to a world far from New England happily set down roots in the region: Mark Twain built a sprawling mansion in Hartford, Connecticut, and transported a representative native of the state to medieval England in *A Connecticut Yankee in King Arthur's Court.*

Modern trends

By 1900, New England had long since ceased to be the most socially and economically vigorous part of the United States, but it still provided fertile ground for writers. Edward Arlington Robinson (1869–1935) drew upon characters of his native small-town Maine to create incisive portraits of often darkly conflicted individuals. Robert Frost (1874–1963), born in California of an old

tayana's darker analysis of a similar scion of the old order in *The Last Puritan* (1936). John Cheever may have moved from his native Massachusetts to New York, but his morally struggling suburbanites traded heavily in the old New England themes of guilt and redemption; John Updike, a New Englander by choice, presented the quandaries of his characters in early novels and stories set in the suburbs of Boston. And, far from the middle class of Cheever and Updike, Jack Kerouac set several autobiographical novels in the French-Canadian quarter of his native Lowell, Massachusetts.

With its scores of colleges and universities, and its many writers' workshops, the region has attracted authors not necessarily rooted in the region and its traditional concerns. Even a small state like Vermont can boast internationally recognized names such as Julia Alvarez, Jamaica Kincaid, and David Mamet. Native or not, though, many writers fasten quickly to New England locales and themes. Boston lawyer George V. Higgins gave us the rough side of his city's life and language via *The Friends of Eddie Coyle* (1972). In *Empire Falls* (2001) Richard Russo serves up his characters in the matrix of a decaying Maine mill town. John Irving, who lives in Vermont, made the quirks of New Englanders part of *The Hotel New Hampshire* (1981) and *The Cider House Rules* (1985).

Carter's *New England White* (2007), and Philip Roth's *The Human Stain* (2001), both dealing with the complexities of race on campus; and Donna Tartt's *The Secret History* (1992), about a murder committed by precocious classicists at a bucolic Vermont college.

In the realm of literate popular reading, Robert B. Parker's Spenser detective novels have a vivid Boston setting. And, up in Bangor, in a big Victorian house behind an iron fence festooned with bats and spiderwebs, lives a native son who uses nondescript Maine settings while scaring his readers out of their wits. His name is Stephen King.   ❏

Howard Frank Mosher, also a Vermonter, lovingly portrays the vanishing world of the backcountry yeomen and eccentrics of the state's remote Northeast Kingdom in *Where the Rivers Flow North* (1978), *Northern Borders* (1994), and *On Kingdom Mountain* (2007). Another Vermont author, Chris Bohjalian, has set moral dilemmas in small-towns in novels such as *Midwives* (1996) and *The Law of Similars* (1998).

New England academia has provided the setting for works such as Yale professor Stephen L.

FAR LEFT: Mark Twain, wit and master storyteller.
LEFT: John Irving with the Oscar he won for adapting his novel *The Cider House Rules* for Hollywood.
ABOVE: Stephen King, pictured with bike in 1986.

STEPHEN KING'S MAINE

King, who has sold more than 350 million books, has done for his native Maine, say critics, what Dickens did for Victorian London, and fans of the prolific writer have fun trying to identify the real-life locations that turn up, thinly disguised, in his creepy tales. Indeed, there's a nascent Stephen King Trail, taking in Kezar Lake, near Lovell (Dark Score Lake in *Bag of Bones)*, Bridgton (setting for *The Mist* and *The Body)*, Hampden *(Carrie)*, Orrington *(Pet Sematary)*, Long Lake *(The Shining)* and Durham *(Salem's Lot)*. King, born in 1947, has a summer lodge near Lovell and an old lumber baron's mansion near Bangor (a town disguised as Derry in *IT)*. To locate the mansion, look for a locked gate decorated with a bronze vampire.

THE TRADITION OF EDUCATION

What cars are to Detroit, so colleges are to Boston.
Not only do they help give New England its character,
they also bring in billions of dollars a year

New England is the cradle of American education, and the home of many of the nation's oldest and most distinguished institutions of higher learning. Four of the colleges and universities that make up the storied "Ivy League" – Harvard, Yale, Brown, and Dartmouth – are located here, as are scores of smaller colleges and six respected state universities. But although the popular perception of education in New England tends to focus on the most elite collegiate institutions, the region's commitment to learning began at a far humbler level.

In an age when literacy was largely a luxury, the religious reformers who created the first settlements in New England firmly believed that every church member – every citizen, in other words – should be able to read Scripture. By 1639, Boston and its neighboring communities of Charlestown and Dorchester had hired schoolmasters. By 1672, every colony except Rhode Island had adopted systems of compulsory elementary education.

In 1636, the Great and General Court of Massachusetts Bay had appropriated the sum of £400

John Harvard left his library of 400 books and half of his estate to the new college, which would thereafter bear his name (*see box, right*).

Yale's beginnings

In Connecticut, a group of 10 clergymen met in 1701 to found an institution called the "Collegiate School," which was located at first in Saybrook but in 1716 moved to the larger community of New Haven. Their impetus was in part a reaction against the perceived liberalization of the Harvard curriculum. The Collegiate School, too, soon benefited from a philanthropic gesture – not from the

In New York, said Mark Twain, they ask how much money a man has; in Philadelphia, what family he's from; in Boston, how much he knows.

for "a schoale or colledge," which was established the following year at New Town, across the Charles River from Boston. The first class assembled two years later, and around the same time New Town was renamed Cambridge in honor of the English University city.

In that same year of 1638, a young minister in nearby Charlestown died of consumption. Rev.

ABOVE: fencing lesson at Yale in the early 20th century.
RIGHT: serious study at Boston Public Library.

modest will of a churchman but from an immensely wealthy, Boston-born ex-governor of the East India Company. His name was Elihu Yale, and so generous were his donations to New Haven's fledgling school that it was named in his honor in 1718.

New England's third-oldest college was the fruit of a growing ecumenical spirit. It isn't surprising that a representative of the relatively new Baptist sect should have chosen to establish a college in Rhode Island, a colony devoted from its infancy to religious freedom. Rev. James Manning secured a charter for a "College of Rhode Island" in 1764, arranging that not only

Baptists but also Congregationalists and Episcopalians would be represented in its corporation. Established on its College Hill campus in Providence by 1770, the college counted among its 1783 class of 15 graduates Nicholas Brown, Jr., son of one of the four Brown brothers who dominated Rhode Island commerce in that era. Nicholas Jr. would give his alma mater some $160,000 over his lifetime. Hence the institution's new name, from 1804 onward – Brown University.

One of the more unlikely locations for a college in the 18th century was the New Hampshire wilderness. In the 1760s, one Rev. Eleazar

HOW HARVARD MADE ITS MARK

Although it was technically not a religious but a civic institution, Harvard College served primarily to train ministers throughout the 17th century – a century which saw only 465 documented graduates. It wasn't until 1708 that a layman was elected president. Harvard's greatest strides were taken during the four-decade presidency of Charles William Eliot (1869–1909), who introduced the elective system, modernized the teaching of law and medicine, and created a graduate school of arts and sciences. Born into an old Boston family himself, Eliot did more than any Harvard educator to elevate the university beyond its onetime status as a school largely attended by the local Brahmin class.

Wheelock was looking for a place to relocate a Christian school for Indians which he had established in Connecticut. Having secured a pledge of £11,000 and the patronage of the Earl of Dartmouth, Wheelock's next step was to find a community that wanted the school. The most eager candidate was tiny Hanover, New Hampshire, which offered 3,000 acres (1,200 hectares). The school, Dartmouth College, received its royal charter in 1769.

Years later, Dartmouth adopted as its motto the Latin phrase *Vox Clamantis in Deserto* ("A Voice Crying in the Wilderness"), an apt suggestion of what the place must have been like in its earliest years, when classes were held in a log cabin. Rev. Wheelock's Indians never

> *"William F. Buckley Jr. once remarked that he would rather be governed by the first 100 names in the Boston telephone book than by the faculty of Harvard University."*
> —*Richard Nixon*, The Real War *(1980)*

showed up in significant numbers, but Dartmouth did attract upcountry New England boys, for whom Boston or New Haven might have been too far away. One of them, Daniel Webster (class of 1801), would one day defend Dartmouth in a charter dispute that threatened the school's existence. It was this case that inspired

Webster's famous statement, "It is a small college, but yet there are those who love it."

Thinking small

New England is peppered with the campuses of small and not so small colleges beloved by many – Bowdoin in Maine, Middlebury in Vermont, and Amherst and Williams in Massachusetts are the nucleus of an informal "Little Ivy League" that shares the standards if not the breadth of graduate offerings of its larger counterpart. The region also pioneered in higher education for women, with Radcliffe (now integrated with Harvard), Smith, Wellesley, and Mount Holyoke all having 19th-century roots. That century also saw the rise of the great public universities; each

New England state supports one, with the University of Vermont (1791) occupying an unusual semi-private status. The Jesuit institutions Boston College and College of the Holy Cross (Massachusetts) and Fairfield University (Connecticut) are among the leaders in church-sponsored higher education.

New England also played a major role in the development of scientific education, with the Massachusetts Institute of Technology enrolling its first students in 1865. Originally located in Boston, MIT now occupies an expansive campus along the Charles River in Cambridge. The Institute's graduates have been instrumental in making Boston a hub of the computer and other high-technology industries, an eastern counterpart to California's Silicon Valley.

The funding predicament

Long before the modern era of public education began in the late 19th century, New England's village schools had multiplied and followed settlement out into the hinterlands, where the legendary "one-room schoolhouses" offered the rudiments of mathematics, language skills, and civics to rural children. An example is preserved at the Bennington Museum in Bennington, Vermont; it's the one attended by folk artist Grandma Moses as a young girl in nearby New York State, c. 1870.

Even in an era when public education largely fits a national rather than a regional mold, one strong aspect of the old colonial legacy robustly survives: a passionate grass-roots involvement in education issues. Drop in at any New England town meeting, and you'll likely hear spirited debates about school budgets, or state versus community control.

In the recent past, Vermont and New Hampshire have grappled with the problem of school funding, with courts ruling that reliance upon local property taxes is unfair to children in towns with meager tax bases, and that revenue-sharing systems must be initiated. Even in more populous and urban Massachusetts, where professional educators are more likely to insulate citizens from education policy decisions, there have been heated public discussions over issues such as teacher competency tests; and the question of English-only instruction actually reached the ballot box in 2002 (it won). ❑

LEFT: graduation day at Harvard University.

Sporting traditions

Ever since football was introduced to the nation on Boston Common in 1862 and basketball was devised in Springfield, Mass., in 1891, New England has trailblazed in sports.

Back when there were far fewer teams overall, Boston could boast major league teams in baseball (Red Sox and Braves), basketball (Celtics), and ice-hockey (Bruins). The Braves decamped after 1952, but football expansion led to the 1960 appearance of the Patriots.

Until recently, only the Celtics, with 17 National Basketball Association titles, and the Bruins, with five Stanley Cups in the National Hockey League, carried on a winning tradition in New England – although the Bruins haven't won the Cup since 1986, and the Celtics only ended a two-decade-long NBA title drought in 2008. That title, plus three recent Super Bowl triumphs for the Patriots, and victories for the Red Sox in the 2004 and 2007 World Series, have renewed the faith of New England fans.

The Sox won the first World Series, in 1903, and clinched it four times between then and 1918. But for the next 86 years – some say they were cursed for selling Babe Ruth to the New York Yankees – the Sox came up dry. Then came 2004, when the Sox beat the Yankees for the American League title and went on to a four-game sweep of the St Louis Cardinals in the World Series. In 2007, they similarly swept the Colorado Rockies.

The major-league Sox aren't the only professional base-

ball attraction in New England. Minor-league teams ("farm" clubs for the majors) include the Pawtocket Red Sox, Portland Sea Dogs, Lowell Spinners, and Vermont Lake Monsters – all offering a chance to watch exciting baseball in small stadiums at bargain ticket prices.

Football's once hapless Patriots won the Super Bowl in 2002, 2004 and 2005. In 2008, they came within two minutes of a fourth Super Bowl victory – but following an undefeated 2007 season, they lost a squeaker to the New York Giants.

New England teams have always been generous in turning out heroes: Ted Williams, Carl Yastrzemski, Jim Rice and Manny Ramirez in baseball; Bobby Orr and Phil Esposito in hockey; Bob Cousy, Bill Russell, and Larry Bird in basketball; and Tom Brady in football. Home-grown sports greats include Rocky Marciano of Brockton, Mass., the only undefeated heavyweight boxing champion in history; Carlton Fisk, the Red Sox catcher who made his way from small-town New Hampshire and Vermont ballfields to the Hall of Fame; and John LeClair, a Vermonter who enjoyed a stellar hockey career.

New England's college teams are followed avidly, but most have little national impact. Exceptions are Boston College (football, hockey, and basketball) and the universities of Connecticut and Vermont (basketball); Vermont also excels in hockey.

Since 1965 oarspeople from around the globe have come to Cambridge in October for the Head of the Charles, the world's biggest one-day regatta. And each Patriot's Day in April, thousands of runners compete in the celebrated Boston Marathon (tel: 617-235 4505). It's the world's oldest annual marathon, having been first run in 1897. ❏

ABOVE AND RIGHT: baseball fans and player at Fenway Park.

THE TRADITION OF GOOD FOOD

Seafood remains one of the New England classics,
but the influence of immigrants and new
traditions have been making their mark

The Pilgrims wouldn't have known what to make of our mania for lobster. They considered the crustaceans fit only for pig food, or bait; well into the 1800s, boatloads of lobsters sold for pennies, and prisoners rioted at the prospect of yet another lobster dinner. But lobster has gone upscale, and today's harvest is a lucrative enterprise. And while creative preparations abound, menus retain traditional boiled lobsters and "lobster rolls" – toasted hot dog buns filled with chunks of lobster meat, tossed with celery and mayonnaise or melted butter.

The settlers weren't quite so blind to the appeal of oysters. As early as 1601, Samuel de Champlain had singled out the area now known as Wellfleet, on Cape Cod, for its exceptional beds. He named the harbor "*Porte aux huitres*." And to this day, Wellfleet and Cotuit, on Cape Cod, are world-renowned for their oysters.

New England's fabled clam chowder got its name from the French settlers of Canada, who simmered their soups in a *chaudière* (cauldron). Such long, slow cooking is needed to render large hard-shell quahogs (pronounced "co-hogs") palatable. Small and medium-size clams – cherrystones

> The United States leads the world in per capita ice cream consumption, and New Englanders are said to eat 14 pints more of the stuff every year than the average American.

and littlenecks – are delectable served raw, on the half-shell. Soft-shell, longneck clams – commonly known as "steamers" – are a favored repast all along the coast, dipped first in their own broth (to wash off the grit), then melted butter. Clam shacks fire up their fry-o-lators to prepare another favorite: clams batter-coated or simply rolled in cornmeal and fried.

Clambakes were once a New England tradition, especially on Cape Cod. The customary procedure was to dig a pit on the beach, line it with stones, build a driftwood fire, cover the hot stones with seaweed, add clams and their accompaniments (typically, lobsters, potatoes, corn on the cob), and then top it all off with more seaweed, a sailcloth tarp, and plenty of sand, leaving the whole to bake for about an hour. Most restaurants these days dispense with clambake *per se*, and just serve what's called a "shore dinner" – steamed.

It was the abundant cod, however, that initially lured English fishermen, and eventually settlers, to this land. Fillet of young cod, called scrod (from the Dutch *schrood*, for "a piece cut off"), still graces traditional menus.

Exposure to European traditions has introduced two relatively new seafood treats. Mussels, long ignored by New England restaurants, are now very nearly ubiquitous, usually served *marinière* or poached in white wine. Seasonal bay scallops have always enjoyed greater gourmet cachet than the larger, tougher sea scallop but, until recently, restaurants invariably threw away the tastiest part, serving only the adductor muscle. Bay scallops are now available year-round, and the more adventurous fine

commonly found nowadays on breakfast menus influenced by French Canadians in northern Maine and New Hampshire. For dessert, try Indian pudding, based on cornmeal and molasses, or grape-nut ice cream, made with the crunchy cereal. And New England might be the home of America's favorite comfort food: Louis' Lunch in New Haven, Connecticut claims to have invented the hamburger.

Bright berries from the bogs

Cranberries – so named by Dutch settlers who thought the flowers resembled cranes – are one of the few fruits native to North America (others

restaurants have begun serving them whole, on the half-shell or cooked.

Northern comfort

Not all New England culinary standards come from the sea. This is the land of Yankee pot roast, still found on the menus of traditional restaurants specializing in "comfort food." Made today with fresh beef, it's a throwback to the days when families got through winter by hunkering over hearth-simmered pots of preserved beef and root vegetables.

Boston has its famous baked beans, more

include Concord grapes and blueberries, a cash crop in Maine). Native Americans used the sassamanesh – "bitter berries" – as a dye, a poultice, and as food, pounded with fat and dried venison to make "pemmican" or sweetened with maple sap. Long before Vitamin C was lauded, whalers would set off to sea with a barrel of cranberries to prevent scurvy. Today, visitors can tour Massachusetts cranberry bogs and celebrate fall festivals from Plymouth to Nantucket.

Maple syrup

New Englanders have also continued the Indian practice of boiling maple sap into syrup, and Vermont is America's leading producer of maple syrup. The trees of the "sugarbush" are tapped in

LEFT: Cape Cod is world-renowned for its oysters.
ABOVE: serving since 1868 in Boston's theater district.

early spring, when just the right combination of cold nights and warm days sets the thin sap rising. However modern the equipment, it still takes 40 gallons of sap to boil down to just one gallon of syrup. Visitors can watch the process at commercial sugar houses.

Specialty products

A new wave of "back-to-landers" has created a trendy land of plenty, raising deer for venison, goats for farmstead chèvre, trout and salmon for smoking. In Connecticut, the actor Paul Newman has followed up on his "Newman's Own" salad dressing success with lines of pasta sauce, popcorn, fig bars, and other foodstuffs – with all profits going to charity. In Vermont, specialty food producers whip up everything from "Putney pasta" to salsa and tortilla chips; the entrepreneurs behind Ben & Jerry's ice cream empire, in Waterbury, parlayed a $5 correspondence school diploma into a business grossing more than $200 million a year. When Ben & Jerry's was sold to Unilever in 2000, many Vermonters reacted as if outsiders had bought Mount Mansfield.

Despite its relatively short growing season, New England has become a center for the "locavore" movement, which stresses the environ-

WHY BEER MAINTAINS A PILGRIM TRADITION

With safe drinking water no certainty in close-packed settlements, the Pilgrims, adults and children alike, drank beer – the alcohol content kept the microbes in check. Today they could travel around New England and never wander far from a microbrewery. Popular regional beer makers include Vermont's Long Trail, Magic Hat, Catamount, Rock Art, Trout River, and Wolaver's (organic); New Hampshire's Old Man Ale and Smuttynose; Maine's Allagash, Shipyard, and Katahdin; and Massachusetts' Boston Beer Company (makers of Sam Adams), Ipswich, Harpoon, and Atlantic Coast (home of Tremont brews). Many of these producers open their doors to visitors.

It's even possible to find good locally produced wine.

Many vineyards are still in the fledgling stage, but several have a proven track record: Stonington Vineyards in Stonington, Connecticut; Sakonnet Vineyards in Little Compton, Rhode Island; Chicama Vineyards on Martha's Vineyard, Massachusetts; and, in Vermont, Snow Farm in South Hero and Shelburne Vineyards in Shelburne.

Apple seeds, which came to New England with the Pilgrims in 1620, contributed another popular beverage – apple cider. President John Adams claimed that a tankard of alcoholic cider every morning calmed his stomach and alleviated gas. Hard cider has enjoyed a trendy revival in the 1990s, led by New England brands such as Woodchuck from Cavendish, Vermont.

mental benefits of eating locally grown foodstuffs to avoid fossil-fuel-consuming long-distance distribution networks. Visitors can enjoy the local bounty at farmstands and farmers' markets that proliferate throughout the region from midsummer through early autumn (pick-your-own strawberries, in late June and early July, and apples in September, are special treats).

Artisan cheesemaking is all the rage in upcountry New England, particularly in Vermont. Shelburne Farms and Grafton cheddars, Bayley-Hazen and Green Mountain blue cheeses, and sheep's milk cheese from Willow Hill Farms and Three Shepherds of the Mad

Franklin Avenue – add more contemporary Italian regional cooking.

In several Rhode Island and Massachusetts cities, Portuguese-Americans have transformed the land of the bean and the cod into the home of the feijão and the bacalhau. They have popularized doughy sweet bread, spicy linguiça (pork sausage), and all manner of salt cod preparations.

Since 1960, almost 80 percent of immigrants to the US have come from Asia, Latin America, and the Caribbean. New England towns boast Chinese, Japanese, Thai, Vietnamese, Puerto Rican, Mexican, Haitian, and many other ethnic eateries, where clams in black bean sauce and

River Valley are all worth seeking out. And you'll never be far from a crusty, locally-baked loaf to enjoy them with.

New traditions

Throughout New England, flavors once considered "exotic" have entered the mainstream, propelled by immigration. The Italian immigrants of a century ago left an indelible stamp on the region's food with pizzerias and spaghetti houses, while urban enclaves – including Boston's North End, Providence's Federal Hill, and Hartford's

lobster sautéed with ginger and scallions blend local ingredients into the classic cuisines of their home countries.

On the urban cutting edge, celebrity chefs transform traditional New England products into creative new "fusion" preparations. Adventurous eaters can have salad of Maine rock crab with lobster knuckles and fried taro, crispy squash risotto cakes, pumpkin ravioli with mussels *marinière*, lightly fried lobster with lemongrass and Thai basil, or seared scallops in cider sauce.

But tradition endures. Those boiled lobsters, that baked cod, and that paper cup overflowing with fried clams, washed down with a cool frappé (that's Massachusetts-speak for milk shake), remain New England culinary favorites. ❑

LEFT: Boston's Cheers Bar, inspiration for the classic television series *Cheers* (1982–93). **ABOVE:** traditional atmosphere at the White Barn Inn at Kennebunkport.

THE DINER

New England is the true home of the classic diner, and scores of these roadside icons still draw hungry travelers in all six states

Ask anyone where the diner capital of the United States is, and they're liable to answer, "New Jersey." It's true that the Garden State is famous for shiny chrome eateries strung along busy highways, but New England claims to be the birthplace of American dinerdom.

It was in 1872 that Walter Scott began serving sandwiches and pie out of a covered horse-drawn cart in Providence, Rhode Island, picking up business from workmen and carousers who were out and about after conventional restaurants had closed. A decade later, in Massachusetts, a Worcester entrepreneur named Sam Jones took the concept one step further, adding indoor customer seating to his cart. By the 1890s, a Worcester firm was building standardized lunch carts, and selling them to mobile restaurateurs throughout New England.

Despite their lunch-on-wheels origins, it's a misconception that early diners were mostly converted railroad cars or trolleys; the idea probably came about because railway dining cars are called "diners," and because some early operators did in fact "recycle" retired streetcars. But well before 1920, most diners were stationary structures. They were delivered to their sites on wheels, but were then installed in place.

So what, exactly, is a diner? Purists insist that a true diner must be a prefabricated building, factory-built and equipped with everything needed for business – food preparation areas, serving counters, and booths, stools, or both. Factory construction meant substantial use of metal paneling inside and out, often enameled in early diners, and later taking the form of brilliant expanses of stainless steel. And although fancier modern establishments often offer extensive menus – or even gourmet specialties – a diner must first and foremost serve the staple repertoire of burgers, sandwiches, pies, and "comfort foods" such as meat loaf with gravy. And, of course, a big satisfying breakfast, washed down by oceans of good hot coffee, should be available all day long.

ABOVE: The Chelsea Royal Diner in West Brattleboro, Vermont, is a 1938 model built by the Worcester Lunch Car Company. As well as traditional all-day breakfasts (pancakes, waffles, eggs benedict), it offers Mexican fare or prime rib as evening meals.

LEFT: Unlike conventional restaurants, diners are mobi and can become museum pieces. Newport's well-know Miss Newport Diner was sol in 2003 and is now in a private Massachusetts collection

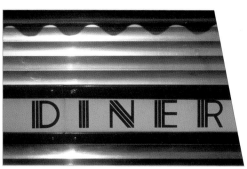

ABOVE: Presidential candidates frequently demonstrate their common touch by staging photo opportunities in diners. Here, during his successful 2008 campaign, Barack Obama raises the sartorial standards of a diner while grabbing breakfast.

THE COMPANIES BEHIND THE CLASSIC DINERS

By the middle of the 20th century, the dominant diner manufacturers were headquartered in the greater New York area. But two Massachusetts firms were instrumental in carrying on a homegrown New England tradition, and turned out some of the most distinctive of the diners that still dot the region's roadways.

The Worcester Lunch Car Company, of Worcester, started business in 1906, when diners were still lunch carts hauled, literally, by horse power. The diners of its classic period, from the 1920s through the 1940s, usually featured porcelain panels, handsome woodwork, and marble counters. Several still operate in the company's home town, where its factory – idle since the firm's closing in 1961 – stands across from the Miss Worcester Diner, one of its own creations.

Farther east, in the little Massachusetts town of Merrimac, the J. B. Judkins Company's Sterling Diners were famous for their "streamline moderne" designs, with sloping ends that resembled the latest sleek locomotives. Sterlings were made for only six years, from 1936 to 1942, but a few are still around. Pawtucket, Rhode Island's Modern Diner and Salem, Massachusetts' Salem Diner are two fine examples.

ABOVE: The restored 1920s Miss Bellows Falls Diner was moved from Massachusetts to its current Vermont location in 1942.

BELOW: Rhode Island's Modern Diner, in Pawtucket, is one of the few remaining sleek Sterling designs from the late 1930s.

BELOW: The Midway Diner in Rutland, Vermont, has been a popular truck stop since 1948. It specializes in steaks, but there's also seafood and the usual diner fare.

THE ARCHITECTURAL TRADITION

Shingles and clapboards, gables and steeples –
New England's buildings reflect the beauty
of its landscape and the practicality of its people

Buildings capture the essence of New England's character; they sum up what was at once noble and humble about the ambitions of generations of its inhabitants. And the charm of historic architecture is not lost on today's New Englanders, whose tireless efforts have preserved much of what was built in centuries past. To learn New England, read its buildings, for they tell rich tales about the lives of their builders and inhabitants.

Puritan practicality

Seventeenth-century New England homes were not built with an eye towards beauty, although there is something attractive about their stark simplicity. None of the earliest New England buildings survive, although they have been faithfully re-created at Plimoth Plantation in Plymouth, Massachusetts. Steep-gabled, almost toylike, these one-room houses look like peasants' huts in a fairy tale, and it is no wonder that their inhabitants built something more substantial as soon as they could.

What they did build – the "first period" houses, some of which have survived – are heavy and medieval, reflecting the Puritans' unaffected motivations. Stylistic vestiges of English country homes governed building design and construction, but none of these was applied solely for decorative effect: there is virtually no ornamental indulgence in the 1640 Whipple House in Ipswich or the *c.*1641 Wing Fort House in East Sandwich, both in Massachusetts.

These two houses and the handful like them were nothing more than offspring of homes the Pilgrims had left behind in southeastern England. Simple oblong boxes, they were framed painstakingly and filled with the wattle-and-daub

that on half-timbered English country homes was left visible. Clapboards, providing a blanket of protection against New England winters, created a stern look, relieved only by small, randomly placed windows. The steep roof and the massive central chimney, shared by the two lower and two upper rooms, crowned the house with an authoritative air.

In very early homes, the upper floor extended slightly beyond the lower. The 1683 Capen House in Topsfield, Massachusetts, offers a marvelous example. This overhang, recalling English townhouses where the lower floor stepped back in deference to the street, was dropped as designs began to allow for expansion and reflect the colonists' growing sense of security.

Many 17th-century meetinghouses, also unadorned and otherwise simple, remain throughout New England – the Old Ship Meetinghouse in Hingham is a fine example. The large meetinghouses often served as the village's town hall and religious nucleus, reflecting early ties between church and state.

Coming of age

With a growing sense of confidence and prosperity, the colonists began adding flourishes to their humble homes. At the turn of the 18th century, commerce was growing beyond town borders, encouraging a more adventurous spirit and a

Italian architect Andrea Palladio. In the United States, Palladian ideas spread in a new style that is as often termed Colonial as it is Georgian; the modern American landscape certainly attests to its staying power.

Symmetry, a sense of strength and a quality of ease characterize the Georgian style. (The term Georgian was derived from the three English King Georges, 1714–1820.) Georgian homes, with wood-paneled walls and broad stairways, had larger rooms and more privacy. Four full rooms both upstairs and down were the norm. Two separate chimneys serviced the two, now larger, halves of the house. These two leaner tow-

weakening of the religious principles that had dampened individual expression. Along the coast, where maritime trading and fishing were making their mark, money and exposure to influences from abroad combined to produce splendid mansions.

The Georgian style

The inspiration for the new Georgian style, as the pre-Revolutionary period of 18th-century design is known, stemmed from misfortune in England. London burned in 1666, and out of the ashes rose tributes to the classical ideas of the 16th-century

ers added to exterior elegance and richness while leaving room for a deep hallway where the massive central chimney had been.

Old Deerfield, Massachusetts, has several charming renderings of early Georgian ideals. At the north end of a marvelous mile of 18th-century historical structures stand the 1733 Ashley House and the 1743 Hawks House. While the precise Georgian proportions and details exude a calm and assurance, their dark, unpainted clapboards suggest a ruggedness absent in later painted facades. Indians were regularly raiding Deerfield, but when one's eyes rest upon these buildings, there is no sense of trepidation, and the doorways welcome visitors warmly.

By mid-century, coastal ports were very prof-

LEFT: the 1683 Capen House, Topsfield, Massachusetts.
ABOVE: classic Georgian style in Deerfield Village.

itable, as sea captains' and merchants' houses showed. Many of these were later remodeled to keep up with architectural fashions, making it difficult to find the purely Georgian. Portsmouth, New Hampshire, is blessed with unsullied originals in its 1763 Moffatt-Ladd House – as handsome as any – and the delightfully understated 1760 Wentworth-Coolidge House.

Aspects of Georgian architecture, particularly Palladian motifs, remained in the vernacular of New England design beyond the 18th century, but the style had almost run its course by the Revolutionary War. One exception is the handsome town of Litchfield, Connecticut, where pristine homes

with his dainty stucco reliefs. McIntire introduced these same embellishments to Salem, as can be seen inside the Gardner-Pingree house. Classical detailing, free-standing curved stairways and delicate fireplace mantels characterize Federal interior design.

The full impact of McIntire's work on the rest of Salem is best grasped on Chestnut Street, which in its entirety has been designated a National Historic Landmark. Up and down both sides of this majestic street are stunning Federal-style mansions, built in the early 1800s when the sea captains decided to move away a little from the noise and clutter of the port.

lining the village green compose the perfect picture of idyllic New England.

The Federal style

Following the revolution, optimism was palpable in the harbors of Salem and Boston. Even inland, whaling, shipbuilding and the expansion of trade brought the sea to many New Englanders as the coastal merchants commanded the goods and natural resources of the whole region. But no country carpenter could rival the skills of Salem's Samuel McIntire or Boston's Charles Bulfinch, whose combined work represents the finest of the period. McIntire's inspiration was Robert Adam, the Scottish architect who raised the art of interior decoration to exquisite heights

Elsewhere in Salem, a 1970s facelift not only turned around a declining city but saved many threatened Federal-era buildings and put them to new uses. A similar turnabout occurred in nearby Newburyport, where life and charm were reintroduced to the c.1811 commercial district. Since the 1980s, preservation-minded private owners have been buying up residential properties in these communities, bringing block after block of irreplaceable Georgian and Federal homes back to life.

The brilliance of Bulfinch

The Federal era peaked with the work of Charles Bulfinch (1763–1844), who pursued architecture first as a leisure activity and then as a profession

– the first native-born American to do so, some would say. Unfortunately, many of his more daring buildings have been destroyed, but the jewel among those standing, the Massachusetts State House, rests atop Beacon Hill. Here is as grand a composition as any Bulfinch realized, and to picture it surrounded by open land is to begin to appreciate what a dazzling paean to the promise of government it must have appeared to the Bostonian of 1798.

The classical State House, very Palladian in inspiration, has been extended twice in two contradictory styles. The 1890 addition to the back of the building is a lumpish but highly mannered

ety for the Preservation of New England Antiquities, is the least developed, a harmonious albeit basic expression of Federal-style concepts. In his 1802 house, Bulfinch took a few cautious steps to animate the street facade – the first-floor windows are recessed inside well-defined brick arches.

By his third house, completed around 1805, Bulfinch's confidence was established. This Beacon Street residence, of noble proportions and refined detail, set a tone of sophistication for the entire neighborhood, which Bulfinch also graced with several surviving row houses on Chestnut Street.

baroque echo of its opposing side. The second addition of 1914 totally neutralized the first by blotting it out, at least from the front, behind two thoroughly impassive marble wings – dull perhaps, but a mute backdrop to the golden-domed Bulfinch original.

Bulfinch was in on the beginning of Beacon Hill speculation, and the three homes he built for the developer and politician Harrison Gray Otis summarize not only his growth but the maturation of the Federal residential style. The 1796 house, now the headquarters for the Soci-

LEFT: Federal style home in Newburyport.
ABOVE: aspects of Boston – the Massachusetts State House, and Back Bay brownstones.

Greek grandeur

New England is a peaceful place, and among the emblems of this serenity are scores of white steeples, visible on every horizon as landmarks for travelers. This ubiquitous New England image can be traced back to Asher Benjamin, an influential force in New England architecture circa 1800. It was Benjamin's first of seven widely read architectural handbooks, in which he rendered a steepled church, that became the basis for decades of church design. The simple classicism changed little over time, but the detailing, particularly of the steeple, incorporated changing architectural fashions, giving a clue to the era in which a church was built.

It was Benjamin who, in his final 1830 volume, judged New England ready for the Greek Revival style, a style that elsewhere in America was already vying with the newer Gothic Revival of architects such as Alexander Jackson Davis. The economy of Greek architecture gives it a superior air, and scale is the key to its grandeur. Civic buildings, institutions and halls of commerce lent themselves to the heroic Greek scale, usually constructed of either marble or granite; houses were dwarfed by it. (There were two residential benefits, however: tall windows and high ceilings.)

Although New England is not particularly rich in examples of the style, two exemplary Greek

ture.) The renovation was carried out with care and charisma; although the sober Greek references of Alexander Parris's 1826 domed building are generally overwhelmed by their surroundings, it seems fitting that this hive of activity be housed in such splendor.

Form overtakes function

The opening of the industrial age marked the closing of an era of architectural innocence in New England. For 200 years, the principles of the region's architecture had been governed by function; form existed to serve the central purpose of shelter. While European ideas had clearly dictated

Revival buildings, both marketplaces, are among the cleverest examples of recently restored 19th-century buildings.

Providence's 1828 Arcade has been described as "something worthy of London or Paris," an apt compliment to its crisply colonnaded and handsomely detailed facade. Inside, the two-story, sky-lit interior has been beautifully restored, its cast-iron balconies once again offering an elegant setting for shops.

The most celebrated New England project of its kind, Boston's Faneuil Hall Marketplace, is now a consumer's cornucopia, with food and specialty stores galore. (The Marketplace occupies the arcaded structure called Quincy Market; Faneuil Hall itself is an adjacent Georgian struc-

WHEN MILLS TURNED INTO TOWNS

Harrisville, New Hampshire, shows how pervasive the textile industry became after 1830. The town comprises handsome granite and brick mills, boarding houses and storehouses. Today, these buildings house a weaving school and offer an abridged version of the rapid rise and fall of New England's mill towns, a story that began with cottage industries and climaxed with the building of entire towns designed around textile mills.

In Lowell, Massachusetts, the Lowell National Historic Park and the Lowell Historic Preservation District celebrate factory buildings designed in the boxy, brick, frugal industrial version of the Federal style. Today they line the city's intricate canal system.

design, they had been tempered by restraint. But by 1850, something had changed. Perhaps for no other reason than boredom with symmetry, scale and four-square plans, architecture took off in a riot of historicist revivals.

Gothic, Italianate, Renaissance and Romanesque are among the eclectic labels attached to the late 19th-century architectural revivals. The Gothic Capitol building in Hartford is particularly asymmetrical, while the "gingerbread" carpenter Gothic style of Martha's Vineyard cottages represents a more quaint interpretation. Newport mansions exemplify a dizzying range of styles, from the shingled Hammersmith Farm "cottage" to the gilded Breakers (Italian Renaissance), the Victorian Château-sur-mer to the beaux-arts Marble House (*see pages 232–3*).

In the hands of architects such as Henry Hobson Richardson (who designed Boston's Trinity Church in a bold Romanesque style) and McKim, Mead and White (the Renaissance Revival Boston Public Library), these styles could be expressed with panache. But the spiritual link to early New England began growing remote, and these buildings – with massive stones and ornamentation – have only a distant kinship with the carefully proportioned, cautiously decorated creations of New England's early centuries. In effect, they represent mainstream trends in American architecture, rather than a homegrown New England school.

International input

Non-native architects played an important part in the look of 20th-century New England. Harvard University boasts the only LeCorbusier building in the United States (the Carpenter Center), and Walter Gropius built a model Bauhaus house in the Boston suburb of Lincoln. At MIT, Eero Saarinen designed the striking Kresge Auditorium and Chapel. I.M. Pei designed Boston's John Hancock Tower, a cool glass 60-story rhomboid that reflects its surroundings and the constantly changing cloudscapes above; other Pei projects in the city include an addition to the Boston Public Library which quotes the original's mass without copying its rich ornamentation, and the Christian Science Center, centered upon an oversized infinity pool.

LEFT: Lowell's sturdy, practical industrial buildings.
RIGHT: Boston's Trinity Church, built in 1872–77, contrasts with the 1970s John Hancock Tower.

More recently, British architect James Stirling chose a postmodernist-Egyptian motif for Harvard's Sackler Museum of ancient, Islamic, and Asian art; and Japanese architect Tadao Ando took his inspiration from mid-century's austere International Style in his 2008 Stone Hill Center at the Clark Art Institute in Williamstown, Massachussetts. Like Ando, the New York firm of Diller Scofidio + Renfro placed great emphasis on sleekly framed outdoor vistas in its 2006 Institute of Contemporary Art (ICA) on the Boston waterfront. With its top floor cantilevered over the harbor's edge, the ICA is, in the words of *Boston Globe* architecture critic Robert Campbell, "intensely involved with the sea." As, indeed, nearly all New England once was. ❏

PLACES

A detailed guide to the six New England states,
with principal sites clearly cross-referenced
by number to the accompanying maps

lthough America's industrial revolution started in New England, it's the region's flaming fall leaves and charming white-steepled churches that local tourist boards promote. Certainly, the six states are bursting with 300 years of historical sights and influence – considerably more than any other place in America. But they are also remarkably vital: attend a town meeting in one of the superficially sleepy rural communities and you'll find that the robust tradition of democracy bequeathed by the founding fathers lives on, making many a town manager's life little easier than the president's.

It is precisely this juxtaposition of past influence and present prestige that is so compelling. What's more, each state has retained a well-defined identity, teasing visitors into testing their preconceptions against 21st-century reality – Maine associated with solitude and contemplation, Massachusetts with bustle and culture, Vermont with beauty and peace, Connecticut with carefully kept white clapboard homes, Rhode Island with its renowned sailing, and tranquil New Hampshire, whose bellwether presidential primary every four years encourages the pollsters to predict the political fortunes that are about to be won and lost.

A trip to New England can mean finding a priceless antique in an out-of-the-way backwoods store, or dining in a sophisticated Boston bistro. It can mean rafting down a Maine river and skiing down a New Hampshire mountain, lounging on a Nantucket beach or picnicking on the harbor in Newport, Rhode Island. Yet the region is surprisingly compact.

State boundaries have more political significance than practical importance to the visitor. But, for convenience, each state is explored in depth in the following pages as a self-contained unit. Massachusetts, the most populous, has been divided into sub-sections: Boston, the areas to the north, west and south, Cape Cod and the islands of Martha's Vineyard and Nantucket, Central Massachusetts, the Pioneer Valley, and the Berkshires. ❑

PRECEDING PAGES: Camden, Maine, from Mount Battie; scenic railroad at Hart's Location, New Hampshire; Boston's skyline, seen from the Prudential Building. **LEFT:** Boston Light on Little Brewster Island. **ABOVE:** celebrating Halloween.

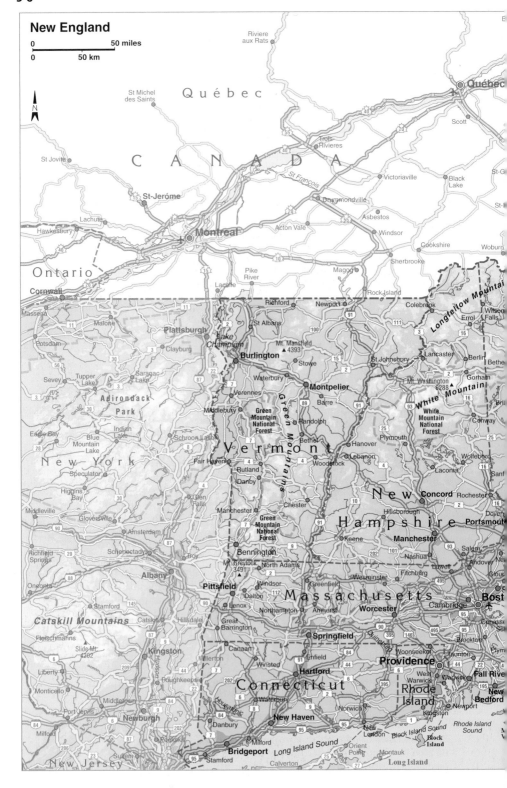

New England

0	50 miles
0	50 km

N

Riviere aux Rats

Québec

St Michel des Saints

St Jovite

Q u é b e c

Scott

St-Jerôme

C A N A D A

Victoriaville

Black Lake

St-G

Trois-Rivières

St François

Drummondville

Asbestos

St-

Lachute

Hawkesbury

Acton Vale

Windsor

Cookshire

Woburn

Montreal

Ontario

Pike River

Lacolle

Magog

Sherbrooke

Cornwall

Rock Island

Richford

Newport

Colebrook

Longfellow Mountain

Massena

St Albans

Wilson Falls

Malone

Plattsburgh

Lake Champlain

Mt. Mansfield 4393

Errol

Potsdam

Clayburg

Burlington

Stowe

St Johnsbury

Lancaster

Berlin

Bethe

Sevey

Tupper Lake

Saranac Lake

Waterbury

Montpelier

Mt. Washington 6288

Gorham

Bric

Adirondack Park

Middlebury

Verennes

Green Mountain National Forest

Barre

White Mountain National Forest

Conway

Eagle Bay

Indian Lake

Randolph

Blue Mountain Lake

Schroon Lake

Bethel

Plymouth

New York

Speculator

Fair Haven

V e r m o n t

Hanover

Lebanon

Woodstock

Wolfeboro

Laconia

Higgins Bay

Rutland

Sanf

Middleville

Glen Falls

Danby

N e w

Concord

Rochester

Gloversville

Manchester

Chester

Hillsborough

H a m p s h i r e

Portsmout

Amsterdam

Green Mountain National Forest

Keene

Manchester

Dover

Richfield Springs

Schenectady

Troy

Bennington

Nashua

Salem

Andover

Mt Greylock 3491

North Adams

Westminster

Fitchburg

Glou

Oneonta

Albany

Pittsfield

Windsor

Greenfield

Lowell

Stamford

Dalton

M a s s a c h u s e t t s

Cambridge

Bost

Catskill Mountains

Catskill

Hillsdale

Lenox

Northampton

Amherst

Worcester

Cohasse

Fleischmanns

Great Barrington

Springfield

Brockton

Slide Mt 1282

Kingston

Canaan

Quinebaug

Woonsocket

Taunton

Plym

Liberty

Illerton

Winsted

Enfield

Providence

Fall Rive

Monticello

Poughkeepsie

Hartford

West Warwick

Warwick

New Bedford

Middletown

C o n n e c t i c u t

Waterbury

Rhode Island

Newport

Port Jervis

Newburgh

Norwich

Kingston

Milford

Danbury

New Haven

New London

Rhode Island Sound

New Jersey

Peekskill

Milford

Bridgeport Long Island Sound

Orient Point

Block Island

Sutten

Stamford

Calverton

Montauk

Long Island

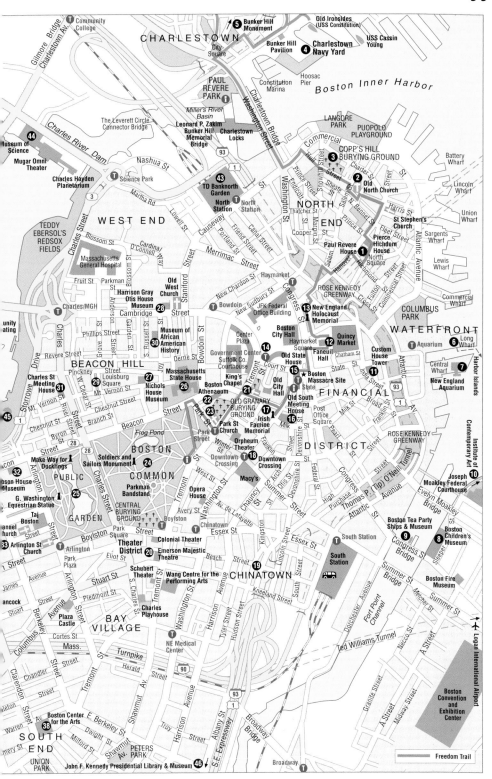

BOSTON

The city has always taken itself seriously. But it does, after all, all, have unequaled Revolutionary history, famed universities, vibrant arts, creative cuisine, and the Red Sox

The poet and essayist Ralph Waldo Emerson wrote: "This town of Boston has a history… It is not an accident, not a windmill, or a railroad station, or a crossroads town, but a seat of humanity, of men of principle, obeying sentiment and marching to it…"

New York may be more dynamic, Washington more imposing, Seattle more gorgeously situated, but no city in America so nobly mingles its past with its present, tradition with innovation.

A walking city

Despite urban development, Boston changes so abruptly in mood and nuance from one street to another that it cries out to be explored on foot. The city is charmingly, perversely bereft of a main drag, and its streets practice the old European vices of waywardness and digression. The visitor should, too.

Every day hundreds of visitors walk the red line on the sidewalk that marks the 2½-mile (4-km) **Freedom Trail**, a self-guided, or narrated 90-minute tour (tel: 617-357 8300; freedomtrail.org) that takes in the major sites of the city's momentous Revolutionary history *(see pages 102–5)*. Note that the Freedom Trail guided tour price does not include admission to sites along the way. If you want to visit several locations, buy a combination, reduced-price admission ticket.

Check the website for other walking

tours, including the enjoyable Tuesday evening Historic Pub Crawl.

The National Park Service conducts a free walking tour along the 1.6-mile (2.5-km) **Black Heritage Trail** (tel: 617-742 5415; nps.gov/boaf) which winds through Beacon Hill and Boston Common, past two dozen historic sites relating to the life of the city's free African-Americans prior to the Civil War. Other walking tours include Michele Topor's popular gourmet tasting forays to the **North End** and **Chinatown** (tel: 617-523 6032; northend markettours.com). *page 106* ▷

Main attractions
THE FREEDOM TRAIL
THE BLACK HERITAGE TRAIL
PAUL REVERE HOUSE
USS CONSTITUTION MUSEUM
BUNKER HILL MONUMENT
NEW ENGLAND AQUARIUM
QUINCY MARKETPLACE
OLD STATE HOUSE
OLD GRANARY BURYING GROUND
PUBLIC GARDEN
CHRISTIAN SCIENCE CENTER
BOSTON PUBLIC LIBRARY
MUSEUM OF FINE ARTS
MUSEUM OF SCIENCE
CAMBRIDGE
MIT MUSEUM
HARVARD UNIVERSITY

LEFT: the new – high-rise office buildings.
RIGHT: the old – Acorn Street, Beacon Hill.

THE FREEDOM TRAIL

Boston is both rich in history and small enough to navigate on foot. The Freedom Trail is a handy way to take in the most important sites

The Freedom Trail, which is a 2½-mile (4-km) painted path linking 16 historic locations that all played a part in Boston's Colonial and Revolutionary history, was born in 1951 and, in 1974, part of it became Boston's National Historical Park. Although its individual attractions are centuries old, it was not until 1951 that newspaperman and author William Greenough Schofield suggested that the most notable sites be linked in a numbered sequence. Until then, according to Schofield, "tourists were going berserk, bumbling around and frothing at the mouth because they couldn't find what they were looking for. Nobody knew where anything was or how to get there."

A leisurely pace

It may be tempting to see the city by tour bus, sightseeing trolley or the amphibious vehicles called duck boats. All provide quick introductions to some of the major sites, and the costumed guides on some tours will deliver their information in the guise of 18th-century characters. But only by walking can you set your own pace, decide when to eat, or explore other interesting buildings close to the itinerary.

Good walking shoes and a map are a necessity – free Freedom Trail maps are available at the National Park Visitor Center at 15 State Street next to the Old State House. The entire trail, whose route is shown on the map on the inside back cover of this book, can be walked in one day, but it's probably wiser to cover it in a more leisurely fashion over two days.

These four pages give a broad overview of the Freedom Trail. The individual attractions are covered in detail in the subsequent pages (see cross-references). For more details, view the Freedom Trail Foundation's website, thefreedomtrail.org

RIGHT: The Freedom Trail Players enliven tours by assuming the characters of Bostonians who lived through the American Revolution. The 90-minute tours attract 3 million tourists a year.

ABOVE: An actor impersonates Benjamin Franklin at Faneuil Hall, adjacent to Quincy Market. Franklin (1706–90) was born in Boston, although he ran away to Philadelphia when he was 17.

ABOVE: Colonial tales are told on **Boston Common**, bounded by Tremont, Beacon, Charles and Boylston streets. British troops camped here before heading to Lexington and Concord in 1775.

LEFT: Now a history museum dwarfed by skyscrapers, the **Old State House** *(page 111)* contains historic artifacts, from ship models to a vial from the Boston Tea Party. Outside, a star within a circle of cobblestones marks the site of the Boston Massacre of March 5, 1770, when British soldiers fired into a hostile crowd.

ABOVE: Books by Hawthorne, Stowe, Emerson, and Thoreau were edited and first printed in the **Old Corner Bookstore** *(page 111)*, on the corner of School and Washington streets. It was built in 1712 as an apothecary shop, office and home. A bookshop in the 1990s, it now sells jewelry.

RIGHT: Charles Bulfinch designed the magnificent red brick and domed **Old State House** ("the hub of the solar system") when he was only 24. A guided tour is available. *See page 111.*

BELOW: The first floor of the magnificent **Faneuil Hall** *(page 110)* is a lively marketplace, and the second-floor assembly room is still used for debates, lectures and readings. Dating from 1742, the "Cradle of Liberty" was rebuilt in 1762 and again in 1898–99.

ABOVE: The **Paul Revere House** *(page 106)*, built around 1680, is the oldest house in downtown Boston. Its frame is mostly authentic, but the interior is a recreation of a colonial household. It was from here that Revere left for his renowned "midnight ride" in 1775 *(page 42)*.

BELOW: The **USS** *Constitution (page 107)*, familiarly known as "Old Ironsides," is the oldest commissioned ship in the United States Navy and is consistently the most visited site on the Freedom Trail. An adjacent museum details the navy's early history.

ABOVE: King's Chapel *(page 113)*, at the corner of Tremont and School streets, was built in its present form in 1749–54 and its bell, recast by Paul Revere, still rings on Sunday morning. Its adjacent burial ground contains the graves of John Winthrop and Mary Chilton, who arrived as a child aboard the *Mayflower*.

ABOVE: A statue of Colonel William Prescott, who led the troops at the Battle of Bunker Hill and was said to have given the legendary order "Don't fire until you see the whites of their eyes," stands in front of the 221-ft (67-meter) **Bunker Hill Monument** (page 108).

BELOW: John Hancock, Paul Revere, Samuel Adams, and James Otis are all interred in the **Old Granary Burying Ground** (page 113). However, many headstones have been moved so often that they no longer correspond with the locations of the original graves.

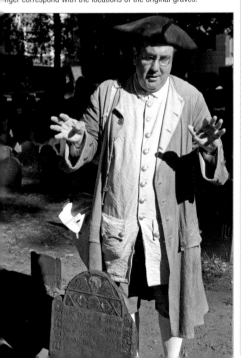

PAUL REVERE RIDES AGAIN

Boston misses few opportunities to relive its stirring history. On March 5, Boston Massacre Day, the Charlestown Militia leads a parade from the Old State House to City Hall Plaza. Patriots' Day, on the third Monday in April, is the year's biggest celebration. Paul Revere's and William Dawes' rides are re-enacted the previous evening. On the day itself, after a parade in Back Bay, the first two battles of the Revolution are staged with gusto at Lexington Green and Concord (pages 148–50). The Boston Marathon (page 75) is also run on that day.

● On the first Monday in June, the Ancient and Honorable Artillery Company gathers at Faneuil Hall and parades to Copley Square.

● On June 17, following a parade from Charlestown, the Battle of Bunker Hill (page 43) is re-enacted at the Monument.

● On July 4, the Declaration of Independence is read from the balcony of the Old State House.

● On December 16, the Boston Tea Party of 1773 is re-enacted (pages 109).

ABOVE: Old North Church (page 106) is Boston's oldest place of worship, dating from 1723. The Episcopal church housed the signal lanterns that told Paul Revere the British were heading for Concord. Its interior high box pews and brass chandeliers are original.

RIGHT: The infant Benjamin Franklin was baptized at **Old South Meeting House** (page 111), which was built in 1879, It was the site of many incendiary debates leading to the American Revolution, including a famous rally against the hated tea tax.

along with fragrant Italian grocery stores, bakeries, restaurants, and festivals.

A stroll through the North End can start at the **Paul Revere House ❶** (19 North Square; tel: 617-523 2338; open daily year-round; entrance fee) in North Square. Built around 1680, it is the city's oldest building, and its period furnishings include some items owned by the Reveres. The age and architecture of the place are the main attractions; for Revere's exquisite work in silver, visit the Museum of Fine Arts *(see page 132–3)*.

From here, head north toward Hanover Street and the Revere Mall, with its equestrian statue of Revere. At the end of the tranquil, tree-shaded mall stands Boston's oldest church, the 1723 **Old North Church ❷** (officially Christ Church, 193 Salem Street; tel: 617-523 6676; open daily), where beneath the graceful spire the sexton Robert Newman famously hung two lanterns on April 18, 1775, on the orders of Paul Revere, to signify to the citizens the British plan to move troops inland by boat rather than on foot. Inside, the stately pulpit and a bust of George Washington preside over the original box pews. The beauty of this

A Sicilian festival in North End garlands the Madonna with dollar bills.

TIP

The name's the same: Boston's trolley, trams trains and ferries are all known as the "T."

The North End

This picturesque neighborhood is Boston's original heart, and to walk its streets is to walk among legends. The Freedom Trail threads through the North End on its way between Boston Common and the Bunker Hill Monument in Charlestown.

The North End was the original nub at the end of the Shawmut peninsula where the first settlers planted their town. Later, it became Boston's immigrant core: once Irish, then Jewish, and now Italian. Gentrification has homogenized this ancient quarter, but many older Italians remain –

Brahmins and blue-collar workers: Boston's history in brief

Founded in 1630 by Puritan émigrés looking for a site with safe drinking water, Boston early on felt that "the eies of all people are upon us," as their first leader, John Winthrop, said. Driven by this relentless self-consciousness and the certainty that God, too, was watching, the little "Bible Commonwealth" quickly made something of itself.

By 1700, thanks to cod fishing and the maritime trade made possible by Boston's natural harbour, the colony was burgeoning: its fleet was the third largest in the English-speaking world, its population the largest in North America.

In the mid-18th century, the English Crown began to tighten its hold on its precocious offspring, imposing taxes and commercial restrictions

that cooled relations between the colonies and the motherland. Tensions escalated; the Boston Massacre of 1770 and the Boston Tea Party protest *(see page 42)* three years later eventually flared into the American Revolution.

During the decades following the Revolution, Boston merchantmen sailed the

ABOVE: Boston's thriving seaport in 1855.

globe. The fishing fleet increased tenfold between 1789 and 1810, and created a "codfish aristocracy" of fortunes netted from the sea. A seemingly unending flow of riches lifted Bostonians with names such as Cabot, Lowell, and Forbes into a new American aristocracy. These were the "Boston Brahmins," a name borrowed from the Hindu priestly caste.

By 1850, industry had replaced trade as a maker of fortunes. And by 1900, in one of the great testimonies to the American knack for making something from nothing, Boston had tripled its size with landfill.

Mid-19th-century Boston also found itself at the center of America's intellectual life, earning the nickname "The Athens of America" as cultural institutions were nour-

space finds lovely accompaniment in the "royal peal" of its eight bells, one of which is inscribed, "We are the first ring of bells cast for the British Empire in North America, Anno 1774." The church is certainly worth a visit; if time is a factor, skip the small adjacent museum.

Nearby, between Hull and Charter streets, stand the weathered headstones of **Copp's Hill Burying Ground ❸** (open daily), where many early Bostonians are buried and where several gravestones bear evidence of British soldiers' musket practice.

Charlestown

Across Charlestown Bridge from the North End a famous bit of history lies at anchor in the **Charlestown Navy Yard ❹**, which opened during the War of 1812 and functioned until 1974. The **USS Constitution** (tel: 617-242 5601; ussconstitution .navy.mil; open daily), the venerable frigate known as "Old Ironsides" was built in 1797 and is the world's oldest commissioned vessel. It fought over 40 battles in the War of 1812 and won them all. Tours of the vessel, given by US Navy sailors, illustrate the cramped and dangerous

world of a man o' war in the days of sail. On July 4, when the *Constitution* makes its annual turn-around cruise (no public allowed), there's a 21-gun salute; on July 5, the public is invited to a sunset parade.

Other sites in the Navy Yard include: The **USS Constitution Museum** (tel: 617-242 5670; ussconstitutionmuseum.org), which tells the ship's story in an engaging fashion; the **Boston Marine Society** (tel: 617-242 0522; bostonmarinesociety.org), housed in the old octagonal Muster House, which contains a diverse collection of nautical art and artifacts; and the **Commandant's House**, preserved as it

The USS Constitution *in Charleston Navy Yard. Owned and operated by the US Navy since 1797 and a museum ship since 1907, the wooden-hulled, three-masted frigate is still fully seaworthy.*

---

ished by Boston money and Boston brains. Among these were the Boston Public Library, the Boston Symphony Orchestra, the Massachusetts Institute of Technology (MIT) and Boston University, the first American university to admit women on an equal basis with men. Harvard, founded in 1636, had already become one of the world's great universities.

When the Irish Potato Famine began in 1845, Boston was at the apogee of its gleaming social and cultural pre-eminence. Suddenly, thousands of impoverished Irish immigrants arrived, promptly constituting a new underclass.

With the arrival of waves of Italians, Poles and Russians, Boston's population swelled to more than half a million by 1900. Newcomers and incumbents clashed, and Boston was divided into two

ABOVE: 19th-century immigrants at work in the port.

distinct cultures. The established elite withdrew into its world of Harvard degrees and Back Bay addresses – but while the new citizens sweated in factories and did handwork, they remade Boston, and its politics, in their own image.

Once dominated by descendants of English colonists, the Puritan "City upon a Hill" became a mainly Catholic metropolis of Irish and Italians.

For all Boston's glory and growth during the 1800s, the century's end brought decline, an economic deterioration that would continue until the 1960s. New York superseded Boston as a port; the textile mills and shoe factories headed south for cheaper labor and lower taxes. By the 1940s and 1950s, Boston was shrinking.

But then the city woke up. For the first time, Boston's Protestant elite, possessing wealth, and its Irish Catholics, possessing political power, cooperated in a program of rejuvenation. Government Center, the Prudential and Hancock towers, and a score of skyscrapers changed the face of the city. The ambitious multi-billion dollar "Big Dig," completed in 2005, eliminated downtown's unsightly elevated highway by diverting traffic underground.

The Bunker Hill Monument seen from Charlestown Marina.

was when last occupied in 1876. Of these three, children will most enjoy the Constitution Museum, with its interactive exhibits. Also in dock: the World War II destroyer **USS** *Cassin Young* (nps.gov; below deck tours in summer at 11 am and 2 pm). Inside the Yard, stop for information at the **Boston National Historical Park Visitors Center** (tel: 617-242 5601; nps.gov/bost; open daily).

The Freedom Trail continues to the **Bunker Hill Monument** ❺ (Monument Square; tel: 617-242 5641; open daily), a granite needle 221 ft (67 meters) high, commemorating the battle. There are 294 steps to the top; the view, while showing the layout of the city and some of the harbor, isn't what it was before the downtown skyscrapers went up. The **Charlestown Visitor Center** (nps.gov; open daily) across from the monument recounts the history of the monument and the city.

The Waterfront

The eastern boundary of the North End is the Waterfront District. The great wharves of windjammer days remain,

many now supporting apartments, shopping arcades and upscale restaurants. At the center of it all is Columbus Park, part of a greenspace linking the Waterfront with the downtown area.

Close to the Aquarium subway station, **Long Wharf** ❻, the hub of Boston's shipping industry in the 17th century, is now the starting point for harbor cruises and the high-speed harbor islands ferry. Or you can get harbor views for free by strolling along the walkway southwards to Rowes Wharf. This is a section of the 47-mile (76-km) **HarborWalk** (harbor walk.com), more than 38 miles (61 km) of which have been completed. Stretching from Chelsea Creek to the Neponset River, it passes through East Boston, Charlestown, the North End, downtown Boston and South Boston, and Dorchester.

The Aquarium

The **New England Aquarium** ❼ is at Central Wharf; tel: 617-973 5200; neaq .org; open daily; entrance fee; discount combination ticket to aquarium and IMAX Theater). It has a gargantuan three-story, 200,000-gallon (900,000-liter) cylindrical tank in which sharks, sea turtles, moray

How to reach the Harbor Islands

Thirty-four islands and peninsulas, ranging from little more than piles of rock (The Graves) to 214-acre (87-hectare) Long Island make up the **Boston Harbor Island National Recreation Area** (tel: 617-223 8666; bostonharborislands.org), where visitors can camp, swim, hike, visit Fort Warren, and tour a lighthouse.

For centuries the islands were a dumping ground for Boston's sick and homeless. In 1996 Congress decided to support local and state efforts to turn them into a recreational state park.

The high-speed Harbor Express (617-222 6999; harborexpress.com) runs from Boston's Long Wharf (and the Quincy Shipyard) to **Georges Island**, the area's nucleus and site of an interesting Civil War-era fort. A free ferry operates between Georges Island and **Spectacle Island**, and

water taxis ($) travel to other islands, some of which feel as remote and unspoiled as those off the coast of Maine, except for that great view of the Boston skyline.

The National Park Service also operates a three-hour (round trip) boat cruise aboard a landing craft vessel to the country's oldest lighthouse, **Boston Light**, where visitors can climb 76 steps to the top. Views along the way, and of the city from the lighthouse, are worth the trip. The boat leaves from both Fan Pier (28 Northern Avenue) and Georges Island (tel: 800-979 3370 or 212-209 3370 for tickets).

ABOVE: visiting Boston Light, built in 1782, on Little Brewster Island.

Recommended Restaurants and Bars on pages 128–31

eels and other tropical species glide in never-ending circles. By its base African and rockhopper penguins play on the Ocean Tray. The Aquarium operates three- to four-hour whale-watch cruises from early April through late October, with researchers and naturalists on board, and its **Simons IMAX Theater** (tel: 866-815 4629) shows 3-D movies with digital sound on New England's largest screen.

The Aquarium, founded in 1969, is one of the city's most popular attractions, and can be extremely crowded. The best days to visit are weekdays; try to arrive when the museum opens at 9am.

Children's Museum

Follow HarborWalk southwards past Rowes Wharf and cross old Northern Avenue Bridge to Museum Wharf, home of the **Children's Museum** ❽ (300 Congress Street; tel: 617-426 8855; bostonkids.org; open daily; Fri till 9pm ; entrance fee). Housed in a renovated warehouse, it is a hands-on adventure, where children can climb a three-dimensional maze, and visit an authentic Japanese house transplanted from Boston's sister city, Kyoto. New England's maritime traditions are reflected in hands-on boating exhibits and environmental exhibits. Like the Aquarium, the museum makes a good, if not centrally located, respite for kids getting "historied out" by Freedom Trail attractions. Admission is only $1 per person on Friday nights from 5pm to 9 pm.

Nearby, on Congress Bridge, is **the Boston Tea Party Ships & Museum** ❾ (Congress Street; tel: 617-338 1773; bostonteapartyship.com; entrance fee), due to reopen in 2009 after a serious fire. It has full-size replicas of three 18th-century ships – *Beaver*, *Dartmouth* and *Eleanor* – whose cargo of tea was thrown overboard on the chilly night of December 16, 1773 by 60 whooping patriots dressed as Mohawk Indians. They were protesting Britain's having imposed taxes on such cargos without granting the colonists representation in Parliament.

Contemporary art

The four-story **Institute of Contemporary Art** ❿ cantilevers starkly over the

New England Aquarium.

TIP

The Reef, the aquarium's outdoor restaurant overlooking Boston Harbor, is a great place for lunch; after 4pm it becomes a popular spot for cocktails.

LEFT: the Children's Museum.
BELOW: Institute of Contemporary Art.

ABOVE: Custom House Tower.
BELOW: Quincy Marketplace.

waterfront at 100 Northern Avenue (tel: 617-478 3100; icaboston.org; open Tues–Sun, Thur and Fri until 9 pm; entrance fee). The first new art museum to be built in Boston in almost 100 years, it opened in 2006 and provides 65,000 sq. ft (6,000 sq. meters) of exhibition and performing arts space, as well as a media center, and gives recent artworks their due in a city whose major museums have a more traditional focus. Check the website for information on its summer concert series.

Admission is free on Thursdays from 5pm to 9 pm, and free to families on the last Saturday of each month.

Just west of the New England Aquarium rises the **Custom House Tower** ⓫ (3 McKinley Square; tel: 617-310 6300; marriott.com), for many years Boston's tallest building. It's certainly the city's quaintest high-rise, with the c. 1910 clock tower placed somewhat incongruously on the 1847 Greek Revival-style building. It's now a Marriott Hotel, with an open-air observation deck and small museum on the 26th floor. Free guided tours are offered daily at 2pm. The harbor view is also magnificent from the Counting Room Lounge.

Faneuil Hall

Close by is **Faneuil Hall** ⓬ (tel: 617-523 1300; faneuilhallmarketplace.com), donated to Boston in 1742 by merchant Peter Faneuil and enlarged in 1805 by Charles Bulfinch. In this "Cradle of Liberty," Patriot orators stirred the embers of Revolution in the early 1770s.

Facing it is the domed granite arcade called Quincy Market, built in 1826. In 1976, the complex was reborn as **Quincy Marketplace**, a chic, wildly successful array of flower stalls, jewelery emporia and shops. Several dozen food stands line the long hall of the central building, offering everything from freshly shucked oysters to French pastry. Jugglers, mimes, acrobats and other performers contribute to the festive atmosphere.

The upper floor of Faneuil Hall is open daily. Historical talks are every half-hour, 10am–3pm, and the museum houses regimental memorabilia of the Ancient and Honorable Artillery Company. Two of Boston's landmark restaurants, **Durgin Park** and the **Union Oyster House** – both old and picturesque, but hardly temples of gastronomy – are close by.

Beside Union Street, six glass towers

comprise the **New England Holocaust Memorial** ⓭, the "windows" etched with rows of numbers in memory of 6 million Jews murdered by the Nazis.

Every Friday and Saturday fruit and vegetable vendors pack nearby **Haymarket Square**'s outdoor marketplace to sell their wares. Smart shoppers can get some nifty buys, but be careful: those shiny red apples may not always be as fresh as they appear.

Government Center

Looming just inland from Faneuil Hall is **Government Center** ⓮. Here, in the 1960s, the Boston Redevelopment Authority razed buildings and removed streets to create a huge open space – some 56 acres (23 hectares). The centerpiece of this plaza is a massive concrete **City Hall** in the cheerless brutalistic style, described as an "Aztec temple on a brick desert."

To the southeast rise the banks and office towers along Franklin, Congress, Federal, State and Broad streets. Soaring confidently from a primitive warren of tumbled byways, these behemoths constitute the Hub of Business. A resurrected early Bostonian might marvel at their architecture, but would nod appreciatively to learn that they are counting-houses.

Old State House

To the southwest lies downtown's retail heart, as well as some buildings illuminated brightly in history.

At Washington Street's intersection with Court and State streets stands the **Old State House** ⓯ (206 Washington Street; tel: 617-720 1713; open daily; entrance

fee), once the seat of British rule. The Bostonian Society has a small museum inside, charting aspects of the city's history with changing displays. It was here, in 1761, that James Otis first fulminated against the British Writs of Assistance in a spellbinding speech that prompted John Adams to write that "then and there the child Independence was born."

In 1770, the infamous Boston Massacre *(see page 41)* took place just outside the State House. After the Revolution, the building served as the meeting place for the Commonwealth Government until the present State House was built in 1798.

The handsome, gambrel-roofed brick building, currently a jeweler's, at the corner of School and Washington streets was once the **Old Corner Bookstore**, a gathering spot for such writers and thinkers as Hawthorne, Emerson and Thoreau.

Old South Meeting House

Continue down Washington Street to the **Old South Meeting House** ⓰ (617-482 6439; open daily; entrance fee), scene of

ABOVE: the New England Holocaust Memorial. **TOP LEFT:** Samuel Adams statue, Faneuil Hall. **BELOW:** Old State House.

scores of protest meetings denouncing British policy. From here on December 16, 1773, that the 60 patriots set off to conduct the Boston Tea Party. A stunning state-of-the-art audio exhibit, "If these Walls Could Speak," sets the scene. Bibliophiles, however, may well find Goodspeed's antiquarian bookstore, located in the church's basement, even more interesting (Mon–Sat; closed Sat July–Sept).

Nearby, at Washington and School streets, the **Irish Famine Memorial** , a pair of sculptures by Robert Shure, commemorate the immigrants driven to America by the potato famine of the 1840s. Set in the round, with seating for passers-by, one sculpture depicts a desperate family about to leave Ireland, and the other shows the three hopeful and determined immigrants arriving in Boston.

Downtown Crossing

A little further to the south on Washington Street is the city's mercantile heart, the pedestrian-friendly **Downtown Crossing** ⑱. It used to be anchored by the legendary Filene's Basement, the country's first offprice megastore, but Filene's has temporarily relocated to

497 Boylston Street to make room for a $625 million renovation which will include a 38-story tower, condominiums, a hotel, and shops. Meanwhile, the Crossing, with several large retailers, numerous pushcarts, and the city's jewelry district, pushes on in spite of the loss of its star attraction.

Chinatown

Continue on Washington Street to Beach Street into the heart of **Chinatown** ⑲. The country's third largest Asian quarter has seen its population boom in recent years with the arrival of citizens from countries including Vietnam, Thailand, and Cambodia. The narrow, crowded streets are packed with tiny restaurants and shops selling everything from back scratchers to thousand-year-old eggs, and is a wonderful place to wander for a few hours.

Theater District

A short distance to the west, the **Theater District** ⑳ begins. Over the years many Broadway hits have had their debuts here. Among the more opulent stage venues are the **Opera House** at 539 Washington Street, renovated at a cost of $38 million

BELOW: the Irish Famine Memorial, unveiled in 1998 and located where the Irish refugees first crowded into tenements along Boston's waterfront.

Eating in Chinatown

No visit to Chinatown would be complete without having lunch at one of its myriad restaurants, and the dim sum "palaces" – always good value – are among the most authentic. Waitresses push carts laden with appetizer-size dishes such as steamed buns, spare ribs, and yes, chicken feet, through vast, cavernous rooms packed with tables. Diners point at the dishes they want, are charged for each (it's OK if you don't speak the language, because pointing is universal), and pay at the end of the meal. Most dishes are $2–$3, and patrons can dine heartily for $12–$15 each (a small tip is appreciated). Literally, dim sum means "touch your heart."

Favorite dim sum eateries include Empire Garden at 690 Washington Street, and China Pearl at 9 Tyler Street.

in 2004, and the 1925 **Wang Center for the Performing Arts** (270 Tremont Street): inspired by the Paris Opera House, it is now one of the city's major performing arts venues.

Nearby **Bay Village** is a six-block neighborhood whose homes are diminutive versions of those on Beacon Hill. The reason: many of the Hill's craftsmen and builders lived in the Village and designed their homes in a similar fashion.

King's Chapel

Back on School Street, pass the **Old City Hall**, a grand affair that out-Second Empires the French Second Empire, and at Tremont Street turn right to look into **King's Chapel** ㉑ (64 Beacon Street; tel: 617-227 2155; open daily in summer; limited hours rest of year; services Wed. 12:15pm and Sun at 11am). Built in 1754 of Quincy granite, it retains its crisp white box pews as well as Paul Revere's largest bell. Its burial ground is Boston's oldest and, in 1713, it was the first church in New England to acquire an organ. The interior is a neoclassical gem.

On Tuesdays at 12:15pm you can attend a 30–45-minute recital series featuring a variety of performers and repertoires from jazz to medieval. A Sunday evening concert series begins at 5 pm. Admission to both is by donation.

Crossing over Tremont Street, head left to the **Old Granary Burying Ground**, founded in 1660, a pleasant glade where Peter Faneuil, John Hancock, Samuel Adams, Paul Revere, and the victims of the Boston Massacre are interred.

Boston Athenaeum

Overlooking the burial ground are the windows of a private library, the **Boston Athenaeum** ㉒ (10½ Beacon Street; tel: 617-227 0270; bostonathenaeum.org; first floor open Mon–Fri in summer; tours of entire building 3pm Tues, Thur; 24-hour minimum advance reservation required). There are reading rooms, marble busts, and prints and paintings, as well as books from George Washington's library. The Athenaeum is one of the best places to spot specimens of the species known as the Proper Bostonian, short of joining an exclusive Beacon Hill club.

An intimation of mortality in the Old Granary Burying Ground. Three signers of the Declaration of Independence are buried here, as are five victims of the Boston Massacre.

BELOW:
the Albert Gordon reading room at the Boston Athenaeum.

An 1869 bronze of George Washington presides over the Commonwealth Avenue entrance to the Public Garden.

BELOW:
pedal-powered (and wheelchair-accessible) swan boats, a tradition since 1877, can carry up to 20 people around the Public Garden's lagoon on a 15-minute cruise.

A few more paces down Tremont Street, at one corner of the Boston Common, is Peter Banner's elegant 1809 **Park Street Church** ㉓ (1 Park Street; tel: 617-523 3383; open for tours mid-June–Aug Tues–Sat 9 am–3 pm). On July 4, 1829, William Lloyd Garrison made his first anti-slavery speech here, launching his far-reaching emancipation campaign. Visitors are invited to attend Sunday services at 8:30am and 11am for traditional service, and at 4pm and 6pm for contemporary service and discussion.

Boston Common

Every American city has a great park, but only Boston can claim the oldest, the venerable **Boston Common** ㉔, a magical swath of lawn and trees and benches. Sitting in the sun-mottled shade, watching pigeons strut and children frolic around Frog Pond, out-of-towners can understand how Bostonians might mistake this spot for the very center of the world.

The land that was to become the Common originally belonged to Boston's first English settler, one Reverend William Blaxton, who had made his home in 1625 on the western slope of what is now known as Beacon Hill. His life was interrupted in 1630 by the arrival of a band of settlers led by Governor John Winthrop of the Massachusetts Bay Company. The new Bostonians were nobly determined, as Winthrop had written, to "be a Citty upon a hill," and in 1634 he sold his land to the town for around $150 and fled farther into the wilderness.

The 45 acres (18 hectares) he left behind quickly became a versatile community utility. During the next 150 years it was used for pasturing livestock, as a militia drilling ground, and a convenient place to whip, pillory, or hang people. As a military post, the Common put up the Redcoats all through the Revolution.

Now the Common is "just" a park, glorious when the magnolias bloom, or when snow at sunset evokes the impressionist paintings of Childe Hassam.

Public Garden

Just across Charles Street, the elegant **Public Garden** ㉕ strikes a more formal pose. These variegated trees, meandering paths, and ornate beds of flowers were

Recommended Restaurants and Bars on pages 128–31

once part of the fetid Back Bay marshes; but by 1867, the Garden had taken its present graceful shape, complete with weeping willows, a bridge for daydreamers, and a shallow 4-acre (1.6-hectare) pond.

In summer, swan boats (swanboats.com; open mid-Apr–mid-Sept daily; entrance fee) carry happy tourists across the placid waters. At the Commonwealth Avenue entrance, an equestrian George Washington bronze by Thomas Ball presides, while a row of bronze ducks on the north side pays tribute to Robert McCloskey's classic 1941 children's picture book *Make Way for Ducklings*. Real ducks, too, inhabit an island in the pond and paddle about to toddlers' delight.

Beacon Hill

Back up at the east end of the Common, the gold dome of the **State House** ㉖ (24 Beacon Street; tel: 617-727 3676; cityofboston.gov; open weekdays; free tours 10am–4pm) gleams atop Beacon Hill. Completed in 1798, this peerless Federal-style design by Charles Bulfinch, with less successful but happily unobtrusive additions by several others, symbolizes the eminence of politics in Boston. The approach to the legislative chambers passes through a series of splendid halls leading to the Senate Staircase Hall and the Hall of Flags, both symphonies of fin e siècle marble opulence.

But one of the highlights is the House Chamber, a paneled hall under a two-stage dome. Great moments of Massachusetts' history decorate the walls in a series of Albert Herter paintings, while above circles a frieze carved with a roll-call of the state's super-achievers. The

portentous codfish known as the "Sacred Cod," a sleek, stiff carving in pine that commemorates Boston's great Federal-era fishing industry, was first hung in the Old State House. Without this old mascot, the house refuses to meet.

At the beginning of the 19th century, the Trimount became the subject of land speculation. It was quite ingeniously leveled and quickly became the idyllic gaslit neighborhood of bow-fronted townhouses now known as "The Hill." At first, everyone expected that the new residences of Beacon Hill would be urban estates along the lines of Bulfinch's free-standing No. 85 Mount Vernon Street (1800) – his second house for developer

ABOVE LEFT: the Sacred Cod, a symbol of prosperity, presides over the House of Representatives in the State House.
ABOVE: stained glass in the 1798 building's State Hall.
BELOW: the State House, built on land used as a cow pasture by John Hancock, the first governor of the Commonwealth of Massachusetts.

The first Harrison Gray Otis House. Otis (1765–1848) was a lawyer, senator, mayor of Boston, and a leader of America's first political party, the Federalists. He commissioned architect Charles Bulfinch to design three mansions at various times.

and politician Harrison Gray Otis – which is to this day one of Boston's most majestic houses. But the mansion plans were quickly scaled down to today's smaller blocks.

At No. 55 Mount Vernon Street is the 1804 Bulfinch-designed **Nichols House Museum** ㉗ (tel: 617-227 6993; nicholshousemuseum.org; open May–Oct Tues–Sat pm; Nov–Apr Thur–Sat pm; tours every half hour; entrance fee). The former home of the philanthropist and landscape designer Rose Standish Nichols, it is a splendidly accurate portrayal of an early 19th-century Beacon Hill interior.

Federal-era tastes

To get a sense of The Hill, walk west down Beacon Street from the State House. At numbers 39 and 40 stand twin 1818 Greek Revival mansions, one built for Daniel Parker, owner of the Parker House, Boston's oldest hotel. At 42 and 43, the Somerset Club, built in 1819 as a mansion for prominent merchant David Sears, was bought by the most exclusive of Boston social clubs in 1872. At number 45 Beacon Street is the third house designed by Bulfinch for Otis (1805).

The first (1797) **Harrison Gray Ot House** ㉘ at 141 Cambridge Street, ju outside Beacon Hill proper (tel: 617-22 3956; open Wed–Sun 11–4:30 pm; tou on the hour and half-hour; entrance fee is headquarters for Historic New Englan and a National Historic Landmark. offers a glimpse into the elegant life Boston's governing class immediatel after the American Revolution.

Louisburg Square ㉙ develope between Pinckney and Mount Verno streets around 1840, epitomizes th Beacon Hill style and its urban delicac Louisa May Alcott (1832–88), author *Little Women*, once lived here.

Another charming example of Beac Hill's spirit is at numbers 13, 15 and 1 Chestnut Street, one of America's mo beautiful residential streets, whe Bulfinch built for the daughters of h client Hepzibah Swan three exquisi townhouses in a prim little row.

African-American History

During the 19th century much Boston's free African American popul tion lived on the north side of Beac Hill. The **Museum of African-America**

History ③⓪ (46 Joy Street; tel: 617-725 0022; afroammuseum.org; open Mon–Sat year-round) encompasses four historic sites, including two generally open to the public. The African Meeting House (8 Smith Court), dedicated in 1806 and the oldest black church building still standing in the United States. It was here was where William Lloyd Garrison founded the New England Anti-Slavery Society in 1832. The Abiel Smith School (46 Joy Street) served as the country's first publicly-funded grammar school for African Americans from 1834 until 1855, when Boston's schools were integrated.

The Museum also oversees a site on Nantucket *(see page 173)*, and Boston's Black Heritage Trail *(see page 101)* with the assistance of the National Park Service (nps.gov; tel: 617-742 5415).

Charles Street

On the west side of Beacon Hill, Charles Street, with its restaurants, coffee houses, bakeries, and boutiques, is a prime spot to stroll, shop and snack. Café Bella Vita (30 Charles Street) serves coffee and pastries, but the real draw is people-watching.

The street's principal landmark is the **Charles Street Meeting House ③①** at the corner of Charles and Mount Vernon streets. Built for the Third Baptist Church in 1807, it later served as the home of the First African Methodist Episcopal Church and the Unitarian-Universalist Church; over the years luminaries including Frederick Douglass and Sojourner Truth spoke here. It was converted into offices and retail space in the 1980s.

Wander off Charles onto the shady, peaceful streets that trail toward the Charles River or lead back up the hill. Many houses here are noteworthy for their former occupants. Polar explorer Admiral Richard E. Byrd (1888–1957) lived in Nos. 7–9 Brimmer Street, while No. 44 in the same street was the lifelong home of the great historian Samuel Eliot Morison. The Victorian clergyman and philosopher William Ellery Channing lived at No. 83 Mount Vernon Street, next door to the second Otis mansion.

Back Bay

From Beacon Hill, it's an easy transition both in distance and architectural feeling to the handsome streets of Back Bay. Although it epitomizes "Old Boston," this neighborhood dates only to the 1850s filling of a noxious tidal mudflat declared, in 1849 "offensive and injurious" by the Board of Health.

The legislature's grand 1857 plan for Back Bay, influenced by Baron Haussmann's recent rebuilding of central Paris, called for long vistas down dignified blocks, and a wide boulevard with a French-style park down the middle. In 1858 the first load of fill arrived by train from Needham, 10 miles (16 km) to the southwest. During the next 20 years, 600 acres (240 hectares) of dry land emerged from the muck that was Back Bay.

Back Bay's imposing rowhouses, now nearly all divided into condominiums or apartments, showcase the successive revival styles of the late 19th century, from Italianate to Colonial. The verdant mall of **Commonwealth Avenue** centers things, and the houses along it, as well as those on Marlborough and Beacon, reveal choice architectural cameos. (Starting near

The attractions of the Back Bay were not appreciated by some conservatives. Even in the 20th century, one Beacon Hill gentleman told his prospective son-in-law, who was hoping to build a house in the Back Bay, that he could not allow his daughter to live on "made land." He got his way: the couple elected to settle on Beacon Hill.

BELOW: Charles Street Meeting House, where anti-slavery activists once preached.

The view from Top of the Hub restaurant, on the 52nd floor of the Prudential Tower (see review on page 129). The adjoining Skywalk Observatory offers 360° views.

BELOW:
open-air jazz on
Newbury Street.

In the block between Clarendon and Dartmouth, Commonwealth Avenue displays its most memorable structures. The romantic houses that march down this stretch perfectly justify the avenue's reputation as America's Champs-Elysées.

Along Newbury Street

Newbury and Boylston streets are the only part of the Back Bay zoned for commerce. **Newbury Street** ㉝ begins at the Garden with the stately Taj Hotel (formerly the Ritz-Carlton), a lovely spot for tea or a martini if you're not wearing jeans. The chic avenue is lined with jewellers, day spas, restaurants, sidewalk cafés, designer boutiques, and art galleries, including the venerable Vose Galleries of Boston at No. 238, which specializes in American painting from 1669 to 1940. Louis Boston, just off Newbury Street at 234 Berkeley Street, is Boston's most elegant men's clothing shop. For a dose of reality, detour a short distance to Marshall's (500 Boylston Street), one its leading discount stores.

the Charles River and going right to left, the axial thoroughfares are Beacon Street, Marlborough Street, Commonwealth, Newbury Street, and Boylston Street).

Head west to No. 137 Beacon Street, between Arlington and Berkeley (the cross-streets ascend in alphabetical order), to visit the **Gibson House Museum** ㉜ (tel: 617-267 6338; thegibsonhouse.org; open Wed–Sun, tours 1pm, 2pm and 3pm; entrance fee). Built in 1859, the brick rowhouse has been left much as it was; it houses a museum whose furniture, paintings, books, clocks and textiles recreate the feel of Back Bay living in its heyday, including the servants' "downstairs" world of kitchen and laundry.

Copley Place

Copley Place ㉞ (100 Huntington Avenue; tel: 617-369 5000; simon.com) is a megaplex occupying more than 9 acres (3.6 hectares) atop the Massachusetts Turnpike, with an 11-screen cinema, hotel, and dozens of inviting restaurants and upmarket shops. Although many of the latter are similar to those found in other upscale malls (Neiman-Marcus, Saks Fifth Avenue, Lord & Taylor), a few are unique, such as the Artful Hand Gallery (exceptional crafts).

The **Prudential Center** encompasses the John B. Hynes Veterans Memorial Convention Center, a hotel, several department stores, and a lively mix of shops and restaurants.

Connected to Copley Place by a "skyway" is Boston's original skyscraper, the 52-story **Prudential Tower** ㉟ (800 Boylston Street; prudentialcenter.com), dating from the early 1960s and looking it age. Its 50th-floor Skywalk Observatory (tel: 617-859 0648; open daily 10am–10 pm in summer, 10am–8pm in winter

entrance fee) provides an exhilarating, map-like, four-way view of the city. An Antenna Audio Tour details points of interest far below. The Top of the Hub is a magical spot to have lunch, or enjoy a cocktail and watch the sunset.

The Mother Church

The religious movement that Mary Baker Eddy began in 1879 today has its world headquarters on 22 acres (9 hectares) immediately south of the Prudential Center on Huntington Avenue. The **Christian Science Center** ❸❻ (tel: 617-450 2000; tfccs.com; Sunday services at 10am, noon and 7pm; testament meeting Wed at noon and 7:30 pm) complex includes three older buildings – the Romanesque Mother Church (1894), the Italianate Mother Church Extension (1904) and the Publishing Society (1933) – as well as I.M. Pei's 1973 additions.

In the publishing wing, the **Mapparium** (tel: 617-450 7000; open daily except Mon; fee) is an extraordinary stained-glass walk-in representation of the globe, constructed between 1932 and 1935 to symbolize the Christian Science Publishing Company's worldwide outlook. Illogical it may be – you stand inside the sphere surrounded by the map in concave form – but it is certainly one of the sights of Boston. The weird acoustics compound the hallucinogenic effect.

Copley Square

Follow Dartmouth Street to Boylston for one of the city's most stimulating displays of architecture: **Copley Square** ❸❼. First, there's Charles McKim's 1895 **Boston Public Library** (700 Boylston Street; tel: 617-536 5400; bpl.org; free, one-hour art and architecture tours begin at the Dartmouth Street Lobby entrance Mon at 2:30pm, Tues and Thur at 6pm, and Fri and Sat at 11am). This Renaissance Revival masterpiece might well be the center of the Boston that claims to be the "Athens of America." With more than 6 million volumes and a vast, ornate reading room, it is one of the great libraries in the world. But it's more than a building of books. There's art everywhere – murals by Sargent and Puvis de Chavannes, statues by Saint-Gaudens and Daniel Chester French – and, at the center of a maze of stairs and passages, a peaceful inner courtyard. Philip Johnson's massive 1972

TIP

An excellent luncheon buffet is served in Novel, Boston Public Library's restaurant Mon–Fri. Breakfast and lunch are served in Sebastian's Map Room Café Mon–Sat, and tea from 2:30 to 4 pm.

LEFT: the Christian Science Center, surrounded by a long reflecting pool that serves as part of the building's air-conditioning system.
BELOW: Boston Public Library, visited by 2¼ million people a year.

addition "quotes" the original structure in a vastly simplified modern vernacular.

Across the square stands H. H. Richardson's 1877 masterpiece, **Trinity Church** (206 Clarendon Street; 617-536 0944; trinitychurchboston.org; open daily 8am–6pm for self-guided tours; guided tour Sun after 11:15am service, and throughout the week: call for hours). This is a tour de force in Romanesque inventiveness and a striking medievalist contrast to the Public Library's classicism. Inside, what impresses is the wealth of murals, mosaics, carvings and stained glass. This is Boston's most sumptuous interior space. Organ concerts (by donation) are held Fridays 12:15–12:45 pm.

The John Hancock Tower

Above everything looms I. M. Pei & Partners' magnificent blue-green mirror, the **John Hancock Mutual Life Insurance Tower**, built in 1976. The Tower initially had a propensity in windy weather to lose the huge sheets of glass covering it; miraculously, no one was hurt when the glass fell. That problem was solved after the tower was completed when all 10,344 panes were replaced, and the building's core stiffened.

The South End

To the south and east of the Christian Science Center and Copley Square sprawls the South End, an ethnically diverse but much gentrified quarter of Victorian bowfront townhouses. Particularly pleasing architecturally are the areas around Worcester Square, Rutland and leafy Union Park Square, where it's evident that London – rather than Paris, as in the Back Bay – was the developers' inspiration.

On Sundays from May through late October the parking lot at 540 Harrison Avenue is transformed into an **Open Market** as local artists and growers display their wares. Look for unique handbags and jewelry, paintings, and antiques plus fresh produce and baked goods.

The **Boston Center for the Arts** ㊳ is at Clarendon and Tremont streets (tel 617-426 5000; bcaonline.org). This lively performing and visual arts complex encompasses the **Mills Gallery** (open Sun, Wed–Thur noon–5pm; Fri and Sat. noon–9pm), which mounts five large-scale expositions each year, and four theaters which present more than 50 productions yearly. The popular bistro, Hammersley's, is in the plaza complex.

Boston's greatest hall

From the South End, Huntington Avenue leads southwest past several of Boston's greatest institutions. At the northwest corner of Massachusetts Avenue stands the majestic gable-roofed **Symphony Hall** ❸ (301 Massachusetts Avenue; for tickets tel: 888-266 7575; bso.org; walk-up tours fall through spring on the first Saturday of the month: call for hours). The acoustically impeccable 1900 building is home to the renowned Boston Symphony Orchestra and, in summer (when the BSO performs at Tanglewood in Lenox) and during the Christmas holidays, its less formal offshoot, the Boston Pops Orchestra. Tickets can be hard to come by.

The MFA

Continue down Huntington Avenue to reach the **Museum of Fine Arts** (MFA) ❹ (465 Huntington Avenue; tel: 617-267 9300; mfa.org; open Sat, Sun, Mon, and Tues 10am–4:45pm; special exhibits open Wed–Fri until 9:45pm; entrance fee. Built in 1909 and enlarged with an I.M. Pei-designed wing in 1981, this incredible museum is perhaps best known for its Impressionists – including the largest number of Monets outside France – but it also has the most complete assemblage of Asian art under one roof; the world's best collection of 19th-century American art; and the finest collection of Egyptian Old Kingdom objects outside Cairo.
● *See margin note (right) and MFA photo feature on pages 132–3.*

Mrs Jack's Palazzo

Close to the MFA, the **Isabella Stewart Gardner Museum** ❹ (280 The Fenway; tel: 617-566 1401; gardnermuseum.org; open Tues–Sun, 11am–5pm; entrance fee) is an exquisite 1903 neo-Venetian palazzo assembled by Boston's most flamboyant grande dame. The unstoppable "Mrs Jack" may have scandalized Brahmin Boston when she paraded two pet lions down Beacon Street), but she proved an astute patron of the arts.

MFA TIPS

● Admission to the MFA is free on Wed 4–9:45 pm (except for special exhibits); reduced admission on Thur–Fri after 5pm.

● Bravo Restaurant, serving progressive American cuisine at lunch, dinner, and Sat–Sun brunch, offers free parking after 5 pm. Lighter fare is served in The Galleria and the Courtyard Café.

● Pay for parking at automated kiosks in the West Wing coatroom before leaving the museum.

LEFT: the John Hancock Tower.
BELOW: Trinity Church's altar.

Feeding the hungry at Fenway Park.

BELOW: bug-eyed attraction at the Museum of Science.
RIGHT: a bust of conductor Arthur Fiedler near the Hatch Shell.

During the 1890s, she set her sights on such masterpieces as Titian's *Rape of Europa*, Rembrandt's *Storm on the Sea of Galilee*, and Vermeer's *The Concert*. In 1896, when her collection was outgrowing her home, she commissioned her fantasy palace at the very edge of town. Today her eclectic collection, displayed in galleries that frame a four-story glass-roofed courtyard, constitutes one of the world's great small museums.

Cocktails, conversation, and live music in the courtyard are on tap at "Gardner after Hours", the third Thursday of each month, 5–9pm. Tickets are on sale at the box office (tel: 617-278 5156).

Fenway Park

North of the museums is another of Boston's shrines, **Fenway Park** ❷ (4 Yawkey Way; tel: 617-267 8661 or 617-267 1700; bostonredsoxmlb.com). Built in 1912 and famously called a "lyrical bandbox" by novelist John Updike, the Red Sox's home field is the oldest ballpark in the major leagues. Behind-the-scenes 50-minute tours (tel: 617-226 6666; $12) daily 9am–4pm on the hour – if there's a game, the last tour is 3½ hours before game time. There are 90-minute twilight tours ($25) on non-game days at 5 pm and 6 pm for groups of 10 or more.

The home of the Boston Celtics (tel: 617-624 1000; nba.com/celtics), who have been National Basketball Association champions 17 times, and the Bruins (tel: 617-624 1000; bostonbruins.com), Boston's National Hockey League team, is the state-of-the-art **Banknorth Garden** ❸ near North Station.

The Charles River

Like many great cities, Boston lies in the embrace of a great river. Along Back Bay, the Charles River widens into a large basin, like a giant mirror held up to the city's profile. It was designed to do just that, by the civic-minded citizens who created the Charles River Dam in 1908

The dam itself is home to Boston's **Museum of Science** ❹ (tel: 617-723 2500; mos.org; open daily; Fri till 9pm entrance fee). Here, visitors can watch simulated lightning, become sleuths at CSI: the Experience, climb into a model

of the Apollo lunar module, cower under a plastic Tyrannosaurus Rex, and enjoy a wide variety of ever-changing hands-on exhibits and live animal and bird demonstrations. For reasonably inquisitive kids over 7, this temple of science and technology surpasses even the Children's Museum as a respite from history and art.

A combination ticket includes admission to the five-story, domed **Omni Theater**, planetarium, and laser show. On-site parking is available for a fee. On Fridays, 6–10pm, the museum's Science Street Café serves up gourmet appetizers, dinner, drinks, and live jazz.

Boston Pops

The river's edge is one of the city's favorite places to stretch its legs. Roller skaters wired for sound, joggers, bike riders and sunbathers all migrate here. So do the great crowds that turn out to hear the Boston Pops (tel: 617-266 1492) at free concerts under open summer skies at the **Hatch Memorial Shell** ⑮. Their Fourth of July concert with fireworks is spectacular; get there very early and bring a blanket or chairs.

Every Wednesday evening from early July through early September the Boston Landmarks Orchestra (tel: 617-520 2200; bostonlandmarksorchestra.org) performs classical music at the Shell. It also puts on concerts for children and neighborhood concerts throughout the city.

JFK's legacy

A short subway ride away is a point of pilgrimage for many people, the **John F. Kennedy Presidential Library and Museum** ⑯ (Columbia Point; tel: 617-514 1600 or 866-JFK-1960; jfklibrary.org; open daily; entrance fee; free parking; MBTA red line south to JFK/UMass and free shuttle bus marked "JFK" – or, in summer, boat from Long Wharf). Set dramatically beside the ocean, the museum, dedicated to the life and legacy of JFK, makes excellent use of film, videos and recreated settings (including the Oval Office) to create a masterful portrait of politics and society half a century ago. The building, designed by I.M. Pei, has a very large library and archive, and is surrounded by a 9½-acre (3.8-hectare) park.

Exhibits in the John F. Kennedy Presidential Library and Museum.

BELOW: Duck Tours depart from the Prudential Center and the Museum of Science Mar–Nov and spend 20 minutes of the 80-minute tour on the river. Tel: 617-267-DUCK bostonducktours.com

TIP

MIT tours: Info Center open Mon–Fri at 77 Mass. Avenue; free 75–90-min tours at 11am and 3pm Mon–Fri from lobby of Building 7 during academic year. Tel: 617-253-4795; mit.edu

Harvard: one-hour tours from Holyoke Center Arcade, 1350 Mass. Avenue, Mon–Fri at 10am and 2pm; Sat at 2pm during academic year; late June–mid-Aug at 10am, 11:15am, 2pm and 3:15pm Mon–Fri; no tours mid-Aug–mid-Sept. Tel: 617-495 1573; harvard.edu

TOP: MIT campus.
BELOW: Stata Center for Computer Information and Intelligence at MIT.

CAMBRIDGE

Literary critic Elizabeth Hardwick once described Boston and Cambridge as two ends of the same mustache. Indeed, across the Charles lies a separate city that is absolutely inseparable from its companion metropolis.

Just across Harvard Bridge is the **Massachusetts Institute of Technology** (MIT) **Ⓐ**. Housed in solid neoclassical buildings with the trim logic of natural laws, MIT reliably produces Nobel laureates, new scientific advances and White House science advisors.

The Finnish architect Eero Saarinen designed two of its highlights: the inward looking, cylindrical **MIT Chapel**, illuminated by light reflected from a moat, and the tent-like **Kresge Auditorium** which rises from a circular brick terrace, its roof apparently balanced by slender metal rods on three points.

Exhibits at the **MIT Museum** (265 Massachusetts Avenue; tel: 617-253 4444; open daily 10am–5pm; mit.edu/

museum; entrance fee; free admission Sundays 10am–noon) explore inventions, ideas, and innovations in creative interactive exhibits, and include the world's largest holography collection. Admission is free to the **Hart Nautical Gallery** (ship models; mainly for enthusiasts).

Harvard Square Ⓑ, at the heart of Cambridge, is home to Harvard University and the playground of book stores, coffee houses, and shops to the west and north of the Yard. At its center is the international Out of Town News, housed in a historic kiosk, and beside it, Dmitri Hadzi's gently humorous stone sculpture Omphalos, suggesting that Harvard is, as its supporters have long held, the center (or navel) of the universe.

The venerable Harvard Cooperative Society ("Coop" for short) was founded in 1882 as an alternative to overpriced local shops; today the prices are pretty much at a par (except for affiliated students and faculty, who enjoy a discount)

Harvard University

Standing proudly above the red brick and green ivy are the spires of America's oldest institution of higher learning, **Harvard University**. Self-confident and backed by enormous wealth – its endowment exceeded $30 billion at last count – Harvard has been a world index of intellectual accomplishment almost since its 1636 founding. Eight American presidents have studied at Harvard, and it remains a formidable force.

The heart of the place is **Harvard**

Recommended Restaurants and Bars on pages 128–31

Yard **C**, withdrawn tranquilly behind the walls that separate it from Harvard Square outside. Passing through the gate that proclaims "Enter to Grow in Wisdom," the visitor encounters a hallowed world of grass and trees, ghosts and venerable brick – a living, eminently walkable museum of American architecture from colonial times to the present.

Massachusetts Hall (1720), Harvard's oldest standing building, has quartered Revolutionary troops, as well as housed a lecture hall, a famous drama workshop and, since 1939, the offices of the University president. Nearby stands little **Holden Chapel** (1744), once described as "a solitary English daisy in a field of Yankee dandelions."

At the Yard's center stands Charles Bulfinch's **University Hall**, built of white granite in 1815. In front is Daniel Chester French's 1814 statue of John Harvard (1607–38), the young Puritan minister for whom the college was named after he left it half his estate and all his books. Since no likeness of John Harvard existed, French used a student as his model.

East of University Hall, three massive buildings set off the central green on which commencement is celebrated each June. These are H. H. Richardson's 1880 masterwork **Sever Hall**, with its subtle brick decorations; **Memorial Church** (1932), with its Doric columns; and the monumental **Widener Library**. Given by the mother of alumnus and bibliophile Harry Elkins Widener, who died on the *Titanic* in 1912, the library is the center of Harvard's network of 92 libraries, which together house over 12 million volumes, America's third largest book collection.

To the east of the Yard stands the **Carpenter Center for the Visual Arts D** (24 Quincy Street, tel: 617-495 3251; open Mon–Sat; Sun pm; Sert Gallery open Tues–Sun pm) a cubist, machine-like building built in 1963 that represents the only American work of the great French architect Le Corbusier. The five levels, a "synthesis of the arts", include the top-floor Sert Gallery exhibiting works by contemporary artists, and the Harvard Film Archive, which shows rare and experimental films (tel: 617-495 4700; ves.fas.harvard.edu).

Of special interest to visitors are the university's museums. A major renovation of the three art museums – the **Fogg**

The inauthentic 1814 statue of John Harvard.

BELOW:
Simmons Hall, a dormitory at MIT with more than 5,500 windows.

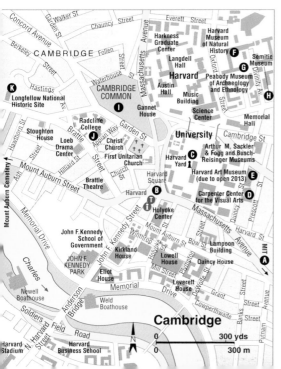

Cambridge

(European and American art), the **Busch-Reisinger** (northern European), and the **Arthur M. Sackler** (ancient, Islamic, and Oriental) – is currently underway and scheduled for completion in 2013. Selected works from the Fogg and the Busch-Reisinger are currently on exhibit at the Sackler Museum (485 Broadway; tel: 617-495 9400; artmuseums.harvard.edu) open Mon–Sat, Sun pm; entrance fee).

When the project is completed, the three museums will occupy the Fogg's premises at 32 Quincy Street and will be collectively known as the **Harvard Art Museum** ⒺE. While each will retain its own identity, there will be larger galleries and a study center.

A few blocks north on Oxford Street stands the **Harvard Museum of Natural History** ⒻF (26 Oxford Street; tel: 617-495 3045; hmnh.harvard.edu; open daily; entrance fee) a huge complex housing several museums. A major draw is the **Botanical Museum** with its famous "Glass Flowers," a collection of astoundingly accurate models of more than 700 plant species executed by Leopold Blaschka and his son Rudolph in 19th-century Dresden.

In the same building, the **Museum of Comparative Zoology** includes George Washington's stuffed pheasants as well as the world's oldest reptile eggs. Also on the site is the **Mineralogical and Geological Museum** (daily 9am–5pm).

The **Peabody Museum of Archaeology and Ethnology** ⒼG (11 Divinity Avenue; tel: 617-496 1027; open daily; entrance fee) was founded in 1866. It houses one of the most comprehensive records of human cultural history in the Western Hemisphere.

Nearby, the University's collection of Near Eastern archaeological artifacts is housed in the **Semitic Museum** ⒽH (6 Divinity Avenue; tel: 617-495 4631; open Mon–Fri, Sat pm; free).

Cambridge Common

On July 4, 1775, George Washington assumed command of the Continental Army on **Cambridge Common** ⒾI. A trio of cannons abandoned by the British when they left Boston in 1776 stand close to a bronze relief of Washington on horseback under an elm tree. On the south side of the Common, just across Garden Street, Christ Church (1761) was used as

BELOW: one of two 3-ton rhino statues, Elizabeth and Victoria, outside the Bio Labs Building.

TIP

It's easy to get to the Kennedy National Historic Site by public transportation (mbta .com). All routes require a walk of about four blocks from the "T" stop: hop aboard the MBTA's Green Line "C" Cleveland Circle train to Coolidge Corner; take the "B" Boston train to Babcock Street; the Route 66 Bus from Harvard Square also goes to Coolidge Corner.

barracks by patriots, and its organ pipes were made into bullets. Close by is an entrance to **Radcliffe College** ❶, (radcliffe.edu) the women's college that merged with Harvard in 1975.

Longfellow's legacy

In the 18th century, Brattle Street was home to so many British loyalists that it was known as Tory Row. Its handsome homes include No. 90, designed by H. H. Richardson of Trinity Church fame, and No. 94, the 17th-century Henry Vassall House. Look out for the yellow clapboard Longfellow House at the **Longfellow National Historic Site** ❿ (105 Brattle Street; tel: 617-876 4491; nsp.gov/long; open May–Sept: May 1–early June, tours Thur–Sat 10:30am–4 pm; early June–Sept, tours Wed–Sun 10:30am–4pm; guided tour only; entrance fee). This was the idyllic wedding present given to the poet Henry Wadsworth Longfellow and his wife, Fanny, by her father in 1843.

Little has changed inside; Longfellow's library and furniture are here, including a chair made from the "spreading chestnut-tree," which stood at No. 56 Brattle Street and was immortalized in his poem *The Village Blacksmith*. Unhappily, Fanny was fatally burned in the house in 1861.

A free summer festival at the site *(check website for schedule)* includes poetry, live music, and living history events.

John F. Kennedy National Historic Site

The nation's 35th president was born at 3 Beals Street in Brookline, now the **John F. Kennedy National Historic Site** ⓱ (tel: 617-566 7937; nps.gov/ofi; open late May–late Sept, Wed–Sun 10:30am–4:30pm; entrance fee) where his family lived from 1914 to 1920. In 1967 his mother, Rose Kennedy, returned to the house and restored it to the way she recalled it looked in 1917, the year of his birth. An unprepossessing house typical of turn-of-the-century homes in Boston's then-new "streetcar suburbs," the birthplace is surprisingly modest for a family later associated with its exclusive Hyannisport compound on Cape Cod – but then, even patriarch Joseph P. Kennedy had to start somewhere.

Visitors can take a half-hour ranger-led tour on the half hour, or opt for a self-guided tour from 3:30 to 4:30pm. ❑

ABOVE: Harvard's Botanical Museum.
BELOW: cultural history recalled at the Peabody Museum.

RESTAURANTS AND BARS

Restaurants

Prices for a three-course dinner per person with a half-bottle of house wine:

$ = under $20
$$ = $20–45
$$$ = $45–60
$$$$ = over $60

Boston

Aquitaine
569 Tremont Street
Tel: 617-424 8577
aquitaineboston.com $$–$$$
A lively French bistro and wine bar (although the "bar" is tiny) in trendy South End restaurant district. L Mon–Fri; D nightly; Sat–Sun brunch.

Artu
6 Prince Street
Tel: 617-742 4336
artuboston.com $$
Friendly, bustling tratto-

ria/rosticceria in North End offers good value for fresh pastas, updated classics. (Also at: 89 Charles Street, Beacon Hill.) L Tue–Sat; D nightly.

Azure
Lenox Hotel, 61 Exeter Street
Tel: 617-933 4800
azureboston.com $$$$
Contemporary American menu, with an emphasis on fresh seafood. B, L, D Mon–Fri; D Sat–Sun.

Barking Crab
88 Sleeper Street,
at Northern Avenue
Tel: 617-426 2722
barkingcrab.com $–$$
Seaside clam shack transported to the city. Fried clams and other simple seafood, and great harbor and city vistas. L and D daily.

Betty's Wok and Noodle
250 Huntington Avenue
Tel: 617-424 1950
bettyswokandnoodle.com
$–$$
Asian-Latino inspired noodle and rice-based dishes and sake cocktails in a sophisticated "diner" across from Symphony Hall. L and D daily.

Clio/Uni
Eliot Hotel, 370A Commonwealth Avenue
Tel: 617-536 7200
cliorestaurant.com $$$$
Elegant New French dishes such as cassolette of sea urchin and lobster. Uni, next door, is an intimate sashimi bar. B and D daily; Sat from 11am; Sun from noon.

Cottonwood Café
222 Berkeley Street
Tel: 617-247 2225
cottonwoodboston.com
$$–$$$
Upscale Tex-Mex fare and a huge tequila selection served in a trendy setting. L and D daily.

The Daily Catch
323 Hanover Street
Tel: 617-523 8567
dailycatch.com $$
Tiny eatery known for superb calamari and Sicilian-style seafood. No credit cards. (Also at: John Joseph Moakley Federal Courthouse Arcade, Two Northern Avenue.) L and D daily.

Durgin Park
Faneuil Hall Marketplace
Tel: 617-227 2038
durgin-park.com $$
One of the city's oldest restaurants offers reliable classics (chowder,

pot roast, baked beans), with good-natured service. L and D daily.

East Ocean Seafood
25 Beach Street
Tel: 617-542 2504
eastoceancity.com $–$$
More than 600 lbs of fresh-from-the-tanks Hong Kong-style seafood is served daily in a low-key Chinatown eatery. L and D daily.

Empire Garden
690 Washington Street
Tel: 617-482 8898 $–$$
Cavernous room serving snack-size dim sum. L and D Mon–Sat.

Excelsior
The Heritage on the Garden, 272 Boylston Street
Tel: 617-426-7878 $$$$
excelsiorrestaurant.com
The cuisine at this elegant dining room overlooking the Public Garden is contemporary American; the three-story wine tower has 7,000 bottles. Pub menu too. D nightly.

Ginza Japanese Restaurant
16 Hudson Street
Tel: 617-338 2261
ginzaboston.com $$
One of Boston's best sushi spots. The unusual *maki* rolls are particularly tasty. L and D daily.

Grill 23
161 Berkeley Street,
Back Bay
Tel: 617-542 2255
grill23.com $$$–$$$$
Upscale steak house. Specialties including a 24-ounce porterhouse steak, and a 3 lb. baked stuffed lobster. D nightly.

Hamersley's Bistro
553 Tremont Street
Tel: 617-423 2700
hamersleysbistro.com $$$
Imaginative touches
dress up sophisticated
comfort food at this pio-
neer on South End's now-
hopping restaurant row.
D nightly; Sun brunch.

House of Siam
542 Columbus Avenue
Tel: 617-267 1755
housesiam.com $
More than 130 Thai
dishes. Go with one of
the 35 house specialties
such as garlic shrimp, or
the signature crispy pad
Thai. L and D daily.

Legal Sea Foods
Boston Park Plaza Hotel,
64 Arlington Street
Tel: 617-426 4444
legalseafoods.com $$-$$$
The ever-popular chain
serves only freshly-
caught and freshly-
prepared seafood. (Also
at: Prudential Center,
Copley Place, Logan Air-
port, Long Wharf, and
Cambridge's Kendall Sq.)

L'Espalier
30 Gloucester Street
Tel: 617-262 3023
lespalier.com $$$$
Ultra-romantic Victorian
townhouse stays two
steps ahead of the culi-
nary cutting edge with its
classic French menu. L
Mon–Fri; D nightly.

Meritage
Boston Harbor Hotel,
70 Rowes Wharf
Tel: 617-439 3995
meritagetherestaurant.com
$$$-$$$$
Superb harbor views and
superior contemporary
American cuisine, with
small and large plate
portions. Great wine list.
D Tue–Sat; Sun brunch.

No Name Restaurant
17 Fish Pier
Tel: 617-338 7539 $-$$
Since the 1920s, this
casual waterfront spot
has been one of of the
best and least expensive
places in Boston to get
off-the-boat fresh sea-
food. L and D daily.

Oishii Boston
1166 Washington Street
Tel: 617-482 8868
oishiiboston.com $$$-$$$$
Chic, contemporary,
crowded, and popular for
sublime sushi. L and D
Tue–Sun. (Also in Chest-
nut Hill and Sudbury.)

Ristorante Toscano
47 Charles Street
Tel: 617-723 4090
toscanoboston.com $$-$$$
True Tuscan delicacies in
a handsome upscale trat-
toria on Beacon Hill.
L and D daily.

Sage
1395 Washington Street
Tel: 617-248 8814
sageboston.com $$$
Modern Italian cuisine in
cozy, intimate South End
spot. Rabbit is a house
specialty. D Mon–Sat.

Sakura-bana
57 Broad Street
Tel: 617-542 4311
sakurabanaonline.com $$
Unparalleled sushi as
well as a full Japanese
menu in the financial dis-
trict. L and D daily.

Sasso Restaurant and Bar
116 Huntington Avenue
Tel: 617-247 2400
sassoboston.com $$$-$$$$
The owners of the North
End's popular Lucca
Restaurant now offer
their contemporary
regional Italian menu at
this handsomely fur-
nished South End out-
post. D nightly.

Skipjack's
199 Clarendon Street
Tel: 617-536 3500
skipjacks.com $$$
Native seafood with a
modernist bent close to
the John Hancock tower.
Free two-hour parking in
garage beneath restau-
rant. (Also in Newton and
Natick.) L and D daily.

Sonsie
327 Newbury Street
Tel: 617-351 2500
sonsieboston.com $$-$$$
International fare in a
trendy spot with a popu-
lar sidewalk patio and
European-style lounge
with comfy chairs and
sofas. L Mon–Fri; D
nightly; Sat–Sun brunch.

Sorellina
1 Huntington Avenue
Tel: 617-412 4600
sorellinaboston.com
$$$-$$$$
Gracious dining with high-
concept Italian fare pre-
pared with a hint of the
Asian, offering dishes
such as grilled octopus
with black pearl cous-
cous. D nightly.

Top of the Hub
Prudential Center
800 Boylston Street
Tel: 617-536-1775
www.topofthehub.net $$$
A romantic spot on the
Pru's 52nd floor. Candle-
light and linen, a lively
bar, live jazz, and danc-
ing. Menu is classic
upscale American (steak
and swordfish are old
favorites). Sun prix fixe
brunch is a treat. L & D
daily until 1am or 2am.

29 Newbury St
29 Newbury Street
Tel: 617-536 0290
29newbury.com $$-$$$
Hip and popular bistro
with a strategic sidewalk
cafe for assessing the
passing fashion parade.
L and D daily.

Tremont 647
647 Tremont Street
Tel: 617-266 4600
tremont647.com $$-$$$

LEFT: informal fast food at Faneuil Hall Marketplace.
RIGHT: treats at Top of the Hub, Prudential Center.

Specialties such as buttermilk fried chicken, and pork schnitzel at this South End restaurant specializing in American "melting pot" cuisine.

Sultan's Kitchen
116 Broad Street
Tel: 617-570 9009
sultans-kitchen.com $
A popular take-out shop (with a few upstairs tables) serving Turkish/ Middle Eastern *shish kebabs*, salads, and the Greek sweet *baklava*. L Mon–Sat; D Mon–Fri.

Union Oyster House
41 Union Street
Tel: 617-227-2750;
www.unionoysterhouse.com $$
"America's Oldest Restaurant" (est. 1826), said to have been a favorite of Daniel Webster and John F. Kennedy. Steaks and seafood are served in atmospheric rooms with creaky floors, low ceilings, and wooden booths. A popular raw bar. L & D daily.

Cambridge

Atasca
50 Hampshire Street
Tel: 617-354 4355
atasca.com $$
Solid Portuguese fare in a charming, cozy spot in the Kendall Square/MIT area. L Mon–Sat, D daily.

Café Mami
1815 Massachusetts Avenue
Tel: 617-547 9130 $
Burgers Japanese style (no bun): handpacked patties with secret blend of spices, topped with a fried egg. L and D daily.

Casablanca
40 Brattle Street
Tel: 617-876 0999
casablanca-restaurant.com $$
Harvard Square's oldest restaurant offers cheap Turkish/Moroccan menu. L Mon–Sat; D nightly; Sun brunch.

Chez Henri
1 Shepard Street
(off Massachusetts Avenue)
Tel: 617-354 8980
chezhenri.com $$$

Modern French fare with a Cuban accent in a snug bistro north of Harvard Square. The spinach salad fired up with spicy duck *tamale* is a classic. D nightly.

Cuchi Cuchi
795 Main Street
Tel: 617-864 2929
cuchicuchi.cc $$–$$$
Antique lighting, stained glass and Victorian tiles set the mood at this "belle epoque" establishment that serves appetizer-size portions of dishes such as "swallowed clouds" (shrimp wantons) and "Cuban cigars" (beef short ribs in dough). D Mon–Sat.

East Coast Grill and Raw Bar
1271 Cambridge Street (Inman Square)
Tel: 617-491 6568
eastcoastgrill.net $$$
Innovative grilled seafood, creative salads, barbecue, and "pasta from hell". Margaritas help ease the often long waits for tables. D nightly; Sun brunch.

Green Street Grill
280 Green Street
Tel: 617-876 1655
greenstreetgrill.com $$–$$$
New England comfort food such as Yankee pot roast and corn chowder, along with some twists like macaroni and cheese with duck confit. The old-fashioned cocktails are definitely a comfort. D nightly.

Harvest
44 Brattle Street
Tel: 617-868 2255
harvestcambridge.com $$–$$$
One of Harvard Square's most reliably innovative bistros, with prime meat and seafood dishes and an award-winning wine list. The garden terrace is delightful. L and D daily; Sun brunch.

Helmand Restaurant
143 First Street
Tel: 617-492 4646
helmandrestaurant cambridge.com $–$$
Authentic Afghani cuisine in muted, tasteful surroundings. The extensive menu has many vegetarian options. D nightly.

Jasper White's Summer Shack
149 Alewife Brook Parkway
Tel: 617-520 9500
summershackrestaurant.com $$–$$$
Lobster served in numerous ways – including pan roasted – at this clam "shack". (Also: Back Bay and Logan Airport.) L and D daily.

Le's
35 Dunster Street
Tel: 617-864 4100 $
A sometimes hectic but generally first-rate spot for traditional Vietnamese fare, including a large selection of *pho* (noodle soup). L and D daily.

Mr. Bartley's Burger Cottage
1246 Massachusetts Avenue
Tel: 617-354 6559 $
For five decades this casual eatery has served up terrific burgers, sweet potato fries, and onion rings. L and D Mon–Sat.

Rialto
Charles Hotel,
I Bennett Street
Tel: 617-661 5050
rialto-restaurant.com $$$–$$$$
Sophisticated and whimsical interpretations of regional and Italian dishes. Four-course tasting menu. D nightly.

Sandrine's Bistro

sandrines.com **$$**
For more than a decade the area's only French-Alsatian restaurant has been a romantic outpost for specialties such as *flammekueche* and *boudin blanc*. L and D Mon–Sat; D Sun.

Charlestown

Figs

67 Main Street
Tel: 617-242 2229
toddenglish.com **$–$$**
Olives' pizza-parlor cousin, still up-scale, only slightly less mobbed. (Also at 42 Charles Street, Boston.) D nightly.

Olives

10 City Square
Tel: 617-242 1999
toddenglish.com **$$–$$$**
Patrons endure long lines and noisy surroundings to savor Todd English's first-class Tuscan country cuisine. D nightly.

Somerville

The Burren

247 Elm Street
Tel: 617-776 6896
burren.com **$**
Comfortable Davis Square Irish pub draws locals, yuppies and students for Guinness, fish and chips, and nightly traditional Irish music. L and D daily; weekend brunch.

The Elephant Walk

2067 Massachusetts Avenue
Tel: 617-492 6900
elephantwalk.com **$$–$$$**
Cambodian and French dishes meet in a light and airy restaurant of wood and brick. D nightly. (Also: 900 Beacon Street, Boston (Lunch weekdays; D nightly; Sun brunch.)

Redbone's

55 Chester Street
(off Elm Street)

Tel: 617-628 2200
redbones.com **$–$$**
Massive plates of barbecued ribs and a cold beer. L and D daily.

Sabur Restaurant

212 Holland Street
Tel: 617-776 7890
saburrestaurant.com
$$–$$$
Cuisine of Bosnia, Greece, Italy, North Africa and the Balkans in a handsomely decorated establishment in Teele Square. D nightly; B Sat and Sun.

Bars

Boston

Beacon Hill Pub, 147 Charles Street. Tel: 617-625 7100. One of the last of its type on the Hill: a neighborhood pub with reasonably priced beer.
Drink, 348 Congress Street. Tel: 617-695 1806. This Fort Point bar with cocktails crafted by "mixologists," gourmet canapés, and restrained atmosphere has become a favorite watering hole.
Game On, 82 Lansdowne Street. Tel: 617-351 7001. In the shadow of Fenway Park and the next best thing to box seats, this sports bar has 90 screens. Bar classic such as quesadillas, nachos, and pizza.
The Greatest Bar, 262 Friend Street. Tel: 617-367 0544. This sports bar just across from TD Banknorth Garden (home to the Celtics and Bruins) really ramps up before and after home games.
Oak Bar, Fairmont Copley Plaza, 138 St. James. Tel: 617-267 5300. Dark wood paneling, marble, mirrors, and comfy seating make for a sedately elegant retreat.

Red Hat Café, 9 Bowdoin Street. Tel: 617-523 2175. One of Boston's oldest drinking places, in historic Scollay Square, has a bustling downstairs neighborhood bar, and an upstairs restaurant.
Sanctuary, 189 State Street. Tel: 617-573 9333. It's a club; it's a lounge; it's a restaurant; it's a "nightery". Open Tues–Sat. Free taco buffet 5–7pm Tues–Fri.
Sunset Cantina, 916 Commonwealth Avenue. Allston. Tel: 617-731 8646. Students from nearby Boston University pack in for a huge range of beers, margueritas, heroic portions of food, and 21 pool tables.

Cambridge

Bukowski's Tavern, 1281 Cambridge Street. Tel: 617-497 7077. A cozy spot in Inman Square famous for its large selection of beers, sweet potato fries, and loud rock. Some hate it here, others love it.

Grendel's Den, 89 Winthrop Street. Tel: 617-491 1160. This landmark bar/restaurant has a huge selection of beers, and international dishes.
Noir, Charles Hotel, One Bennett Street. Tel: 617-661 8010. This upscale bar in Harvard Square uses dramatic lighting and old films projected on louvered screens to create a mood described as "decadent but sophisticated".
River Gods, 125 River Street. Tel: 617-576 1881. Hip, tiny, and usually jammed with a youthful crowd who pack in for the loud music and convivial atmosphere. The bar menu includes a tasty steak sandwich.
Shea's Pub & Wine Bar, 58 JFK Street. Tel: 617-864 9161. A terrific find in Harvard Square – a small, unpretentious bar with European and American beers, wines by the glass, and tasty pub grub, including terrific nachos and burgers.

LEFT: Union Oyster House has been going since 1826.
RIGHT: a venerable venue on Massachusetts Avenue.

THE MUSEUM OF FINE ARTS, BOSTON

Few museums in the world rival the MFA for the quality and scope of its decorative and fine art collections. Every one has something exceptional

One of America's first museums, the MFA opened at Copley Square in 1876 and moved into its present building in 1909. Cyrus Edwin Dallin's bronze statue *Appeal to the Great Spirit* (left) was placed in the forecourt in 1913.

The cultured citizens of 19th-century Boston were keen collectors. Many were passionate about things Asian, and their treasures in due course came to the MFA, forming the nucleus of an outstanding collection. Others travelled to Europe, and the museum acquired one of the foremost holdings outside Paris of Impressionist painting, in particular works by Monet, Pissaro, Sisley, Renoir and Manet. It has nearly 70 works by Jean-François Millet. The American art collection is one of the best in the US; the European and American decorative arts rooms display superb silver, porcelain, furniture and musical instruments. The Nubian and Egyptian collections are unrivaled in the world.

There's so much to see, the first-time visitor would be well advised either to pick out just one collection, or take a free tour focusing on highlights of the collections.
● *For location and opening times, see page 121.*

Above: the museum's 22,000 European artworks encompass 1,600 paintings, with one of the largest collections of Monets outside France.

Right: the building's orginal neoclassical design allowed for sections to be added as funding was obtained, and the museum is still expanding.

THE ANCIENT WORLD

For 40 years from 1905 Harvard University and the Museum of Fine Arts collaborated on an archeological excavation in Egypt, based at the Great Pyramids at Giza. From this, the museum acquired a world-famous collection of Egyptian treasures. Among many Old Kingdom sculptures is this beautiful statue of King Mycerinus, who built the Third Pyramid at Giza, and his queen, dated to c.2548–30BC. Other treasures include gilded and painted mummy masks, and some amazingly well preserved hieroglyphic inscriptions. The Giza expedition's director, Dr George Reisner, also worked in the Sudan and brought home a dazzling collection of Nubian artifacts, the best outside Khartoum. Particularly awe-inspiring is the exquisite gold jewelry, inlaid with enamel and precious stones, and the sculptures, varying in size from huge statues of Nubian kings to tiny shawabtis (funerary statuettes).

ABOVE: the New England landscape is captured in works such as Edward Hopper's watercolour *Lighthouse and Buildings, Portland Head, Cape Elizabeth* (1927).

LEFT: Renoir's *Dance at Bougival* (1883) shares wall space with equally important works by such European painters as Titian, van Gogh, Degas, and Gauguin.

RIGHT: *The Letter* by Mary Cassatt (1890). More formal are the portraits by colonial painters Gilbert Stuart and John Singleton Copley, and the society portraitist John Singer Sargent (1856–1925).

ABOVE: Jonathan Borofsky, born in Boston 1n 1942 and famous for his large Hammering Men sculptures, created *Walking Man* at the MFA.

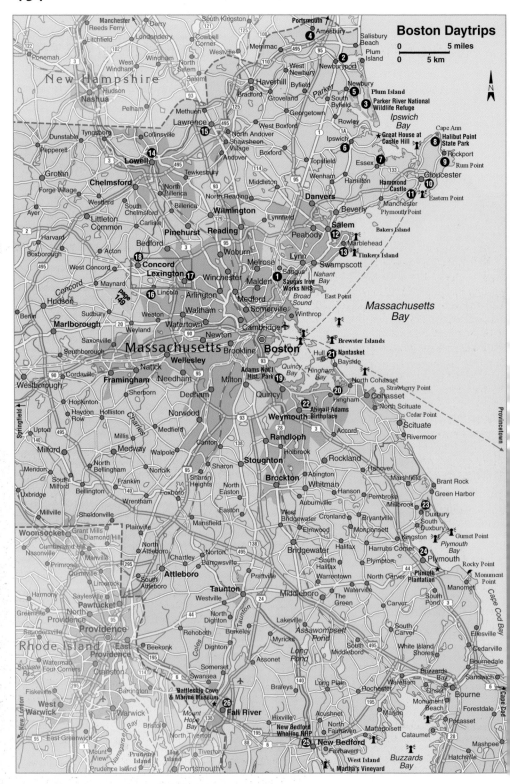

Boston Daytrips

Recommended Restaurants and Bars on pages 144–5

MASSACHUSETTS: NORTH OF BOSTON

The ragged coastline between Boston's northern suburbs and the New Hampshire border offers a rich amalgam of colonial history, seafaring towns, old-money retreats, artists' colonies, and inviting beaches

Just a few miles north of Boston via Route 1 is the **Saugus Iron Works National Historic Site ❶** (244 Central Street; tel: 781-233 0050; open daily Apr–Oct). The buildings have been reconstructed as they were from 1646 to 1668, with a blast furnace, forge, slitting mill, iron house, ironworks house, a blacksmith's shop, and a restored 17th-century home. The site was established by John Winthrop Jr., and, though ultimately unprofitable, launched America's ironworking industry. Modest in size and scope, the site nevertheless offers a worthwhile glimpse at a vital in the days before the industrial revolution.

Newburyport

Continue north on Route 1 (or hop onto I-95) to **Newburyport ❷**, 35 miles (56 km) north of Boston. The "Clipper City," once home to a magnificent merchant fleet and a thriving shipbuilding industry, has benefited from careful preservation. After the city was devastated by a fire in 1811, the rebuilding gave downtown its uniform Federal-era appearance. But by the early 20th century, the arrival of

Main attractions
NEWBURYPORT
PARKER RIVER NATIONAL
  WILDLIFE REFUGE
IPSWICH
CRANE WILDLIFE REFUGE
ESSEX
ROCKPORT
GLOUCESTER
HAMMOND CASTLE
SALEM
MARBLEHEAD

BELOW: North Shore boat builder.

The state in snapshot

Known as: The Bay State.
Motto: *Ense Petit Placidam Sub Libertate Quietem* (By the sword we seek peace, but peace only under liberty).
Origin of name: May derive from an Algonquian Indian village meaning "place of big hills".
Entered Union: 6 February 1788, the sixth of the 13 original states.
Capital: Boston.
Area: 10,555 sq. miles (27,337 sq. km).
Highest point: Mount Greylock.
Population: 6.1 million.
Population density: 570 people per sq. mile (220 per sq. km).
Economy: Financial services; high technology; healthcare; academe.
Annual visitors: 33 million.
National representation: 2 senators and 10 representatives to Congress.
Famous citizens: Samuel Adams, Louisa May Alcott, Emily Dickinson, Ralph Waldo Emerson, John Hancock, Nathaniel Hawthorne, Oliver Wendell Holmes, Edgar Allen Poe.

Lowell's Boat Shop, America's oldest working boat builder.

BELOW: Plum Island in the Parker River National Wildlife Refuge.

freighters had reduced the once-proud shipbuilding community to an aging relic.

An exemplary renewal program begun in the 1960s has restored Newburyport's architectural beauty, and made it a popular destination. The **Market Square** district is a symphony of brick and bustle, with fine shops and restaurants, adjacent to a waterfront promenade and piers where whale watching tours embark several times a week (Prince of Whales, tel: 978-499 0832). Exhibits at the **Custom House Maritime Museum** (25 Water Street, tel: 978-462 8681; open Thur–Sat, Sun pm; entrance fee) chronicle the history of the US Coast Guard and the area's shipwrecks, as well as displaying maritime art.

On High Street successful sea captains built an imposing string of Federal-style mansions. The **Cushing House**, (tel: 978-462 2681; open May–Oct Tues–Sat; entrance fee) at No. 98 High Street, belonged to Caleb Cushing (1800–79), a lawyer and diplomat who became Newburyport's first mayor and America's first ambassador to China. Visitors to the 1808 house, now home to the Historical Society of Old Newbury, can view the exotic booty he brought back.

Parker River National Wildlife Refuge

On the way out to **Plum Island** along Water Street, the Massachusetts Audubon Society offers interpretive displays at their 54-acre (22-hectare) **Joppa Flats Education Center** (tel: 978-462 9888; open Tues–Sun and Mon holidays).

Just across the road, the **Parker River National Wildlife Refuge** visitor center ❸ (open daily; tel: 978-465 5753) offers a fine introduction to the 4,662-acre (1,887-hectare) refuge just 3 miles (5 km) away. Depending on the season, the 6 miles (10 km) of sand dunes and ocean beach yield a riot of false heather, dune grass, scrub pine and beach plums. Geese, pheasants, rabbits, deer, woodchucks, turtles and toads roam freely over the preserve. In March and October the skies are dark with migrating geese and ducks. From April 1 through mid-August, large areas of the beach are roped off to permit the piping plovers –

endangered species of shorebirds – to
st and feed in peace. Fishing, hiking
d bird-watching are encouraged.
Only a limited number of visitors (300
rs; parking fee) are allowed into the
fuge at one time. This makes the un-
oiled strand even more appealing, and
s well worth arriving early.

mesbury

nearby **Amesbury** ❹ is the National
ndmark **Lowell's Boat Shop** (495
ain Street, tel: 978-834 0050; open
emorial Day–Labor Day Tues–Sun).
nis is the oldest continuously operating
oat shop in the US, and birthplace of
e fishing dory. It continues to make
ories and skiffs much as it did when it
rst opened its doors in 1793.

Close by is the **Whittier Home** (86
riend Street; tel: 978-388 1337; whittier
me.org; open May–Oct, Tues–Sat; en-
ance fee). It was here that the "Quaker
oet" and abolitionist John Greenleaf
hittier (1807–92) lived as an adult. The
ouse and furnishings have been pre-
rved as they were during his life.

he road to Ipswich

eading south out of Newburyport on
oute 1A, city and country meet about 4
iles (7 km) out of town in **Newbury**
❺, whose National Historic District of
7 buildings built between 1650 and
927 is centered around a pre-Revolu-
onary Common. Two historic proper-
es are managed by Historic New
ngland (tel: 617-227 3956; historic
wengland.org).

The **Coffin House Museum** (14 High
oad) is open June–Oct 15 on the first
d third Saturday of the month. With its
riginal furnishings, it chronicles the
olution of three centuries of domestic
e in rural New England.

The National Historic Landmark
encer-Peirce-Little Farm (5 Little's
ane; tel: 978-462 2634; tours June–
id-Oct, Thur–Sun; entrance fee), is a
anor house built around 1675–1700 of
one and brick. It was a distinctively
urdy building for its day and is now a
ime site for architectural archaeology.

Ipswich

Continue on Route 1A, a lazy, tree-lined
road, into **Ipswich** ❻, which has more
homes built between 1625 and 1725 that
any other community in the country. On
Main Street, the 1640 **John Whipple
House** (tel: 978-356 2811; open Apr–
mid-Oct Wed–Sat, Sun pm; entrance fee)
is a fine example of a Puritan homestead,
furnished in period style and with a colonial herb garden.

Just out of town, the **Crane Wildlife
Refuge** (tel: 978-356 4354; thetrustees
.org) was part of a vast estate owned by
plumbing fixtures magnate Richard
Crane, who in 1927 built the magnificent, 59-room, Stuart-style **Great House
at Castle Hill** (310 Argilla Road; tel:
978-356 4351; one-hour tours late
May–mid-Oct, Wed–Sat; entrance fee).
Historic landscape tours are offered at
10am Thur and Sat late May–mid-Oct.

The refuge's 4-mile (6-km) **Crane
Beach** (tel: 978-356 4354; parking fee) is
one of New England's finest. Boat tours
to nearby **Choate Island** (also known as
Hog Island), home to a farm that has
remained virtually intact for more than
250 years, depart from Crane Beach. For

TIP

Like any paradise, the
Parker River National
Wildlife Refuge has its
bugbears – in this case,
small, flying insects
called greenhead flies,
whose bite is very
painful. They're most
common from July
through mid-August.
Avon Skin So Soft is
an excellent deterrent.
Also, watch out for
poison ivy and deer
ticks carrying lyme
disease.

BELOW: the Great
House at Castle Hill
on the Crane
Estate, Ipswich.

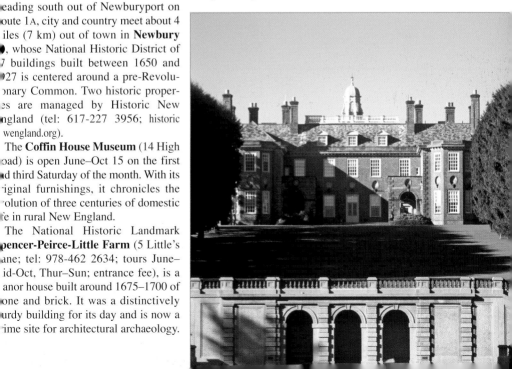

those who want the complete experience, the **Inn at Castle Hill** offers luxurious overnight accommodations.

Essex

Although Ipswich is known for its fried clams, it was in the neighboring town **of Essex ❼**, 5 miles (8 km) southeast on Route 133, where, folk legend has it, the fried clam was born. It was at Woodman's restaurant (tel: 978-768 6451) that clams were first dipped in cornmeal and fried. Today the restaurant still serves up clams in a noisy but relaxed self-serve spot on Route 133.

The **Essex Shipbuilding Museum** (66 Main Street; tel: 978-768 7541; open June–Oct Wed–Sun, Nov–May weekends; entrance fee) traces the region's rich boatbuilding history through thousands of photographs, documents and shipbuilding tools. A 1927 schooner, *Evelina M. Goulart*, sits in the shipyard. Most of the collections are housed in an 1835 schoolhouse, next to which is a burial ground full of interestingly designed 18th- and 19th-century gravestones. A carriage hearse and a sleigh hearse, both 19th-century, are on display.

Cape Ann

Named for the mother of England's King Charles I, Cape Ann is practically an island, compact enough to explore in a day. From Annisquam, at the mouth of Ipswich Bay, to Pigeon Cove, the landscape is quintessential New England – quaint fishing villages and a picturesque rockbound coast.

The quarries at **Halibut Point State Park ❽** (Gott Avenue off Route 127; tel 978-546 2997; entrance fee) once provided granite for Boston's buildings. Within the granite-strewn dwarf woods, the original quarry is now a huge pool edged by sheer cliffs; trees open out into heathland and scrub to reveal views over the rocky shore towards Plum Island. There are majestic views from the top of the Visitors Center, in a renovated, World War II fire-control tower,

Rockport

The granite was shipped to ports around the world in the 19th century, from **Rockport ❾**, a bustling former fishing village-turned-artists' colony and tourist attraction. The seagoers' cottages that crowded onto Bearskin Neck have become tourist-oriented shops. The red fishing shack on the harbor is known as **Motif No. 1** because it is said to be more frequently painted and sketched than any other building in America.

Signposted off Curtis Street on the edge of the village, the **Paper House** (tel: 978-546 2629; 52 Pigeon Hill Street; open daily spring–fall; entrance fee) is an endearing oddity, built entirely of rolled-up newspaper reinforced with glue and varnish. Begun in 1924 by an inventor of office supplies, the project took 20 years, and includes a desk made of copies of the *Christian Science Monitor*. Touristy it may be, especially in summer, but Rockport is disarmingly picturesque, and offers plenty of seaside accommodations and dining.

Gloucester

Take Route 127 or Scenic Route 127A **Gloucester ❿**. Here, Leonard Craske's famous statue, **Fishermen's Memorial**

BELOW: the much-painted Motif #1 fisherman's shack at Rockport harbor. This is a replica of the 1840s original which was swept into the harbor by a blizzard in 1978.

Recommended Restaurants and Bars on pages 144–5

oute 127) grips the wheel and peers eanward, a moving tribute with the ords from the 107th Psalm "they that o down to the sea in ships." The city still s an active fishing fleet, immortalized Sebastian Junger's 1997 bestseller and e subsequent movie *The Perfect Storm.* ne bar where the movie was shot, the row's Nest, still looks much as it did ring filming a decade ago.

On the last Sunday in June, the fish-men, predominantly of Portuguese and alian ancestry, participate in the Bless-g of the Fleet ceremony. The unusual, ission-style **Our Lady of Good Voy-ge Church** (142 Prospect Street, tel: 78-283 1490), overlooking the harbor, as built for the Portuguese community.

Landlubbers get into the act, too, by king one of the whale-watching cruises at leave daily from the **Cape Ann arina**. To learn more about the heyday ' whaling, visit the **Cape Ann Museum** 7 Pleasant Street; tel: 978-283 0455; ues–Sat & Sun pm; entrance fee) for its nall but select collection of furnishings d artwork, ranging from the luminist ascapes of 19th-century painter Fitz ugh Lane to semi-abstractions by mod-

ernist Milton Avery. Exhibits trace the history of local granite quarrying, once an important industry here. To check out the work of living artists, visit the galleries and studios lining the narrow way along **Rocky Neck**, just off East Main Street.

Facing Gloucester across the harbor are two intriguing exam-ples of monomaniacal nesting instincts. On Eastern Point Boule-vard is the early 1900s National Historic Landmark **Beauport**, also known as the Sleeper-McCann House (tel: 978-283 0800; open Tues–Sat June–Oct 15, until 7pm Thur in July–Aug; tours on the hour; entrance fee). This is a romantic labyrinth of cottagey rooms, using architectural fragments from other buildings. The house served as a setting for the summer parties of col-lector and interior designer, Henry Davis Sleeper (1878–1934). The themes vary entertainingly: one bedroom is in chapel style, the belfry is rich in chinoiserie, and the book tower has wooden "damask" curtains salvaged from a hearse.

The Fisherman's Memorial, erected in 1925, looks out to sea at Gloucester.

BELOW:
visiting the galleries at Rocky Neck.

Hammond Castle

Just south of Gloucester, off Route 127 on Hesperus Avenue stands the imposing **Hammond Castle** (tel: 978-283 7673; hammondcastle.org; open Memorial Day–Labor Day Tues–Sun; after Labor Day–mid-Oct and Apr–Memorial Day, Sat & Sun; entrance fee). This was the 1920s fantasy abode of the prolific inventor John Hays Hammond Jr. – remote control via radio waves was his most important idea – who plundered Europe for elements to work into his dreamhouse, including a medieval village facade to overlook the indoor pool.

The entire castle was built around the monumental 8,200-pipe organ (the largest organ in a private home in the US) that Hammond designed – although he is not the Hammond of Hammond Organ fame. Check the museum's website for a schedule of organ concerts.

Salem

All year round – but particularly during October, leading up to Hallowe'en – the old seaport of **Salem** promotes occult events. Salem's web site (www.salem.org) provides gory details on attractions such

as "Terror on the Wharf" and where to buy a "Fright Pass" for admission to three haunted houses. Although the civil rights of witchcraft practitioners have been upheld in Massachusetts, the focus is on the notorious witch trials of 1692 *(see page 143)*.

It's a shame that witch kitsch dominates, because the area has much else to recommend it. "Witch City" (on Route 1A south of Route 128; 40 minutes' train journey from North Station) owes its grandeur, now carefully restored, to its former prominence as a seaport.

A red line along the sidewalks marks the route linking the historic sites, which are also connected by trolley services. Begin a tour with a visit to the **National Park Service Regional Visitor Center** (2 New Liberty St.; tel: 978-740 1650; nps.gov/sama; open daily), which shows an excellent film, *Where Past is Present*, detailing the area's history.

Nearby, the Park Service's **Salem Maritime National Historic Site** at the Derby Street Waterfront shows another fine film, *To the Farthest Parts of the Rich East*, which explains how Salem opened up trade with the Orient. Here

BELOW: Salem Maritime National Historic Site includes the replica tall ship *Friendship*.

Recommended Restaurants and Bars on pages 144–5

7pm; Oct weekends until 11pm; rest of year 10am–5pm; entrance fee), The structure is famous for more than mere antiquity, though, having been the inspiration for the house in the classic 1851 novel of the same name by Salem native Nathaniel Hawthorne. The c. 1750 house in which Hawthorne was born has been moved next door, and visitors can tour both houses as well as the handsome colonial revival gardens.

Peabody Essex Museum

No visit should omit the **Peabody Essex Museum D** (East India Square; tel: 866-745 1876 or 978-745 9500; pem.org; open daily; entrance fee), whose outstanding collections includes a fully re-erected Qing Dynasty merchant's house, numerous displays related to the maritime trade (particularly memorable are the ships' figureheads), maritime paintings, and a superb collection of artifacts brought back from the Far East.

sitors may tour the Derby Wharf, a plica of the 1797 ship *Friendship*, the 319 Custom House, and Derby House, merchant's mansion built in 1762. here is a fee to enter buildings and oard the ship.

On Turner Street is New England's dest remaining 17th-century wooden ansion, the forbidding-looking 1668 ational Register of Historic Places ouse of the Seven Gables **C** (tel: 978-44 0991; open July–Oct daily 10am–

On Essex Street, the Museum preserves six houses that span two centuries of New England architecture; the McIntyre Historic District preserves Georgian and Federal-period houses designed or

Seafaring symbol on display at the Peabody Essex Museum in Salem.

TOP LEFT:
Hawthorne's
House of the
Seven Gables.

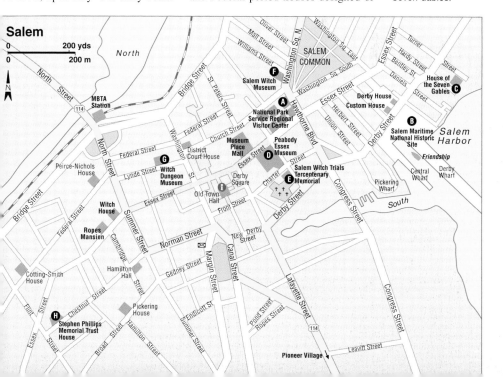

Recommended Restaurants and Bars on pages 144–5

One of the best ways to get your bearings is aboard the Salem Trolley (8 Central Square; tel: 978-744 5469; salemtrolley .com; fee). After the one-hour tour, you can use it as a shuttle as it makes 12 stops along its route.

BELOW: statue outside the Salem Witch Museum.

inspired by architect and master builder Samuel McIntire. The district offers a tour-de-force for anyone interested in both architecture and in American cultural history: this is where, and how, the nation's first millionaires lived.

The witch trail

Salem's maritime glory notwithstanding, most visitors will want to tour the scenes of the infamous witchcraft trials of 1692, in which "hysteria" conveniently abetted political repression, allowing the gentry, personified by the convicting judges, to fall back on the time-honored method of attacking political and social upstarts as moral deviants.

Most moving is the **Salem Witch Trials Tercentenary Memorial** ❺, a stark granite court adjoining **Charter Street Burying Point**, the final resting place of Witch Trials Court magistrate John Hawthorne. Incised along the paving stones and walls are passages from the accused women's pleas of innocence.

The **Salem Witch Museum** ❻ (Washington Square North; tel: 978-744 1692; open daily; fee) reenacts, accurately if sensationally, key scenes to recorded commentary, while the **Witc Dungeon Museum** ❼ (Lynde Street; te 978-741 3570; open Apr–Nov dail entrance fee) presents a well-researche live show evoking the persecutions. F a less melodramatic but historical accurate presentation of the times, vis the **Witch House** (310 Essex Street; te 978-744 8815), home of witch tria judge Jonathan Corwin.

Chestnut Street ranks among Ame ica's finest shows of domestic archite ture. The **Stephen Phillips Memori Trust House** ❶ (34 Chestnut Street; te 978-744 0440; open June–Oct Tues–Sa Nov–May, Sat and Sun) is furnished wi the belongings of five generations of th Phillips family. Antique cars and ca riages are displayed in the Carriag House. The elegant gardens at the late 1720s **Ropes Mansion** (318 Esse Street) are open to the public.

Marblehead

Take a short detour from Salem on rout 1A south and 114 to **Marblehead** ❿ founded as a fishing village in 1629 an today the "Yachting Capital of America The narrow streets of the Historic Di trict are lined with pre- and post-Rev lutionary homes – many now chic B&B shops, and galleries.

The **Marblehead Museum & Hi torical Society** (170 Washington St.; te 781-631 1768; open June–Oct, Tues–Sa preserves the city's history with art ar artefacts; exhibits include a delightf collection of folk art. It also oversees th elegantly preserved **Jeremiah Lee Ma sion** (161 Washington Street; open Jun Oct Tues–Sat 10am–4pm, Thur un 7pm; entrance fee), one of the most op lent homes of the mid-1700s.

The original of Archibald Willard painting *The Spirit of '76* (a.k.a. *Yanke Doodle)* is displayed in the selectmen room of **Abbot Hall** (Washington Stree tel: 781-631 0000; open daily).

Be sure to visit **Old Burial Hill**, ove looking the harbor and sea. Establishe in 1638, it is the final resting place f 600 soldiers of the Revolution.

Salem's witches

Behind the tawdry merchandising and overwrought re-enactments lies one of New England's darkest episodes of religious intolerance.

Since its founding in 1626, the town (whose name derives, ironically, from *shalom*, the Hebrew word for peace) had never been a bastion of tolerance and good will: it was from Salem that Roger Williams, the founder of Rhode Island, had been exiled for preaching religious freedom.

The townspeople's rigid ways took a destructive turn when Tituba, a Barbados slave serving the household of Salem's minister, Samuel Parris, began regaling his daughter, Elizabeth, and niece, Abigail Williams, with vivid accounts of voodoo. Fascinated, Elizabeth and Abigail invited a handful of their friends to listen to Tituba's tales.

Meetings of such a nature, being strictly forbidden in Puritan Salem, held an illicit appeal that the girls must have found difficult to resist, but no doubt they also found their guilty pleasure difficult to live with, for all soon began to exhibit bizarre behavior: they would crawl on the floor, making choking sounds, and cry out that needles were piercing their flesh. The town doctor was called in to examine the girls and, after medicine failed to cure them, he diagnosed them as victims of witchcraft.

The Rev. Mr Parris suggested that Tituba might be their tormentor, and the slave was charged with witchcraft. In confessing, un-

der pain of torture, she gave a lurid account of how a tall man from Boston, accompanied by witches, had molested the girls.

Satan himself, she claimed, had ordered her to murder the girls, and other witches had beaten her for her refusal to comply; she merely tormented them, trying to abate her own pain. In her stories, she pointed a finger at two women unpopular in the village, Sarah Osborne and Sarah Good, who were charged with everything from bewitching cattle to using voodoo dolls.

Enflamed by the oratory of such self-promoting preachers as Cotton Mather, subsequent accusations spread like wildfire. Ultimately, 400 people ended up accused – many of them marginal members of society, whose lack of prosperity the Puritans took to mean a lack of godliness.

Imprisoned in cold, damp cells, several of the accused women died while awaiting trial. Of those found guilty in Salem, 19 were hanged and one man was pressed to death beneath a wooden plank piled with rocks. These executions took place between June and September, and the terror might have continued through the fall had Governor General Sir William Phips not returned from the north woods, where he had been fighting an alliance of French and Native Americans, and put a stop to the madness. In December 1692, he ordered all the suspects released – including his own wife. ❏

ABOVE: today, kitsch toys boost the economy.
RIGHT: the reality of a 1692 persecution – *The Duckingstool*, by Charles Stanley Reinhart.

RESTAURANTS AND BARS

Restaurants

Prices for a three-course dinner per person with a half-bottle of house wine:
$ = under $20
$$ = $20–45
$$$ = $45–60
$$$$ = over $60

Amesbury

Ristorante Molise
1 Market Square
Tel: 978-388 4844
ristorantemolise.com
$$–$$$
Italian specialties include homemade gnocchi and risottos, veal parmesan. (Also at 464 Main Street, Wakefield.) D Tues–Sun.

Essex

Woodman's
The Causeway
Tel: 978-768 6451
woodmans.com **$**

Home of the original fried clam, invented in 1915. Also on the menu at this very informal spot: fresh fish, a raw bar, and chowder. No credit cards. L and D daily.

Gloucester

65 Main and Dog Bar
65 Main Street
Tel: 978-281 6565 **$–$$**
A casual, candlelit restaurant with a contemporary American menu ranging from huge hamburgers to seared duck breast. D Tues–Sun.

The Rudder
73 Rocky Neck
Tel: 978-283 7967 **$–$$**
A rollicking tavern/restaurant in the Rocky Neck artists' colony. D nightly in season; Thur–Sun off season.

Passports
110 Main Street
Tel: 978-281 3680 **$$–$$$**
Foods from around the world, including fresh fish dishes from the Adriatic, sushi from Japan, creative pastas, and great popovers. L and D daily.

Ipswich

The Clam Box
246 High Street
Tel: 978-356 9707 **$–$$**
ipswichma.com/clambox
Serving fabulous fried clams and other native seafood for 60-plus years. Self-service either indoors or on the deck. L and D daily in season.

Marblehead

The Landing
81 Front Street
Tel: 781-639 1266 **$$–$$$**
New England seafood in a cheerful dining room overlooking the harbor. Opt for the deck in nice weather. L and D daily. (Also: 7 Central Street, Manchester; L Sat–Sun, D nightly.)

Maddie's Sail Loft
15 State Street
Tel: 781-631 9824
maddiessailloft.com **$$**
Fried or broiled seafood and landlubber options in a lively, often-crowded casual room. The bar, with a pub menu, is a favorite with seafaring folks. L and D Mon–Sat.

Newburyport

Glenn's Restaurant and Cool Bar
Merrimack Street
Tel: 978-465 3811
glennsrestaurant.com **$$**
"World class cuisine in a funky casual atmos-

phere" – actually a former shoe factory. Try a dish from the wood-fired grill. D Tues–Sat.

The Grog
13 Middle Street
Tel: 978-465 8008
thegrog.com **$–$$**
For more than 30 years the city's premier rendezvous for burgers, seafood, chowder, and drinks in a laid-back atmosphere. Live music (rock, folk, blues) Wed–Sun. L and D daily; Sun brunch.

Jewel in the Crown
23 Pleasant Street
Tel: 978-463 0956
newburyportjewel.com **$**
A large menu of classic Indian dishes, including lamb dosa, curries, and firey vindaloos. The dinner sampler is a good bet. L and D daily.

Michael's Harborside
Tournament Wharf
Tel: 978-462 7785
michaelsharborside.com **$$**
A long-time riverfront favorite, with a varied menu including sandwiches, fresh fish, and baby baby ribs. Live music upstairs. L Mon–Sat; D nightly. No reservations.

Szechuan Taste, Sushi Yen and Thai Café
19 Pleasant Street
Tel: 978-463 0686
szechuantaste.com **$–$$**
A handsomely-furnished room with a superb selection of ethnic dishes, and a particularly deft touch with seafood dishes and sushi. L and D daily.

tourist bustle specializes in chowder, but serves up sandwiches, burgers, and seafood plates, too. L and D daily.

Salem

Fresh Taste of Asia
118 Washington Street
Tel: 978-825 1388
freshtasteofasia.com $$
Sushi is the star in a menu that mixes Chinese and Japanese cuisines. L and D daily.

Grapevine
26 Congress Street
Tel: 978-745 9335
grapevinesalem.com
$$–$$$
A peaceful, elegant spot for northern Italian fare sparked with an occasional fusion influence. D nightly.

Lyceum Bar and Grill
43 Church Street
Tel: 978-745 7665
lyceumsalem.com $$–$$$
Seafood, chowder and grilled meats in a converted, 19th-century theater overlooking the Green. L Mon–Fri; D nightly; Sun brunch.

Red's Sandwich Shop
15 Central Street
Tel: 978-745 3527
redssandwichshop.com $
For more than 35 years this landmark spot has been popular for breakfasts, classics such as American chop suey, and homemade desserts. Mon–Sat 5am–3pm; Sun 6am–1pm.

Salem Beer Works
278 Derby Street
Tel: 978-745 2337
beerworks.net $–$$
Salem's contribution to microbreweries. Upscale bar food and fresh-

Rockport

Brackett's Oceanview Restaurant
25 Main Street
Tel: 978-546 2797
bracketts.com $–$$
The small storefront opens up into a spacious harborfront dining room. Seafood is the specialty, and the emphasis is on solid Yankee fare. L and D Apr–Oct.

The Lobster Pool
329 Granite Street
Tel: 978-546 7808 $–$$
lobsterpoolrestaurant.com
For more than 60 years one of the area's best waterfront "in the rough" dining destinations. Among specials are the "no celery lobster rolls", chowders, and homemade pie. L and D Apr–Oct.

Portside Chowder House
Bearskin Neck
Tel: 978-546 7045 $
A basic eatery in the heart of Rockport's

brewed beers are served in a renovated warehouse building. L and D daily.

Bars

Barking Dog Bar & Grill, 21 Friend Street, Amesbury (tel: 978-388 9537). Care for a carrot cake martini? How about coconut almond? If not a martini, order from the extensive beer and wine menus. There's live music Tues and Wed nights; but this place – which also serves terrific American food – is always packed.
Crow's Nest, 334 Main Street, Gloucester (tel: 978-281 2965). The funky waterfront bar that Sebastian Junger made famous in his book (and the subsequent movie) *The Perfect Storm* looks just as it did in October 1991, when the crew of the *Andrea*

Gail set out on their fateful voyage.
Park Lunch, 181 Merrimac Street, Newburyport (tel: 978-465 9817). With two large-screen TVs tuned to sports, this bar is in a very busy, very good, and very moderately priced establishment a short distance from downtown.
The Peddler's Daughter, 45 Wingate Street, Haverhill, (tel: 978-372 9555). A dimly lit Irish pub with cold pints, and great fish 'n' chips wrapped in newspaper. Live music Thur–Sat nights. The menu offers classic bar fare and more creative fusion dishes. Also in Nashua, New Hampshire.
Salem Beer Works, 278 Derby Street, Salem (tel: 978-741 7088). A place to quench your thirst with Boston microbrews, and the burgers and sandwiches are okay.

LEFT: welcome to The Rudder in Gloucester.
ABOVE: sushi in Salem's Fresh Taste of Asia.
RIGHT: lobsters on offer at Woodman's in Essex.

MASSACHUSETTS: WEST OF BOSTON

West and northwest of Boston are vivid reminders
of two American revolutions – the one that gave
the nation its independence, but also the Industrial
revolution, financed by Brahmin capital and
powered by the waters of the Merrimack River

Main attractions
LOWELL
LAWRENCE
LINCOLN
LEXINGTON
MINUTE MAN NATIONAL
    HISTORICAL PARK
CONCORD
WALDEN POND

BELOW:
Lowell National
Historical Park.

The one-time model mill town of Lowell ⑭, 34 miles (55 km) northwest of Boston via Route 3, is enjoying a renaissance as a major tourist attraction, and is arguably America's best brick-and-mortar chronicle of industrial history. Sightseeing ferries ply the old canals, trolleys clang through the streets, and looms pound again at the **Boott Cotton Mills Museum** (115 John Street; open daily; entrance fee) operated with the **Lowell National Historical Park Visitor Center** (246 Market Street; tel: 978-970 5000; nps.gov/lowe; open daily;

fee for walking and trolley tours), where a film and exhibits trace the town's history, and trolley and walking tours begin. There is also an excellent exhibit, *Mill Girls and Immigrants*, at the nearby **Patrick J. Morgan Cultural Center** (40 French Street; open Mon–Fri).

Jack Kerouac, the Beat Generation icon, was born, raised, and buried here. The **Kerouac Memorial**, in Kerouac Park on Bridge Street, is a series of metal tablets displaying his most poignant quotes. The lowellcelebrateskerouac.org website is informative about his local links.

The artist James Abbott Whistler (1834–1903), spent the first three years of his life in what is now the **Whistler House Museum of Art** (243 Worthen Street; tel: 978-452-7641); open Wed–Sat; entrance fee), now home to the Lowell Art Association. The collection of 19th- and 20th-century New England representational arts includes etchings by Whistler.

Exhibits at the vast **American Textile History Museum** (491 Dutton Street; tel: 978-441 0400; open Thur–Sun; entrance fee), housed in an 1860s canal-front factory, include the world's largest collection of spinning wheels and several re-created 18th- and 19th-century mills.

It's appropriate that the center of the nation's textile industry is home to the **New England Quilt Museum** (18 Shattuck Street; tel: 802-452 4207; open Tues–Sat; Sun pm May–Dec; entrance fee). It recounts the history of American quiltmaking with more than 150 traditional and contemporary quilts.

Recommended Restaurants and Bars on page 151

Hop aboard New Orleans #99, the trolley that inspired playwright Tennessee Williams, for a 2-mile (3-km) ride at the **National Streetcar Museum** (25 Shattock Street; tel: 207-967 2712; open Tues–Sun; streetcar rides weekends May–Oct). This outpost of the Trolley Museum in Kennebunkport, Maine, tells the story of urban rail transportation.

Lawrence

About 15 miles (24 km) miles east via Route I-495 is **Lawrence** ⓯, one of the country's first planned industrial cities. Over the years more than 30 immigrant populations have moved here to work in the city's mills, and their story is ably recounted at **Lawrence Heritage State Park** (1 Jackson Street, Tel: 978-794 1655; mass.gov; open daily). Exhibits at the Visitor Center, housed in a restored boarding house, also document the Great Strike of 1912, also called the "Bread and Roses" strike. That year a state law reduced the work week from 56 to 54 hours, and mill owners reduced pay at the same time, making the average weekly wage just $8.76. Workers eventually won, but not without much suffering.

Lincoln

Tiny, upscale **Lincoln** ⓰, just a half-hour from Boston via Route 2, has an unusual number of attractions for its size, including the superb **DeCordova Sculpture Park** (51 Sandy Pond Road; tel: 781-259 8355; decordova.org; open Tues–Sun; entrance fee). With around 75 large-scale contemporary outdoor American sculptures, the 35-acre (14-hectare) museum is the largest of its kind in New England. The house of the one-time estate, known as "the castle," is now a museum of modern and contemporary American art. The café serves light lunches.

Summer jazz concerts are held in the outdoor theater. The grounds are free when the house is not officially open.

Historic New England (historicnewengland.org; tel: 781-259 8098) oversees two properties within a few miles of each other. Furnishings in the palatial, c. 1740 **Codman House** (The Grange, 34 Codman Road) reflect the five generations that lived on this expansive farm. The c. 1900 Italianate and 1930s English gardens are gems. The **Gropius House** (68 Baker Bridge Road), built by the renowned 20th-century architect who

LEFT: the Boott Mill in Lowell National Historical Park.
BELOW: DeCordova Sculpture Park.

helped launch the Bauhaus school, built his house here in 1938 when he came to teach at the Harvard Graduate School of Design. Both houses are open June–Oct 15 on the first and third Saturday of the month, with tours 11am–4pm on the hour (entrance fee).

Drumlin Farm (208 South Great Road; tel: 781-259 2200; massaudubon.org/drumlin; open Tues–Sun and some Monday holidays; entrance fee) is a working farm and wildlife sanctuary, with a lively barnyard.

Lexington

On April 19, 1775 British regulars clashed in a battle with Massachusetts militia and Minutemen in Lexington and Concord, and "the shot heard round the world" launched the eight-year War for Independence. The route of the British advance from Boston is designated the **Battle Road**, and, although mostly a highway, has many historic attractions.

The best place to start a visit to the area is at one of **Minute Man National Historical Park**'s (tel: 978-369-6993; nps.gov/mima) visitor centers: the **North Bridge Visitor Center** (174 Liberty Street, Concord; open daily); **Minuteman Man Vis-**

itor Center (270 North Great Road, Lincoln; open daily); and the **Hartwell Tavern** (Route 2A. Lincoln; open daily lat May–late Oct), a restored, 18th-centur home and tavern where park rangers i Colonial attire offer 20-minute program daily at 11:15am, 2:15pm; 3:15pm, an 4:15pm. The excellent film *The Road t Revolution* is shown here throughout th day. From Boston, all of the revolution ary sites in and around Lexington an Concord can be reached via Route 2.

A weekend of parades and historica re-enactments takes place aroun Patriot's Day (the Monday closest t April 19) at the park.

Chronologically, a visit to the Battl Road sites should go east to west. In **Le ington** ⑰, just south of the town cente the **National Heritage Museum** ⓐ (3 Marrett Road, Route 2A; tel: 781-86 6559; open Mon–Sat; Sun pm) focuse on the history of American freemasonr and fraternalism, as well as the perio surrounding the American Revolutior

The c. 1690s **Munroe Tavern** ⓑ (133 Massachusetts Avenue; tel: 781-86 1703; open June–Oct, call for hours entrance fee) served as headquarters fc

TIP

The Liberty Ride (liberty ride.us), a 90-minute narrated trolley tour that departs from the National Heritage Museum in Lexington, is a good way to see Lexington and Concord's sites. It stops at all major attractions, and passengers can disembark and reboard at no additional charge. Tours are given at noon, 1:30pm, and 3 pm.

BELOW: the iconic statue of Captain John Parker on Battle Green, Lexington.

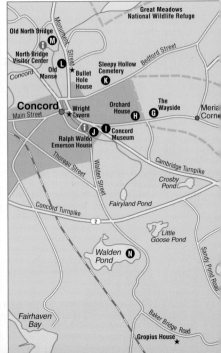

Brigadier General Earl Percy and his British troops for one-and-a-half hours during their retreat from Concord.

At the heart of Lexington a statue of Captain John Parker stands on **Battle Green** ☉, where on Apr 19, 1775, the first shot was fired; of the Minutemen, vastly outnumbered, eight were killed. The **Lexington Visitor Center** (tel: 781-862 2480; lexingtonchamber.org; open daily) is next to the Green.

Buckman Tavern ☉ (1 Bedford Street; tel: 781-862 5598; open Apr-Nov daily; entrance fee; tours every half-hour), built in 1710, has been restored to look as it did in 1775 when Captain Parker and his Minutemen sipped beer while awaiting Paul Revere's warning; a bullet hole is visible in one door.

The **Hancock-Clarke House** ☉ (Hancock Street; tel: 781-862 1703) open July–Oct; entrance fee), where John Hancock and Samuel Adams were woken by Revere on the eve of the battle with news of the British advance, displays the furnishings of two ministers who lived here for a period of 105 years.

At the **Ebenezer Fiske House Site** ☉, a historical trail explains the course of the fierce fighting that broke out there; a section of the Battle Road here is unpaved and closed to traffic, giving an idea of its original appearance.

Concord

As you enter **Concord** ⑱ the theme digresses for a time into literature. From 1845 to 1848 the writer Louisa May Alcott and her father, Bronson Alcott, lived in **The Wayside** ☉ (455 Lexington Road, Route 2A; tel: 978-318 7863; nps.gov/mima; open May–Oct; 40-minute tours Wed–Sun at 11am, 1pm, 3pm; and 4:30pm; limited to 10 people; phone reservations accepted; fee for tour). In 1852 it was bought by writer Nathaniel

The British are back: a Patriots Day re-enactment on Concord's replica Old North Bridge. It was here that General Gage's British troops, crowded into the narrow pathway, were easily routed in 1775 by the ragtag Americans. An obelisk marks where the first British soldier fell.

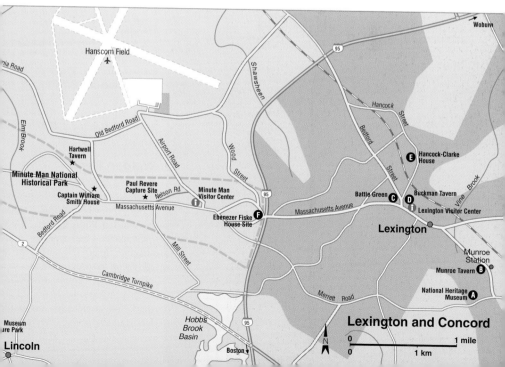

Lexington and Concord

Walden Pond, considered to be the birthplace of the conservation movement.

BELOW: statue of Thoreau outside a replica of his cabin at Walden Pond.

Hawthorne – he added the tower, but found it unsatisfactory for working in, and said he would happily see the house burn down.

The Alcott family lived from 1858 to 1877 at **Orchard House** ⓗ (399 Lexington Road, Route 2A; tel: 978 369 4118; louisamayalcott .org; open Mon–Sat; Sun pm; closed Jan 1–15; guided tour only, tickets on a "first come, first served" basis; entrance fee) where Louisa May set and penned the hugely popular *Little Women* and *Little Men*. The house still has most of the family's furnishings and looks as it did when they lived here. There's an excellent orientation video, and a self-guided tour of Bronson's School of Philosophy, which functioned from 1880 to 1888.

Thoreau and Emerson

Near the junction of the Battle Road with Route 2, **Concord Museum** ⓘ (200 Lexington Road, Route 2A; tel: 978-369 9763; open Mon–Sat; Sun pm; entrance fee) has excellent displays relating to Revolutionary and literary Concord, includ-

ing one of the two lanterns hung by Robert Newman in Old North Church in Boston. A gallery devoted to Concord's Henry David Thoreau (1817–62) has a superb collection of artifacts associated with the great author and naturalist including furnishings from his cabin by Walden Pond.

The philosopher and author Ralph Waldo Emerson lived most of his adult life nearby; his house, furnished as it was when he died in 1882, is preserved as the **Ralph Waldo Emerson House** ⓙ (28 Cambridge Turnpike; tel: 978-369 2236 open mid-Apr–mid-Oct Mon–Sat; Sun pm; entrance fee).

Sleepy Hollow Cemetery ⓚ (Bedford Street, Route 62; tel: 978-318-3233 is the resting place of most of the Concord big names, among them Hawthorne the Alcotts, Emerson and Thoreau.

The Old Manse ⓛ (269 Monumen Street; tel: 978-369 3909; open Apr–Oc Mon–Sat; Sun pm; entrance fee) was bui by minister William Emerson aroun 1770, and was used to shelter women an children during the battle. It became hom to his grandson Ralph Waldo, who wrot *Nature* (1836) here, and was rented fo three years to Nathaniel Hawthorne It houses a huge book collection an Hawthorne's desk.

Cross **Old North Bridge** ⓜ (se *picture and caption, page 149),* pas Daniel Chester French's *Minut Man* statue, unveiled for the cen tennial of the famous fight, an walk up to the Minute Ma National Historical Park's Nort Bridge Visitor Center.

Walden Pond

South of Concord off Route 12 Thoreau spent 26 months in a on room cabin (there's now a replic by **Walden Pond** ⓝ (tel: 978-36 3254; parking fee; open year-roun striving to be self-sufficient an recording the progress of nature, of which he recounted in *Wald* (1854). A National Historic Lan mark, the pond and surroundi land are now a state reservation.

RESTAURANTS AND BARS

Restaurants

Prices for a three-course dinner per person with a half-bottle of house wine:
$ = under $20
$$ = $20–45
$$$ = $45–60
$$$$ = over $60

Concord
Colonial Inn
48 Monument Square
Tel: 978-369 2000
concordscolonialinn.com
$$–$$$
A 1716 inn serving traditional New England fare plus international dishes. High tea Fri–Sun 3–5pm. B, L, D daily; Sun brunch.

La Provence
105 Thoreau Street
Tel: 978-371 7428
laprovence.us **$–$$**
A self-serve, informal bistro with treats such as salmon in champagne sauce, beef bourgougnon, and quail. Mon–Fri 7am–7pm; Sat 7am–5.30pm.

Walden Grille
24 Walden Street
Tel: 978-371 2233
waldengrille.com **$$–$$$**
Creative American dishes like wild mushroom ravioli, and crab macaroni and cheese, in a handsomely renovated 1903 firehouse. L and D daily.

Lawrence
Lawton's
606 Canal Street.
Tel: 978-686 9603. **$**
Deep fried hot dogs are the specialty at this tiny, hole-in-the-wall eatery. Hungry? Opt for "the works" – a dog topped with chilli and cheese. L Mon–Sat.

Lexington
Dabin
10 Muzzey Street
(Off Mass Avenue)
Tel: 781-860 0171 **$$**
Japanese and Korean cuisine. Small patio for outdoor dining when it's warm. L and D Mon–Sat.

Lemon Grass
1710 Massachusetts Avenue
Tel: 781-862 3530 **$–$$**
A low-key Thai storefront café where the food is tempered for American palates. L and D daily.

Mario's Restaurant
1733 Massachusetts Avenue
Tel: 781-861 1182 **$**
Family favorite for large portions of homemade Italian-American treats including pasta and calzones. BYOB. L, D daily.

Lowell
La Boniche
143 Merrimack Street
Tel: 978-458 9473
laboniche.com **$$–$$$**
An intimate French-style bistro serving creative fare in a landmark Art Nouveau building. L Tues–Fri; D Tues–Sat.

The Olympia
453 Market Street
Tel: 978-452 8092
olympia.com **$–$$**
Lowell's oldest restaurant, a friendly, family-run traditional Greek spot. L Mon–Fri, D nightly.

Natick
Casey's Diner
36 South Avenue.
Tel: 508-655 3761. **$**
Established in 1805, this tiny diner seats just 10. Good home cooking and great hot dogs.

Maxwells 148
148 E. Central Street
Tel: 508-907 6262. **$$–$$$$**
A melting pot of cuisines includes ribeye, gravlax, Pho Max soup, and homemade ricotta gnocchi with Maine lobster. A prix-fixe dinner (**$$$**) Tues–Fri. L & D Tues–Sat.

Sudbury
Longfellow's Wayside Inn
72 Wayside Inn Road
Tel: 978-443 1776. **$$–$$$**
Longfellow really did visit this 1716 inn and might recognize many of the New England specialties. L and D Mon–Sat; D menu from noon Sun.

Waltham
The Tuscan Grill
361 Moody Street
Tel: 781-891 5486. **$$–$$$**
Local favorite for Northern Italian cuisine. Chefs in the open kitchen whip up wood grilled monkfish and herb-crusted lamb chops. D nightly.

Wellesley
Blue Ginger
583 Washington Street
Tel: 781-283 5790. **$$$–$$$$**
In celebrity chef Ming Tsai's elegantly-furnished establishment, shiitake-leek spring rolls share the menu with rack of lamb and garlic black pepper lobster. L Mon–Fri; D Mon–Sat; closed Sun.

Bars
The Claddagh Pub & Restaurant, 399 Canal Street, Lawrence. A serious spot for darts, pool, and live bands (Thur–Sun evenings). Free pizza and chicken Fri 4pm–6pm.
J.J. Boomers, 705 Pawtucket Boulevard (Route 113), Lowell. Karaoke, pool, and darts keep patrons happy when the Red Sox and Patriots aren't on the house TVs. Specials include Thursday corn beef and cabbage.
Sadie's Saloon & Eatery, 5 Pine Street, Waltham. More of a bar than a restaurant, but the steak tips (turkey, pork, or beef) here are outstanding. L Tues–Sat; D nightly.
Watch City Brewing Company, 256 Moody Street, Waltham. The beer and wine are brewed on the premises, and the menu – with dishes such as fire-grilled chicken – is reasonably priced.

MASSACHUSETTS: SOUTH OF BOSTON

The southeastern corner of Massachusetts, often overlooked by travelers heading for Cape Cod, is rich in a legacy that includes Pilgrims, presidents and whalers

Main attractions
HINGHAM
NANTASKET
DUXBURY
PLYMOUTH
PLIMOTH PLANTATION
NEW BEDFORD WHALING
  MUSEUM
FALL RIVER HERITAGE
  STATE PARK
BATTLESHIP COVE

BELOW:
the battleship
Salem at Quincy.

From Boston, head south on Route 1 for 8 miles (13 km) to **Quincy** and the **Adams National Historical Park** (Visitor Center at 1250 Hancock Street; tel: 617-770 1175; nps.gov/adam; open mid-Apr–mid-Nov, daily; Visitor Center – not houses – open year-round with limited hours; last tour at 3:15pm; entrance fee). This was home to four generations of Adamses from 1720 to 1927. The site includes the birthplace of America's first father-and-son presidential pair, John Adams (second President of the US), about 10 ft (3 meters) away, the birthplace of his son, John Quincy Adams (the sixth); and Peacefield, the elegant home that John and his wife, Abigail, moved to in 1787.

High points of the tour are J.Q. Adams's stone library, with 14,000 volumes, and the formal garden, especially appealing when the daffodils bloom. A free trolley connects the houses. A 2008 HBO mini-series about John Adams based on David McCullough's Pulitzer Prize-winning book, rekindled interest in the historical site. Entrance to the buildings is by guided tour only, first-come first-served: on weekends and holidays waits of one to two hours are common.

Hingham

Further down the coast off Routes 1 and 3A, is **Hingham** ⑳, beautified by Frederick Law Olmsted, creator of Boston's "Emerald Necklace" of parks and Central Park, New York; his handiwork here is the bucolic **World's End Reservation** (250 Martin's Lane; tel: 781-740-6665; open daily; entrance fee), a 250-acre (100-hectare) harborside preserve that is a protectorate of the Trustees of the Reservations (thetrustees.org). Walking trails provide views of the Boston skyline and Hingham Harbor.

At the center of town is the **Old Ship Church** (90 Main Street; tel: 781-749-1679; open seasonally) one of the country's oldest continuously-used wooden church structures (1681). Built by ship's carpenters, the interior, resembles a giant hull turned upside down.

Recommended Restaurants and Bars on page 157

Nantasket

Enclosing Hingham Bay and curving toward Boston like a beckoning finger is the sandy spit of **Nantasket ㉑**, a long-time summer playground of which only a carousel has survived redevelopment. The classic 1928 **Paragon Carousel** (205 Nantasket Avenue; tel: 781-925 0472; open daily Memorial Day–Labor Day 10am–10pm; entrance fee) is a gem. An "adopt a horse" program helps fund the restoration of the 66 horses that prance to the music of a Wurlitzer organ.

The **Hull Lifesaving Museum** (1117 Nantasket Avenue; tel: 781-925 5433; open daily, year-round; entrance fee), in a restored 19th-century lifesaving station at the mouth of Boston Harbor, gives visitors a good idea of the heroic measures required when the lighthouse warnings failed to stave off disaster. Hands-on exhibits focus on storms, lighthouses, wrecks, and rescues, and there are fabulous views of Boston Light (America's oldest operating lighthouse) and Graves lighthouse from the observation cupola.

At the end of the Hull peninsula, the observation deck at the top of the water tower in **Fort Revere Park** (tel: 617-727 4468; Memorial Day–Labor Day; entrance fee) offers a panoramic view from Cape Ann to Provincetown. There's also a small military museum.

The second first lady, John Adams's wife Abigail, was born at the **Abigail Adams Birthplace ㉒** (180 Norton Street; tel: 781-335 4205; abigailadamsbirthplace.org; call for tour information) in **Weymouth** in 1744. The house, built in 1685 and once referred to as "the mansion" has been restored to its mid-1700s appearance.

Duxbury

Just off gently meandering Route 3A to the south is **Duxbury ㉓**, one of the state's loveliest and most carefully conserved towns. It was settled in 1628 by Pilgrims, and they are well remembered here. A 14-ft (4.3-meter) monument to Captain Myles Standish, *Mayflower* passenger and Plymouth colony leader, crowns a 125-step observation tower at the top of Captain's Hill in **Myles Standish Monument State Reservation** (Crescent Street; tel: 508-208 0676; open mid-June–late August, closed Wed and Thur). Fellow *Mayflower* passengers

John Adams (1735–1826) served as ambassador to the Netherlands and Britain and became the second president of the United States. In helping to frame the Constitution, he ensured that rigorous checks and balances were included.

BELOW: two of the family homes in the Adams National Historical Park.

Interpreting the past at Plimoth Plantation.

BELOW: the replica *Mayflower II.*

John and Priscilla Alden lived at the finely preserved 1653 **Alden House** (105 Alden Street; tel: 781-934 9092; open mid-May–mid-Oct Mon–Sat pm; entrance fee), and are buried, along with Myles, at the **Old Burying Ground** on Chestnut Street.

A wealthy shipbuilder/merchant, Ezra Weston, Jr., affectionately nicknamed King Caesar (New England's then-largest ship, *The Hope*, was constructed in his shipyard in 1841), built a stately Federal mansion in 1809 that today stands as a testament to his wealth and good taste. Highlights at the **King Caesar House** (120 King Caesar Road; tel: 781-934 6106; open July–Aug Wed–Sun pm; Sept Sat and Sun pm; entrance fee) include rare French scenic wallpaper and a variety of 19th-century furnishings.

Carl A. Weyerhaeuser, the grandson of the founder of the hugely successful lumber company, began collecting art with a discerning eye while a student at Harvard. Today the **Art Complex Museum** (189 Alden Street; tel: 781-934 6634; open Wed–Sun; entrance fee) houses his superb collection, including prints by masters such as Dürer, Turner, and Corot; Shaker furniture; American paintings by artists such as Sargent, Cropsey, and Bellows; and Asian art. A Japanese tea house hosts traditional tea ceremonies.

Plymouth

Directly southward, on Route 3, lies **Plymouth** ㉔, which styles itself "America's Home Town." Here **Plymouth Rock** Ⓐ, legendary 1620 landing place of the Pilgrims, enjoys a place of honor under an elaborate harborside portico. The rock is… well, a rock, but even if taken with a grain of salt as the actual landfall, it's an interesting example of origin mythology.

A stone's throw from the monument is the *Mayflower II* Ⓑ (State Pier, Water Street; tel: 508-746-1622; open late March–Nov daily; entrance fee). A replica of the original *Mayflower*, this was built in England and sailed to Plymouth in 1957. Actors on board the 104-ft (32-meter) long vessel portray the original passengers and field visitors' questions with accuracy and wit, vividly conveying the hardships that its 102 passengers must have suffered on their 66-day voyage.

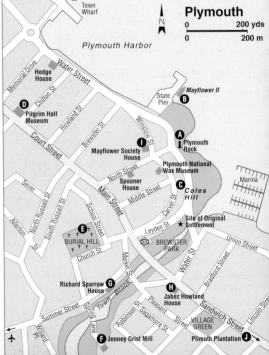

Plymouth

0 ——— 200 yds
0 ——— 200 m

Across the road from the Rock is **Coles Hill** , where, during their first winter, the Pilgrims secretly buried their dead at night to hide the truth about their fast dwindling numbers from the Indians. Nearby is the original settlement's site.

Pilgrim Hall Museum (75 Court Street; tel: 508-746 1620; open Feb–Dec daily; entrance fee), America's oldest public museum in continuous use (1824), gathered the more outstanding memorabilia of Pilgrim life early on (though they are rather unimaginatively displayed). Relics include John Alden's halberd, Myles Standish's sword, razor and Bible, and the cradle of Peregrine White, born aboard the *Mayflower*.

Farther east, beyond Main Street, is **Burial Hill**, with gravestones dating back to the colony's founding. "Under this stone rests the ashes of Willm Bradford, a zealous Puritan and sincere Christian, Governor of Plymouth Colony from April 1621–57 [the year he died, aged 69] except 5 years which he declined." The hill was the site of the Pilgrims' first meeting house, fort and watchtower.

South of Burial Hill is the replica **Jenney Grist Mill** tel: 508-747 4544; open April-December; entrance fee), where corn is still ground as it was by the Pilgrims in 1636. A costumed guide gives 30-minute tours (advance reservations are appreciated).

Plymouth's historic houses

Plymouth also has a number of historic houses worth visiting.

The oldest is the **Richard Sparrow House** (42 Summer Street; tel: 508-747 1240; open Apr–Thanksgiving Day weekend Thur–Tues; donations). Built in 1640, it contains exhibits of crafts and 17th-century pottery.

The **Jabez Howland House** (33 Sandwich Street; tel: 508-746 9590; open late May–mid-Oct daily; entrance fee) originated in 1667 as a home for the son of one of the original Pilgrims and contains some fine 17th-century furniture.

The **Mayflower Society House** (4 Winslow Street; tel: 508-746 2590; open July–mid-Sept daily; spring and fall Fri–Sun; entrance fee) is an elegant mansion built in 1754. It has a graceful flying staircase and a variety of period rooms.

Plimoth Plantation

About 3 miles (5 km) south of town, on Route 3, **Plimoth Plantation** (Warren Avenue; tel: 508-746 1622; plimoth.org; open late March–Nov daily; entrance fee) is a painstaking reconstruction of the 17th-century Pilgrim village; its every detail has been meticulously researched. It is inhabited by actor/interpreters who so convincingly enact the quotidian rituals of the original village – and converse with visitors in Jacobean English – that visitors can easily lose themselves in the fantasy of those heady days full of hardship and dreams. Perhaps nowhere in the US is history recounted with such accuracy and verve. *More details: page 38.*

New Bedford

Southwest of Boston, via routes 3, 6, 495 and 195, is **New Bedford**, onetime whaling capital and today the East Coast's busiest fishing port. The narrow cobblestone streets and historic buildings of the old quarter have been incorporated

TIP

● A combination ticket, good for two consecutive days with the Plimoth Plantation, and a third day at the *Mayflower II*, is on offer. Couples with up to four children can buy a Plimouth Pass.

● Call a day in advance to book one of Jenney Grist Mill's 60-minute walking tours of Plymouth's Historic District (tel: 508-747 4544). They're offered every day but Tuesday Apr–Nov at 9am and 5pm.

BELOW: the replica Jenney Grist Mill.

Anchor aweigh at Battleship Cove.

TIP

New England Fast Ferries (tel: 866-683 3779; nefastferry.com) run from New Bedford's State Pier to Martha's Vineyard.

BELOW: submarine at Battleship Cove.

into the **New Bedford Whaling National Historical Park** (33 William Street; tel: 508-996 4095; nps.gov/nebe). At weekends in July and August, park rangers conduct Underground Railroad tours of the city, relating the history of the escaped slaves who fled to New Bedford for freedom and jobs.

The big attraction is the **New Bedford Whaling Museum** (18 Johnny Cake Hill; whalingmuseum.org; open daily year-round; entrance fee). In addition to informative sections evoking the lifestyles of the whalers and fishermen, there is a huge show of ship models – most memorably the *Lagoda*, a half-size replica of a 19th-century whaling vessel – and some fine paintings on the theme, plus a collection of scrimshaw, intricately carved out of whalebone by the sailors on their long voyages.

Across from the museum is the **Seamen's Bethel** (open Memorial Day–Columbus Day Mon–Fri; entrance fee)) with the "Whaleman's Chapel" portrayed by Herman Melville in *Moby-Dick*. The 156-ft (57-meter) Grand Banks fishing

schooner *Ernestina* (tel: 508-992 4900) launched in Essex in 1894, was grounded by the US Coast Guard in 2004, but the historic sailing ship has been restored and is moored at the State Pier.

Taking up a full city block, the 183- **Rotch-Jones-Duff House & Garden** (396 County Road; tel: 508-997 1401 open Mon–Sat, Sun pm; entrance fee) i a National Landmark. A prominent whaling merchant's home, it was designed by renowned architect Richard Upjohn and is a superb example of residential Greek Revival architecture. It chronicles life in New Bedford from 1834 to 1981.

Fall River

At the mouth of the Taunton estuary 9 miles (6 km) west from New Bedford **Fall River 26** is dominated by huge mills reminders of the city's long-defunct cotto industry. Some of these Victorian relic now house factory outlets. The city's lif before outlets is told at **Fall River Heritage State Park** overlooking Battleshi Cove (Davol Street; tel: 508-675-5759 open daily). You can ride on a 192 **carousel** (open late June–early Sept daily late May–late June weekends; fee housed in a Victorian pavilion.

Battleship Cove (tel: 508-678 1100 800-533 3194 in New England; battleshi cove.org; open daily 9am–5pm; entranc fee) has the world's largest collection of historic naval ships. Among them are th submarine USS *Lionfish;* the 46,000-to battleship USS *Massachusetts*; and th world's only restored pair of PT boat The submarine and the battleship – "B Mamie," a fighting veteran of World W II – can be visited. The former fascinate in a claustrophobic way; the latter is a amazing, labyrinthine floating steel cit bristling with firepower.

Virtually adjacent, the **Marin Museum** (70 Water Street; tel: 508-67 3533; open Wed–Fri, Sat pm, Sun an entrance fee) traces the history of the Fa River Line from 1847 to 1937, and packed with nautical paraphernali including the model of the *Titanic* use in a 1953 film, *Titanic* memorabilia, a more than 150 steamship models.

RESTAURANTS AND BARS

Restaurants

Prices for a three-course dinner per person with a half-bottle of house wine:
$ = under $20
$$ = $20–45
$$$ = $45–60
$$$$ = over $60

Fall River
Estoril
1577 Pleasant Street
Tel: 508-677 1200 **$–$$**
A white-tablecloth introduction to classic Portuguese fare at very moderate prices.
L and D Wed–Sun.

Tabacaria Açoriana Restaurant
408 S Main Street
Tel: 508-673 5890 **$–$$**
A casual Portuguese café with authentic dishes such as kale soup, marinated pork and steamed octopus, and a fine selection of regional wines. L and D daily.

Hingham
Nino's Steak & Chop House
415 Whiting Street
Tel: 781-340 7300. **$$–$$$**
Housed in an old mill, this local favorite has a reputation for good service and large portions of well-prepared American, Greek, and Italian dishes. D Tues–Sun.

Hull
Jake's Seafood Restaurant & Market
Steamboat Wharf, 50 George Washington Boulevard
Tel: 781-925 1024. **$–$$**
A large assortment of flopping-fresh fish dishes, but fried clams are the specialty at this

waterfront spot on Nantasket Beach.
L Mon–Sat; D Mon–Sat and Sun from noon.

Plimoth Plantation
Patuxet Café
Warren Avenue
Tel: 508-746 1622 **$**
You can wash down a venison burger or bowl of turkey and cranberry soup with a Mayflower Golden Ale, brewed by Boston Brewing Company to replicate beer consumed by the English in the 17th century.

Plymouth
14 Union Dockside Bar and Grill
14 Union Street
Tel: 508-747 4503 **$$–$$$**
Seafood and beef specialties at a pleasant spot with a deck looking out on the *Mayflower II*. Live entertainment Thur–Sun; jazz and reggae brunch weekends.
L and D daily.

Lobster Hut
Town Wharf
Tel: 508-746 2270 **$**
Basic fried seafood served on the waterfront.

Stoneforge
140 Warren Avenue, Route 3A
Tel: 508-747 7887
stoneforge.net **$$–$$$**
The extensive raw bar and waterfront view are major attractions, as are fish dishes such as wasabi tuna and tangerine teriyaki salmon.
L and D daily.

Quincy
Quincy Dynasty
49 Billings Road
Tel: 617-328 3288. **$**

ABOVE: the art of preparing oysters.

Chinese-American favorites share the menu with traditional dishes such as lobster with glass noodle hot pot. There's a week day luncheon buffet; Sunday brunch buffet includes dim sum. L and D daily.

Bars

Alumni Café, 708 Hancock Street, Quincy. A terrific place to mingle with the locals, watch a game, have one of its acclaimed pizzas, and wash it down with a beer.
British Beer Company, 6 Middle Street, Plymouth. This Massachusetts-based chain recreates the "locals" of Great Britain, serving (cold) craft and international beers and traditional pub fare such as bangers & mash, fish 'n' chips, pasty pies. Entertainment, ranging from blues to country, is a bit less Merrie Olde England. Also locations in Cedarville, Hyannis, Pembroke, Plymouth, Sandwich, and Walpole, Massachusetts.
Cronin's Publick House, 23 Des Moines Road, Quincy Point. A relaxed, informal Irish-themed pub/restaurant with an expanded bar menu which includes the house specialty pound of grilled sirloin tips; and a fine spicy Cajun chicken soup.
Union Brewhouse, 550 Washington Street, Weymouth. The "Home of the 99 Club" truly does have 99 kinds of bottled beer as well as seven draft beers, along with broadcasts of local sports and an expanded pub menu served until midnight.

CAPE COD AND THE ISLANDS

This sandy summer playground has fine clam shacks, historic B&Bs, undeveloped National Seashore beaches, and a lively arts scene – plus the sharply contrasting little islands of Martha's Vineyard and Nantucket

Main attractions
SANDWICH GLASS MUSEUM
SANDY NECK BEACH
BARNSTABLE
CAPE COD NATIONAL
  SEASHORE
WELLFLEET
PROVINCETOWN
CHATHAM
HYANNIS
WOODS HOLE
MARTHA'S VINEYARD
NANTUCKET

BELOW:
fishing charters are
readily available.

Bostonians consider Cape Cod their own private playground, but its fame has spread so far that it attracts international travelers. In high season (July and August), lodgings are filled to capacity, traffic on the Cape's few highways is heavy, and local merchants work hard to make the profits that will carry them through the virtually dormant winters. (The pleasures of the Cape off-season, however, are much less of a secret than they were even a few years ago.) Even at the height of its summertime popularity, when the roads, restau-

rants, and beaches tend to be jamme Cape Cod manages to preserve its wi charm and dramatic beauty.

Much of this quality is protecte within the boundaries of the Cape C National Seashore, a vast 27,000-ac (11,000-hectare) nature reserve esta lished by foresighted legislators in 196 Precisely because it has not been co mercially exploited, this huge expanse untouched dunes survives as one of t Cape's most alluring features.

Getting your bearings

Note the nomenclature. "Upper Cap refers to the portion nearest the mai land; "Mid-Cape" is roughly from Bar stable County eastward to Chatham a Orleans, where the "arm" bends; "Low Cape" is the "forearm" jutting northwa to Eastham, Truro and Provincetown.

Technically, Cape Cod is an islar The **Cape Cod Canal** was built by N York financier August Belmont in 19 to eliminate the need for ships to rou the Cape via the often stormy Atlant Belmont ran the canal as a priva endeavor until 1928, when it was p chased by the US Government. The U Army Corps of Engineers supervised building of the two bridges, whi opened in 1935, and improvements to t waterway: by 1940 it was the widest se level canal (there are no locks) in t world. Two 7-mile (11-km) service roa which parallel the canal are great f bicycling or hiking.

The **Cape Cod Canal Visitor Cent**

❶ (60 Ed Moffitt Drive, Sandwich; tel: 08-759 4431; nae.usace.army.mil/recreati/ cc/recreation/recreation.htm; open May–Oct daily) off Route 6A recounts the history of the canal and the bridges. Park rangers conduct a guided tour daily at 2pm, and also offer numerous excellent programs throughout the summer.

Choose a bridge

Expressways funnel traffic to the two access bridges over the Canal. At the waterway's eastern end, Route 3 comes south from Boston and crosses the **Sagamore Bridge** to join Route 6, the Mid-Cape Highway.

The other span, the **Bourne Bridge**, is handy if you're approaching the Cape from the west via Routes I-95 and 495. This is the crossing to use if you want to head south toward Falmouth and Woods Hole via Route 28.

Which route? It depends…

Itineraries on the Upper and Mid-Cape offer a choice of speedy, featureless highways or scenic, meandering roads. Those intent on reaching the Outer Cape in a hurry generally opt for Route 6, the four-

lane, limited-access Mid-Cape Highway; those headed for Falmouth, Woods Hole, and points along Nantucket Sound can take the equally speedy Route 28.

Anyone wishing to get a true sense of the Cape, however, will be well rewarded by taking the prettier non-highway counterparts. Roughly parallel to the Mid-Cape Highway, two-lane Route 6A starts in Sagamore and runs eastward along the Bay through old towns full of graceful historic houses, crafts and antique shops.

The same can be said of Route 28, hugging the shore en route to Falmouth. As Route 28 veers northeastward from Falmouth to Chatham, though, it's marred by recurrent stretches of overdevelop-

The four-lane Sagamore Bridge over the Cape Cod Canal opened to traffic in 1935.

TIP

For information about Cape Cod arts events, galleries, and artists, log onto: capecod culturalexplorer.org

The unpromising peninsula that became a playground

Shaped like a bodybuilder's flexed arm, Cape Cod extends 31 miles (50 km) eastward into the Atlantic Ocean, then another 31 miles to the north. Well rested up to about the "elbow," then increasingly reduced to scrub oak and pitch pine, this sandy peninsula is lined with more than 310 miles (500 km) of beaches. The crook of the arm forms Cape Cod Bay, where the waters are placid and free of often treacherous ocean surf. Lighthouses guide mariners plying the cold Atlantic waters. Geologically the Cape is relatively new, a huge mass of debris dumped after the melting of a last ice sheet.

Before the advent of modern transport, Cape Cod was a hardscrabble area peopled by the Wampanoag

tribes, hardy Yankees and industrious immigrants from the coasts and islands of Portugal. Since the land supported only subsistence farming, most people earned their living from the sea.

In 1602, Bartholomew Gosnold, a British

ABOVE: Cape Cod earned its living from the sea.

mariner sailing by this long arm of sand, noted a great many codfish in the waters and added the name "Cape Cod" to his map. In 1620, the *Mayflower* pulled into the harbor of what is now Provincetown and, before debarking to explore, its passengers drew up the Mayflower Compact for self-government. This early "constitution" grew into the government of the Commonwealth of Massachusetts.

The first hordes of tourists arrived in the late 19th century, brought by steamship and railroad. Escaping the summer heat of Boston, Providence and New York for the cool sea breezes along the shore, they found low prices, inexpensive real estate and simple pleasures in abundance.

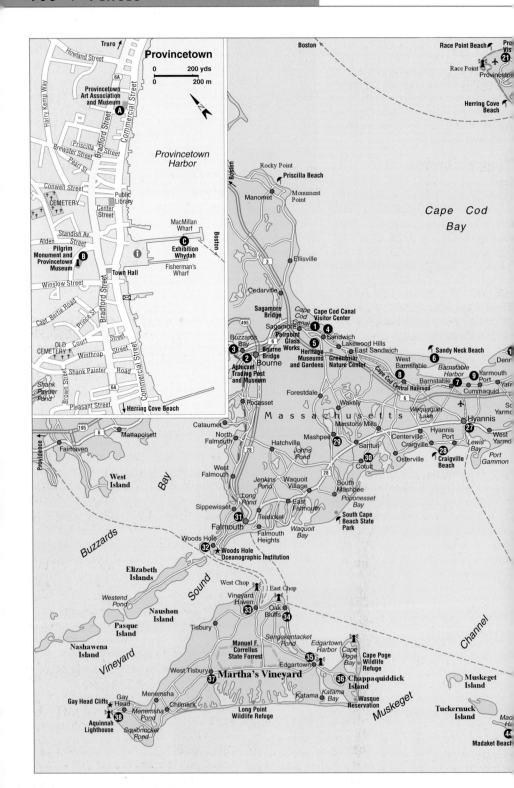

Truro

Provincetown

| 0 | 200 yds |
| 0 | 200 m |

Howland Street

Harry Kemp Way

6A

Commercial Street

Provincetown
Art Association
and Museum Ⓐ

Bradford Street

(Priscilla
Brewster Street
Pearl St

Conwell Street

Public
Library

CEMETERY

Center
Street

Standish Av.

Alden

Pilgrim
Monument and
Provincetown
Museum Ⓑ

Winslow Street

Capt. Bertie Road

Prince St.

OLD
CEMETERY

Court

Winthrop

Street

Street

Shank Painter

Road

Shank
Painter
Pond

6A

Pleasant Street

195

6

Mattapoisett

Providence

Fairhaven

West
Island

Buzzards

Bay

Elizabeth
Islands

Westend
Pond

Naushon
Island

Pasque
Island

Nashawena
Island

Vineyard

Gay Head Cliffs

Gay
Head

Aquinnah
Lighthouse

Menemsha

Menemsha
Pond

Squibnocket
Pond

Ⓒ

Provincetown
Harbor

Boston

MacMillan
Wharf

Exhibition
Whydah

Fisherman's
Wharf

Town Hall

Herring Cove Beach

Boston

Provincetown
Harbor

Rocky Point

Priscilla Beach

Manomet

Monument
Point

Ellisville

Cedarville

Sagamore
Bridge

Cape
Cod
Canal

495

Sagamore

Cape Cod Canal
Visitor Center

⓵ ⓸

Buzzards
Bay

6

Pairpoint
Glass
Works

⓹ Sandwich

Lakewood Hills

⓷

⓶

Bourne
Bridge
Bourne

Heritage
Museums
and Gardens

East Sandwich

Greenbriar
Nature Center

West
Barnstable

⓺ Sandy Neck Beach

Denr

Aptucxet
Trading Post
and Museum

Forestdale

Wakely

Cape Cod Central Railroad

⓼

Barnstable
Harbor

Barnstable ⓻

⓽ Yarmouth
Port

Cummaquid

Yar

Pocasset

Massachusetts

Wequaquet
Lake

Sc
Yarmo

Cataumet

North
Falmouth

Marstons Mills

Mashpee

⓾

Centerville

Santuit

Hyannis
Port

Hyannis Ⓩ

West
Yarmo

Hatchville

28

Johns
Pond

Craigville

Osterville

Lewis
Bay

Port
Gammon

West
Falmouth

Jenkins
Pond

Waquoit
Village

South
Mashpee

Cotuit

Ⓒ Craigville
Beach

28

Long
Pond

Sippewisset

Ⓩ

Teaticket

East
Falmouth

Poponesset
Bay

South Cape
Beach State
Park

Falmouth

Woods Hole

Ⓩ

Waquoit
Heights

Waquoit
Bay

Woods Hole
Oceanographic Institution

West Chop

Vineyard
Haven

East Chop

Oak
Bluffs Ⓩ

Ⓩ

Tisbury

Sound

Manuel F.
Correllus
State Forrest

Sengekontacket
Pond

Edgartown

Edgartown
Harbor

Cape
Poge
Bay

Cape Poge
Wildlife
Refuge

West Tisbury

Ⓩ Martha's Vineyard

Edgartown

Ⓩ

Chilmark

Long Point
Wildlife Refuge

Katama

Katama
Bay

Ⓩ Chappaquiddick
Island

Wasque
Reservation

Muskeget
Island

Muskeget

Tuckernuck
Island

Mac
Ha

Ⓩ Madaket Beach

Cape Cod
Bay

Race Point Beach

Race Point

Herring Cove
Beach

Pro
Vis

Ⓩ

Provinceto

Boston

Channel

Cape Cod and the Islands

0   5 miles
0   5 km

N

19 Cape Cod
Highland
Lighthouse

Cranberry Bog Trail

Truro
Truro Center
for the Arts

Cape Cod

17 Wellfleet
Great
Wellfleet
Harbor   **18**
Island Wellfleet Bay
Wildlife
Sanctuary

South
Wellfleet

16 Marconi Beach

Nauset Light Beach

Billingsgate
Island   North
Eastham   **15** National

13   Coast Guard Beach

Eastham

First Encounter
Beach   **14** Salt Pond
Visitor Center

Skaket Beach   Tonset

Museum   Orleans   **22** French Cable
History   **12**   Station Museum

Nickerson   Orleans
East   State Park
Brewster   South   Seashore
st Brewster   Orleans   **23** Nauset Beach

Pleasant   Pleasant
Lake   Bay
Hawksnest
State Park

North Chatham
West
Chatham

Harwich   Chatham

Harwich   **24**
Port
Chatham Lighthouse

Sequetucket
Harbor

ATLANTIC

Monomoy National
Wildlife Refuge   **25**

OCEAN

Monomoy Island

cket
nd

Great
Point

40 Coatue-Coskata
Wildlife Refuge

Wauwinet   **41**

Nantucket Life-Saving
Museum
Sankaty Head

Monomoy

tucket Island   Siasconset

Nantucket   **42**
State Forest

---

ment but, again, one has only to venture off the main road a bit to discover such towns as Osterville and Centerville, Harwich Port and Chatham itself.

Once Route 28 and Route 6 merge in Orleans, Route 6 north is pleasant all the way to Provincetown, if traffic-clogged in summer. For those wishing to avoid the drive, there are summer ferries between Provincetown and Boston, Provincetown and Plymouth, and flights into Hyannis and Provincetown.

Attractions near the bridges

On the Cape side of the Sagamore Bridge are **the Pairpoint Glass Works** (Route 6A; 800-899 0953; open daily in season), where glassblowers give demonstrations weekdays. Right nearby is the **Cape Cod Factory Outlet Mall** (Route 6; tel: 508-888 8417; open daily). It's not the most exciting mall, but with 20 stores, it's the largest on the Cape.

West of the Bourne Bridge, on the mainland side near the canal, the Bourne Historical Society's **Aptucxet Trading Post and Museum** ❷ (Aptucxet Road, Bourne; 508-759 9487; open Tues–Sat Memorial Day/end-May–Columbus Day/Oct; entrance fee) is a replica of the first English-speaking trading post in North America, set up in 1627 to trade with the Wampanoag Indians, the Dutch in New York and the Plymouth settlement.

The society also maintains several other historic sites in town, including the National Register of Historic Places **Briggs-McDermott House**; and **Gray Gables Railroad Station**, built for the personal use of President Grover Cleveland, who had a summer home here.

In nearby **Buzzards Bay** ❸ displays and animal exhibits at the **National Marine Life Center** (120 Main Street; tel: 508-743 9888; nmlc.org; open late May–early Sept, Mon–Sat and Sun pm) focus on the rescue and rehabilitation of stranded marine animals.

The Bay Side: Sandwich to Brewster

This region gained world renown for its glass after Boston merchant Deming Jarvis founded a glass factory in **Sandwich** ❹ in 1825. It thrived until threatened by coal-powered plants in the Midwest; that, and a strike by exploited workers, shut the enterprise down in 1888. However, examples of their output, in an astounding range of styles, can still be found in the **Sandwich Glass Museum** (tel: 508-888 0251; Main Street; open Apr–Dec daily; Feb–March Wed–Sun; entrance fee), which also shows an excellent, 23-minute multi-media program portraying life in 18th-century rural New England.

Sandwich, the first town to be founded on the Cape, in 1637, is one of the prettiest and best-preserved. At

Glass blowing is a tradition in the area, dating back to the 1825 founding of the Boston and Sandwich Glass Company.

BELOW: relaxing near Sandwich, the oldest town on Cape Cod – it was incorporated in 1639 and today has 23,000 residents.

its center stands the restored 1680 **Dexter Mill** (stone-ground cornmeal available in summer) and the c. 1637 **Hoxie House** (Water Street; tel: 508-888 1173; open mid-June–mid-Oct, Mon–Sat; Sun pm; entrance fee), a remarkably well-preserved saltbox reputed to be the Cape's oldest dwelling.

Peter Rabbit, Reddy Fox, Jimmy Skunk and all of the other whimsical characters created by the author and naturalist Thornton Burgess (1874–1965) come to life at the **Thornton Burgess Museum** (4 Water Street; tel: 508-888-6870; thorntonburgess.org; open May–Oct Mon–Sat; Sun pm; donation). Sometimes they come to life literally as summer storytelling sessions include the live animal featured in a story. The museum is housed in an 18th-century home once owned by his aunt Arabella.

Another property supervised by the Burgess Society, Peter Rabbit's favorite briar patch – a 57-acre/23-hectare conservation area – is adjacent to **Greenbriar Nature Center** (6 Discovery Hill Rd; open daily April–Dec; Tues–Sat Jan–March; donation) in East Sandwich. The center's 1903 Jam Kitchen prepares and sell jams and relishes.

Heritage Museum & Gardens

For more glimpses into the American past, follow the signs – past a lovely historic cemetery overlooking Shawme Pond – to **Heritage Museums and Gardens** ❺ (67 Grove Street; 508-888 3300; heritagemuseumsandgardens.org; open Apr–Oct daily; Nov–Dec Fri–Sun; entrance fee), a spacious complex of three museums of Americana that includes toys, military artifacts, and folk art. A round stone barn (copied from the Shaker original in Hancock, Massachusetts) houses an outstanding array of early cars, including one particular beauty, Gary Cooper's 1931 Duesenberg. In spring the grounds are awash in the vivid pinks and purples of flowering rhododendrons.

Museum admission includes a ride on the antique carousel hand-carved by the renowned Charles Looff (1852–1918).

Sandy Neck and Barnstable

Motoring east along Route 6A into Barnstable County you'll pass the turn-off for the 6-mile (9-km) **Sandy Neck Beach** ❻.

Recommended Restaurants and Bars on pages 182–5

which is a favored habitat of the endangered piping plover. Hikers and swimmers are welcome to explore, provided they don't disturb the birds' nesting sites. There's a $15 daily parking fee.

Barnstable ❼ is also home to 4,000-acre (1,620-hectare) **Great Marsh**, the Cape's largest salt water marsh. **Hyannis Whale Watcher Cruises** (tel: 508-362-6088 or 888-942-5392) depart from Barnstable Harbor May through October.

Just up the hill from the harbor is the **Trayser Memorial Museum** (3353 Route 6A; tel: 508-362 2092; open June–mid Oct, Thur–Sun pm), the former 1856 Custom House, which now focuses on maritime life and culture.

In **West Barnstable ❽**, **West Parish Meetinghouse**, built in 1646, is an outstanding example of early colonial architecture and has a Paul Revere bell cast in 1806. The weathervane, a gilded cock, was ordered from England in 1723.

East of Barnstable, **Yarmouth Port ❾** is a delightful village with fine old houses to tour. These include the **Captain Bangs Hallett House** (Strawberry Lane; tel: 508-362 3021; open June–mid–Oct Thur–Sun; tours at 1, 2 and 3pm; entrance fee), an 1840 Greek Revival showcase; and the **Winslow Crocker House** (250 Route 6A; tel: 508-227 3957; open June–mid Oct, first Sat of month; entrance fee), a 1780 Georgian manse filled with colonial furniture, hooked rugs, ceramic and pewter.

The **Edward Gorey House** (8 Strawberry Lane; tel: 508-362 3909; open July–early Sept, Wed–Sat, Sun pm; call for off-season hours; entrance fee) exhibits possessions of the artist/illustrator who lived here focuses on one of his lifetime passions: animal welfare. For a pleasurable glimpse of more recent history, stop for an ice cream soda at **Hallett's Store** (139 Main Street; tel: 508-362 3362), a well-preserved 1889 drugstore/soda fountain with a small "down home" second-floor museum.

Cape Playhouse

In the town of **Dennis ❿**, follow signs for the **Scargo Hill Tower**, a stone turret

from which, on a clear day, you can see Cape Cod laid out like a map, with Provincetown visible at the northern tip. Dennis is home to America's oldest, and most outstanding, professional summer theater, **Cape Playhouse** *(see margin tip)*.

On the playhouse grounds, at the **Cape Cod Museum of Art** (tel: 508 385-4477 open end-May–late Oct, daily; rest of year, Tues–Sun; entrance fee), works interpreting the role of the Cape and islands in American art are exhibited in seven galleries and a sculpture garden. Guided tours of the museum are offered Thursdays at 2 pm and Saturdays at 11am and 1 pm; Thursdays, when the museum stays open until 8pm, admission is by donation.

East to Brewster

In **Brewster ⓫**, home to numerous fine old houses and Inns, the **Stony Brook Mill** (Stony Brook Road southwest off Route 6A) grinds cornmeal Saturdays and Sundays 10am–2pm June–Aug; there's a small museum upstairs. Each spring, from mid-April to early May, the mill hosts an eye-catching event when schools of herring leap up a series of

TIP

Performances take place mid-June–mid-Sept at Cape Playhouse (Route 6A; tel: 508-385 3838 or 877-385 3911. Aspiring thespians such as Bette Davis (an ambitious usher) and Henry Fonda started their careers here. Productions are skilled and lavish, and movies at the adjoining Cape Cinema (tel: 508-385 2503; capecinema .com), with leather armchairs and Art Deco frescoes by Rockwell Kent (1882–1971), are a sensory treat.

BELOW:
the Gulf Stream keeps the Cape's temperatures warmer for longer.

Scalloping at Wellfleet. Bay scallops are found at low tide in eelgrass and tidal pools. The three-day Bourne Scallop Festival, held each September at Buzzards Bay, attracts 50,000 people. Details: bournescallopfest.com

ladders to spawn in the freshwater pond behind the mill.

The **Cape Cod Museum of Natural History** (869 Main Street, Route 6A; tel: 508-896 3867 or 800-479-3867 in Mass; open Oct–May, Wed–Sun; June–Sept, daily; entrance fee) explores the local habitat through hands-on exhibits and nature trails.

Railroad magnate Roland Nickerson once owned 2,000 acres (800 hectares) of open land in Brewster, using them as a personal hunting and fishing preserve. In 1934 his widow donated most of this tract to the state; today **Nickerson State Park ⑫** (Route 6A; tel: 508-896 3491) is a popular spot for camping, swimming, picnicking, and walks. The 8-mile (13-km) bicycle trail connects with the **Cape Cod Rail Trail** *(see box, below)*.

Eight sparkling "kettle ponds" at the park are among more than 300 on the Cape formed as the glaciers retreated.

The Lower Cape: Eastham

Eastham ⑬, easily recognized by its 1793 windmill on the town green, also has several historic buildings of note,

The Cape Cod Rail Trail

In the Cape's early heyday, summertime visitors arrived by train. But except for the excursion trains run between Hyannis and the Cape Cod Canal by the Cape Cod Central Railroad (tel: 508-771 3800; 800-797 7245) rail travel has disappeared from the Cape. However, at least one lengthy section of roadbed has been put to an energy-saving, pleasure-making use: the Cape Cod Rail Trail is a 25-mile (40-km) paved recreational path ideal for bicycling, skating, walking and jogging. Along the way, it passes lakes and marshes, woods and a harbor. The most scenic or dramatic sections are the National Seashore spur trails in Eastham and Wellfleet that terminate at the Atlantic Ocean. The trail runs from just off Route 134 in South Dennis through Nickerson State Park and on to Wellfleet. You can rent bicycles at a number of places along the way, including Barbara's Bike & Sport (tel: 508-760 4723) at the trailhead, Idle Times Bike Shop (tel: 508-255 8281) in North Eastham, and Little Capistrano Bike Shop (tel: 508-255 6515) across from the National Seashore headquarters in Eastham.

including two National Register of Historic Landmarks properties: the period-furnished **Swift-Daley House** (Route 6, next to post office; tel: 508-240 0871; open July–Aug, Mon–Fri pm; Sat pm in Sept), built in 1741 by a ship's carpenter; and, across from the Salt Pond Visitors Center *(see below)*, a **one-room schoolhouse** built in 1869 (tel: 508-255 6896; open July–Aug, Tues–Wed pm, Fri 10am–4pm; Sat pm in Sept).

For a deeper side trip into Cape Cod's history, head west to **First Encounter Beach**. It's here that a Pilgrim scouting party out of Provincetown first encountered a band of Indians, who, wary after earlier encounters with kidnappers, attacked the Pilgrims and were rebuffed by gunfire. This uneasy meeting is one of the reasons why the Pilgrims pressed on to Plymouth. Today the historic site is a peaceful town beach (which, like most, charges a parking fee in summer).

Cape Cod National Seashore

Established in 1961 when part-time Cape resident John F. Kennedy was president, **Cape Cod National Seashore** (headquarters: 99 Marconi Site Road, Wellfleet; tel: 508-349 3785; nps.gov/caco) extends from Eastham to Provincetown and protects 27,000 acres (10,930 hectares) of land, including 40 miles (65 km) of pristine beaches, lighthouses, cranberry bogs, marshes, ponds, hiking and biking trails, and sand dunes.

The **Salt Pond Visitor Center ⑭** (tel: 508-255 3421; open daily) provides an excellent introduction to the area. Interpretive films and exhibits explain the ecology of the Cape, and a bicycle trail (bikes can be rented nearby) winds through pine forests and marshes to end at Coast Guard Beach, where, in 1928, writer-naturalist Henry Beston produced his classic book *The Outermost House*, chronicling a year spent living on the dunes. Park rangers offer numerous guided tours, including a visit to the 1730 **Atwood Higgins House**, a typical early settler's home in nearby Wellfleet.

Farther north is **Nauset Light Beach** ⑮, graced with an 1877, 48-ft lighthouse which was rescued from an eroding cliff in nearby Eastham in 1996 and moved to its present site. Tours (tel: 508-240 2612; nausetlight.org; donation) are given Sundays from early May through October, and Wednesdays in July and August.

At the Seashore's **Marconi Beach** ⑯, Guglielmo Marconi set up the first wireless station in the United States and transmitted the first trans-Atlantic wireless message to Europe in 1903. (In 2003, Marconi's daughter marked the event's centennial by speaking with International Space Station astronauts via satellite from here.) The **Atlantic White Cedar Swamp Trail**, starting from the Marconi site, is especially beautiful.

Wellfleet

Famous for its oysters, **Wellfleet** ⑰ is one of Cape Cod's most appealing towns, full of fine galleries and fun restaurants, and surrounded by inviting wildlife areas. Just south of town, off Route 6, the Audubon Society maintains the 1,100-acre (445-hectare) **Wellfleet Bay Wildlife Sanctuary** ⑱ (tel: 508-349 2615; massaudubon. org; open 8am–dusk, Columbus Day–early May, Tues–Sun; entrance fee); a net-work of delightful walking trails leads from the visitor center, which displays natural history exhibits.

That's not a mirage you see when heading north on Route 6: the **Wellfleet Drive-In Theatre** (tel: 508-349 7176; wellfleetcinemas.com), the only drive-in on the Cape, shows first-run double features nightly Apr–early Oct. On Saturdays, Sundays, and holiday Mondays – and on Wednesdays and Thursdays in July and August – the drive-in turns into a huge flea market as 300 vendors set up booths.

Truro

Farther north, the landscape becomes ever more wild and barren. Scrubby vegetation gives way to desert-like sand dunes. This is **Truro**, whose light and scenery led realist painter Edward Hopper (1882–1967) to make his summer home here for 30 years.

East of Truro, the **Cranberry Bog Trail** (within the Cape Cod National Seashore) accesses the natural habitat of the tiny red fruit that proved such a boon to Cape Cod agriculture. Another road east leads to **Highland Light**, towering over Head of the Meadow Beach.

TIP

A beach entrance fee is collected from late June through early September, and on weekends and holidays from Memorial Day through September. Vehicles are charged $15; bicyclists, motorcyclists, and pedestrians, $3. If you're going to be visiting for an extended period, a $45 vehicle pass covers all beaches on the National Seashore for the season.

BELOW: top temperatures in July and August average 79°F (26°C).

Cape Cod Highland Lighthouse ⓳ (tel: 508-487 1121; capecodlight.org; tel: 508-487 1121; open mid-May–mid-Oct, daily; entrance fee) is a much photo-graphed landmark; erected in 1857, it is the peninsula's oldest lighthouse.

The **Highland House Museum** (truro historical.org; tel: 508-487 3397; open June–Sept, Mon–Sat 10am–4:30pm, Sun 1–4:30; admission fee) on the grounds was built as a hotel in 1907. The museum offers an interesting look at the hard-scrabble life of the Lower Cape before tourism, and even has a pirate's chest.

The **Truro Center for the Arts** (10 Meetinghouse Road; tel: 508-349 7511; castlehill.org) hosts a summer-long festi-val of crafts, concerts, and forums.

Provincetown

Contrast the subtle beauties and serenity of the National Seashore lands with the raucous and sometimes tawdry atmos-phere along Commercial Street in **Provincetown** ⓴. Sidewalk artists will run off a pastel portrait, or perhaps a car-toon caricature. Shops emblazoned with advertisements sell fine works of art, bad works of art, kitsch souvenirs and an infi-nite variety of snacks. There are good restaurants and bad ones, delightful old inns and inexpensive guest houses, tacky shacks and beautiful landscaped cap-tains' mansions. The artiness of "P-town" (a term never used by locals) has coin-cided with its status of one of the most overtly gay capitals of the East Coast.

With its well-protected harbor, Prov-incetown started out as a natural fishing port – long before the Pilgrims came along. So it remains to this day. Portu-guese fishermen, many from the Azores, came here in the heyday of the whaling trade and stayed on for the good fishing. Their descendants still make up a sizable proportion of the town's year-round resi-dents. Led by painter Charles Hawthorne, who in 1899 founded the Cape Cod School of Art, hordes of artists and writers flocked to Provincetown in the early decades of the 20th century, drawn partly by the area's stark beauty and largely by the cheap rents and food to be found here (thanks to the tourist boom they inspired, the latter are of course history).

Among the notables who passed through here, if only briefly, are drama-tists Eugene O'Neill and Tennessee Williams, and writers Sinclair Lewis, John Dos Passos, and Norman Mailer. A dozen or more illustrious painters, such as the abstract expressionist Robert Motherwell (1915–91), have left their mark, with new contenders cropping up year after year in such galleries as the Bertha Walker (208 Bradford Street). A number of galleries now specialize in Provincetown art from the early 1900s onward.

Another place to catch outstanding early work is the **Provincetown Art Association and Museum** Ⓐ founded in 1914 (460 Commercial Street; tel: 508-487 1750; paam.org; open Memorial Day–Sept, daily; Oct–May, Thur–Sun pm; entrance fee).

The lofty Italianate tower looming above the town is the **Pilgrim Monu-ment** Ⓑ (High Pole Hill Road; tel: 508-487 1310; open Apr–Nov, daily; entrance fee). It was built in 1892 to commemo-rate the *Mayflower* Pilgrims' first landing in the New World: they touched down

here in November, 1620. The determined climber (252 steps) will be rewarded with a panoramic view of the town and the entire Cape. At the monument's foot is the **Provincetown Museum** (same opening times as monument), whose intriguing exhibits document the town's colourful history. One ticket admits visitors to both sites.

Spoils from the *Whydah*, a pirate ship that sank in 1717 and was discovered off Wellfleet in 1984, are displayed at **Exhibition Whydah** Ⓒ on MacMillan Wharf (tel: 508-487 8899; whydah.com; open May–Oct, daily; entrance fee).

The very tip of Cape Cod – which is almost entirely within National Seashore boundaries – has a desolate beauty. Two vast beaches, **Race Point** and **Herring Cove**, invite exploration – by bike, on horseback, on foot, and via off-road vehicle tours. Open houses are held throughout the summer at the 1897 **Old Harbor Life Saving Station** on Race Point Beach.

For information, stop at the **Province Lands Visitor Center** ㉑ (Race Point Road; tel: 508-487 1256; open mid-May–Oct, daily), which has a good viewing platform. This is the best place to get information about the **Dune Shacks of the Peaked Hill Bars Historic District**: 18 tiny dwellings (inhabited: please respect privacy) scattered throughout the Province Lands. There is a lottery for rentals of these bare-bones lodgings, several of which were once inhabited by seclusion-seeking writers and artists.

THE SOUND: Chatham to Falmouth

At the junction of Routes 6 and 28, turn left onto Route 28 to **Orleans**, called by its Indian name of Nauset until it was incorporated in 1797 and renamed for the Duke of Orleans (the future king of France), a recent visitor. Orleans has another "French connection" – it was the stateside terminus for a transatlantic telegraph cable to Brest in France.

The cable performed well from 1891 to 1959 before it become obsolete, and is now commemorated in the **French Cable Station Museum** ㉒ (41 South Orleans Road; tel: 508-240 1735; open June and Sept Fri–Sun pm; July and Aug, Thur–Sat pm). This is a small, technology-specific museum, worth a look for "look-how-they-did-it-then" enthusiasts.

ABOVE: the Pilgrim Monument.
BELOW LEFT: the easiest way to get around Provincetown.

Provincetown's art colony

Bay and ocean, sand and sky: the natural beauty of Provincetown at the tip of Cape Cod has attracted artists since the town was little more than a fishing pier at the end of a sand spit. Today, Provincetown has dozens of art galleries, many of which specialize in contemporary works by local painters, photographers, and sculptors such as Joel Meyerowitz, Paul Bowen, and Paul Resika.

Today's artists are drawn to the area by its pure, Mediterranean-like light – the same light that nearly a century ago inspired a group collectively known as the "Provincetown Art Colony," as renowned as those in Taos in New Mexico, Carmel in California, and East Hampton in New York State.

The colony began in the late 1800s, when a new railroad bed made Provincetown more easily accessible to artists in search of inexpensive lodging and studio space. In 1899, impressionist painter Charles Webster Hawthorne opened the Cape Cod School of Art, which was followed by the Summer School of Painting. By the summer of 1916, more than 300 artists and students – associated with six schools of art – were thriving in the town, inspiring the *Boston Globe* to dub it "the Biggest Art Colony in the World."

In summer, visitors need to guard against overexposure to the sun, wind and biting insects.

BELOW: Chatham's Old Godfrey Windmill, built in 1797 to grind corn, was moved to its present location in Chase Park in 1956.

Turn onto Route 6A through East Orleans to Nauset Beach Road and **Nauset Beach** (parking fee) ㉓. Almost 10 miles long, this is one of the Cape's best stretches of coast, popular for bathing as well as surf-casting for stripers and bluefish. Facilities include a concession stand and public restrooms. Gentler **Skaket Beach** (parking fee) on the bay side is popular with those who prefer calmer waters, and with families.

Chatham

Cape Cod's southern shore, from Chatham to Falmouth, is a zone where the battle for – and against – commercialization has raged for decades. Some pockets of subdued gentility still reign just off the honky-tonk stretches.

Chatham ㉔ is one of the aristocratic enclaves. The handsome **Chatham Bars Inn** (chathambarsinn.com) was built as a private hunting lodge early in the 20th century. The nearby Fish Pier is a perfect spot to watch the fishing fleet bring in the daily catch. The **Chatham Railroad Museum** (153 Depot Road; tel: Chamber of Commerce at 508-945 5199; mid-June–mid-

Sept, Tues–Sat) is housed in the town's ornate but defunct Victorian railroad station. Rail buffs will be interested in reminders of the days when passenger trains ran all the way to Provincetown. **Chatham Light**, an active Coast Guard station, overlooks South Beach. Check the website (lighthouse.cc/chatham) for tour dates and schedules.

Bird fanciers will want to make a visit to **Monomoy National Wildlife Refuge** ㉕, a 7,600-acre (3,100-hectare) preserve which is a stopping point for hundreds of species of birds traveling the Atlantic Flyway. Continue past Chatham Light to the refuge headquarters (Morris Island Road, Chatham; tel: 508-945 0594; monomoy.fws.gov; open daily), where a 1,200-meter nature trail begins. But most of the refuge is accessible only by boat: Monomoy Island Ferry (tel: 508-945 5450; monomoyislandferry.com) offers transportation Apr–Oct, and also offers walking tours to Monomoy Lighthouse, as well as seal-watching tours. Reservations for all services are essential.

Harwichport to Hyannis

Picturesque Harwich and Harwich Port are the last peaceful settlements east of the Cape's commercial belt. From West Harwich to Hyannis, Route 28 is lined with motels, restaurants, businesses and amusements. It's a long, tawdry stretch, where traffic usually crawls all summer.

Detour a short distance to visit **South Dennis** ㉖, nicknamed "Sea Captain's Village". Many of the handsome homes built by prosperous 19th-century sea captains are preserved in the Historic District.

Hyannis

Hyannis ㉗, the Cape's year-round commercial center, has more than a score of worthwhile restaurants and nightclubs. The **Cape Cod Melody Tent** features top-name musicians and comedians (West Main Street; tel: 508-775 5630; melodytent.com). In the old Town Hall, the highlight is the **John F. Kennedy Hyannis Museum** (397 Main Street; tel: 508-790 3077; jfkhyannismuseum.org; open mid-Feb–mid-April and Nov–Dec, Thur–

at; Sun pm; mid-April–Oct Mon–Sat, un pm; closed Jan; entrance fee). The useum displays photos and mementos f the President who summered in adjoin-g Hyannis Port. For a deeper historical verview, the JFK Library in Boston *(see age 123)* is a must. (Although the ennedy Compound is the object of any a pilgrimage, it is not open to the ublic and very little of it can be seen om the road.) A small park dedicated to ennedy's memory adjoins Veterans each, on Hyannis's harbor.

An "old-fashioned swashbuckling dventure" awaits kids and parents oard the **Pirate Adventure on Sea ypsey** (Ocean Street Docks; tel: 508-30 0202; pirateadventurescapecod.com; id-June–Labor Day, eight sailings daily; servations essential; entrance fee).

Alternatively, you can take to the rails oard one of **Cape Cod Central Rail-ad**'s excursions (252 Main Street; tel: 08-771 3800; capetrain.com). These in-ude a scenic, two-hour trip, an adults-nly five-course dinner train, a Sunday runch ride, and a family supper train.

More than 50 classic sports cars – ostly British, and mostly red – are on

show in **Hyannis Port** on the grounds of the Simmons Homestead Inn (288 Scud-der Avenue; tel: 508-778 4934; daily 11am–5 pm; entrance fee). "Bored wives can sit in the chairs and play with the cats at no cost," says the management.

Craigville Beach

West of Hyannis, the tide of commercial-ism subsides occasionally to provide glimpses of Cape Cod's beauty. Make a southward detour for Centerville. Here, relatively warm-watered **Craigville Beach** ❷❽ (1050 Craigville Beach Road; tel: 508-775 9695; fee in summer) on Nantucket Sound, with lifeguards and bath houses, is one of the Cape's most popular.

Memorial at the John F. Kennedy Hyannis Museum. "I always go to Hyannisport to be revived," said Kennedy.

LEFT:
waiting for the Hyannis ferry.
BELOW:
playing at pirates.

The Cahoon Museum covers American art from pre-Revolutionary times to the present.

BELOW: the Cahoon Museum of American Art.

Mashpee sidetrip

Heading toward Falmouth, take a side trip north to **Mashpee ㉙**, located amid Wampanoag tribal lands which have been carved up by development. The **Old Indian Meetinghouse** (Meeting House Road at Route 28), the oldest church building on the Cape, built in 1684, and the burial ground next door, are well worth a look.

Cahoon Museum

The contemporary primitive and very charming paintings of Ralph and Martha Cahoon are on show, along with 19th- and early 20th-century American marine art, in **Cotuit ㉚** at the **Cahoon Museum of American Art** (4676 Falmouth Road; tel: 508-428 7581; open Tues–Sat, Sun pm; closed Jan). The building is a 1775 Georgian Colonial farmhouse.

Falmouth

Falmouth ㉛ is a microcosm of Cape Cod life. The pretty town green, a Revolutionary militia training ground, is ringed by fine old houses, including sev-

eral delightful B&Bs, and the Historical Society's **Museums on the Green** (Village Green; tel: 508-548 4857; open mid-June–mid-Oct, Tues–Fri; Sat 10am–1pm; entrance fee). These are two 18th-century houses with period furnishings and an historic barn (free admission).

Falmouth Harbor is filled with pleasure craft; swimmers and windsurfers favor the beaches and guest houses of Victorian-era Falmouth Heights, overlooking Nantucket Sound. Spring, when thousands of daffodils and rhododendrons bloom, is the best time to visit the 6-acre (2.4-hectare) **Spohr's Gardens** (45 Fells Road; tel: 508-548 0623) overlooking a scenic oyster pond.

Woods Hole

One of the most pleasant activities in Falmouth is to rent a bicycle and follow the old railroad bed, now a bike path, down to **Woods Hole ㉜**. Most travelers come here merely to board the ferry for Martha's Vineyard, a 45-minute voyage away, but Woods Hole itself warrants a stopover, It is devoted almost exclusively to maritime activities. and has several excellent seafood restaurants.

The world-famous **Woods Hole Oceanographic Institution** maintains a visitor center (15 School Street; tel: 508-457 2180; open May–Oct, Mon–Sat) to describe its fascinating research. Weekdays in July and August the institution offers free 75-minute tours of the dock area and restricted village facilities. Tours begin at 10:30am and 1:30pm from 93 Water Street; it's wise to reserve – tel: 508-289 2252.

With an advance reservation of at least a week, visitors can tour the **Marine Biological Laboratory** which houses marine organisms used in research (MBL Street at Water Street; tel: 508-289 7623; mbl.edu; tours late June–Aug Mon–Fri at 1pm and 2pm; note: children under the age of five cannot take the tour). The Pierce Visitors Center is open July–Aug, Mon–Sat, and Sun pm (check the website for varying off-season hours).

The small but intriguing **Woods Hole Science Aquarium** (Albatross and Water streets; tel: 508-495 2001; open June–Aug, Tues–Sat 11am–4pm; school year Mon–Fri) is home to 140 species of marine animals. A highlight is the outdoor seal pool, with Coco and LuSeal.

plains and many-fingered ponds. And Martha herself? She was the daughter of Thomas Mayhew, who in 1642 bought a large tract of land, including Nantucket Island, for £40. (Mayhew named the nearby Elizabeth Islands after another daughter.) The "Vineyard" part of the name refers to once-abundant wild grapes.

Vineyard Haven, Oak Bluffs and Edgartown, the three protected harbor towns of the northeastern portion of the island, have always been active and prosperous, although the main order of business is no longer shipping and whaling, but tourism and summer homes. By contrast, the sparsely populated "up-island" (that is, to the west and south) towns of West Tisbury, Chilmark, Menemsha, and Gay Head remain determinedly rural.

It may come as a disappointment to many visitors to find that, as a rule, Martha's Vineyard's extensive beaches are not accessible to outsiders but have been reserved for homeowners; the major exception, beyond the placid Joseph Sylvia State Beach on the bay side, is South Beach, fronting the rolling Atlantic south of Edgartown; other public beaches are Katama (good for surf-

MARTHA'S VINEYARD

Over the decades, Vineyard residents have grown blasé about the celebrities in their midst, and precisely because of that laissez-faire attitude, the roster just keeps growing. It took a presidential visit – the Clintons' during the mid-1990s – to shake things up a bit, but, despite the hordes lining the roadways, most people went about their business, and leisure, as usual.

Islanders have worked too hard to create and preserve a relaxed way of life to let a little glitz and glamour throw them. For many, the island represents a true escape from the stresses of high-powered careers. Though the price of admission may be high, once one has arrived, a kind of barefoot democracy prevails.

Like Cape Cod, Martha's Vineyard is a geological remnant of the last Ice Age. Two advancing lobes of a glacier molded the triangular northern shoreline, then retreated, leaving hilly moraines, low

TIPS

● Parking in Woods Hole is metered and can be extremely hard to find. During the summer a trolley runs between Falmouth (free parking) and Woods Hole on the half hour (Tel: 800-352 7155).

● Pie in the Sky Bakery and Internet Café at the end of the bike path in Woods Hole (10 Water Street) opens at 5 am with freshly brewed coffee and homemade croissants.

BELOW: Falmouth. An Unwired Village program provides free wireless broadband access in public places.

ing and for strong swimmers), Moshpu, Oak Bluffs and Menemsha.

Vineyard Haven

Known until 1870 as Holmes Hole, **Vineyard Haven** ㉝ (the official name of the town is Tisbury, but everyone calls it by the name of its primary village) blossomed into a busy port during the 18th and 19th centuries, with both maritime businesses and farmers profiting from the constant movement of ships. Today, the homey **Black Dog Tavern** (Beach Street Extension; tel: 508-693 9223), with its offshoot bakery, store, and catalog business, enjoys a similar relationship with the legions of vacationers who arrive by ferry from Woods Hole.

Handsome houses dating from the years before the great fire of 1883 grace Williams Street, a block off Main Street. Nearby, the 1829 **Old Schoolhouse Museum** (110 Main Street), was the island's first schoolhouse; the building was also once a carpentry shop and a church.

Covering a swath of more than 5,000 acres (2,000 hectares) in the middle of the island, **Manuel F. Correllus State Forest** (tel: 508-693 2540), site of one of the largest environmental restoration projects in the country, is laced with 15 miles (24 km) of walking, bicycling, and bridle paths. Take Edgartown Road out of Vineyard Haven to Barnes Road, then turn right (south) to the forest entrance.

Oak Bluffs

Religion tinged with tourism produced an unusual community in **Oak Bluffs** ㉞, a town renowned for its engaging cottages built in "carpenter gothic" style. In 1835, Edgartown Methodists chose a secluded circle of oak trees here as a site for a camp meeting. Twenty years later, there were more than 320 tents at Wesleyan Grove, as it was named, and many thousands of people gathered here each summer. Small houses soon replaced the tents, laid out along circular drives that rimmed the large central "tabernacle" where the congregation assembled.

Today this camp meeting site is known as **Trinity Park**. Tiny gingerbread cottages are a riot of color and jigsaw carvery, with all manner of turrets, spires, gables and eaves.

Visitors can tour **Cottage Museum** (One Trinity Park; mvcma.org; open Mon-

Sat and Sun pm in summer), an 1867 home representative of the more than 300 here. The huge cast iron-and-wood tabernacle in the center of the campground, built in 1879, still hosts community gatherings. **Grand Illumination,** held on a Wednesday night every August, recreates the camp's traditional closing-night ceremony, when colorful glowing lanterns were strung up throughout the park.

Interdenominational worship services are held in the tabernacle Sundays at 9:30am in summer.

The acoustically-acclaimed **Union Chapel,** built in 1870 as a non-sectarian place of worship, is overseen by the Martha's Vineyard Preservation Trust (tel: 508-627 4440; mvpreservation.org).

Circuit Avenue and Lake Street mark the hub of town and the site another Preservation Trust property, the 1876, National Historic Landmark **Flying Horses Carousel,** one of America's oldest (Circuit Avenue; tel: 508-693 9481; open mid-Apr–mid-Oct, daily; fee). Nearby, **Linda Jean's Restaurant** (25 Circuit Avenue) serves up terrific diner-type fare.

Several of the 16 sites included in the Island's **African-American Heritage Trail** (tel: 508-693 2729; mvheritagetrail.org) are located in the area.

East Chop Lighthouse (East Chop Drive; tel: 508-693 8104)), erected in 1878 and nicknamed "the chocolate light" because of its brown color, can be visited in summer Sundays just before sunset.

Edgartown

South of Oak Bluffs on Beach Road, Edgartown ❸ is the oldest settlement in Martha's Vineyard. In 1642, missionary Thomas Mayhew, Jr, son of the Watertown, Massachusetts, entrepreneur who bought the islands off the Cape for a pittance, arrived at Great Harbor, now Edgartown, and set about converting the island's native population.

The Martha's Vineyard Preservation Trust oversees several properties in Edgartown. The Federal-style **Dr Daniel Fisher residence** was built in 1840 by a whale-oil magnate who once supplied all

US lighthouses with Edgartown's oil.

The imposing Greek Revival **Old Whaling Church** of 1843, with enormous pillars and a soaring tower, is a rare instance of monumental scale in Edgartown. The church is now the venue for concerts, a film series, and community events. Tucked behind the church is the **Vincent House Museum,** the oldest house on the island (1672).

The Martha's Vineyard Historical Society operates the **Martha's Vineyard Museum** (59 School Street; marthasvineyardhistory.org; tel: 508-627 4441; open early June–early Oct Tues–Sat; early Oct–early June Wed–Fri pm and Sat 10am–4pm; entrance fee). Its 30,000 items include agricultural equipment, weapons, clothes, boats and sailors' artwork, as well as old maps and manuscripts.

The Society also oversees several lighthouses, historic buildings and sites including the **Ross Fresnel Lens Building,** housing a 19th-century first order Fresnel lens; the **Francis Foster Maritime Gallery,** exhibiting logbooks, ship models and other nautical treasures; and the c.1845 **Captain Francis Pease House,** with exhibits about the island's

Prosperity eluded Edgartown until the 18th century, when it became a capital in the worldwide whaling trade, vying with Nantucket and, later, New Bedford. The captains who made their fortunes from the sea left behind a treasure: their elegant Federal and Greek Revival houses, especially those lining North and South Water streets.

BELOW: riding the Flying Horses Carousel in Oak Bluffs.

The shore at Chappaquiddick.

BELOW: Edgartown, an old whaling port first settled by the English in 1642.

history, a Native American Gallery, a book shop, and local crafts.

The Museum oversees **Edgartown Lighthouse**, open summer weekdays (entrance fee) 11am–5pm, and Thursday nights for sunset tours.

Chappaquiddick Island

A stone's throw away from Edgartown, across a narrow neck of the harbor, is **Chappaquiddick Island** ㊱. The island's native name means "The Separated Island," which it steadfastly remains, although the *On Time* open barge regularly ferries cars (three or four at a time) and clusters of pedestrians over the 200-yard (180-meter) crossing (tel: 508-627 9427).

The main attraction on "Chappy," several miles from the ferry landing, is the **Wasque** (pronounced *wayce-kwee*) **Reservation** (east end of Wasque Road; thetrustees.org; tel: 508-627 7689; open year round; entrance fee Memorial Day–mid Oct), a 200-acre (80-hectare) preserve with walking trails and beach (be careful: there's a strong current).

Cape Poge Wildlife Refuge at the island's eastern end, offers 6 miles (10 km) of dunes, woods, salt marshes ponds, tidal flats, a lighthouse, and beach. A variety of narrated tours are offered, including a 1½-hour lighthouse trip, and a 2½-hour overland exploration (tel: 508-627 3599; the trustees.org).

If you want to visit both the reserva tion and the refuge, request a vouche when you pay admission at the first site and present it at the second site – yo won't have to pay again.

Up-island escape

Tiny **West Tisbury** ㊲ is home to several properties of the Martha's Vineyar Preservation Trust (tel: 508-627 8017 mvpreservation.org), including: **Alley** **General Store**, which opened in 185 and still deals in "most everything (open daily); the 1859 **Grange Ha** where there's a lively farmer's market o Wednesday and Saturday mornings ; an the Second Empire **Old Library** (1870

The popular **agricultural fair** is he' in town each August, and the island only **youth hostel** (25 Edgartown-We Tisbury Road; tel: 508-693 2665; hihoste .com) is here. The **Granary Gallery** the Red Barn (636 Old County Road exhibits photographs by Margar Bourke-White and Alfred Eisenstaedt, summer regular.

Highlights of a visit to **Long Poi Wildlife Refuge** (tel: 508-693 367 thetrustees.org; open mid-June–mid-Sep entrance fee), part of a sand barre ecosystem which exists in patches fro New Jersey to Maine, include a love beach and an easy 2-mile nature trail.

You can explore the refuge in a cance or kayak with expert naturalists, wh lead 90-minute tours daily in season 8:30am, 11am, and 1:30pm. Space limited to 12 people (children welcome so you need to book (tel: 508-693 7392

Chilmark to Gay Head

Of the parallel roads traveling from We Tisbury to Chilmark, Middle Road tr verses the most rugged, interesting glaci terrain. At **Chilmark Center** is Beet

oung Corner, a stand of tupelo trees from which "beetles" (mallets) and "bungs" (wooden stoppers) were once made. The residents of Chilmark (incorporated in 1694) built their dwellings at a generous distance from one another, and the once inexpensive property and evocative natural settings attracted an influx of artists such as Jackson Pollok.

Nearby **Menemsha** is a tiny fishing village on Vineyard Sound, famed for its appearance in Steven Spielberg's ever-popular 1975 movie *Jaws* and prized for its Technicolor sunsets. Fishing charters operate from the harbor, which has a number of shops and restaurants.

One of the most spectacular natural sights on Martha's Vineyard is at its westernmost tip, looking out to the untamed sea. From Chilmark, follow the single hilly road that at several points offers breathtaking views of Menemsha Pond northward and Squibnocket Pond to the south.

At the end, **Aquinnah Lighthouse ㊳** (Lighthouse Road; tel: 508-627 4441; mvmuseum.org; sunset tours mid-June–mid-Sept, Fri, Sat and Sun; entrance fee) marks the western terminus of the island

and the location of the stunning, ancient geologic strata that compose the majestic **Gay Head cliffs**. Clays of many colors – from gray to pink to green – are most vibrant towards late afternoon and represent eons of geological activity: fossils found amid the ever-changing contours of this 150-ft (46-meter) promontory have been dated back millions of years. For sailors returning from a voyage, this magnificently coloured embankment was the first sign they were home, thus giving Gay Head its "gaiety."

Gay Head is one of only two Native American communities in Massachusetts; it has been more successful than the related Wampanaoag settlement at Mashpee in asserting its land ownership rights, and remains a cohesive social entity despite three centuries of colonizing forces.

On Indian Hill Road, heading back toward Vineyard Haven, is the site of Christiantown, settled by "praying Indians" in 1659; a plaque fixed to a boulder honors the missionary efforts of Thomas Mayhew (*see page 171*).

Bringing a good catch into Menemsha, where much of Steven Spielberg's Jaws *was filmed.*

BELOW:
Gay Head cliffs.

NANTUCKET

An Indian word meaning "that faraway land," Nantucket isn't too far away for the thousands of people who visit each year by ferry and airplane. The winter population of 7,000 increases sevenfold when the "summer people" take over the sidewalks of town.

In sharp contrast to Martha's Vineyard, Nantucket's mid-island moors and miles of beautiful, unspoiled beaches are open to visitors, most of whom use the preferred island mode of transportation: bikes (several shops stand ready to equip tourists near the ferry dock). Though smaller residential neighborhoods dot the island's coast, the harbor town of Nantucket, centrally located on the north shore, is unquestionably the focal point of the island and its only commercial center.

Nantucket town

One can spend days walking through the town of **Nantucket 39** and always be sure of seeing something new. The community is a gem of 18th- and 19th-century architecture, from the dominant clapboard-and-shingle Quaker homes to the grandeur of the buildings lining

Upper Main Street. Because the twist and turns can prove disorienting, it's be to tour with a street map (available from the bike shops, or in the free local news papers distributed on the ferry).

As in whaling days, the waterfront the focus of life in Nantucket town. Sev eral wharves extend into the harbor, th most central of which – **Straight Wha** – is an extension of Main Street. Fir built in 1723, rebuilt after the 1846 fir and renovated in the late 1950s accommodate shops and restaurants, it now like a small village unto itself, su rounded by luxury yachts and sailboat some of which are available for charte (The untouched barrier beach of Coat is an ideal destination.)

Old South Wharf has also bee spruced up and rendered tourist-friend with boutiques and cafés; it's possible for a tidy sum – to rent tiny but pi turesque wharfside cottages here.

Along Main Street up from Straig Wharf, a picturesque shopping distri lines the gently rising cobblestone stree Although the square-mile (2.5 sq. kr **National Landmark Historic Distri** contains 800 pre-1850 buildings, the re

BELOW: Brant Point Lighthouse at Nantucket Harbor.

ick facades lining Main Street are rel-
ively "young," post-fire replacements.
'ith its tree-lined, brick-paved side-
alks, Main Street is a hub of activity in
immer, offering distractions from col-
ctibles to edibles.

Nantucket is proud of its history, espe-
ally its grand old homes and museums.
he **Nantucket Historical Association**
el: 508-228 1894; nha.org; fee) oversees
ore than a dozen properties on the
land, and sells a Visitor Pass good for
dmission to those open to the public (or
dividual tickets). Most are open daily
lemorial Day–mid-Oct: call ahead for
f-season hours.

Among their properties in town are the
/haling Museum (13 Broad Street),
oused in a former spermaceti candle
ctory, which commemorates Nan-
cket's seafaring days with impressive
splays, including the skeleton of a 43-
(13.1-meter) finback whale. If your
ily exposure to old-time whaling was
a a high-school reading of *Moby-Dick*,
e museum will bring the hardship and
eroics of the "fishery" vividly to life.
The 1686 **Jethro Coffin House** on the
orthwest edge of town on Sunset Hill
ane, is the oldest on the island. This
ain saltbox design reflects the austere
iestyle led by the island's earliest set-
ers. Other Association holdings include:
e 1746 **Old Mill**, the oldest functioning
ill in the country; the 1805 **Old Gaol**;
id the 1838 **Quaker Meetinghouse**.
Climb up the tower of the **First Con-**
regational Church (50 Prospect Street;
)8-228 0950) for a spectacular view of
e island; Sunday service is at 10am.
The three-story red-brick **Jared Coffin**
ouse (tel: 800-248 2405; jaredcoffin
ouse.com), at the corner of Centre and
'road streets, made its 1845 debut as the
land's showiest dwelling; within two
ears it became a hotel, and today it
mains one of the island's finest inns.
The family was so prolific that it
ccounted for half the island's popula-
on by the early 19th century, and two
ore Coffin residences stand at No. 75
id No. 78 Main Street, examples of the
ick Federal style of architecture.

Farther up Main Street are the
"**Three Bricks**," architectural
triplets built by wealthy whaler
Joseph Starbuck for his three sons.
Across the street, and worlds apart
in style, stand the "**Two Greeks**,"
Greek Revival mansions built by
Frederick Coleman for two Star-
buck daughters. One, the Associa-
tion's **Hadwen House** (96 Main
Street, showcases the affluent lifestyle of
a wealthy whaling family.

Ralph Waldo Emerson gave the inau-
gural address at the 1847 Greek Revival
Nantucket Atheneum, now a public
library and cultural center, at the corner
of Lower India Street.

The **Museum of African American**
History (29 York Street; tel: 508-228
9833; afroamemuseum.org; July–Aug,
Tues–Sat 11am–3pm or by appointment)
maintains two historic sites document-
ing the history of the island's African-
American community. The **African**
American Meeting House and the **Flo-**
rence Higginbotham House are included in a tour which begins at the
Whaling Museum.

No. 99 Main Street, with its detailed

The 1805 Old Gaol,
with its unassuming
shingled facade,
contained four
barred cells, two
with fireplaces. Most
of its prisoners were
allowed to go home
each night, having
no real chance of
escaping from the
island.

BELOW:
sea view from the
White Elephant Inn.

Nantucket's stormy past

The island's golden age didn't last long, but the handsome little town that whaling fortunes had built found new prosperity in tourism.

In 1830 the whaling ship *Sarah* returned home to Nantucket island, carrying 3,500 barrels of valuable whale oil after a voyage of nearly three years. On the island, stately mansions, decorated with silks and china from faraway lands, awaited the returning captains of such vessels. Schools, hotels, a library and the commercial activity on Main Street were indications of a prosperous people.

There was no more glorious way for young men to seek their fortunes than aboard a whaling ship, but it was dangerous work. "For every drop of oil, a drop of blood," the whalemen's saying went.

Chasing the whales

Since its earliest days, Nantucket has been populated by determined and spirited people. The first colonists, who arrived in 1659, were emigrants who chafed at the Puritan severity of towns on the North Shore of Massachusetts. Taught "onshore"

whaling by the native Algonquins, they traveled out in open boats to chase and harpoon whales sighted from land. By the beginning of the 18th century, offshore whaling had begun and, with each generation of larger, more seaworthy craft, the whaling industry grew.

The natives, however, lost out. Although they sailed on whaling boats, their way of life on the island was irreversibly changed by the colonists. By 1855, disease (introduced to the country from Europe) and alcohol had taken the last of Nantucket's original residents.

Both the Revolutionary War and the War of 1812 battered Nantucket's whaling industry, but the islanders' tenacity brought it back to life. Nantucket ships again sailed throughout the world and brought back record quantities of oil. It was during this period that the town acquired much of its urbanity, but the islanders' prosperity was short-lived: the Great Fire of 1846 razed the port, and in the 1850s kerosene replaced whale oil. Too heavily dependent on whaling, Nantucket was left high and dry.

Tourism arrives

From a peak of around 10,000, Nantucket's population dropped to 3,200 in 1875. Those who remained applied their ingenuity to a new venture, one that thrives today and continues to capitalize on the gifts of the sea. Tourism took off toward the end of the 19th century, as steamboats made the island more readily accessible. Land speculators built hotels and vacation homes.

Quaint Siasconset (pronounced "Sconset"), linked to the town by a narrow-gauge railroad built in 1884, was especially popular, drawing such luminaries as the popular actress Lillian Russell. The railroad is gone now – it was used for scrap metal during World War I – but tourism lives on. ❑

ABOVE: offshore whaling began in the early 1700s.
LEFT: harvesting cranberries, the focus of a Nantucket festival that kicks off the harvesting season each October. Details: nantucketconservation.com

Recommended Restaurants and Bars on pages 182–5

nd finely proportioned facade, is one of the most handsome wooden Federal-tyle buildings on Nantucket; it was built y forebears of Rowland Macy, who left ne island to seek his fortune and ounded a well-known namesake store.

Overlooking the harbor from **Brant oint** is one of America's oldest light-ouses. Visitors departing by sea often oss the traditional penny into the water ff Brant Point to ensure that they'll eturn to the shores of Nantucket.

A few blocks out of town, at the corner f Vestal and Milk streets, is the **Maria 1itchell Science Center** (4 Vestal treet; tel: 508-228 9198; mmo.org; mid-une–mid-Oct, most facilities open 1on–Sat; entrance fee). It honors the ocal savant – and Atheneum librarian – vho discovered a comet at the age of 29 1 1847, garnering international acclaim. he became the first woman admitted to ne American Academy of Arts and Sci-nces, and America's first female college rofessor, teaching astronomy at Vassar. 'he somewhat scattered complex en-ompasses several facilities open to the ublic, including her childhood home, uilt in 1790 and showing what 19th-

century island Quaker life was like; an aquarium (closes mid-Sept), and two observatories. The Center offers several field trips, including bird, wildflower, and marine ecology.

The classic and unique arts of the island, including basket making and scrimshaw carving, are displayed at the **Nantucket Lightship Basket Museum** (49 Union Street; tel: 508-228 1177; nantucketlightshipbasket museum.org; late May–early Oct, Tues–Sat; call for off-season hours; entrance fee).

Outside Nantucket town

"Nantucket! Take out your map and look at it," urged Herman Melville in *Moby-Dick*. An inspection of the map reveals an island with hamlets and hideaways sprinkled across its 14-mile (23-km) length. Despite some mid-island devel-opment in recent decades, about one-third of the island is under protective stewardship, Although environmental restrictions limit activities on dunes and moors, much of the land can be explored. Wear long pants and use insect repellent; deer ticks carry Lyme disease.

The island has long attracted painters. The Artists' Association of Nantucket, formed in 1945, has more than 500 members and runs a gallery.

BELOW: Nantucket's harbor.

A well-mannered garden in Nantucket.

BELOW: cranberries, cultivated in Cape Cod since 1816.

Stretching northeast from the town of Nantucket is a 6-mile (10-km) inner harbor, protected from Nantucket Sound by **Coatue**, a thin spit of land with flat white beaches accessible only by boat. This sweep of land, encompassing the 1,117-acre (453-hectare) **Coatue-Coskata Wildlife Refuge**  (Wauwinet Road; thetrustees.org; tel: 508-228 5646) extends north **to Great Point**, where a lighthouse – a solar-powered 1986 replica of the 1818 original, swept away by a 1984 storm – warns boats away from the sandbars of Nantucket Sound. Gray and harbor seals rest here after they have fed on fish provided by the riptide.

The Trustees of Reservations, which administers the refuge, offers 2½-hour naturalist-led excursions June–Columbus Day weekend. They depart daily at 9:30am and 1:30pm and are limited to 8 persons: reservations are needed.

The excellent **Nantucket Life-Saving Museum** (158 Polpis Road; tel: 508-228 1885; open mid-June–Columbus Day weekend, daily; entrance fee), en route to Great Point, presents fascinating exhibits, including artifacts from the Italian liner *Andrea Doria*, which sank not far from here in 1956.

Monomoy, the most populous settlement other than Nantucket town, affords spectacular views from its bluffs. From here, the Polpis Road leads across the rolling and delicate Nantucket Moors, which are carpeted with bayberry, beach plum, heather and other lush vegetation – a lovely green and flowering pink in summer, brilliant red and gold in the fall.

Wauwinet , a tiny community of cottages tucked amid the beach grass at the head of the harbor, is home to the ultra-elegant (and ultra-expensive) Wauwinet (tel: 800-426 8718; wauwinet .com), a finely refurbished and very elegant 1850 hostelry within splashing distance of both ocean and harbor. (It's located on the "haulover" where fishing boats used to avoid the long trip around Great Point.)

Siasconset

Tourists discovered **Siasconset** , the easternmost town on Nantucket, in the 1880s. Theater people from the mainland mingled with local fishermen; the resulting architecture ranges from Lilliputian cottages to large rambling shingle-style houses along the bluffs.

Nantucket's most popular beaches are located on the flat, windswept south shore, open to the cold, spirited waters of the Atlantic Ocean. **At Surfside Beach** , a colorful Victorian lifesaving station serves nowadays as the island's only Youth Hostel. Surfers favor the beach **Cisco**, a bit more remote, at the end of Hummock Pond Road, while **Madaket Beach** , at the southwestern tip of Nantucket, is popular for swimming, fishing and, especially, sunset-gazing.

The northern coast east of Madaket Harbor, heading back toward town, offers the gentle surf of **Dionis** and Jetties beaches. **Children's Beach**, tucked well inside the West Jetty, near Steamship Wharf, is especially placid and enhanced by a playground. Free concerts here begin at 6pm Thursday and Saturdays in summer.

Whale Watching

Every summer crowds flock to see one of the world's greatest gatherings of humpback whales off the coast of Massachusetts

The painting *(below)* by Robert Walker Weir, Jr., on show at the Kendall Whaling Museum in Sharon, Massachusetts, is a dramatic reminder of New England's whaling history. The whales are still a source of income, but today's hunters are tourists armed with cameras and the proceeds go to the owners of the large whale-watching boats that leave Boston, Provincetown and Gloucester on three-hour sightseeing trips. The season lasts about six months; humpbacks and minkes begin arriving in April and May and the numbers peak from June to October.

The boats head for Stellwagen Bank, a shallow underwater deposit of sand and gravel, to which humpbacked whales return after spending the winter in their Caribbean breeding grounds. Experts recognize the different humpbacks, which often reach lengths of 40–50 ft (15 meters) and weights of 30 tons, by their distinctive body markings, especially those on their tail flukes.

It's fairly rare for a visitor not to see at least one whale during a trip. More often than not, the whale-watching boats are able to approach within 50 ft (15 meters) of at least half a dozen humpbacks. Frolicking dolphins often keep people entertained until a whale surfaces.

The humpback is a bulk feeder who dives deep below the schools of sand eels and then lunges upward through the school with its mouth open to engulf large quantities of fish and water. These vora-cious eating machines are capable of capturing hundreds, if not thousands, of small fish with every lunge they make.

The boat companies

Sightseeing boats generally depart two or three times daily in summer and on weekends in spring and fall. Take jackets and seasickness pills, even on calm and seemingly warm days.

Many companies are based in Provincetown on Cape Cod: the Dolphin Fleet (tel: 508-349 1900, 800-826 9300) has an on-board biologist from the Center for Coastal Studies. In the mid-Cape's Barnstable Harbor, call Hyannis Whale Watcher Cruises (tel: 508-362 6088).

From Boston, the New England Aquarium (tel: 617-973 5200) sponsors whalewatching trips, as does Boston Harbor Cruises (Rowes Wharf; tel: 617-227 4321).

On the North Shore in Gloucester, call Cape Ann Whale Watch (415 Main Street; tel: 978-283 5110, 800-877 5110) and Yankee Fleet Whale Watch (Route 133; tel: 978-283 0313, 800-942 5464). In Plymouth, Captain John Boats (tel: 508-746 2643, 800-242 2469) and Captain Tim Brady and Sons (tel: 508-746 4809) leave from Town Wharf. ❑

RESTAURANTS AND BARS

Restaurants

Prices for a three-course dinner per person with a half-bottle of house wine:
$ = under $20
$$ = $20–45
$$$ = $45–60
$$$$ = over $60

Cape Cod and The Islands

Barnstable

Mattakeese Wharf
271 Mill Way
Tel: 508-362 4511
mattakeese.com **$$–$$$**
A classic wharfside seafood haven featuring bouillabaisse and baked, stuffed lobster. L and D May–Oct.

Brewster

Chillingsworth
2449 Route 6A
Tel: 508-896 3640/

800-430 3640
chillingsworth.com **$$$$**
The seven-course *prix-fixe* menu, a feast of classic French/American cuisine, is among the Cape's ultimate dining experiences. Lunch, dinner and Sun brunch are served in the less formal Green House. Open Mother's Day–Nov D Tues–Sun. Reservations essential.

Bramble Inn
2019 Route 6A
Tel: 508-896 7644
brambleinn.com **$$$–$$$$**
Four-course dinners featuring continental dishes with an emphasis on fresh seafood are served in the intimate rooms of a restored 1861 house. D nightly April–New Year's Eve. A la carte bistro menu until 6.30pm.

Brewster Fish House
2208 Route 6A
Tel: 508-896 7867 **$$**
Creative fresh seafood and pasta, snazzy desserts, and long waits. L and D Tue–Sun.

Chatham

Chatham Bars Inn
Shore Road
Tel: 508-945 0096/
800-527 4884
chathambarsinn.com **$$$$**
A grand old inn dining room serving French and regional cuisine with an emphasis on seafood in a leisurely and elegant fashion. B and D daily; Sun brunch.

Impudent Oyster
15 Chatham Bars Avenue
Tel: 508-945 3545 **$$–$$$**
International takes on local seafood, with specialties such as sole piccata. Beef lovers will enjoy the steak au poivre. Reservations recommended.

Vining's Bistro
595 Main Street
Tel: 508-945 5033 **$$$**
The second-floor European-style bistro serves an eclectic menu ranging from warm lobster tacos to pan-roasted sea scallops from April–Dec. D nightly.

Wild Goose Tavern
512 Main Street
Tel: 508-945 5590
wildgoosetavern.com **$$$–$$$$**
A diverse menu such as lobster-scallop ravioli, beef short ribs, and flatbread pizza served inside or on the deck. B, L, D daily.

Cotuit

Regatta of Cotuit at the Crocker House
4631 Falmouth Road
Tel: 508-428 5715
regattaofcotiut.com **$$–$$$$**
Sophisticated New American cuisine with French, Continental and Asian accents in an 18th-century stagecoach inn with eight intimate candlelit dining rooms. Lighter menu in the tap room. D nightly.

Dennis

Captain Frosty's
219 Route 6A
Tel: 508-385 8548
captainfrosty.com **$**
A casual clam shack with exceptional lobster rolls and fish 'n' chips. L and D Apr–Sept.

Gina's by the Sea
134 Taunton Avenue
Tel: 508-385 3213 **$$–$$$**
Hearty northern Italian classics such as home-made ravioli characterize this long-standing favorite where reservations are not accepted and peak-time waits can be long. D nightly; closed Mon–Wed Oct–Nov, closed Dec–Mar.

The Red Pheasant
905 Route 6A
Tel: 508-385 2133
redpheasantinn.com **$$$**
This romantic spot in an historic barn has been a favorite for innovative New American cuisine for over 25 years. D nightly.

Scargo Cafe
799 Route 6A
Tel: 508-385 8200
scargocafe.com **$$–$$$**

Traditional New England favorites, plus a few eclectic wild cards, in a retro-fitted captain's house. L and D daily.

Eastham

Eastham Lobster Pool
4360 Route 6
Tel: 508-255 9706 $$$
No frills, just unbeatable fresh fish.

Falmouth

Chapoquoit Grill
Route 28A
Tel: 508-540 7794
chapoquoitgrill.com $$–$$$
New American cuisine, grilled seafood, and wood-fired, brick oven pizza in a casual environment. The desserts are homemade. D nightly.

Clam Shack
227 Clinton Avenue (off Scranton Avenue)
Tel: 508-540 7758 $
A shack (albeit picturesque) right on the water. Picnic tables outside, and roof deck.

Coonamessett Inn Cahoon Dining Room
311 Gifford Street
Tel: 508-548 2300
capecodrestaurants.org
$$$–$$$$
Elegant fare, with an accent on fresh seafood and prime meats, in a classic country inn. Dress is semi-formal, and Sunday brunch is superb. D nightly.

Hyannis

Alberto's Ristorante
360 Main Street
Tel: 508-778 1770
albertos.net $$–$$$
Northern Italian fare with a flair: homemade pastas and entrées such as seafood ravioli stuffed with lobster, scallops, shrimp and ricotta. Jazz

piano Fri–Sat night. L and D daily.

Baxter's Boathouse
177 Pleasant Street
Tel: 508-775 4490
baxterscapecod.com $$
A 1950s harborfront clam shack with an extensive menu of fish platters. Piano entertainment Thur–Sun. L and D late May–Sept.

Naked Oyster Bistro and Raw Bar
20 Independence Drive
Tel: 508 778 6500
nakedoyster.com $$–$$$
Fresh fish and prime grilled beef are specialties, plus a good raw bar. L Tues–Fri; D nightly July–Aug, and Mon–Sat the rest of year.

The Original Gourmet Brunch
517 Main Street
Tel: 508-771 2558
gourmetbrunch.com $–$$
Omelets are the specialty, but there are also Belgian waffles, eggs Benedict,and a full luncheon menu. Open Mon–Sat 7am–midday; Sun until 2pm.

Tugboats
21 Arlington Street
Tel: 508-775 6433
tugboatscapecod.com $$
The lobster bisque/lobster roll special, a large outdoor deck, and a kids' menu make this harborfront spot popular with families. L and D daily.

Mashpee

Bleu
Mashpee Commons,
7 Market Street
Tel: 508-539 7907 $$–$$$
Classic French bistro cuisine such as cassoulet, planked salmon, and chicken Provençal. For

dessert? A caramelized apple tart tatin. L and D daily; Sun jazz brunch.

North Truro

Adrian's
Route 6
Tel: 508-487 4360
adriansrestaurant.com $$
Irresistible neo-Italian treats plus spectacular views. B and D daily mid-May–mid-Oct.

Orleans

Captain Linnell House
137 Skaket Beach Road
Tel: 508-255 3400
linnell.com $$$$
One of the Cape's most respected restaurants, housed in an 1811 sea captain's home, serves dishes such as bourbon lobster bisque, scrod in parchment, and rack of lamb. D nightly.

Mahoney's Atlantic
28 Main Street
Tel: 508-255 5505 $$$$
Classy, contemporary US cuisine. Signature dish is Tuna Sashimi. Live jazz is played Thursday nights.

Land Ho!
38 Main Street
Tel: 508-255 5165
land-ho.com $$
A pub and casual eatery popular with locals. L Mon–Fri; D nightly; Sun brunch.

Lobster Claw
Route 6A
Tel: 508-255 1800
lobsterclaw.com $–$$
Big, touristy, and good. Excellent fried clams and lobster rolls. Family-owned since 1970. L and D.

Provincetown

Cafe Edwige
333 Commercial Street
Tel: 508-487 2008 $$–$$$
The contemporary dishes, with specialties such as crab cakes and Wellfleet scallops over pasta, are among the best in town. B and D May–Oct.

Cafe Heaven
199 Commercial Street
Tel: 508-487 9639 $
Terrific burgers and good breakfasts, too.

LEFT: old-style soda fountain restaurant.
RIGHT: fresh lobster is a regular on Cape Cod menus.

Front Street
230 Commercial Street
Tel: 508-487 9715
frontstreetrestaurant.com
$$$–$$$$
Mediterranean-American
fusion food in an intimate
dining room. Look for
lobster cappuccino, tea-
smoked duck, and gor-
gonzola-stuffed rack of
lamb. D nightly.

Mews and Cafe Mews
429 Commercial Street
Tel: 508-487 1500
mews.com **$$–$$$**
Two levels of creative,
beach-side cuisine: inter-
continental fare on the
first floor; an American
bistro menu upstairs. D
nightly; Sun brunch
Mother's Day–Oct.

Napi's
7 Freeman Street
Tel: 508-487 1145
napis-restaurant.com **$$$**
A colorful institution built
of architectural salvage.
Menu spans the world.
L Oct–April; D nightly.

Provincetown Portu-
guese Bakery
299 Commercial Street
Tel: 508-487 1803 **$**
Fried dough creations,
freshly-baked breads and
pastries, and treats such
as linguica crossants and
meat pies have made
this longtime landmark a
popular spot for snacks.
B and L. Open Mar–Nov;
until 11pm in summer.

Sal's Place
99 Commercial Street
Tel: 508-487 1279

salsplaceofprovincetown.com
$$$
Classic southern Italian
dishes; dine indoors
overlooking the water, or
on patio. D nightly Apr–
Oct; Sat–Sun Oct–Apr.

Spiritus
190 Commercial Street
Tel: 508-487 2808
spirituspizza.com **$**
Popular pizzas draw the
late-night crowd.

Sandwich
Dan'l Webster Inn
149 Main Street
Tel: 508-888 3622
danlwebsterinn.com **$$–$$$**
The candlelit, fireside
dining room at this tradi-
tional inn has surprisingly
sophisticated fare. B, L,
D, Sun brunch buffet.

Dunbar Tea Shop
1 Water Street (Route 130)
Tel: 508-833 2485
dunbarteashop.com **$**
An English tearoom
housed in a 1740 home
serves pastries, light
lunches, and ports and
sherries inside and on
the garden patio.

Wellfleet
Bayside Lobster Hut
Commercial Street
Tel: 508-349 6333 **$**
Shore dinners in an
1857 oyster shack.

Woods Hole
Fishmonger Café
56 Water Street
Tel: 508-540 5376 **$$**
Lively wharfside café with
inventive natural foods,
fresh seafood. Seasonal.

Landfall
Luscombe Avenue
Tel: 508-548 1758
woodshole.com **$–$$**
A popular waterfront stop
for seafood for more than
60 years. L and D early
April–late Nov.

Shuckers World Famous
Raw Bar and Café
91A Water Street
Tel: 508-540 3850
woodshole.com **$$**
The freshest of seafood,
to be slurped dockside.
The raw bar and lobster
boil are particularly popu-
lar. L and D May–Oct.

Yarmouthport
Inaho
157 Route 6A
Tel: 508-362 5522 **$$$**
A superb Japanese
restaurant, with the
freshest sushi imagin-
able. L and D daily.

Jack's Outback
161 Main Street
Tel: 508-362 6690 **$**
Looking for local color?
You'll find it here in
spades, along with tasty,
affordable old-favorites
food. B Sun; L daily.

Cape Cod Islands
Martha's Vineyard
Edgartown
Among the Flowers
Cafe
Mayhew Lane
Tel: 508-627 3233 **$**
Omelets, quiches, pasta,
and other filling, inexpen-
sive fare. B, L, and D late
April–Columbus Day.

Atria
Old Post Office Square
Tel: 508-627 5850
atriamv.com **$$$**
Contemporary fare in a
house just out of town.
Specialties include ahi
tuna tempura, and
seared filet mignon. A
lighter menu is served in
the lively pub. Terrace

Prices for a three-course
dinner per person with
a half-bottle of house
wine:
$ = under $20
$$ = $20–45
$$$ = $45–60
$$$$ = over $60

dining in the summer.
D nightly.

L'Etoile
Charlotte Inn,
27 S Summer Street
Tel: 508-627 5187
letoile.net **$$$$**
Superlative French cuisine
served in a candlelit
conservatory. Three-
course tasting menu or à
la carte. A bar menu is
available too. D nightly
in season.

The Newes from
America
Kelley House, 23 Kelley Street
Tel: 508-627 4397
kelley-house.com **$**
Well-prepared pub grub in
a 1742 tavern. A vast
range of beers is avail-
able in sampler "racks".
L and D daily.

Menemsha
Homeport
512 North Road
Tel: 508-645 2679
homeportmv.com **$$–$$$**
Overlooking the harbor
and one of the best
spots on the island for
fresh fish: eat on the
lawn or the deck. No
credit cards. BYOB. D
nightly mid-Apri–mid-Oct.

Oak Bluffs
Offshore Ale Company
30 Kennebec Avenue
Tel: 508-693 2626
offshoreale.com **$–$$**
Homemade brews, an
expanded pub menu with
items such as seafood
gumbo and wood-fired
pizzas (try the chicken
pesto); plus a children's
menu. Entertainment.
L and D daily.

LEFT: relaxing by the sea at Provincetown.

Vineyard Haven

Black Dog Tavern and Bakery
Beach Street Extension
Tel: 508-693 9223
theblackdog.com **$–$$$**
One of the island's most popular restaurants serves up fresh seafood, homemade breads and pastries, and offers a children's menu. B, L and D daily.

Le Grenier
96 Main Street
Tel: 508-693 4906
legrenierrestaurant.com **$$$$**
A Vineyard favorite for classical French cuisine for more than 25 years. Tableside preparations include lobster Normande flambéed with calvados, and banana flambé. L and D daily. BYOB.

Nantucket

American Seasons
80 Centre Street
Tel: 508-228 7111
americanseasons.com **$$$$**
Adventurous dining from around the country in a romantic atmosphere. The award-winning all-American wine list complements the fare. Outdoor patio. D nightly June–late Dec.

Boarding House
12 Federal Street
Tel: 508-228 9622
boardinghouse-pearl.com **$$$–$$$$**
Mediterranean cuisine with an emphasis on "comfort served in a romantic candlelit dining room, in the bar, or at the island's most sophisticated sidewalk café. D nightly mid-April–Dec; brunch Memorial Day–Labor Day.

Chanticleer Inn
9 New Street, Siasconset
Tel: 508-257 6231
$$$–$$$$
High-class traditional

French cuisine in an opulent auberge-like setting. D nightly in season.

Rope Walk
Straight Wharf
Tel: 508-228 8886
theropewalk.com **$$$$**
Seafood with *nouvelle* splashes, on the harbor. Raw bar daily 3–10pm. L and D daily.

Straight Wharf Restaurant
Straight Wharf
Tel: 508-228 4499
straightwharfrestaurant.com **$$$–$$$$**
The elegant regional menu, served in a handsome loft space, might include panko-crumbed Chatham halibut with whole milk ricotta agnolotti. Bar menu. D nightly.

21 Federal
21 Federal Street
Tel: 508-228 2121
21federal.com **$$$–$$$$**
Excellent new and traditional American fare cuisine in a tastefully spare 1847 Greek Revival house with a seasonal patio. D nightly mid-May–mid-Oct.

Brotherhood of Thieves
23 Broad Street
Tel: 508-228 2551
brotherhoodofthieves.com **$$**
Great burgers, live music, and an appreciative crowd in an 1840 whaling bar. L and D daily.

Espresso To Go
1 Toombs Court
Tel: 508-228 6930
nantucketespresso.com **$**
Cheap, scrumptious international grazing. B and L daily.

Bars

Atlantic House, 6 Masonic Place, Provincetown. The town's most famous gay bar – located in a 1798 tavern – is

actually three bars, a dance club, a "Macho Bar" big on leather and Levi's, and the fireplaced Little Bar, a cozy hangout once frequented by Tennessee Williams.
The Beachcomber, Wellfleet. Tel: 508-349 6055. Watch the sun set while sipping a frozen Mudslide and feasting on a dozen oysters from the raw bar. The restaurant/bar, overlooking Cahoon Hollow Beach, also has live entertainment.
The Chicken Box, 14 Daves Street, Nantucket. Tel: 508-228 9717. A local institution for more than 50 years, this hot spot serves up a fine menu of local and nationally-known jazz and blues bands.
Crown & Anchor Inn, 247 Commercial Street, Provincetown. The complex's six bars offer something for most adventurous tastes, including the town's largest nightclub (Paramount), its only video bar (Wave), a cabaret venue, a poolside bar with heated pool, a piano bar and a landmark, cruisy leather bar (The Vault).
Grand Cru Wine Bar & Grill, 1225 Lyanough Road, Hyannis. Located at the Cape Codder Resort, this upscale retreat specializes in fine wines by the glass, and

features vintages from around the world. Dining options range from light snacks to full meals, and there's live jazz on Friday and Saturday nights.
The Lampost/Rare Duck, 111 Circuit Avenue, Oak Bluffs, Martha's Vineyard. A lively night spot with a split personality – upstairs features live bands and DJs with dancing (and more expensive drinks); the homier "basement" is the place to hear acoustic acts. Open all night in season. Closed Nov–Mar.
Liam Maguire's Irish Pub & Restaurant, 273 Main Street, Falmouth. Tel: 508-548 0285. There really is a Liam Maguire, and he really is from Ireland. He and his wife have exported the best of their native land to their pub, and serve it up with live entertainment and six big-screen TVs. Corned beef and cabbage is on the menu nightly.
The Squealing Pig, 335 Commercial Street, Provincetown. One of the straight (or "straighter") bars in town, the snug Pig features an extensive selection of draft and bottled beer, excellent fish and chips and lobster rolls, and decent jukebox selections for when the bands aren't playing.

CENTRAL MASSACHUSETTS

Tucked between metropolitan Boston and the more tourism-oriented western region of the state, the mid-section of Massachusetts harkens back to an earlier era of agriculture and small-town industry

Main attractions
FRUITLANDS MUSEUMS
BLACKSTONE RIVER VALLEY
WORCESTER
SOUTHWICK'S ZOO
OLD STURBRIDGE VILLAGE
QUABBIN RESERVOIR

BELOW:
the past preserved
at Fruitlands
Museums.

The vigor and sincerity of early Americans' social vision is vividly on display from mid-May to mid-October at **Fruitlands Museums ❶** (102 Prospect Hill Road; 978-456 3924; fruitlands.org; open mid-May–mid-Oct daily; entrance fee). These four museums are set in 210 acres (85 hectares) in the little town of **Harvard**, an hour west of Boston via Route 2.

In the mid-19th century, transcendentalist Amos Bronson Alcott, father of Louisa May Alcott (author of *Little Women*), left his Concord home with political activist Charles Lane and a group of followers to found an anti materialist utopian community on a farm in Nashoba Valley. Vegetarianism, asceti cism and a philosophical return to nature – living off the "fruits of the land" – were their mandates but, despite the best inten tions, the commune soon dispersed.

Between 1914 and 1945 Clara Endi cott Sears, who had been born into a privileged Boston Brahmin background in 1863, assembled an astonishing col lection of more than 6,000 artifacts an artworks in six historic buildings. Th result was one of America's first outdoo museums, now a National Register His toric District.

Along with presentations on the tran scendentalists, and Hudson River paint ings, there are a 1794 Shaker house an an Indian Museum. Beyond its art an history attractions, Fruitlands will in trigue anyone interested in the paralle between 19th-century and modern soci betterment movements. There are als 3¼ miles (5 km) of trails, giving fir views of the Nashua river valley an passing a site recreating the landscape of a Native American seasonal camp.

Wachusett State Reservation

For a bird's-eye view of the geograph center of the state, begin your visit at th **Wachusett State Reservation and S Area ❷** (tel: 413-464 2300; wasa.wachus .com; fee for events and chairlift), just o Route 140 in **Princeton** (an hour west Boston). If you visit during one of th

pring or fall special events (posted on heir website), you can ride the chairlift to the summit of the 2,006 ft/649 meters) mountain. Otherwise, the reservation's **Visitor Center** (open daily year round), just a mile past the base lodge, provides maps of the hiking trails, which are open year round. This is the nearest ski and snowboard center to Boston.

Blackstone River Valley

Beginning in the mid-1800s, a swath of Central Massachusetts extending from Worcester into Rhode Island was a bustling industrial center whose factories made everything from monkey wrenches to the whimsical Mr Potato Head toy.

This area, now called the **Blackstone River Valley National Heritage Corridor**, is a non-traditional national park — a living landscape whose people and their environs tell a fascinating story of early industrial America. There are visitor centers in Massachusetts at the 1,000-acre (400-hectare) River Bend Farm in Uxbridge *(see below)* and, in Worcester *(see below)* at Broad Meadow Brook Wildlife Sanctuary and the Worcester Historical Museum.

When completed the 48-mile (77-km) Blackstone River Bikeway (nps.gov/blac) will run from Worcester to Providence, Rhode Island. So far 8 miles (13 km) have been opened.

Worcester

About 15 miles (24 km) south is **Worcester ❸**, the state's second-largest city. This gritty industrial center spawned the country's first park, first wire-making company, first steam calliope, first carpet loom, first diner manufacturer, first Valentine, and (suitably enough) first birth-control pill, not to mention the beginnings of liquid-fuel rocketry, female suffrage and the Free Soil Party, precursor of the Republican Party.

Notable residents have included Dr Robert H. Goddard, born here in 1882 (a fine collection of his rocketry patents, drawings and other memorabilia is on exhibit at the **Goddard Library ❹** at Clark University (990 Main Street; tel: 508-793 7711; open Mon–Sat, Sun pm); composer Stephen Foster; socialist leader Emma Goldman; humorist Robert

A 1938 sculpture of Wo-peen, "The Dreamer," in the Native American section of Fruitlands Museums. Visitors can enter a wigwam and see how dugout canoes were made.

BELOW:
the ski scene on Wachusett Mountain.

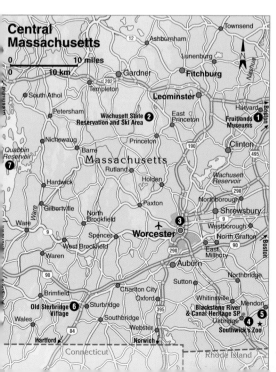

Worcester Art Museum, opened in 1898, contains 35,000 pieces.

BELOW: Higgins Armory Museum.

through 1876 (tel: 508-755-5221; one-hour tours Wed 3pm). Tours include an especially interesting visit to the document preservation laboratories.

The city, despite its reincarnation as an educational and medical center, is itself a trove of antiquarian delights. The **Worcester Historical Museum** ● (30 Elm Street; tel: 508-753 8278; worcesterhistory.org; open Tues–Sat; Thur until 8:30 pm; Sun pm; entrance fee) traces the city's industrial and cultural history, and maintains the splendid 1772 Georgian **Salisbury Mansion** (40 Highland Street: open for guided tours only Thur 1–8:30 pm, Fri and Sat 1–4 pm; entrance fee). The museum is also a visitor center for the Blackstone River Valley National Heritage Corridor *(see above)*.

The four-story **Higgins Armory Museum** ● (100 Barber Avenue; tel 508-853 6015; higgins.org; open Tues–Sat; Sun pm; entrance fee), the only museum in the Western Hemisphere solely dedicated to exhibiting arms and armor. It features a vast collection of artifacts, including some dating back to 6th century BC Greece. Children (and small people) can try a suit on for size.

Benchley; and 1960s radical Abbie Hoffman. Sigmund Freud gave his only US lecture at Clark University.

Publisher Isaiah Thomas, a Son of Liberty who fled Boston in advance of the British Army in 1770 and continued to publish his rabble-rousing revolutionary newspaper, the *Massachusetts Spy*, was from Worcester. In 1812 he established the **American Antiquarian Society** ●; its Worcester headquarters, at 185 Salisbury Street, is now a research library whose vast collection focuses on American history, literature and culture

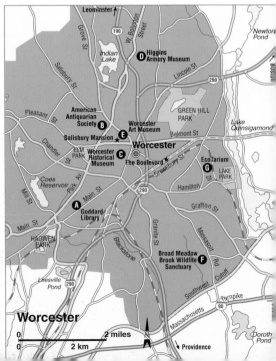

Recommended Restaurants and Bars on page 191

Adventurous art

With more than 35,000 works of art, the **Worcester Art Museum** ❸ (55 Salisbury Street; tel: 508-799 4406; worcesterart.org; open Wed–Sun; third Thur of the month until 8pm; entrance fee except Sat 10–noon) is the second largest in New England and arguably the most adventurous: its sponsorship of excavations at Antioch, Syria, in the 1930s yielded a remarkable collection of 2nd-century AD Roman mosaics. It also has fine collections of European and Eastern art. But perhaps most appealing is the extensive gallery of 17th-, 18th- and 19th-century American art, including paintings by John Singleton Copley, Winslow Homer, and John Singer Sargent. The museum's café is a good place for lunch.

More than 78 species of butterflies make their home at the 400-acre (160-hectare) **Broad Meadow Brook Wildlife Sanctuary** ❻ (414 Massasoit Road; tel: 508-753 6087; massaudubon.org; open Tues–Sat, Sun pm; entrance fee), run by the Massachusetts Audubon Society. There are nature trails and picnic sites.

Two miles (3 km) from downtown Worcester, you can walk through tree tops, visit a digital planetarium, ride on a narrow-gauge railway, and see great horned owls and a polar bear at the **EcoTarium** ❼ (222 Harrington Way; tel: 508-929 2700; open Tues–Sat; Sun pm; entrance fee). The unique, 60-acre (24-hectare) property introduces visitors to the region's ecosystem and wildlife.

The best-known diner in the city where they were originally made *(see photo feature, pages 80–1)* is **The Boulevard** (155 Shrewsbury Street; tel: 508-791 4535). Built in 1936, "The Bully", with stained-glass windows and formica-topped tables, is open 24 hours a day.

Canals and camels

South of Worcester, close to the Rhode Island border, tiny **Uxbridge** ❹ is home to the **Blackstone River and Canal Heritage State Park** (287 Oak Street; tel: 508-267 7604; open daily) on **River Bend Farm**. Displays at the visitor center tell the story of the area's canals; visitors can walk along restored sections of the canals and towpaths, and explore 1,000 acres (400 hectares) of natural area, including Rice City Pond, rich in wildlife.

There's also an abundance of wildlife

TIP

For six weeks each summer the EcoTarium hosts a Friday night Sunset Jazz series (for tickets, tel: 508-929 2703) under the stars – or in a tent if it rains. Ticket prices include admission to the facility, and children 12 and under are free.

BELOW: rowing is popular on the Blackstone River.

Old Sturbridge Village, opened in 1946, grew out of a collection of early New England artifacts, including tools, utensils, furniture, and clocks, assembled by Albert B. and J. Cheney Wells who ran the American Optical Company in nearby Southbridge.

BELOW: demonstrating how to raise a barn in Old Sturbridge Village.

– albeit a bit more contained – 5 miles (8 km) northeast in **Mendon** ❺ at **Southwick's Zoo** (4 miles/6 km off Route 16; tel: 800-258 9182; southwickszoo.com; mid-Apr–Oct, daily; entrance fee). This is a delightful stop for families with children: although it's relatively small, there are more than 100 kinds of animals, including Bengal tigers, camels, and elephants; there are lots of rides; and shows throughout the day.

Old Sturbridge Village

Off Route 20, **Old Sturbridge Village** ❻, a recreated community of more than 40 period buildings and 60,000 historic artifacts scattered over 200 acres (80 hectares), offers a "you are there" take on New England rural life between 1790 and 1840 (tel: 508-347 3362 or 800-733 1830; osv.org; open mid-April–late Oct daily; rest of year Tues–Sun; entrance fee includes two days' admission within 10 consecutive days).

Visitors are given illuminating explanations, couched in modern parlance, as the interpreters go about the daily business of farm and town life: cobbling shoes, making tin lanterns, leading prayers.

Of special interest is the Pliny Freeman Farm, where, depending on the season, workers in period dress engage in making soap, shearing sheep, and laboriously building stone walls. Concepts of political freedom and discourse grew, in part, from the emergence of a free and vibrant press, and the activities of the Isaiah Thomas Printing Office are designed to show how printed communication became an integral part of the new nation's growth.

Quabbin Reservoir

Lying northwest of Sturbridge amidst rolling hills that are especially beautiful in autumn is the huge **Quabbin Reservoir** ❼ (Visitor Center; Route 9, Belchertown tel: 413-323 7221; open daily). One of the country's largest man-made public water supplies, it comprises 128 sq. miles (331 sq. km) of flooded valley that hold 412 billion gallons and supplies the drinking water to Greater Boston.

Four towns were flooded in 1939 to create this great body of water. Quabbin is prized as a place to fish, hike and admire the rare bald eagles that breed here. ☐

RESTAURANTS AND BARS

Restaurants

Prices for a three-course dinner per person with a half-bottle of house wine:
$ = under $20
$$ = $20–45
$$$ = $45–60
$$$$ = over $60

Mendon

Alicante Mediterranean Grille
84 Uxbridge Road
Tel: 508-634-7888
Seafood with a Spanish/Portuguese flavor is the star here, although veal and beef – as in a sirloin graced with a Rioja and roasted garlic sauce – shouldn't be overlooked. The wine list offers a chance to get acquainted with various Iberian vintages. D Wed–Sun.

Sturbridge

Cedar Street
12 Cedar Street
Tel: 508-347 5800. $$$
Creative international fare in the heart of downtown. House specialties include mushroom risotto and cedar plank salmon; the wine list includes some very reasonable bottles.

Publick House
295 Main Street
Tel: 508-347 3313. $$–$$$
This gracious 1771 inn and tavern, once a stop for Boston–New York stagecoaches, serves New England fare with a contemporary flair. The Sunday breakfast buffet is excellent; the weekday three-course twilight dinner ($) 4–6pm is a bargain. B & L Mon–Sat; D nightly, Sun. from noon.

The Whistling Swan
502 Main Street
Tel: 508-347 2321. $$–$$$
Continental cuisine in three formal dining rooms of a Greek-Revival mansion; casual fare is served in the converted barn. L & D Tues–Sun.

West Brookfield

Salem Cross Inn
260 W Main Street (Route 9)
Tel: 508-867 2345. $$–$$$
New England fare is featured at this handsomely-restored, 1705 home amid 600 acres. Prime rib slow-roasted in a pit is served at special Drover's Roasts.

Worcester

Charlie's Diner
32 West Main Street
Tel: 508-885-4033. $
Hearty, classic fare in a 1941 diner. B & L Mon–Sat; D Thur–Sat; Sun B.

Coney Island Lunch
158 Southbridge Street
Tel: 508-753 4362. $
Folks have been flocking here for hot dogs since 1918: look for the sign – a hand holding a wiener. L & D Wed–Mon.

Five & Diner
525 Lincoln Street
Tel: 508-852 6100. $
The national chain's first Massachusetts outpost is truly a blast from the past: a 1950s setting, and a large menu of comfort foods including meat loaf with mashed potatoes, and the Big Bopper double decker burger. B, L, & D daily.

Viva Bene
144 Commercial Street
Tel: 508-799 9999. $–$$$
The menu at this casual downtown Italian restaurant ranges from basic pizza and calzones to creative chicken and veal dishes. L & D daily.

Tribeca
92 Shrewsbury Street
Tel: 508-754-7600
Choose between formal restaurant and bistro grill dining at this sophisticated spot, with a menu built around beef and seafood favorites and a remarkably imaginative starter selection. Extensive wine list; piano dessert bar. L & D Tues–Fri; D Mon & Sat; call for special Sun openings.

Wholly Cannoli
490 Grafton Street
Tel: 508-753 0224. $
The popular bakery/restaurant also serves breakfast, lunch and dinner, including a large selection of pizza; but patrons flock to this shrine for 20 flavors of cannoli, from the traditional sweet ricotta, to mint chocolate chip. B, L & D daily.

ABOVE: breakfast with waffles and maple syrup.

Bars

The Compound, 281 Lunenburg Street, Fitchburg. Two levels of entertainment nightly: live bands upstairs, and a DJ down. There are also pool tables and other forms of amusement. Open nightly 7 pm–2am.
Blackstone Tap, 81 Water Street, Worcester. A classic sports bar with TVs, a pool table, and occasional live entertainment (no cover).
The Boynton Restaurant & Spirits, 117 Highlands Street, Worcester. Half-bar, half-restaurant, and always a popular hangout for students from nearby Worcester Polytech. Giant TVs broadcast sports, there are 28 beers on tap, and turkey dinners for $10.
Dive Bar, 34 Green Street, Worcester. No frills, just a small and simple place with a large selection of craft beers.

MASSACHUSETTS: THE PIONEER VALLEY

As the Connecticut River wends its way south, it passes through several counties in the western Massachusetts lowlands. In 1939 a group of local businessmen dubbed this area the Pioneer Valley in honor of its 17th-century settlers

Main attractions

SPRINGFIELD
AGAWAM, SIX FLAGS
HOLYOKE
SMITH COLLEGE MUSEUM
OF ART
HADLEY FARM MUSEUM
AMHERST COLLEGE
EMILY DICKINSON HOMESTEAD
HISTORIC DEERFIELD

BELOW: exhibits in the Basketball Hall of Fame.

Springfield ❶, the Pioneer Valley's largest city, was established as a trading post in 1636. Throughout its history Springfield has been a manufacturing hub. Indian motorcycles, Rolls-Royces, and Smith & Wesson revolvers have all been made here. But it was in 1892, at the local YMCA, that Dr James Naismith invented a game that would make possible the city's major attraction: the new $103 million, interactive, state-of-the art **Basketball Hall of Fame** ❹ (1000 West Columbus Avenue; tel: 413-781 6500; hoophall.com; open daily;

entrance fee). The 48,000-sq-ft (4,460 sq meter), three-level facility fascinates th sport's aficionados: others may experienc an information overload. Max's Taver (good steaks) is on site, as is McDonald'

In 1779 George Washington chos Springfield as the site of one of th nation's first two arsenals. The **Spring field Armory National Historic Site** ❶ (Armory Square; tel: 413-734 647 nps.gov/spar; open Tues–Sun) now hous a museum featuring the world's large museum collection of historic US mil tary shoulder arms, including Springfiel

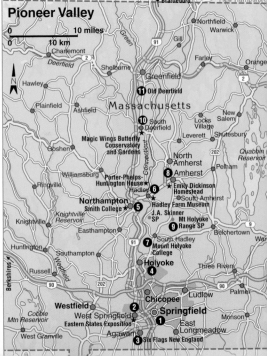

rifles manufactured here. The Organ of Muskets, made famous by Longfellow's 1845 anti-war poem *The Arsenal at Springfield*, is particularly poignant.

Springfield supports four more outstanding museums, all clustered around "the Quad" – the **Springfield Museums at the Quadrangle** ⓒ (Chestnut and State streets ; tel: 413-263 6800 or 800-625 7738; springfieldmuseums.org; open Tues–Sun, Welcome Center open daily; entrance fee; one ticket covers all four):

■ The **George Walter Vincent Smith Art Museum** features oriental decorative arts, from Persian rugs to Japanese netsuke and Chinese cloisonné.

■ The **Science Museum** contains the first American-built planetarium and plenty of intriguing, hands-on exhibits; consider it "dessert" for kids who have made it through the art museums.

■ The **Connecticut Valley Historical Museum** showcases local artifacts, from folk paintings to fine furniture.

■ The **Michele and Donald D'Amour Museum of Fine Arts** has an impressively broad collection, including portraits by noted itinerant painter Rufus Porter; contemporary shows are also mounted.

Surveying all this culture is the **Dr Seuss National Memorial Sculpture Garden** (catinthehat.org), a fanciful outdoor park with life-size bronze sculptures of characters created by the city's favorite son, the children's author and cartoonist Theodore Seuss Geisel (1904–91).

The 735-acre (300-hectare) **Forest Park** ⓓ (Sumner Avenue; open daily; fee) has a zoo (tel: 413-733 2251) with more than 100 species, and a seasonal, child-size train tour.

The city's rich cultural life is reflected in the music, from classical to popular, of the Springfield Symphony Orchestra, based in **Symphony Hall** ⓔ (1350 Main Street; tel: 413-733 2291; springfieldsymphony.org). Its stage also hosts theatre and headliner performances.

African exhibits in Springfield's Science Museum.

The Big E

Across the river, in **West Springfield** ❷, the Theater Project at the Majestic Theater (131 Elm Street; tel: 413-747 7797) mounts live performances. Down the

BELOW: Dr Seuss National Memorial Sculpture Garden.

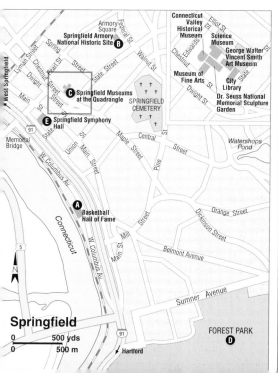

Springfield

0 _____ 500 yds
0 _____ 500 m

FOREST PARK ⓓ

That sinking feeling at the Six Flags amusement park.

BELOW: cartoon classics at Six Flags.
RIGHT: Holyoke's merry-go-round.

road is the 175-acre (71-hectare) fairgrounds for the **Eastern States Exposition** (the "Big E"), New England's major agricultural fair (tel: 413-737 2443; thebige.com). Every September, prize livestock and top-name talents entertain the crowds for 2½ weeks. Permanently ensconced on the grounds is the **Storrowton Village Museum**, nine transplanted 18th- and early 19th-century buildings surround a traditional town green (1305 Memorial Avenue; tel: 413-737 2443; open late June–late Aug Tues–Sat; entrance fee). The on-site restaurant serves New England fare in a lovely dining room.

Six Flags

In nearby **Agawam**, **Six Flags New England ❸** (1623 Main Street; tel: 413-786 9300 or 877-474-3524; sixflags .com; open weekends in spring and fall, daily in summer; entrance fee) is New England's largest amusement park. The four dozen rides are varied. But at peak times the lines can be long and, when you add parking charges and pricey food, the total cost can be far from amusing.

Holyoke

Head 8 miles (13 km) north from Spring field on Route 5 or I-91 (exit 16) to **Holyoke ❹**, home to **Wisteriahurst Museum** (238 Cabot Street; tel: 413-53 2216; open Apr–Oct, Wed, Sat and Sun pm; entrance fee). The elegantly fur nished mansion where one family lived from 1875 to 1959 is a fine example of the classical revival architecture of the Beaux Arts movement.

In the center of town, the Visitor Cen ter at **Holyoke Heritage State Park** (221 Appleton Street; tel: 413-534 1723 open Wed–Mon) recounts the history of the city and its industrial heritage. Next to the center is a 1929 **merry-go-round** (July and August, Tues–Sun) with rides for just $1. It was saved when a local amusement park closed in 1987.

In the same complex, the young can enjoy hands-on activities at the **Chil dren's Museum** (444 Dwight Street; tel 413-536 5437; open Wed–Sat; Sun pm entrance fee). In the same building, the **Volleyball Hall of Fame** (open Thur–Sun pm; tel: 413-536 0926) immortalizes William G. Morgan, who invented the game at the Holyoke YMCA in 1895.

Recommended Restaurants and Bars on page 199

Northampton

Continue north alongside the Connecticut River to **Northampton ❺**. Surrounded by colleges – Amherst, Mount Holyoke, Hampshire, the University of Massachusetts ("U-Mass"), and **Smith College** (tel: 413-584 2700), right in town, Northampton's lively bistros, restaurants, and galleries reflect the youthful, energetic company it keeps. The area has attracted hundreds of artisans and artists, who showcase their wares at craft shops all over town and in the multi-story **Thornes Marketplace** complex (150 Main Street).

Smith College Museum of Art (Elm Street, Route 9; tel: 413-585 2760; smith.edu/museum; open Tues–Sat; Sun pm; entrance fee) exhibits one of the finest collections in the country, with a special focus on American art and on French impressionists including Degas, Seurat, Picasso, Cassatt, and Cézanne. It also exhibits an impressive collection of Asian and African and Asian pieces. The college's **Lyman Plant House** (tel: 413-585 2740; open daily), a delicate 1896 greenhouse, makes a lovely rainy-day retreat. On clear days, tour their 127-acre (51-hectare) **arboretum and gardens**.

Calvin Coolidge (1872–1933), the governor of Massachusetts who became the 30th US President, began his law practice in Northampton, was the town's mayor, and eventually died there. A collection of his papers is on exhibit in the **Coolidge Memorial Room** in the **Forbes Library** (20 West Street; tel: 413-587-1011; open Mon–Thur pm; Sat 9am–noon). *(For more on Coolidge, see page 278.)*

Hadley

To the east along Route 9, between Northampton and Amherst, is **Hadley ❻**, whose long history of farming is documented at the **Hadley Farm Museum** (jct. routes 9 and 47; open May–Oct, Tues–Sat; Sun pm; donation).

Exhibits are housed in a 1782 barn moved to its present location from the **Porter-Phelps-Huntington Historic House Museum** (130 River Drive, Route 47N; tel: 413-584 4699; pphmuseum.org; open mid-May–mid-Oct Sat–Wed pm; entrance fee). This Georgian-style house, built in 1752 and structurally unchanged since 1799, was home to seven generations of the same family.

The museum hosts "A perfect spot of

Calvin Coolidge's reputation as a man of few words once prompted a matron at a society banquet to coax him: "Mr President, I have a wager with a friend that I can persuade you to say more than two words." His reply: "You lose."

BELOW: interior and exterior of Wistariahurst Museum, Holyoke, a Beaux Arts gem.

A family excursion in lanes near Hadley.

BELOW:
biking over the Connecticut River near Hadley.

tea," live music, and conversation on Saturday afternoons at 2:30 and 3:30pm in July and August ($10 per person). If you're in the area Wednesday evenings in June and July, pick up some picnic goodies at Whole Foods Market (Route 9, Hadley) and catch a concert beginning at 6:30 pm in the Sunken Gardens.

Just off Route 47 in nearby **J.A. Skinner State Park** (tel: 413-586 0350) a road (open Apr–Nov) climbs to a viewpoint immortalized in Thomas Cole's 1830 painting, *The Oxbow*. The **Summit House**, a former 19th-century hotel, is open for tours on weekends from Memorial Day to Columbus Day.

South on Route 116, in nearby **South Hadley**, **Mount Holyoke College** ⑦ (tel: 413-538 2000) is America's oldest women's college. Its 400-acre (160 hectare) campus was the work of landscape architect Frederick Law Olmsted. Students run regular campus tours (details: mtholyoke.edu/adm/tours).

Amherst

Continue east on Route 9 to **Amherst** ⑧, long a hotbed of intellectual vigor and social independence. Lexicographer Noah Webster lived here, as did a reclusive genius of American poetry.

Visitors to the **Emily Dickinson Homestead** can experience the spartan environment that housed a self-confined soul who poured her emotions solely into her poetry (280 Main Street; tel: 413-542 8161; emily dickinsonmuseum.org; open Mar–Dec, Wed–Sun 11am–5pm; June–Aug until 6pm). Guided tours leave from the Visitors' Center on the hour. As New England offers a wealth of period homes of greater architectural interest, this should be considered a literary pilgrimage site first and foremost *(see margin note, facing page)*.

Just off the spacious central green

Amherst College's (amherset.edu) stately fraternity houses flank a campus quadrangle that is a classic of early 19th-century institutional architecture. At the college's **Mead Art Museum** (tel: 413-542 2335; open Tues–Sun; free) more than 16,000 works include a superb collection of American art, as well as Russian modernist paintings, and West African sculptures. The addition of more than 2,500 Japanese woodblock prints has made this one of the major collections of ukiyo-e in the country.

The skeleton of a woolly mammoth is the centerpiece at the college's **Museum of Natural History** (tel: 413-542 2165; open Tues–Sun; free), showcasing a trove of fossils and geological history.

South on Route 116, children of all ages will want to visit the home of *The Very Hungry Caterpillar*: the **Eric Carle Museum of Picture Art** (125 West Bay Road; tel: 413-658 1100; picturebookart.org; open Tues–Sat and Sun pm; entrance fee). The children's author and illustrator opened the large facility in 2002. It is next to **Hampshire College**, a small liberal arts college.

Yiddish spoken here

Hampshire College alumnus Aaron Lansky is the motivating force and director of the **National Yiddish Book Center** (Hampshire College, Route 116; tel: 413-256 4900 or 800-535 3595; yiddishbookcenter.org; open Mon–Fri 10am–3:30pm; Sun 11am–4pm). This is a collection of more than a million Yiddish books housed in a wooden complex designed to resemble an Eastern European *shtetl* (village). The center hosts art exhibits and special performances. As an heroic exercise in the preservation of an imperiled language and the tradition it represents, the center will interest not only the heirs of that tradition, but also those interested in social history.

Encompassing a 7-mile (11-km) ridge that stretches from Hadley to Belchertown, **Mount Holyoke Range State Park ❾** (Route 116; tel: 413-586 0350; visitor center open daily) offers some of the Pioneer Valley's best scenery.

South Deerfield

Backtrack to Route 5 (or hop on I-91) and head north to **South Deerfield ❿**. Here it's always Christmas in the Disneyesque Bavarian Village and Santa's Workshop at "the world's largest candle store," **Yankee Candle Company** (Route 5; tel:877-636 7707; open daily). This is one of the area's major attractions for children, who have the chance to dip their own candles, colonial-style. Also, Chandler's Restaurant at Yankee Candle Company hosts a concert series and all-you-can-eat BBQ on their patio many evenings from late June through August.

Less than 3 miles (5 km) up Route 5 is **Magic Wings Butterfly Conservatory and Gardens** (tel: 413-665 2805; open daily; entrance fee), where thousands of butterflies flutter about in an 18,400-sq ft (1,710 sq-meter) indoor – and, in summer, outdoor – conservatory garden.

Historic Deerfield

Farther northwest, just off Route 5 in the well-preserved pioneer village of **Old Deerfield ⓫** – 13 museum houses make up Historic Deerfield (Main Street; tel: 413-774 5581; historic-deerfield.org; open

Emily Dickinson (1830–86), unknown in her lifetime, is now considered a major American poet. Extremely reclusive, she lived her life in Amherst. Recurring themes in her prolific poetry are death and immortality. A complete collection of her work was not published until 1955.

BELOW: antiques shows are big attractions in Pioneer Valley.

The 1730 Ashley House in Deerfield.

BELOW:
candle-making at
Historic Deerfield.

daily; entrance fee good for two consecutive days, includes 11 homes plus the Flynt Center of Early Life).

Deerfield has a fascinating history that dates from its settlement in 1669. The Pocumtuck Indians, who farmed the fertile valley, were not pleased to see their land usurped, and massacred the entire population (by then 125 strong) in 1675. That deterred settlers, but the lure of the land was irresistible, and the interlopers eventually won out, despite a French-instigated Indian raid in 1704 in which half the village was burned, 100 colonists carried off to captivity in Quebec, and 50 slaughtered.

Tomahawk marks can be seen on one sturdy wooden door, but the town's lurid history is not what attracts most visitors. The draw is an extraordinary architectural cache: the carefully restored Colonial and Federal structures along "The Street," Deerfield's mile-long main thoroughfare. The treasures inside the houses, representing decades of changing decorative styles, easily equal the exteriors.

Among the buildings open to the public are the **Ashley House** (1730), a former parson's home with intricately carved woodwork and antique furnishings; the **Asa Stebbins House** (1810) with early paintings, Chinese porcelain and Federal and Chippendale furniture; and the **Hall Tavern** (1760), where Historic Deerfield maintains its information center. Deerfield doesn't offer the costumed interpreters and crafts demonstrations of a Sturbridge Village, and so may not hold children's interest to the same extent; but history buffs – and anyone enamored of the restrained elegance of colonial design – will find it fascinating. Gravestones in the **Old Burying Ground** at the end of Albany Road make for interesting reading.

Memorial Hall Museum (Memorial Street; tel: 413-774 3768; open May–Oct daily; combination ticket or separate admission), houses a wonderful hodge-podge of folk art, Native American relics, needlework, and the eclectic collection of town historian George Sheldon. The **Channing Blake Meadow Walk** (May–Dec) passes a working farm and through meadows to the Deerfield River. ❑

RESTAURANTS AND BARS

Restaurants

Prices for a three-course dinner per person with a half-bottle of house wine:

$ = under $20
$$ = $20–45
$$$ = $45–60
$$$$ = over $60

Amherst

Amherst Chinese
62 Main Street
Tel: 413-253 7835 **$**
A casual restaurant known for hearty portions of traditional dishes. L and D daily.

Lord Jeffrey Inn
30 Boltwood Avenue
Tel: 800-742 0358
lordjefferyinn.com **$$–$$$**
Continental fare in the formal, dark-paneled, fireplaced restaurant at this historic inn. A casual menu is served in the tavern. D Wed–Sun; B, L and D in tavern.

Deerfield

Deerfield Inn
81 Old Main Street
Tel: 413-774 5587/
800-926 3865
deerfieldinn.com **$$$**
The Continental menu in this antiques-filled, historic inn is surprisingly forward-thinking. B daily; D Thur–Mon.

Sienna
6 Elm Street, South Deerfield
Tel: 413-665 0215
siennarestaurant.com **$$$**
An informal but intimate atmosphere and a changing but consistently good menu with dishes such as wild-mushroom crêpes, grilled duck breast, and creative desserts. D Wed–Sun.

Northampton

East Side Grill
19 Strong Street
Tel: 413-586 3347
eastsidegrill.com **$$**
Wildly popular Cajun-influenced grill. The food may not convince you that New Orleans has come north, but the room is always bustling. D nightly.

Spoleto
50 Main Street
Tel: 413-586 6313
spoletorestaurants.com
$$–$$$
New and traditional Italian fare in a lively contemporary cafe. A four-course special ($20) changes daily. Spoleto Express is at 225 King Street. D nightly.

South Deerfield

Chandler's Restaurant
Yankee Candle, Route 5.
Tel: 413-665 1277. **$$–$$$**
A welcome oasis in one of the area's largest tourist attractions, serving creative New England dishes, along with classic favourites such as prime rib. Excellent kids' menu. Dinner is served by candlelight. L Sun–Sat; D Wed–Sun.

Springfield

Chef Wayne's Big Mamou
63 Liberty Street
Tel: 413-788 6628
chefwaynes-bigmamou.com
$–$$
Highlights of the Cajun and Southern fare include fried oysters, crawfish quesadillas, and sweet potato pie. L and D Mon-Sat. There's a second location at 15

ABOVE: one of New England's most popular beers.

Main Street in Williamsburg (northwest of Northampton).

Student Prince and Fort Restaurant
8 Fort Street
Tel: 413-788 6628
studentprince.com **$$–$$$**
This reliable downtown spot, popular since the 1940s, offers stout German cuisine and an authentic beer-hall ambience. L and D daily.

West Springfield

Viva Bene
144 Commercial Street
Tel: 508-799 9999
viva-bene.com **$–$$$**
The menu at this casual downtown Italian restaurant ranges from basic pizza and calzones to creative chicken and veal dishes. L & D daily.

White Hut
280 Memorial Avenue
Tel: 413-736 9390
whitehut.com **$**
It's usually standing room only in this tiny eatery that has been serving hot dogs and hamburgers (and now french fries) to devoted patrons for almost 70 years. L daily.

Bars

Hugo's, Pleasant Street, Northampton. Cozy student hangout with pool tables, darts, jukebox.
Moan & Dove, 460 West Street, Amherst. Popular beer bar, well situated on Route 116 between Amherst and Hampshire colleges. Hard-to-find labels include Old Rasputin Imperial Stout and Avery Maharaja.
Northampton Brewery Bar & Grill, 11 Brewster Court, Northampton. A venerable brewpub with an outdoor rooftop beer garden. Full menu.
Theodore's, 201 Worthington Street, Springfield. "Blues, booze, and BBQ" are staples at this popular club which hosts local, regional, and national blues bands Friday and Saturday nights.
The Tunnel, Union Station Restaurant, 125A Pleasant Street, Northampton. It really is a renovated railroad tunnel, but a luxurious one, with plush couches and leather easy chairs in which to sip one of the bar's signature martinis or single malt scotches.

MASSACHUSETTS: THE BERKSHIRES

Berkshire County encompasses valleys dotted with shimmering lakes, rolling farmlands punctuated by orchards, deep forests abundant with deer, and powerful rivers that cascade into dramatic waterfalls

Main attractions
COL. JOHN ASHLEY HOUSE
NEW MARLBOROUGH
GREAT BARRINGTON
STOCKBRIDGE
ASHINTULLY GARDENS
TANGLEWOOD
HANCOCK SHAKER VILLAGE
PITTSFIELD
WILLIAMSTOWN
THE MOHAWK TRAIL
SHELBURNE FALLS

BELOW:
kayaking on the
Deerfield River.

Everywhere one turns in this westernmost corner of Massachusetts, the horizon is piled and terraced with mountains. Though less dramatic than the mountains of New Hampshire or Vermont, these gentle ranges have nonetheless provided the Berkshire Hills with an insularity that has historically set them apart from the rest of the state.

With the Hoosac and Taconic mountains forming a natural barrier to the early settlers, the Berkshires remained a wilderness until 1725, when Matthew Noble built a cabin in what is now the town of Sheffield. Later, farmland was cleared and towns were established along the Housatonic River and its tributaries. During the 19th century, the Industrial Revolution brought prosperity to the Berkshires: its iron foundries smelted ore for the country's first railroads, while marble quarried from its hills graced the dome of the US Capitol.

As farming declined in the late 1800s, the Berkshires receded into a sleepy silence. But city dwellers seeking pretty scenery and respite from summer heat have periodically rediscovered the region. During the 1890s, the county became a playground for such wealthy families as the Carnegies and Vanderbilts, who built their mansions in the hills surrounding Stockbridge and Lenox. More recently, visitors have come for the renowned summer music festivals, the splendor of fall foliage, or the fun of winter skiing.

The first settlers reached the Berkshires through the Housatonic Valley from Connecticut. The modern traveler can do the same, following US Highway 7 north along the Housatonic, or by taking the Massachusetts Turnpike from the eastern part of the state.

THE SOUTH BERKSHIRES

Just inside the Connecticut border on Route 7A is **Ashley Falls ❶**, a village surrounded by hayfields and dairy farms. The village was named for Colonel John Ashley (1709–1802), a prominent lawyer and Revolutionary War officer.

Off Route 7A, the **Colonel John Ash-**

ley House**, built in 1735, is the oldest structure in Berkshire County. It was here the Sheffield Declaration protesting British tyranny and advocating for individual rights was drafted (published 1773). Now on the National Register of Historic Places, it has been restored as a colonial museum (Cooper Hill Road; tel: 413-229-8600; thetrustees.org; grounds open year round; guided house tours Sat and Sun Memorial Day weekend– Columbus Day weekend; entrance fee to house). Although the furnishings are not all true to the home's earliest period; it's worth a visit as an example of serenely proportioned early country Georgian architecture.

Up the road is the 329-acre **Bartholomew's Cobble** (105 Weatogue Road; tel: 413-229 8600; the trustees.org; open daily; entrance fee), a natural rock garden with hiking trails that meander along the banks of the Housatonic. It contains more species of fern – at their most prolific in June – than any other area in the continental United States. There's a small natural history museum.

Guided three-hour canoe tours, led by expert naturalists, explore Bartholomew's

Cobble and river in the summer. Children 12 and older are welcome, and advance reservations are mandatory.

Sheffield to Great Barrington

North on Route 7, **Sheffield ❷**, established in 1733, is the oldest town in Berkshire County. In 1994 the state's oldest covered bridge, just off Route 7, was destroyed by vandals. A new one (pedestrians only) replaced it a few years later.

The Berkshires' true beauty lies in its backroads and small villages. **Mill River** and **New Marlborough**, small communities that prospered in the heyday of the Industrial Revolution, are gems.

In New Marlborough, the **Old Inn on**

Cross-country skis are sometimes the best form of transport in winter.

LEFT: fall foliage in the Berkshires.

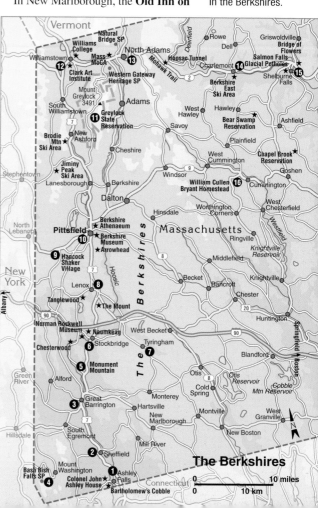

The Berkshires

In the terraced grounds at Naumkeag, Steele's Blue Steps is a series of deep blue fountain pools flanked by four flights of stairs ascending a hillside and overhung by birch trees.

BELOW: the Mission House, Stockbridge.

the **Green and Gedney Farm** (tel: 413-229 7924; oldinn.com) was once a stagecoach stop en route from New York to Boston.

Great Barrington ❸ offers an excellent base from which to explore the towns and villages of the southern Berkshires. Although it does not have the architectural treasures of towns farther north such as Stockbridge and Lenox, Great Barrington has long been a popular vacation destination for sophisticated New Yorkers, and upscale galleries, shops, and restaurants line the main and side streets.

Fans of singer Arlo Guthrie's *Alice's Restaurant Massacree* will want to see the **Guthrie Center** (4 Van Deusenville Road; tel: 413-528 1955), where Alice once lived. Built as a church in 1829, it is now an interfaith center.

Folks at the **Saint James Episcopal Church** on Main Street (Tel: 413-528 1460) truly do "make a joyful noise unto the Lord," with the help of a magnificent Ahlborn-Galanti organ and a wonderful chorus. The public is invited to attend Sunday morning service (10am), which incorporates everything from spirituals to historic hymns, and the free weekly chamber music program in July.

Head west on Route 23 and south on Route 41 to the tiny hill hamlet of **Mount Washington**, in the state's southwestern corner. This smallest of Berkshires towns offers some of the finest fall-foliage viewing and the most dramatic natural waterfall in New England: at **Bash Bish Falls State Park** ❹ (Falls Road; tel: 413-528 0330), in Mount Washington State Forest, water plummets 80 ft (24 meters) into a deep gorge.

Stockbridge

North of Great Barrington on Route 7 is **Monument Mountain** ❺, a craggy peak whose summit is a pleasant half-hour hike from the parking lot at its base. The mountain is a Berkshire literary landmark of considerable repute. The poet William Cullen Bryant sang its praises while practicing as a local attorney in the 1830s.

Stockbridge ❻ was incorporated as an Indian mission in 1739. Its first missionary was John Sargeant, a young tutor from Yale who lived among the natives for 16 years. He slept in their wigwams, shared their venison and spoke their language, while introducing them to the colonists' ways. Eventually, Sargeant helped them establish a town, build homes and cultivate the land. Some among the Mohican tribe held public office, serving alongside whites in the town government. But as more colonists moved into the area, the tribes were slowly deprived of their land.

By 1783, the mission was history, and surviving Indians were forced to settle on the Oneida reservation in New York State. All that remains is the 1739 National Historic Landmark **Mission House**, now a museum on Stockbridge Main Street (tel: 413-298 3239; the trustees.org; open daily late May–mid-Oct; entrance fee). It is furnished with a superb collection of 18th-century American furniture and decorative arts and has a unique Colonial Revival garden.

If Stockbridge's Main Street looks familiar, it may be because its New England essence was captured on the canvases of that remarkable illustrator of American life, Norman Rockwell, who created more than 300 covers for the *Saturday Evening Post*. He kept a studio and made his home here for a quarter of a century, until his death in 1978. Located in Route 183 is the stunning **Norman Rockwell Museum** (9 Glendale Road, Route 183; tel: 413-298 4100; nrm.org; open daily; entrance fee). Designed by Robert A.M. Stern, it showcases his work and even recreates his Stockbridge studio (open May–early Nov).

The **Red Lion Inn** (Tel: 413-298 5545; redlioninn.com), on Main Street, is one of the *grandes dames* of New England country inns. Its flower-laden front porch, complete with rocking chairs, is a place of pilgrimage for Berkshires travelers.

Naumkeag, a half mile off Route 7 and Route 102 (Prospect Hill; tel: 413-298 3239; open daily Memorial Day weekend through Columbus Day; entrance fee), is a 44-room, Norman-style mansion designed by Stanford White for Joseph Choate, the US ambassador to Great Britain, in 1899. The furniture and artworks are outstanding, as are the 8 acres (3.2 hectares) of terrace gardens and grounds.

Chesterwood, the meticulously-preserved summer home of sculptor Daniel Chester French (1850–1931), is 3 miles (5 km) west of Stockbridge (4 Williamsville Road, off Route 183; tel: 413-298 3579; open mid-May–mid-Oct daily; entrance fee). It was here that he created his masterpiece, *The Seated Lincoln*, focal point of the Lincoln Memorial in Washington, DC. Many of his pieces are on exhibit, and displays in the Barn Gallery document his outstanding career.

Tyringham

To the southeast, off Route 102, the tiny unspoiled village of **Tyringham 7**, became an artists' colony in the early 20th century. **Ashintully Gardens** (Sodem Road; tel: 413-298 3329; thetrustees.org; mid-June–mid-Sept, Wed and Sat pm; entrance fee), a charming assemblage of fountains, ponds and statuary, is all that remains of the magnificent estate of the

The Norman Rockwell Museum recreates the studio used by the Saturday Evening Post *illustrator.*

BELOW: music makers celebrate fall in the Berkshires.

Food and music mix at Tanglewood.

Egyptologist and politician Robb de Peyster Tytus (1875–1913), which was destroyed by fire.

Santarella, the fairytale "Gingerbread house" and studio of Sir Henry Hudson Kitson, sculptor of the Minuteman statue in Lexington, is at 75 Main Road. Although only open for functions, it is worth a drive-by.

Lenox

Further north, off Route 7, in **Lenox ❽**, are novelist Edith Wharton's grand neo-Classical, 1902 mansion and magnificent formal gardens at **The Mount**, (2 Plun-

kett Street; tel: 413-637 1899; edith wharton.org; open early-May–late Oct daily; entrance fee). After a $9 million restoration, they now look much as they did when she wrote *Ethan Frome, The House of Mirth,* and other works here.

Just out of town, **Tanglewood,** the 550-acre (220-hectare) summer home of the Boston Symphony Orchestra (297 West Street, Route 183; tel: 413-637 5165 or 888-266 1200; bso.org; open July–Aug.: entrance fee) has been a haven for performers, students and music lovers since 1937. The BSO, the Boston Pops and special guest artists also perform throughout the summer season in the 6,000-seat Music Shed, designed by architect Eero Saarinen. Tickets to Saturday morning rehearsals are offered at a reduced price

There are a café and grille on the grounds, but picnicking is a huge part of the Tanglewood experience. The on-site Meals to Go offers several options, including the Picnic Tote for Two, which includes food, wine, a corkscrew, glasses and a tablecloth. Menus are posted on Tanglewood's website (or tel: 413-637 5240)

Also in the grounds is a replica of the little red cottage where Nathaniel

Summer festivals in the Berkshires

Tanglewood is the best-known of several Berkshires summer festivals. The South Mountain Concerts (tel: 413-442 2106), featuring chamber music by renowned performers on most Sunday afternoons at 3pm in Sept and Oct, take place south of Pittsfield, on Route 7. For Renaissance and Baroque music, head for the Aston Magna Festival (tel: 413-528 3595; astonmagna.org), at St James Church in Great Barrington and at the Clark Museum in Williamstown; the church has free concerts on Sundays in July.

When the Jacob's Pillow Dance Festival *(pictured)* was launched in the early 1930s in the hilltown of Becket, southeast of Pittsfield on State 8, modern dance was in its infancy. Today, it's a national institution and hosts a 10-week summer program (tel: 413-243 9919).

Also impressive is the Williamstown Theater Festival (tel: 413-458 3200; 413-597 3400 box office), which stages summer theater ranging from Greek tragedy to Restoration comedy, and from Chekhov to Pirandello.

At Berkshire Theater Festival (tel: 413-298 5576), in Stockbridge, the emphasis is on American classics. For fans of the Bard, there's Shakespeare & Co (tel: 413-637 1199) in Lenox, performing throughout the year.

awthorne lived and wrote *The House of e Seven Gables* and *Tanglewood Tales.* Continue on Route 183 past the trance to Tanglewood to visit **Kripalu** l: 866-200 5203; kripalu.org), the coun-'s largest center for yoga and holistic alth. "Shadowbrook" was once the ate of Andrew Carnegie. Day passes – st generally available off-season and ekdays—include use of all facilities.

ancock Shaker Village

Tis a gift to be simple," says the old aker hymn, and the **Hancock Shaker llage** ❾ (tel: 413-443 0188 or 800-817 37; hancockshakervillage.org; open year-ind; entrance fee) on Route US 20, 3 les (5 km) west of Pittsfield, testifies to virtues of simplicity.

The 20 buildings in the village are en for self-guided tours daily from ly April through the weekend after lumbus Day. The rest of the year nission is by guided tour only – week-vs at 1pm, and weekends at 11am and 1 1pm – and includes some of the jor attractions here.

The Shakers *(see page 47)* settled in ncock in the late 1780s. The commu-

nity prospered through farming, printing, selling garden seeds and herbs and making their distinctively designed furnishings. Shakers lived in Hancock until the 1950s, when the community had dwindled to a few staunch survivors, celibacy and changing times having led to their decline.

Pittsfield

Returning to Route 7, continue north into **Pittsfield** ❿, the Berkshire County seat and largest city (population 52,000). Herman Melville completed *Moby-Dick* (1851) while living at **Arrowhead** (off Route 7 at 780 Holmes Road; tel: 413-442 1793; open Memorial Day–Columbus Day Fri–Wed. First tour 11am, last tour 3pm; tours available off-season by appointment; entrance fee). He lived in the 1780 farmhouse from 1850 to 1863; the view of the distant hills, he claimed, reminded him of the rolling ocean as he labored at his masterpiece.

A room in the **Berkshire Athenaeum** (1 Wendell Avenue; tel: 413-449 9480; open Mon–Sat) exhibits photographs, documents and memorabilia of Melville.

The **Berkshire Museum** (39 South Street; tel: 413-443-7171; berkshire

The elegance and functionalism of Shaker architecture is exemplified by Hancock's famous 1826 round stone barn, visible in the photograph below. Its design enabled one farmhand, standing at its center, to feed an entire herd of cattle.

BELOW: Hancock Shaker Village.

The Veterans' Memorial Tower.

BELOW: hiking in Greylock State Reservation.

museum.org; open Mon–Sat; Sun pm; entrance fee) presents an eclectic collection of natural science and history exhibits, ranging from a 143-pound (65kg) meteorite to shards of Babylonian cuneiform tablets. Its art collection is equally eclectic: it was the first gallery to exhibit Norman Rockwell, but it also showcased Andy Warhol and Robert Rauschenberg.

NORTH TO WILLIAMSTOWN

Off Route 7, just north of Lanesborough, turn right to **Greylock State Reservation ⓫** (tel: 413-499 4262; mass.gov/dcr/parks). Rising to 3,491 ft (1,064 meters), Mount Greylock is the tallest peak in Massachusetts. At the top is a distinctive granite monument, the 92-ft (28-meter) Veterans' Memorial Tower, commemorating the casualties of all America's wars.

From the top, the writer Nathaniel Hawthorne looked down upon Williamstown – "a white village and a steeple set like a daydream among the high mountain waves." The Visitor Center at the base of the mountain is open daily.

Route 7 continues north past the turn-off for **Jiminy Peak** and **Brodie Mountain** ski areas. The latter is the highest skiing mountain in the state.

Williamstown

In the state's northwest corner **Williamstown ⓬**, among the most beautiful of New England villages, is home to two excellent art museums. The **Williams College Museum of Art** (Main Street; tel 413-597 2429; wcma.org; open Tues–Sat Sun pm), under the auspices of **Williams College** (founded in 1793) houses more than 12,000 works from diverse eras and cultures, with a special emphasis on modern and contemporary art.

Just down the street is the exceptional **Sterling and Francine Clark Art Institute** (225 South Street; tel: 413-458 2303 clarkart.edu; open daily July–Aug; Tues–Sun rest of year; entrance fee June–Oct

Between 1918 and 1956, the Clark amassed a superb private collection that included silver and porcelain, as well as European and American paintings, including works by Botticelli, Goya, Gainsborough and Fragonard. The museum is best known, however, for its French Impressionist collection. There are additional

galleries in the new Stone Hill Center, designed by the Japanese minimalist architect Tadao Ando *(see page 87).*

ALONG THE MOHAWK TRAIL

The **Mohawk Trail** (Route 2) winds for 63 miles eastwards from Williamstown, cross Interstate 91 (I-91), to Orange. The ection from North Adams to Greenfield (I-91) is a designated scenic drive. An old ndian path-turned-roadway, it offers ome of the most rugged and romantic cenery in the Berkshires. It is a popular eaf-peeping route in the fall.

Stop in **North Adams** ⑬ to visit one f the state's newest museums, the **Mass-chusetts Museum of Contemporary rt (MoCa)** (jct. Route 2 and Marshall treet; tel: 413-662 2111; daily July–abor Day; Labor Day–June, Wed–Mon; ntrance fee). The vast, renovated 19th-entury factory complex houses a fine ollection of contemporary art, including ome pieces so large they've not been xhibited before. The large space is also performance arts center, presenting a ear-round program of dance, cabaret, lms, and avant-garde theatre. The luseum's **Kidspace**, a contemporary art

gallery and workshop for the young-sters, is open Sat–Sun noon–4pm.

Western Gateway Heritage State Park (115 State Street, Building 4; tel: 413-663 6312; open daily), in a restored freight yard, chronicles the town's history, including the build-ing of the nearby 4¾-mile/7.6 km Hoosac railroad tunnel.

Just north on Route 8, in **Natural Bridge State Park** (tel: 413-663 6392; open daily Memorial Day–Columbus Day; entrance fee), a water-eroded bridge that was formed in the last ice age spans a vast chasm.

Charlemont

In **Charlemont** ⑭, the Mohawk Trail winds past **Berkshire East** ski area and a stunning statue of a Mohawk warrior. *Hail to the Sunrise* was erected in 1932 to commemorate the Native Amer-icans who used the trail as a migration route back when it was a dirt road through the forest.

Crab Apple Whitewater (Route 2; Tel: 800-553 7238; crabapplewhitewater .com) offers half- and full-day rafting trips on the Deerfield and Millers rivers.

In Hail to the Sunrise, *a 900-pound (400-kg) Mohawk Indian lifts his arms to the Great Spirit.*

BELOW: rafting on the Deerfield River.

miles (5 km) of hiking trails, and **Chape Brook Reservation**, whose Pony Moun tain is popular with technical climbers Both are properties of the Trustees o Reservations (tel: 413-684 0148; th trustees.org). The pools that form at th base of Chapel Falls are a delightful spc to cool off on a hot summer's day.

The Bryant Homestead

Turn west where routes 112 and 9 merg to **Cummington** and yet another Trustee property, the **William Cullen Bryan Homestead** ⑯ (Bryant Road off Rout 112; tel: 413-634-2244; June–Columbu Day, Sat–Sun; Mon holidays, pm entrance fee to house). This was the boy hood home of Bryant (1794–1878), widely published poet, editor/publishe of the *New York Evening Post*, and men tor to Walt Whitman. Bryant used th house as a summer retreat, converting from Colonial style to Victorian. Toda it is filled with objects he purchased whil travelling overseas. There are footpath and hiking trails round the property.

Continue west on Route 9 back t Pittsfield and Route 7, or east on Route to Northampton and I-91.

The Bridge of Flowers at Shelburne Falls, tended by the local Women's Club.

Bridge of Flowers

In **Shelburne Falls** ⑮, turn onto 2A East to visit the one-of-a-kind **Bridge of Flowers**, a trolley bridge until 1928, now pedestrian only, which displays more than 500 varieties of flowers, vines, and shrubs. When the flowers are in bloom, it's truly worth a stop. At the **Shelburne Falls Trolley Museum**, climb aboard for a spin on an 1896 trolley car (May–Oct, Sat, Sun and holidays; July and August, Sun pm; fee). The glacial-carved **Salmon Falls Glacial Potholes** at the base of Shelburne Falls are great fun to explore.

Head south on Route 112, passing by the **Bear Swamp Reservation**, a 285-acre (115-hectare) wilderness area with 3

BELOW:
fishing on the Deerfield River, best known for its trout.

RESTAURANTS AND BARS

Restaurants

Prices for a three-course dinner per person with a half-bottle of house wine:

$ = under $20
$$ = $20–45
$$$ = $45–60
$$$$ = over $60

Great Barrington

Castle Street Cafe
10 Castle Street
Tel: 413-528 5244
castlestreetcafe.com
$$–$$$
An American/Continental bistro with big-city flair and award-winning wine list. Entertainment most weekends. D Wed–Mon.

Pearl's
47 Railroad Street
Tel: 413-528 7767
pearlsrestaurant.com $$$
Huge steaks and thick chops are specialties at this upscale and bustling restaurant with pressed-tin ceilings and exposed brick walls. L Wed–Sat; D nightly; Sun brunch. Closed Mon in winter.

Lenox

Blantyre
16 Blantyre Road
(off Route 20)
Tel: 413-637 3556
blantyre.com $$$$
Contemporary French cuisine in the formal dining rooms of one of the Berkshires' most elegant lodgings, a Tudor mansion open year round. L and D Tue–Sun. Jacket and tie at dinner.

Prime Italian Steak-house & Bar
15 Franklin Street
Tel: 413-637 2998
primelenox.com $$–$$$

Candlelight, reasonable prices, and fine service have made this a local favorite. Look for classic Italian dishes, along with savory beef offerings including a superb rib eye and braised short ribs. D nightly.

Rumplestiltzkin's Restaurant
Village Inn, 16 Church Street
Tel: 413-637 0020
villageinn-lenox.com $$$
Modern fare with American touches, such as mushroom Napoleon, and Shaker-style cranberry pot roast, in a venerable 1771 inn. D Thur–Sun.

Church Street Cafe
65 Church Street
Tel: 413-637 2745
churchstreetcafe.biz $$–$$$
Regional American bistro fare and whimsical decor in three dining rooms and on an outdoor deck. L and D daily; closed Sun–Mon in winter.

New Marlboro

Old Inn on the Green
Village Green (Route 7), 01230
Tel: 413-229 7924
oldinn.com $$$
Chef/owner Peter Platt serves dishes such as roast duck and lamb shank in the candlelit, fireplaced dining rooms of a c. 1760 stagecoach inn. A four-course, *prix fixe* dinner is offered Sat evenings. D nightly.

West Stockbridge

The Taste of Germany Restaurant
Williamsville Inn, 286 Great Barrington Road (Route 41)
Tel: 413-274 6118 $$–$$$

ABOVE: where B&B includes breakfast in bed

Candlelight, fireside dining featuring German and other European specialties. D Wed–Sun; Fri–Sat off-season.

Truc Orient Express
3 Harris Street
Tel: 413-232 4204 $–$$$
A handsome dining room, fine service and creatively presented Vietnamese fare, with specialties such as Shaking Beef and Happy Pancake. L and D summer; D only Wed–Mon winter.

Williamstown

Hobson's Choice
159 Water Street
Tel: 413-458 9101. $$–$$$
For more than 15 years, a popular choice for steaks, prime rib, seafood, and a terrific salad bar. "Death by Chocolate" is a sublime way to end up. D nightly.

Bars

Barrington Brewery and Restaurant, Jennifer House Commons, Rte. 7, Great Barrington. Hand-crafted beers made in a barn on the premises – Barrington Brown is a rich, English-style ale; also try stouts, lagers, IPAs, and seasonal spe-

cialties. Tasty pub menu, including an updated "plowman's lunch."

Brick House Pub, 425 Park Street, Great Barrington. Popular local hangout with a broad selection of beers on tap. Locals swear by the burgers and wings.

Old Heritage Tavern, 12 Housatonic Street, Lenox. An inexpensive, casual spot in an atmospheric 125-year-old building. Locals and the Tanglewood crowd belly up for expertly poured Guinness; pub fare includes vegetarian items.

Pittsfield Brew Works, 34 Depot Street, Pittsfield. The stouts and porters brewed on site at this big, friendly establishment have an avid following. Inexpensive "pub grub" includes burgers, fried calamari.

The Purple Pub, 8 Bank Street, Williamstown. Williams College students have hoisted their cold ones here since 1973. The baked-not-fried appetizers are served till midnight, and there's a burger on the menu for under $3. Free Friday night buffet 5–7pm when school is in session.

Recommended Restaurants and Bars on pages 230–1

RHODE ISLAND

With Providence's downtown, Newport's mansions, sailing in Narragansett Bay, and Block Island's rolling pastures and beaches, this tiny state packs a diverse punch

he smallest state in the nation, Rhode Island has nonetheless managed to hold on to a disproportionate share of wealth and clout. Certainly, the millionaires who built their legendary summer "cottages" in Newport at the end of the 19th century recognized natural wealth when they saw it: the dramatic vistas of the Rhode Island Sound, the refreshing westerly breezes wafting in to relieve summer doldrums. The mansions they left behind still gleam atop the cliffs, jewels left over from the Gilded Age.

The reclusive Reverend William Blax-ton was an early British settler; he moved here from the site of Boston when the Puritans arrived and crowded his one-man neighborhood. But Rhode Island's official founder was a clergyman, Roger Williams. Driven out of Salem in 1635 for preaching religious tolerance, Williams headed south to establish a settlement where all were free to practice their own faith: traveling by canoe with a cadre of followers, he arrived in what is now Providence. In 1663 Charles II granted a charter to the rather wordily named Colony of Rhode Island and

Main attractions

PROVIDENCE
SLATER MILL, PAWTUCKET
GREEN ANIMALS TOPIARY
 GARDENS
NEWPORT'S MANSIONS
JAMESTOWN
BLOCK ISLAND
FLYING HORSE CAROUSEL,
 WATCH HILL

PRECEDING PAGES:
Snug Harbor, Block Island Sound.
LEFT: The Elms.
BELOW: Newport's Second Beach.

The state in snapshot

Known as: The Ocean State.
Motto: Hope.
Origin of name: Unknown. Perhaps it reminded an early explorer of Rhodes in Greece. Or maybe derived from the Dutch for "red" after the color of its soil.
Entered Union: May 29, 1790, the last of the 13 original states.
Capital: Providence.
Area: 1,545 sq. miles (4,002 sq. km).
Highest point: Jerimoth Hill, 812 ft (247 meters).
Population: 1 million.
Population density: 649 people per sq. km (251 per sq. km).
Economy: manufacturing (fabricated metals, precision instruments, apparel and textiles, printed materials, rubber and plastic items, industrial machinery, primary metals, electronic goods, transportation equipment, chemicals, and processed foods.
Annual visitors: 29 million
National representation: 2 senators and 2 representatives to Congress.
Famous citizens: George M. Cohan, Nelson Eddy, Christopher and Oliver La Farge.

Castle Hill Light-
house, Newport.
Rhode Island has 21
lighthouses, 15 of
them active. The first,
Beavertail Light-
house, built in 1747,
is near Jamestown.

Poles, French, Swedes, Greeks, Armenians, Chinese and Cape Verdeans. Today,
with a population in excess of 1 million
crowded into its 1,214 sq. miles (3.144 sq.
km), Rhode Island is a bustling, multicultural cross-section of New England life.

Revitalized Providence

Rhode Island's capital has much in its
favor: it has outstanding 18th and 19th
century architecture on Benefit Street, an
excitingly rejuvenated downtown, and
appealingly diverse neighborhoods – Italian, Portuguese, Ivy League university
and funky places such as Hope Street. It's
also easily reached from Boston, a feasi-
ble day trip by car, train or bus.

In its early days, **Providence ❶** was
the port of call for ships engaged in the

Providence Plantations – a name it still
officially retains as a state.

Soon people from even farther afield
flocked to Rhode Island's shores. Many
Quakers, fleeing Puritan persecution,
made Newport their home, and as early
as the 18th century, Jews from Portugal
and Holland settled here. In the ensuing
centuries came Italians, Irish, Russians,

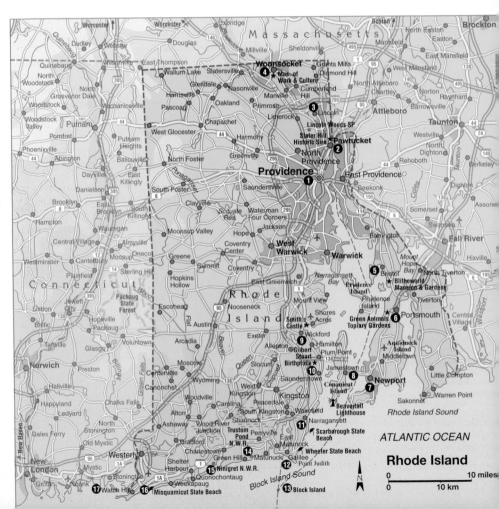

Rhode Island

lucrative Triangular Trade: New England rum for African slaves for West Indies molasses. In 1781, John Brown, one of four brothers whose family would dominate Providence for some years to come, sent the first of many ships to China. The maritime trade began to decline, however, following a series of international wars which resulted in embargoes and protectionism, and public interest and investment shifted toward industry.

As a major manufacturing center in the 19th century, Providence was dubbed "the cradle of American industry." The 20th century brought hard times. With the Great Depression and the textile industry's exodus to the south, Providence lost its industrial pre-eminence. Today Providence is home to five colleges and universities, and has enjoyed a certain revitalization of business.

The city has in turn lavished restorative attention on its variegated downtown. Artists have been given tax-free incentives to set up here; old warehouses and department stores have found new uses; I-195 is to be moved to free up more land for development close to the downtown area; and the ignored river has been beau-

tified and made more accessible. The man responsible for much of the revitalization, flamboyant mayor Buddy Cianci, was jailed for corruption in 2002.

Providence is a city best seen on foot. Like Rome, it was built on seven hills, the three best-known being College (officially, Prospect), Federal, and Constitution. The other four have melted in the metropolitan sprawl.

Center of town

Constitution Hill is pretty much impossible to miss because of the **State Capitol A** that dominates its crest (Smith Street; tel: 401-222 3983; state.ri.us; reserve ahead for tours Mon–Fri at 9, 10 & 11am). Exhibits inside this imposing 1891–92 McKim, Mead, and White structure include an historic portrait of George Washington by Rhode Island native Gilbert Stuart.

Just across the way, **Providence Place B** (tel: 401-270 1000; providenceplace.com) has more than 140 stores, restaurants,

Fireworks illuminate the State Capitol, which has the world's fourth-largest self-supporting marble dome. It is crowned with a bronze statue, Independent Man, representing the spirit of freedom that led Roger Williams to establish Rhode Island in 1636.

What makes the Ocean State different

As Rhode Island's license plate attests, Narragansett Bay dominates the state. Taking a dinosaur bite out of the New England coast, it gives the state a shoreline out of all proportion to its land area. Rhode Island is only 48 miles long and 37 miles wide (77 by 60 km), yet it claims 400 miles (640 km) of coastline.

With such an abundance of water at their disposal, Rhode Islanders have long turned to the sea for their livelihood. Two of the nation's leading seaports in the early days of the republic were Providence and Newport. Using Rhode Island as a base, pirates raided merchant ships in the North Atlantic until a clampdown in the 1720s. Later, Newport was the birthplace of the modern US Navy: President Chester Alan Arthur devel-

oped a new fleet – built of steel, rather than wood – there in the early 1880s.

Among the state's distinctions are: America's first textile mill, in Pawtucket, and America's only operational water-powered snuff mill, in Saunderstown. The state boasts the country's first synagogue, its first department store, and its

ABOVE: Roger Williams, Rhode Island's founder.

oldest enclosed shopping mall, built in the early 19th century.

Rhode Island, in the singular, is actually a misnomer. In fact, there are 35 islands within the state. Within and without Narragansett Bay are the four principal islands of Aquidneck (also called Rhode, just to keep things confusing), Block, Conanicut and Prudence; others include Hen, Hog, Rabbitt, Boat, Old Boy, Patience, Hope and Despair.

Despite the concentrated population, parklands are plentiful. And precisely because the state is so small – it takes less than two hours to drive from one end to the other – a visitor can walk historic city streets in the morning, picnic in an idyllic grove at noon and savor the delights of the seashore by moonlight.

and leisure options, including the six-story **Feinstein IMAX** theater (tel: 401-453 4446, ext. 200; imax.com/providence).

The 4-acre (1.6-hectare) **Waterplace Park and Riverwalk** is evidence of a waterside renaissance. The long neglected riverside was cleaned up, equipped with an Italian-inspired piazza, walkways, and descriptive panels with photos of the old port. At **WaterFire** (waterfire.org; May–Oct), performers ride down the river on gondolas, igniting wood fires that light up the night sky *(see margin tip)*.

Kennedy Plaza , in the shadow of the art deco skyscraper affectionately dubbed the Superman Building (not that *Superman* was ever filmed here), is the arrival point for buses from Boston and elsewhere. To the east stands the restored Providence Station, an Amtrak stop.

Around the corner from Kennedy Plaza is the **Turk's Head Building**, a 1913 landmark with an ornate stone head over its entrance; and the **Customs House** (1856), with a dome and lantern that once welcomed ships returning from China.

For shopping or snacking and a bit of history, visit the **Arcade** (65 Weybosset Street; tel: 401-598 1199; open Mon–Fri, 10am–5pm; Sat 11am–4pm This Greek Revival "temple of trade" an the nation's first indoor shopping ma was built in 1828. Its three-story grani columns (said to be the second largest America, after those at the Cathedral of ! John the Divine in New York) were c from single pieces of stone, whic required 15 yokes of oxen to move.

The Mile of History

In historic East Side, **Benefit Street**, th "Mile of History," deserves walking from one end to the other. There are more tha 200 restored 18th- and 19th-centur buildings (many now private homes) bui by sea captains and merchants; man houses, churches and schools bear bronz plaques identifying their original owne and dates of construction. In the la 1960s and early 1970s the street was ru down, and nearly demolished as part of renewal program; only the efforts of th Providence Preservation Society (pp .org) saved the day. Staff at the Joh Brown House Museum *(see below)* off 90-minute walking tours Tues–Sat 11am mid-June–mid-Oct.

Benefit Street was once a twisting di path informally known as Bac Street because it led around th back side of homes to the fami graveyards. When at last a comm nal burial ground was marked o and ancestral bones duly transferr to it, Back Street was straighten out and "improved for the bene of the people of Providence."

In 1638 Roger Williams estab lished the **Meeting House of th First Baptist Church in Ameri** (75 North Main Street; tel: 40 454 3418; fbcia.org; guided and se guided tours June–Oct, Mon–F 10am–noon and 1–3pm; Sat 10an 1pm; Nov–May, self-guided tou Mon–Fri; donation). Designed Joseph Brown, it was restored 1775 and is a fine example of th Colonial style. You can hear th magnificent Foley-Baker orga during the 10am Sunday servic

The **Old State House** (te

TIP

La Gondola offers a unique way to tour the river: on a genuine, Venetian gondola. Rides are offered evenings May–Oct, and the gondoliers provide cheese, ice buckets, glasses, and, of course, music. Tel: 401-421 8877; gondolari.com

BELOW: a statue of Rhode Island founder Roger Williams surveys modern Providence.

Recommended Restaurants and Bars on pages 230–1

401-222 3103; open weekdays) is at 150 Benefit Street, between North and South Court streets. It's worth a peep, if only to see the modest size of the former capitol, where the Rhode Island General Assembly renounced allegiance to King George III in May 1776.

Prospect Terrace , on Congdon Street a block east of the Old State House, is a tiny park that gives a fine view of the city; a statue of Roger Williams, the city's founder (who is buried here), presides. The streets hereabouts are full of imposing 19th-century industrialists' mansions.

The bookstacks of **Providence Athenæum** (251 Benefit Street; tel: 401-421 9970; open Mon–Fri; Sat am) reputedly witnessed the courtship of Edgar Allan Poe and a local resident, Sarah Whitman. She refused to marry him, however, because she claimed he couldn't stay sober. Such literary associations apart, the 1836 Greek Revival structure is well worth a visit for its collections of rare books, prints, and paintings.

Virtually opposite is the museum of the prestigious **Rhode Island School of Design (RISD) Museum** (224 Benefit Street; tel: 401-454 6500; risdmuseum.org; open Tues–Sun; entrance fee except Sun 10am–1pm, Fri noon–1:30pm, third Thur of each month 5pm–9pm; and last Sat of month). It has more than 80,000 works of art, including paintings by American masters and French Impressionists, a major Oriental collection, American furniture, and decorative arts.

Brown University (College Hill; tel: 401-863 1000; brown.edu) dominates this part of Providence. The Ivy League establishment was founded as Rhode Island College in Warren in 1764, and moved to Providence in 1770. Among

Marina on the Providence River. The river is 8 miles (13 km) long and has a barrier near the city to guard it against tidal floods.

BELOW: Portuguese store in Providence.

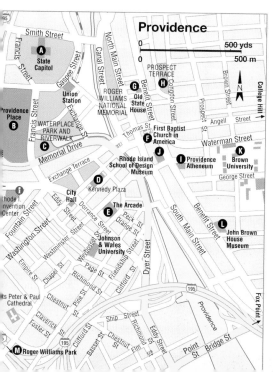

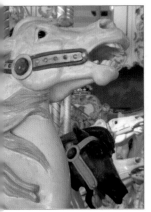

Rhode Island has several Victorian carousels, including the Crescent Park Looff Carousel in East Providence, a National Historic Landmark (open Easter–Columbus Day Thur–Sun, tel: 401-435 7518

BELOW:
Brown University.

the buildings of interest on the campus: the 1770 University Hall (on the Quadrangle), used as a barracks during the Revolutionary War; the 1904 Beaux-Arts John Carter Brown Library (corner of George and Brown streets); and the Annmary Brown Memorial (21 Brown Street; open weekdays pm) with European and American paintings from the 16th to early 20th centuries.

The heart of the **College Hill** shopping area is Thayer Street, four blocks east of Benefit, packed with interesting restaurants, bars, shops, and bookstores.

"The most magnificent and elegant private mansion that I have ever seen on this continent," said John Quincy Adams of the 1786 **John Brown House Museum** ⓛ (52 Power Street; tel: 401-273 7507; rihs.org/museums.html) open for tours Tues–Fri at 1pm and 3pm; Sat at 10:30am, noon, 1:30 pm and 3pm; entrance fee). You can see period furniture, paintings, pewter, silver, porcelain, and mementos of the China Trade; a later resident added an astonishingly showy bathroom. The museum staff also gives tours of the area, including Ben-

efit Street *(see above)*. There's free parki at the lot on the corner of Charlesford a Benefit streets. (If you visit just one hi oric home in Rhode Island (outside Newport), this should be the one.

Federal Hill, just to the west on t other side of I-95, is Providence's "Litt Italy." Wander along Atwells Avenue a enjoy the aroma of crusty Italian brea cheeses, pastas, herbs and spices. Son people come to stock up on tradition delicacies such as gorgonzola, Roman homemade pork sausages and prosciut others for the restaurants, espresso sho and festive ambiance.

One of Providence's best-kept secre is **Fox Point**, home to the city's Po tuguese community. The area spea with an Old World accent. On holy day celebrants parade with statues of the V gin Mary while children dressed in the best suits and crinolines follow alon Early morning brings to Fox Point t tantalizing scent of Portuguese swe bread wafting from small bakeries.

Before leaving town, head south I-95 to exit 17 and follow signs to **Rog Williams Park** ⓜ (Elmwood Avenu tel: 401-785 9450; admission to rides)

435-acre (176-hectare) complex which encompasses the state's only **Museum of Natural History and Planetarium**, a Botanical Center with New England's largest public indoor gardens, a carousel, a children's train, and a highly rated **zoo** (tel: 401-785 3510; open daily; entrance fee) which is home to more than 1,000 animals, including an African elephant.

BLACKSTONE RIVER VALLEY

Called "America's hardest working river", the Blackstone runs for 46 miles (74 km) from Worcester, Massachusetts to Providence. It was here, in the Blackstone Valley, that the country's Industrial Revolution began.

Techniques of mechanized textile production were pioneered with the construction of **Slater Mill** in **Pawtucket ❷** (5 miles/8 km northeast of Providence) in 1793 by Moses Brown. The riverfront **Slater Mill Historic Site** (67 Roosevelt Avenue; tel: 401-725 8638; slatermill.org; open March and April, Sat and Sun, May–Nov, Tues–Sun; closed Jan–Feb; entrance fee) offers visitors a rare look into the earliest days of the Industrial Revolution. The Sylvus Brown House (1758), the Slater Mill (1793) and the Wilkinson Mill (1810) show how textiles progressed from being handcrafts to a major industrial undertaking.

The **John H. Chafee Blackstone River Valley National Heritage Corridor** (Visitor Center, 175 Main Street; tel: 800-454 2882 or 401-724 2200; open Mon–Fri; tourblackstone.com), preserves the birthplace of America's Industrial Revolution. The center's **Blackstone Valley Explorer** (which departs from Central Falls and Woonsocket) gives informative 45-minute boat tours. Rides are free on the first Sunday of each month from June through September.

You can sleep aboard America's only British-built canal boat, the *Samuel Slater* (Central Falls; tel: 401-724 2200; ourblackstone.com. Run as a B&B, the boat also offers river cruises.

Eight generations of one family lived in the 1685 **Daggett House** (16 Second Street, Slater Park; tel: 401-722 6931;

open June–Sept, Sat and Sun pm; entrance fee). The oldest house in Pawtucket, it is filled with period antiques, including Colonial-era pewter.

Lincoln

Seven miles (11 km) to the northwest, in **Lincoln ❸**, Lincoln Woods State Park has one of the largest freshwater beaches in the area. Blackstone River State Park (Lower River Road; tel: 401-723 7892; riparks.com). Exhibits at the **Wilbur Kelly House Museum** (Lower River Road; tel: 401-333 0295; open April–early Oct, daily) narrate the history of the river and canal, and how it was long used for transportation by Native Americans. The museum is named after a sea captain who moved from seafaring to textiles.

Eight miles (13 km) of a proposed 17-mile (27-km) **Blackstone River Bikeway** (riparks.com; tel: 401-333 0295) which will eventually stretch along the Black River Corridor from Providence to Worcester are now completed between Lincoln and Cumberland.

Twin River (100 Twin River Road; tel: 877-827 4837) is one of the state's two video slots casinos.

The resilient Rhode Island Red was originally bred in the 1830s in Adamsville, now part of Little Compton, where a monument to it was erected in 1925.

BELOW:
Slater Mill, Pawtucket.

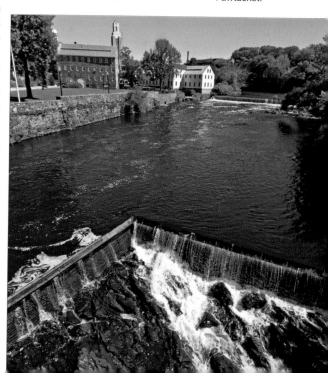

BELOW: Green Animals Topiary Gardens.

Woonsocket

For more local history, head north to **Woonsocket** ❹, on the Massachusetts border, to the **Museum of Work and Culture** (42 South Main Street, Market Square; tel: 401-769 9675; rihs.org; open Mon–Sat, Sun pm; entrance fee). Two floors of displays, many interactive, provide the story of local culture, immigration, labor, and enterprise, and of the French Canadians who migrated here from Quebec to work from the 1840s. (By 1900, 60 percent of Woonsocket's population was French-Canadian).

EAST BAY

Head east out of Providence on I-195 to Route 114 south, which winds along the eastern shore of East Bay, an offshoot of Narragansett Bay. In **Bristol** ❺, about 15 miles (24 km) south, visitors can tour **Blithewold Mansion, Gardens and Arboretum** (101 Ferry Road; tel: 401-253 2707; blithewold.org; grounds open daily; mansion open mid-Apr–mid-Oct, Wed–Sun and most Mon holidays; limited hours, Dec; entrance fee). The 45-room mansion was built by Pennsylvania coal magnate Augustus van Wickle in 1908 to resemble

a 17th-century English country manor. The 33 acres (13 hectares) of landscaped grounds are a riot of colour in spring.

More than 50 yachts from 1859 to 1947 and the America's Cup Hall of Fame are displayed at **Herreshoff Marine & America's Cup Museum** (1 Burnside Street; tel: 401-253 5000; open May–Oct daily; entrance fee). Artifacts from native peoples of the Americas, Africa, Asia and the Pacific are housed at Brown University's **Haffenreffer Museum** (300 Tower Street; tel: 401-253 8388; open June–Aug Tues–Sun; Sun rest of year; entrance fee).

The National Register of Historic Land marks **Mount Hope Farm & Governor Bradford House Country Inn** (250 Metacom Avenue; tel: 401-254 1745; mounthopefarm.com) is a 200-acre (80 hectare) estate dating back to a 1677 King Charles II land grant. Tours are given May–late Oct, Wed–Sat noon–4pm (fee).

Topiary Gardens

Six miles (10 km) south, just off Route 114 in **Portsmouth** ❻ at **Green Animal Topiary Gardens**, (Cory's Lane; tel: 401-847 1000; open late May–mid Oct, daily; combined admission ticket with Newport mansions). Eighty sculpted trees and shrubs represent everything from an ostrich to a camel. The main house of the gardens' creator, Thomas Brayton (1844–1939), has period furnishings.

NEWPORT

During World War II an anti-submarine net was strung across the entrance of the bay guarding **Newport** ❼. It was effective. But then, the elite of the city had long been expert at protecting their privacy. In the halcyon days of the Gilded Age, huge palaces built by the rich on expansive grounds were surrounded by mammoth fences and patrolled by guards and dogs. Now, however, a great many of these fiercely guarded fiefdoms are open to all comers, having become Newport's foremost tourist attractions.

A good place to begin a visit is downtown at the **Visitor Information Center** (23 America's Cup Avenue; tel: 800-976 5122; gonewport.com). They have exten

Recommended Restaurants and Bars on pages 230–1

sive information on the area, including maps – be sure to pick up detailed directions to **10-mile drive**, the stretch of Ocean Avenue that combines great Atlantic views with glimpses of Newport's grand mansions. Free, 30-minute parking (have your ticket validated in the visitor center) is available in the parking lot adjacent to the center.

Thames Street along the harbor is lined with shops and restaurants, many concentrated on **Bowen's Wharf**, lined, like many other wharves in town, with handsome craft tied up at yacht club slips.

Get your historical bearings at the **Museum of Newport History** Ⓐ in Washington Square (127 Thames Street; tel: 401-846 0813; newporthistorical.org; open spring-summer, daily; donation) in the restored, 1762 Brick Market building. Museum staff offer walking tours lasting from 30 to 90 minutes.

The **White Horse Tavern** (26 Marlborough Street; tel: 401-849 3600) is the country's oldest operating tavern (1673). It claims to be the birthplace of the "businessman's lunch" because, in 1708, city councillors would charge their meals to the public treasury.

Newport has a remarkable legacy of colonial architecture: some 200 houses pre-date 1800 – the biggest concentration in the nation. Many are to be found in the neighborhood off Washington Square. At 85 Touro Street, the Georgian **Touro Synagogue** Ⓑ (tel: 401-847 4794; tours year-round except Sats and Jewish holidays; entrance fee) is the nation's oldest Jewish house of worship (1763). The mysterious **Old Stone Mill** in nearby **Touro Park**, an unexplained open-sided structure once thought to have been left behind by the Phoenicians, Vikings, Portuguese, or Irish, is now known to be

Bowen's Wharf at Christmas. In season, the Jamestown & Newport Ferry (tel: 401-423 9900) runs a passenger service between here and Jamestown Village, Rose Island, Fort Adams, and Perrotti Park. Ride-all-day passes are available.

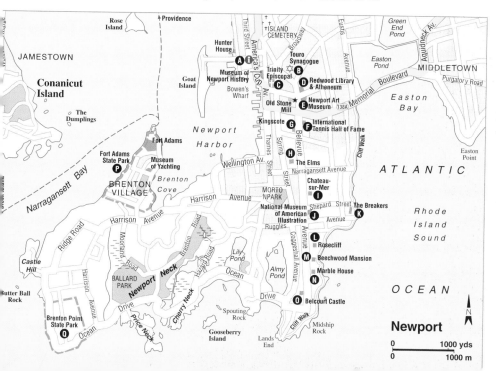

16th- or 17th-century, and was probably built by a Colonial farmer.

A landmark of Colonial Newport is the white clapboard 1725–26 **Trinity Episcopal Church** (tel: 401-846 0660; services Sun at 8am and 10am) on Queen Anne Square. It is said to be based on the designs of Sir Christopher Wren.

If you're planning to tour several mansions, the **Preservation Society of Newport** (242 Bellevue Avenue; tel: 401-847 1000; newportmansions.org) sells a variety of tickets for admission to up to 11 properties and offers tours; seasons and hours vary greatly – call or check website. One ticket includes admission to the National Historic Landmark, dockside **Hunter House** (54 Washington Street; entrance fee), a prosperous merchant's 1748 home.

Many of Newport's attractions line Bellevue Avenue, one of the town's major thoroughfares. The 1748–50 **Redwood Library and Atheneum** (50 Bellevue Avenue; tel: 401-847 0292; open Mon–Sat, Sun pm; donation) took its inspiration from Roman temple architecture; it is thought to be the oldest continuously used library building in the US and contains a noted collection of portraits, including works by Gilbert Stuart.

The 1862 "Stick Style" **Newport Art Museum** (76 Bellevue Avenue; tel: 401-848 8200; open Mon–Sat; Sun pm; entrance fee) exhibits paintings by luminaries including Winslow Homer and George Innes as well as works by regional artists.

The state-of-the-art **International Tennis Hall of Fame** (194 Bellevue Avenue; tel: 800-457 1144 or 401-849 3990; tennisfame.com; open daily; entrance fee), is the country's largest tennis museum. A must for tennis fans, it is housed in the Newport Casino, which never had anything to do with gambling but was America's most exclusive country club when it opened in 1880 and hosted the first US National Tennis Championships the following year. Also here is the Casino Theater, designed by Stanford White, which hosts performances.

The mansions

Continuing along Bellevue Avenue, the first mansion open to the public is **Kingscote** (PSN, *see margin tip on facing page*). This was the first of the summer cottages, built in Gothic Revival

---

BELOW: Trinity Episcopal Church, which has pew boxes paid for by members of the original 1726 congregation.

The barons who built Newport's mansions

S ummering in Newport first became fashionable before the Revolution among Southern plantation owners intent on escaping the heat of Georgia and the Carolinas. After the Civil War, the nation's wealthiest families – Astors, Morgans, Fishers, Vanderbilts – discovered its charms. Arrivistes hoping to legitimize their newfound wealth with indisputable good taste duplicated the palaces and châteaux that had so awed them in Europe.

Coal magnate Edward Berwind (*pictured*), the son of poor German immigrants, managed to enter the ranks of this self-appointed aristocracy with The Elms. Extravagance became obligatory. Harry Lehr hosted a formal dinner at which a monkey, complete with tuxedo and princely title, numbered among the guests. James Gordon Bennett, the man who bought a Monte Carlo restaurant when it refused him a table, rode stark naked in his carriage through Newport's streets. The Coogans invited everyone who was anyone to a grand ball to celebrate the completion of their "summer cottage." When no one showed up, the Coogans simply walked out – leaving all the food, drink and furniture – never to return.

Stick Style" – making playful use of symmetry and varied textures, sprouting wealth of pendants, lattices and gables. has glass paneling by Tiffany and exquisite porcelain.

The coal-rich Edward Julius Berwind commissioned **The Elms** (PSN) built French Renaissance style, based on hâteau d'Asnières near Paris. It borrows from a range of styles, including hinese, Venetian and Louis XIV.

William S. Wetmore built **Château-sur-Mer** (PSN) in 1852, a confection of Victorian lavishness, and Newport's lowiest mansion when built. Richard Morris Hunt enlarged it in the 1870s.

Works by artists including Norman Rockwell, Maxfield Parrish and N.C. Wyeth are exhibited at the **National Museum of American Illustration** 92 Bellevue Avenue; tel: 401-851 049; general admission late May–Aug, at 10am–4pm, Sun 11am–4pm; guided tour by advance reservation Fri at 2pm; entrance fee $25, ages 5–12, $10).

The Preservation Society of Newport pays the grand sum of $1 a year to rent the **Breakers** (PSN). Considered the most magnificent of the Newport cot-

tages, this opulent Italian Renaissance palace, completed in 1895, took only two years to build. Cornelius Vanderbilt II commissioned American architect Richard Morris Hunt to design the mansion, whose 70 rooms are extravagantly adorned with marble, alabaster, gilt, mosaic, crystal, and stained glass. The kitchen alone is the size of a small house.

Further along Bellevue Avenue, Mrs Hermann Oelrichs hired Stanford White to design **Rosecliff**, (PSN), an imitation of Versailles' Grand Trianon. It has a huge French-style ballroom and a heart-shaped staircase.

Caroline Schermerhorn Astor, the *grande dame* of New York society, held court at one of the oldest "cottages," now the **Astors' Beechwood Mansion and Victorian Living History Museum** (tel: 401-846 3772; astorsbeechwood.com; open daily; entrance fee). Costumed actors show you around in your assumed role as a guest of the family. From early November to mid-December, the mansion is open for Victorian Christmas.

Rough Point was one home of the heiress and horticulturalist Doris Duke (1912–93).

TIP

Opening times for Newport's mansions vary. Check the schedules and admission fees for Preservation Society of Newport (PSN) at 401-847 1000 or newportmansions.org.

BELOW:
the Music Room at The Breakers.

TIPS

● A **Newport Summer Pass** offers discounted admission to: Amazing Grace harbor tours, the Astor's Beechwood, Fort Adams, and the Tennis Hall of Fame.

● Tuesday nights the **Beechwood Theater Company** at the mansion offers candlelight tours: guests are urged to sing, dance, and party as if it was 1894 – but at today's prices.

TOP RIGHT: the Cliff Walk.
BELOW: a bedroom at Marble House.

Marble House  (PSN), another of Hunt's designs, was built in 1892 for William K. Vanderbilt and styled after the Grand and Petit Trianons of Versailles. With scenes and figures from ancient mythology, it even manages to upstage The Breakers for ostentation, though it is not as large. A Chinese tea house stands in the grounds.

Belcourt Castle (tel: 401-846 0669; one-hour guided tours 10am–4pm daily June–Aug; Sept Wed–Mon; Oct Thur–Mon; closed Jan; also candlelight, ghost, and champagne tours) is at 657 Bellevue Avenue. A 1894 Gothic Revival mansion styled on a Louis XIII hunting lodge at Versailles, it is owned by Harle Hope Hanson Tinney, who may guide you on your tour. The castle has the largest collection of objets d'art of any of the mansions, including a full-size gold Coronation Coach.

Strollers can examine the backyards of the Bellevue Avenue mansions from the **Cliff Walk** (cliffwalk.com), a 3½-mile (5.5-km) path that overlooks Rhode Island Sound. Crusty local fishermen saved this path for public use by going to court when wealthy mansion owners tried to close it. Visitors who don't wish to walk the length of this path can start the end of Narragansett Avenue an reach the water by way of the Fort Steps, part-way along the route.

■ *For more on the mansions, see th photo feature on pages 232–3.*

Music events

During the summer, Newport hosts number of major outdoor music event such as the Dunkin' Donuts Folk Festiv and the JVC Jazz Festival, both held i August at **Fort Adams State Park** (Fort Adams Drive; tel: 401-841 070 guided tours daily mid-May–mid-Oc entrance fee). The National Histor Landmark, built between 1824 and 185 and decommissioned after World War I was once a key coastal defense, ar offers magnificent views from its obse vation deck.

While there, take a look at the **Museu of Yachting** (Ocean Drive; tel: 401-84 1018; open mid-May–Oct, daily; entran fee), which examines the pursuit throug the centuries and across continents. Ne port is the scene of many yachting even The prestigious America's Cup was he in Newport waters 24 times from 18 through 1983, when the Cup was lost (f the first time) to the Australians. T 685-mile (1,100-km) Bermuda–Newp Race, held every other year, begins at t fort, and the grueling Single-Hand Transatlantic Race, which starts in Pl mouth, England, ends in Newport.

The **Rhode Island Public Saili**

Recommended Restaurants and Bars on pages 230–1

Center, on the grounds of the fort (60 Fort Adams Drive; tel: 401-849 8385; sailnewport.org), rents sailboats and sit-on-top kayaks.

A mile out to sea, the **Rose Island lighthouse** (tel: 401-847 4242; open 9am–1pm Mon–Fri; roseislandlighthouse .org; tours daily in season; fee) was abandoned after the Newport Bridge was built. Now visitors can be "keepers" for a night, renting one of the two bedrooms in the facility that was restored to its 1912 appearance and is a museum by day.

Ocean Drive

One of the region's most magnificent drives extends for 10 miles (16 km) around Narragansett Bay, passing by numerous oceanfront public access points, and, at the tip, where the bay meets the Atlantic Ocean, **Brenton Point State Park ①**. There are sweeping views from the vast lawns. The rocky shores are great for exploring tidal pools and sunset-watching.

Other mansions along Ocean Drive include **Hammersmith Farm**, the 28-room childhood home of Jacqueline Bouvier Kennedy. She and John F. Kennedy were married here in 1953 and it was later known as the "Summer White House." It is no longer open to the public.

At the western end of the drive, the elegant **Castle Hill Inn** (590 Ocean Drive; tel: 888-466 1355; castlehillinn.com) sits atop a 40-acre (16-hectare) peninsula overlooking the sea. Lunch, dinner and a Sunday jazz brunch are served, but for twilight magic, order a drink at the Sunset Grill (open 3:30pm daily June 30–Labor Day; weekends pre- and post-season), grab one of the Adirondack chairs on the lawn, and watch the sun go down.

Jamestown

Just across the Newport Bridge (toll), follow signs to historic **Jamestown ③** on Conanicut Island. The southern tip of the island offers New England scenery at its most picturesque. In **Beavertail State Park** (Beavertail Road; tel: 401-423 9941; riparks.com), the Atlantic coast's third oldest lighthouse is commemorated in **Beavertail Lighthouse and Museum** (open weekends Memorial Day–June 15; daily June 16–Labor Day; weekends Labor Day–Columbus Day; fee).

The 275-acre (110-hectare) **Watson Farm** (445 North Road; tel: 401-423

TIPS

● At Fort Adams, you take the Jamestown & Newport ferry (tel: 401-423 9900; conanicut-marina.com) for a sail to Jamestown, Rose Island, and Bowen's Wharf. Passengers can stay aboard for the round trip; or go ashore, then reboard.

● The Block Island Ferry (tel: 401-783 7996 or 866-783 7996; blockislandferry .com) sails from Fort Adams to Block Island at 9:15am, and returns at 4:45 pm, making for an enjoyable day trip.

BELOW: Newport Bridge leads to Jamestown.

Active vacations

New England offers a wide choice, and the "shoulder" months of May–June and September–October are both cooler and less crowded.

With 400 miles (640 km) of coastline, Rhode Island looks to the sea for recreation. Newport, known as "The Sailing Capital of the World" for its years hosting the America's Cup, is a good base for harbor sailing or learn-to-sail vacations.

At America's oldest sailing school, Boston's Community Boating, skiffs cruise the Charles River against a backdrop of brick bowfronts and downtown office towers. For longer adventures – with a professional crew doing most of the work – many head for the Maine coast, where several outfitters offer multi-day sailing expeditions on magnificent "windjammers" featuring hearty meals and cozy accommodations *(see page 408)*.

Maine has also become a center for sea kayaking, with over 2,000 coastal islands and their protected waters, The Maine Island Kayak Company *(see page 406)* offers sea kayaking lessons and tours. Rhode Island kayakers are rewarded with seaside views of Newport's grand Ocean Drive estates.

West of Boston, canoeists on the lazy Sudbury and Concord Rivers can visit Revolutionary-era sights, while on Cape Cod, naturalist guides lead canoe tours of salt marshes and tidal rivers. The Deerfield River in western Massachusetts is a good spot for whitewater rafting trips.

Connecticut's Housatonic River is a favored destination for canoeing and rafting. North American Outdoor Adventure (tel: 800-727 4379) organizes trips on the Housatonic and on Maine's Kennebec and Penobscot Rivers.

Swimmers will find beaches on Cape Cod or Nantucket Sound warmer and calmer than those on the Atlantic. But the Atlantic can offer reasonable surfing, especially after an offshore storm.

Fishermen head for the trout-filled Battenkill River, near Manchester in Vermont, where the Orvis Company runs a fly fishing school. Orvis also teaches saltwater fishing on Cape Cod. Near New Hampshire's Mount Washington, Great Glen Trails (tel: 603-466 2333) offers introductory fishing classes and arranges guided fly fishing excursions.

There's hiking for all abilities, from leisurely strolls on conservation land – such as the 11 self-guided nature trails within Cape Cod's National Seashore – to rugged mountain climbs. The 2,000-mile (3,200-km) Appalachian Trail crosses Maine, New Hampshire, Vermont, Massachusetts and Connecticut on its way south to Georgia. Serious hikers also follow the Long Trail (270 miles/435 km) across Vermont's highest peaks. The Appalachian Mountain Club (tel: 617-523 0655; outdoors.org) has a network of overnight huts for walkers in New Hampshire's White Mountains.

Many ski resorts, including Vermont's Mount Snow and Killington, have also become summer mountain biking centers. The self-guided Franconia Notch Bike Tour in New Hampshire starts at Echo Lake, continues through the scenic notch, and ends at Loon Mountain's ski area. ❑

ABOVE: water sports are a big draw in New England.
LEFT: hiking on Mount Greylock in the Berkshires.

0005; open June–mid-Oct, Tues, Thur and Sun pm; entrance fee) on Narragansett Bay has been a working farm since 1787. Visitors can take a self-guided tour, and hike the 2 miles (3 km) of scenic trails. Just down the road is the 1787 **Jamestown Windmill** (North Main Street; tel: 401-423 1798; open Sat and Sun pm in summer).

SOUTH COUNTY

From Jamestown, continue west on Route 138 to Route 1A, and turn north to **Wickford** ❾, whose historic waterfront, lined with galleries, shops, and restaurants, is one of the loveliest in Rhode Island. Many of the buildings in towndate to the 18th century. The 1707 **Old Narragansett Church** is the oldest Episcopal Church north of the Mason-Dixon Line.

Just a mile north of town is the inappropriately-named **Smith's Castle** (55 Richard Smith Drive; tel: 401-294 3521; smithscastle.org; open June–Aug, Thur–Sun pm; Sept Fri–Sun pm; entrance fee). One of the country's oldest plantation houses, it was originally built in 1678 to garrison soldiers, and was rebuilt in 1692 by the Updike family. It now preserves four centuries of Rhode Island history, which docents in period clothing bring to life.

South along the Narragansett Bay

Backtrack south on Route 1A to **Saunderstown** ❿. One of early America's most famous portrait artists was born in 1755 at the **Gilbert Stuart Birthplace** (815 Gilbert Stuart Road; tel: 401-294 3001; open mid-May–mid-Oct, Thur–Mon; entrance fee). The property encompasses an authentically restored and furnished workingman's house of the period, the country's first snuff mill, a partially-restored grist mill, and a fish ladder that teems in spring.

Organic produce for homes in the area is raised by farm managers at the mid-18th century **Casey Farm** (tel: 401-295 1030; open June–mid-Oct, Sat pm; entrance fee) on Route 1A.

To the south on Route 1A, at the town beach in **Narragansett** ⓫, you can stroll along the pier and admire the Twin Towers

Jamestown Windmill, which ground corn from 1787 until 1895.

BELOW: two Rhode Island products, pumpkins and wine.

Block Island sells itself as a hideaway destination, unsullied by developers and fast-food chains.

– the stone structures that are the remains of a casino destroyed by fire in 1900.

Between Narragansett and Point Judith are a skein of fine, sandy state-owned beaches (parking fee).

Whale watching tours depart from **Point Judith** (woonsocket.org/galilee), where there's a US Coast Guard Station and lighthouse. Backtrack a short distance on Route 108, past the entrance for **Captain Roger B. Wheeler State Beach** (tel: 401-789 3563; parking fee) and follow signs to **Galilee** , the departure point for the ferry to Block Island.

The **Block Island Ferry** (tel: 401-783 7996 or 866-783 7996; blockislandferry

.com) offers high-speed and traditional passenger ferry service from Galilee and Newport's Fort Adams.

Block Island

When Rhode Islanders want to get away from it all, they head for **Block Island** ⑬ a 3 by 7-mile (5 by 11-km) island some 12 miles (19 km) south of the entrance to Narragansett Bay. Whereas Newport is packed to the gills with hotels, shops, restaurants, and tourists, Block Island – named by the Nature Conservancy as "one of the 12 "last great places" in the Western Hemisphere – remains a hideaway that holds its own, quite successfully, against developers and fast-food chains.

Block Island, discovered in 1614 by a Dutch navigator, Adriaen Block, is the least accessible of the state's islands: although regular or chartered planes fly out of Westerly, R.I., and points in Connecticut (a 10-minute hop), most people take the ferry. It docks in **Old Harbor** the island's only town, a charming, small-scale resort where one can rent everything from mopeds to bicycles to convertibles to explore the island. Charter

fishing boats line the dock near the ferry.

Visitors come to Block Island for fine beaches, fishing, tranquility and the romantic allure of aging Victorian hotels with huge verandahs and a sense of bygone splendor. The **Spring House** (tel: 401-466 5844; springhousehotel.com), on a 5-acre (6 hectare) promontory, opened its doors in 1852; and in 1888 the **National House** (tel: 401-466 2901 or 800-225 2449), a majestic wooden ark of a building, opened in the heart of Old Harbor. To spend time in either of these two lodgings is to be caught in a time warp.

The island's maritime claim to fame is its large number of shipwrecks. Many luckless captains saw their vessels come to misery on the submerged rocks and sandbars around "The Block." Tourism arrived in 1842.

The **Block Island Historical Society** (Old Town Road; tel: 401-466 2481; blockislandinfo.com), in an 1850 farmhouse, does a good job of recreating the island's farming and seafaring history. The latter is elaborated upon at the Interpretive Center **in North Lighthouse** (Corn Neck Road; tel: 401-466 3200 for opening hours). It was first lit in 1956.

The island's beaches include **Surfers Beach**, popular with surfers, as its name suggests; **State Beach** and others on the east are calmer and attract the most visitors. The westerly strands are windswept and usually deserted. One trek not to be missed is the hike to the magnificently scenic **Mohegan Bluffs**, where the 1874 **Southeast Lighthouse** perches above the cliffs. Here, the entire Mohegan tribe met its doom at the hands of the Manasees, who enslaved them or drove them over the 200-ft (60-meter) cliffs.

The Nature Conservancy (nature.org) and local groups help to preserve more than 40 percent of the island, including, on the island's south side, **Rodman's Hollow**, a 230-acre (90-hectare) swath of conserved land formed more than 10,000 years ago by glacial meltwater.

When the kids have had enough ice cream and body surfing, visit **Manisses Farm** (1 Spring Street; tel: 401-466 2421), behind the Manisses Hotel. It has an exotic menagerie, including camels, llamas, emus, sheep, and donkeys.

Back on the mainland

Head north on Route 108 to US Route 1 and continue south along the Block Island Sound. In **South Kingston**, the **Trustom Pond National Wildlife Refuge ⓮** (1040 Matunuck Schoolhouse Road) protects the state's only undeveloped salt pond.

To the south, in **Charlestown**, at the **Ninigret National Wildlife Refuge ⓯**, a visitor center (50 Bend Road; tel: 401-364 9124) just off the highway tells about the more than 250 bird species that visit this diverse habitat.

In **Westerly**, the half-mile **Misquamicut State Beach ⓰** (tel: 401-322 8910; riparks.com; parking fee) is one of the state's most popular; get there early on a hot summer day. The village of **Watch Hill ⓱**, with its Victorian cottage mansions, shops, and the circa 1876 landmark **Flying Horse Carousel**, the oldest in the country, is well worth seeing.   ❏

One of Block Island's attractions is its many fine beaches. Fred Benson Town Beach and Ballard's Beach have lifeguards on duty.

BELOW: Block Island's Southeast Lighthouse, opened in 1875, has a small museum.

RESTAURANTS AND BARS

Block Island

Eli's Restaurant
Chapel Street
Tel: 401-466 5230 **$$–$$$**
A small bistro with a big reputation and a deft hand with fresh fish. D nightly in season.

Finn's
Ferry Landing, Water Street
Tel: 401-466 2473 **$–$$$**
Good food and incomparable views. Burgers, chowder, fried seafood platters, and "stuffies"–clams topped with

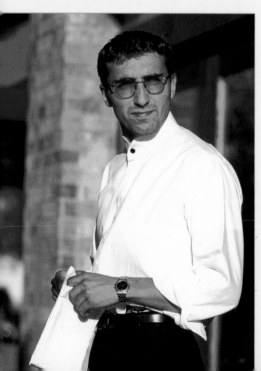

melted jack cheese and bacon. No reservations. L and D daily in season.

Hotel Manisses
1 Spring Street
Tel: 401-466 2421
blockislandresorts.com **$$$$**
Sophisticated fare such as seared fois gras, roasted rack of wild boar, and bouillabaise. D nightly May–early Oct; Tues–Sun early Oct–Thanksgiving. Summer breakfast buffet. Lighter menu in Gatsby Room.

Bristol

DeWolf's Tavern
Thames Street Landing
Tel: 401-254 2005
dewolftavern.com **$$–$$$**
Contemporary American dishes with an Indian twist in an historic, waterfront warehouse. Look

for duck confit with peanut-red chili sauce, and charcoal tandoor roasted chicken. D nightly.

Lobster Pot
119–21 Hope Street,
Route 114
Tel: 401-253 9100
lobsterpotri.com **$$**
This local harborfront institution has served up fresh American fare since 1929. L and D daily.

Quito's
411 Thames Street
Tel: 401-253 4500 **$–$$**
Well-established casual spot overlooking the bay specializes in seafood. L and D daily in season.

Jamestown

Bay Voyage Inn
150 Conanicus Avenue
Tel: 401-423 2100
bayvoyageinn.com **$$$**
Classic American food and a bountiful Sunday brunch in an 1859 harborfront inn. L and D Mon–Sat Memorial Day–Labor Day; D Tues–Sat rest of year.

Trattoria Simpatico
13 Narragansett Avenue
Tel: 401-423 3731
trattoriasimpatico.com
$$$–$$$$
Superb Italian fare, al fresco dining, and a jazz trio in good weather. L Mon–Fri, D nightly.

Little Compton

Commons Lunch
Tel: 401-635 4388 **$**
A downhome diner fit for gentleman (and lady) farmers and a particu-

larly welcome sight for an early breakfast. Open daily 5am–8pm.

Narragansett

Aunt Carrie's
1240 Ocean Road,
Point Judith
Tel: 401-783 7930
auntcarriesri.com **$**
A classic seaside clam shack since 1920. L and D in season.

Basil's
22 Kingstown Road
Tel: 401-789 3743 **$$–$$$**
Continental fare, with an accent on French, in an elegant Victorian restaurant near the pier. D Tues–Sun in summer; Wed–Sun year round.

Turtle Soup Restaurant
113 Ocean Road
Tel: 401-792 8683 **$–$$$**
Bayfront restaurant with an eclectic menu. No reservations. L Sat–Sun; D Tues–Sun.

Newport

The Black Pearl
Bannister's Wharf
Tel: 401-846 5264
blackpearlnewport.com
$$–$$$$
A renowned harborside tavern serving classic French and American fare, including the house special clam chowder. Jackets and reservations required in Commodore Room. L and D daily.

Brick Alley Pub and Restaurant
140 Thames Street
Tel: 401-849 6334
brickalley.com **$$–$$$**
For more than 25 years a

LEFT: waiting for custom in Providence.

favorite for steaks, pasta, seafood, and reliable bar foods, including the ultimate nacho plate. Extensive wine list. L and D daily; Sun brunch.

Castle Hill Inn
590 Ocean Avenue
Tel: 401-849 3800
castlehillinn.com **$$$–$$$$**
This magnificent 1874 summer "cottage" overlooking Narragansett Bay specializes in New England cuisine and offers several prix fixe options.

Clarke Cooke House
Bannister's Wharf
Tel: 401-849 2900
bannisterwharf.net **$$$$**
Formal, waterview dining in a 1790 colonial house. Eclectic Continental fare is served by waiters in tuxedos. Outdoor dining in warm weather.

Newport Dinner Train
19 America's Cup Avenue
Tel: 401-841 8700
newportdinnertrain.com **$$$–$$$$**
Multi-course, cooked-on-site lunches and dinners served aboard a beautifully restored train which travels 22 miles/35 km along Narragansett Bay. Lunch trips include a tour of Rosecliff Mansion.

The Mooring Restaurant
Sayer's Wharf
Tel: 401-846 2260
mooringsrestaurant.com **$$–$$$**
Award-winning chowder is on the menu at this family-friendly restaurant with an enclosed patio overlooking the harbor. L and D daily.

Puerini's Restaurant
24 Memorial Boulevard West
Tel: 401-847 5506
purinisrestaurant.com **$$**
An extensive menu of innovative Italian specialties includes homemade

pastas, tortellini with seafood, veal, and a reasonably priced wine list. No reservations. D only.

Scales and Shells
527 Thames Street
Tel: 401-848 9378
scalesandshells.com **$$–$$$**
A large selection of fresh fish dishes, including wood-grilled specialties. Upstairs is quieter but pricier. D nightly.

White Horse Tavern
26 Marlborough Street
Tel: 401-849 3600
whitehorsetavern.com **$$–$$$**
The country's oldest continually operating tavern (est. 1687) serves classics such as Chateaubriand and grilled lobster in candlelit rooms with cavernous fireplaces. Jackets required at dinner. L Mon–Sat; D nightly; Sun brunch.

Providence
Al Forno
577 S Main Street
Tel: 401-273 9760
alforno.com **$$$–$$$$**
Arguably New England's preeminent temple of *nuova cucina*, with Northern Italian specialties. D Tues–Sat.

Angelo's Civita Farnese
141 Atwells Avenue
Tel: 401-621 8171
angelosonthehill.com **$**
A friendly and boisterous place serving large portions of low-priced Italian classics since 1924. Reservations accepted Mon–Thur only. L and D daily; closed Sun late May–early Sept.

The Capital Grille
1 Union Station
Tel: 401-521 560
thecapitalgrille.com **$$$–$$$$**
Premium dry-aged beef, fresh seafood, and an

ABOVE: in September, Providence's Food for Thought Festival showcases local chefs and vineyards.

extensive wine list in a renovated railroad station. L Mon–Fri; D nightly.

Hemenway's Seafood Grill and Oyster Bay
1 Providence Washington Plaza. Tel: 401-351 8570
hemenwaysrestaurant.com **$$$**
Superb seafood, steak, chicken and pasta in upscale place overlooking the Providence River. L and D daily.

Rue de L'Espoir
99 Hope Street
Tel: 401-751 8890
therue.com **$$–$$$**
Chic, modern bistro fare in a pretty room near Brown University. B daily, L Mon–Fri; D nightly.

Watch Hill
Olympia Tea Room
Bay Street
Tel: 401-348 8211
olympiatearoom.com **$$**
A classic 1916 luncheonette. Specialties include stuffed quahogs and the "world-famous Avondale swan" with puff pastry, ice cream and chocolate sauce. L and D daily.

Westerly
Shelter Harbor Inn
10 Wagner Road, Route 1
Tel: 401-322 8883

shelterharbor.com **$$$**
A changing menu of well-priced regional specialties and an outstanding Sunday brunch. B, L, and D daily; Sun brunch.

Bars
Celtica Public House,
95 Long Wharf, Newport.
Tel: 401-847 4770.
High-definition TVs, surround sound, and a full menu of live music from Irish to soul, along with a limited bar menu featuring paninis and chowder. Free buffet Fridays 5pm–7pm.
Johnny's Atlantic Beach Club Outdoor Bar,
53 Purgatory Road, Middletown. Tel: 401-847 2750. Grab a table on the outdoor deck of this oceanfront bar, order a frosty tropical drink, and listen to the surf.
Trinity Brewhouse Pub and Bar,
186 Fountain Street, Providence.
Tel: 401-453 2337.
Little Rhody's biggest brewery handcrafts beers, ales, porters, and stouts, and serves them up alongside everything from Cajun sweet fries and chicken wings, to beef stew.

Newport's "Gilded Age" Mansions

Newport, a 19th-century summer playground for the rich and famous, became a showplace for America's greatest architects and designers

With the coming of the railways in the mid-19th century, vacationing became ever more popular, and the delights of Newport, set on an island with a fine summer climate, became readily accessible from New York and Philadelphia. Wealthy and influential families, began to spend their summers here. Many had made vast fortunes from industry and began to lavish unstinting funds on creating opulent summer homes, where they would entertain and impress all those who mattered. The country's most innovative architects – names such as Stanford White and Richard Morris Hunt – were employed, creating designs that reflect the full range of styles in vogue at the time *(see also pages 222–4)*. Building materials and furnishings were often imported from Europe (for Marble House, for instance, different coloured marbles were imported from Italy to be worked by Italian craftsmen in Newport). Interior decor frequently borrowed from European or Far Eastern styles; fine paintings, furnishings and objets d'art collected from around the world filled the rooms.

Eight of these mansions are now maintained by The Preservation Society of Newport County and are open to the public, as is the Astor family's Beechwood Mansion.

Above: a ball held at Beechwood.
Right: Ochre Court, a Beaux-Arts mansion built in 1892. It is now owned by the local Salve Regina University. Only The Breakers is larger.

Above: The Elms, at 367 Bellevue Avenue, replicates a two-story château near Paris, with the servants' quarters placed behind the roof balustrade and the kitchens located in a cellar. It was built in 1901 for the coal baron Edward Julius Berwind, the son of German immigrants.

LEGACY OF THE VANDERBILTS

The Breakers was commissioned in 1893 by Cornelius Vanderbilt II *(right)* to replace an earlier house destroyed by fire. Vanderbilt, chairman of the New York Central railway and a director of 49 other railways, was the head of America's wealthiest family. His younger brother, William, had inherited equal shares in the family fortunes, some part of which he spent building Marble House, on nearby Bellevue Avenue. A serious, modest and gentle man, Cornelius II gave free rein and an unlimited budget to Richard Morris Hunt, the architect of Marble House and of the grand Vanderbilt houses on Fifth Avenue in New York. Hunt followed the Italian Renaissance layout adopted for 16th-century palaces, where rooms were grouped symmetrically around a central courtyard. With 70 rooms, including 33 for resident staff and visitors' servants, The Breakers is Newport's largest "cottage." Vanderbilt died in 1899, aged 55, four years after the house was completed.

ᴀʙᴏᴠᴇ: Marble House, whose ballroom is shown here, was built in 1888–92 for William K. Vanderbilt, brother of Cornelius *(see panel, right)*. It took its inspiration from the Petit Trianon at Versailles.

ʀɪɢʜᴛ: With their ornate carvings, the mansions were designed to resemble the castles and palaces of Europe. Styles such as Beaux Arts, Renaissance, Romanesque, and Rococo merged together.

ʙᴇʟᴏᴡ: The Breakers was designed by architect Richard Morris Hunt, who took his inspiration from the 16th-century palaces of Genoa and Turin, and employed an international team of builders.

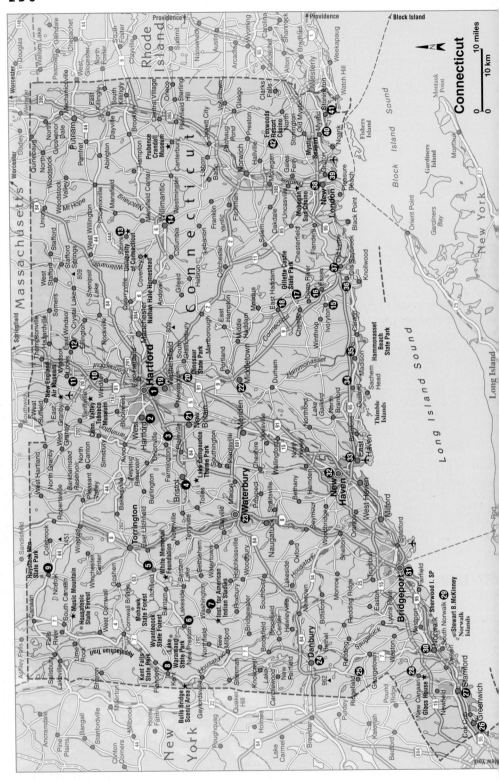

Connecticut

Recommended Restaurants and Bars on pages 262–5

CONNECTICUT

This historic state encompasses Yale University in New Haven, maritime traditions in Mystic Seaport, antiquing and art in the Litchfield Hills – and, unexpectedly, two of America's biggest casinos

Driving through the neat-as-a-pin village of Guilford, a one-time resident once remarked: "Connecticut ~~al~~ways looks as if the maid has just been ~~in~~ to clean." There, as in so many of Connecticut's picturesque colonial villages, ~~th~~e carefully kept, white clapboard homes ~~an~~d manicured lawns evoke an image of ~~qu~~iet wealth, propriety and old school ties. Connecticut's original image, created ~~by~~ the state's dollar-savvy Puritan founders, has not changed. It has, however, ~~be~~en tempered with pride for the place ~~an~~d a heartfelt sense of its history.

With Long Island Sound as its southern border, Connecticut roughly forms a rectangle measuring 90 miles (145 km) from east to west and 55 miles (89 km) north to south. The Connecticut River, New England's longest, bisects the state; along with the Thames and Housatonic rivers, the Connecticut was a vital avenue of settlement and industrialization.

The state capital

Hartford **1** (pop. 124,500) is America's Insurance City. The skyline of Connecticut's capital is dominated by the tower-

Main attractions

HARTFORD
BRISTOL
THE LITCHFIELD HILLS
LAKE WARAMAUG
WEST CORNWALL
ESSEX STEAM TRAIN
GILLETTE CASTLE
GREENWICH
NEW HAVEN
MYSTIC SEAPORT
MASHANTUCKET PEQUOT
  MUSEUM

PRECEDING PAGES
fall at Litchfield.
BELOW:
the State Capitol.

The state in snapshot

Known as: The Constitution State, because of its delegates' role in framing the US Constitution in 1787.
Motto: *Qui Transtulit Sustinet* (He who transplanted still sustains)
Origin of name: may derive from Algonquian Indian term meaning "place of the long river"
Entered Union: 9 January 1788, the fifth of the original 13 states.
Capital: Hartford.
Area: 5,544 sq. miles (14,358 sq. km).
Highest point: Mt Frissell, 2,380 ft (725 meters).
Population: 3.29 million.
Population density: 593 people per sq. mile (229 per sq. km).
Economy: Hartford is a major insurance centre. Also aircraft engines, helicopters, submarines, and firearms.
National representation: 2 senators and 6 representatives to Congress
Famous citizens: Phineas T. Barnum, Samuel Colt, Katharine Hepburn, J. Pierpoint Morgan, Harriet Beecher Stowe, Mark Twain, Noah Webster, Eli Whitney.

A statue in the State Capitol of the Connecticut patriot Nathan Hale, who was hanged in 1776. His famous last words: "I only regret that I have but one life to lose for my country."

ing headquarters of the nation's largest insurance companies. Several dozen are located in greater Hartford and, together with related financial services, employ approximately 10 percent of the total work force. The first insurance policy, covering losses in the event of shipwreck, was written in the 18th century.

Settled in 1635 and Connecticut's oldest city, Hartford has parlayed its location on the navigable Connecticut River into political, economic and social pre-eminence. In 1662, a royal charter was drawn up uniting the colonies of Hartford and New Haven, and guaranteeing their independence. Sir Edmund Andros, appointed governor of all New England in 1687, had the charter revoked. In defiance, the Hartford patriot John Wadsworth stole the charter and hid it in the trunk of an oak tree at the center of the town. Two years later, on the accession of William III, Andros was recalled to England and the charter was reinstated. A plaque at Charter Oak Place, in the south end of

the city, marks the spot where the mag nificent oak stood until 1856, when windstorm felled it.

The **Greater Hartford Visitors Cen ter** (One Civic Center Plaza; tel: 860-72 6789 or 800-446 7811; enjoyhartford.com distributes a free guide which includes map and walking tour of the city.

Oldest state house

Begin at the **Old State House** ❶, at th intersection of Main Street and Asylur Avenue (800 Main Street; tel: 860-52 6766; open Tues–Sat). Built in 1796 an the nation's oldest state house, it was th first public commission for Charle Bulfinch, who would later design th state capitols of Maine and Massachu setts. The building was the site of th 1839 *Amistad* slave ship mutiny tria which is re-enacted periodically in th Great Senate Chamber.

It's worth looking at the interactiv multi-media presentation *History is A Around Us*; Gilbert Stuart's portrait (George Washington; and the secon(floor **Joseph Steward's Museum (Curiosities** (a two-headed calf, th mummified hand of Ramses, a unicor

How the Constitution State earned its nickname

Adrian Block, a Dutch navigator, was probably the first to understand the possibilities of the region when he sailed along the coast and up the Connecticut River in 1614. Nineteen years later, the Dutch established a trading post, Fort Good Hope, near where Hartford is today.

But it was the British, lured by fertile land and religious freedom, who settled the region in 1635. By that time, good farmland in the coastal areas of the Massachusetts Bay colony had mostly been claimed, and newcomers looked toward the Connecticut River. Added to population pressures were the personalities of strong-willed leaders such as the Reverend Thomas Hooker, who were looking for more theological leeway than Massachusetts divines would allow.

By 1636, settlements had been established in Hartford, Windsor and Wethersfield. These three towns adopted the Fundamental Orders of Connecticut on January 14, 1639. This document is regarded by many historians as the world's first written constitution, giving rise to Connecticut's formal sobriquet "The Constitu-

tion State." New settlements were org nized along the shores of Long Islar Sound. Old Saybrook was first, followed New Haven, Guilford, and Stamford. La towns took such Biblical names Goshen, Sharon, Canaan, and Bethlehe

Connecticut's Revolutionary hero included General Israel Putnam and Eth Allen, who made his fame as a Ve mont guerrilla leader. Most famo was Nathan Hale, the Covent Connecticut, schoolteacher wh when hanged by the British as spy, uttered the immortal words. regret that I have only one life give for my country."

With the end of the Revoluti Connecticut turned increasingly commerce, and from the ye 1780 to 1840, the Yankee pedc

ABOVE: Rev. Thomas Hooker travels to Hartford.

●rn – that sort of thing). A cannon is
ed at opening and closing time.
　While at the Old State House, pick up
●elf-guided tour of the city's oldest his-
●ic site, the **Ancient Burying Ground**
　(corner Gold & Main streets). Around
●00 people are interred here, the oldest
●avestone being from 1648.

●adsworth Atheneum

●irectly to the south, also on Main
●reet, is the **Wadsworth Atheneum of
●rt ●**, America's oldest continually
●erating public art museum (600 Main
●reet; tel: 860-278 2670; wadsworth
●eneum.org; open Tues–Sun; entrance
●). The Gothic Revival-style Atheneum
●as erected to house the library and art
●llery of Daniel Wadsworth.
　Its collection now includes paintings by
●ya, Rubens, Rembrandt and van Dyck,
●s works by American masters such as
●omas Cole and John Singer Sargent
●d Meissen and Sèvres porcelains. The
●stin House**, the former home of the
●seum director from 1927 to 1944 and a
●tional Historic Landmark, is open by
●pointment at 3pm on the first and third
●ursday of each month.

The State Capitol

Perched on Capitol Hill, the white marble, gold-domed National Historic Landmark **Connecticut State Capitol ●**, a
Gothic wedding cake of turrets, gables,
porches, and towers, was designed by
Richard Upjohn and opened in 1878
(210 Capitol Avenue; tel: 860-240 0222).
In typical Victorian manner, its ornate
interiors of hand-painted columns, marble floors and elaborate stained-glass
windows were designed to reflect the
prosperity of the community it served.
　The Capitol overlooks 41-acre (17-
hectare) **Bushnell Park ●** (tel: 860-232
6710; bushnellpark.org), home to a hand-
carved **1914 carousel** (open late Apr–
mid-Oct Tues–Sun 11am–5pm; $1 per
ride) and the **Pump House Park Café
and Gallery** (tel: 860-543 8874; gallery
open Tues–Fri 11am–2pm; café open for
lunch weekdays, dinner Mon–Sat), an art
gallery/outdoor restaurant which hosts
live music most evenings. Free concerts
are held in summer at the outdoor Performance Pavilion on the park's west side.
Free tours of the Soldiers and Sailors
Memorial Arch are given noon–1:30pm
on the first Thur of the month, May–Oct.

TIPS

● You can hop aboard
the free, downtown
Hartford Star Shuttle
which passes every
10–12 minutes Mon–Fri
from 7am to 11pm, and
Sat 3pm–11pm.
● The capitol is open
for self-guided, and one-
hour guided tours,
Mon–Fri: in July–Aug,
tours are hourly
9:15am–2:15pm, the
rest of the year 9:15–
1:15 pm. Admission by
guided tour only on Sat
Apr–Oct, 10:15am–
2:15pm. Tours begin at
the neighboring Legisla-
tive Office Building.

BELOW: a gallery
in the Wadsworth
Atheneum.

●OVE: a 1776 map of Connecticut.

●gned supreme. His sturdy wagon,
●ded with tinware, soap, matches, yard
●ds and tools, was a familiar sight up
●d down the Atlantic seaboard and even
●yond the Appalachians. Some of the
●s scrupulous peddlers allegedly sold
●den nutmegs, thus giving Connecticut
●other nickname, "The Nutmeg State."

But it was in manufacturing that the
Connecticut Yankees truly excelled. Eli
Whitney, inventor of the cotton gin, first
introduced the use of standardized parts
at his firearms factory in New Haven.
Colt revolvers were made in Hartford,
Winchester rifles in New Haven, hats in
Danbury, clocks in Bristol, and fine brass
in Waterbury. Today the state continues
to rely on industry for its economic good
fortune. Airplane engines are manufactured in East Hartford, and helicopters in
Stratford; nuclear submarines are
designed and built in Groton.
　Nevertheless, Connecticut has remained a largely rural enclave. With
manufacturing concentrated along the
South Shore and in Hartford, 75 percent
of the state is given over to small towns
and dense woodlands. Narrow, winding
roads lead the visitor from one charming village to another.

Bushnell Park, named after local pastor Horace Bushnell (1802–76).

TIP

For "deals and steals" on events throughout the city – discounts of up to 50% offered on the same day as a show is presented – log on to the Greater Hartford Arts Council's website, letsgoarts.org

The National Historic Landmark **Bushnell Center for the Performing Arts ⑤** (166 Capitol Avenue; tel: 860-987 5900; 888-824 2874 outside CT; bushnell.org), Connecticut's premier performing arts center, has an impressive program of concerts, ballet, opera and theatre all year. A free, 45-minute tour (by appointment only; tel: 860-987 6000) takes visitors behind the scenes.

To the south of the Capitol is the State Library, the **Museum of Connecticut History ⑥** (231 Capitol Avenue; tel: 860-757 6535; open Mon–Sat). Exhibits include the state's 1662 Royal Charter and the Colt Collection of Firearms manufactured in Hartford. Fans of "The World's Right Arm" and of the Old West, where Colts played such a prominent role, will find the collection fascinating.

Constitution Plaza, a 12-acre (5-hectare) 1960s complex, provides Hartford with an open mall, a vast array of shops, office buildings and the starkly

modern, elliptically shaped Phoen Mutual Life Insurance Building.

St Paul Travelers' Tower ⑪, the city second tallest building (City Place is t tallest), has an **Observation Deck** givi offers a good view of the Hartford area Tower Square; tel: 860–277 4208; to mid-May–late Oct, Mon–Fri 10am–3pr

Hartford's oldest house, the **Butle McCook House and Garden and Ma Street History Center ①** (396 Ma Street; tel: 860-522 1806; Jan–Apr, S and Sun pm; May–Dec, Wed–Sat, S pm; entrance fee), was in the same fan ily from 1782 to 1971. It is one of t best-documented homes in America a visiting is like entering a time capsu

Mark Twain House

Hartford's most famous resident, Ma Twain (1835–1910), lived in a 19-roo Victorian mansion in a part of town call Nook Farm, which in his time was a ru area and the intellectual center of Ha ford. Today, Nook Farm is a develop area, but there's a special charm to t National Historic Landmark **Ma Twain House ①** (351 Farmington A\ nue; tel: 860–247 0998; marktwainho

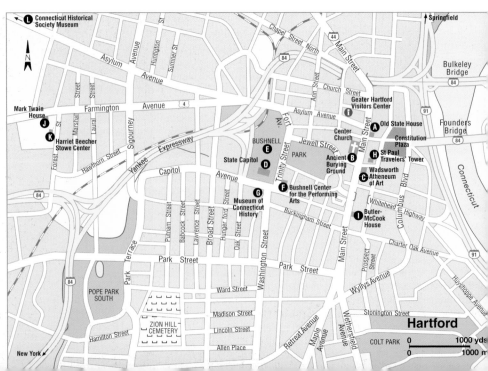

Recommended Restaurants and Bars on pages 262–5

org; open Apr–Dec Mon–Sat and Sun pm; Jan–Mar, Wed–Mon; guided tours only; allow two hours for a visit; entrance fee). The author's home from 1874 to 1891, designed by Edward Tuckerman Potter and decorated by Louis Comfort Tiffany, reflects his quirky character.

Outdoor porches and balconies give the impression of a Mississippi riverboat, while the interiors are grand and whimsical. Of interest is the upstairs billiard room, where Twain wrote his most successful novels, including *The Adventures of Tom Sawyer* and *The Adventures of Huckleberry Finn*. To visit, take Interstate 84 north to exit 46 and turn right at the traffic light onto Sisson Avenue. Continue to the end and turn right at the next ight onto Farmington Avenue.

Harriet Beecher Stowe Center

Mr Twain's neighbor was Harriet Beecher Stowe, author of *Uncle Tom's Cabin*. She lived next door in a 17-room Gothic-Revival home from 1873 until she died in 1896. Her restored house is a part of the **Harriet Beecher Stowe Center** ❸ (77 Forest Street; tel: 860-522 9258; harrietbeecherstowe.org; open for tours Tues–

Sat; Sun pm; Memorial Day–Columbus Day, daily; combined ticket available). The center also includes the Katharine Seymour Day House, whose library contains volumes about the women's suffrage movement and African-American history; and the Victorian grounds and gardens.

Both the Twain and Stowe houses are recommended not only for their literary associations, but for a peek at genteel 19th-century life in what Twain called the most beautiful city in America.

More than 3 million manuscripts and a fine genealogy collections are held by the research library at the **Connecticut Historical Society Museum** ❿ (off Asylum Avenue on campus of Connecticut Law School, 1 Elizabeth Street; tel: 860-236 5621; open Tues–Sat pm; entrance fee; free first Sat of every month 10am–1pm). Exhibits document Connecticut history.

West Hartford

A few miles from downtown, in **West Hartford** ❷, a half-acre of rosebushes is the centerpiece of **Elizabeth Park**

Hartford's Riverfest, which includes concerts and parades, is held every July.

BELOW:
Mark Twain House.

(915 Prospect Avenue; tel: 860-231 9443), whose 100 acres (40 hectares) includes greenhouses (open weekdays), a pond, meadows, and fields. The park's free summer concert series (Wed from 6pm, late June–late Aug; indoors on rainy evenings), is worth catching and features music ranging from swing to jazz to zydeco.

Noah Webster House

The author of the first American dictionary (1828) lived at what is now the National Historic Landmark **Noah Webster House & West Hartford Historical Society** (227 South Main Street; tel: 860-521 5362; open Thur–Mon 1–4pm; call for extended summer hours; entrance fee). The dictionary, now revered, was not initially a big seller and Webster had to mortgage his home to bring out a second edition. The house has been restored to reflect 18th-century Connecticut life. To visit, take I-84 north to exit 41 and follow signs north for 1 mile (1.6 km).

The Children's Museum

A perfect rainy-day destination, **The Children's Museum** (950 Trout Brook Drive; exit 43 off I-84; tel: 860-231 2824; open Tues–Sat; Sun pm; Mon holidays, school vacations, and during Jul–Aug; entrance fee) has lots of creative hands-on exhibits, live animals, and digital space and science shows.

WEST OF HARTFORD

Take Route 84 south to exit 39 to **Farmington ❸**, 10 miles (16 km) west of Hartford. Often called one of the loveliest towns in New England, its elegant 18th- and 19th-century mansions display a clarity of architectural detail seldom equaled in the area.

A particular gem is the National Historic Landmark **Hill-Stead Museum** (35 Mountain Road; tel: 860-677 4787; hillstead.org; open by guided tour only May–Oct Tues–Sun 10am–5pm, last tour at 4pm; Nov–April Tues–Sun 11am–4pm, last tour at 3pm; entrance fee). Designed by Stanford White, the Colonial Revival home on 150 acres (60 hectares) was the retirement home of industrialist Alfred Atmore Pope, a friend of the artist Mary Cassatt and a great admirer of French Impressionism. Scattered throughout the mansion are a number of familiar canvases, including paintings from Monet

TIP

If attending an Elizabeth Park concert, either bring a picnic to the concert, or make reservations at the Pond House Café (Tel: 860-231 8823; lunch and dinner Tues–Sat; Sun brunch). This moderately priced restaurant on the park grounds offers an eclectic menu and al fresco dining.

BELOW: a summer festival in the grounds of Hill-Stead Museum.

Haystack series, Manet's *The Guitar Lady*, and Degas's *The Tub*. Whistler and Cassatt are also well represented. The gardens are magnificent.

Exhibits at the National Historic Landmark **Stanley-Whitman House** (37 High Street; tel: 860-677 9222; tours May–Oct, Wed–Sun pm; Nov–Apr, Sat and Sun pm; entrance fee) focus on everyday objects from 1642 to 1810.

Bristol

Continue south on Route 84 to exit 34 to the turn-off for **Bristol ❹**, 18 miles (29 km) west of Hartford. The town was a 19th-century clockmaking capital, producing more than 200,000 clocks in a single year. The **American Clock and Watch Museum** (100 Maple Street; tel: 860-583 6070; Apr–Nov, daily; entrance fee), is housed in an 1801 mansion. It displays some valuable timepieces, and has the country's largest collection of American production clocks.

Hand-carved, antique and contemporary carousel pieces and band organs are featured at the **New England Carousel Museum** (95 Riverside Avenue, Route 72; tel: 860-585 5411; Apr–Nov, Mon–Sat, Sun pm; Dec–Mar, Thur–Sat, Sun pm; entrance fee). The museum is housed in the **Bristol Center for Arts and Culture**, which is also home to the **Museum of Fire History** and several art galleries. A 1927 wooden roller coaster, rated the best of its type in the world, is the highlight of 50 rides at **Lake Compounce Theme Park** (822 Lake Avenue; exit 31 off I-84; tel: 860 583 3300; open July–Aug, daily; call for off-season hours). Splash Harbor Water Park (open noon–7pm; entrance fee), the state's only water park, is located here.

THE LITCHFIELD HILLS

In the northwest corner of Connecticut, the wooded Litchfield Hills are dotted with quintessential New England villages, covered bridges, and the tumbling stone walls of forgotten farms. Through runs the **Housatonic River**, crystal clear and freckled with trout, and excellent for canoeing. Hikers may want to follow the Appalachian Trail from Kent to Salisbury and Mount Frissell.

Litchfield ❺, 35 miles (56 km) from Hartford is dominated by a spacious green, graced by the tall-steepled Congregational Church. The town's rich history is documented at the excellent **Litchfield History Museum** (7 South Street; tel: 860-567 4501; open mid-Apr–Nov Tues–Sat; Sun pm; entrance fee). Admission includes entrance to the **Tapping Reeve House and Litchfield Law School**, the nation's first school of law (82 South Street, Route 63), where visitors learn about student life in the early 19th century.

Just east of town, off Route 118, Connecticut's first winery, **Haight-Brown Vineyard** (29 Chestnut Hill Road; tel: 860-567 4045; open Mon–Sat; Sun pm) is one of 19 vineyards on the **Connecticut Wine Trail** (tel: 860-267 1399; ctwine.com). Free tours and tastings are offered in the vineyards, which are divided for ease of driving into a western group and an eastern group. Commercial wineries were sanctioned in the state only in 1978. They produce a surprisingly wide range of wines, ranging from a dry

Town merchants in Litchfield prospered during the early days of the China trade when their money backed the sailing ships of Mystic and New Haven. But industry faltered when a new railroad bypassed the town center and Litchfield was left nestled in the past.

BELOW: the First Congregational Church of Litchfield.

Lake Waramaug, named after an Indian chief of the Wyantenock tribe, has an average depth of 22 ft (7 meters).

BELOW:
old agricultural implements at the Sloane-Stanley Museum.

barrel-fermented Chardonnay to late-harvest Vidals and Vignoles.

Head south out of Litchfield center for 3½ miles (6 km) on Route 63 to **White Flower Farm** (tel: 860-567 8789; open Apr–Oct, daily), where English tuberous begonias flourish amid 10 acres (4 hectares) of display gardens at their peak June–Sept.

White Memorial Foundation, 2 miles (3.2 km) south of town on Route 202 (tel: 860-567 0857; open Mon–Sat; Sun pm; entrance fee to museum), the state's largest nature center, encompasses 4,000 acres (1,600 hectares) and includes 35 miles (56 km) of trails and the **White Memorial Conservation Center Museum**, which has informative displays and a nature store.

Lake Waramaug

Continue south on Route 202 for approximately 6 miles (10 km) to **New Preston ❻**, a tiny town with several fine antique shops. Continue north on Route 45 for 5 miles (8 km) to **Lake Waramaug State Park** (30 Lake Waramaug Road; tel: 860-868-2592; entrance fee May–Oct weekends and holidays), a tranquil hideaway

with boating and swimming. Several fine inns, including the **Hopkins Inn** (tel: 860-868 7295) and the **Boulders Inn** (tel: 860-868 0541); and **Hopkins Vineyard** (2 Hopkins Road; tel: 860-868 7954; open Jan–Feb, Fri–Sun; Mar–Apr, Wed–Sun; May–Dec, daily) overlook the lake.

Washington

To the southeast, on Route 47 is the magnificently-preserved town of **Washington ❼**, home to three historic districts, five private schools (including The Gunnery, founded in 1850), and one of the country's finest lodgings/spas: the historic **Mayflower Inn** (tel: 860-868 9466; mayflowerinn.com).

Continue past the inn onto Route 199 to the turn-off for the **Institute for American Indian Studies** (38 Curtis Road; tel: 860-868 0518; open year-round, Mon–Sat; Sun pm; entrance fee), where artifacts and a simulated archaeological site interpret the 10,000-plus-year history of the region's native American

West to Kent

The Housatonic Valley has one of its most dramatic moments to the west in the

Recommended Restaurants and Bars on pages 262–5

now-chic town of **Kent ❽** at **Kent Falls State Park** (Route 7; tel: 860-927 3238; entrance fee May–Oct weekends and holidays), where water tumbles 200 ft (65 meters) down a natural stone staircase.

A short distance south on Route 7, ruins of the **Old Kent Furnace** recall the 18th-century discovery of iron ore in the Litchfield Hills. Adjacent, the **Sloane-Stanley Museum**, (tel: 860-927 3849; open May–Oct, Wed–Sun; entrance fee) displays an extensive collection of early American tools, and the artwork of Eric Sloane (1905–85), chronicler of early American life, including the re-created studio where he wrote and illustrated works such as *An Age of Barns*.

Dip south on Route 7 to visit the handsome covered bridge and rapids at **Bulls Bridge Scenic Area.** A hiking trail connects with the Appalachian Trail (which runs from Maine to Georgia).

To the north on Route 7, in **West Cornwall**, a much photographed 1836 covered bridge spans the Housatonic.

At **Falls Village**, Music Mountain Gordon Hall; tel: 860-824 7126; music mountain.org; fee) hosts the country's oldest continuing summer chamber music

festival. The 120-acre (48-hectare) National Register of Historic Places property, built by Sears, Roebuck and Company in 1930, encompasses a concert hall and magnificent grounds. Most of the chamber music concerts are held Sunday afternoons; Saturday evenings, jazz and choral concerts are presented.

Norfolk ❾, almost on the southern border of Massachusetts, is another classic town with handsome 18th-century homes clustered around a tidy green. The Ellen Battell Stoeckel Estate (Routes 44 & 272; tel: 860-542 3000; yale.edu/norfolk; entrance fee to concerts) hosts Yale Uni-

You can canoe, kayak, or raft down the Housatonic from Clarke Outdoors' headquarters on Route 7 in West Cornwall (tel: 860-672 6365). It offers 6-mile (10-km) or 10-mile (16-km) trips.

BELOW:
the covered bridge
at West Cornwall.

versity's renowned **Norfolk Chamber Music Festival**. Buy tickets well in advance, and bring a picnic.

On a clear day you can almost see forever – or at least to Long Island Sound and the Berkshires – from the top of the 34-ft (12.4-meter) tower at the top of 1,716 ft (523-meter) Haystack Mountain. A road in **Haystack Mountain State Park** (Route 272; tel: 860-424 3200; entrance fee) goes half-way up the mountain, and from there it's a rather rugged half-mile hike to the summit.

NORTH OF HARTFORD

In the 1920s and '30s, more than 35,000 acres (14,000 hectares) of land along the Connecticut River Valley between Hartford and the Massachusetts border were devoted to growing shade tobacco for cigar wrappers. Today, much of the land is covered by houses, but a few farmers carry on; Connecticut wrappers are still considered the world's best. Some of the state's earliest settlements are here, along with several excellent museums.

The history of the region is well told a few miles north of the city in **Windsor** at the **Luddy/Taylor Connecticut Valley**

Tobacco Museum (Northwest Park, 135 Lang Rd, exit 38 off I-91; tel: 860-285 1888; open March–mid-Dec, Tues–Thur and Sat pm). Nearby is the beautifully preserved 1780 **Oliver Ellsworth Homestead** (778 Palisado Avenue, Route 159; tel: 860-688 8717; open mid-May–mid-Oct, Wed, Thur, Sat, and last Sun of the month, pm; entrance fee). It remained in the hands of the same family until 1903.

Cheek by jowl with Bradley International Airport in **Windsor Locks** is the **New England Air Museum** (36 Perimeter Road, exit 40 off I-91; tel: 860-623 3305; neam.org; open daily; entrance fee). It has more than 80 aircraft on display, is the largest of its kind in the Northeast and a must for plane buffs.

Just down the road, the **Connecticut Firefighters Memorial** (34 Perimeter Road) commemorates those who died in the line of duty.

In **East Windsor** , the history of fire fighting is chronicled at the **Connecticut Fire Museum** (58 North Road, Route 140; tel: 860-623 4732; July and August Mon and Wed–Sat; Sun pm; call for off season hours; entrance fee). A ticket to the museum also includes a visit to the **Con**

Norfolk's Loon Meadow Farm organizes horse-drawn carriage rides through the village and countryside – not to mention wedding carriages and funeral vehicles. It's just off Route 44 – turn into Loon Meadow Drive at the junction with State road 182. Tel: 860-542 6085; loonmeadowfarm.com

BELOW: serenity at Tyler Lake, Goshen.

necticut **Trolley Museum** (same address and summer hours; tel: 860-627 6540), where passengers board an antique trolley for a 3-mile (5-km) journey.

Although there isn't much to see, the now abandoned **Old Newgate Prison and Copper Mine** (115 Newgate Road; tel: 860-653 3563; open mid-May–Oct, Wed–Sun; entrance fee) in **East Granby**, is a National Historic Landmark. It was New England's first copper mine, and later served as a prison.

The Quiet Corner

The Nutmeg State's relatively unheralded northeastern region has been dubbed the "quiet corner." The best way to enjoy the small, scenic villages is to "shun pike" – avoid the well-traveled highways and explore the meandering byways.

For a small town, **Storrs** ⑬ has much to offer. The extensive campus of the **University of Connecticut** is located here, and it encompasses numerous museums and places of interest, including: the **William Benton Museum of Art**; the **Connecticut Museum of Natural History**; the **Ballard Museum of Puppetry**, and the **Jorgensen Center for the Performing Arts**. For information, tel: 860-486 4900; uconn.edu.

Dip southwest to **Coventry** and the **Nathan Hale Homestead** (2299 South Street; tel: 860-742 6917; open mid-May–mid-Oct, Wed and Fri–Sun; entrance fee), the family home of the official state hero, hanged as a spy by the British in 1776.

Route 31 goes south past the 1730 **Strong-Porter House Museum** (tel: 860-742 1419; limited hours, call ahead) to **Willimantic** ⑭, home to the **Connecticut Eastern Railroad Museum** (55 Bridge Street; tel: 860-456 9999; open May–Oct, Sat and Sun; entrance fee). Exhibits, housed in vintage railroad buildings, include locomotives, rolling stock, and a reconstructed roundhouse. **Willimantic Brewing Company** (967 Main Street; tel: 860-423 6777; lunch Tues–Sun, dinner nightly) is the oldest operating pub brewery in the state. It serves lunch, dinner, and late-night

snacks along with handcrafted brews in a converted 1909 post office.

The **Windham Textile and History Museum** (411 Main Street; tel: 860-456 2178; Fri–Sun pm; entrance fee) houses a factory, rooms for a worker's rowhouse, and owner's mansion.

To the east in **Canterbury**, the **Prudence Crandall Museum** (Junction Routes 14 & 169; tel: 860-256 2800; open Apr–mid-Dec, Wed–Sun; entrance fee) was New England's first academy for black women. The National Historic Landmark features period rooms and changing exhibits.

ALONG THE RIVER VALLEY

Beginning as a mountain stream near the New Hampshire–Canada border, the Connecticut River travels 410 miles

A Boeing B-29A Superfortress on show in the New England Air Museum.

BELOW: Thread City Crossing in Willimantic is known as Frog Bridge.

(660 km) through four states and ends its journey to the sea as a broad and majestic tidal estuary. The Native Americans named it "Quinnituckett," which means "the long, tidal river." Throughout history, the Connecticut River has linked valley residents with the outside world. A fertile floodplain nourishes crops, and water power has generated energy for small industries.

Begin a tour of the valley in **Ivoryton** ⓯, a center of piano-making 100 years ago which takes its name from the substance used to make the keys.

The historic **Ivorytown Playhouse** (103 Main Street; tel: 860-767 7318) presents year-round professional theatre. Down the road, the **Museum of Fife and Drum** (62 North Main Street; tel: 860-399 6519; open July–Labor Day weekend, Sat and Sun pm; donation) presents a visual and musical history of America on parade from the Revolutionary War to the present. Free concerts are presented Tuesday evenings in July–Aug.

The 1890 **Copper Beech Inn** (46 Main Street; tel: 888-909 2056; copperbeechinn.com) offers elegant lodging and French country fare nightly.

Essex

Essex ⓰, a seaport founded in 164 developed as an important shipbuildi center during the 18th century. The *Oliv Cromwell*, America's first warship, w launched here in 1776. Yachts and cab cruisers still berth here, and tall masts a yards of tackle lend the town a distinct nautical air. The **Connecticut Riv Museum** (67 Main Street; tel: 860-7 8269; open Tues–Sun; entrance fee), Steamboat Dock, highlights the town maritime heritage with exhibits, boa and a replica of the *Turtle*, the nation first submarine, invented by Connec cut's David Bushnell (*see margin note*

The 1776 **Griswold Inn** (tel: 860-7 1776; griswoldinn.com) on Main Street one of New England's oldest hostelric

For a close look at the Connectic River, take an old-fashioned journey steam locomotive and/or riverboat means of the **Essex Steam Train a Riverboat Ride** (1 Railroad Avenue; t 800-377 3987 or 860-767 0103; ess steamtrain.com; open May–Dec with va ied schedule; fee). You board a 192 coach and ride along the river throu; the villages of **Chester** and **Deep Riv**

Recommended Restaurants and Bars on pages 262–5

At Deep River, passengers may board a riverboat for a hour-and-a-half cruise. The round trip takes about 2½ hours and is recommended. A dinner train runs from May through October.

Head north on Route 154 and east on Route 148 to the **Chester-Hadlyme Ferry** (54 Ferry Road; tel: 860-526 2743 to book; open Apr–Nov; fee). It has been transporting people across the Connecticut River to East Haddam since 1769.

In **Chester**, original works by local artists are on show at the Connecticut River Artisans Cooperative (5 West Main Street; tel: 860-526 5575; open Jan–June and Sept–Oct, Wed–Sun; July/Aug and Nov/Dec, daily).

Gillette Castle

From the opposite shore it's a short drive to the spectacularly eccentric **Gillette Castle** at **Gillette Castle State Park**  (67 River Road; tel: 860-526 2336; castle open Memorial Day–Columbus Day, daily; grounds open daily; entrance fee to castle). William Gillette (1853–1937) was a much admired American actor whose stage portrayal of Sherlock Holmes brought him fame and fortune.

For his dream house, the actor selected a hilltop aerie overlooking the Connecticut River and its surrounding countryside. Work on the 122-acre (49-hectare) site with its stone-and-concrete castle began in 1914 and took five years and more than $1 million. The results are whimsical and bizarre. He installed hidden mirrors so that he could spy on public rooms from the master bedroom. The park's 184 acres (75 hectares) have hiking trails and fine views of the river.

North on Route 82, is the charming Victorian town of **East Haddam** ⑱. The 1876 **Goodspeed Opera House** (tel: 860-873 8668; goodspeed.org), which sits majestically on the banks of the Connecticut River, was a popular stopover in the heyday of steamboat travel. Beautifully restored, the Opera House presents revivals of Broadway musicals, as well as original productions, Apr–Dec. Half-hour tours are offered mid-June–late Oct, Sat 10:30am–1pm (fee).

It's worth stopping for a quick visit at the one-room **Nathan Hall Schoolhouse** (29 Main Street; tel: 860-873 3399; open May–Oct, Wed–Sun pm), where Connecticut's celebrated patriot once taught.

William Gillette's will stated that his castle should not be sold to any "blithering saphead who has no conception of where he is or with what surrounded." In 1943 it was bought by the State of Connecticut.

BELOW:
Essex Steam Train.

SOUTH OF HARTFORD

Take Route 91 south to exit 27, and Route 314 to **Wethersfield** , one of the oldest villages in the state, on the Connecticut River. More than 150 of the 17th- and 18th-century "downtown" homes have been preserved. Three can be toured at the **Webb-Deane-Stevens Museum** (211 Main Street; tel: 860-529 0612; open May–Oct, Wed–Mon; Nov–Apr, weekends; entrance fee). Note: George Washington slept here.

One gem is the meticulously restored, *c.*1710 **Buttolph-Williams House** (249 Broad Street; tel: 860-247 8996; open mid-May–mid Oct Wed–Mon; entrance fee). Its architecture reflects the influence of medieval English building styles.

The **Wethersfield Historical Society** (150 Main Street; tel: 860-529 7656; entrance fee) maintains the *c.* 1790 Hurlbut-Dunham House at 212 Main Street (entrance fee) and maritime exhibits at the Cove Warehouse (both open mid-May–mid-Oct, Sat 10am–4pm; Sun pm).

Look for 800-plus varieties of seeds – including a huge selection of heirlooms – at **Comstock, Ferre & Co.** (263 Main Street; tel: 860-571 6590), America's oldest continuously operating seed company and a National Historic Landmark.

Dinosaur State Park

Continue south on Route 91 to exit 23 to **Rocky Hill** and the National Historic Landmark **Dinosaur State Park**  (400 West Street; tel: 860-529 8423; dinosaurstatepark.org; open daily; exhibit center open Tues–Sun; casting area open daily May–Oct; entrance fee). Here, 200-million-year-old dinosaur tracks are housed under a geodesic dome.

Visitors can make plaster casts of the tracks, but must bring materials such as cooking oil and Plaster of Paris (call or check website for details). Dinosaur-mad youngsters will appreciate this stop.

New Britain to Middletown

In **New Britain** , over 5,000 works by artists including Cassatt, Church, Whistler, Wyeth, and Sargent are on exhibit at the excellent **New Britain Museum of American Art** (56 Lexington Street; tel: 860-229 0257; open Tues–Sat, Sun pm; entrance fee). **Free concerts**, featuring everything from jazz to country to rock and roll, are presented

The Connecticut Valley may not have the allure of Jurassic Park, but dinosaur footprints have been found here since the 1840s. Fossils have also been found but few skeletons, so a certain amount of guesswork has gone into determining which types of dinosaur walked in the valley 200 million years ago.

BELOW: Dinosaur State Park.

at the Davis Miller Band Shell in Walnut Hill Park on Monday and Wednesday evenings in July–Aug, starting at 7pm.

Southeast of New Britain on Route 9, **Middletown ㉒** is home to Wesleyan University and the elegant, Beaux-Art-style **Wadsworth Mansion at Long Hill Estate**, 421 Wadsworth Street; tel: 860-347 1064; wadsworthmansion.com; tours Wed 2–4pm). The Olmsted brothers designed the magnificent, park-like grounds, open daily. A free concert series is held on the mansion lawn in summer. Check the website for the schedule.

The **Sculpture Mile**, featuring works of American sculptors, begins at the South Green on Main Street. The gallery at the non-profit, cooperative **Wesleyan Potters** (350 South Main Street; tel: 860-347 5925; open Wed–Sat, Sun pm) displays works by juried craftspeople throughout the country.

West to Waterbury

In **Waterbury ㉓**, creative exhibits at the excellent **Mattatuck Museum** (144 West Main Street; tel: 203-753 0381; open Tues–Sat, Sun pm; entrance fee) in Waterbury document the industrial, social, architectural and cultural history of the Naugatuck Valley.

The doors of the Renaissance Revival **Palace Theater** (100 East Main Street; tel: 203-755 4700; palacetheater.ct.org) opened in 1922, closed in 1987, and are now reopened as the city's Center for Performing Arts, with a variety of shows scheduled from September through May.

Danbury

To the west along I-84 **Danbury ㉔** attracts train buffs to the **Danbury Railway Museum** (120 White Street; exit 5 off I-84; tel: 203-778 8337; open Jan–Mar, Wed–Sat, Sun pm; Apr–Dec, Tues–Sat, Sun pm). It offers 20-minute tours of the rail yard aboard vintage trains and has a good collection of artifacts.

Danbury's hat industry is documented at the **Danbury Museum and Historical Society** (43 Main Street; open May–Oct, call for hours); tel: 203-743 5200; entrance fee). It also oversees the birth-

place of composer Charles Ives, and the studio of the famous contralto Marian Anderson.

To the south in **Ridgefield ㉕**, catch a rising star at the **Aldrich Contemporary Art Museum** (258 Main Street; tel: 203-438 4519; open Tues–Sun pm; entrance fee; free on Tues). The museum, with no permanent collections, exhibits works by emerging and mid-level artists.

Just down the street, the National Register of Historic Places **Keeler Tavern Museum** (132 Main Street; tel: 203-438 5485; open Wed, Sat and Sun pm; garden open daily; entrance fee) exhibits late 18th-century furnishings. A British cannonball from 1777 can be seen embedded in its exterior.

THE SOUTHWESTERN SHORE

From the harbors of New Haven, New London, Mystic and Stonington, China clippers and Yankee whalers sailed out to seek their fortunes. People along Connecticut's coast still retain a fondness for the sea, and most towns have at least one marina. On a clear summer's day the horizon of Long Island Sound is filled

Tarrywile Mansion, a community center for Danbury in the city-owned Tarrywile Park, a large recreation area with picnic spots and 21 miles (34 km) of hiking trails.

BELOW: the wealthy Gold Coast has a big appetite for antiques.

Visitors from Long Island can cross the Sound to the Connecticut shore by ferry from Orient Point to New London. The car ferry takes 80 minutes. The passenger-only ferry takes 40 minutes and has a coach connection with Foxwoods Resort Casino (see page 260). Ferry details: tel: 860-443-5281 or 631-323-2525 (LI). longislandferry.com

BELOW: a tug at Stamford.

with billowing sails. Greenwich, Cos Cob, Stamford, Darien and Rowayton – to the thousands of Connecticut residents who work in New York City, this is a railroad conductor's litany. About an hour from Manhattan by train, the Connecticut suburbs are among the nation's smartest bedroom communities.

The "Gold Coast"

The coastal area that parallels I-95 from Greenwich to Westport – lower Fairfield County – is sometimes referred to as the "Gold Coast" because of the many wealthy communities it encompasses.

In **Greenwich** ㉖ the **Bruce Museum** (One Museum Drive; tel: 203-869 9697; open Tues–Sun; entrance fee), features exhibits ranging from fine and decorative arts, to natural science, to anthropology. Nearby, **Cos Cob's Bush-Holley Historic Site** (39 Strickland Road; tel: 203-869 6899; open Tues–Sun pm; entrance fee), a National Historic Landmark, was home to the state's first art colony. A worthwhile American Impressionist art collection is on exhibit in the circa 1730 period-furnished home.

In **Stamford** ㉗, take a stroll through the **Bartlett Arboretum and Gardens** (151 Brookdale Road; tel: 203-322 6971; open daily; donation), a 91-acre (37-hectare) swath of wildflower meadows, wetlands, boardwalks, and trails. Nature-lovers will also want to visit **Stamford Museum and Nature Center** (39 Scofieldtown Road; tel: 203-322 1646; open daily; closed Mon Jan–Mar; entrance fee), whose 118 woodland acres include a New England working farm. Free **concerts on the Green** are hosted by First Presbyterian Church (1101 Bedford Street; tel: 203-324 9522) Thursdays beginning at 7pm in July.

The **United House Wrecking Co.** (535 Hope Street; tel: 203-348 5371; Mon–Sat, Sun pm), the state's largest antiques store, fills more than 40,000 sq. ft (3,700 sq. meters) with architectural salvage and antique and reproduction furniture.

New Canaan

At the junction of I-91 and Route 123 you can take a detour by turning north to **New Canaan** ㉘ to visit Philip Johnson's 1949 **Glass House** (199 Elm Street; tel: 203-966 8167 or 866-811 4111; philipjohnsonglasshouse.org; tours May–Oct; fee) This is the architect's minimalist masterpiece – once his private (if glass-walled retreat – on 47 magnificently-landscaped acres (19 hectares). Tours include the house, grounds, and outbuildings.

Note that tours of the Glass House and other buildings on the former Johnson property are limited and sell out very early in the season: book at least six months in advance. Visitors can choose from a 90-minute tour ($25) or a two hour tour ($40).

Nearby attractions include the **New Canaan Nature Center** (144 Oenoke Ridge; open Mon–Sat; Sun pm), with walking trails and a raptor exhibit; and the **New Canaan Historical Society** (1 Oenoke Ridge; tel: 203-966 1776; open Tues–Sat), whose complex encompasses an 1845 pharmacy, an old schoolhouse, sculpture studio, and a tool museum. Works of contemporary professional artists are on exhibit at the **Silvermin**

Guild Arts Center (1037 Silvermine Road; tel: 203-966 9700; open Tues–Sat, Sun pm).

The Norwalks

South Norwalk ㉙, with its upscale galleries and shops, has been dubbed "SoNo" for its emulation of New York's SoHo district. Once a gritty, run-down neighborhood, it's now a stimulating place to while away a day.

The huge **Maritime Aquarium** (10 North Water Street; tel: 203-852 0700; maritimeaquarium.org; open daily; entrance fee) on the banks of the Norwalk River has more than 1,000 marine animals and plenty of hands-on displays relating to the marine life and maritime culture of Long Island Sound. Seal feedings are at 11:45am, 1:45pm and 3:45pm. There's also an IMAX movie theater. The aquarium's research vessel takes passengers on a 2½-hour excursion daily in July and August, and weekends from Apr–June and Sept–Oct. Riders must be over 42 inches (1.07 metres) tall.

You can hop on board the ferry at Hope Dock for a scenic cruise to Sheffield Island and a guided tour of an 1868, 10-room lighthouse (tel: 203-838 9444; seaport.org; cruises daily late June–mid-Sept; shoulder season, weekends and holidays; fee). **The Stewart B. McKinney National Wildlife Refuge** is also here. On Thursday nights in summer (rain or shine), a cruise includes the lighthouse tour and dinner on the island.

In nearby **Norwalk** ㉚, tours are offered of "America's first chateau", the partially-restored, 62-room Victorian National Historic Landmark **Lockwood-Mathews Mansion Museum** (295 West Avenue, Matthews Park; tel: 203-838 9799; open mid-Mar–Dec Wed–Sun pm; entrance fee). Stop at **City Hall** (125 East Avenue; tel: 203-866 0202; Mon–Fri) to view one of the country's largest collection of Works Progress Administration murals *(see margin note)*.

Children 10 years old and younger will enjoy the hands-on activities at **Stepping Stones Museum for Children** (303 West Avenue; Matthews Park; tel: 203-899 0606; open daily Memorial Day–Labor Day; Wed–Sun, and Tues pm the rest of year; entrance fee). A tropical rainforest exhibit is fun, and sections on health and conservation are educational.

The Works Progress Administration funded employment for artists during the Great Depression of the 1930s, creating over 5,000 jobs. In addition, the Treasury Department's Section of Fine Arts funded murals in post offices to make art "accessible to all people." These murals can be seen in dozens of post offices throughout New England.

BELOW: feeding time at South Norwalk's Maritime Aquarium.

Westport

One of the country's most affluent communities, **Westport** is perhaps best known for its **Westport Country Playhouse** (25 Powers Court; tel: 203-227 4177; westportplayhouse.org), which mounts award-winning experimental plays as well as reinterpretations of the classics. The outdoor **Levitt Pavilion for the Performing Arts** (40 Jesup Road; tel: 203-221 2153 hosts more than 50 free events throughout the summer, including bands, movies, and children's shows (Wed at 7pm). Rain location: 170 Riverside Avenue.

If it's hot, you can swim at the beach in **Sherwood Island State Park** by Long Island Sound (Sherwood Island Connector; tel: 203-226 6983; open daily; fee in season).

Westport's Levitt Pavilion for the Performing Arts.

Bridgeport

To the east, **Bridgeport ㉛**, a major industrial center, is an exception to the coast's general aura of ease and affluence. But there are several attractions of note. **Barnum Museum** (820 Main Street; tel: 203-331 1104; open Tues–Sat; Sun pm; entrance fee), is a showcase for memorabilia connected to circus pioneer P.T. Barnum (1810–91), with a 4,000-piece miniature circus, clown props, bogus "oddities" like the Feejee Mermaid, and items relating to the diminutive Bridgeport native General Tom Thumb.

Highlights at **Connecticut's Beardsley Zoo** (1875 Noble Avenue; tel; 203-394 6565; open daily; entrance fee), the state's only zoo, include North and South American species including some rarities, a tropical rainforest, and a carousel.

Captain's Cove Seaport (1 Bostwick Avenue; tel: 203-335 1433) on Black Rock Harbor has harbor cruises, a maritime history museum, charter fishing and dive boats, shops, a restaurant, and terrific views. There are free band concerts Sunday afternoons in summer.

New Haven

New Haven ㉜, 18 miles (29 km) to the north, settled by Puritans in 1638, was an independent colony until 1662, when it merged with the Hartford settlement At first a seafaring community, New Haven later embraced industry and pioneered such inventions as the steel fish

ook, the meat grinder, the corkscrew, nd the steamboat.

New Haven is best known, however, or **Yale University** (Visitor Center, 149 lm Street; tel: 203-432 2300; yale.edu; ours Mon–Fri 10:30am and 2pm; Sat nd Sun 1:30pm). Founded in 1701 by a roup of Puritan clergymen, it was origally located in nearby Saybrook. In 716, the school was moved to New laven, and two years later it took the ame of benefactor Elihu Yale.

Alma mater to famous personalities uch as Nathan Hale, Noah Webster, and oth Presidents Bush, Yale has pursued a olicy of commissioning leading archicts to design its buildings. But the domant style on the Yale campus is Gothic evival – much of it evoking the British niversities of Oxford and Cambridge.

Any visit to the university should clude its excellent museums and braries. Start from the **Beinecke Rare ook and Manuscript Library** at 121 all Street (tel: 203-432 2977; open lon–Sat year-round), where an edition f the Gutenberg Bible and original udubon bird prints are displayed.

Two blocks south, the **Yale University Art Gallery** (1111 Chapel Street; tel: 203-432 0600; open Tues–Sat; Sun pm) exhibits well over 100 paintings by patriot artist John Trumbull (1756–1843), impressive collections of African and pre-Columbian art, canvases by Manet, Van Gogh, Corot, Degas, and Matisse; and a superb collection of American paintings and decorative arts.

Across the street, is the **Yale Center for British Art** (1080 Chapel Street; tel: 203-432 2800; open Tues–Sat; Sun pm). It has a vast collection of British paintings (including works by Constable and Turner), drawings and sculpture donated in 1966 by industrialist Paul Mellon.

Collections at the university's **Peabody Museum of Natural History** (170 Whitney Avenue; tel: 203-432 5050; open Mon–Sat; Sun pm; entrance fee) include dinosaur fossils, native birds, meteorites and minerals.

Western and non-Western instruments are displayed at the **Yale Collection of Musical Instruments** (15 Hillhouse Avenue; tel: 203-432 0822; open Sept–June Tues–Thur pm except during uni-

Sherwood Island State Park has facilites for shore fishing and saltwater swimming in Long Island Sound.

BELOW: students heading for Yale University.

The Thimble Islands are supposedly named for the the thimbleberry, though the plant is more frequently found in parts of northern New England. There are between 100 and 365 islands, depending on how you distinguish an island from a rock, and the complex currents are a big challenge for sailors. The 23 inhabited islands have just 81 houses in total.

BELOW: the Thimble Islands.

versity vacations; entrance fee). It has one of the world's best collections, and concerts are given throughout the year.

Adjacent to the university, New Haven Green is surrounded by a trinity of churches constructed in Gothic Revival, Georgian, and Federal styles.

New Haven's cultural offerings include **Yale University's Institute of Sacred Music** (409 Prospect Street; tel: 203-432 6052), which presents concerts, art exhibitions, and films; the **Yale Repertory Theater** (1120 Chapel Street; tel: 203-432 1234), the **Long Wharf Theater** on the downtown waterfront (222 Sargent Drive; tel: 203-787 4282), and the **Shubert Theater** (247 College Street; tel: 203-562 5666), the "Birthplace of the nation's greatest hits". The **New Haven Symphony Orchestra** (tel: 203-865 0831) performs at Woolsey Hall on the Yale campus.

ALONG THE EASTERN SHORE

Just off Route 95 in **East Haven ㉝**, the National Register of Historic Places **Shore Line Trolley Museum** (17 River Street; tel: 203-467 6927; open Sun in Apr; Sat–Sun May; Memorial Day–

Labor Day daily; Sat and Sun Sept–Oct Sun in Nov; entrance fee) preserve some 100 trolleys, the oldest rapid tran sit car and a rare parlor car. Hop aboar for a 3-mile (5-km) ride on one of th vintage cars.

A short jog to the east on Route 14 off Route 1 in **Branford**, cruise boat (including Thimble Islands Cruise & Charter ; tel: 203-488 8905; and Captai Bob Milne; tel: 203-481 3345) sail fror the town's nearby **Stony Creek** dock fc interesting narrated tours of the **Thimbl Islands**, a cluster of islands, 23 of ther inhabited, just offshore *(see margin* They also offer seal watches in seasor

A mile east on Route 146, **Guilford ㉞** was settled in 1639 by the Reveren Henry Whitfield. His home, built tha year, is the oldest stone dwelling in Nev England and now the **Henry Whitfiel State Museum** (248 Old Whitfield Roa tel: 203-453 2457; open Apr–mid-De Wed–Sun; entrance fee). The house give visitors a feel for how early settlers live

Guilford has one of the largest an prettiest town greens in New Englanc it's famous for its Christmas tree ligh ing ceremony (first weekend in Dec

Nearby are several historic house museums, including the *circa* 1690 **Hyland House** (84 Boston Street; tel: 203-453 9477; open June–Labor Day Tues–Sat, Sun pm; Sept–mid-Oct weekends; entrance fee) and the *circa* 1774 **Thomas Griswold House** (171 Boston Street; tel: 203-453 3176; open mid-June–Sept Tues–Sun; weekends in Oct; Nov–May by appointment; entrance fee), with a restored blacksmith shop and Colonial garden. The **Dudley Farm** (2351 Durham Road; tel: 203-457 0770; open Apr–Oct, Mon–Sat 10am–1pm), a 19th-century working farm and living history museum, has a farmers' market Saturday mornings June through October.

Five miles (8 km) east, **Madison** ㉟ has some of the state's most beautiful summer and year-round homes. The *circa* 1685 **Deacon John Grave House** (581 Boston Road; tel: 203-245 4798; call for hours; entrance fee) has been a school, wartime infirmary, inn, tavern, and courtroom.

Hammonasset Beach State Park (Route 1; tel: 203-245 2785; weekend parking fee mid-Apr–Memorial Day and Labor Day–Oct), just 2 miles (3 km) east, is the state's longest public beach.

At **Old Saybrook** ㊱, by the western mouth of the Connecticut River, **Fort Saybrook Monument Park** (Saybrook Point, Route 154) has storyboards chronicling Saybrook Colony from 1635, and offers fine estuary views, with opportunities for bird watching from the boardwalk. Stop in for a Miss James Sundae at the **James Gallery & Soda Fountain** (2 Pennywise Lane; tel: 860-395 1229; open June–Aug, daily; Sept–May, Wed–Sun pm), once managed by Connecticut's first licensed African-American pharmacist. It retains many turn-of-the-19th-century furnishings.

Summer concerts on the Green are presented Wednesday evenings at 7pm from late June through August.

Old Lyme to New London

Of all the towns on the shore, **Old Lyme** ㊲ boasts the richest artistic heritage – thanks in large part to Florence Griswold, the daughter of one of the town's many sea captains and a devoted, if impecunious, patron of the arts. Her 1817 Georgian mansion, now the **Florence Griswold Museum** (96 Lyme Street; tel: 860-434 5542; open year-round Tues–Sat and Sun pm; entrance fee) contains a stunning array of works by her illustrious American Impressionist boarders, including such notables as Childe Hassam. Some were so moved by her laissez-faire hospitality, they left painted mementos on the doors, mantels and paneled walls. Don't miss the gardens.

The **Lyme Art Association** (90 Lyme Street; tel: 860-434 7802; open Tues–Sat, Sun pm), is one of the oldest in the country and a National Historic Landmark. It exhibits traditional works of art.

New London

New London ㊳ was one of America's busiest 19th-century whaling ports. More than 80 ships sailed from its docks, and many a vast fortune was accumulated by its merchants. Evidence of this wealth can be seen in Whale Oil Row on Huntington Street, where four Greek Revival mansions were built in the 1830s.

The Florence Griswold Museum has been restored to how it looked around 1910 when the local art colony was the center of Impressionism in America.

BELOW: breath of fresh air for a vintage vehicle.

Mystic Aquarium.

BELOW: this 1998 statue on New London's City Pier shows playwright Eugene O'Neill as he was when he spent his boyhood summers here.

When petroleum began to replace whale oil, manufacturing became New London's chief occupation. But the city maintained its ties to the sea and today is the home of the **US Coast Guard Academy** (the base is not open to the public).

It was also the boyhood home of Eugene O'Neill (1888–1953), the Nobel Prize-winning playwright whose works include *Long Day's Journey Into Night* and *Ah, Wilderness*. The O'Neill family's **Monte Cristo Cottage** (325 Pequot Avenue; tel: 860-443 5378, ext. 290; open Memorial Day–Labor Day, Thur–Sun pm; entrance fee), is now a National Historic Landmark. It has been restored to reflect the setting of the author's autobiographical work, *Long Day's Journey into Night*, first performed in 1956.

Nearby, **Ocean Beach Park** (1225 Ocean Avenue; tel: 800-510 7263; open daily; parking fee in summer) on Long Island Sound offers excellent swimming, a boardwalk, and a swimming pool.

The two restored **Hempstead Houses** (11 Hempstead Street; tel: 860-247 8996; open mid-May–mid-Oct, Thur–Sun pm;

entrance fee) were built in 1678 and 1759. They are furnished with period pieces tracing the evolution of colonial lifestyles.

American Impressionist paintings and 18th- to 20th-century decorative arts are highlighted at the **Lyman Allyn Art Museum** (625 Williams Street; tel: 860-443 2545; open Tues–Sat, Sun pm; entrance fee). There is no admission to the Outdoor Art Park and September 11th Memorial Gardens.

USS *Nautilus*

Across the Thames River from New London is the city of **Groton** , known as the "Submarine Capital of the World" – the manufacture of nuclear submarines is its major industry. Non-claustrophobes who wish to view the interior of a submarine may visit the USS *Nautilus* at the **US Naval Submarine Force Museum** (1 Crystal Lake Road at exit 86, off I–95; tel: 800-343 0079; ussnautilus.org; open May–Oct Wed–Mon and Tues pm; Nov–May 13, open Wed–Mon). The only submarine museum operated by the US Navy has working periscopes, mini-subs and mini-theaters.

Fort Griswold Battlefield State Park (Monument Street and Park Avenue; tel: 860-449 6877; museum and monument open Memorial Day–Labor Day, Wed–Sun) displays the remains of a Revolutionary War fort, and has a collection of Civil War memorabilia in the museum. Visitors can climb to the top of the monument for remarkable views.

Mystic

Five miles (8 km) east, at exit 90 off I-95 is **Mystic** , an old maritime community of trim white houses, sitting at the tidal outlet of the Mystic River. For generations Mystic was the home of daring mariners and fishermen, and was feared by the British during the Revolution as a "cursed little hornets' nest" of patriots. The village teemed with activity during the Gold Rush days of 1849, when shipbuilders vied to see who could construct the fastest clipper ships to travel round Cape Horn to the boom town of San Francisco. It was the *Andrew Jackson*, a Mystic-built clipper

launched in 1860, that claimed the world's record: 89 days, 4 hours.

Beluga whales, sharks, penguins, and sea otters are just a few of more than 3,500 creatures at the **Mystic Aquarium and Institute for Exploration** (55 Coogan Boulevard; mysticaquarium.org; tel: 860-572 5955; open daily; entrance fee). The Hidden Amazon exhibit recreates a rain forest, complete with crawly creatures and frogs. At the Institute for Exploration, visitors utilize the latest deep-sea technology, including live cameras, robots, and a live web feed to dive under the sea, visit kelp beds, and watch sea otters romp. Sea explorer Dr Robert Ballard displays many of the treasures he has brought up from the ocean floor in the Challenge of the Deep exhibit. The Aquarium operates seasonal seal, eagle and whale-watching cruises.

Olde Mistick Village, across from the aquarium, has lots of cute "shoppes" but its promised 18th-century ambience is not immediately apparent.

Mystic Seaport

Down Route 27 just a mile, **Mystic Seaport** (75 Greenmanville Avenue; tel:

888-973 2767; mysticseaport.org; open daily; entrance fee) is a living replica of a 19th-century waterfront community during the heyday of sailing ships. The project includes a complex of over 60 buildings covering 17 acres (7 hectares), and is so authentic that it was used as the 1839 setting for New Haven's harbor in Steven Spielberg's 1997 movie *Amistad*, about a revolt aboard a slave ship sailing from Africa. A recreation of the freedom schooner was designed, built here, and launched from the seaport in June 2000. An exhibit details the project.

A full day and plenty of stamina are required to tour the entire seaport properly. Visitors can wander along the wharves and streets of the village, and taste the old seafaring way of life. (Note: The *Charles W. Morgan*, the last surviving vessel of America's 19th-century whaling fleet, is scheduled for a major restoration.) Visitors can board the *Joseph Conrad*, built in 1882 by the Danish as a training vessel, and now a student dormitory. You can take to the water in a rented boat or study navigation in the planetar-

Spinning a yarn at Mystic Seaport.

BELOW:
the whaling ship
Charles W. Morgan
at Mystic Seaport.

Recommended Restaurants and Bars on pages 262–5

Ascending the lighthouse at Stonington.

BELOW: a rodeo on the Mashantucket Pequot Reservation.

ium. A Collections and Access Research Room (10am–5pm Mon–Fri) provides access to huge collections of maritime materials.

Passengers who opt for the 90-minute Friday or Saturday 6:30pm downriver cruise aboard the 1908 *Sabino*, one of the oldest wooden, coal-fired steamboats still operating, don't need to pay museum admission to board; they're permitted to enter the grounds 20 minutes before departing. There are also 30-minute cruises, available from mid-May through Columbus Day.

Stonington

Five miles (8 km) further east is the charming old whaling port of **Stonington** ⓪, one of the prettiest coastal enclaves in New England. An 1823 lighthouse, the first government-operated one in Connecticut, is now the **Old Lighthouse Museum** (7 Water Street; tel: 860-535 1440; open daily May–Nov; entrance fee). It has artifacts from the Oriental trade, whaling gear and a children's room.

Admission to the museum includes a visit to the National Historic Landmark,

1853 **Captain Nathaniel B. Palme House** (Palmer Street, Route 1A; tel 860-535 1440; open May–Oct, Thur Sun pm; entrance fee), built by the sea hunter and clipper ship designer who i 1820 discovered "land not yet laid dow on my chart" – it turned out to be Antarc tica. The house contains memorabili of that trip as well as family portrait artifacts and furnishings.

Massive casinos

Ten miles (16 km) north of Stonington on the Mashantucket Pequot Reservation the massive **Foxwoods Resort Casino** ⓸ (Route 2; open 24 hours) has grown t become the nation's largest (*see facing page*), welcoming gamblers by the bus load. On the grounds is the **Mashan tucket Pequot Museum and Research Center** (110 Pequot Trail; tel: 800-41 9671; open daily 1–4pm; last admissio 3pm; entrance fee). The museum include a walk-through 16th-century woodlan Indian village, a 17th-century Pequot for and an outdoor 18th-century farmstea

The **Mohegan Sun casino**, a worth rival to Foxwoods, is just to the south west in **Uncasville**.

The coming of the casinos

Despite its Puritan traditions, New England has boldly challenged the the more famous gaming venues of Las Vegas and Atlantic City.

For a region associated with Puritan mores and a distaste for gaudy display, New England has experienced a surprising casino revolution. The catalysts have been even more unlikely: New England's Indian tribes, Native American nations long thought to have been subsumed into the general population but rising with a new sense of identity – and the legal muscle to make their fortunes as big-time players in the gaming industry.

In the mid-1980s, eastern Connecticut's Mashantucket Pequots emerged to take advantage of new legislation exempting tribal reservation land from local laws against gambling. The Pequots began developing hundreds of acres of ancestral land in sleepy Ledyard, Connecticut, creating a vast casino-and-hotel complex, Foxwoods. By 1998, just six years after it opened, Foxwoods had become the world's highest-grossing casino, part of a resort complex that offers – in addition to high-stakes bingo, slot machines, and dozens of other games – a regular schedule of concerts and performances by America's entertainment elite, half a dozen restaurants ranging from casual to high-roller high-style, and ultra-plush hotel towers that rise, Ozlike, from the rolling countryside.

Honoring its past, the tribe opened the Mashantucket Pequot Museum and Research Center as part of the resort complex. Visitors journey back in time through a "World of Ice" that sets the glacial scene of the first peoples' arrival, 11,000 years ago, and proceed to exhibits including a re-created 16th-century Pequot village, a computer re-creation of a 17th-century Pequot fort excavated on the site, and a film explaining how the tribe achieved Federal recognition in 1983.

Just up the road in Uncasville, the Mohegan tribe has its own casino, the Mohegan Sun. A bit smaller than Foxwoods but similar in its glamorously seductive style, the Sun offers another winning hand: a slick combination of gambling, resort amenities, and Vegas-style concerts by big-name stars in its new 10,000-seat arena.

Not to be left behind, the state of Rhode Island now features two giant casinos of its own. The Newport Grand, located in the yachting capital's former jai alai arena, features more than 1,000 slot machines; video poker, keno, and blackjack; and betting on simulcast races. Twin River, in Lincoln, boasts nearly five times that many slots, along with blackjack tables.

Massachusetts is also getting into the act. In 2007, voters in Middleborough, an exurban town 40 miles (64 km) southwest of Boston, approved construction of a $1 billion casino to be run by the Mashpee Wampanoag tribe. Proposals for gambling palaces large and small occasionally surface in northern New England, although more hesitant upcountry voters and political leaders have so far resisted the casino temptation.

Whether or not the lure of gaming dollars will turn the whole region into Vegas East is a question that will be answered by the health of the overall economy, by the possible saturation of an industry that already has footholds in upstate New York and in nearby Montreal... and by the influence, not to be dismissed, of those eroding but still extant Puritan mores. ❏

ABOVE: part of the gigantic Foxwoods complex.
RIGHT: Bill Clinton performs at the grand opening of a new hotel at the Mohegan Sun resort.

RESTAURANTS AND BARS

Restaurants

Prices for a three-course dinner per person with a half-bottle of house wine:

$ = under $20
$$ = $20–45
$$$ = $45–60
$$$$ = over $60

Avon

Max A Mia
70 East Main Street (Rte 44)
Tel: 860-677 6299
maxrestaurantgroup.com
$–$$$
A lively northern Italian spot; good for pizza, risotto, and seafood. L and D daily.

Seasons Restaurant
Avon Old Farms Hotel, 1 Nod Road, Routes 44 and 10
Tel: 860-677 0240
avonoldfarmshotel.com **$$$**
Continental favorites

including roast duck, in an elegant room overlooking a stream. Sunday brunch is a standout. A lighter menu in The Pub. B, L Mon–Fri; D Tues–Sat; Sun brunch.

Bethel

Roadside Chili House
44 Stony Hill Road
Tel: 203-790 5064 **$**
Fry a foot-long wiener, put it on a soft bun, and top it with spicy chili, melted cheese, and raw onion: hot dog perfection.

Chester

Restaurant du Village
59 Main Street
Tel: 860-526 5301
restaurantduvillage.com
$$$–$$$$
Superb formal French cuisine, with specialties such as filet mignon and

escargot, served in a charming country auberge. D Wed–Sun.

East Lyme

Flanders Fish Market and Restaurant
22 Chesterfield Road, Route 161
Tel: 860-739 8866
flandersfish.com **$$–$$$**
This humble roadside restaurant wins regular accolades for its ultra-fresh, good-value fish, including an outstanding lobster pot pie. Sunday seafood buffet 11am–3pm. L and D daily.

Essex

Griswold Inn
36 Main Street
Tel: 860-767 1776
griswoldinn.com **$$–$$$**
New England fare with a sophisticated touch in a historic country inn. The Tap Room offers a lighter menu, and a three-course fireside supper is offered Mon–Fri ($20). L and D daily.

Farmington

Apricots Restaurant
1593 Farmington Avenue
Tel: 860-673 5405 **$$–$$$$**
Creative contemporary American dishes in an elegant colonial home with river and garden views. Casual pub fare is available downstairs.

Glastonbury

Glas Restaurant
2935 Main Street
Tel: 860-657 4527
hottomatos.net **$$$**
Chic, upscale restaurant specializing in New American cuisine with an accent on steaks and chops. Also a raw bar,

and streetside bar. L Mon–Fri, D nightly.

J. Gilbert's

185 Glastonbury Boulevard
Tel: 860-659 0409
jgilberts.com **$$$**
Steakhouse with southwestern and Mediterranean influences. Club-like dining room done in dark woods. D nightly.

Max Amore
Somerset Square Shopping Arcade
Tel: 860-659 2819 **$$–$$$**
maxrestaurantgroup.com
The Connecticut-based chain delivers again, this time with a lively bistro whose menu emphasizes northern Italian dishes and oak-grilled meats. L and D daily.

Groton

Norm's Diner
171 Bridge Street
Tel: 860-445 5026 **$**
A 1950s diner serving breakfast all day. Good house cheesecake.

Paul's Pasta Shop
223 Thames Street
Tel: 860-445 5276
paulspastashop.com **$**
Homemade pasta and sauces made daily, riverfront views, and tempting desserts. Specialties include lasagna and spaghetti pie. L and D Tues–Sun.

Hartford Area

Arugula
953 Farmington Avenue, West Hartford
Tel: 860-561 4888 **$$$**
Contemporary Italian cuisine – from roasted eggplant Napoleon to

wild mushroom lasagna – served in a small, intimate dining room. L and D Mon–Sat.

Carbone's Ristorante
588 Franklin Avenue
Tel: 860-296 9646
carbonesct.com **$$–$$$**
The city's premier Italian restaurant has been winning awards since it opened in 1938. Tableside preparations are a specialty, as is the "bocce ball" dessert. L Mon–Fri; D Mon–Sat.

Costa Del Sol Restaurant
901 Wethersfield Road
Tel: 860-296 1714
costadelsolrestaurant.net **$$$**
Spanish cuisine, with dishes such as paella, garlic soup, and the house special flan, in a pleasant spot near the airport. L Tues–Fri; D Tues–Sun.

Grants Restaurant, Bar and Patisserie
977 Farmington Avenue, West Hartford
Tel: 860-236 1930
billygrant.com **$$–$$$**
Sophisticated Italian/ French fusion fare in one of the city's hottest destinations range from Mom's meatloaf to gorgonzola-encrusted filet mignon. L Mon–Sat; D nightly; Sun brunch.

Max Downtown
185 Asylum Street, Hartford
Tel: 860-522 2530
maxrestaurantgroup.com **$$–$$$**
Upscale power dining. The contemporary menu emphasizes fish, pasta, and meat dishes. The cigar room draws a business crowd. L Mon–Fri; D nightly.

Quaker Diner
319 Park Road, West Hartford
Tel: 860-232 5523 **$**
Restored 1931 diner cooking up "made from scratch" breakfasts and homestyle favorites. B and L daily.

Ivorytown
Copper Beech Inn
46 Main Street
Tel: 860-767 0330/ 888-809 2056
copperbeechinn.com **$$$$**
One of the state's best-known restaurants serves classic French cuisine with studied elegance. Specialties include *moules aux épinards*, *homard à la Provençale*. Jacket and tie. D Tues–Sun.

Lakeville
Morgan's
Interlaken Inn, 74 Interlaken Road, Route 112
Tel: 860-435 9878/ 800-222 2909
interlakeninn.com **$$$**
New American cuisine, with organic/hormone and antibiotic-free ingredients, in the dining room of elegant country inn. B and D daily, L Mon–Fri; Sun brunch.

Litchfield
Village Restaurant
25 West Street
Tel: 860-567 8307 **$–$$**
Ample portions of reasonably priced New England standbys and homemade desserts at this popular local eatery. L and D daily.

West Street Grill
43 West Street (Route 202)
Tel: 860-567 3885
weststreetgrill.com **$$$**
American fare with a note of sophistication in an elegantly finished room decorated in black and

white and splashes of color. L and D daily.

Madison
Café Allegre
Inn at Lafayette, 725 Boston Post Road (Route 1)
Tel: 203-245 7773
allegrecafe.com **$$$**
Once a church meeting house, now an elegant spot for great southern Italian food with a French flair. L and D Tues–Sun.

Manchester
Cavey's Restaurant
45 East Center Street
Tel: 860-643 2751
caveysrestaurant.com **$$$–$$$$**
Two award-winning restaurants under one roof: casual northern Italian menu upstairs and French cuisine in the more formal setting downstairs. D Tues–Sat.

Mystic
Flood Tide Restaurant
The Inn at Mystic, 3 Williams Avenue (Routes 1 and 27)
Tel: 860-536 8140
innatmystic.com **$$$**

Contemporary continental food served with water views. L (in lounge) and D daily; Sun brunch.

Sea Swirl
30 Williams Ave (junction Routes 1 and 27)
Tel: 860-536 3452
seaswirlofmystic.com **$**
Order a plate of the whole belly fried clams, grab a seat at an outdoor picnic table, and watch the sun set. Then have an ice cream cone. L and D in season.

New Haven
Bentara Restaurant
76 Orange Street
Tel: 203-562 2511
bentara.com **$$–$$$**
Authentic Malaysian dishes (hot and spicy) in a tranquil downtown setting. L and D daily off season; L Mon–Fri; D nightly in summer.

Claire's Corner Copia
Chapel Street
Tel: 203-562 3888
clairescornercopia.com **$**
Serving a diverse menu

LEFT: Apricots in Farmington offers riverside dining.
RIGHT: traditional fare at the Griswold Inn, Essex

of organic, gluten-free, light vegetarian dishes, including nachos, pitas, and burritos, since 1975. B, L, D daily.

Frank Pepe's Pizzeria
157 Wooster Street
Tel: 203-865 5762 **$**
Since 1925 a favorite pizza stop, legendary for white clam pie. Be prepared to wait in line. Their sister location, next door (The Spot) is open Wed–Sun. L and D daily.

Ibiza Tapas Café
39 High Street
Tel: 203-865 1933
ibizanewhaven.com **$$–$$$**
Authentic Spanish tapas elevate group grazing to an art. L Thur; D Mon–Sat.

Union League Café
1032 Chapel Street
Tel: 203-562 4299
unionleaguecafe.com
$$$–$$$$
Imaginative contemporary touches to classic bistro fare, with dishes such as roasted Nova Scotia lobster, and wild

mushroom risotto.
L Mon–Fri; D Mon–Sat.

New London
Adrienne
218 Kent Road (Route 7)
Tel: 860-354 6001
adriennerestaurant.com **$$$**
Fine fireside New American dining in a pretty white, 19th-century farmhouse. D Tues–Sat; Sun brunch.

Timothy's at the Lighthouse Inn
6 Guthrie Place
Tel: 860-443 8411/
888-443 8411
lighthouseinn-ct.com
$$–$$$
Traditional American fare in a restored waterfront Victorian mansion. House specialties include crabmeat bisque and homemade pastas (Wed night pasta bar: **$**). L and D daily; Sun brunch.

New Preston
Boulders Inn
Route 45
Tel: 860-868 0541
bouldersinn.com **$$$**

At this inn overlooking Lake Waramaug, the menu changes with the season, but might include chicken breast stuffed with goat cheese, or braised lamb shanks. D Wed–Sat; Sun brunch.

Hopkins Inn
22 Hopkins Road
Tel: 860-868 7295
www.thehopkinsinn.com
$$–$$$
Austrian and Swiss specialties – including sweetbreads – are offered in an 1847 Victorian inn overlooking Lake Waramaug. L Tues–Sat; D Tues–Sun; closed Jan–late March.

Norwalk
Meigas
10 Wall Street
Tel: 203-866 8800
meigasrestaurant.com **$$$**
Tapas, fish and other artfully prepared Spanish dishes. L Tues–Fri; D Tues–Sun.

Noank
Abbott's Lobster in the Rough
117 Pearl Street
Tel: 860-536 7719
abbotts-lobster.com **$–$$**
Classic waterfront lobster shack with "in the rough" counter service and outdoor picnic tables. L and D in season.

The Fisherman
937 Groton Long Point Road
Tel: 860-536 1717
fishermanrestaurant.com
$$–$$$
Seafood, with some creative offerings as well as standard fried platters. Good steaks and a water view, too. L and D daily.

Old Lyme
Bee and Thistle Inn
100 Lyme Street
Tel: 860-434 1667/
800-622 4946
beeandthistleinn.com
$$$–$$$$

Prices for a three-course dinner per person with a half-bottle of house wine:
  $ = under $20
  $$ = $20–45
  $$$ = $45–60
  $$$$ = over $60

Award-winning American cuisine is elegantly served in romantic historic inn. L Wed–Sat; D Wed–Sun; Sun brunch.

Old Lyme Inn
85 Old Lyme Street
Tel: 860-434 2600
oldlymeinn.com **$$$–$$$$**
Creative American dishes served with aplomb in the lovely dining room of a white clapboard 1850s farmhouse in the historic district. D Fri–Sat; grill menu nightly.

Old Saybrook
The Terra Mar Grille
Saybrook Point Inn and Spa, 2 Bridge Street
Tel: 860-388 1111
saybrook.com **$$$–$$$$**
Traditional decor, continental fare with emphasis on fresh fish and prime meats, and lovely water views. Try the blue corn-encrusted oysters. D nightly.

Plantsville
Deli 66
1152 Meriden-Waterbury Rd
Tel: 203-271 2464 **$–$$**
A New York-style deli specializing in corned beef, pastrami, and homemade chicken soup. B and L Mon–Sat.

Ridgefield
Elms Restaurant and Tavern
500 Main Street
Tel: 203-438 9206
elmsinn.com **$$$–$$$$**
Sophisticated American dishes such as pulled wild boar BBQ on Johnnycake and an award-winning wine list in a 1799 Colonial inn. Terrace dining in season.

Salisbury
White Hart Inn
Village Green (Routes 44 and 41)
Tel: 860-435 0030/ 800-832 0041
whitehartinn.com $$$–$$$$
Dishes such as osso bucco (braised lamb shank) served in the Colonial-era Tap Room, the fireplaced Garden Room, and on the porch. B, L, and D in Tap Room and Garden Room; L and D on porch.

South Norwalk Area
Barcelona Restaurant and Wine Bar
63 N Main Street, South Norwalk
Tel: 203-899 0088
barcelonawinebar.com $$
Tapas are on offer at this stylish restaurant and sidewalk café in a converted factory in the SoNo (South Norwalk) district. (Also: Greenwich, West Hartford, and New Haven.) D nightly.

Pasta Nostra
116 Washington Street, South Norwalk
Tel: 203-854 9700 $$
A convivial contemporary Italian café. D Wed–Sat.

Silvermine Tavern
194 Perry Avenue, Norwalk
Tel: 203-847 4558
silverminetavern.com $$–$$$
An historic country inn serves up New England classics beside a mill pond. Live jazz Thur–Sat; buffet dinner Thur. L and D Wed–Sun.

Vernon
Rein's New York-Style Delicatessen
435A Hartford Turnpike, Route 30 (I-84, Exit 65)
Tel: 860-875 1344
reinsdeli.com $
The most authentic deli fare available north of Manhattan. B, L, D daily.

Washington
G.W. Tavern
20 Bee Brook Road, Washington Depot
Tel: 860-868 6633
gwtavern.com $$
A restored colonial tavern honoring the first president with updated New England classics: clam chowder, slow-roasted duck, cherry pie. L and D daily; Sun brunch.

Mayflower Inn
118 Woodbury Road, Route 47
Tel: 860-868 9466
mayflowerinn.com $$$–$$$$
The regional American menu at this Relais and Chateaux country inn includes slow-roasted osso bucco, and Kobe beef carpaccio. You can sit on the terrace overlooking the garden. Lighter menu in the Tap Room. L and D daily.

Westport
Acqua
43 Main Street
Tel: 203-222 8899
acquaofwestport.com $$–$$$
Italian/Mediterranean fare and signature dessert soufflés in a wildly popular, sometimes clamorous, restaurant in a two-story riverside villa. L and D Mon–Sat.

Sakura
680 Post Road East
Tel: 203-222 0802
sakurarestaurant.com $$–$$$
One of Connecticut's favorite sushi spots also serves hibachi-style tableside dishes and a terrific tempura. L Mon–Fri; D nightly.

Woodbury
Good News Café
694 Main Street
Tel: 203-266 4663
good-news-cafe.com $$
Carole Peck uses local bounty to prepare modern American dishes such as onion bundles, and braised veal shanks at her highly acclaimed restaurant. L and D Wed–Mon.

Bars
The Federal Café, 84 Union Place, Hartford. Tel: 860-527 0394. The only snack at one of the city's oldest watering holes is peanuts in the shell, but it remains one of the most popular spots in town for a reasonably-priced pitcher of beer, some darts or pool, or to watch a game.
McKinnon's Irish Pub, 114 Asylum Street, Hartford. Tel: 860-524 8174. Talented Celtic musicians play (no cover) to a mellow crowd on weekends. Fri 4pm–7pm there's a free buffet.

Rudy's Bar & Grill, 372 Elm Street, New Haven. Tel: 860-865 1242 New Belgian owners now offer *frites* with dipping sauces, but they haven't changed the down-home charisma that has made this neighborhood spot a popular hangout for more than three decades. Live music many nights.
Stonewall Tavern, Route 32, Mansfield. Tel: 860-487 9785. A popular spot for both University of Connecticut students and bikers, who turn out for live bands Wed–Sun nights and decently prepared American comfort food.
West Wings, 310 Prospect Avenue, Hartford. Tel: 860-570 9858. Forty-two beers on tap, 40 in the bottle, 28 plasma TV screens (including one in the men's room), and 18 kinds of chicken wings. All this, plus pool tables and dart boards, make this 150-seat bar one of the city's most popular venues.

LEFT: fresh croissants for breakfast.
RIGHT: eating out in South Norwalk's SoNo district.

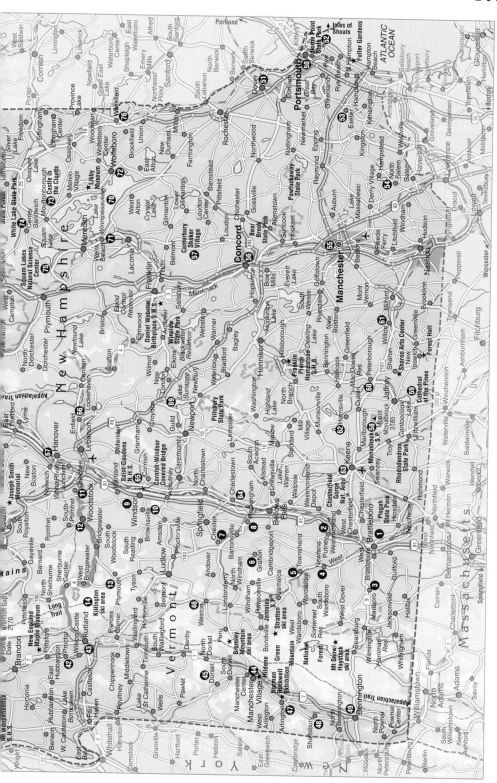

Recommended Restaurants and Bars on pages 300–3

VERMONT

The Green Mountain State is alive with the sound
of leaves crunching under foot; the sight of
red barns and white steeples; the smell of
country lanes and maple sugar boiling

magine New England, and you will
very likely imagine Vermont. When
you round a bend to find a valley
ainted in a thousand shades of green, or
and atop Mount Mansfield to see a quilt
farm and forest rumpled against Lake
hamplain, or drop down from the
ountains into a white village framed in
e glorious colors of autumn, your pre-
nceptions will become reality.

___

RECEDING PAGES: Weathersfield Meeting
ouse. **LEFT:** a farm family.
GHT: sleigh ride near Stowe.

Lakeside retreats

Tourism in Vermont dates to before the
Civil War – Manchester, where President
Abraham Lincoln's wife and children
summered in 1863, was an early resort
town. Vermont lakeside retreats were
popular during the late 19th century, and
there was even a small hotel on top of
Mount Mansfield, the state's highest
peak. The word was out: Vermont was a
splendid place to rusticate.

Vermont may have been able to offer
fresh air, fine scenery, and good fishing,
but what really kicked the state's tourism

Main attractions
BRATTLEBORO
NEWFANE
QUECHEE GORGE
BILLINGS FARM & MUSEUM
KILLINGTON SKI AREA
MONTPELIER
BEN & JERRY'S, WATERBURY
STOWE
THE NORTHEAST KINGDOM
ST JOHNSBURY
LAKE CHAMPLAIN ISLANDS
BURLINGTON
SHELBURNE FARMS
VERMONT COUNTRY STORE,
    WESTON
NORMAN ROCKWELL
    EXHIBITION, ARLINGTON
BENNINGTON

The state in snapshot

Known as: The
Green Mountain
State.
Motto: Freedom
and unity.
Origin of name:
from the French
vert (= green) and *mont* (= mountain).
Entered Union: March 4, 1791, the 14th state.
Capital: Montpelier
Largest city: Burlington
Area: 9,615 sq. miles (24,903 sq. km).
Highest point: Mount Mansfield, 4,393 ft
(1,339 meters).
Highest recorded temperature: 105°F (41°C)
at Vernon in 1911
Population: 621,250 (4.3% of region)
Population density: 65 per sq. mile (26 per
sq. km).
Economy: once agricultural, now relies
increasingly on tourism.
Annual visitors: 7.9 million.
National representation: 2 senators and
1 representative to Congress.
Famous citizens: Ethan Allen, President Calvin
Coolidge, President Chester A. Arthur, Rudy
Vallée, and Admiral George Dewey.

Maple sugar is produced in the Green Mountains.

industry into overdrive was the selling of winter. The ski boom began during the 1930s, when the first mechanical lifts and cut trails appeared. By the early 1970s, dozens of ski areas had given rise to a burgeoning second-home industry, and to new worries over runaway development.

That same era brought an influx of new Vermonters, mostly young people looking for a simpler way of life. The cliché is that they were hippie communards, but the vast majority were tradespeople, artisans, and soon-to-be professionals. What they shared was a sense that they had found someplace special, and that they wanted to keep it that way.

In alliance with progressive natives, the new Vermonters crafted a far-reaching array of environmental regulations, from a ban on highway billboards to controls on development in rural areas. It hasn't all gone down smoothly; there is still considerable chafing between conservative natives and the "flatlanders" whom they feel have taken

over the state. Stop in at a town meetin first week of March, and you might he a good argument or two – usually civ

THE LOWER CONNECTICUT RIVER VALLEY

The long, lazy Connecticut River forr the entire boundary between the states Vermont and New Hampshire. Cover today by a hydroelectric dam, Vermon first permanent settlement – Fort Du mer, founded in 1752 – has been reduc to a mere marker on the shore.

A few miles north, however, **Bratt boro ❶**, the town it was meant to pr tect, enjoyed resort status from 1846 1871, when a local physician parlay its pure springs into a "water cure." the 1960s and '70s, some of the mo dedicated of the back-to-the-land crov settled here, and sunk their roots de into the community.

Some turned their talents to the ar and their works are now displayed **Vermont Artisan Designs & Galle** (106 Main Street), southern Vermon largest arts/crafts gallery. Others dete mined to live off the land, and still s their produce at the summer **farmer**

New England's last frontier

Tucked as it was in a corner of New England precariously close to New France and its Indian allies, Vermont was among the last parts of the region to be settled. Even after the French threat was eliminated, the lands between the Connecticut River and Lake Champlain were uncertain ground, contested by New Hampshire and New York. This is where Ethan Allen and his staunchly independent Green Mountain Boys, an informal militia, fought off "Yorker" surveyors in order to protect the interests of the original settlers. Then Allen's forces turned their attention to repulsing the British during the Revolution.

Even after the war, Vermont was chary about joining the union – it had never been one of the 13 original colonies. For 14 years, beginning in 1777, the Repub-

lic of Vermont, initially known as New Connecticut, stood alone. Not until 1791 did Vermont become the 14th state.

Much of what appeals in Vermont's human-crafted environment – the small farms, the neat villages – harks back to

ABOVE: a 1927 stamp salutes Vermont.

the state's "golden age" between th early federal era and the Civil War. Tho were the peak years of self-sufficie largely based on sheep farming, wh the state's image and character we largely created.

Things began to change in the mid of the century. The 1849 California G Rush lured some young Vermonters fr their farms, and the Civil War lured ma more. "Put the Vermonters ahead a keep the column well closed up," s General John Sedgewick at the Battle Gettysburg; no other state gave as larg share of its sons to the cause of Unic Nor did all the survivors return home: t many of them had heard tales of bet land out west. Between 1865 and 19 Vermont's population declined, thou today it is rising again.

markets on Saturday (by the Route 9 covered bridge) and Wednesday (Co-op Plaza off Route 9) mornings.

The 1938 **Latchis Building** on Main Street, which houses a movie theater and the **Latchis Hotel** (802-254 6300; latchis. com), is one of only two Art Deco buildings in Vermont (the other is in Rutland). The **Brattleboro Museum and Art Center** (tel: 802-257 0124; open Wed–Mon 11am–5pm; entrance fee) is in the Union Railroad Station. A "non-collecting" museum, it hosts changing art exhibits

Kipling's Naulahka

North of the city 2½ miles (4 km), off Route 5, **Naulahka**, the shingle-style manse where Rudyard Kipling wrote the first two *Jungle Books* and *Captains Courageous* in the 1890s, has been restored by Great Britain's Landmark Trust, which rents it by the week (tel: 02-254 6868 in the US, 01628-825925 in the UK; landmarktrust.usa.org). Kipling, an Englishman born in India, built his home here after his honeymoon in 1892, and immediately warmed to the life of a country squire. His grand airs, however, didn't endear him to the locals, and in

1896 when a property dispute with his roguish brother-in-law hit the headlines, destroying his rural idyll, he and his wife fled, never to return.

Putney to Rockingham

A few miles further north on US 5, **Putney ❷** predated the social experiments of the 1960s by a good 150 years: in the early 19th century, it was the site of a short-lived but sensational commune espousing free love *(see margin note)*. The countryside is still populated in part by '60s counterculture types.

Master puppeteers at the **Sandglass Theater** (17 Kimball Hill Road; tel: 802-387 4051; sandglasstheater.org) perform here in their 60-seat theatre as well as at venues throughout the region. Students and professors at the **Yellow Barn Music School and Festival** (63 Main Street; tel: 800-639 3819; yellowbarn.org) perform chamber music concerts throughout July and the first week in August.

Follow US 9 (also known as the Molly Stark Trail) west to **Marlboro ❸** – hilltop home of small, liberal arts **Marlboro College**, which every summer hosts the world-renowned, chamber music **Marl-**

John Humphrey Noyes, a Yale-educated preacher, set up the Putney Association in 1840. His group of three dozen embraced Perfectionism, sharing property, embracing sexual freedom and bringing up children communally. They were soon chased out of town and set up a more durable community in New York State.

BELOW: watching for hawks on Putney Mountain.

Making life easier for snowboarders, Mount Snow uses hundreds of fan guns that combine compressed air and water to create additional snow.

boro Music Festival, founded by the late Rudolf Serkin (book early for tickets; tel: 802-254 2394 in summer; 215-569-4690 rest of year; marlboromusic.org).

A few miles further west at Wilmington, turn north to reach **West Dover**, home to **Mount Snow/Haystack** (tel: 802-464 3333 or 800-245-SNOW; mount snow.com), a behemoth ski area and summer resort. It's a popular spot for hikers and mountain bikers; on weekends throughout the summer, and daily in fall, scenic chairlift rides are available.

Route 30 northwest out of Brattleboro follows the West River, past the 1872 West Dummerston Covered Bridge (there's a fine swimming hole here) to the postcard-perfect town of **Newfane ❹**. Its broad common is lined with shady elms and surrounded by stately Greek Revival public buildings – a white-columned courthouse with Congregational church to match, the luxurious Four Columns Inn, and some worthwhile antique stores. A flea market is held on summer Sundays in a field north of town.

Further up Route 30 the handsome town of **Townshend ❺** has a 2-ac common whose focal point is the 179 Congregational Church. The **Big Blac Bear Shop and Museum** (tel: 802-36 4160) sells stuffed toys made next do at Mary Meyer Stuffed Toys, the state oldest stuffed toy maker. In the fr museum, kids get to play with th exhibits. North on Route 30, Sc Bridge – the state's longest single-sp covered bridge – was built in 1870.

Just past it is the turn for **Townshe Lake Recreation Area** (tel: 802-3 7703; open late May–early Sept dai entrance fee). Created by a dam built the 1960s, it's a fine spot to take a swi

There's another opportunity for swi ming up the road in **Jamaica**, **Jamaica State Park** (off Route 30; 802-874 4600; open late May–Colu bus Day; entrance fee). One trail he leads to a 125-ft (38-meter) waterf

Grafton

About 10 miles (16 km) north of Tov shend on Route 35, **Grafton ❻** i Greek Revival town in an 1840s ti warp: visitors wander about in bliss disbelief, sampling a slice of chedda

the **Grafton Village Cheese Company** (tel: 800-462-3866 or 802-843 2210; open daily), and perhaps claiming a rocker on the porch of the 1801 **Old Tavern at Grafton** (tel: 802-843 2231; old-tavern.com), whose guests have included notables from Thoreau and Kipling to Ulysses S. Grant and Teddy Roosevelt. Once a thriving agricultural center, the town was preserved in the 1960s through the efforts of the Windham Foundation.

There are more than 2,000 acres (800 hectares) of trails at the inn's **Grafton Ponds Nordic Ski and Mountain Bike Center** (783 Townshend Road; tel: 802-843 2400; graftonponds.com).

The **Grafton Historical Society Museum** (147 Main Street; tel: 802-843 010; graftonhistory.org; open Fri–Mon Memorial Day–Columbus Day; daily during foliage season, and by appointment; donation) is housed in a homestead built in 1845 and relates the town's fascinating history. Collections range from soapstone objects to musical instruments.

Chester

Route 35 winds north about 7 miles (11 km) to **Chester** ❼, a curious little strand of Victoriana on the Williams River. An 1850s stone village-within-a-village features 30 homes faced in gneiss ledge-stone, built before the Civil War. The town (pop. 3,000) is a good base for cyclists and boating enthusiasts.

Chester is also the northern terminus for the **Green Mountain Flyer** (54 Depot Street; tel: 800-707 3530 or 802-463 3069; rails-vt.com; open Thur–Sun in summer, daily in fall; fee), a vintage diesel-powered excursion train that journeys 13 miles (21 km) to the southeast in Bellows Falls. Elsewhere in the state, the company operates the Champlain Valley Flyer and the White River Flyer, plus seasonal and holiday excursion trains.

Between the two towns, just off Route 103 in **Rockingham** ❽, is Vermont's oldest unchanged public building, the 1787 Federal-style **Rockingham Meeting House** (tel: 802-463 3964; open Memorial Day weekend–Columbus Day, daily; entrance fee). The **Vermont**

Country Store (tel: 802-463 2224; open daily), headquartered in Weston, has a branch store, along with an 1810 gristmill, on Route 103.

UPPER CONNECTICUT VALLEY

A center of invention during the 19th century, **Windsor** ❾, along with nearby Springfield, became home to Vermont's machine tool industry. The **American Precision Museum** at 196 South Main Street (Route 12 East; tel: 802-674 5781; open late May–Oct daily; entrance fee), is housed in a National Historic Landmark, the 1846 Robbins and Lawrence Armory. It has a fascinating array of the machinery that made "Yankee ingenuity" a byword. A brief visit will yield plenty of information about the American industrial revolution; for diehard paleo-techies, there are plenty of retired machine tools to ponder.

Windsor is also famed as the birthplace of Vermont, because it was here in the **Old Constitution House** (tel: 802-828 3051; open late May–mid-Oct, Sat and Sun, 11am–5pm; entrance fee) that delegates met in 1777 to draw up a constitution for the prickly little republic,

The Green Mountain Flyer has its origins in Vermont's earliest railroads, built from 1843. Rail became important for transporting freight, from milk to lumber, and in the early 20th century up to 16 passenger trains a day traveled through Bellows Falls. The current tourist operation began in 1984.

BELOW: mixed traffic in Grafton.

BELOW: in theory,
Vermont has
enough land to
produce all its food.

which was as wary of the other states as of the Crown. The building is now a museum, worthwhile for those interested a local slant on revolutionary history. Just up the road, the **Cornish Colony Museum** (Old Firehouse Building, 147 Main Street; tel; 802-674 6008; open late May–Oct, Tues–Sat, Sun pm; entrance fee) houses an excellent collection of Maxfield Parrish paintings, as well as works by other artists of the early 20th-century Cornish Colony across the river in New Hampshire.

Just up Main Street, the **Windsor-Cornish Covered Bridge**, spanning the Connecticut River to lovely Cornish, New Hampshire *(see page 318)*, is the longest covered bridge in the United States. Note that the **Saint-Gaudens National Historic Site** *(see page 318)* is just across the bridge in New Hampshire.

North, just off Route 5 in the Windsor Industrial Park, **Harpoon Brewery** offers tours and tastings (Ruth Carney Drive, Windsor Industrial Park; tel: 802-674 5491; 45-minute tours Fri and Sat at 3pm; must be 21 or older). Lunch is served in the outdoor beer garden Tuesday through Saturday. **Simon Pearce Glass** (109 Park Road; tel: 802-674 6280; open daily) h. an outpost (their main store is Quechee; see below), where glass blow ing demonstrations are given.

North to Woodstock

"I live in New Hampshire so I can get better view of Vermont," explained arti Maxfield Parrish from his home in Co nish. He did sneak a considerable pie of that view into most of his painting notably Mount Ascutney, which loom to the southwest of Windsor. **Brownsville** , **Ascutney Mounta Resort** (tel: 800-243 0011; ascutney.con one of the state's major downhill s resorts, offers a full roster of outdo activities in the summer months.

Sixteen miles (26 km) to the nort **White River Junction,** a major cros roads since railroad days, still serves an Amtrak stop and marks the interse tion of Interstates 91 and 89.

A few miles west on Route 4, **Quechee** ⑪, 162-ft (49-meter) de **Quechee Gorge**, "Vermont's Littl Grand Canyon," is best viewed from t bridge which spans it, or from the 0 mile trail at the **Quechee State Pa** (fee). The mile-long gorge is a legacy the last ice age.

In town, Irish artisan Simon Pearce h transformed **The Mill at Quechee** (t 802-295 1470; open daily), an abandon flannel factory, into an inviting compl with a distinctive glassworks. The m sells pottery and furniture, and has delightful restaurant. The sprawli **Quechee Gorge Village** (Route 4, t 802-295 1550) includes the Cab Quechee store (with lots of cheese sa ples), an antiques mall, and several g shops. The **Quechee Polo Cl** (Dewey's Mill Road; tel: 603-443 200 entrance fee) holds matches most Sat days beginning at 2pm from mid-Ju through Labor Day at its field a half-m (1 km) north of Route 4.

Woodstock

Woodstock ⑫, just to the west, was c of the first Vermont towns to be disco ered – and given a high polish – by o

...ders. Upscale shopping sprees along
...e refurbished downtown blocks of
...abot and French streets may have
...placed placid strolls up Mount Tom as
...e fashionable summer pastime, but in
...eneral the enlightened despotism of the
...nancier and philanthropist Laurance
...ockefeller (1910–2004) has preserved
...e tone of the town much as it must
...ve been in the 1930s, when he met his
...ture wife, Mary French, while sum-
...ering here.

A passion for maintaining a graceful
...lance between society and nature has
...ng been the keynote to Woodstock's
...nown. Mary's grandfather, Frederick
...illings, returned from his lucrative law
...actice in San Francisco in the 1890s to
...come a pioneer in reforestation and a
...ealous model farmer. The slopes of
...ount Tom and Mount Peg and the
...stored **Billings Farm and Museum**
...Route 12 East; tel: 802-457 2355;
...lingsfarm.org; open May–Oct daily,
...eekends Nov–Feb; entrance fee) are
...staments to his love for rural Vermont
...d his adherence to the principles of
...'oodstock native George Perkins
...arsh, a linguist, diplomat, and author

of the seminal conservationist tract *Man
and Nature*. Daily life on a late 19th-
century dairy farm is depicted in the
barns and farm house. Children will
enjoy the experience of a working farm,
with plenty of barnyard animals.

In 1998 the Billings family mansion
and its surrounding 500 acres (200
hectares) were bequeathed by Laurance
Rockefeller as the **Marsh-Billings-
Rockefeller National Historical Park**
(Route 12; tel: 802-457 3368; nps.gov/
mabi; mansion tours by advance reservation Memorial Day–Oct; entrance fee;

*The Quechee Polo
Club plays on
Saturdays at 2pm
during the summer.*

BELOW:
updating news
of Woodstock's
cultural attractions.

A country lane near Tunbridge, whose annual agricultural event is grandly known as "Tunbridge World's Fair."

BELOW RIGHT:
the Coolidge
State Historic Site.

grounds open free year-round). This is Vermont's only national park and the only park in the system to concentrate specifically on conservation (one reason why mountain bikes are banned). The Queen Anne mansion houses more than 400 paintings, including a superb collection of Hudson River art. Tours of the grounds are also offered.

Tip: if you plan to visit both the Billings Farm and the Historical Park, purchase a combined ticket good for two days.

For further glimpses of Woodstock's past, visit the **Woodstock Historical Society** headquarters, nine rooms of period furnishings, fine art, clothing, textiles, silver, ceramics, photographs, and early American toys in the 1807 Dana House (Elm Street; tel: 802-457 1822; late June–Columbus Day, Tues–Sat; entrance fee).

The **Woodstock Inn and Resort** (tel: 802-457 1100; woodstockinn.com) on the green is one of the state's finest lodgings, and its Robert Trent Jones golf course and **Suicide Six** ski area (tel: 802-457 6661) offer year-round amusements. On

the other side of the green, a cover bridge leads to Mountain Avenue redoubt of old summer cottages, an park at the base of Mount Tom. Trails the summit overlook a guided floral w through the Rockefeller estate.

The Coolidge homestead

The nation's 30th president was born a is buried at the **President Cal Coolidge State Historic Site** (off Ro 100A; tel: 8092-672 3773; open May–mid Oct daily; entrance fee; v tor center open Mon–Fri year round **Plymouth ⑬**, 15 miles (24 km) sou west of Woodstock. Coolidge (18 1933) was a taciturn man, best reme bered for his remark "The business America is business." *(See page 1*

The site preserves not only "Si Cal's" home, but his entire boyhood lage, including the general store with upstairs office that served as his sum White House, and a barn holding a sup collection of 19th-century agricultu equipment. One of the nation's m authentic presidential sites, this is lau by Vermonters as showing "what life small-town America used to be like."

Why Vermont excels at crafts

With over 1,500 professional artisans, Vermont has more artists and craftspeople per capita than any other state. Thanks in part to a bucolic setting but also to state support – the Vermont Crafts Council in Montpelier has designated three "Vermont State Craft Centers" – shops and galleries exhibit and sell pottery, woodwork, jewelry, textiles, glassware, quilts and anything else you can think of.

Frog Hollow (as each of the State Craft center shops is called, after the original Middlebury location) has locations in Burlington, Manchester, and Middlebury (tel: 802-388 3177). Hundreds of "juried" artisans (those whose work has been judged to be of the highest quality) show their work at these venues.

In summer and fall, large craft fairs are held throughout the state *(see listing in the Travel Tips section)*, and on Memorial Day weekend artists participate in a statewide "Open Studio" weekend. The Vermont Crafts Council (tel: 802-223 3380; www.vermontcrafts.com) publishes a free annual studio and gallery guide, and a calendar of fairs. For full information, see www.vermontcrafts.com.

Killington

North and west via Routes 100 and 4, New England's largest ski area, **Killington** ⑭ (4763 Killington Road; tel: 802-422 3333 or 800-621 6867; killington.com), covers seven peaks and encompasses 200 trails. "The Beast of the East" also ranks top among the Northeast ski resorts for nightlife. With a 4,241-ft (1,296-meter) peak reached by gondola, for sightseers as well as skiers, the resort is active year-round – the skiing often lasts from October through June and then in summer, the area turns into a giant fun park, with 45 miles (72 km) of mountain biking trails, a golf course, an alpine slide, and, at nearby **Pico Peak**, an Adventure Center.

There's a free summer concert series at Killington's Sherburne Memorial Library Thursday evenings in July and August beginning at 6pm. A full schedule of activities is posted on killington.com.

The tiny village of **Strafford** ⑮ was the birthplace of Vermont representative and senator Justin Morrill, author of the 1862 Morrill Acts which established America's system of land grant colleges and universities. He built his **Justin Morrill Homestead** (Route 132; tel: 802-765 4484; open Memorial Day–Labor Day, Sat and Sun 11am–5pm, tours on the hour; entrance fee), a 17-room pink Carpenter Gothic home, between 1848 and 1851. The nearby 1799 **Town House** was built for town meetings and interdenominational church services. Its steeple is one of the most beautiful in Vermont.

Mormon connections

"A man can easily hear strange voices," said Kipling of the lonely Vermont winter, "the Word of God rolling between the dead hills; may see visions and dream dreams…" Joseph Smith, a visionary of another sort who went on to found the Mormon religion, was born a few miles away in **South Royalton** in 1805. Just off Route 14, Mormons maintain the **Joseph Smith Memorial and Birthplace** (Dairy Hill Road; tel: 802-763-7742; open Mon–Sat; Sun pm), with a 38½-ft (11.5-meter) obelisk made from a single block of Barre granite, and a museum. (*See margin note.*)

North of South Royalton on Route 10, four covered bridges span the First Branch of the White River in **Tunbridge**, which hosts the Vermont History Expo each June, and the Tunbridge World's Fair, a decidedly non-glitzy event held every September since 1867.

Brookfield

North on Route 14, the tranquil village of **Brookfield** ⑯ is in the geographical center of the state. In 1812, a 320-ft (98-meter) **Floating Bridge**, supported by 380 tarred barrels, was built across Sunset Lake at the center of town, and an eighth version, in place today, has been declared unsafe and is currently closed to vehicles. It is, however, open to pedestrians and is a popular for fishing. One of the last ice harvests in the east is now the occasion for an annual festival on the lake, held the last Saturday in January. The town's Free Public Library, founded in 1791, is the oldest in Vermont.

To continue on Route 65, follow detour signs for 2.7 miles (4.3 km).

Joseph Smith (1805–44) claimed that God had begun revealing the true nature of Christianity to him when he was 15, and he published these revelations in 1830 as The Book of Mormon. He said he would run for the presidency in 1844, but instead was jailed in Illinois. A mob broke into the jail and shot him dead.

BELOW: the Justin Morrill Homestead.

Rock of Ages

About 10 miles (16 km) to the north, between Brookfield and Barre, is the town of **Graniteville** ⑰, site of the largest granite quarry in the world, the **Rock of Ages Quarry** (Visitors Center, 773 Graniteville Road; tel: 802-476 3119; rockofages.com; visitor center and shuttle tours May–Oct, Mon–Sat daily; entrance fee; free self-guided tours of historic, inactive quarry daily May–Oct).

Mining began soon after the War of 1812, and boomed with the influx of skilled immigrant stoneworkers between 1880 and 1910. Fed up with poor wages and working conditions (many died of silicosis), the granite workers managed to elect a Socialist mayor of Barre – many decades before liberal Burlington was ready to do the same.

Today, the Rock of Ages firm owns nearly all of the Graniteville quarries, which provide the nation with one-third of its memorial stones, offers shuttle tours skirting the fully operational quarry, and a new Cut-in-Stone Center (open Mon–Sat) where visitors can test stoneworkers' tools. There's a granite bowling lane outdoors.

The discovery of granite drove Barre's growth, increasing its population from 2,060 in 1880 to 10,000 by 1894 as immigrants arrived from Italy, Scotland, Spain, Scandinavia, Greece, Lebanon, and Canada. The Italians' militancy over labor practices helped elect a socialist as town mayor in 1916.

BELOW: fall comes to the area around Montpelier.

Barre

Many of the workers in the quarries were Italian immigrants, as evidenced by the names on the headstones at **Hope Cemetery** (off Route 14) in **Barre** ⑱ (pronounced *Barry*). Quarry workers commemorated their own with often touching artwork. Among the standouts: a half-scale racing car, and the life-sized statue of labor leader Elia Corti shot down in 1903 at a Socialist rally

The workers' heritage and politics are much in evidence in downtown **Barre**. The larger-than-life statue of a mustachioed Italian stonecutter at the corner of North Main Street and Maple Avenue looks toward Granite Street, site of the National Historic Landmark, Socialist headquarters **Old Labor Hall** now being renovated by the Barre Historical Society (46 Granite Street; tel: 802-476 0567).

Barre's 1891 **Spaulding Graded School**, home to the Vermont Historical Society's **Vermont History Center** (60 Washington Street; tel: 802-479 8500, open Tues–Fri, and second Sat of each month) reflects in its Romanesque grandeur the most prosperous days of the granite industry. The granite **Robert Burns Memorial** in front of the school was erected in 1899 by Scots, who also worked in the quarries.

Montpelier

Home to about 8,200 people, **Montpelier** ⑲ (pronounced *Mont-peel-yer*) the nation's smallest state capital. The lively little downtown is dominated by the gold-leaf dome of the **Vermont State House** (State Street; tel: 802-828 2228 or 828-0386; tours July–Oct Mon–Fri 10am–3:30pm; Sat 11am–2:30pm; self-guided tours Mon–Sat 8:30am–4:30pm; audio tours available at office).

Initially, Vermont's capital rotated through the state, but, with the completion of the original nine-sided building in 1808, the seat of power settled here. When an imposing stone successor, built in 1838, was gutted by fire in 1857, the Doric portico and native granite walls withstood the flames to form a shell for the present structure. The Senate Chamber

ber is rightfully considered the most beautiful room in the state.

The Italianate Pavilion Building replicates a hotel – in its day a virtual dormitory for legislators – that stood on this site adjacent to the State House. The new structure houses government offices and the **Vermont Historical Society & Museum** (109 State Street; tel: 802-828 2291; vermonthistory.org; open Tues–Sat; May–Oct, also Sun pm; entrance fee). The extensively renovated museum contains an attractively presented collection of Vermont artifacts.

Montpelier is home to the **New England Culinary Institute**, whose students and teachers staff two excellent dining spots on Main Street – the **Main Street Grill and Bar** (118 Main Street; tel: 802-223 3188; open for lunch Tues–Sat; dinner Tues–Sun; and Sat and Sun brunch buffet) and **La Brioche Bakery and Cafe** across the street, open for breakfast and lunch daily.

The **City Hall Arts Center** (39 Main Street) is the venue for numerous events throughout the year, including productions of the **Lost Nation Theatre** (tel: 802-229 0492; lostnationtheatre.org).

North out of town via Main Street for 2½ miles (4 km), the **Morse Farm Sugar Works** (1168 County Road; tel: 800-242 2740; open daily), more than 200 years old, offers free tours of the sugar house, tastings of maple products, and sugar-on-snow (warm maple syrup poured over snow or ice shavings).

Sugarbush to Waterbury

Some 20 miles (32 km) west of Montpelier, the Green Mountain range attains heady heights that tempt skiers – as well as mountain climbers and bikers. South of I-89, the Mad River Valley towns of **Waitsfield** ⓴ and **Warren** support two ski areas, the rustic, but challenging **Mad River Glen** (madriverglen.com), opened in 1948 and run by a cooperative, and the more developed and extensive **Sugarbush** (sugarbush.com), opened in 1958. Both towns are full of the pleasures – inviting restaurants and cozy inns – that outdoors enthusiasts enjoy in off-hours.

Spectators are welcome at the **Sugarbush Polo Club (Carpenter Field, East Munger Street;** tel: 802-496 8938 for information), which plays Wed at 5pm (rain date Thur) in summer; the original

The "folk art" statue atop the State House is the Roman goddess of agriculture, Ceres. It was carved in 1938 by the 87-year-old Dwight Dwinell, the building's chief usher.

BELOW: Vermont State House.

Mount Mansfield, Vermont's highest peak, has hiking trails and ski slopes, and alpine tundra survives here from the ice ages.

BELOW:
hot-air balloon festival at Stowe.

players, in 1962, used ski poles and a volleyball).

To get an unusual perspective on the countryside, consider a soaring excursion in a sailplane towed by **Sugarbush Soaring** (Warren-Sugarbush Airport, Route 100; tel: 802-496 2290; flights May–Oct), or continue north on Route 100 to the **Vermont Icelandic Horse Farm** (3061 North Fayston Road, Fayston; tel: 802-496 7141), where you can take a half or full-day trail ride or a two-to-six day trek.

For a more conventional scenic tour, head for one of the nearby "gaps" (glacially-formed passes through the mountains). The road to **Lincoln Gap** begins on Route 100 near Warren Village and climbs for 3 miles (5 km) to 2,424 ft (739 meters) before descending into tiny Lincoln. The road through **Appalachian Gap** begins on Route 17 and winds past Mad River Glen to the 2,365-ft (721-meter) crest before its descent into the Champlain Valley (note: gaps can't accommodate trailers, and Lincoln Gap is closed in winter).

Waterbury

Fourteen miles (22 km) north via Route 100, in **Waterbury ㉑**, a pair of "flatlander" entrepreneurs turned this famous dairy state into ice cream heaven. **The Ben & Jerry's Homemade Ice Cream Factory** offers tours and tastings daily (tours daily; tel: 866-258 6877 for schedule; benjerry.com; entrance fee for tour). If you want to actually see ice cream being made, schedule a weekday visit. The company's "small is beautiful" image was seriously dented when Ben Cohen and Jerry Greenfield sold out in 2000 to the multinational giant Unilever.

Just up the road, stop for samples of the "Best Cheddar in the World" at the **Cabot Annex Store complex** (2653 Waterbury-Stowe Road; tel: 802-244 6334; open daily). Lake Champlain Chocolates, Vermont Teddy Bear and Snow Farm Winery also have stores here. Farther north, watch cider being pressed, and browse through the huge gift shop at the **Cold Hollow Cider Mill** (3600 Waterbury-Stowe Road; tel: 800-327 7537; open daily).

The headquarters of the **Green Mountain Club** (4711 Waterbury Road; tel 802-244 7037; greenmountainclub.org Memorial Day–Labor Day, Mon–Sat rest of year, Mon–Fri) is the best place to pick up information about the **Long Trail**, Vermont's "footpath in the wilderness," which follows the ridges of the Green Mountains for 270 miles (430 km from the Massachusetts border to the Canadian line.

Stowe

In **Stowe ㉒**, the **Ski Museum** (5 South Main Street; tel: 802-253-9911; vermont skimuseum.org; open Wed–Mon daily entrance fee) chronicles the development of skiing in Vermont as well as of the sport's ever-changing technology, from the days of wooden skis and leather boots to the present. But even before skiing arrived in the 1930s, the town enjoyed a reputation as a stylish summer place. Summer or winter, sports opportunities abound, particularly along the **Stowe Recreation Path**. Ideally suited

or skiers, cyclists, skaters, wheelchair acers, runners, walkers, and stroller ushers, the 5.3-mile (8.5-km) paved ath skirts the West Branch river from own all the way out to the **Topnotch esort and Spa** (topnotchresort.com), assing a number of appealing inns, estaurants, and shops en route. Other otable Stowe inns, such as the Austrian-yle **Trapp Family Lodge** (trappfamily om), founded by the Baroness Maria on Trapp of *Sound of Music* fame (*see ox below*). The 2,700-acre (1,100-ectare) resort has Vermont's oldest ross-country ski trail system, part of one f the biggest networks in New England. On **Mount Mansfield** ㉓ Ralph Valdo Emerson had a bracing vacation a 1823 at the Summit House, where, he ecounts, his "whole party climbed to the op of the [mountain's] nose and watched e sun rise over the top of the White Mountains of New Hampshire."

Hikers still favor this craggy human rofile, and two shortcuts at the **Stowe Mountain Resort** (Route 108; tel: 800-53 4754; stowe.com) are popular: the 4½-ile (7.5-km) **Auto Road** (fee), a entury-old toll road that offers an easy

way to ascend to the "nose," and an eight-passenger gondola (fee) zips to 3,625 ft, close to the 4,393-ft (1,338-meter) "chin," the state's highest point.

On the right is **Stowe Mountain Lodge** (7412 Mountain Road; tel: 802-253 3560 or 888-478 6938), the resort's luxury hotel/home ownership development. Nearby is an alpine slide and climbing wall. The handsome Cliff House at the upper terminus of the gondola serves an elegant lunch along with spectacular views when the lift is operating.

Other big summertime draws are the hot air balloon festival and a midsummer classic car rally; in mid-January, during the Stowe Winter Carnival, the whole town parties (*see margin caption*).

Over Smugglers Notch

The nearby ski area at **Smuggler's Notch Resort** ㉔ (Route 108 South; tel: 800-451 8752 or 802-644 8851; smuggs .com) was so named for its role during the War of 1812 when trade with Canada was forbidden. Wintertime visitors hoping to fit in a visit are in for a surprise – and a drive: the connecting road from Stowe is closed in winter, and those

Stowe's winter carnival, first held in 1921, is now a major nine-day fair in late January and early February. Events include a range of competitive sports (including snow golf and snow volleyball), ice carving, and "the world's coldest parade." For details, check stowewinter carnival.com

Climb every mountain: the tuneful saga of Maria von Trapp

Maria Augusta Kutschera was born on a train in Austria in 1905. After a lonely childhood, she was sent to be governess to a sickly daughter of a retired naval captain, Georg von Trapp. In 1927, as in the best romances, she married the captain. In 1938 the entire family – by this time Maria was pregnant with their tenth child – fled from the Nazis across the Alps into Italy.

As poor refugees, they tried to earn a living by singing and, while touring the US in 1939, they discovered Stowe, Vermont. Because it reminded them of home, they used their savings of $1,000 to buy an old farm. In 1947 they set up the Trapp Family Music Camp and later added a lodge to accommodate guests. Maria told the family's story in a book, published in 1949. Later she sold the film rights for just

ABOVE: Maria von Trapp and some of the clan at the Trapp Family Lodge in 1965.

$9,000 to a German producer, who made *Die Trapp Familie*. This meant she made little money from the lucrative Rodgers and Hammerstein Broadway version, *The Sound of Music*. When 20th Century Fox later adapted the musical, it ignored her demands for a more realistic portrayal of

her family, and she wasn't even invited to the film's premiere in 1965.

After spending some time on missionary work in the South Pacific, Maria returned to Stowe, where she died in 1987. She lies in the family cemetery next to the Lodge.

who've traveled it in summer will understand why. Hundred-foot cliffs and giant boulders crowd the narrow, winding roadway – a popular staging point for mountaintop hikes.

On the other side, "Smuggs" offers downhill skiing on three peaks, as well as cross-country trails, and is popular with families for its well-thought-out children's programs. In summer the attraction is hiking, horseback riding, and an assortment of water slides.

The town closest to the resort, **Jeffersonville**, has a restaurant, the historic Smugglers Notch Inn (smuggsinn .com), and a well-equipped general store with a liquor outlet.

About 8 miles (13 km) east on Route 15, the town of **Johnson**  has been all but taken over by the **Vermont Studio Center**, a working retreat for artists that attracts many prominent instructors. **Johnson Woolen Mills** (Main Street; tel: 877-635 9665; open daily) has been manufacturing the green woolen work pants preferred by Vermont farmers and loggers since 1842, and its retail store is filled with sturdy outerwear. The **Forget-**

The library in St Johnsbury's Athenaeum.

BELOW:
St Johnsbury, with a population close to 8,000, is known locally as St Jay.

Me-Not Shop (Route 15; tel: 802 63 2335; open daily) to the west of town with deeply discounted clothing, is must-stop for bargain hunters.

The Northeast Kingdom

North of Route 15 is a remote and remarkable region. The **Northeast Kingdom** is nearly 2,000-sq.-mile (over 5,000-sq.-km) swath of crystal lakes and deep forests, region known for greater natural wealth and homegrown poverty than any other area in the state. The counties of Caledonia, Essex and Orleans are sparsely populated and make up Vermont's least industrialized area. *Where the Rivers Run North* is the title Orleans writer Howard Frank Mosher gave his 1978 collection of short stories in honor of a region known for its backwater quirks.

Continue south on Route 15, through Morrisville and Hardwick, to **Cabot** and the turn-off for the **Cabot Creamery Co-operative** (2878 Main Street; tel: 800-837 4261; open June–Oct, daily; Nov–May, Mon–Sat; cheese isn't made every day; fee). Founded in 1919, the co-op draws on some 500 member farms for the milk that goes into its award-winning

cheddar cheese. Factory tours include cheese tastings – a good way to select picnic favourites.

St Johnsbury

The city of **St Johnsbury** ㉖, the largest community in northeastern Vermont, remains a vibrant pocket of Victorian charm. From the bank buildings downtown to the Fairbanks mansion on the Plains overlooking the valley, the stamp of architect Lambert Packard (1832–1906) and his wealthy patrons is visible everywhere. Thaddeus Fairbanks started making the world's first platform scale here in the 1830s, and he and his sons were great civic benefactors.

The handsome, Second Empire **St Johnsbury Athenaeum** (1171 Main Street; tel: 802-748 8291; open Mon–Sat; Mon and Wed till 8pm) built in 1871–73, houses both the city library and an art gallery (open library hours; fee) dominated by the huge skylit panorama *Domes of the Yosemite* by artist Albert Bierstadt. This is one of the oldest intact art collections in the country ("Welcome to the nineteenth century," reads a sign at the entrance) and one of the most inviting.

The Romanesque **Fairbanks Museum and Planetarium** is at Main and Prospect streets (tel: 802-748 2372; open Mon–Sat, Sun pm mid-April–mid-Oct; rest of year closed Mon; planetarium shows July and Aug, daily at 1:30pm; Sept–June, weekends at 1:30pm; entrance fee). With more than 4,500 stuffed birds, mammals and reptiles, old toys, exotica from around the globe, local history displays, a children's activity room, and a vintage planetarium, the museum, built by the Fairbanks family in 1890, is a temple to Victorian curiosity. Often considered a bit musty, it's planning a major modernization.

East out of downtown St Johnsbury on route 2, watch for the sign for **Stephen Huneck's Dog Mountain** (143 Parks Road off Spaulding Road; tel: 800-449 2580), where the well-known artist and woodcarver has created a chapel to memorialize man's best departed friends (dogs, of course, are welcome). He also maintains a gallery here.

Nearby, visit the museum at **Maple Grove Farms** (1052 Portland Street, Route 2; tel: 802-748 5141; tours Mon–Fri 8am–2pm; fee) to learn how syrup is made, and then take a 15-minute tour of the factory where specialty products, including maple candy, are created.

East Burke

About 10 miles (6 km) north of St Johnsbury, **Burke Mountain Ski Area** (tel: 802-626 3322; skiburke.com) in **East Burke** ㉗ offers challenging downhill trails. **Kingdom Trails** (Route 114; tel: 802-626 0737; kingdomtrails.org; fee), whose welcome center (open daily spring, summer, and fall) is in town behind Bailey & Burke Store, has more than 100 miles (160 km) of mountain biking trails (cross-country skiing and snowshoeing in winter). **East Burke Sports** (tel: 802-626 3215), across the street from the welcome center, rents bikes.

Around St Johnsbury

West and north of St. Johnsbury via routes 15 and 16, **Greensboro** on Caspian Lake, is a peaceful retreat long

Stained glass in the chapel at Stephen Huneck's Dog Mountain.

BELOW: Stephen Huneck's chapel comes complete with a dog flap.

BELOW:
a hay ride near
Burke Mountain.

favored by writers, academics, and professionals. **Willey's Store** – the heart of the tiny village – dispenses local information and carries an astounding inventory ranging from boots to Beaujolais to the *New York Times*.

A few miles to the north, **the Craftsburys** begin. There are three: East Craftsbury, Craftsbury, and the Shangri-La of Vermont villages, **Craftsbury Common ㉘**, a tidy collection of beautifully preserved, 19th-century homes surrounding a town green on a ridge overlooking the valley.

The area is a magnet for serious athletes – the **Craftsbury Outdoor Center** (535 Lost Nation Road; tel: 802-586 7767; craftsbury.com) offers dormitory-style accommodations, family-style meals, and year-round instruction in a variety of sports, including sculling and running.

Back toward I-91, in **Glover ㉙** the **Bread & Puppet Theater Museum** (Route 122; tel: 802-525 3031; breadand puppet.org; open June–Nov 1 daily 10am–6pm; donation) is home base for an amazing collection of huge and fantastical creatures created by German immigrant Peter Schumann *(see margin note)* to illustrate

the horrors of war and wonders of life. They perform many Sunday afternoons throughout the summer: check their website for the schedule.

Further north, off I-91, is another village that feels as if it's in a time warp. **Brownington ㉚**, a thriving community in the early 1800s when the Boston–Montreal stage stopped here, is best known for its elegant old homes and the **Old Stone House Museum** (off Route 58; tel 802-754 2022; open mid May–mid-Oct, Wed–Sun 11am–5pm; entrance fee). Its collection of local miscellania is housed in the former county grammar school, built in 1827–30 by "Uncle" Alexander Twilight. He is claimed by Middlebury College as America's first black college graduate, Class of 1823, and said to be the first black legislator in the nation. The remarkable building itself is more of an attraction than the exhibits.

Newport

Straddling the US-Canadian border, 30 mile long (48-km) **Lake Memphrema gog** snakes between steep wooded hills. **Newport ㉛**, the "Border City" at the southern end of the lake," is noted for it

easy mingle of Canadian day-trippers, locals, and sports fishermen in search of trout and landlocked salmon. There is a lovely boardwalk along the waterfront. **Louis Garneau USA** (1352 East Main Street; tel: 802-334 7346), a manufacturer of cycling clothing and accessories, has an outlet store here. **Newport Marine Services** (197 Farrant Point; tel: 802-334 5911) rents pontoon boats on the lake; **Up the Creek Paddle Sports** (tel: 802-673 9995) rents canoes and kayaks for exploring the lake and the large **South Bay Wildlife Management Area**. Be sure to obey border regulations if you cross into Canada, where the lakeside town of Magog is attractive.

About 20 miles (32 km) to the west, Route 242 climbs to the ski area of **Jay Peak** 32 (tel: 802-988 2611 or 800-451 4449 out of area; jaypeakresort.com), where an aerial tramway transports skiers, foliage peepers and summer sightseers to its 3,861-ft (1,177-meter) summit. The resort also has an 18-hole championship golf course. The views into Canada are magnificent, and the mountain receives Vermont's greatest snowfalls. Look for great changes here in the next few years as new owners upgrade facilities.

The northwestern corner

Vermont's northwestern corner is defined by the Canadian border and the jagged, picturesque shoreline of Lake Champlain. The Vermont "mainland" here is gently rolling dairy country, growing flatter and more open as it nears the border and the great alluvial plain of the St Lawrence River. The big lake is bisected here by the Alburg peninsula descending from Quebec (the town of Alburg is connected to the rest of the US only by a causeway) and by a 22-mile (35-km) skein of islands, likewise linked by bridges and causeways.

This is where Samuel de Champlain (567-1635) first ventured out upon the waters that would bear his name; where Iroquois raiders canoed north via Lake Champlain's outlet, the Richelieu River, to terrorize early French settlements, and where bootleggers' speedboats barreled

south to the thirsty speakeasies of Prohibition days. Such excitement is long past, and today's northwest corner is one of Vermont's most enticing watery playlands.

Lake Champlain Islands

The **Lake Champlain Islands** 33 are strewn with arcadian preserves, lakeshore drives and sleepy little towns. Several state parks have fine-sand swimming beaches, including **Sand Bar** (Route 2; Milton; tel: 802-893 2825; open Memorial Day–Labor Day; entrance fee) and **Alburg Dunes** (off Route 129, Alburg; tel: 802-796 4170; open Memorial Day–Labor Day; entrance fee).

South Hero, roughly on the same latitude as Bordeaux, France, is home to Vermont's first winery, **Snow Farm Vineyard** (190 West Shore Road; tel: 802-372 9463; snowfarm.com; tasting room and tours May–Dec). You can bring a picnic and enjoy a free concert under the stars at the farm's Thursday evening Music in the Vineyard concert series, mid-June–late Aug.

Turn onto South Street to visit **Allen-**

Ice windsurfing on the frozen margins of Lake Champlain. In some years, the big lake freezes entirely across its 10-mile (16-km) width at Burlington.

BELOW: Fourth of July parades are a highlight in the state's small towns.

holm **Farms** and **Hackett's Orchards**, where visitors can pick their own apples in the fall.

Food, fiber, and crafts are highlights of the farmers' markets held June–Oct, Wed 4pm–7pm on Route 2 in South Hero, and Saturdays 10am–2pm at **St Joseph's Church** on **Grand Isle**.

Grand Isle is also home to the circa 1783 **Hyde Cabin** (Route 2; open late May–mid-Oct, Thur–Mon 11am–5pm; fee), one of the nation's oldest. Next to it is the 1814 **Corners Schoolhouse**.

The Vermont Shakespeare Company (tel: 877-874 1911) performs at **North Hero's Knight Point State Park** (tel: 802-372 8389).

Driftwood Tours (tel: 802-373 0022) gives tours of Lake Champlain from its home base at the **North Hero House** (tel: 888-525 3644; northherohouse.com), one of the island's finest inns.

On **Isle La Motte** "the oldest coral reef in the world" was left behind 10,000 years ago, when the Atlantic covered the Champlain Valley; the formations are visible at a preserve on the West Shore Road. **St Anne's Shrine** (West Shore Road; tel: 802-928 3362; open mid-

May–mid-Oct, daily) honors America's first French settlement (1664).

Swanton

East on Route 78 in **Swanton** ③, more than 201 avian species, including ospreys and blue heron, have been identified at the 6,345-acre (2,568-hectare) **Missisquoi National Wildlife Refuge** (headquarters on Route 78; tel: 802-868 4781). Swanton is home to many of the Abenaki people. The **Abenaki Tribal Museum** (100 Grand Avenue; tel: 802-686 2559 or 868 3808; usually open Mon–Fri, but call ahead) also serves as a cultural center and clearing-house of information on the various powwows throughout New England (powwowschedule.com).

St Albans

For many years **St Albans** ③, 10 mile (16 km) south on Route 7, was head quarters of the Central Vermont Railway and its glory days are reflected in its fine town green, imposing brick buildings and handsome Victorian homes. S Albans was the scene of the Civil War most northerly skirmish: in 1864 a ban of Confederates infiltrated the town

TIP

Lake Champlain offers great scope for cruises. You can take a one-hour sea voyage (each way) on the Lake Champlain Ferry (tel: 802-864 9804; ferries.com) which sails to Port Henry, NY, from Burlington's King Street dock. The 65-ft *Moonlight Lady* has overnight voyages, including a gourmet wine cruise (tel: 802-863 3350; vermont discoverycruises.com

BELOW: farming chores in South Hero. **RIGHT:** a local farmers' market.

Recommended Restaurants and Bars on pages 300–3

bbed the banks and hightailed it to anada. There they were caught and ought to trial; however, their exploits ere excused as "legitimate" acts of war. The city's history is ably recounted in xhibits at the **St Albans Historical luseum** (corner Church and Bishop treets; tel: 802-527 7933; open May– id-Oct, Tues–Sat pm; entrance fee).

urlington and environs

The most miserable of one-horse wns," complained the young wife of an rmy recruiting officer stationed here in e 1840s. "Startling incidents never ccur in Burlington. None ever occurred ere, and none probably ever will." hings have livened up along "New Eng- nd's West Coast" since then. By the ivil War, fiercely competitive steamboat nes and a busy lumber trade were turn- g **Burlington ❸** into a plucky little land port of entry. By 1900, the harves were teeming with businessmen, ekers of pleasure and ships' crews.

Today, trendy restaurants and the vely **Church Street Marketplace**, a edestrian mall, have further improved urlington's outlook. But the view remains the same. From Battery Park or the Cliffs, the sunset over Lake Champlain and the Adirondacks is still – as novelist William Dean Howells (1837–1920) maintained – "superior to the evening view over the Bay of Naples," and the old workaday waterfront has been reborn with a park, bike path, marina, and sailboat rentals.

A growing influx of industry, notably IBM, and the new metropoli- tan tone mingle to make the core of Vermont's "Queen City" (population 40,000) a commercial and cultural nexus that keeps turning up on polls as being one of the US's "most liv- able cities." Thanks in part to the pres- ence of the University of Vermont (called "UVM" for its Latin name, *Universitas Viridis Montis*, University of the Green Mountains), the city enjoys a year-round array of cultural events, including annual Mozart and jazz festivals.

The **Flynn Center for the Performing Arts Ⓐ**, a 1930 Art Deco movie palace on Main Street, hosts an impressive line- up of dance, music and theater (153 Main Street; tel: 802-652-4500; flynncenter.org).

Bronze statue of Civil War General William W. Wells in Burling- ton's Battery Park. After the war, Wells (1837–92) moved to Burlington and became one of its most prominent businessmen.

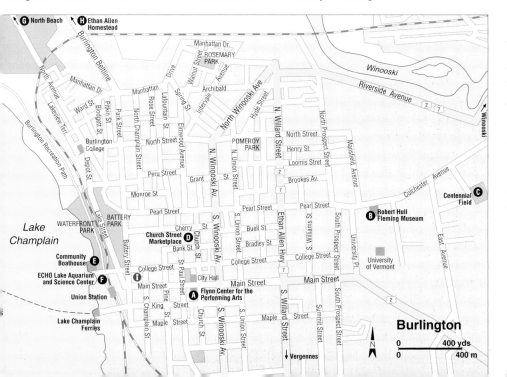

Church Street Marketplace in Burlington, showing the First Unitarian Universalist Society church.

BELOW: Ethan Allen Homestead.

Most of the city's activity is concentrated between the UVM campus and the bustling waterfront. Many of the buildings on and surrounding the campus are architectural gems. The university offers tours (tel: 802-656 3370 for schedule). European and American paintings are displayed in the school's **Robert Hull Fleming Museum** Ⓑ (61 Colchester Avenue; tel: 802-656 2090; open May–Labor Day Tues–Sun pm; Labor Day–April Tues–Fri 9am–4pm and Sat & Sun pm; closed mid-Dec–mid-Jan; entrance fee). It includes works by painters of the Hudson River School as well as Sargent, Homer and Fragonard.

The Vermont Lake Monsters, a Washington Nationals Farm Club, plays home games at UVM's **Centennial Field** Ⓒ throughout the summer.

Church Street Marketplace Ⓓ, in the heart of downtown, is a lively four-block promenade lined with galleries, shops and restaurants. At the waterfront, visitors can go for a sunset sail or a lake excursion, and or dine at the Splash Café at the **Community Boathouse** Ⓔ (tel:

877-964 4858); rent a sailboat at nearby **Lake Champlain Commun Sailing Center** (tel 802-864 2499; h aboard a ferry for a lovely day trip scenic Essex, New York, or take a str along the **Burlington Recreation Pa**

The lakeside **ECHO Lake Aquariu and Science Center** Ⓕ (1 College Stre 802-864 1848; echovermont.org; open da 10am–5pm; entrance fee) uses hands-exhibits to explore the history and ec ogy of the Lake Champlain region.

Nearby is **Union Station**, where y hop aboard the **Champlain Valley Fly** (tel: 802-463 3069; rails-vt.com).

On Burlington's northern outskir near the bike path, **North Beach** Ⓖ (Institute Road; tel: 802-852 0942; f has a sandy beach, snack bar, and char ing rooms.

Nearby, off Route 127, the **Eth Allen Homestead** Ⓗ (tel: 802-865 45. open late May–Labor Day for guid tours Fri and Sat; Sun pm; off seaso limited self-guided tour; entrance fe with its restored 1787 farmhouse, w the home of Vermont's Revolutiona hero *(see margin note, facing pag* There's an excellent exhibit on the stat

Recommended Restaurants and Bars on pages 300–3

story and miles of walking trails along the Winooski River.

In nearby **Winooski**, **St Michael's Playhouse** (Allen Street, Route 15; tel: 02-654 2000), on the campus of Saint Michael's College, has mounted professional summer theater shows since 1951.

Continue up Route 15 to **Essex** and the **Essex Outlet Mall** (21 Essex Way; tel: 02-657 2777). National names including Orvis, Brooks Brothers, and Polo Ralph Lauren have outposts here. There's also a cinema multiplex.

Shelburne

Head south out of Burlington to **Shelburne** ❸, home to a number of attractions including **Vermont Teddy Bear** (6655 Shelburne Road; tel: 800-985 001; open daily), where you can take a short tour of the factory (weekdays) and then create your own bear.

A short distance up Route 7 is one of Vermont's major destinations, **Shelburne Museum** (tel: 802-985 3346; shelburne museum.org; open mid-May–late Oct, daily; late-Oct–mid-May but hours can vary, guided tour of selected buildings daily at 1 pm; entrance fee). This beauti-

fully assembled 45-acre (18-hectare) complex reflects the tastes of one very passionate and well-funded collector. Electra Havemeyer Webb (1888–1960) developed an eye for Americana and folk art long before anyone else was paying attention, and managed to amass 80,000 exemplary objects – 37 buildings full, plus some train cars, a carousel and a Lake Champlain side-wheeler, the *Ticonderoga*. It takes more than a casual stroll to do the collection justice; hence admission, though pricey, is good for two days.

Just south of the museum, you can learn about the art of winemaking Vermont-style at **Shelburne Vineyard Winery and Tasting Room** (6308 Shelburne Road, Route 7; tel: 802-734 8700); the grapes are grown right at Shelburne Farms.

Another Shelburne landmark is the Webbs' 100-room Queen Anne-style "cottage" (now an inn and restaurant) on the lake. Its surrounding estate was carved from 22 lakeside farms by Frederick Law Olmsted, designer of New York City's Central Park. This 1,400-acre (570-hectare) property, **Shelburne Farms** (off Route 7; tel: 802-985-8686; shelburnefarms.org; visitor center and

Vermont hero Ethan Allen (1738–89) and his Green Mountain Boys resisted the attempts of New York and New Hampshire to gain control of the region. With Benedict Arnold, he captured Fort Ticonderoga in 1775, but soon after was jailed by the British for three years. He died two years before Vermont became a state.

LEFT: going nowhere – the *Ticonderoga* on dry land.
BELOW: the Shelburne Museum's Round Barn visitor center.

Taking aim at the Lake Champlain Maritime Museum.

BELOW: kayaking on Lake Champlain.

grounds open year-round; guided tours daily mid-May– late Oct), is now a National Historic Landmark. It is a model ecological farmstead with an award-winning cheese-making facility, extensive grounds, and a children's farmyard. The Webb mansion offers superb accommodations and dining throughout the summer.

Charlotte ㊳, 6 miles (10 km) south of Shelburne, is home to the unusual **Vermont Wildflower Farm,** a 6-acre (2.5-hectare) preserve and learning center that offers delightful strolling (Route 7; tel: 802-425 3641; open Apr–Oct daily; entrance fee to gardens).

Charlotte is also a Lake Champlain crossing point; a ferry to the charming little town of Essex, New York operates from spring to late autumn.

Quakers, farmers, abolitionists, authors, and artists – four generations of one family – lived in **Ferrisburg** at what is now the **Rokeby Museum** (4337 Route 7; tel: 802-877 3406; open mid-May–mid-Oct,

Thur–Sun by guided tours only at 11am, 12:30 pm, and 2pm; entrance fee). The museum tells the story of the family, including author Rowland Robinson (1833–1900), and recreates rural farm life in Vermont from 1790 to 1961.

Maritime attractions

Lake Champlain's maritime traditions are preserved just west of **Vergennes** the **Lake Champlain Maritime Museum ㊴** (4472 Basin Harbor Road; tel: 802-475 2022; lcmm.org; open late May–Oct, daily; entrance fee). The museum, which conserves artifacts brought up from the lake bottom, chronicles its military, mercantile and recreational history with hands-on exhibits, including a replica of the Revolutionary War gunboat *Philadelphia II*.

The **Basin Harbor Club** (4800 Basin Harbor Road; tel: 802-475 2311) next to the museum, is a classic and elegant lakefront family resort.

Vermont spawned the world-famous Morgan horse, a barrel-chested steed which, as one celebrant boasted, "can out run, outpull, and outlast any other breed just as you would expect a Vermont horse

to do." The **UVM Morgan Horse Farm**, off Route 23 in the village of **Weybridge**, is a working farm with training demonstrations and tours (off Route 23; tel: 802-388 2011; open May–Oct daily, tours on the hour; entrance fee).

Middlebury ㊵, just southeast of Weybridge or directly down Route 7 for 13 miles (21 km) from Vergennes, is the ideal college town, a verdant campus of grand, well-spaced 19th-century buildings, accompanied by a lively community of shops and restaurants. The traditional arts of Vermont are highlighted at the **Vermont Folklife Center** (88 Main Street; tel: 802-388 4964; gallery open Tues–Sat). A superb collection of late 18th and 19th-century Vermontiana, is housed in the **Henry Sheldon Museum of Vermont History** (1 Park Street; tel: 802-388 2117; open Tues–Sat; entrance fee).

The **Vermont State Craft Center at Frog Hollow** (1 Mill St, tel: 802-388 3177; open Mon–Sat; Sun pm) showcases and sells work by Vermont artisans (*see box, page 278*). Collections at the **Middlebury College Museum of Art** (Route 30 South; tel: 802-443 5007; open Mon–Fri pm; some Sats am) include Asian art, photography, 19th-century American and European paintings, and contemporary prints.

In search of Robert Frost

The poet Robert Frost spent his summers writing in a log cabin 7 miles (11 km) east on Route 125 in **Ripton** ㊶, in the northern section of the 400,000-acre (120,000-hectare) **Green Mountain National Forest**, which stretches across two-thirds of the state. The cabin is not far from **Bread Loaf Mountain**, home of the prestigious 10-day Bread Loaf Writers' Conference, founded in 1926.

The mile-long **Robert Frost Interpretive Trail**, beginning at his home, the Homer Noble Farm, leads to the Bread Loaf campus by way of the cabin, which has been left untouched. For great scenery, continue on State 125, through steep **Middlebury Gap**; you can return to Route 7 by following Route 100 for 6

miles (10 km) south and heading back west on equally scenic Route 73 through **Brandon Gap**.

The entire core of **Brandon** – more than 200 buildings – is listed on the National Register of Historic Places. Stephen A. Douglas was born in the white cottage next to the Baptist Church north on Route 7; he was the Illinois senator whose famous seven debates with Abraham Lincoln, the rival for his seat in 1858, focused on the issue of slavery.

The lobby of the 1786 **Brandon Inn** (tel: 800-639 8685) on the Village Green appears to have been frozen in time.

In **Pittsford** is the **New England Maple Museum** (tel: 802-483 9414; open daily Mar–Dec; entrance fee). It bills itself as "the world's largest maple museum" and has a huge gift shop.

Proctor

Just off Routes 7 and 3, the town of **Proctor** ㊷ ("Marble Center of the World") is the logical spot for the **Vermont Marble Museum** (52 Main Street; tel: 80-427 1396; open mid-May–Oct daily; entrance fee to exhibit). It offers a glimpse into the workings of the Ver-

TIP

Of interest to Revolutionary War buffs is a side trip south from Middlebury to visit Mt Independence (off Rte. 22A, Orwell; open late May–mid Oct 9:30am–5pm; fee). Here, American forces massed against a British incursion along Lake Champlain. Nearby is the ferry to Ticonderoga, New York (spring–late autumn), a handsomely restored fortress that saw action during the French and Indian war and the Revolution.

BELOW: the Vermont Marble Museum.

Covered bridges

Masterpieces of folk technology, they were the work of largely self-taught craftsmen who acted as designers, engineers and builders.

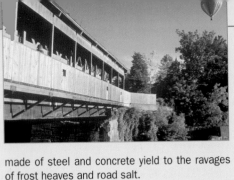

There are covered bridges throughout the United States, but they are a special icon in New England, where they help define the landscape as much as the rushing streams they span. Vermont alone has more than 100, New Hampshire more than 50; Maine has nine, and even the states of southern New England boast a few surviving examples – not counting modern replicas.

Why were bridges covered? The explanation commonly offered – that the barnlike structures mollified horses who might otherwise have been spooked by the prospect of crossing open water – isn't really accurate. The bridges were provided with walls and roofs simply because they were made out of wood, and New England weather would have long since made short work of them if their structural members weren't protected. Give a covered bridge a good roof – usually metal – and it will stand up through the decades, even as spans made of steel and concrete yield to the ravages of frost heaves and road salt.

The worst enemy of wooden covered bridges is vandalism, usually in the form of fire. But they are so well loved by their communities, and by aficionados, that it's a rare occasion when a bridge lost to vandals (or to a colossal snow load, as happened in Johnson, Vermont, in 2001) isn't promptly replaced with a replica.

New Englanders didn't invent covered bridges – they have been built in European countries with ample timber supplies for centuries – but they did perfect their design and engineering. Working with centuries-old truss designs, Yankee bridge builders devised systems of load-bearing that still stand up to traffic, although some spans succumb to the need for steel-girder underpinnings.

One simple design is the "kingpost," in which diagonal braces lead from a central upright towards the opposite shores. The "queenpost" elaborates on this design with two parallel uprights, allowing a longer distance to be spanned. The Long and Howe designs are X-braced box trusses, while the Burr and Paddleford incorporate wooden arches.

Perhaps the most elegant approach was that devised in the early 19th century by Ithiel Town. The "Town Lattice" truss incorporates a pair of crisscrossed diagonal members, assembled on site or hauled to the streamside, then opened out like an old-fashioned laundry rack and made rigid with wooden pegs. There are a half-dozen Town Lattice bridges in the town of Montgomery, Vermont alone. The Cornish-Windsor Bridge, spanning the Connecticut River between Vermont and New Hampshire, is a Town Lattice type and is the second longest covered bridge in the US (a longer Ohio bridge was completed in 2008).

To learn more about these bridges, you can pick up Ed Barna's *Covered Bridges of Vermont* (Countryman Press), or visit vermont bridges.com, website of the National Society for the Preservation of Covered Bridges. ❑

ABOVE: the covered bridge at Quechee, Vermont.
LEFT: Cornish-Windsor bridge, New Hampshire.

mont Marble Company factory, which flourished here for more than 100 years. There are marble samples from around the world, including the local product.

The region west of Vermont's second biggest city, Rutland, was a popular summer spot in the Victorian era, but faded after World War II, when the trains stopped coming. But wandering the back roads that link towns such as Middletown Springs, Fair Haven, and the tiny agricultural hamlets near Lake Champlain can be rewarding; there's a scattering of comfortable B&Bs; also fishing and swimming at state parks alongside lakes Bomoseen and St Catherine.

Off Route 3, Dr John Johnson built a home for his wife, a wealthy English aristocrat, in 1867. **Wilson Castle** (West Road; tel: 802-773 3284; open late May–late Oct daily; entrance fee) is an opulent stone mansion with 32 rooms, 12 fireplaces and such elegant appointments as a Louis XVI crown jewel case. The castle and its manicured walkways covering 115 acres (46 hectares) are open for tours. What might not seem terribly extravagant in a big city makes for a curious diversion in rural Vermont.

Rutland **43**, a once thriving industrial city, is struggling hard to revitalize its downtown and improve its image. It's an amalgam of period architecture, ranging from palatial Victorian homes to an Art Deco mini-skyscraper to 1960s-era shopping malls. The HQ for the **Green Mountain National Forest** is at 231 North Main Street (tel: 802-747 6700).

The Manchesters

Franklin Orvis gave the local tourist industry a boost in 1849 when he began taking in summer guests at his father's house, located next to the famed 1769 Marsh Tavern in **Manchester Village 44**, where Ethan Allen and his "Green Mountain Boys" had plotted the Tories' overthrow. The hotel kept expanding bit by bit until it grew into the **Equinox Resort & Spa** (3567 Main Street, Route 7A; tel: 802-362 4700), a grand resort hotel (with the adjacent Charles Orvis Inn) named for the mountain that presides over the town. It can be reached 4 miles (6.5 km) south of town via the 5-mile (8-km) **Skyline Drive** toll road (Route 7A; tel: 802-362 1114; open 9am–dusk May 1– October 31, weather

TIP

Since 1993, the wide variety of food has been the main attraction in early August at the one-day Rutland Region Ethnic Festival. Entertainment includes multi-ethnic performers and crafters, children's activities, and bargain shopping. For details, tel: 802-773 9380.

BELOW:
horse breeding is well established in Vermont.

Robert Todd Lincoln (1843–1926) was 21 when his father, Abraham Lincoln, was assassinated. A lawyer, he ran the Pullman Palace Car Company, conducting business from Hildene, his stately home in Vermont, in summer and from Washington, D.C. in winter. In Vermont, he also pursued his hobbies of astronomy and golf.

BELOW: fly fishing in the Housatonic near Manchester.

permitting). Vintage sports cars such as Bugattis and Bentleys stage the **Mount Equinox Hill Climb** (equinoxmountain .com) here each summer, negotiating 20 hairpin bends in the grueling 5.2-mile (8.4-km) ascent. Several hiking trails begin at the Toll House.

Franklin Orvis's younger brother, Charles, also had a clever idea – why not teach the leisured class to catch their supper along the banks of the abundant Battenkill River? Less than 10 years after he sold his first bamboo fly rod, Manchester had become the place to get away from it all.

By the mid-20th century, the Equinox had deteriorated into white elephant-hood, but in the early 1980s it was restored, along with its 18-hole golf course. And **Orvis** (4180 Main Street, Route 7A; tel: 802-362 3750), with its core emphasis on fly fishing equipment and schools, has grown into an outdoor-lifestyle powerhouse: today it operates a thriving mail-order business, and its huge retail store is billed as "Vermont's largest retail attraction." There are indoor and outdoot trout ponds; at the latter, patrons can test equipment.

Next door to Orvis is the **American**

Museum of Fly Fishing (Route 7A; tel: 802-362 3300; amff.com; open daily May–Dec; closed Sun Jan–Apr; entrance fee). It documents the history of the sport and its exhibits will engross aficionados.

All this brisk commerce notwith-standing, Manchester Village remains as tranquil and elegant as ever, with its mar-ble-slab sidewalks and showy summer homes, many now inns and restaurants.

Orvis's success inspired a raft of other upscale companies such as Ralph Lau-ren, Brooks Brothers, Joan & David, and Giorgio Armani, to open outlets in nearby **Manchester**, turning that one-time quaint town into a wall-to-wall shopping mall.

A highlight to the town includes a visit to the **Southern Vermont Arts Center** (West Road; tel: 802-362 3274; svac.org; open Tues–Sat; Sun pm; entrance fee). "Vermont's premier home for the arts" includes a 400-seat performing arts center, several galleries, and a sculpture garden.

Although Abraham Lincoln never made it to The Equinox (several other presidents did), Mary Lincoln and son Robert *(see margin note)* cherished fond memories of the mountains; they returned to build a 24-room estate near

Manchester. **Historic Hildene** (Route 7A; tel: 802-362 1788; hildene.org; open daily; entrance fee), now displays its richly appointed Georgian Revival rooms to history buffs and opens its 412-acre (167-hectare) grounds to cross-country skiers and summer strollers.

Out of Manchester

The picturesque, marble-paved village of **Dorset** ⑮, 8¼ miles (13 km) northwest of Manchester, is home to the **Dorset Playhouse** (tel: 802-867 5777; dorset theatrefestival.org). It hosts a summer festival from June to August in a rustic barn with offerings as diverse as Agatha Christie and Stephen Sondheim.

Just 6 miles (10 km) east of Manchester, on Route 11, is the downhill ski area at **Bromley Mountain** (tel: 802-824 5522; bromley.com; open Memorial Day–mid-Oct, daily mid-June–early Sept, weekends spring and fall). It becomes the Thrill Zone in the warmer months, with a bevy of activities including a water ride, an alpine slide, a scenic chairlift. There's a special park for children six and under. A special Adventure Pass is available for all the attractions.

Weston

One of Vermont's other venerable summer playhouses is about 15 miles (24 km) east of Bromley via routes 11 and 100, in the hill village of **Weston** ⑯. **Weston Playhouse** (tel: 802-824 5288; weston-playhouse.org; admission fee), the oldest professional theater in Vermont, has been in operation for over 65 years. The Café at the Falls overlooking the waterfall at the Weston Playhouse serves bistro fare on performance evenings.

The town has also been home to another of the state's major attractions, the **Vermont Country Store** (tel: 802-824 3184; open daily) a purveyor of cracker-barrel atmosphere and useful and arcane) merchandise since 1946. Its Brands From the Past such as Raggedy Ann dolls, Fuller brushes and Guittard's chocolate nonpareils evoke instant nostalgia. The family-owned business now has 1 million customers a year, mainly through its catalog and the internet (vermontcountrystore.com).

Arlington

Nine miles (14 km) south of Manchester on Historic Route 7A, **Arlington** ㊼ is a former Revolutionary capital and one-time home to America's most beloved illustrator. The **Norman Rockwell Exhibition** (3772 Main Street, Route 7A; tel: 802-375 6423; open May–Oct, daily; entrance fee) displays a large number of *Saturday Evening Post* covers and lesser-known prints; several locals who posed for Rockwell serve as docents.

Rockwell (1894–1978), born in New York City, lived on a farm in Arlington from 1939 until 1953. Although best known for his sentimental magazine illustrations, he tackled everything from mail order catalogues to presidential portraits *(see also page 203)*.

Works and papers by Rockwell and local author Dorothy Canfield Fisher are in the **Dr George A. Russell Collection of Vermontiana** (open Tues and by

The Vermont Country Store in Weston.

BELOW: *Breaking Home Ties* (1954) in the Norman Rockwell Exhibition. It hangs alongside a forgery that nobody had detected until the original was found in 2006.

Anna Mary Robertson Moses (1860–1961), took up painting in her seventies and, as "Grandma Moses," became a renowned naïve artist, painting 1,500 canvases in the next three decades. Her works alone make the Bennington Museum worth a visit. The schoolhouse she attended as a child in Eagle Bridge, New York, was moved to the museum's grounds in 1972 and has activities to interest kids.

appointment), behind the town's Martha Canfield Public Library on Main Street.

It was in a circa 1769 stone house on Main Street in **Shaftsbury** ❽ that the poet Robert Frost wrote his poems "Stopping by Woods on a Snowy Evening", and "New Hampshire," which concluded, "At present I am living in Vermont." His home is now the **Robert Frost Stone House Museum** (tel: 802-447 6200; frostfriends.org; open May–Dec, Tues–Sun; entrance fee), with exhibits about the poet on one floor, and an art gallery on another.

Bennington

Robert Frost is buried just to the south on Route 7 in **Bennington** ❾, at the Old Burying Ground in the town's Historic District. His epitaph reads simply, "I had a lover's quarrel with the world." The cemetery is next to the 1805-06 **Old First Church** (tel: 802-447 1225; open Mon–Sat; Sun pm; donation), with its unusual three-tiered steeple.

Bennington, home to Bennington College, looms large in Vermont's history, and a crucial 1777 skirmish is commemorated by the 306-ft (93-meter) **Bennington Battle Monument** (15 Monument Circle; tel: 802-447 0550; open mid Apr–Oct, daily; entrance fee). The battle actually took place a few miles to the west in New York State, where General John Stark and 1,800 ragtag troops forced the Redcoats back across the Walloomsac River. But it was a colonial supply dump on this site that General John Burgoyne was after, and his failure to attain it proved a turning point in the British campaign.

Nearby, the **Bennington Museum** (West Main Street, Route 9; tel: 802-447 1571; benningtonmuseum.org; open Thur–Tues; daily Sept and Oct; entrance fee) exhibits an exceptional collection of regional history and art, including the largest public collection of works by Grandma Moses *(see margin note)*. There are fine collections of Vermont furniture and pottery.

Near Route 67A in **North Bennington** is the 35-room **Park-McCullough House** (tel: 802-442 5441; open mid May–Oct daily; entrance fee). On the National Register of Historic Places, it is a time capsule of of the family that lived here for more than 100 years. Its furniture and decorative arts are among the most outstanding in Vermont.

BELOW: Bennington Battle Monument.

The ski scene

Scandinavian immigrants brought skiing to New England logging camps in the 1870s. Today it is a major part of the winter economy.

The Norwegian-speaking Nansen Ski Club was founded in Norway Village, near Berlin in New Hampshire, about 1872. With six other clubs, it founded the US Eastern Amateur Ski Association in 1922, and survives to this day. The sport spread to the college circuit after Dartmouth's Outing Club was founded in 1909. Just five years later, Dartmouth college librarian Nathaniel Goodrich was the first to descend Vermont's highest peak, Mount Mansfield in Stowe.

The sport was essentially confined to "touring" (comparable to today's cross-country), jumping off wooden chutes, and the odd foray into the woods. In 1926 Appalachian Mountain Club hutmaster Joe Dodge was the first to hurtle down Mount Washington's Tuckerman Ravine.

By then, skiing was well on its way to popularity. In 1929, fresh from a Switzerland ski trip, Katharine Peckett opened the country's first organized ski school at her family's resort in Sugar Hill, New Hampshire. Soon, the Boston and Maine Railroad began running ski trains to the state and, in 1934, New England's first rope tow was constructed at Gilbert's Hill, in Woodstock, Vermont.

The sport was dormant during the gas-rationing of the early 1940s, but area after area sprouted up in the late '40s and '50s, among them Vermont's Mount

Snow (tel: 800-245 7669), Smuggler's Notch (tel: 800-451-8752), Stratton (tel: 800-787 2886), Sugarbush (tel: 800-537 8427) and Killington (tel: 877-458 4637). For current slope conditions, call for an around-the-clock snow report (tel: 802-229 0531). The Vermont Ski Museum (Main Street, Stowe; tel: 802-253 9911) documents the state's alpine history with vintage equipment, old movies, and the Ski Hall of Fame.

At Killington, in the mid-1960s, the Graduated Length Method was introduced, easing the way for the general public to approach this often intimidating sport: tyros could start on short skis, gradually increasing the length as their prowess improved.

Just to keep the challenge fresh, though, a Stratton bartender came up with an innovation in the mid-'60s that has changed the landscape of skiing. Jake Burton Carpenter started experimenting secretly at night with ways to improve the "Snurfer" (as an early ancestor of the snowboard was called). It would take years, but his Vermont-based Burton snowboard company would become a leader in the field and create a whole new skiing subculture. Today, more than one in four ticket-buyers at most resorts is a snowboarder.

Today, Maine's big downhill resorts are Sugarloaf/USA (tel: 800-843 5623) in the Carrabassett Valley and Sunday River (tel: 207-824 3000) in Bethel. Sugarloaf has 43 miles (69 km) of trails and a vertical drop of 2,820 ft (860 meters); Sunday River has 121 trails. Snowmaking is excellent at both. There are almost 20 mountains developed for skiing in New Hampshire, but the two biggies are Loon Mountain, Lincoln (tel: 800-229 5666) and Waterville Valley (tel: 800-468 2553). "Skiophiles" will want to check out the New England Ski Museum, Franconia, NH (tel: 603-823 7177), for a full regional history. ❑

ABOVE: slope at Greensboro, Vermont.
RIGHT: Bretton Woods slope, New Hampshire.

RESTAURANTS AND BARS

Restaurants

Prices for a three-course dinner per person with a half-bottle of house wine:

$ = under $20
$$ = $20–45
$$$ = $45–60
$$$$ = over $60

Arlington

Arlington Inn
Route 7A
Tel: 802-375 6532
arlingtoninn.com $$$
A formal candlelit restaurant with continental and traditional American dishes – rack of lamb, roast duck, and lobster pie. D Tues–Sun.

West Mountain Inn
River Road (off Route 313)
Tel: 802-375 6516
westmountaininn.com $$$
Fixed-price, New American cuisine featuring fresh fish and prime meat in a low-beamed paneled dining room at a romantic but family-friendly inn. B & D daily; Sun breakfast buffet.

Bennington

Four Chimneys
21 West Road (Route 9)
Tel: 802-447 3500
fourchimneys.com
$$$–$$$$
American and continental cuisine in the gracious dining room of a restored 1910 Colonial Revival inn. D nightly.

Pangaea
1&3 Prospect Street, North Bennington
vermontfinedining.com
$$$–$$$$
A sophisticated menu that changes with what's

fresh. Award-winning wine list. Outdoor terrace. D Tues–Sat.

Brattleboro

Peter Havens
32 Elliot Street
Tel: 802-257 3333 $$–$$$
The locals' favorite New American bistro is a tiny art-filled space. Dishes include roasted boneless duck breast, homemade pastas. D Tues–Sat.

Riverview Café
Bridge Street
Tel: 802-254 9841
riverviewcafe.com $
A child-friendly place with two levels of outdoor decks overlooking the Connecticut River. All-you-can-eat fish and chips, and macaroni and cheese. B, L, D daily.

T.J. Buckley's
132 Eliot Street
Tel: 802-257 4922 $$$
Upscale cuisine in a tiny 1920s diner. Four entrées – usually fish, chicken, beef, and vegetarian. D Wed–Sun in summer; Thur–Sun winter.

Burlington Area

Daily Planet
15 Center Street
Tel: 802-862 9647
dailyplanet15.com $$
Mediterranean with Asian influences in a cheerful restaurant with a delightful solarium. Specialties include soups and tapas. D nightly.

Pauline's Cafe and Restaurant
1834 Shelburne Road, (Route 7 S), South Burlington
Tel: 802-862 1081
paulinescafe.com $$–$$$

Deft American dishes and regional specialties in an elegant little restaurant just out of town. The early-bird dinner for two ($30) is a real deal. Children's menu. L Mon–Sat; D nightly; Sun brunch.

Peking Duck House
79 West Canal Street, Winooski
Tel: 802-655 7474
pekingduckhousevt.com
$–$$
Located just over the Winooski Bridge, it wins awards for the best Chinese food around. Dishes and atmosphere are upscale; prices down to earth. L & D daily.

Penny Cluse Café
169 Cherry Street
Tel: 802-651 8834
pennycluse.com $
The only problem here are the crowds, who pack in for creative breakfast and lunch creations such as gingerbread pancakes, and chorizo and egg tacos. B & L.

Sakura
2 Church Street
Tel: 802-863 1988
sakuravt.com $$–$$$
Skillfully prepared Japanese specialties include *tempura* and *sashimi*. Sushi bar and tatami room. (Also a smaller outpost at Tafts Corners Shopping Center). L Mon–Sat, D nightly.

Souza's Brazilian Restaurant
55 Main Street
Tel: 802-864 2433
souzas.org $$
All-you-can eat meats and poultry delivered on

skewers to your table. An elaborate salad bar and dessert are included. L & D Tues–Sun.

Trattoria Delia
152 Street Paul Street
Tel: 802-864 5253
trattoriadelia.com **$$–$$$**
Award-wining Italian trattoria. Specialties include handmade pastas, hardwood-grilled chops, and authentic veal dishes. D nightly.

Chester
Old Town Farm Inn
665 VT Route 10
Tel: 802-875 2346
otfi.com **$$$**
Authentic Japanese cuisine at an 1861 B&B in the Green Mountains. D Wed–Sun.

Craftsbury
Craftsbury Inn
Main Street
Tel: 802-586 2848
craftsburyinn.com **$$$**
The nightly table d'hôte at this 1850 Greek Revival village inn features Continental fare. D Tues–Sun by reservation.

Dorset
Chantecleer Restaurant
Route 7A, East Dorset
Tel: 802-362 1616
chantecleerrestaurant.com **$$$–$$$$**
The Swiss chef at one of the area's favorite restaurants prepares Swiss and French provincial cuisine in a handsomely renovated dairy barn. Reservations required. D Wed–Sun.

Dorset Inn
Route 30
Tel: 802-867 5500
dorsetinn.com **$$–$$$**
Superb regional cooking. Formal dining or tavern

feasting in a 1796 hostelry. B, L & D daily.

East Burke
River Garden Café
Route 114
Tel: 802-626 3514
rivergardencafe.com **$$–$$$**
Artichoke dip, succulent porterhouse steaks, and *tiramisu*, plus rack of lamb and local smoked trout. Kids' menu. L & D Wed–Sun; Sun brunch.

Grafton
Old Tavern at Grafton
Route 121
Tel: 802-843 2231
old-tavern.com **$$–$$$**
International dishes with a New England slant served in two dining rooms: one more formal, the other rustic tavern-style. L in café; D nightly.

Killington
Choices
2820 Killington Road
Tel: 802-422 4030 **$$–$$$**
Chef Claude specializes in rotisserie, with entrées such as filet mignon with Saga blue cheese, and prime rib. Lively 30-something bar scene. D Tues–Sun.

Hemingway's
Route 4
Tel: 802-422 3886
hemingwaysrestaurant.com **$$$$**
In an 1860 country house, New American cuisine with international flavor. Hailed as among nation's best restaurants. Prix-fixe options. D nightly in season.

Lake Champlain Islands
Blue Paddle Bistro
Route 2, South Hero
Tel: 802-372 4814
bluepaddlebistro.com **$$–$$$**
Cozy spot for gorgonzola-

stuffed meatloaf, half-pound burgers with hand-cut fries, and, at Sunday brunch, lobster Benedict. Call for hours.

Lower Waterford
Rabbit Hill Inn
48 Lower Waterford Road, Route 18
Tel: 802-748 5168
rabbithillinn.com **$$$–$$$$**
Dazzling New American cuisine served in an atmosphere of understated elegance in a 1795 country inn. Features prix-fixed choices. D nightly Apr–Nov; Thur–Mon rest of year.

Manchester
The Equinox
Route 7A
Tel: 802-362 4700
equinoxresort.com **$$$–$$$$**
Spectacular regional cuisine in a formal barrel-vaulted dining room looking out on Mount Equinox. Live entertainment in lounge; L and D daily; Sun brunch.

Ye Olde Tavern
5183 Main Street, Manchester Center
Tel: 802-362 0611
yeoldetavern.net **$$–$$$**
Yankee classics and more ambitious offerings such as venison medallions. Gracious 1790 Colonial inn. D nightly.

Middlebury
Fire and Ice
26 Seymour Street
Tel: 802-388 7166/ 800-367 7166
fireandicerestaurant.com **$$**
Prime rib, fresh fish, a huge salad bar, and an intimate atmosphere attract couples. Families opt for the "Children's Corner", complete with cartoons. L Fri–Sat; Sun from 1pm; D nightly.

Tully & Marie's
7 Bakery Lane
Tel: 802-362 0611
tullyandmaries.com **$$–$$$**
New American and multicultural comfort food in an art deco-inspired spot with a deck overlooking Otter Creek. The pad Thai

LEFT: chef at work in the Craftsbury Inn.
RIGHT: lobster pie at the Old Inn, at Grafton.

is a knockout. L Mon–Sat; D nightly.

Montgomery Center

The Belfry Restaurant & Pub
Route 242
Tel: 802-326 4400
thebelfryrestaurant.com **$–$$**
Vermont microbrews and unpretentious fare in a one-time school house. Wednesday is Italian night. D nightly.

Montpelier

Main Street Grill
118 Main Street
Tel: 802-223 3188
necidining.com **$$**
Adventurous grazing courtesy of students of the New England Culinary Institute. Sunday brunch buffet features a "cold kitchen" of smoked sausages, meats, and homemade pâtés. L & D Tues–Sun; Sun brunch.

Sarducci's
3 Main Street
Tel: 802-223 0229
sarduccisrestaurant.com **$–$$**

The capital's best Italian fare, including pastas, pizza, and panini from a wood-burning oven; opt for the enclosed deck overlooking the river. L Mon–Sat; D nightly

Newfane

Four Columns Inn
230 West Street
Tel: 802-365 7713
fourcolumnsinn.com **$$$–$$$$**
New American cuisine with Asian and French touches and fresh ingredients in formal dining room of an historic country inn. D nightly with advance reservations.

Newport

The East Side Restaurant
47 Landing Street
Tel: 802-334 2340 **$–$$**
Popular lakefront restaurant serves American dishes in several large, cheerful dining rooms.

Lago Trattoria
95 Main Street
Tel: 802-334 8222

lagotrattoria.com **$–$$**
A genuine Italian trattoria with creative dishes, an open kitchen, and reasonable prices. D nightly.

Putney

Curtis' Barbecue
Just off Route 5, and Route 103, Chester
Tel: 802-387 5474
curtisbbqvt.com **$–$$**
Barbecue, slow-cooked and served up from an old school bus. Seating is at outdoor picnic tables. Open April–Oct, Wed–Sun 10am–dusk. The Chester location, with indoor seating, is open Wed–Sun all year.

Quechee

Simon Pearce Restaurant
The Mill, Main Street
Tel: 802-295 1470
simonpearce.com **$$–$$$**
Fine country cuisine, with Irish touches, in modern café in an old riverside mill/glassblowing, and gift complex. Extensive wine list. L & D daily.

St Johnsbury

Anthony's Restaurant
50 Railroad Street
Tel: 802-748 3613 **$**
Burgers and other American fare. Family-friendly spot. L daily; D Tues–Sat.

Elements Food & Spirit
98 Mill Street
Tel: 802-748 8400
elementsfood.com **$$**
"Creative comfort food" in a 150-year-old mill might include red curry mussels or smoked trout and apple cakes. D Tues–Sat.

Shelburne

Café Shelburne
Route 7
Tel: 802-985 3939
cafeshelburne.com **$$$**
Has been serving French bistro fare for more than 30 years. D Tues–Sun; nightly in foliage season.

Prices for a three-course dinner per person with a half-bottle of house wine:
$ = under $20
$$ = $20–45
$$$ = $45–60
$$$$ = over $60

Inn at Shelburne Farms
Harbor Road
Tel: 802-985 8498
shelburnefarms.com **$$$**
Gourmet dining in the elegant dining room of a Queen Anne-style manor overlooking Lake Champlain. Sunday brunch is a local institution. Reservations required. Open early May–late Oct for B & D daily; Sun brunch.

Stowe

Cliff House
Mount Mansfield
Tel: 802-253 3000
gostowe.com **$$**
Board the gondola to the top of the mountain for a menu built around Vermont meats, cheeses and bread. Elegant surroundings and the best view in Vermont. L only.

Edson Hill Manor
1500 Edson Hill Road
Tel: 802-253 7371
edsonhillmanor.com **$$$–$$$$**
American cuisine with French and Italian influences. Charming inn with majestic views. D nightly.

Trapp Family Lodge
Luce Hill Road.
Tel: 802-253 8511
trappfamily.com **$$–$$$$**
Gemütlich atmosphere, fine valley views, light meals and *torten* in the Austrian tea room. Candlelight and harp music accompany Austrian and American fare in the handsome main dining room.

Trattoria La Festa
La Toscana Country Inn, Mountain Road
Tel: 802-253 8480

stowetrattoriafesta.com **$$**
Red oilcloth table cover-
ings and candlelight set
the mood for regional
Italian dishes served in a
c. 1819 farmhouse/
country inn. D nightly.

Waitsfield
The Spotted Cow
Bridge Street Marketplace
Tel: 802-496 5151 **$$–$$$**
Classical French prepara-
tions with regional over-
tones in small, cheerful
spot. L & D Tues–Sun.

Warren
Pitcher Inn
Warren Village
Tel: 802-496 6350
pitcherinn.com **$$$$**
Elegant dining in one of
the area's finest inns.
Lighter fare served in
lounge. B & D daily.

Waterbury
**Hen of the Wood
Restaurant**
92 Stowe Street
Tel: 802-244 7300
henofthewood.com **$$**
An acclaimed restaurant
in a 19th-century mill,
features seasonal ingre-
dients from local farms,
boutique North American
wines, and artisan
cheeses. D Mon–Sat.

Waterbury Centre
Michael's on the Hill
Route 100 (between Stowe
and Waterbury)
Tel: 802-244 7476
michaelsonthehill.com **$$$**
Award-winning European
cuisine in a classic c.
1820 farmhouse with an
enclosed porch and piano
lounge. D Wed–Mon.

Weathersfield
The Chef's Table
Inn at Weathersfield,
Route 106
Tel: 802-263 9217
weathersfieldinn.com **$$$**

Sophisticated fare such
as Maine black mussels,
roast duck, and porcini
dusted Atlantic salmon
served by candlelight. D
Wed–Sun.

West Dover
Inn at Sawmill Farm
Off Route 100
Tel: 802-464 8131
theinnatsawmillfarm.com
$$$$
Chef/proprietor Brill
Williams has ingredients
flown in daily to prepare
his highly-acclaimed
cuisine served in the
elegant dining room of
one of Vermont's finest
inns. The wine list is outstanding. D nightly.

West Townshend
Windham Hill Inn
Windham Hill Road
Tel: 802-874 4080
windhamhill.com **$$$$**
The best way to sample
the eclectic cuisine at
this romantic inn is the
four-course prixe-fixe
menu, which might
include ricotta and bacon
stuffed quail, and pheas-
ant roulade. A la carte
menu available. D nightly
6–8.30pm.

Windsor
Juniper Hill Inn
Juniper Hill Road
Tel: 802-674 5273
juniperhill.com **$$$**
A four-course menu of
updated classics offers
three entrée selections,
served by candlelight at
this traditional inn. D
Tues–Sat at 7pm.

Windsor Station
Depot Avenue
Tel: 802-674 2052
windsorstation.com **$$**
Bistro fare in a family-
oriented spot in a con-
verted c.1900 railroad
station. D Tues–Sat.

Woodstock Area
Prince and the Pauper
24 Elm Street, Woodstock
Tel: 802-457 1818
princeandpauper.com **$$$**
Fine Nouvelle and Conti-
nental fare and exquisite
desserts in a candlelit
but comfortably rustic
atmosphere. D nightly.

Kedron Valley Inn
Route 106, South Woodstock
Tel: 802-457 1473
kedronvalleyinn.com
$$$–$$$$
One of the area's finest
inns. Regional specialties
with a Vermont accent.
Superb wine list. B & D
daily in season; closed
Tues–Wed off-season.

Bars
Charley O's, 70 Main
Street, Montpelier. Tel:
802-223 6820. Small,
Spartan, often crowded,
has pool tables and a juke
box. Clientele ranges from
legislators to students.
McGrath's Irish Pub, Inn
at Long Trail, 709 Route
4, Sherburne Pass,
Killington. Tel: 802-775

7181. Celtic ambiance.
Children welcome. Live
music Sun 5–7pm.
Pickle Barrel Nightclub,
1741 Killington Road,
Killington. Tel: 802-422
3035. Central Vermont's
most popular spot for
big-name entertainment
has a dance floor and
live music most nights.
Red Square Bar & Grill,
136 Church Street Mar-
ketplace, Burlington. Tel:
802-859 8909. A favorite
spot for the Queen City's
non-student population,
who gather for martinis
and live music. No cover
charge. Patio packed in
summer.
Rusty Nail Bar & Grille,
1190 Mountain Road,
Stowe. Tel: 802-253
6245. Martini bar, après-
ski hot spot, sports bar,
dance club... Great range
of Vermont microdrafts.
Three Needs, 207
College Street, Burling-
ton. Tel: 802-658 0889.
Laid-back hangout with
freshly-brewed German-
style lagers. Schwarzbier
is a house specialty.

LEFT: the Blue Paddle Bistro in South Hero.
RIGHT: the Windham Hill Inn, West Townshend.

NEW HAMPSHIRE

This tradition-minded state serves outdoor
pleasures on a platter, making the most
of the dramatic and rugged White
Mountains and dozens of deep lakes

Just when you are about to conclude that even New England is inching towards homogenization, you come up against New Hampshire. It is the contrarian in a contrary region, the state that has to do things just a little bit differently. It's the only state in New England that won't hear of a sales or income tax. It harbors the most conservative newspaper (the *Manchester Union Leader*) in a famously liberal region. And it defies any state to hold its quadrennial party primaries so much as a day before its own.

In a region famous for its reserved neighborliness, New Hampshire often stands out in stark contrast to Vermont, though they lie across the Connecticut River from each other. Vermont often seems to wring its hands over its state liquor sales and its lottery; New Hampshire was first in the nation with a state lottery, and runs liquor stores the size of Wal-Marts right on its interstate highways. And, yes, there are billboards in New Hampshire – not enough to spoil the view, but enough to let Vermont types know that business dislikes officialdom.

What made New Hampshire different?

Main attractions

PORTSMOUTH
ISLES OF SHOALS
CHRISTA MCAULIFFE
  PLANETARIUM, CONCORD
CANTERBURY SHAKER VILLAGE
CORNISH-WINDSOR BRIDGE
DARTMOUTH COLLEGE
MOUNT WASHINGTON COG
  RAILWAY

PRECEDING PAGES:
Hart's Location.
LEFT: Cornish-
Windsor bridge.
BELOW: Stark, a
typical small town.

The state in snapshot

Known as: The
Granite State.
Motto: Live free
or die.
Origin of name:
Named in 1629
by Captain John
Mason of Plymouth Council for his home
county in England.
Entered Union: June 21, 1788, the ninth of
the 13 original states.
Capital: Concord.
Area: 9,351 sq. miles/24,219 sq. km.
Highest point: Mount Washington, 6,288 ft
(1,917 meters).
Population: 1.172 million.
Population density: 119 people per sq. mile
(46 per sq. km).
Economy: Manufacturing (industrial
machinery, precision instruments, and
electronic equipment) and services
including tourism).
National representation: two senators and
two representatives to Congress.
Famous citizens: Mary Baker Eddy, Robert
Frost, Horace Greeley, Grace Metalious,
Alan B. Shepard Jr, and Daniel Webster.

Strawbery Banke is open for self-guided tours May–Oct daily; garden tours at 1pm; Nov, guided 90-minute tours Sat & Sun 10am–2pm, tours on hour with last tour at 2pm; Dec, guided 90-minute tours Mon–Fri 10am–2pm, tours on hour with last tour at 2pm; Jan–Apr, closed. Entrance fee.

New Hampshire's tourism industry h been long since been transformed automobile travel, shorter vacations, a a more energetic style of outdoor rec ation. And the White Mountains are the only draw – boaters and anglers ha an array of rivers and lakes to choc from, crowned by huge Lake Winne saukee in the center of the state; plen of tidy villages and back roads lie w beyond the southeastern urban spra and that short but scenic coastline strewn with state parks.

Also, lovers of antiques and fine arch tecture can still enjoy the gracious wor the Wentworths and their contemporar created in Portsmouth. And remember you want to take one of those antiqu home: there still isn't any sales tax.

For one thing, it has a seacoast – all 16 miles (26 km) of it. That was just enough to get colonization started much earlier, and launch an aristocratic merchant class in Portsmouth. Later, it used water power to develop a concentration of industry, at Manchester, far beyond anything dreamed of in Vermont. It had bigger lumber interests, bigger railroads, and Boston money closer at hand to finance it all.

Tourism today

Although wonderful old arks such as the Balsams, Mountain View Grand, and Mount Washington remain in business,

Portsmouth

Portsmouth ⑳ stands at the mouth the Piscataqua River. Graced with superb natural harbour, the town is nation's third oldest English settleme (after Plymouth and Jamestown).

Strawbery Banke Ⓐ (Marcy Stre tel: 603-433 1100; strawberybanke.org; s margin note for opening times) is

How pioneers and revolutionaries built the state

Like the rest of New England, New Hampshire had little to offer in the way of good soil and easy farming. The main assets of the region at the beginning of the colonial period were the deepwater port and surrounding shores of what is now Portsmouth; and the tall, straight pines, which became highly prized in the construction of ships. Fisheries established along the coast prospered from the sale of salt cod and other catches, hauled from the Atlantic as far north as the Grand Banks off Newfoundland.

The impetus behind these first forays was provided by Sir Ferdinando Gorges, head of the council established by King James to govern all of New England, and Captain John Mason, an early governor of Newfoundland. They obtained grants to an ill-defined territory lining the coast from

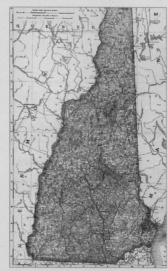

ABOVE: map of New Hampshire, 1881.

the Naumkeag to the Sagadahock riv and extending roughly 60 miles (100 k inland. Gorges and Mason propose variety of commercial enterprises a promised healthy dividends to investo The venture never really paid off. Lacl supplies limited the scheme's progre the company eventually collapsed, and settlers simply divided the land up am themselves and proceeded to amass th own fortunes, without giving very m thought to the niceties of property la

Strong-willed settlers, gradually pu ing their way inland from Portsmouth up the Connecticut River from the so laid claim first to the lush valleys, the the harsher hillsides, and finally to the bidding mountains in the north. The man to lend the colony some cohesion John Wentworth, a prosperous merch

urban quarter preserved in amber. The English named their 1623 colony for the profusion of wild strawberries that greeted them; today the 10-acre (4-hectare) living history museum tells the story of the evolution of the city's oldest neighborhood from 1650 to 1950. Restored and refurnished homes, ranging from humble to grand, illustrate changes in architectural and living styles.

Several of the lesser abodes serve as workshops for artisans whose work harks back to the past: open on a revolving schedule, there are studios for a cabinet-maker, cooper, potter, and weaver. Here, also, one of the oldest boat shops in America continues to produce dories, skiffs, and other vessels, using archaic copper clench nails. Strawbery Banke is literally an open-air museum: tours are self-guided and open-ended, permitting visitors to proceed at their own pace.

Just across from Strawbery Banke, **Prescott Park** stretches for more than 10 acres (4 hectares) along the Piscataqua River. Each summer the **Prescott Park Arts Festival** (prescottpark.org) hosts a free series of concerts, ranging from dance to theatre to music.

Several other worthy historic manses are scattered about this enchanting, compact town. (All are worthwhile for those interested in historic architecture and early Americana, but will likely be tedious for children, who are more likely to appreciate the crafts demonstrations at Strawbery Banke.)

Among these is the 1763 National Historic Landmark **Moffatt-Ladd House & Garden B** (54 Market Street; tel: 603-436 8221; one-hour tours mid-June–mid-Oct, Mon–Sat; Sun pm; entrance fee), an imposing three-story Georgian mansion topped with a captain's walk and graced

Open-air theater in Prescott Park.

TIP

You can traverse New Hampshire fast by driving I-95. But the state's seacoast is best discovered by meandering along the slower Route 1A, with its ocean vistas and state park beaches.

ppointed by the King in 1717 to govern the province of New Hampshire. Though hardly an altruist his land grants always reserved a portion for himself, a token 500 acres/200 hectares), he did begin the process – carried on by his son and nephew – of stabilizing the province, encouraging settlement and promoting commerce.

When the Revolution came, New Hampshire joined early in the fight – although alone of the 13 original colonies, it was spared the ravages of battle within its boundaries. Among its Revolutionary credits, New Hampshire was the first colony to assert its independence from England (establishing its own government on January 5, 1776) and the first to suggest the idea to the Continental Congress in Philadelphia (in 1775). Following the Revolution, people went

ABOVE: an old-fashioned New Hampshire toboggan ride.

back to the task of coming to terms with their land. The push inland was by now extending up into the White Mountains, a New England "last frontier" where the logger's ax would always be more useful than the plow. Even early in the 19th century, though, the success of rough hostelries such as the one run by Ethan Allen Crawford in Crawford Notch pointed the way for the mountains' eventual economic path.

By the mid-1800s, there were already two New Hampshires, with a buffer of small towns and farms between them. Along the Merrimack River in the south, the textile mills of Manchester and Nashua were growing in output and economic power; theirs would be an urban New Hampshire, an extension of Lowell and Lawrence in Massachusetts. But up north, a far different economy was growing around a resource every bit as important as water power – mountain scenery.

By the 1850s, "summer people" were a well-established industry. The retreats that drew them were modest at first, but as the railroads reached farther into the mountains, palatial resort hotels were built to serve clients who would arrive, servants and steamer trunks in tow, to spend summer days in the lap of luxury.

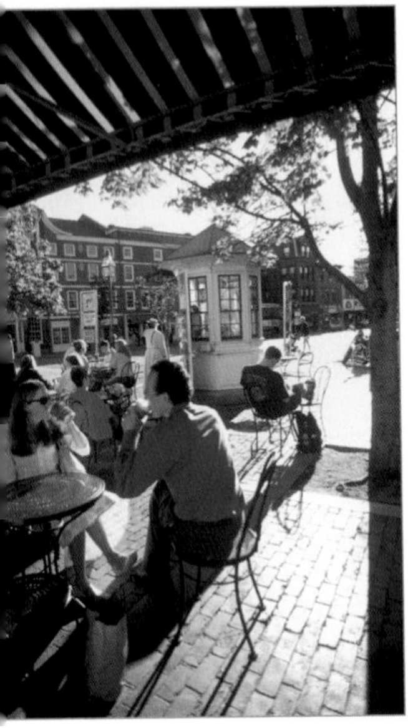

The Market Square in Portsmouth, which was incorporated in 1653 and now has a population of more than 20,000.

with terraced English-style gardens, a splendid carved staircase, a Gilbert Stuart portrait and choice examples of the furniture for which 18th-century Portsmouth was famous.

Seek out, too, the 1716 **Warner House** Ⓒ (150 Daniel Street; tel: 603-436 5909; open mid-June–mid-Oct 11am–4pm Thur–Sat and Mon and Tues, Sun pm; entrance fee). America's first house to be registered as a National Historic Landmark (1962), it was the first of Portsmouth's many brick houses, and the stair hall is endowed with an intriguing array of early 18th-century murals. Each room in the mansion is decorated in the style of one of the six generations who lived here. There are craft demonstrations on Thursdays throughout the summer.

Historic New England oversees several properties in Portsmouth (historicnewengland.org; tel: 603-436 3205; houses open June–mid Oct on first and third Saturdays of the month; tours 11am through 4pm; entrance fee). The 1614 **Jackson House** Ⓓ (76 Northwest Street) is the state's oldest surviving wood frame house. The Federal-style **Rundlet-May House** Ⓔ (364 Middle Street; tel: 603-436 3205; open June–mid Oct, Wed–Sun pm; entrance fee), built by a wealthy textile merchant in 1807, is filled with many of the technological advances of the day.

McKim, Mead & White designed a wing for the 1794 **Governor John Langdon House** Ⓕ (143 Pleasant Street; open Fri–Sun) to house modern conveniences.

The 1760 Georgian **Wentworth-Gardner House** Ⓖ (50 Mechanic Street; tel: 603-436 4006; open June–mid-Oct, Tues–Sun pm; entrance fee) is on the banks of the Piscataqua River. It displays photographs by Wallace Nutting, a founder of the Colonial Revival movement, who bought the house in 1915.

Portsmouth's Historical Society maintains the **John Paul Jones House** Ⓗ (43 Middle Street; tel: 603-436 8420; open mid-May–mid-Oct, Thur–Tues, 11am–5pm; entrance fee). The Revolutionary War naval hero once rented a room here. The 1758 Georgian home has period furnishings and chronicles the city's history

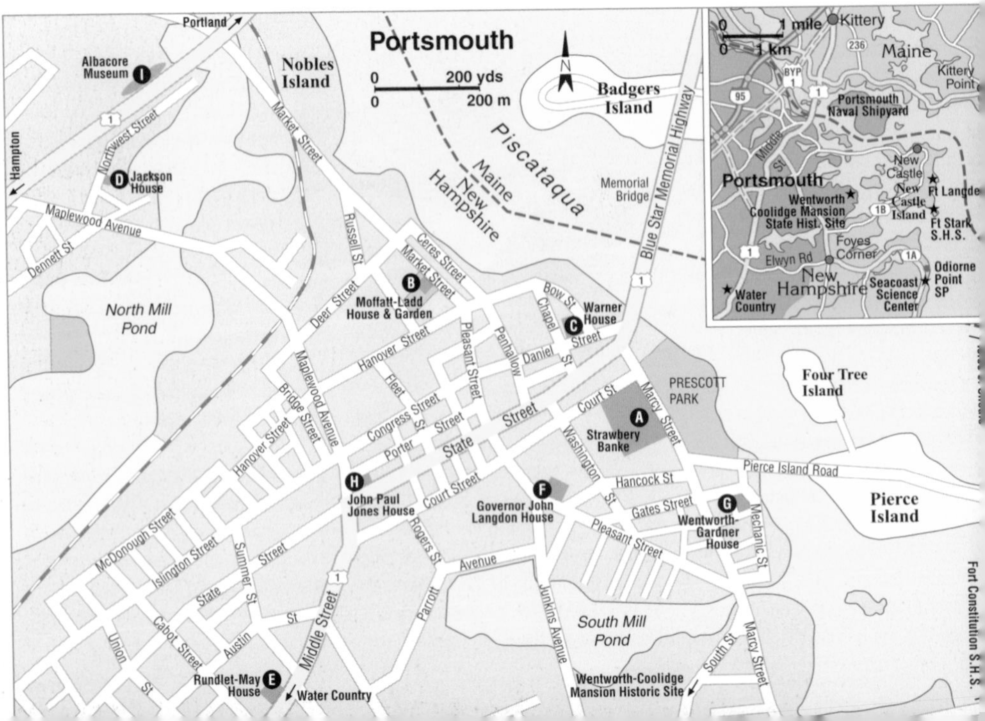

Recommended Restaurants and Bars on pages 331–3

Also well worth a visit is the Port of Portsmouth **Albacore Museum**  (600 Market Street; tel: 603-436 3680; uss albacore.org; open Memorial Day–Columbus Day daily; rest of year, Thur–Mon; entrance fee). The *Albacore* is a grounded 1952 submarine, 205 ft (62 meters) long, which for two decades carried a crew of 55 in sardine-like quarters.

Isles of Shoals

For a more pleasant experience on the water, consider a cruise to **the Isles of Shoals**, 6 miles (10 km) offshore; "barren piles of rock" charted in 1614 by Captain John Smith and long haunted by pirates and other outcasts. Improbably enough, an arts colony blossomed here at the end of the 19th century, after poet Celia Thaxter, the daughter of an innkeeper, created a miraculous garden on Appledore which inspired no fewer than 400 paintings by the noted American Impressionist Childe Hassam.

Kids can take a break from historic sites with a visit to New England's largest water park, **Water Country** (2300 Lafayette Road; tel: 603-427 1111; open mid-June–Aug; entrance fee).

Head out of town on Route 1B to the Portsmouth neighborhood of **New Castle**, a quaint fishing village settled in the late 1600s and home to **Fort Constitution State Historic Site** (tel: 603-436 1552). In 1774, the fort was raided by Portsmouth patriots for British guns and powder to use at the Battle of Bunker Hill. After visiting the site, it's pleasant to wander New Castle's narrow streets, lined with tidy colonial homes.

Just off Route 1A, at 375 Little Harbor Road, is the rambling, 40-room **Wentworth-Coolidge Mansion Historic Site** (tel: 603-436 6607; open for guided tours late June–Aug; mid-Sept–mid-Oct, Fri and Sun pm; entrance fee). Built between 1720 and 1760, it was the rambling, 40-room home of the state's first Royal Governor and displays five distinct periods of architecture and an impressively furnished interior.

North to Dover

Dover , 10 miles (16 km) northwest of Portsmouth, is the home of the **Children's Museum of New Hampshire** (6 Washington Street; tel: 603-742 2002; open

This 200-year-old stone chapel is on Star Island in the Isles of Shoals.

BELOW: Portsmouth by the Piscataqua River, the third fastest-flowing navigable river in the world.

spring, fall and winter, Tues–Sat, Sun pm, and Mon school holidays; July–Labor Day, Mon–Sat, Sun pm; entrance fee). Hands-on exhibts teach children about subjects from dinosaurs to flying machines. They can work in the museum's post office and handle footwear, costumes and masks from foreign countries, from Bolivia to Japan.

One of New Hampshire's most eclectic museums is also in town: the **Woodman Institute Museum** (182 Central Avenue; tel: 603-742 1038; open Wed–Sun pm; Dec and Jan, weekends; closed Feb and March; entrance fee). It encompasses three buildings: the main building, with more than 800 relics of colonial and natural history, including everything from a polar bear to dolls; the 1813 Hale House, and the 1675 Damm Garrison, the state's oldest Garrison house.

South of Portsmouth

Three miles (5 km) south, on Route 1A in **Rye**, is the 331-acre (134-hectare) **Odiorne Point State Park** (570 Ocean Boulevard; tel: 603-436 7406; parking fee in summer months). It has the largest undeveloped shoreline on the state's 16 miles (26 km) of coastline. Visitors can explore the remains of a World War II fort, and hike through the dunes.

The **Seacoast Science Center**, concentrating on the marine and coastal environments, on the grounds of the park (603-436 8043; open daily; entrance fee) is run by the state's Audubon Society.

Continue south on Route 1A to **North Hampton** and **Fuller Gardens** (10 Willow Avenue; tel: 603-964 5414; open mid-May–mid-Oct; entrance fee). This magnificent turn-of-the-century estate garden has more than 1,700 rose bushes, English perennial gardens, and a tropical conservatory.

There are several fine public beaches along Route 1A from Portsmouth to the Massachusetts border, including **Wallis Sands State Beach** (Rye), **North Hampton State Beach**, and **Hampton Beach State Park**.

Historic Exeter

Five miles (8 km) inland, just off Route 101, the handsome town of **Exeter** one of the state's earliest settlements, was founded in 1638. It's home to Phillips Exeter Academy, a prestigious college

BELOW: tugboat at Portsmouth.

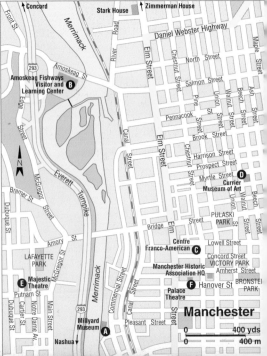

Recommended Restaurants and Bars on pages 331–3

preparatory school whose alumni include 19th-century statesman Daniel Webster.

The **American Independence Museum** (One Governors Lane; tel: 603-772 2622; open mid-May–last Sat in Oct, Wed–Sat, guided tours on the hour), is housed in a handsome 1721 building that once served as the state's state treasury and then a governor's mansion. The museum documents the country's and town's experiences during the Revolutionary War, and also offers tours of the historic **Ladd-Gilman House**, which focuses on life in 18th-century Exeter.

The Merrimack Valley

Flowing south from the foothills of the White Mountains, the swift Merrimack River brought to life one of America's earliest and most successful industrial centers. Still the state's most populous region, the Merrimack Valley is a center of government, business, and the arts.

America's Stonehenge is an outdoor museum in **North Salem**  (off Route 111 on Haverhill Road; tel: 603-893 8300; open daily; entrance fee). Long known as "Mystery Hill," it has purportedly been carbon-dated to about 2000 BC. Though considerably scaled down from its British namesake – its circle of standing stones measures only 3 ft (1 meter) tall – the site is thought to have served much the same purpose as Stonehenge: as a giant calendar tracing celestial movements. The identity of the builders and the purpose the site served remain matters of pure speculation.

Manchester

Further north on I-93 is **Manchester** , which together with Nashua and several other New Hampshire cities, were centers of textile manufacturing. The massive, red-brick **Amoskeag Mills** was, in the early 20th century, the world's largest textile enterprise, employing 17,000 workers in 64 buildings that stretched for 1½ miles (2.5 km) along the Merrimack River. The **Manchester Historic Association** (headquarters at 129 Amherst Street; tel: 603-622 7531; manchesterhistoric .org; open Tues–Sat) has exhibits about the area's history, offers walking tours, and operates the **Millyard Museum**  in Mill #3 (corner of Commercial & Pleasant Streets; open Wed–Sat; entrance fee). The

Manchester, the largest city in northern New England with a population of more than 109,000, has had to find new uses for old industrial buildings.

BELOW: a farming community near Manchester.

TIP

Located at 30 Park Street in Concord, the New Hampshire Historical Society's Tuck Library (open Tues–Sat 8:30am–4pm; tel: 603-856 0641; nhhistory.org /library; fee payable) is an invaluable resource for students of the state's history. It is named for the Society's greatest benefactor, financier Edward Tuck (1842–1938).

BELOW: the solidly built Concord stagecoaches, described by Mark Twain as "a cradle on wheels," were first built in 1827.

See Science Center, upstairs from the Museum (tel: 603-669 0400; open daily; entrance fee), offers a host of hands-on activities for toddlers to teens.

Amoskeag Fishways Visitor and Learning Center at Amoskeag Dam (6 Fletcher Street tel: 603-626 3474; open Mon–Sat; daily in May and June; donation) has exhibits on the history of the river and falls. Between late April and early June, their fish ladder teems with fish making their way upstream.

The mills attracted large numbers of French-Canadian immigrant workers, and comprehensive archives on French-speaking Canadians are held in the **Centre Franco-American** (52 Concord Street; tel: 603-669 4045; open Mon–Fri 9am–4pm). The cultural centre includes an art gallery and bookstore.

The **Currier Museum of Art** (201 Myrtle Way; tel: 603-669 6144; open Mon, Wed–Sun; Thur till 8pm; entrance fee; free admission Saturday 10am–noon) has fine collections of European and American paintings, New England decorative arts, and contemporary crafts. It also offers modern architecture buffs access to the **Zimmerman House**, a 1950 design by Frank Lloyd Wright. The home, located on Manchester's outskirts and filled with the owners' modern art, pottery and sculpture, is considered a work of art in itself. The museum offers a variety of tours to the Zimmerman House Apr–Dec. Vans, which hold 12 passengers, depart from the museum. Reservations should be made well in advance.

You can catch a live performance at the **Majestic Theatre** (281 Cartier Street; tel: 603-669 7469; majestictheatre.net) or at the elegantly-restored, 1915 **Palace Theatre** (80 Hanover Street; tel: 603-668 5588; palacetheatre.org) which also presents a summer children's series.

"Live free or die", New Hampshire's official motto, is attributed to General John Stark, the commander at the Battle of Bennington *(see page 298)*. His boyhood home, the 1736 **Stark House** (2000 Elm Street; tel: 603-647 6088; by appointment), is now owned by the Daughters of the American Revolution.

Concord

Some 15 miles (24 km) north of Manchester is **Concord** , New Hampshire's capital. The gold-domed 1819 **State House** (107 North Main Street; tel: 603-271 2154; open Mon–Fri), was built of Concord granite by state prisoners and is fronted by statues of New Hampshire's political luminaries – Daniel Webster, Franklin Pierce, General John Stark and others – striking imperial poses in bronze. Its Hall of Flags contains 88 Civil War standards carried into battle.

The **Museum of New Hampshire History** (Eagle Square off Main Street; tel: 603-228 6688; open Tues–Sat, Sun pm, July-mid–Oct and Dec, Mon–Sat, Sun pm; entrance fee) houses the collection of the New Hampshire Historical Society, from furniture and folk art to tools and toys. Worth the admission fee all by itself is an original Concord Coach, the 19th-century vehicle built here and known as "the coach that won the West." (Park in the lot across from the museum and present the entry ticket at the reception desk for a free parking token.)

Also worth a visit is **the League**

New Hampshire Craftsmen gallery at 205 North Main Street (tel: 603-224 3375) – this was the first state officially to support its artisans, with the establishment of the New Hampshire Commission of Arts and Crafts in 1931.

One of the world's most advanced digital planetarium projection systems, capable of simulating space travel in three dimensions, is installed at the **Christa McAuliffe Planetarium** (3 Institute Drive, tel: 603-271 7827; starhop .com; open Mon–Sat, Sun pm; entrance fee; advance tickets recommended). This highly interactive planetarium is dedicated to the New Hampshire teacher who perished in the 1986 space shuttle *Challenger* disaster. There's a free Skywatch on the museum lawn on the first Friday of the month, beginning at dusk.

North of Concord

Head north on I-93 about 17 miles (27 km) to exit 18 and follow signs to **Canterbury Shaker Village** ⑤ (Shaker Road; tel: 603-783 9511; open May–Oct, daily; Apr, Nov, early Dec, weekends; entrance fee), an eloquent testament to the ingenuity and gentle faith of the Shak-

ers, one of the religious sects that sought asylum in the New World *(see page 47)*. Guided tours of a part of the 694 acres (281 hectares) of grounds, 25 restored buildings, and 4 reconstructed structures provide a glimpse of the skill and faith of this remarkable community. Crafts on display (some reproductions of which are for sale) include basketry, tin-smithing, wood-working and "the sewing arts."

Daniel Webster Birthplace

The orator and statesman Daniel Webster (1782–1852) was born in a tiny farmhouse near **Franklin** in 1782. Today

Crafting a traditional broom at Canterbury Shaker Village, founded in 1969.

BELOW: Concord's 1819 State House.

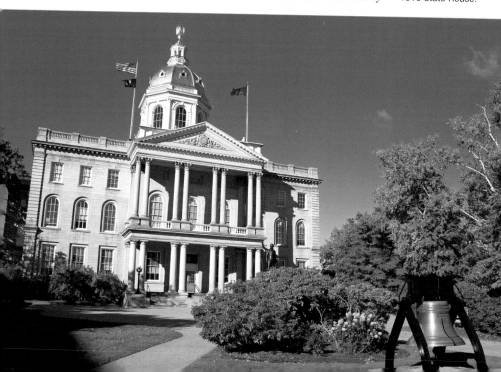

BELOW: birders in Monadnock State Park take part in a competition to see who can find the highest number of birds in 12 hours.

the restored **Daniel Webster Birthplace** (off Route 127; tel: 603-934 5057; open mid-June–Sept 1 Sat and Sun), filled with period furnishings and family memorabilia, gives visitors an idea of the rigors of 1700s farm life.

MOUNT MONADNOCK REGION

Crowned by **Mount Monadnock**, a rocky 3,165-ft (968-meter) peak whose 360° views attract record numbers of climbers (the relatively gentle ascent is surpassed in popularity only by Mount Fuji), this is a region of meandering back roads past prim white churches, innumerable antique stores, and historic inns.

Trails to the peak begin at **Monadnock State Park** ⑤⑧ (Visitor Center, off Route 12, Jaffrey Center; tel: 603-532 8862; entrance fee). A few miles to the south, the large **Rhododendron State Park** (Route 119W, Fitzwilliam; tel: 603-532 8862; open mid-May–early Nov; entrance fee) boasts a 16-acre (6-hectare) grove of the flowers, which bloom from early spring until the first frost.

To the east, the small town of **Rindge** hosts the 2,000-seat **Cathedral of the Pines** ⑤⑨ (Prescott Road; tel: 603-899 3300; cathedralofthepines.org; open daily May–Oct; July & Aug Tues–Thur, outdoor meditations 11am–3:30pm; check website for services). This open-air war memorial chapel has a set of Norman Rockwell bas-reliefs. It began when the Sloane family planned a small chapel to their son, a bomber pilot killed in Germany in 1944, and later became an interdenominational place of worship. Every President since Harry Truman sent a stone to build the altar, which is backed by a view of Mount Monadnock.

The 1979 Merchant-Ivory film *The Europeans* was shot at the elegant Federal-style **Forest Hall (the Barrett House)** (Main Street; tel: 860-928 4074; open June–mid-Oct on first and third Sat of month; tours on the hour 11am–4pm) in the former mill town of **New Ipswich**. The terraced grounds rise to a Gothic Revival summerhouse.

Peterborough

To the north, the handsome town of **Peterborough** ⑥⓪ is home to the country's most prestigious artists' retreat, the McDowell Colony. The village inspired *Our Town,* Thornton Wilder's 1938 Pulitzer Prize-winning play *(see margin note).*

Stop at the **Chamber of Commerce** (junction Routes 101/202; tel: 603-924 7234) for a copy of *A Walking Tour of Peterborough*, which includes the town's numerous historic sites and buildings. The **Peterborough Historical Society** exhibits intriguing relics and photographs as well as two mill houses and an early general store (19 Grove Street; tel: 603 924 3235; open pm only weekdays; entrance fee). The renowned **Sharon Art Center** has several exhibition galleries and a store which sells handmade craft and fine art (30 Grove Street; tel: 603-924 7676; store open daily).

To the east, **Frye's Measure Mill** (12 Frye Road; tel: 603-654 6581; shop open Tues–Sat, Sun pm in summer; Thur–Sat Sun pm in winter) in **Wilton** ⑥① is one of the country's few remaining water-powered mills and its only active measure mill (since 1858, Frye's has been making boxes designed for accurate

measurement of quantities of items such as nails). On Sat at 2pm June–Oct, a 90-minute tour of the mill includes a demonstration by Harland Savage, former Measure Mill owner and master box maker (fee; reservations recommended).

Head west on Route 101 from Peterborough to **Dublin,** home of *Yankee* Magazine and the *Old Farmer's Almanac*, America's oldest continuously published periodical. Turn right at the flagpole in the center of town to the National Historic Landmark village of **Harrisville ⑫**, one of New Hampshire's best-preserved 19th-century mill towns. A self-guided tour of its beautifully proportioned brick buildings, one of which is now a renowned weaving center, is worth taking.

Twelve miles (20 km) to the west, **Keene ⑬**, the largest city in this region, was a thriving mill town at the turn of the 19th century. Today it is primarily a market center: the restored **Colony Mill Marketplace** houses several multi-dealer antique shops, stores, and restaurants. Keene claims to have America's widest Main Street, crowned at one end by the handsome spire of the United Church of Christ (23 Central Square). The handsome

1806 Federal home at the **Horatio Colony House Museum & Nature Preserve** (199 Main Street; tel: 603-352 0460; open May–mid-Oct Wed–Sun 11am–4pm) is filled with early18th- to late 19th-century American and European furnishings. Three-and-a-half miles (5 km) of trails wind through the 415-acre (168-hectare) preserve. In April 1775, 29 Minutemen departed from the *circa* 1762 **Wyman Tavern** (339 Main Street; tel: 603-352 1895; open June–Aug, Thur–Sat 11am–4pm for guided tours; entrance fee) to join the battles in Lexington and Concord, Massachusetts. The tavern reflects the 1770–1820 period.

The city is also home to **Keene State College**, whose excellent **Thorne-Sagendorph Art Gallery** (tel: 6030358 2720) exhibits works by 19th-century artists who worked around Mount Monadnock.

Just few miles to the south, **Swanzey** has the state's largest collection of **covered bridges**. Stop in at the **Swanzey Historical Museum** (Route 10, West Swanzey; tel: 603-352 4579; open June–mid Oct, Mon–Fri 1pm–4:30pm; Sat and Sun 10am–4:30pm) for information.

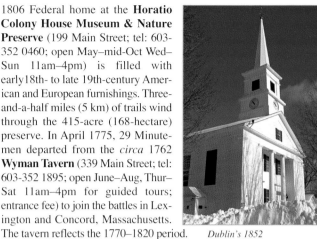

Dublin's 1852 Community Church. A hurricane in 1938 snapped the steeple off the building.

BELOW: a covered bridge at Swanzey.

Amor Caritas in the garden of Augustus Saint-Gaudens' home. The sculptor created many variations on this motif.

BELOW: the Saint-Gaudens National Historic Site.

Ten miles (16 km) west of Keene off Route 9 in **Chesterfield**, a half-mile trail meanders along the rim of **Chesterfield Gorge** (River Road; tel: 603-684 0148; open daily; entrance fee), carved by glacial meltwater. Other trails wind through the 166-acre (67-hectare) Natural Area.

Between Keene and Concord, off Route 9E, in **Hillsborough**, is the boyhood home of the country's 14th president, the **Franklin Pierce Homestead** (Route 31N; tel: 603-478 3165; open July and Aug, Mon–Sat, Sun pm; June and Sept, Sat and Sun; entrance fee). The Federal-style home was built in 1804 by his father, Benjamin, a two-term governor of New Hampshire.

CONNECTICUT RIVER VALLEY

Like its counterpart on the Vermont side of the river, New Hampshire's portion of the Connecticut River Valley is a realm of small towns, meandering roads, and rolling meadows and pastures – but with an Ivy League College at its heart.

In **Charlestown** ❻, about 22 miles (35 km) northwest of Keene, the **Fort at**

Number 4 Living History Museum (Route 11 West; tel: 603-826 5700; open June–Oct, Wed–Sun, 10am–4:30pm; entrance fee) recreates a 1740s settlement. In its day, it was the northernmost frontier of New England colonization. Within its stockade, interpreters demonstrate such crafts as candle-dipping, weaving, and the molding of musket balls; and, at certain dates, re-enact skirmishes. The entire **Main Street** of downtown Charlestown – with 62 buildings (including 10 built before 1800) – has been designated a National Historic Landmark.

Some 10 miles (16 km) farther north on Route 12A in **Cornish**, the **Cornish-Windsor bridge** on the Connecticut River *(picture, page 306)* connects New Hampshire to Vermont and is the world's longest two-span covered bridge.

Cornish was a thriving artists' colony at the turn of the 20th century, and one of the most prominent to put down roots here was Augustus Saint-Gaudens (1848–1907), the celebrated classical sculptor whose works included Boston's Robert Gould Shaw Memorial and several representations of Lincoln. Today, his handsome home, gardens and studios are the **Saint-Gaudens National Historic Site** ❻ (off Route 12A; tel: 603-675 2175; sgnhs.org; open late May–Oct, daily; entrance fee). Carrying on a a Saint-Gaudens tradition, Sunday afternoon concerts are held on the lawn in front of the Little Studio in summer.

Enfield

In Lebanon, jog east on Routes 4 and 10 to **Enfield** ❻ and the **Enfield Shaker Museum** (447 Route 4A; tel: 603-632 4346; shakermuseum.org; open Mon–Sat, Sun pm; entrance fee) which preserves the settlement that thrived here from 1793 to 1923. The "Great Stone Dwelling" was designed by Ammi Burnham Young, later the architect for the US Treasury in Washington, D.C. The deconsecrated Mary Keane Chapel next to it, with its 26-rank Casavant pipe organ, and magnificent German stained-glass windows, is a jewel (concerts and recitals are held in summer and a fine place for quiet contemplation

Dartmouth College

Another 5 miles (8 km) north along the Connecticut River is **Hanover 67**, home of Ivy League **Dartmouth College** (tel: 603-646 1110; dartmouth.edu; one-hour campus tours depart from McNutt Hall Apr–Dec). Dartmouth was founded in 1769, primarily for "the education and instruction of youth of the Indian tribes in this land."

The college retains much of its colonial appearance while accommodating such modern touches as the **Hood Museum of Art** (tel: 603-646 2808; open Tues–Sat; Wed until 9pm; Sun pm), whose collections run from Assyrian relief to Revere silver to Winslow Homer, and the **Hopkins Center for the Arts** (Wilson Hall; tel: 603-646 2422; hop.dartmouth.edu), with an impressive performing arts roster. **Baker-Barry Library** (on the Green; tel: 603-646 2560; open daily) houses an impressive collection of rare volumes as well as a series of murals on an anticolonialist theme by Mexican artist José Orozco.

The Terrace (lunch and dinner daily; Sunday from 1:30pm) at the historic **Hanover Inn** (tel: 603-643 4300; hanoverinn.com) offers al fresco dining overlooking the Green.

Just across the river in **Norwich**, the wonderful **Montshire Museum of Science** (Montshire Road; tel: 802-649 2200; open daily; entrance fee) is a hit with children. It has exhibits on natural history, physics and astronomy.

Fifteen miles (24 km) north on Route 10 in **Orford 68** a string of seven mansions built between 1773 and 1889 stretch along "The Ridge" in one of the state's loveliest towns.

THE LAKES REGION

Canoes, loons, rustic family camps along wooded shores... all the classic icons of easy days in the lake-dappled New England forest come to the fore in this scenic swath of New Hampshire.

New Hampshire's "Lakes Region" straddles the state's central section and boasts dozens of inviting lakes and ponds. One of the prettiest, **Lake Sunapee 69** in **Newbury** has been a summer resort since the late 1800s. **Mount Sunapee Resort** (Route 103; mtsunapee.com; tel: 603-763 2356; fee for lifts) includes the ski area, with a chair-

Famous alumni of Dartmouth College include Daniel Webster (1801), Theodor "Dr Seuss" Geisel (1925), Vice-President Nelson Rockefeller (1930) and writer Louise Erdrich (1976).

LEFT: Baker-Berry Library, Dartmouth College.
BELOW: keeping cool at Lake Sunapee.

lift open on select days throughout the summer and fall; from the summit, a short trail makes the most of the views across to Mount Washington and other points some 75 miles (135 km) distant. The League of New Hampshire Craftsmen *(see below)* holds its annual August fair at the base of the lift. There's a fine, sandy beach in **Sunapee State Park** (Route 103; tel: 603-271 3628; entrance fee in season).

Lake Winnipesaukee

To the northeast, **Lake Winnipesaukee** sprawls in convoluted splendor with 183 miles (294 km) of shoreline and 274 islands. According to legend, Winnipesaukee means "the smile of the Great Spirit," the name Chief Wonotan gave it when his daughter married a young chief from a hostile tribe. Wonotan saw the overcast sky on their wedding day as a bad omen but, just as the two lovers were departing, the sun broke through the clouds and sparkled over the lake.

A number of towns dot the shoreline, offering various tourist attractions and services. On the western shore, **Weirs Beach** ❼ (named for the weirs, or fish-

nets, which Indians once stretched across a narrow channel there) brings a touch of Atlantic City to Winnipesaukee's western shore, with its boardwalk, arcade, marina, water parks, and elaborate miniature golf links.

Weirs Beach is homeport for the **M/S *Mount Washington***, which offers day, evening dinner dance, and island cruises *(see margin tip)*.

A few miles to the north, the resort town of **Meredith** is home to the **Winnipesaukee Railroad** (154 Main Street; tel: 603-279 5253; hoborr.com; fee), which offers a scenic ride alongside the lake to Lakeport. A dinner train which departs at 6pm features cuisine of the popular Hart's Turkey Farm Restaurant. The **League of New Hampshire Craftsmen** (279 Daniel Webster Highway; tel: 603-279 7920) has a retail gallery here with products ranging from hand-made jewelry and wood-carving to baskets and furniture.

Wolfeboro

One of the *Mount Washington*'s ports of call is **Wolfeboro** ❼❷, on the eastern shore, the oldest summer colony in the nation. In 1769, John Wentworth, the last

TIP

If you take the 10am cruise on the *Mount Washington* from Weirs Beach, you can stop off at one of the other lakeside towns for lunch and shopping and return by a later cruise. The vessel operates from early May through the end of October. Tel: 888-843 6686 or, in NH 603-366 5531. cruisenh.com

BELOW:
a trip on Lake Winnipesaukee.

of New Hampshire's colonial governors, built a summer home here, and comfortable old money has been following his example ever since; a stroll around reveals a wealth of architectural styles, including Georgian, Federal, Greek Revival, and Second Empire.

The **Wolfeboro Historical Society** (233 South Main Street; tel: 603-569 4997; open July–Aug Wed–Sat; by appointment in spring and fall) maintains the Clark House Museum Complex which encompasses three historic buildings. The state's rich boating history is preserved at the **New Hampshire Antique and Classic Boat Museum** (397 Center Street; tel: 603-569 4554; open Memorial Day weekend–Columbus Day weekend, Mon–Sat; Sun pm; entrance fee); exhibits include a magnificent collection of vintage mahogany and antique boats, canoes, and sailboats.

The first-rate **Wright Museum of American Enterprise** (77 Center Street; tel: 603-569 1212; open May–Oct, Mon–Sat, Sun pm; entrance fee) documents World War II, both home and abroad, with two floors of cleverly assembled exhibits, from parlor radios to tanks.

Throughout the summer, **Great Waters Music Festival** (56 North Main Street; tel: 603-569 7710; greatwaters.org) on the lakefront presents a diverse series of entertainment.

Three miles (5 km) north of town on Route 109, exhibits at the small lakeside **Libby Museum** (tel: 603-569 1035; open May–Columbus Day, Tues–Sun; entrance fee) focus on local wildlife and history; an hour's visit is an informative diversion.

Elsewhere on the lake

Looking down over the lake from the north near Moultonborough, the **Castle in the Clouds ⓭** (off Route 171; tel: 800-729 2468; castleintheclouds.org; open early June–mid-Oct, daily; entrance fee) stands as an imposing monument to one man's vision of a tranquil idyll. Built in an inventive amalgam of styles by shoe machinery magnate Thomas Gustave Plant, this 1910 mansion is set in a 3,200-acre (2,100-hectare) estate with

waterfalls, ponds, streams, miles of forest trails, and magnificent views – worth the trip – out over the lake and surrounding countryside. Lunch is served in the Carriage House, which hosts a Thursday evening "jazz at sunset" series on its patio in summer.

At **Moultonborough**, the **Old Country Store**, built as a stagecoach stop in 1781, is one of the oldest continually-operating stores in the US and a trove of New Hampshire-made products. The small museum upstairs exhibits a Concord Coach.

A few miles to the north on Route 109 is the early 19th-century village of **Center Sandwich ⓮**, where the **League of New Hampshire Craftsmen** (32 Main Street; tel: 603-284 6831; open May–Oct) first opened its doors in 1926 as a sales venue for the state's craftspeople. The **Methodist Meetinghouse**, with its unusual free-standing brick chimney, is one of the most photographed buildings in the state. The **Sandwich Historical** Society (4 Maple Street; tel: 603-284 6269; open June–Oct, Tues–Sat; entrance fee), headquartered in the circa 1850, antiques-filled Elisha

A dock on Lake Winnipesaukee, which has more than 250 islands.

BELOW: lakeside concert at Wolfeboro.

Marston House, oversees several sites.

Twelve miles (19 km) southwest, in **Holderness**, exhibits at the 200-acre (80-hectare) **Squam Lakes Natural Science Center** , (Route 113; tel: 603-968 7194; open May–Nov 1, daily; entrance fee) include a nature preserve for injured animals (including black bears, mountain lions, and bobcats) unable to survive in the wild. Visitors can also hike, visit the gardens, and take a 90-minute lake cruise (May–Oct).

The 1981 movie On Golden Pond *with Katherine Hepburn and Henry Fonda was filmed on Squam Lake, famed for its loons. Boat tours are run by Experience Squam (tel: 603-968-3990; experiencesquam.com).*

Wakefield

To the east of Lake Winnipesaukee, Route 153 winds north along the Maine border toward the White Mountains, threading together a skein of tidy small towns set amidst rolling countryside.

More than 200 years ago **Wakefield** , "the center of New England", was the intersection of two stagecoach routes. Twenty-six of the 18th- and 19th-century buildings in **Wakefield Corner National Historical Area** – including the **Wakefield Inn** – are listed in the National Register of Historic Places.

The **Museum of Childhood** (tel: 603-522 8073; open mid-June–Labor Day Mon, and Wed–Sat; Sun pm; entrance fee), offering "memories for all ages", is packed with old dolls, trains, and other children's toys.

Continue through the Effinghams to Effingham Falls, and turn onto Route 25, which skirts **Ossipee Lake** as it merges with Route 16 and heads northwest to the turnoff for Route 113 and **Tamworth** . Grover Cleveland, US President in 1885–89 and 1893–97, summered here, and in 1931 his son founded **Barnstormers Summer Playhouse** (tel: 603-323 8500; barnstormerstheatre.org). It has 282 seats, is the country's oldest professional summer theater and puts on well-chosen plays, from *Tartuffe* to *The Sunshine Boys*.

The **Remick Country Doctor Museum and Farm** (tel: 603-323 7591; open Mon–Fri year round; July–Oct, Mon–Sat; entrance fee) is a working farm museum. It portrays agricultural life from 1790 to the present, and also re-creates the home of a country doctor.

Back on Route 16, continue north through **Chocorua**, in the shadow of rugged, 3,475-ft/1,059-meter **Mount Chocorua**, at the eastern end of the Sandwich Range. Several hiking trails lead to the summit.

THE WHITE MOUNTAINS

Continuing north, travelers now begin their ascent into the **White Mountain National Forest**, a vast tract of almost 800,000 acres (320,000 hectares) encompassing the Franconia Range, clustered along an east-to-west axis (and dipping into Maine for a bit), and the Presidentials, running northeast and culminating in New England's tallest peak, Mount Washington. Long a forbidding wilderness, the White Mountains have evolved into an enormously popular tourist region, equally popular with hikers and motorists (particularly at foliage time).

Most of the tourist infrastructure is contained – by law and convenience – in pockets along the major highways. All the rest is reserved (and preserved) for backwoods purists.

A typical trail will lead from a parking lot along the highway directly into

the forest, over gradually inclining terrain, maybe taking in a viewpoint or waterfall. Trails are well marked, with color-coded blazes cut into tree trunks at regular intervals, so there's little risk of taking a wrong turn. Eventually, towering trees give way to twisted dwarf pines and lichen-encrusted boulders. Above the tree line are the summits, from which adventurers may savor that peculiar sense of accomplishment that comes from finding oneself on top of the world.

Most of these peaks are not, for all their massive beauty, too demanding: summits can be reached within a couple of hours at a fairly leisurely pace. One of the most rewarding excursions (in terms of view obtained relative to energy expended) is the short (45-minute) romp up **Mount Willard**, along an old bridle path. Those reaching the summit are rewarded with a magnificent panorama of **Crawford Notch** – particularly splendid at sunrise.

There are too many trails – some 1,200 miles (1,900 km) all told – to attempt even a partial description here; details can be obtained from White Mountain National Forest offices (various locations in the area; mail address: 719 North Main Street, Laconia 03246; tel: 603-528 8721; fs.fed.us/r9/white) and the Appalachian Mountain Club (headquarters at 5 Joy Street, Boston, Massachusetts 02108; tel: 617-523 0636; outdoors.org and at Pinkham Notch, NH (Rte. 16; tel: 603-466 2721). The AMC also maintains a network of "huts" (some fairly large) offering hikers bunk lodgings and hearty meals; it's wise to reserve well ahead (tel: 603-466 2727). The AMC's White Mountain Guide is the "walker's bible."

The Kancamagus Highway

Alternatively, you can just enjoy the scenery from the car. One of the most rewarding routes begins in **Conway** ⑦⑧, best known as the southern end of a stretch of shopping outlets that extends 5 miles (8 km) to the bustling tourist town of **North Conway**, home to the **Conway Scenic Railroad** (tel: 800-232 5251; conwayscenic.com; call for schedule; entrance fee). The railroad runs excursions either through the countryside or Crawford Notch (far more dramatic) aboard vin-

Ice climbing in the White Mountains.

BELOW: the view from Mount Willard.

The Fall

A revered ritual of New England life is leaf-peeping – driving to see the green leaves of summer turn to vivid oranges, yellows and reds.

Droves of dedicated leaf-peepers come by the car and busload from all over the US and the world – advance reservations at inns and even restaurants are essential during October. In the far north of the region, the leaves usually start turning mid-September, farther south a little later; by the end of October, the show is pretty much over.

New Hampshire and Vermont are most often linked with great foliage, but all six states have favored routes for colorful fall vistas. The advantage the northern states have is their mountains. From certain routes through the Green or White Mountains (a misnomer in fall), the views across valleys to neighboring peaks can be breathtaking.

Each New England state has a toll-free foliage hotline telephone number. There's even a Maine "leaf lady" whose Web page contains frequently updated photos of the show (access the page through the state's website, visitmaine.com).

By trying too hard to pinpoint the absolute peak of foliage, however, you risk missing the majesty of the leaf-changing phenomenon: If you're lucky enough to be in New England in October, you're sure to see peak foliage somewhere, because each tree changes its color according to an inner timetable that's affected by moisture, temperature, and the shorter days of fall.

Botanists call the color change "leaf senescence" – the process by which the green pigment chlorophyll is drawn back into the tree to nourish it, permitting other, brighter pigments in the leaves to shine through. Brightest of all are red swamp maples and sumac. Aspen and birch turn yellow, sugar maples a peachy orange.

While it can be fun to drive back roads in search of great fall color, interstates often have the best foliage. Designed to cut through swaths of forest bypassing populated areas, I-95, for example, offers some of Maine's best leaf-peeping in the 75-mile (120-km) stretch from Augusta to Bangor. Similarly, in northeastern Connecticut, I-395 always puts on a fine leaf show.

Almost any highway route designated as "scenic" on a state map will yield bountiful leaf color. In Massachusetts, one of the best foliage drives is westward along the Mohawk Trail (Route 2, Greenfield to Williamstown) in the northwestern corner of the state. Turn north on Route 7 into Vermont, then east on Route 9 and south on I-91 for an exceptionally pretty loop tour.

New Hampshire's mountains and lakes make it particularly appealing. A 340-mile (550-km) mid-state tour that takes in a little bit of mountain and lake begins at the Massachusetts border on I-93. Take Exit 24 and follow signs to Holderness on Route 25; then take Route 113 east to Route 16 north. At the Kancamagus Highway (Route 112), go west through the White Mountains National Forest back to I-93.❑

● **Foliage hot-lines:** Connecticut, 1-800-282 6863; Massachusetts, 1-800-632 8038; New Hampshire, 1-800-258 3608; Vermont, 1-800-837 6668; Maine, 1-800-533 9595; Rhode Island, 1-800-556 2484.

LEFT: maple foliage in New Hampshire.

tage coaches. Lunch and dinner tours are also offered in the 1929 Chocorua car.

To the north of North Conway, at **Glen**, is **Story Land** (tel: 603-383 4186; storylandnh.com; open weekends Memorial Day–Father's Day and in the fall, daily until Labor Day; entrance fee). There's enough here to keep children aged 2–12 occupied most of a day, with rides in a pumpkin coach, antique car, swan boat or pirate ship, a farm-themed show and several character-filled play areas.

Kancamagus Highway

Conway is the eastern terminus for the 34½-mile (55-km) **Kancamagus Highway** (Route 112), a designated National Scenic Byway. The "Kanc" winds alongside the Pemigewasset and Swift rivers, passing numerous trailheads offering anything from short strolls through the forest to major upland hikes. Seek out especially the signed overlooks at the western end (notably Kancamagus, Pemi and Hancock); views are at their best when the fall foliage reaches its most brilliant phase, but then you may find the traffic bumper to bumper (if you do take the drive in the fall, start early in the morning). Worth-

while short walks include the Champney Falls Trail and the Boulder Loop Trail, while pleasant roadside picnic areas are at Rocky Gorge and Sabbaday Falls.

Lincoln ⓱, at the western terminus, is home to **Loon Mountain ski area** (60 Loon Mountain Road; tel: 745 8111; skyrides daily mid-June–mid-Oct; fee): during the summer and fall a gondola whisks visitors to the summit, where there's an artisans' village, hiking trails, and observation tower. The summit restaurant serves an all-you-can-eat Sunday brunch early June–Aug.

This well-developed tourist area offers several other attractions, including one of the state's oldest attractions, **Clark's Trading Post** (Route 3), where black bears put on a performance; the **Whale's Tale Water Park** (Route 112); and **Hobo Railroad** (64 Railroad St, Lincoln; tel: 603-745 2135; hoborr.com), which runs excursions May–Oct, plus Santa Trains in Nov–Dec, with vintage coaches and diesel locomotives.

Through Franconia Notch

Route 3/I-93 north from **Lincoln** winds for 8 miles (13 km) through **Franconia**

TIP

North Conway's outlet shops are especially attractive because New Hampshire has no sales tax. Be warned that this commercial strip of highway is prone to bottlenecks. For details of stores, visit shopmtwashington valley.com

BELOW: Conway Scenic Railroad has operated in the Mount Washington Valley since 1974.

Above the clouds on Mount Washington. The mountain's erratic weather makes it popular with glider pilots.

BELOW: heading up the mountain.

Notch State Park N (tel: 603-745 8391), between Kinsman and Franconia mountain ranges. Among the highlights en route: **The Flume** (open early May–late Oct, entrance fee to flume), an 800-ft (240-meter) gorge with granite walls attaining 90 ft (27 meters) and ending at a waterfall. It was reportedly discovered in 1803 by 93-year-old Aunt Jess Guernsey, who happened upon it while out fishing. Unfortunately, it's no longer quite as she found it – viewing platforms have been added to accommodate the busloads of sightseers – but some hint of the awe this natural wonder must have inspired remains. Off the main path is **the Pool**, another fine waterfall. In winter the wooden walkways are dismantled as the ice forms a massive layer.

Northward, pull into the parking lot at **Profile Lake** to read a plaque telling of the sad demise of the Old Man of the Mountain, a rock formation that loomed just above the lake. Noteworthy not so much for its size – it measured 40 ft (12 meters) from top to bottom – as for the fine detailing of its features, the Old Man generated a sense of reverence over the years. The jutting brow, regal nose, lips slightly pursed as if in meditation and sharp line of the bearded chin all conspired to produce not merely a likeness, but a real sense of character.

Ten thousand years of freezing and thawing cycles finally proved too much for the Old Man, who had been held together with cables and iron braces. On a spring morning in 2003, the entire formation slid down the mountainside and disappeared in a pile of rubble. The Old Man survives on the New Hampshire quarter coin in a recently issued state series. A monument in his memory is planned for the former viewing site.

Directly to the north is **Cannon Mountain**, a ski area (named for a cannon-shaped rock perched on its ridge). An easy year-round means of ascent is offered by the **Aerial Tramway** (tel: 603-823 8800; open late May–mid-Oct daily; fee) leading to a short trail at the summit. At the base, the **New England Ski Museum** exhibits historical paraphernalia, such as hand-crafted wooden skis from the 19th century, and various audio-visual exhibits (tel: 603-823 7177; open Memorial Day–March daily 10am–5pm; *see page 299*).

Beyond the Notch

Two classic villages await the visitor just past Franconia Notch. **Franconia** N was home to poet Robert Frost in 1915–20; here he "farmed a little, taught a little and wrote a lot." Looking out towards his favorite three New Hampshire mountains is the modest **Robert Frost Place** (off Route 16, Ridge Road; tel: 603-823 5510; open Memorial Day–early July weekends; early July–Oct Wed–Mon pm; donation). "R. Frost" still marks the mailbox, and the house preserves manuscripts and assorted memorabilia, and hosts readings by contemporary poets

Route 117 from Franconia winds to the upscale hill town of **Sugar Hill**, home to several elegant country inns and the **Sugar Hill Historical Museum** (Main Street; tel: 603-823 5336; open

mid-June–mid-Oct, Thur–Sat pm; entrance fee). The museum is a repository of local history, a bit narrowly focused.

Mount Washington

Nathaniel Hawthorne, who played an important role in promoting and preserving the region, accurately pointed out that the White Mountains, and particularly the Presidential Range, are "majestic, and even awful, when contemplated in a proper mood, yet by their breadth of base and the long ridges which support them, give the idea of immense bulk rather than of towering height." **Mount Washington**, at 6,288 ft (1,197 meters), is high enough to qualify as the tallest summit north of the Carolinas and east of the Rockies, and its sheer bulk is impressive, at least from the bottom, but to really appreciate its height, one must tackle the peak.

There are three ways to "climb" Mount Washington: on foot, by car, or by train. The first two options are accessible from **Pinkham Notch**. A trail to the summit via **Tuckerman Ravine**, a large glacial cirque famous for its spectacular scenery and dangerous but thrilling spring skiing,

begins at the Appalachian Mountain Club's **Pinkham Notch Visitor Center** ㉜ (tel: 603-466 2727), which offers lodgings, workshops, and trail information.

Across the way, the gondola at **Wildcat Mountain Ski Area** whisks off-season visitors to the top of this less lofty mountain (tel: 800-255 6439; a four-passenger gondola operates Memorial Day–mid-June Sat and Sun; daily mid-June–mid-Oct; entrance fee). On one thrill ride, the Zip Rider, you soar for a half-mile above the trees at 45 mph (72 km/h); riders must be at least 52 inches/ 1.32 meters tall. Those who prefer to remain tethered to the earth might opt for a round of alpine disc golf.

The 8-mile (13-km) climb up the **Mount Washington Auto Road** ㊸, via endless switchbacks, can be hell on radiators, the return journey tough on the best of brakes (off Route 16; open mid-May–mid-Oct, weather permitting; daily in summer 7:30am–6pm; shorter hours in spring and fall; entrance fee; tel: 603-466 3988; mt-washington.com). But the views along the way and at the summit make the effort worthwhile – provided the summit isn't socked in by fog. For

TIP

More than 130 people have died on Mount Washington and hikers should be aware of its fierce weather. The average daily temperature is 26.5°F (–3.1°C) and has fallen as low as –47°F (–44°C).

BELOW:
Mount Washington Observatory suffers some of the worst weather in the world. A wind speed of 231 mph (372 km/h) was recorded in 1934.

those who'd rather spare their vehicles the ordeal (and forgo the campy "This Car Climbed Mount Washington" bumper-sticker), a tour van departs from the base.

The summit bears chilling markers commemorating those who, like 23-year-old Lizzie Bourne in September 1855, died of exposure only a few hundred yards from the top. The destination she sought, a rustic hotel called the **Tip Top House**, survives as a small museum; visitors can marvel at the cramped dormitories, where travelers bunked down on crude beds cushioned with moss.

Climatically, the summit is classified as arctic. Its topographic isolation results in alarmingly abrupt changes in weather, including blizzards even in summer. The highest-velocity winds ever recorded – 231 miles (372 km) an hour – were measured here in 1934, and some of the older buildings that are part of a weather observatory (founded in 1932) are chained down to keep them from blowing away.

The **Sherman Adams Summit Building** is surrounded by a deck with 70-mile

ABOVE AND BELOW: golf and skiing at the Mount Washington Resort, Bretton Woods.

(112-km) views; inside is the small but fascinating **Summit Museum** (tel: 603-356 2137; seasonal; entrance fee). It focuses on mountaineering history and on the summit's ecology and weather.

Crawford Notch

Head west on Route 302 through **Crawford Notch ❽**, a narrow pass named for two notable early entrepreneurs. The notch was "discovered" in 1771 (more or less accidentally) by Timothy Nash, who was tracking a moose at the time. When Nash informed Governor Wentworth of his discovery, the disbelieving governor offered to grant him a tract of land including the notch if Nash could bring a horse through it and present the animal, intact, at Portsmouth. Nash met the challenge – incidentally opening up the White Hills (as the mountains were then called) to a steady influx of settlers, and eventually tourists.

Among the first to anticipate and capitalize on the area's potential were Abel Crawford and his son, Ethan Allen Crawford. They blazed the first path to the summit of Mount Washington (in 1819), advertised both it and their services as tour guides and established inns to accommodate their clients and other travelers – thereby masterminding the White Mountains' debut as a tourist attraction.

Bretton Woods

Route 302 through **Crawford Notch State Park** (tel: 603-374 2272) passes by the few remaining symbols of the mountains' resort heyday. Its genteel grandeur still surprisingly intact, the colossal **Mount Washington Resort at Bretton Woods ❽** (tel: 800-258 0330 or 603-278 8813; mtwashington.com), which opened in 1902, welcomes well-heeled visitors in a manner to which most people could easily become accustomed.

Circled by a 900-ft (270-meter) verandah set with white-wicker chairs, and topped with red-tiled turrets, this elongated white-stucco wedding-cake contains some 174 rooms (many marked with plaques commemorating guests attending the famed 1944 Bretton Woods monetary conference – *see margin note*) and a voluminous lobby with 23-ft (7-meter) ceilings supported by nine sets of columns and illumined with crystal chandeliers. Nearby is **Bretton Woods ski area**, whose 76 trails cover a wide variety of terrain.

The Cog Railway

Just past the hotel, turn off Route 302 onto the access road for 6 miles (10 km) to ride up Mount Washington on the remarkable 1869 **Cog Railway** (tel: 800-922 8825 or, in NH, 603-278 5404; thecog.com; operates year round, call for schedule; three-hour trip includes 20 minutes at summit; entrance fee). The railway is a testament to American ingenuity in the pursuit of diversion. Powered by tough little steam locomotives, the train, the world's first mountain-climbing cog railway, carts passengers 3½ miles (5.5 km) up and down the mountain, but does so with an admirable inventiveness, relying on a fail-safe rack-and-pinion system. The average grade is 25 percent, the steepest 37.4.

West on Route 2, toward the Vermont border, children may enjoy **Six Gun City** in **Jefferson** (tel: 603-586 4592; open Memorial Day–Labor Day, daily; call for off season hours; entrance fee). It's a small-scale theme park, with rides, a water slide, go karts, and lots of other fun activities.

The North Country

This isolated, sparsely populated region is one of New Hampshire's better-kept secrets. The landscape is as stunning as any in the state: vast stretches of forest cover most of the region and provide its primary industry – logging. A lacework of lakes, rivers, ponds, and streams offers a delicate counterpoint to the craggy hills and mountains. It is up here that the Connecticut River has its source, in a string of lakes just a few miles from the Canadian border, in a corner so out of the way that its allegiance was not decided, nor its boundary fixed (and then, by force), until 1840. The wilderness is a magnet for fishermen in search of salmon and trout; and, in winter, snowmobilers are attracted by miles of trails.

Route 3 is *the* road north past the Connecticut Lakes to the border. Just south of **Colebrook** ⑳, where the Mohawk and Connecticut rivers meet, the Oblate fathers oversee the **Shrine of Our Lady**

In July 1944 delegates from 44 countries met at Bretton Woods to devise a plan to create financial stability after World War II. The meeting gave birth to the World Bank and the International Monetary Fund, and its policies, although later seen by many as instruments of US power, survived until the 1970s.

BELOW: Mount Washington's Cog Railway.

Motorists stop to photograph a young bull moose – but collisions are not uncommon.

of Grace, notable for an unusual, life-size granite carving called "Motorcyclists in Prayer." Past Colebrook, Route 3 meanders alongside the infant Connecticut to **Pittsburg** , the state's largest municipality in acreage with more than 300,000 acres/120,000 hectares but one of its smallest in terms of population.

From here north to Canada, it's a world of forest, water, scattered hunting and fishing camps – well suited to an exploring spirit. Folks at **The Glen** (800-445 4536; open May–Oct), a handsome lakeside retreat on the western shore of the First Connecticut Lake, will be glad to provide information, as will the **Connecticut Lakes Tourist Association** (nhconnlakes.com).

Route 26 east out of Colebrook follows the Mohawk River through **Dixville Notch State Park** (tel: 603-323 2087). Watch for moose: the park is home to much of the state's population of these behemoths. That provides a peg for a chamber of commerce-backed Moose Festival each August, with various events in Colebrook, Canaan and Pittsburg.

In the heart of the Notch is **The Balsams Grand Resort Hotel** (tel:877-225 7267; thebalsams.com), a sprawling 1866 establishment with some 233 rooms and varied recreational facilities (golf, tennis, skiing, trout-fishing, canoeing, riding) spread over a private enclave as large – 15,000 acres (6,100 hectares) – as Manhattan Island; it even has its own small ski area.

Lake Umbagog

At the junction of Routes 26 and 16 in **Errol**, turn north for 5½ miles (9 km) to visit the headquarters of the 13,000-acre (5,300-hectare) **Lake Umbagog National Wildlife Refuge** (tel: 603-482 3415; open Mon–Fri, 8am–4:30pm). It was created in 1992 to conserve wetlands and protect migratory birds. The 7,000-acre (2,850 hectare) lake is 7 miles (11 km) long.

Lake Umbagog has been in danger of becoming too popular. On a summer weekend, as many as 200 boats a day took to the lake, causing the US Fish and Wildlife Service to report that jet skis and off-road vehicles were harming wildlife habitats.

RESTAURANTS AND BARS

Restaurants

Prices for a three-course dinner per person with a half-bottle of house wine:
$ = under $20
$$ = $20–45
$$$ = $45–60
$$$$ = over $60

Bedford

Bedford Village Inn
2 Old Bedford Road
Tel: 603-472 2001
bedfordvillageinn.com
$$$–$$$$
Sophisticated New England regional fare in the elegantly appointed dining room of a gracious inn. Afternoon tea ($20) Friday afternoons. Tavern menu. L and D daily.

Bretton Woods

Mount Washington Hotel
Route 302
Tel: 603-278 1000
mtwashingtonhotel.com $$$
Old-fashioned, sometimes uneven fare in a dining room with an echo of its luxury past. An orchestra plays nightly. Must book. Jacket and tie at dinner. D nightly.

Center Sandwich

Corner House Inn
Main Street
(Routes 109 and 113)
Tel: 603-284 6219
cornerhouseinn.com $$
Continental fare, antiques, and candlelight in a delightful 1849 house. Try the lobster and mushroom bisque, and the double-thick lamb chops. Pub menu. L June–Oct; D nightly; Sun brunch.

Concord

The Barley House Tavern
132 North Main Street, Concord. Tel: 603-228 6363
thebarleyhouse.com $$
This gleaming bar/restaurant across from the State House has Irish whiskey steak, Guinness beef stew and Dublin burgers. Entertainment most nights; outdoor seating available May–Oct; L & D Mon–Sat.

Moritomo Japanese Restaurant
32 Fort Eddy Road
Concord
Tel: 603-224 8363
$$$–$$$
Upscale Japanese cuisine, with a tatami room, habachi grills, and first-rate sushi bar. L and D daily.

Dixville Notch

Balsams Grand Resort Hotel
Route 26
Tel: 603-255 3400/
877-225 7267
thebalsams.com $$$
The sprawling resort hotel offers classic New England cuisine, fabulous views, and an award-winning wine list. Reservations and jackets required at dinner. B and D daily; L in summer.

Eaton Center

Palmer House Pub
Inn at Crystal Lake,
Route 153
Tel: 603-447 2120/
800-343 7336
innatcrystallake.com $$
Belly up to the bar that was once in Boston's Ritz-Carlton for a bone-dry martini, then enjoy fare ranging from a bowl of chili to rack of lamb. D Wed–Sun.

Franconia

Franconia Inn
1300 Easton Valley Road
Tel: 603-823 5542/
800-473 5299
franconiainn.com $$–$$$
Upscale American cuisine in a formal dining room with mountain views. B and D daily.

Lovett's Inn by Lafayette Brook
Profile Road
Tel: 603-823 7761
lovettsinn.com $$
Traditional New England favorites and more adventurous fare in 18th-century inn. D nightly.

Glen

The Bernerhof
Route 302
Tel: 603-383 9132/
800-548 8007
bernerhofinn.com $$–$$$
Alpine delights including spaetzle and Provimi veal, Delice de Gruyere, and cheese fondue. A Taste of the Mountains Cooking School has been an institution here for 20 years. D nightly.

Red Parka Pub
Route 302
Tel: 603-383 4344
redparkapub.com $–$$
The steaks are aged, the prime rib prime, the fish fresh, and the salad bar items all homemade. Couples without kids might prefer the porch or Skiboose, a 1914 railroad car. D nightly.

RIGHT: Mount Washington Hotel, Bretton Woods.

The Hanover Inn at Dartmouth College
Main Street
Tel: 603-643 4300
hanoverinn.com **$$$**
Contemporary American cuisine in "Edwardian elegance," plus outstanding wine list. Sunday brunch is a local tradition. B Mon–Sat; L Mon–Fri; D Tue–Sat.

Colby Hill Inn
3 The Oaks, Henniker
Tel: 603-428 3281
colbyhillinn.com **$$–$$$**
An 18th-century country inn serving Continental cuisine. Try the boneless chicken breast stuffed with lobster, leeks and boursin cheese. D nightly May–Dec; rest of year Tues–Sun; Sun brunch.

The Manor on Golden Pond
Route 3/Shepard Hill Road
Tel: 603-968 3348
$$$–$$$$
manorongoldenpond.com

Excellent New American cuisine and a superb wine list in a baronial setting. *Prix-fixe* four-course dinners. D nightly; bistro menu.

Inn at Thorn Hill
Thorn Hill Road
Tel: 603-383 4242
innatthornhill.com **$$$**
Three-course *prix-fixe* or à la carte menus in romantic country inn. Reservations required. D nightly.

Red Fox Bar and Grille
Route 16
Tel: 603-383 4949
redfoxpub.com **$–$$**
Specialties include wood-fired, grilled steaks and shepherd's pie. Sunday's all-you-can-eat jazz brunch is just $7.95. L Sat–Sun; D nightly.

Thompson House Eatery
Routes 16a and 16
Tel: 603-383 9341
thompsonhouseeatery.com
$$–$$$
Innovative salads and

Prices for a three-course dinner per person with a half-bottle of house wine:
$ = under $20
$$ = $20–45
$$$ = $45–60
$$$$ = over $60

sandwiches, luscious entrées, and the signature chocolate espresso pudding in an 1800s barn. L and D daily.

Wentworth Resort Hotel Dining Room
Route 16a
Tel: 603-383 9700
thewentworth.com **$$$**
Exceptional Continental cuisine with New England ingredients in a French provincial dining room.

Wildcat Inn and Tavern
Route 16a
Tel: 603-383 4245
wildcattavern.com **$–$$**
This popular place serves dishes such as baked scallops, rack of lamb, and lobster fettuccini by candlelight. D nightly. Lighter L and D in Tavern.

Luca's Mediterranean Café
10 Central Square
Tel: 603-358 3335
lucascafe.com **$$**
Small bistro with offerings such as escargots in terra cotta, and salmon tajine. L Mon–Fri; D nightly April–Dec, Mon–Sat rest of year.

Fratello's Ristorante Italiano
155 Dow Street
Tel: 603-624 2022
fratellos.com **$$**
Traditional Italian cuisine in a renovated textile mill. L and D daily. (Also in Laconia and Lincoln).

Red Arrow Diner
61 Lowell Avenue
Tel: 603-626 1118

redarrowdiner.com **$**
A landmark 1903 luncheonette, open 24/7.

The Woodshed
Lee's Mill Road
Tel: 603-476 2311
thewoodshedrestaurant.com
$$
Classics – clam chowder, scrod, prime rib – plus a raw bar in an 1860s barn. D Tues–Sun.

The New London Inn
140 Main Street
Tel: 603-526 2791
newlondoninn.us **$$**
Inventive regional cuisine includes popovers, horse-radish crusted salmon, and prime steaks. D in dining room Tues–Sat; tavern Tues–Sun.

Moat Mountain Smokehouse
Route 16
Tel: 603-356 6381
moatmountain.com **$–$$**
The brew pub, inn and restaurant overlooking Mount Washington specializes in great ribs, pulled pork and wood-fired pizza. L and D daily.

Stonehurst Manor
Route 16
Tel: 603-356 3113
stonehurstmanor.com **$$**
Continental cuisine such as smoked roasted duck, veal Oscar and pastas, plus wood-fired, oven-baked pizzas in a historic inn. B and D daily.

Woodstock Inn
Main Street (Route 3)
Tel: 603-745 3951
woodstockinnnh.com **$–$$$**
A variety of options: Continental cuisine in the Victorian parlor, casual fare at the cafe, and microbrews in the Brewery. On Sun, there's an all-you-can eat brunch.

Peterborough

Cafe at Noone Falls
50 Jaffrey Road (Route 202S)
Tel: 603-924 9486 **$$**
Get a seat overlooking
the falls to watch the
great blue herons dive
for their food, while you
demolish homemade
soups, fresh salads, and
house specialties such
as pad Thai noodles.
B and L Mon–Sat.

Pinkham Notch

Joe Dodge Lodge
Appalachian Mountain Club,
Pinkham Notch Camp,
Route 16
Tel: 603-466 2727
outdoors.org **$**
The modern lodge serves
hearty fare for hikers,
including all-you-can-eat
breakfast, deli lunch, and
solid American dinners.

Portsmouth

**Blue Mermaid Island
Grill**
409 The Hill
Tel: 603-427 2583
bluemermaid.com **$–$$**
Dishes with a Caribbean
flair, great margaritas,
mojitos, lots of beers. L
and D daily; Sun brunch.

Dolphin Striker
15 Bow Street
Tel: 603-431 5222
dolphinstriker.com **$$**
This riverfront tavern in
an 18th-century ware-
house serves New Eng-
land cuisine and offers
an 8-course dinner Tues-
day evenings ($40).
Spring Hill Tavern has live
music Thur–Sun.
D Tues–Sun.

Friendly Toast
121 Congress Street
Tel: 603-430-2154 **$**
Extremely popular for
breakfast, with hearty
treats and 1950s kitsch
decor. Open 24 hours on
weekends. B, L & D daily.

The Green Monkey
86 Pleasant Street
Tel: 603-427 1010
thegreenmonkey.net **$$–$$$**
This restaurant/martini
bar takes traditional
American dishes to new
heights, integrating cook-
ing techniques and ingre-
dients from around the
world. D Mon–Sat.

Jumpin' Jay's Fish Café
150 Congress Street
Tel: 603-766 3474
jumpinjays.com **$$**
It's seafood all the way
at this lively downtown
spot. Extensive raw bar.
D nightly.

Pesce Blue
103 Congress Street
Tel: 603-430 7766
pesceblue.com **$$–$$$**
Contemporary Italian
seafood grill with small
and large plate offerings.
D nightly; Sun brunch.

Portsmouth Brewery
56 Market Street
Tel: 603-431 1115
portsmouthbrewery.com **$**
New Hampshire's original
microbrewery serves up
international munchies
as well as burgers, sand-
wiches, and salads.
L and D daily.

Snowville

Snowvillage Inn
92 Stuart Road
(Off Route 153)
Tel: 603-447 2818
snowvillageinn.com **$$**
New England dishes
served in the candlelit
dining room of a fine
mountain-top country inn.
D Thur–Sun spring and
winter; Thur–Mon in
summer and fall.

Sugar Hill

Polly's Pancake Parlor
Route 117
Tel: 603-823 5575
pollyspancakeparlor.com **$**

The place to go for tasty
– if somewhat expensive
– pancakes, waffles, and
sandwiches. B and L
daily May–Oct.

Temple

Birchwood Tavern
Birchwood Inn, Route 45
Tel: 603-878 3285
thebirchwoodinn.com **$$–$$$**
The English menu at this
historic inn includes
steak and ale pie,
bangers and mash, and,
for dessert, spotted dick
and custard. D Wed–Sun.

Wolfeboro

51 Mill Street
51 Mill Street
Tel: 603-569 3303 **$$**
An eclectic menu com-
bines French dishes such
as veal citron with local
treats including crab
cakes and lobster rolls.
L Mon–Sat; D nightly.

Bars

Coat of Arms Pub, 174
Fleet Street, Portsmouth.
Tel: 603-431 0407. Cozy
pub/restaurant offers "a
taste of Britain", with
imported beers and ales,
bangers and mash, and
the seacoast's only
snooker table.
La Bec Rouge, 73 Ocean
Boulevard, Hampton. Tel:
603-926 5050. There's
an underground pub, a
first-floor restaurant and
bar, and an upper deck
bar with an ocean view.
Library Lounge, 401
State Street, Portsmouth.
Tel: 603-431 5202.
Book-lined, fireplaced
library with country-
estate feel and 100-plus
varieties of vodka.
**Poco's Bow Street
Cantina**, 37 Bow Street,
Portsmouth. Tel: 603 431-
5967. Grab a table on the
outdoor deck overlooking
the waterfront and relax
with one of the Mexican
restaurant's specialty
house drinks. There's
live music Thur nights.
Poor People's Pub, 1
Witchtrot Road. San-
bornville. Tel: 603-522
8378. A fine spot for a
pitcher of Sam Adams or
Pabst Blue Ribbon and a
slice of pizza.

LEFT: distinctive table accessories in Portsmouth.
RIGHT: Jumpin' Jay's Fish Café, Portsmouth.

WILDLIFE

New England's wilderness areas are one of its big draws, attracting campers, hunters, fishermen, photographers and nature lovers

It's obvious from the air and just as clear from the highways: trees cover more than three-quarters of New England, cloaking the mountains of New Hampshire, Maine, and Vermont. These woods and mountains ring with birdsong and are carpeted with wild flowers; particularly enthralling are the alpine flowers on Mount Washington *(see panel, far right)*.

The most exciting animal to see in the forests is moose. Desperately ungainly, and sporting hairy dewlaps beneath large snouts, they can often be spotted in northern New England, especially in and around lakes and marshes – or licking the salt that runs off the roads in winter. A bull can grow to well over 6 feet (2 meters) tall, with huge antlers, and can weigh half a ton – give him a wide berth. You may see moose as you drive around, particularly at dawn or dusk; if not, join one of many moose-watching trips organized locally.

Black bears are shy denizens of the deep forests. They seldom attack humans, but don't feed them or leave food scraps on the ground. Keep food in sealed containers and *never* approach cubs – their mothers are fiercely protective.

In the lakes and streams that lace the forests, beavers fell trees with their teeth, building dams and creating ponds. Their lodges built of mud and sticks, may be up to 6 ft (2 meters) tall. Also look out for raccoons, chipmunks, squirrels, porcupines, and skunks.

ABOVE: Signs along Route 3 from Pittsburg, New Hampshire, to the Canadian border read: "Brake for Moose. It Could Save Your Life. Hundreds of Collisions." They're not kidding: attracted by salt on the road, dozens of the state's 10,000 moose can be seen just before dusk strolling along "Moose Alley." These docile beasts, said to outnumber humans in parts of Vermont's Northeast Kingdom, have spread as far south as Connecticut.

LEFT: Black bears are most common in Maine, which has about 23,000. Hunters in the state shoot ("harvest") an average of 3,600 a year.

ABOVE: The fact that a Massachusetts company called Beaver Solutions dedicated itself to "resolving human/beaver conflicts and flooding-related beaver problems" indicate how North America's largest rodent wreaks havoc. Slow-moving, they take refuge in the ponds they create by building intricate dams.

ALPINE ATTRACTIONS

This cairn on Mount Washington, in New Hampshire, marks an alpine hike across this rugged arctic zone. The treeline occurs as low as 1,400 feet (420 meters). The area supports mammals such as voles and shrews, living in deep crevices, and 100 species of alpine plants, many of which grow only here, on Mount Katahdin in Maine's Baxter State Park, and in Labrador and the Arctic. They have adapted to dessication caused by biting winds, poor soil, minimal sunlight, and a short growing season. Some take 25 years to flower. These exquisite plants, growing in and around the lichen-covered rocks with sedges and dwarfed balsam firs, include gold thread, fireweed, alpine bearberry, starflower, arnica, mountain cranberry, wren's egg cranberry, skunk currant and the dwarf cinquefoil Potentilla robbinsiana, unique to Mount Washington. Their vibrant colors are best seen mid-June to August.

ABOVE: Almost four in five of New England's red foxes were wiped out in the 1990s, hit by rabies and distemper and outflanked by coyotes. But, to the alarm of chicken farmers, they have been making a comeback. They can most easily be seen in summer when they hunt food for their young.
BELOW: The loon is the state bird of New Hampshire. Some believe it is the oldest bird on earth, though scientists say this is a case of mistaken identity. They are known in Europe as "divers," and their American name derives from the aquatic birds' yodel-like cry. They can live for up to 30 years.

ABOVE: Waders include American egret (pictured) and black-crowned night heron. Forest birds include pine siskin, blue jay, golden crowned kinglet and chickadee.

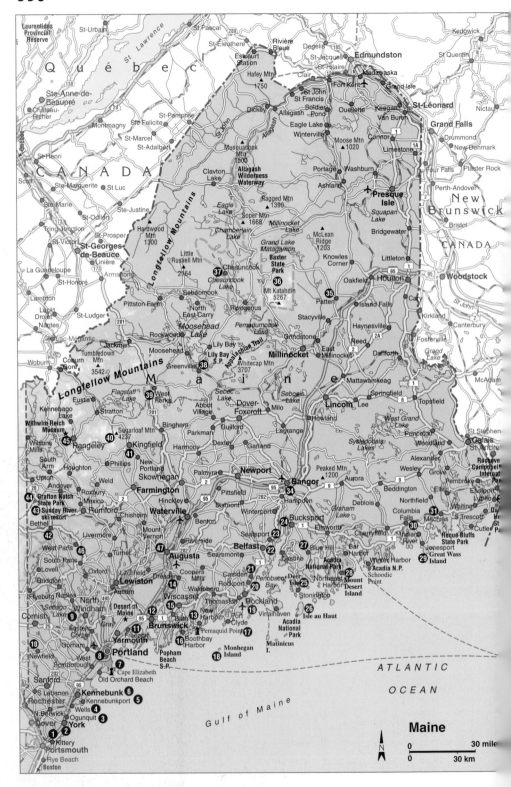

Maine

0   30 miles
0   30 km

Recommended Restaurants and Bars on pages 364–7

MAINE

Maine is a land of jagged coastlines and vast pine woods, of remote peninsulas, fresh lobster and famed outlet shops – a state inimitably evoked in the soft canvases of Winslow Homer

By New England standards, Maine – beyond its heavily trafficked southern coast – remains a vast and mysterious wilderness. Larger in area than the other five New England states combined, the "Pine Tree State" (nine-tenths covered with forest) bears little resemblance to its comfortably settled neighbors and has a savage beauty. It's little wonder, then, that residents pride themselves on their rugged independence and turn a bemused eye on the strange habits of "summer people" – or, in the well used 19th-century term "rusticators."

The two Maines

Maine's economy developed much in the way its future tourism industry would – with a bifurcation of interests based on geography. Coastal Mainers made ample use of the fine natural harbors, and virtually all commerce within Maine, and between Maine and the outside world, was conducted by sea.

Along with trading and boatbuilding, the seaside communities of Maine depended heavily upon the fishing industry, and eventually became home to New England's biggest lobster fleet. Inland

Main attractions
OLD GAOL, YORK
KENNEBUNKPORT
PORTLAND
L.L. BEAN, FREEPORT
BRUNSWICK
BATH IRON WORKS
WISCASSET
PEMAQUID POINT
PENOBSCOT BAY
MOUNT DESERT ISLAND
AUGUSTA

PRECEDING PAGES:
Pemaquid Point
Lighthouse.
BELOW: tribute to
a fishing heritage.

The state in snapshot

Known as: The Pine Tree State.
Motto: *Dirigo* (I direct).
Origin of name: called after old French province.
Entered Union: March 15, 1820, when it was separated from Massachusetts to form the 23rd state.
Capital: Augusta.
Area: 33,215 sq. miles (91,653 sq. km).
Highest point: Mount Katahdin, 5,268 ft (1,606 meters).
Population: 1.24 million.
Population density: 35 people per sq. mile (13 per sq. meter).
Economy: services (including tourism) and manufacturing (paper and paper products, footwear and other leather goods, lumber), plus fishing, agriculture, and forestry.
Annual visitors: 8 million.
National representation: two senators and two representatives to Congress.
Famous citizens: Henry Wadsworth Longfellow, Sir Hiram and Hudson Maxim, Edna St Vincent Millay, and Stephen King.

A floatplane at Chesuncook Lake in the North Woods. Some remote regions are accessible only by boat or by plane.

Maine, where settlement was thin, became a timber empire. The "paper plantations" have, paradoxically, kept much of northern Maine a wild paradise for campers, canoeists, hunters, and anglers, although flux in the industry is turning more land over to potential development and shuttering mills in towns such as East Millinocket, where the overpowering aroma of paper manufacture has long been the perfume of prosperity.

THE SOUTH COAST

The best way to see Maine is to start at the southern tip and head northeast along the old coastal highway, US 1. (I-95 is bigger and faster, for those who have specific destination in mind, but utter lacking in scenery.) Although, geograp ically, the coast represents only a ti fraction of the state, 45 percent of Mai residents call it home, and the ove whelming majority of visitors are a headed for the shore.

The southernmost segment, extendi from Kittery to Freeport, attracted t earliest settlers and to this day is the m heavily traveled, blending histo enclaves with built-up beaches and d count shopping malls. Just across t New Hampshire border from Portsmou is **Kittery ❶**, home to **Kittery Outle** (exit 3 off I-95; tel: 888-548-8379) c of the state's largest concentrations outlet malls. More than 120 stores a clustered around the **Kittery Tradi Post** (tel: 888-587 6246; open daily shopping destination for outdoor equi ment and clothing since 1926.

The town is also home to **Portsmou Naval Yard** – the nation's first, found in 1806. **Kittery Historical and Nav Museum** (Routes 1 and 236; tel: 20 439 3080; open June–Columbus D Tues–Sat 10am–4pm; entrance fee) de

Why harbors were the key to the making of Maine

Geologists refer to Maine's littoral as a "drowned" coastline: the original coast sank thousands of years ago, its valleys becoming Maine's harbors, its mountains the hundreds of islands lying just offshore. As the coastline sank, receding glaciers exposed vast expanses of granite, which not only gave Maine's mountains their peculiar pink coloration, but also provided settlers with a valuable source of building material. The "rock-bound coast of Maine" extends only 400 miles (640 km) as the gull flies, but 3,500 miles (5,600 km) if all the coves, inlets, and peninsulas were magically ironed out.

The first known residents, 11,000 years ago, were paleolithic hunters and fishers who lived along the coast. Other tribes followed, including a race

known as the Red Paint People because lumps of red ocher (powdered hematite), thought to have been part of a religious sacrament, have been found in their grave sites. The earliest European explorers, in the 15th and 16th centuries, were greeted

ABOVE: fishing off the Maine coast in 1882.

by the Abenaki tribe, whose name mea "easterners" or "dawnlanders."

John Cabot visited Maine in 1497– (his explorations established all fut British claims to the land), but it was until after Captain John Smith soune "about 25 excellent harbors" in 16 that the "Father of Maine," Sir F dinando Gorges, was granted a ch ter to establish British colonies. R French explorers also claimed pa of Maine and Canada, and territc disputes that were resolved only the French and Indian Wars of 18th century.

Maine became a part of the Cc monwealth of Massachusetts a remained so until 1820, whe became, as residents still like to it, the State of Maine.

...ments the shipyard's history, from the construction of *Ranger* (the first ship ...er to fly the Stars and Stripes, under ...e command of John Paul Jones in ...777) to today's submarines.

Nearby **Fort McClary State Historic ...ite** (off Route 103, 28 Oldsfield Road, ...ittery Point; tel: 207-384 5160; open ...lemorial Day–Oct 1; entrance fee) was ...rst fortified in 1715 and rebuilt repeat-...lly right up until the 1898 Spanish-...merican War. All that remains is the ...846 hexagonal wooden blockhouse, and ...e granite seawall – a scenic vantage ...oint from which to view racing yachts in ...ortsmouth Harbor and Whaleback Light ...the mouth of the Piscataqua River.

...ork

...few miles to the north, **York ❷**, one of ...laine's first settlements, was a center of ...ssent during the Revolutionary era. The ...ocal chapter of the Sons of Liberty ...ecided to hold their own tea party when ...British ship carrying tea anchored in ...ork Harbor**. Being practical Mainers, ...owever, they "liberated" the tea rather ...an throw it in the harbor.

The **Old York Historical Society** (207

York Street; tel: 203-363 4974, oldyork .org; open early June–mid-Oct Mon–Sat; entrance fee) maintains nine historic sites, including the **John Hancock Warehouse** (a contemporary wrote that the signer of the Declaration of Independence was "more successful in politics than in business"), the 1750 **Jefferds Tavern** and the **Old Gaol**, built in 1719, thought to be the oldest public building in the US. With its 2-ft (60-cm) thick fieldstone walls and tiny windows bordered with sawteeth, the jail served its purpose until 1860. It has now been restored to its 1790s appearance, complete with dungeon, and provides an interesting (sawtoothed) window on penal attitudes of yore. The **Elizabeth Perkins House** is a prime example of Colonial revivalism, an 18th-century farmhouse renovated by descendants of its builders in the early 20th century.

The other side of York, physically and philosophically, is **York Beach**, a narrow mile-long strip of fine sand, lined with every imaginable type of fast-seafood shack and family-entertainment facility. The **Cliff Walk** off York Harbor's boardwalk affords beautiful views

Maine pioneered the temperance movement in 1815 when the world's first Total Abstinence Society was formed in Portland. Support grew, and in 1851 the state banned the manufacture and sale of liquor. It wasn't until Prohibition was repealed nationally in 1933 that the citizens of Maine could legally hit the bottle again.

BELOW: York Beach divides into Short Sands Beach, close to the town's main attractions, and Long Sands Beach, close to the motels along Route 1A.

BELOW: Rachel Carson National Wildlife Refuge, off Route 9, was established in 1966 at Wells to protect salt marshes and estuaries for migratory birds.

of the coastline, and of Cape Neddick's 1879 **Nubble Light** off Route 1A; seasonal information center).

Ogunquit and Wells

The scenic **Shore Road** north from York's Main Street to Ogunquit passes the turn-off for **The Cliff House Resort & Spa** (tel: 207-361 1000), a 70-acre (28-hectare) oceanfront resort and spa founded in 1872. Just ahead, the **Ogunquit Museum of American Art** (543 Shore Road; tel: 207-646 4909; open July–Oct, Mon–Sat; Sun, pm; entrance fee) exhibits works by 20th-century American masters including Reginald Marsh and Maine-inspired Edward Hopper and Rockwell Kent.

Turn right just past the museum to **Perkins Cove** in Ogunquit, the southern terminus for **Marginal Way**, a spectacular, 1-mile (1.6-km) seaside walk along the cliffs. Excursion boats leave from here, and there are some shops and restaurants.

Charles Woodbury "discovered" the tiny fishing village of **Ogunquit** ❸ (whose Indian name meant "coastal lagoon") in 1898, and the word soon spread to artists and vacationers. Today, tourists crowd the galleries, shops, and

eateries that have taken over the fishing shacks, and frolic in the surf at the 3-mile (5-km) **town beach** (parking fee). In summer the town is so packed with visitors that reproduction trolleys are the easiest way to get around (parking is tight). Tallulah Bankhead, Bette Davis and Helen Hayes all trod the boards at the **Ogunquit Playhouse**, a highly regarded summer theater founded in 1933 (Route 1; open June–Labor Day; tel: 207-646 5511; ogunquitplayhouse.org).

A few miles north on Route 1, in **Wells** ❹, the **Wells Auto Museum** (tel: 207-646 9064; open mid-June–Sept daily 10am–5pm; entrance fee) exhibits more than 80 antique and classic cars, including a 1949 Cadillac Fleetwood and a 1907 Stanley Steamer.

Watch for the turn-off to the **National Estuarine Research Reserve at Laudholm Farm** (Laudholm Road; tel: 207-646 1555; wellsreserve.org; visitor center open mid-Jan–early Dec Mon–Fri, Memorial Day weekend–Columbus Day Mon–Sat, Sun pm; parking fee). The preserve has 7 miles (11 km) of hiking trails along coastal marsh, uplands, and pristine beach. There are tours in summer.

The Kennebunks

East of Wells on Route 9, **Kennebunkport ❺**, once the shipbuilding center of York County, has embraced tourism; upscale shops, galleries and restaurants are clustered around downtown **Dock Square**. The Kennebunkport Historical Society (tel: 207-967 2751) maintains several properties. In town, at 8 Maine Street, the **Nott House** (open late June–mid-Oct, Wed–Fri, Sat am; entrance fee), an 1853 Greek Revival, is a time capsule of seacoast life from the late 1700s to the mid-1900s. The Society leads guided walking tours from the house Thur at 11am mid-July–Aug; Sat at 11am from mid-July–mid-Oct. Their second property, a mile-and-a-half from Dock Square (125 North Street; exhibit center open year-round) includes an exhibit center and blacksmith shop.

From Dock Square head up North Street (which becomes Log Cabin Road) 3¼ miles (5 km) to the **Seashore Trolley Museum** (Log Cabin Road; tel: 207 967 2712; open weekends in May and late Oct; Memorial Day–mid-Oct daily; entrance fee). It exhibits one of the world's largest collections of antique trolley cars and offers a 4-mile (6.5 km) ride on vintage streetcars.

From town, take a drive along Ocean Avenue, past the historic **Colony Hotel** (140 Ocean Avenue; tel: 800-552 2363; thecolonyhotel.com) and Walker's Point, the summer home of the first President Bush. After the road converges with Route 9, continue on to visit the charming fishing village of **Cape Porpoise**, site of the region's first settlement. Route 9, which passes the turn-off for **Goose Rocks Beach,** is a scenic – and less crowded – route to Old Orchard Beach (see below). The deck overlooking the ocean at Cape Pier Restaurant, next to Cape Porpoise Town Pier, is a good place for clam chowder and a lobster roll.

Kennebunk ❻, 4¼ miles (7 km) northwest of Kennebunkport, has a rich shipbuilding heritage. This is the focus of the first-rate **Brick Store Museum** (Main Street; tel: 207-985 4802; open Tues–Sat; entrance fee), which also offers tours of the architecturally-diverse downtown

Historic District (May–Oct). At 105 Summer Street (Routes 9A/35) look for the unmistakable 1826 **Wedding Cake House**, festooned with elaborate carved wooden scrollwork. Legend has it that a sea-bound captain who married in haste had it built to compensate his wife for the lack of a cake at their rushed ceremony.

North to Portland

Further up the coast is **Old Orchard Beach**, a seaside resort popular among French Canadians. The 7-mile (11-km) beach is flanked with motels and condos and, at the Ocean Pier, an amusement park makes for a nice old-fashioned way to cap off a beach day.

Eastward, just south of Portland on **Cape Elizabeth ❼**, is the oldest lighthouse on the eastern seaboard, the Portland Head Light (1791). The history of lighthouses is documented at the **Museum at Portland Head Light** (Shore Road, Fort Williams Park; tel: 207-799 2661; open Memorial Day–late Oct, daily; late Oct–Dec, mid-April–Memorial Day, weekends; entrance fee). The sweeping views are largely unchanged since Henry

The Wedding Cake House at Kennebunk. It is said that the Gothic tastes of its creator, shipbuilder George Washington Bourne (1801–56), were inspired by Milan's cathedral.

BELOW: the harbor at Kennebunkport.

TIP

The "CAT" departs from Portland at 8am and crosses to Yarmouth in 5½ hours, and departs from Yarmouth at 4pm, making this a long but pleasant day trip (there are slot machines and movies on board). But there are not a lot of places to sit on the deck, and in inclement weather this can feel like a long voyage, particularly with kids. It's an international cruise, so be sure to bring the necessary documents.

BELOW: the Flat Iron Building, Portland.

Wadsworth Longfellow's day. The Portland-born poet often walked here from town to chat with the keeper. The 90-acre (36-hectare) park is open daily.

Portland

With a population of 230,000 in its greater area, **Portland ⑧**, overlooking Casco Bay, is home to almost one-fourth of the state's population. Founded as Casco in the middle of the 17th century, the city has the advantage of being 100 miles (160 km) closer to Europe than any other major US seaport, and is blessed with a sheltered, deep-water harbor.

Three times the city was burned completely to the ground – by Indians in 1675, by the British in 1775, and by accident in 1866. After the last fire, it was reconfigured. Streets were widened, and an elaborate network of municipal parks instituted. The Portland Trolley (tel: 207-772 0429; mainelytours.com; fee) provides a 90-minute tour of the city's highlights.

The city's skill in urban planning can be seen in the revitalization of the atmospheric **Old Port ⒜** district, a salty warren of old brick buildings and cobbled streets, packed with sophisticated shops

and restaurants. Several whale watch and cruise ships depart from the docks along Commercial Street at the edge of the Exchange. **The CAT** (tel: 877-359 3760; catferry.com), a high-speed catamaran (passengers and cars) operates between Portland and Yarmouth, Nova Scotia Thur–Sun mid-July–Aug; Fri–Sun May 30–mid-July and Sept–mid-Oct; other days, it departs from Bar Harbor (see margin tip). **Casco Bay Lines** (56 Commercial Street; tel: 207-774 7871; cascobaylines.com), the oldest ferry service in America, offers inexpensive cruises as well as a leisurely three-hour ride aboard a mailboat, which delivers mail to islands throughout Casco Bay.

Spread out beyond the harbor are the **Calendar Islands** – so named because John Smith reported that there were 365 of them (in reality, there are only 136). **Eagle Island Tours** (Long Wharf; tel: 207-774 6498; mainelytours.com) runs visitors out to **Eagle Island** to tour the summer home of Admiral Robert Peary, who planted the American flag on the North Pole in 1909 (open late June–Labor Day and weekends in Sept). The company also operates sunset lighthouse cruises.

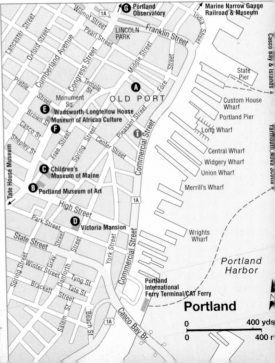

Portland

Portland remains a thriving cultural crossroads, known for its innovative dance and theater troupes. The city also has a designated downtown **Arts District**, home to several museums, including the **Portland Museum of Art** , designed by I.M. Pei and strong on such locally inspired artists as Winslow Homer, Edward Hopper and Andrew Wyeth, as well as Van Gogh, Degas and Picasso (7 Congress Square; tel: 207-775 6148; open Memorial Day–Columbus Day, daily; Tues–Sun rest of year; Fri until 9pm; entrance fee).

Next door is the imaginative **Children's Museum of Maine** (142 Free Street; tel: 207-828 1234; open Memorial Day–Labor Day, Mon–Sat; Sun pm; rest of year, Tues–Sat; Sun pm; entrance fee). It has a camera obscura and appeals mostly to children up to 14.

Several Portland neighborhoods warrant strolling – especially the Western Promenade, a parade of 19th-century architectural styles. By far the most elaborate dwelling in town is the 1859–63 brownstone Italianate villa **Victoria Mansion** (109 Danforth Street; tel: 207-772 4841; open May–Oct Mon–Sat,

Sun pm by 45-minute guided tour; entrance fee). It has showpiece interiors, with painted ceilings and carved walls in the Rococo manner.

By contrast is the somewhat restrained 1785–86 **Wadsworth-Longfellow House** (489 Congress Street; tel: 207-774 1822; open May–Oct, Mon–Fri, Sat pm; entrance fee), built by Longfellow's grandfather, a Revolutionary War officer. Inside are the parlor where the poet's parents were married and the room where he wrote *The Rainy Day*. The house is headquarters for the Maine Historical Society, whose exhibits chronicle five centuries of local history.

The **Museum of African Culture** (13 Brown Street; tel: 207-871 7188; open Tues–Fri; entrance fee) exhibits works by artists from sub-Saharan Africa, and includes more than 1,500 works, including bronzes and masks.

Built in 1807 as a maritime signal tower, the 86-ft (26-meter) high **Portland Observatory** (138 Congress Street; tel: 207-774 5561; open Memorial Day weekend–Columbus Day, daily; entrance fee), which ceased operation in 1923. It offers one of the most magnifi-

Statue to the poet Henry Wadsworth Longfellow (1807–82) in Portland's Longfellow Square.

BELOW: lobsters are big business in Portland.

The Androscoggin River rapids at Brunswick.

cent views in town. Admission includes a 30-minute guided tour.

Hop aboard one of the 2-ft gauge trains that once connected rural Maine to the rest of the world at the **Marine Narrow Gauge Railroad and Museum** (55 Fore Street; tel: 207-828 0814; mngrr.org; open daily May 19–mid-Oct, weekends rest of year; fee). Admission includes a ride along Casco Bay, and entrance to the museum which chronicles the trains' history from 1879 to the late 1930s.

Overlooking the Fore River is the **Tate House Museum** (1267 Westbrook Street; tel: 207-774 6177; open early June–mid-Oct, Tues–Sat and first Sun of the month; entrance fee). A Georgian townhouse, it was built in 1755 for the senior mast agent for the Royal Navy. A guided tour includes the summer gardens.

The Lakes Region

With its easy access from Portland via Route 302, **Sebago Lake** is the state's second largest lake, and the most popular of the Western Lakes, offering swimming, boating, camping, and fishing in 1,400-acre (160-hectare) **Sebago Lake State Park** (State Park Road, between Naples and South Casco; tel: 207-693 6613; open year round; entrance fee May–mid-Oct).

On the causeway which separates Sebago from Long Lake, the *Songo River Queen II* (Route 302; tel: 207-693 6861) provides one-hour tours on Long Lake, and 2½-hour sails up Songo River. Several marinas rent canoes, powerboats, pontoon boats, and jet skis.

Near the New Hampshire border off Route 11, **Willowbrook at Newfield** (Elm Street; tel: 207-793 2784; open Memorial Day weekend–Columbus Day, Thur–Mon; entrance fee) is a reconstituted late 19th-century museum village of 37 buildings which captures aspects of this gentler time, from horse-drawn sleighs to bicycles built for two, from a classic ice-cream parlor to a century-old "riding gallery" – a working carousel.

To the north of Portland via Route 1 or I-95 in **Yarmouth**, Delorme Company, one of the leaders in cartographic technology, has a huge **Map Store** (2 Delorme Drive; tel: 800-642 0970; open daily). The centrepiece is the astoundingly detailed "Eartha," the world's largest rotating globe.

Freeport

The little town of **Freeport** is known worldwide, thanks to the legendary **L.L. Bean** department store (95 Main Street; tel: 800-559 0747 ext. 37222; llbean.com), open 24 hours, 365 days a year. Though a boon to the local economy, Bean's has inspired imitators, so that the entire village is now overrun with upscale discount outlets (freeportusa.com).

Atlantic Seal Cruises (25 Main Street: tel: 207-865 6112 or 877-285 7325: Memorial Day–late Oct daily sails every day at 1:30pm for Admiral Robert Peary's summer home on Eagle Island, with seal and osprey watching en route. If enough people sign up (at least 10), there is also a six-hour voyage to Seguin Island (Thur only). Cruises depart from Main Street Wharf in South Freeport. Advance booking is required.

A rather peculiar attraction in this area is the **Desert of Maine** (95 Desert Road

BELOW:
rail nostalgia at Yarmouth.

2 miles (3 km) of I-295; tel: 207-865 6962; open early May–mid-Oct, daily; entrance fee). This was a farm that was overcultivated, then logged, eventually losing all its topsoil. Sand took over, engulfing entire trees. It's like an overgrown sandbox, interesting mainly for the simple fact of its being there.

THE MID-COAST

Brunswick **⑫** is best known as the home of **Bowdoin College** (tel: 207-725 3000 for tour information). Founded in 1794, Bowdoin was originally slated to be built in Portland, but the college's benefactors found that that city offered too many "temptations to dissipation, extravagance, vanity and various vices of seaport towns." Nathaniel Hawthorne and Henry Wadsworth Longfellow were alumni, class of 1825.

On campus, the **Bowdoin Museum of Art** (Walker Art Building; tel: 207-725 3275; open Tues–Sat; Sun pm; donations) houses a small but astute sampling of paintings by such notables as Stuart, Copley, Homer, Eakins, and Wyeth; as well as the Warren Collection of classical antiquities, and works by European masters.

Also on campus is the fascinating **Peary-MacMillan Arctic Museum** (Hubbard Hall; tel: 207-725 3416; open Tues–Sat; Sun pm). It heralds the accomplishments of North Pole explorers Robert E. Peary and Donald MacMillan, who achieved their objective in 1909.

The **Pejepscot Historical Society** (the Indian name for the Androscoggin River meant "crooked like a snake") oversees several fine museums in town. Their museum and headquarters, at 159 Park Row (tel: 207-729 6606), are open year-round Mon–Sat.

Next door is the **Skolfield-Whittier House** (open June–Columbus Day, Thur–Sat, tours at 11am and 2pm; entrance fee). This brick Italianate "double house" was built in 1859. One side houses the society's collections; the other has the original furnishings of three generations of one family. Civil War hero Joshua L. Chamberlain (1828–1914) was teaching at Bowdoin until he enlisted. The **Joshua L. Chamberlain Museum** (226 Maine Street; open June–Columbus Day, Tues–Sat, guided tours on hour 10am–4pm; entrance fee) exhibits memorabilia of Chamberlain, who

> **TIP**
>
> The Bowdoin International Music Festival (Tel: 207-373 1400; bowdoinfestival.org), from late June through July, features chamber music concerts at sites throughout Brunswick.

BELOW:
the boot that built
the Bean empire.

L.L. Bean's beginnings

In 1912, the 40-year-old Maine-born Leon Leonwood Bean, a keen hunter and fisherman, decided to build a better hunting boot. In a circular, he offered the new, improved waterproof boot with a money-back guarantee. Legend has it that 90 out of the first 100 pairs fell apart: the soles separated from the leather uppers. True to his word, Bean replaced the defective boots with pairs of a newer, improved design and – after absorbing the loss – began building the legendary L.L. Bean empire that he controlled until his death in 1967 at the age of 94.

Bean lived long enough to see his store grow from a humble outdoors outfitter to a purveyor of casual fashion and recreational sporting goods with an enormous mail-order business. Its sales today exceed $1.5 billion a year.

Bath claims to have a slower pace and a friendly pedestrian atmosphere.

Bath

East of Brunswick on US 1, **Bath** ⓭ was once the nation's fifth largest seaport, and still builds ships. For a time in the 19th century, Maine's shipyards were responsible for one-third to one-half of all ships on the high seas. When the days of wooden ships ended, the old yards gave way to the **Bath Iron Works**, today a busy producer of Navy ships.

Visitors can tour the Iron Works aboard a trolley (one-hour tours Tues and Thur at 12.30pm and Sat at 10am) run by the **Maine Maritime Museum** (243

Washington Street; tel: 207-443 1316; bathmaine.com; open daily; entrance fee). This is a 25-acre (10-hectare) riverside complex which preserves the history of shipbuilding in Bath and other coastal towns. Exhibits on nautical tools and gadgets capture the flavor of seafaring days, while a working boatyard demonstrates shipbuilding techniques. The museum also maintains an authentic 142-ft (43-meter) Grand Banks schooner, the *Sherman Zwicker*, which can be boarded when in port, and offers boat rides.

Bath's **historic district** has fine examples of Greek Revival, Georgian and Italianate architecture among its mansions, cozy inns, and restaurants. The **Midcoast Maine Chamber of Commerce** (45 Front Street; tel: 207-443 9751; midcoast maine.com) distributes an excellent self-guided tour brochure.

Fourteen miles (22 km) south of Bath on Route 209 on the **Phippsburg Peninsula** is **Popham Beach State Park** (tel: 207-389 1335; entrance fee in season), a 4½-mile (7-km) stretch of sand which is one of the prettiest and most popular beaches in the state. Just past the park is **Fort Popham State Historic Site** (open

BELOW: there are more than 3 milliion lobster traps in Maine waters.

(column continued above) later served four terms as Maine's governor and became Bowdoin's president.

Recommended Restaurants and Bars on pages 364–7

Memorial Day-Sept), an unfinished 1861 fort with a tower and bunkers.

Just across the Kennebec River from Bath, in **Woolwich**, visitors have several options: turn north on Route 128 for approximately 10 miles (16 km) to the **Pownalborough Courthouse** (tel: 207-882 6817; open July–Labor Day, Tues–Sat; Sun pm; June and day after Labor Day–Sept, Sat, and Sun pm; entrance fee) in **Dresden** ⓴. The state's only remaining pre-Revolutionary courthouse is a handsomely restored and magnificently detailed three-floor riverfront building with a fascinating period cemetery on the grounds. (Note: if continuing north, to avoid backtracking continue north past the courthouse for 2½ miles/ 4 km to Route 27 and head south about 9 miles/14 km to Wiscasset.)

A right turn onto Route 127 south in Woolwich goes to **Georgetown**'s **Reid State Park** (375 Seguinland Road; tel: 207-371 2303; entrance fee), another popular wide, sandy beach.

Maine's prettiest village

Wiscasset ⓯ claims, with some justification, to be the "prettiest village in Maine." Two handsome sea captains' houses are maintained by Historic New England (historicnewengland.org; tel: 207-882 7169; open June–mid-Oct; entrance fee). These are the Federal-era, National Historic Landmark **Nickels-Sortwell House** (121 Main Street; open Fri–Sun; tours on the hour); and the 1807 **Castle Tucker** (2 Lee Street; open Wed–Sun), an 1807 Georgian mansion with Federal and Victorian furnishings.

Another offbeat tourist attraction is the **Old Lincoln County Jail and Museum** Federal Street; tel: 207-882 6817; open July, Aug Tues–Sat, Sun pm; Sat and Sun in June and Sept; entrance fee). This is an 1811 hoosegow with granite walls up to 41 inches (over 1 meter) thick. Considered a model of humane treatment in its day, because prisoners were afforded individual cells, this grim repository was used right up until 1913, and has the graffiti to prove it. It's now headquarters of the Lincoln County Historical Association.

Collectors may want to visit the Merry Music Box Shop in a 32-room 1852 sea captain's mansion, now **Musical Wonder House** (18 High Street; tel: 207-882-7163). It has more than 5000 restored musical boxes, player grand pianos and organs, spring-powered phonographs, musical birds, and the like.

On to Boothbay Harbor

North on Route 1, just over the Sheepscot River, turn onto Davis Island to visit **Fort Edgecomb State Historic Site**, an octagonal fort of 1808–9 with commanding views of the river and beyond. Revolutionary War reenactments take place on some weekends in summer (Fort Road, Edgecomb; tel: 207-882 7777; open Memorial Day–Labor Day, daily; entrance fee).

Although certainly subdued compared to the commercial excesses of the south coast, **Boothbay Harbor** ⓰, to the south on Route 27, is decidedly touristy. In summer, tens of thousands of visitors throng the streets of this former fishing village to inspect the shops, sample seafood delicacies, charter boats to explore offshore

The Nickels-Sortwell House, Wiscasset, built in 1807 by Captain William Nickels, a ship owner and trader.

BELOW: the past on sale in Wiscasset, which was first settled in 1663, abandoned during the French and Indian Wars, and then resettled around 1730.

A photographer's favorite: Pemaquid Point Lighthouse.

BELOW:
Boothbay Harbor, a popular yachting destination.

islands with names such as the Cuckolds and the Hypocrites, and book passage on whale watches and deep-sea fishing trips. There are yacht and golf clubs, flower shows, auctions, and clambakes.

At Boothbay Railway Village (Route 27, 586 Wiscasset Road, Boothbay; tel: 207-633 4727; open June–early Oct, daily; entrance fee), the main attraction is a narrow-gauge, coal-fired railroad, encircling a range of reconstructed buildings of yesteryear, including a barbershop, bank and country store.

In **West Boothbay Harbor**, the state's **Marine Resources Aquarium** (194 McKown Point Road; tel: 207-633 9674; open Memorial Day weekend–late Sept daily; entrance fee) has an 850-gallon fish tank and a gallery echoing the rocky Maine coast. Kids can pet live sharks and view a 23-lb (10-kg) lobster named Fritz.

Pemaquid Point

Farther to the north off Route 1, Route 130 cuts south through Damariscotta to **Pemaquid Point** ⓱, a rocky peninsula

whose Indian name meant "long finger." Early explorers couldn't miss it, and in fact there's some evidence to support a claim that a settlement here may have predated Plymouth. Some 75,000 artifacts dating to the first quarter of the 17th century have been unearthed so far, and many are displayed in an interesting state-run museum, **Colonial Pemaquid State Historic Site**, alongside a diorama recreating the settlement (off Route 130; open late May–early Sept, daily; tel: 207-677 2423; entrance fee to museum).

Admission also includes **Fort William Henry**, a 1907 replica on the site of several failed stockades. The 1630 original was burned by pirates, and a 1677 replacement, thought impregnable, was destroyed in 1689 by the French and Indians.

At the tip of this peninsula on Route 130, in **Lighthouse Park** stands the **Pemaquid Point Lighthouse,** commissioned in 1827 by John Quincy Adams. Visitors can climb the tower and visit the 1857 keeper's house, now a quaint hodgepodge **Fishermen's Museum** (open Memorial Day–Columbus Day, daily; entrance fee). With powerful surf constantly breaking on the rocks, the point is a favorite spot for painters and photographers, as well as families who enjoy poking around the tide pools. The lighthouse is shown on the Maine quarter coin.

The large white mansion on the hill overlooking the St George River at the junction of Routes 1 and 131 in **Thomaston** is the **General Henry Knox Museum** (tel: 207-354 8062; open Memorial Day–Columbus Day, Tues–Sat for guided tours; entrance fee). It's a replica of Montpelier, the home built by the country's first secretary of war after he left his post and moved to Maine in 1795, and is a good place to learn the story of the self-made artillery commander who was vital to America's struggle for independence.

Monhegan Island

An early European explorer, David Ingram, astounded Europe with tales – most rather tall – of the marvelous peoples and cities he encountered on a jour ney from the Gulf of Mexico to Canada. Lured by such promising reports, a group of Germans settled Waldoboro in 1748, with, as a plaque at the center of town attests, "the promise and expectation of finding a prosperous city, instead of which they found nothing but wilderness." Another Ingram allusion, to "a great island that was backed like a whale," was naturally dismissed as fantasy.

However, the cliffs of **Monhegan Island ⑱**, 12 miles (19 km) south of Port Clyde, do indeed lend the island the appearance of a whale. And an otherworldly air still pervades this 700-acre (280-hectare) isle, little changed in the past century. Cars have made no inroads, and many residents are perfectly content without electricity. A magnet first for fishing fleets and later for artists (the most famous summer resident is the painter Jamie Wyeth, son of Andrew Wyeth), most of the island remains undeveloped.

Visitors can explore the Cliff Trail circling the island, and the Cathedral Woods Trail, where the island children are in the habit of constructing tiny "fairy houses" out of twigs and moss.

Monhegan is served by several ferries.

One, **Monhegan Boat Line** (tel: 207-372 8848; moheganboat.com; late May–mid-Oct), departs from **Port Clyde** (Route 131 South off Route 1 in Thomaston), at the tip of the St George Peninsula. In addition to the mailboat run to the island, the company also offers scenic and nature cruises.

Other boats to Monhegan depart from Boothbay Harbor (Balmy Days Cruises, tel: 800-298 2234, balmydaycruises.com; June–late Sept, daily) and New Harbor (Hardy Boat Cruises, tel: 800-278 3346; hardyboat.com; mid May–mid-Oct). Although it's possible to make the round-trip in one day, an overnight is advised for those who wish to ease back into a less stressful age *(lodgings: page 396)*.

Penobscot Bay

On the west end of Penobscot Bay is the town of **Rockland ⑲**, once a great limestone producer and now the world's largest distributor of lobsters, as well as the "Schooner Capital of Maine". These two- or three-masted schooners are a wonderful way to discover the coast as the earliest explorers encountered it. Weekend and weeklong excursions may

TIPS

● Windjammer cruises, lasting a day to a week, depart from Rockland and nearby Camden. For information, contact the Maine Windjammer Association (tel: 207-374 2993; sailmaine coast.com).

● Rockland's annual Maine Lobster Festival (tel: 207-596 0376; mainelobsterfestival .com), held in late July–early August, is one of the state's most popular events.

BELOW: rowing teams in training.

Rockland holds the Maine Lobster Festival at the end of July with parades, a Maine Sea Goddess contest and cooking competitions. Details: www.maine lobsterfestival.com

Thanks to the 1935 bequest of "Aunt" Lucy Farnsworth, a frugal spinster who lived in but three rooms of her family mansion and left the town $1.3 million to start a museum, Rockland has a world-class collection of art. Worth visiting is the **Farnsworth Art Museum and Wyeth Center** (16 Museum Street; tel: 207-596 6457; farnsworthmuseum.org; open late May–mid-Oct, daily; mid-Oct–late May, Tues–Sun; Sun, pm; fee includes admission to all properties; free admission Sun 10am–1pm). It has many noted 19th- and 20th-century works, including paintings by Winslow Homer and John Marin, and sculpture by Louise Nevelson, who grew up in a Bath lumberyard.

be booked aboard more than a dozen vessels, some vintage and others quite new. The **Maine State Ferry Service** (general information: tel: 207-596 2202; state.me.us/mdot/opt/ferry/ferry.htm) transports passengers and vehicles to **Matinicus**, a small, quiet island populated primarily by lobstermen and their families; **Vinalhaven**, where old granite quarries make fine swimming holes and the paved roads are ideal for day-tripping bicyclists, and **North Haven**, mainly given over to vacation homes; the main village has several shops, restaurants and galleries. It's usually easy to board as a foot passenger; but taking a car means advance planning and often a wait in line.

Paintings by all three Wyeths (N.C., Andrew, and Jamie) are exhibited in a former church across from the **Farnsworth Homestead**, an 1850 Greek Revival home next to the museum. The museum's **Olson House**, 14½ miles (23 km) from Rockland in Cushing, was home to Christina Olson, immortalized in Andrew Wyeth's painting, *Christina's World*.

The traditions and history of lighthouses, life saving services, and the US Coast Guard are lovingly preserved at the

Hard-shell or soft-shell lobsters – which tastes better?

The colorful lobster buoys dotting the coast of Maine highlight a $130 million business: more lobster is fished here than in any other state. Yet most lobsters in Maine are still caught by independent fishermen in small boats.

Many lobstermen head out before dawn, when waters are calmer, and return in the late afternoon. Traps need to be checked at least once a week, and many professional lobstermen ("high-liners") have 1,000 to 1,500 traps or more, and may need to check several hundred a day. Although proximity to shore makes lobstering safer than other commercial fishing, it is still dangerous – and particularly grueling in the bitter Maine winter.

Lobsters are crustaceans whose external skeletons do not grow. Every year they molt, shedding their old shells and growing larger ones. This process happens when the water is warmer, in late June or early July. Conveniently for tourists, molting brings the lobsters closer to shore, making them easier to catch.

Without shells, the soft lobsters are vulnerable to predators such as codfish and sharks, so they migrate to shallow waters for safety. Here, they hide, absorbing sea water and expanding 15 to 20 percent in size. Over four to six weeks, the lobsters produce new shells, then return to deep water, where they shrink again. The lobsters are now known in the trade as "new-shell," or in restaurants as "soft-shell," as opposed to "hard-shell" before molting. A hard-shell lobster's meat can be up to 33 percent of its body weight, while a soft-shell's is only 25 percent, so hard-shell lobster tends to be more expensive. The taste is slightly different, and each Maine connoisseur has a preference. Some say new-shell is sweeter, some prefer hard-shell for its stronger taste.

ABOVE: outdoor cooking at Penobscot Bay.

Recommended Restaurants and Bars on pages 364–7

Maine Lighthouse Museum at the Maine Discovery Center (One Park Drive; tel: 207-594 3301; open daily Memorial Day–Columbus Day; Wed–Mon rest of year; entrance fee to museum).

The **Owl's Head Transportation Museum** is housed in a spiffed-up hangar at the Owl's Head airport south of Rockland (off Route 73; tel: 207-594 4418; open daily; entrance fee). It displays a splendid collection of vehicles – 50 cars, 28 planes, plus bikes and motorcycles – ranging from an 1885 Benz to a 1939 Packard to a Model F plane, a Wright Brothers prototype. On summer weekends, some displays are taken off their blocks and sent for a spin – a worthwhile departure from usual museum practice.

Works by some of the state's finest contemporary artists are in the **Center for Maine Contemporary Art** (162 Russell Avenue; tel: 207-236 2875; open year-round Tues–Sat, Sun pm; entrance fee), 6 miles (10 km) up the coast in the quiet village of **Rockport ⑳**. Here also are Maine Media Workshops (70 Camden Street; tel: 877-577 7700; theworkshops .com), which offer courses in photography and all types of film making.

Camden

Camden ㉑ ("Where the Mountains Meet the Sea") has enjoyed a long reign as the ultimate in genteel summering spots. Its picturesque harbor is lined with shops and restaurants; many of the finely preserved, gracious homes of 19th-century ship captains have been converted into upscale B&Bs.

Numerous excursion boats and wind-jammers (sailmainecoast.com) sail from the harbor from late May to mid-October: Contact the Chamber of Commerce for information (tel: 800-223 5459 or 207-236 4404; visitcamden.com).

Rockland native Edna St Vincent Millay once worked at an inn here, and penned one of her verses after climbing to the summit of 800-ft (240-meter) Mount Battie in the **Camden Hills State Park** (north of town off Route 1; tel: 207-236 3109; open mid-May–mid-Oct; entrance fee). The summit is accessible on foot or via a toll road, and the seaward view is one of Maine's loveliest.

Norumbega Inn (63 High Street; tel: 207-236 4646; nurumbegainn.com), the imposing stone castle overlooking the harbor just north of the village, was built

Camden's Chestnut Street Baptist Church.

BELOW: Camden from Mount Battie. Movies filmed or set in the pretty resort town include *Carousel* (1956), *Peyton Place* (1957) and *In the Bedroom* (2001).

Totems for sale in Belfast.

in 1886 by Joseph Stearns, who sold rights to his invention for the duplex telegraphy system to Western Union.

Belfast and Searsport

The 19th-century captains and shipbuilders of **Belfast** ❷ built their stately mansions in a variety of architectural styles that makes the town at the mouth of the Passagassawaukeag River a fascinating place to take a stroll. Stop at the **Belfast Area Chamber of Commerce**'s (tel: 207-338 5900; belfastmaine.org) seasonal booth on Main Street for a Walking Tour brochure.

A few miles north on Route 1, **Searsport** ❷, lined with dazzling white sea captains' homes, calls itself "the antiques capital of Maine." Between 1770 and 1920, this one town produced more than 3,000 vessels, and evidence of its rich history, along with China Trade treasures, can be found on Route 1 in **Penobscot Marine Museum** (5 Church Street; tel: 207-548 2529; penobscotmarine museum.org; open late May–late-Oct, Mon–Sat; Sun, pm; entrance fee). The sprawling complex, on the National Reg-

ister of Historic Places, has a fine collection of marine and folk art, ship models, nautical paintings, and water craft.

Farther along the coastal road, the outskirts of **Bucksport** ❷ are dominated by the new **Penobscot Narrows Bridge** (tel: 207-469-6553; open May–Oct; fee for observatory includes admission to fort). Here visitors can ride an elevator to the world's tallest bridge observatory, 420 ft (128 meters) above sea level, and view sweeping panoramas.

The only observatory access is in the vast **Fort Knox State Park** (Route 174 off Route 1; tel: 207-469 7719; open May–Nov; entrance fee). It was built in 1844–69 to defend Maine from Canada during the Aroostook War (actually a boundary dispute), but never completed.

Penobscot Bay

Intent on getting to the justly famed Mount Desert Island, many tourists never veer from US 1 and thus miss one of the most scenic areas in Maine. The peninsulas along the eastern side of Penobscot Bay well warrant some poking around, but be forewarned: the roads can be confusing, even with a road map.

From Route 1 in Bucksport, wind your way down Routes 175 and 166 (or 166A) to **Castine**. Established as a trading post by the Plymouth Pilgrims, the tiny town became one of the most hotly contested chunks of property in New England. Changing hands nine times, it was owned by the French, Dutch, British, and, eventually, Americans. Plaques around town as well as a free walking-tour brochure available at most local merchants, fill in the details, but it's enough to wander around, beneath a canopy of elms, taking in the array of fine white houses.

Some of these houses belong to the **Maine Maritime Academy** (founded in 1941 and one of five such schools nationwide that train merchant mariners). The academy's 1952 ship, the decommissioned *T/S State of Maine*, serves as a floating classroom (tel:207-326 2364 hourly tours, early-July–Aug, daily).

Take a detour off this detour to make a circuit of **Deer Isle** ❷, where the princi-

pal occupations are lobstering and fishing, and tourists, though welcome, won't find themselves catered to unduly. On the eastern side of the isle is the prestigious **Haystack Mountain School of Crafts**, whose 1960 "campus" is a cluster of small modern buildings perched precipitously on a piney bank overlooking Jericho Bay (Sunshine Road; tel: 207-348 2306; haystack-mtn.org). Special evening presentations are open to the public during the summer, and tours are offered Wednesdays at 1pm.

For a true getaway, take the **Isle-au-Haut Company mailboat** (tel: 207-367 5193; isleauhaut.com; bicycle rentals available) from the picturesque port of **Stonington** to the sparsely inhabited 5,800-acre (2,300-hectare) **Isle au Haut** **㉖**, 6 miles (10 km) out to sea. Half is privately owned and occupied primarily by lobstermen and their families; the other half part of **Acadia National Park**. For details, contact the Park: P.O. Box 177, Bar Harbor 04609; tel: 207-288 3338.

Heading northeast to hook up with US 1 again, you'll pass through **Blue Hill** **㉗**, long the choice of blueblood summerers who didn't care for the showy social season in Bar Harbor. The shipbuilding town is also renowned for its pottery, finished with glazes made from nearby copper mines and quarries. Several potters welcome visitors, including **Rowantrees Pottery** (Union Street; tel: 207-374 5535) and **Rackliffe Pottery** (Route 172; tel: 207-374 2297).

Mount Desert Island

Spotting the 17 exposed pink granite peaks of **Mount Desert Island** in 1604, Samuel de Champlain described the place as *"l'île des monts déserts"* – and the French pronunciation still holds, more or less, so accentuate the final syllable, as in "dessert."

The reason there's so much territory to explore in **Mount Desert Island** **㉘** is that 41,409 acres (16,765 hectares) of the 16 by 13-mile (26 by 34-km) island belong to **Acadia National Park,** which draws more than 5 million visitors a year *(see box below).*

Stop at the **Mount Desert Island Information Center** (on Thompson Island, between Ellsworth and Mt Desert Island; tel: 207-288 3411; open mid-May–mid-Oct) to get general informa-

BELOW: Mount Desert Island.

The making of Acadia

Society notables discovered this remote spot in the mid-19th century, and by the time the stock market crashed in 1929, millionaires had constructed more than 200 extravagant "cottages." (Only a few survive, some as institutions or inns: many were destroyed in 1947's devastating fire.) Harvard University president Charles W. Eliot had the foresight to initiate the park in 1916, and many of his peers contributed parcels. John D. Rockefeller Jr. threw in 11,000 acres (4,400 hectares) crisscrossed with 50 miles (80 km) of bridle paths he built to protest against the admission of horseless carriages onto the island in 1905. The trail network encourages mountain-biking, cross-country skiing, and just plain walking. And Frenchman Bay, to the northeast, is great for sailing.

tion for the entire island. Off Route 3 in **Hulls Cove** is the **Hulls Cove Visitor Center** Ⓐ (open mid-Apr–Oct, daily; tel: 207-288 3338; nps.gov/acad). Pick up a park map and a schedule of naturalist activities here; there are excellent hiking maps on sale.

Most visitors will want to experience the view from Cadillac Mountain, whose form dominates the park, and to drive or cycle the Park Loop Road, but there are many other possibilities, including horse and carriage tours from **Wildwood Riding Stables**, kayaking, sailing, and hiking in the less frequented areas. Even the shorter trails tend to be over uneven rock, so suitable footwear is essential.

The park is open all year. For off-season information, contact the headquarters at P.O. Box 177, Bar Harbor 04069; tel: 207-288 3338.

Car traffic is kept under control by a permit system covering the mostly one-way 27-mile (43 km) **Park Loop Road,** a toll road which makes a clockwise circuit of all the more scenic spots along the eastern coast; the reasonably priced permits are good for a week.

South of the Visitor Center, the **Wild**

TIP

The Island Explorer Shuttle bus (explore acadia.com) offers a free service throughout Mount Desert island from late June through Columbus Day. Check the website for detailed route information.

BELOW RIGHT: riding out on Mount Desert Island.

Gardens of Acadia shows a range of flor found at a variety of park sites, such a mountain heath and bog; adjacent are th **Nature Center**, with exhibits on Acadia' cultural and natural history, and a branc of the **Abbe Museum** (off Route 3 an Park Loop Road; open May–Oct, daily entrance fee). The museum is devoted t Maine's Native American heritage.

Sweeping views follow, from th Champlain Mountain Overlook acros Frenchman Bay to the distant Gouldsbor Hills. The road passes the start of th **Precipice Trail**, which has iron rungs an ladders for the steep sections, and furthe on are Sand Beach – edged by low cliffs and Acadia's one sandy beach – and th **Beehive Trail**, which gets superb panora mas but involves some potentially dizzy ing sections. Thunder Hole needs a win to stir things up; in the right conditions the spray blasts up through this chink o the coastline. Otter Point provide another memorable coastal outloo before the road heads inland, past Jorda Pond, with walks along the lakeside o on the short trail past Bubble Rock, huge boulder transported and dumped b glacier, to South Bubble Summit.

Recommended Restaurants and Bars on pages 364–7

Reached by the toll road or on foot, the tallest peak, 1,530-ft (466-meter) **Cadillac Mountain**, is the highest point along the Atlantic coast north of Rio de Janeiro, and affords glorious 360° views stretching inland as far as Mount Katahdin, Maine's highest summit, and seaward to encompass myriad smaller islands – a particularly lovely vista when bathed in the glow of sunrise (a surprisingly large number of people arrive at this early hour) and sunset.

Bar Harbor

Back on Route 3, continue past the entrance for "The CAT" (tel: 207-288 3395 or 888-249 7245; catferry.com), a high-speed catamaran car and ferry service from Bar Harbor to Yarmouth, Nova Scotia *(also see margin note, page 344).*

Bar Harbor **B** is Mount Desert Island's main town – a bit over commercialized, but with a pretty town green, a marvelous Art Deco cinema, a lovely walk along the ocean, some exceptional crafts stores, appealing restaurants, and a good choice of accommodations. The **Bar Harbor Historical Society** (33 Ledgelawn Avenue; tel: 207-288 0000; open June–Oct, Mon–Sat pm) does a fine job of chronicling the resort town's rich history.

Numerous whale watches, cruise boats and sailing charters set sail from the town's wharf, and the **Abbe Museum Downtown** (26 Mount Desert Street; tel: 207-288 3519; open late May–Oct, daily; Nov–mid-May, Thur–Sat; entrance fee), displays an extensive collection of Indian artifacts from the state's Native people, the Wabanaki.

Elsewhere on the island

Head out of Bar Harbor on Route 3 to **Northeast Harbor C**, known for its scenic, protected harbor. Here, visit the spectacular seaview **Asticou Terraces, Thuya Garden, and Thuya Lodge** (tel: 207-276 5130; open July–Labor Day; donation), the 215-acre (87-hectare) garden and home of landscape artist Joseph Henry Curtis. The **Sea Princess** (tel: 207-276 5352; barharborcruises.com) offers nature cruises as well as sunset dinner cruises to **Little Cranberry Island**, a scenic, 400-acre (160-hectare) island 20 miles (32 km) offshore. The Sea Princess also cruises through **Somes Sound D**, the only fjord on the East Coast.

Bar Harbor's heyday as a fashionable summer resort was in the 19th century, when a railroad from Boston and a steamboat service lured the wealthy. A 1947 forest fire destroyed 60 of the grand summer cottages and finally ended the resort's gilded age.

BELOW LEFT: dockmaster's shed at Bar Harbor.
BELOW RIGHT: Owl's Head Light, Penobscot Bay.

Maine's lighthouses

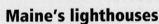

With thousands of miles of deep craggy coastline and treacherously rocky shores, it isn't surprising that Maine has 63 lighthouses. These sentinels guard the entire coast – from East Quoddy Head Lighthouse on Campobello Island at the Canadian border (accessible only at low tide) to the southern Nubble Light on York Beach. You could easily structure a coastal drive with them acting as a focal point. Although several are privately owned, many are open to the public. Portland Head Light, Maine's oldest – built in 1791 under President George Washington's authorization – has a charming museum in the lighthouse keepers' quarters. Pemaquid Point Light, at the tip of the eponymous peninsula, rises 79 ft (24 meters) above the water from a dramatic rock ledge. (You're likely to spot painters at their easels here.) In 1934 it became the first automated lighthouse, and is depicted on the US quarter-dollar coin honouring Maine. Like others, however, it still relies on a Fresnel lens – a technology designed in 1822 that bends the light into a narrow beam by means of a magnifying lens and concentric rings of glass prisms.

Maine's private and state-run ferries provide a vital link to many island communities.

BELOW: puffins on Machias Seal Island, a breeding colony which can be visited. Boats leave from Jonesport and Cutler.

Head south on Route 102 to the "quiet side" of the island – just as lovely and a lot less traveled. **Echo Lake Beach** , part of Acadia National Park, is one of the best spots for fresh water swimming. There's a hiking trail up 839-ft-high (256-meter) **Beech Mountain**.

The charming little town of **Southwest Harbor** has art galleries and restaurants, plus the **Wendell Gilley Museum** (Route 102; tel: 207-244 7555; open June–Oct, Tues–Sun, May, and Nov–mid Dec, Fri–Sun; entrance fee). It exhibits the magnificent works of the world-renowned bird carver. **Cranberry Cove Boating** (Upper Town Dock; tel: 207-244 4040; downeast windjammer.com) operates a ferry to the Cranberry Isles, Isleford, and the Sutton Islands. If you'd rather be captain, rent a power boat at Manset Yacht Services (tel: 207-244 4040).

Isleford, also known as Little Cranberry Island (cranberryisles.com) has the most tourist services. There are restaurants, lodgings, and a few craft shops. **Bass Harbor Head Lighthouse** presents a classic Maine cameo. The

Maine State Ferry (state.me.us/mdot/opt/ferry) runs a ferry from Bass Harbor to Swans Island, 6 miles (10 km) out to sea.

To the Canadian Border

Back on the mainland, continue north on Route 1 and turn south onto Route 186 to the small, unspoiled fishing village of **Winter Harbor** and nearby **Schoodic Point**, a little-visited portion of Acadia National Park with fine views of Cadillac Mountain across the bay.

North on Route 1 in Washington County, also known as "Sunrise County" for its easterly location, tourism takes a back seat to lobstering and growing blueberries and Christmas trees. It's a classic Maine scene.

Head south off Route 1 on Route 187 about 12 miles (19 km), continue through Jonesport and Beals to the 1,540-acre (623-hectare) **Great Wass Island** . The Nature Conservancy (tel: 207-729 5181) property, with several somewhat difficult but very reward trails through the woods and along the coast, is one of the state's natural treasures.

Just off Route 1 in **Columbia Falls** , tour the elegant, 1818 **Ruggles House** (Main Street; tel: 207-483 4637; open June–mid-Oct; entrance fee), which has a magnificent flying staircase. A few miles north, turn south onto Roque Bluffs Road for about 5 miles (8 km) to **Roque Bluffs State Park** (tel: 207-255 3475; open mid-May–mid-Sept; entrance fee). It offers fabulous views, a beach (with incredibly cold water), and a much warmer freshwater pond.

Machias on Route 1, was the site of the first naval battle of the Revolutionary War. In June 1775, a month after the Battle of Lexington, the *Margaretta* set anchor off Machias to stand guard over a freight ship collecting wood with which to build British barracks in Boston. After debating their course of action at **Burnham Tavern** (now restored and open as a museum; Main and Free Streets; tel: 207-255 6930; open mid-June–Sept, daily; entrance fee), the townspeople successfully attacked. *Margaretta*'s captain died of his wounds

when brought back to the tavern, but the crew, nursed back to health there, vowed revenge – and followed through, with subsequent attacks and conflagrations.

North on Route 1 and east on Route 189 about 18 miles (29 km), **Lubec** ㉜ is the easternmost town in the United States, and the easternmost American soil is **West Quoddy Point**, a dramatic landscape of rocky cliffs and crashing surf graced with a candycane-striped 1858 lighthouse (closed to the public).

Hiking trails wander past a peat bog, through stances of wild roses and day lilies. The lighthouse is part of 600-acre (240-hectare) **Quoddy Head State Park** (tel: 207-733 0911; open mid-May–mid-Oct; entrance fee)

From Lubec, you can cross over the Franklin D. Roosevelt Memorial Bridge to **Roosevelt Campobello International Park** ㉝ in Canada (tel: 506-752 2922; visitor center and cottage open late May–Columbus Day; trails open year-round). Franklin Delano Roosevelt summered on New Brunswick's Campobello Island from 1905 to 1921, when he was crippled by polio; he returned only briefly in later years, but his seaside retreat offers a poignant look at the days when the future wheelchair-bound president was a fit, energetic young man.

After a self-guided tour of the 34-room Roosevelt house, which remains as the family left it, visitors can enjoy 8 miles (13 km) of walking trails, including a 2-mile (3-km) stroll along the ocean. Note that New Brunswick is one hour ahead of Maine's Eastern Standard Time.

Bangor

In the 1830s, **Bangor** ㉞, Maine's third-largest city, was the self-proclaimed "lumber capital of the world," with more than 300 sawmills. Today little remains of its glory days except for the huge houses built by lumber barons that line its wide avenues, and a 31-ft (9.4-meter) statue of legendary lumberjack Paul Bunyan, subject of many tall tales, on the outskirts of town.

A push for urban renewal in the 1960s destroyed many downtown landmarks. But the citizens of Bangor are beginning to recreate their city on the Penobscot River. The waterfront is being revitalized, some first-rate museums are attracting tourists, and the city offers some

TIP

Visitors crossing between Maine and Canada must show a passport or certified birth certificate and photo I.D. at the border. Single parents, grandparents, or guardians traveling with children may need proof of custody or notarized letters from the other parent authorizing travel.

BELOW: pie-eating contest at the Machias Wild Blueberry Festival.

*Baxter Peak is con-
nected to nearby
Pamola Peak by a
narrow, mile-long
strip of rock known
as the Knife Edge.
Only a few feet wide
in spots, the Knife
Edge is an acro-
phobe's nightmare –
3,000 ft (900 meters)
straight down on one
side, 4,000 ft (1,200
meters) on the other.
Would a person fall
straight down to the
bottom? No, a park
ranger reassures:
they'd bounce a
couple of times.
Don't attempt to
cross in high winds.*

BELOW: Bangor's
tribute to the
legendary lumber-
jack Paul Bunyan.

great opportunities for live theatre, music, and dance.

The University of Maine, whose main campus is just a few miles away in Orono, has its **Museum of Art** at 40 Harlow Street (tel: 207-561 3350; open Mon–Sat; entrance fee). Among the almost 5,000 work collection are paintings by Wyeth, Picasso, and Winslow Homer. The **Maine Discovery Museum** (74 Main Street, tel: 207-262 7200; open Mon–Sat, Sun pm in summer; Tues–Sat, Sun pm rest of year; entrance fee), is the largest children's museum north of Boston. It has three floors packed with hands-on activities for all ages.

Renowned British architect Richard Upjohn designed several Bangor landmarks, including the **Thomas A. Hill House** at 159 Union Street (Bangor's Historical Society; tel: 207-942 5766; by appointment) and the elegant St. John's Episcopal Church at 225 French Street.

A legendary modern author makes his home in the city. Stephen King's house on West Broadway is easy to spot – it's the handsome 1856 Italianate mansion surrounded by a wrought-iron fence decorated with bats and spiders.

The North Woods

Much of the northernmost part of Maine consists of millions of acres of softwood forest, owned by a couple of dozen corporations who sometimes admit visitors onto their gravel logging roads for a fee. For an overview of the logging boom that swept the area in the mid-19th century, when papermakers turned to timber in lieu of rags, visit the **Lumberman's Museum** (Route 159; tel: 207-528 2650; open Memorial Day–June Fri–Sun; July–mid-Oct, Tues–Sun; entrance fee) in **Patten** ❸. Here nine buildings of exhibits include a reconstructed 1860s cabin and a blacksmith shop. It's all pretty rustic but so was the life it depicts.

Continue west on Route 159 to **Baxter State Park** ❸ (tel: 207-723 5140; baxterstateparkauthority.com), the legacy of Percival Baxter, governor from 1920 to 1925. When the state legislature refused to purchase and protect this land, he bought a total of 201,018 acres (81,21 hectares), and deeded them to the state requiring only that the tract remain "forever wild." The park contains 45 peaks over 3,000 ft (900 meters) high, including 5,267-ft (1,605-meter) Baxter Peak, the tallest of Mount Katahdin's three peaks and the second highest point in New England.

Running northward from the northwest corner of Baxter State Park, the **Allagash Wilderness Waterway** provides 92 miles (150 km) of America's most scenic canoeing; the trip takes a week to 10 days. South of the park, the Penobscot River's West Branch offers hair-raising whitewater rafting, through granite-walled Ripogenus Gorge.

To the west of the park, accessible only by boat or float plane, is the preserved 19th-century logging town of **Chesuncook** ❸. The **Chesuncook Lake House** (tel: 207-745 5330) in this lovely little village welcomes outdoors-oriented guests eager to leave the 21st century behind.

Several dozen such "camps," unchanged for decades, are tucked away in this region pocked with lakes and ponds where fish are plentiful and moose and black bear roam. Many cluster around

Recommended Restaurants and Bars on pages 364–7

Moosehead Lake, the largest body of fresh water entirely in New England, with 320 miles (512 km) of shoreline.

Although tiny **Greenville** ㊳, at the southern end of the lake, has grown into a year-round vacation destination with several fine B&Bs, fishing resorts, and restaurants, it still retains its air of a wilderness hideaway. Three-hour lake tours are offered aboard the National Historic Landmark *Katahdin*, (center of town; tel: 207-695 2716; katahdincruises.com; check schedule for cruise times) a restored 1914 lake steamboat. The vessel also provides three- and five-hour cruises to Mount Kineo, a peninsula whose 763-ft (233-meter) cliff was sacred to early Native Americans. The **Moosehead Marine Museum** (open July–Columbus Day; donation), next to the boat dock, contains fascinating displays on Greenville's history.

Another great way to get a full grasp of this mammoth lake is to take a float-plane tour; several operators offer "fly-and-canoe" packages, including Folsom's Air Service (Greenville; tel: 207-695 2821) and Currier's Flying Service (Greenville Junction; tel: 207-695 2778).

Lily Bay State Park (tel: 207-695 2700; open mid-May–mid-Oct; fee), 8 miles (13 km) north of Greenville, has a fine sandy beach and an excellent spot to picnic.

Whitewater rafting

About 20 miles (32 km) southwest of Greenville as the crow flies (or thrice that distance by car), **West Forks** ㊴ attracts thousands of amateurs eager to try whitewater rafting along the Kennebec and Dead rivers. Suitable for anyone over 10 and in reasonably good health, these thrilling descents take only a day and alternate roiling rapids with placid floats.

Several outfitters organize trips and provide lodging and meals. Among them: Northern Outdoors, Inc. (tel: 800-765 7238; northernoutdoors.com), New England Outdoor Center (tel: 800-766 7238; neoc.com), and Wilderness Expeditions (tel: 800-825-9453; wildernessrafting.com).

Western lakes and mountains

In the heart of Carrabassett Valley, the ski area at **Sugarloaf/USA** ㊵ (Route 27; tel: 207-237 2000; sugarloaf.com), on

Bull moose roam freely in the North Woods. Young males sometimes wander hundreds of miles from their home in search of females.

BELOW: viewing Mount Katahdin in Baxter State Park.

Rangeley was the home of the Freud protégé Wilhelm Reich (1897–1957). His renegade theories on sexual energy ended in his ignominious death in jail – the victim, many believe, of an overzealous Food and Drug Administration. Some of his "orgone energy accumulators" stand at his remote home and laboratory, Orgonon, at the Wilhelm Reich Museum (off Routes 4 and 16; tel: 207-864 3443; open July, Aug, Wed–Sun pm; Sept, Sun pm; entrance fee).

BELOW:
old cars in Bethel.

Maine's second highest peak, has a treeless top offering superb views (including Mounts Katahdin and Washington), and boasts a greater vertical descent (2,820 ft/860 meters) than any other winter resort in New England. The area is a year-round resort, with an 18-hole golf course, fly-fishing, and hiking and mountain-biking trails

A useful base for Sugarloaf is **Kingfield** ④, 18 miles to the south, which has been a magnet for sporting types since the mid-19th century. The renovated but decidedly funky 1918 **Herbert Hotel** (246 Main Street; tel: 207-265 2000 or 888-656 99222; herbertgrand hotel.com) offers basic but comfortable rooms and moderately-priced dining.

The town fostered a family of homegrown geniuses, whose accomplishments are showcased in the **Stanley Museum** (40 School Street; tel: 207-265 2729; open June–Oct Tues–Sun, Nov–May Tues–Fri pm or by appointment; entrance fee). The twins, F.O. and F.E., invented the Stanley Steamer, which wowed enthusiasts at the first New England auto show in 1898 and set a land-speed record of 127 mph (203 km/h) in 1906. Three

restored, working samples are garage this Georgian-style schoolhouse, w the family built for the town in 1903

Grafton Notch

Some of Maine's prettiest and least ited scenery is near the New Hamps border. **Bethel** ④ takes its name, w means "House of God," from the B of Genesis. It gained prominence as a town when Dr John Gehring attracte his clinic many Harvard academic suffering from nervous disorders. hotel he built in 1913 on the pretty t green, the **Bethel Inn** (tel: 800-0125), is still a restorative treat.

Also in town is the National His Register **Moses Mason House** (10 Broad Street; tel: 207-824 2908; o July–early Sept, Tues–Sun pm; entra fee). This 1813 Federal manse, m tained by the Bethel Historical Societ a treasure house of American primi painting: the itinerant muralist R Porter decorated the entryway and ond-floor landing with, respectivel seascape and forest tableau.

North of town, in **Newry**, the **Sun River** ④ **ski resort** (Sunday River R tel: 207-824 3000 or 800-543 2754; dayriver.com) covers seven mountains has the largest snow-making syster New England. Off-season, chairlifts (June–mid-Oct Fri–Sun) carry visitor the top for an exhilarating ride and s tacular views. The nearby 1872 **Arti Covered Bridge** (closed to traffic) delightful spot for a swim or a pic

Head north on Route 26 which cli into the fabulously scenic **Grafton Nc State Park** ④ (tel: 207-824 2912), p ing by numerous trailheads and the p ing lot for Screw Auger Falls. 2,175-mile (3,508-km) Appalachian T cuts across the park on its way to Mc Katahdin, its northern terminus.

Rangeley Lakes region

Although both Routes 4 and 17 lea to the town of **Rangeley** ④, overlool the 9-mile (14-km) long Rangeley L are designated National Scenic Byw Route 17 has the more spectac

scenery. The **Rangeley Lakes region** is actually a collection of 112 lakes and ponds, and has been popular with outdoors enthusiasts for more than a century. Rangeley is the service area for the region.

West Paris

West Paris ㊻, about 12 miles (19 km) southwest of Bethel, might appeal more to those with "get rich quick" inclinations: **Perham's of West Paris** (Jct. Routes 26/219; tel: 207-674 2342), founded in 1919, is a rockhound's mecca, not just for its store, but for the chance to poke around in the five quarries it owns within 10 miles (16 km). Gem-quality tourmaline – striated in a watermelon-like color scheme – is fairly common in these hills, and even gold is not unheard of.

The capital city

Augusta ㊼, Maine's modest-sized capital (population 22,000), stands on the Kennebec River and began its days in 1628 as a trading post. Although its website describes it as "a world-class capital city," the locals tend to head for Portland when they seek urban excitement. It has a gold-domed **State House** (State and Capi-

tol streets; tel: 207-287 1400; open weekdays) designed by Charles Bulfinch in 1832, but substantially altered and enlarged in 1909–10.

The superb **Maine State Museum** in the State House complex (tel: 207-287 2301; open Mon–Sat) has displays on "12,000 years of Maine," plus the "Made in Maine" exhibition, which includes prehistoric arrowheads and a water-powered woodworking mill.

The **Children's Discovery Museum** (265 Water St; tel: 207-622 2209) has a bank, grocery store and restaurant designed to teach children how to cope with such places in later life, and there's a rainforest play area for toddlers.

The city's other major sight is **Old Fort Western**, built close to the river in 1754 and America's oldest wooden fort (City Center Plaza; tel: 207-626 2385; open Memorial Day–Labor Day, daily in pm; Labor Day–Columbus Day, Sat & Sun pm; Nov–Jan, first Sun of month 1–3pm; entrance fee). The stockade and blockhouses have been evocatively re-created, complete with replica cannons. ❑

Old Fort Western.

BELOW:
the State House and the Governor's residence, Blaine House.

RESTAURANTS AND BARS

Restaurants

Prices for a three-course dinner per person with a half-bottle of house wine:

$ = under $20
$$ = $20–45
$$$ = $45–60
$$$$ = over $60

Augusta

Cloud 9
Senator Inn & Spa, 284 Western Avenue. Tel: 207-622 5804.
senatorinn.com **$$–$$$**
Eclectic menu includes crab cakes, and brick-oven pizzas with creative toppings (roasted pear, walnut and gorgonzola).
B, L & D daily; Sun brunch.

Riverfront BBQ & Grille
300 Water Street.
Tel: 207-622 8899. **$–$$**
One of the capital city's nicest surprises: respect-

able Memphis-style barbecue. From the beef brisket with jalapeno corn-bread to slow smoked ribs, it's delicious. L & D daily.

Bangor

Sea Dog Brewing Company
26 Front Street
Tel: 207-947 8009
seadogbrewing.com **$–$$**
Handcrafted ales and solid pub fare close to Penobscot River. L and D daily. (Also in Topsham.)

Bar Harbor

Bar Harbor Lobster Bakes
10 State Highway 3, Hulls Cove
Tel: 207-288 4055 **$$**
barharborlobsterbakes.com
Classic lobster bake with all the sides. Overlooking sea. D nightly in season.

Jordan Pond House

Park Loop Road
Tel: 207-276 3316
jordanpond.com **$$**
Popovers, homemade ice cream, tea, and New England fare served on lawn of a landmark in Acadia National Park. Jackets suggested at dinner. L, D and tea daily in season.

Lompoc Café and Brew Pub
36 Rodick Street
Tel: 207-288 9392
lompoccafe.com **$$**
Brew pub and restaurant serving Maine's own Bar Harbor Real Ale, international dishes, delicious pizza. L and D daily.

Bath

Beale Street Barbecue and Grill
215 Water Street
Tel: 207-442 9514
mainebbq.com **$–$$**
Blues, brews, Memphis-style BBQ, and for the undecided, a sampler platter. L and D daily. (Also in South Portland.)

Mae's Café and Bakery
160 Centre Street (Route 209)
Tel: 207-442 8577
maescafeandbakery.com
$–$$
A popular spot for light, eclectic fare, micro-brews, and pecan sticky buns. Outdoor patio; entertainment. B and L daily; D Thur–Sat; weekend brunch.

Bethel

Bethel Inn and Country Club
Village Common. 04217
Tel: 207-824 2175
bethelinn.com **$$**
Yankee classics, piano

music, and mountain views in the formal dining room and on the verandah of an old-fashioned inn. B and D daily.

S.S. Milton
43 Main Street
Tel: 207-824 2589 **$$–$$$**
A cozy house is the setting for this fine restaurant serving creatively prepared American cuisine. Children's menu.
L and D June–mid-Oct; D Thur–Mon rest of year.

Blue Hill

Arborvine Restaurant
Main Street, Tenney Hill
Tel: 207-374 2119
arborvine.com **$$–$$$**
Traditional American fare and candlelight dining in an 1823 Cape Cod-style house. Lighter dishes and live entertainment next door in The Vinery.
D Tues–Sun in summer; D Fri–Sun in winter.

Boothbay Harbor Area

Ebb Tide
67 Commercial Street
Tel: 207-633 5692 **$–$$**
Restored diner serving a wide variety of comfort foods; breakfast all day.

Robinson's Wharf
Route 27, Southport Island
robinsonswharfinc.net **$–$$**
Traditional lobster pound also offers chowders, fried fish and homemade desserts. Seating is at picnic tables. Seasonal.

Brunswick

The Great Impasta
42 Maine Street
Tel: 207-729 5858
thegreatimpasta.com **$–$$**
A small storefront serving pasta of all types, plus

other Italian treats including stuffed eggplant and homemade lasagna. L and D Mon–Sat.

Atlantica Seafood Bistro
1 Bayview Landing
Tel: 207-236 6011
atlanticarestaurant.com
$$–$$$
This upscale harborfront bistro has a lovely deck and menu emphasizing creative fish preparations. D nightly in season.

Cappy's Chowder House
Main Street
Tel: 207-236 2254
cappyschowder.com $$
Homemade chowders, croissant sandwiches, pasta dishes, and a lively pub atmosphere. For a quieter venue opt for the upstairs dining room. L and D daily.

Cape Neddick Lobster Pound
Shore Road, Route 1A
capeneddick.com $$
A popular riverfront spot with candlelight dining and live entertainment. Lobster and clams are specialties. L and D daily in season.

Clay Hill Farm
220 Clay Hill Road
Tel: 207-362 2272
clayhillfarm.com $$$
Piano music and candlelight in fine restaurant on the grounds of a wildlife refuge/tree farm. Wed–Sat in season. D nightly.

Cape Pier Chowder House Restaurant
79 Pier Road
Tel: 207-967 0123/
800-967 4268

capeporpoiselobster.com
$–$$
Oceanfront lobster shanty cooks up lobsters and fried clams. L and D daily April–early Nov, B weekends.

The Pentagoet Inn
Main Street
Tel: 207-326 8616
pentagoet.com $$–$$$
New England specialties and sumptuous desserts served in the intimate, candlelit dining room and intriguing pub of a turreted Victorian inn. D nightly in season; reservations required.

The Lucerne Inn
2517 Main Road
Tel: 207-843 5123/
800-325 5123
lucerneinn.com $$–$$$
This sprawling old lakefront inn between Bangor and Bar Harbor offers dishes ranging from bistro steak to chicken parmesan. D nightly.

Whale's Rib Tavern
Pilgrim's Inn, 20 Main Street
Tel: 207-348 6615
pilgrimsinn.com $$–$$$
A casual, cozy spot whose menu includes simple fare plus more ambitious offerings. Entertainment. D nightly.

Harraseeket Inn
162 Main Street
Tel: 207-865 9377
harraseeketinn.com
$$–$$$$
Classic tableside preparations such as chateaubriand for two are highlights in the elegant dining rooms of a luxury inn. L and D served in the tavern. D nightly.

Harraseeket Lunch and Lobster Company
36 Main Street,
South Freeport
Tel: 207-865 4888 $–$$
Seafood basics in the rough: lobster dinners, fried clams, and other fried seafood. Picnic tables outside. L and D daily May–Oct.

A-1 Diner
3 Bridge Street, Route 201
Tel: 207-582 4804 $
Classic 1946 diner, south of Augusta. B, L and D daily.

Robinhood Free Meetinghouse
Robinhood Road off Route 127
Tel: 207-371 2188
robinhood-meetinghouse
.com $$–$$$
An historic meetinghouse transformed into a temple of classic and fusion cuisine. Signature dishes include 72-layer cream cheese biscuits. D nightly in summer; Thur–Sat mid-Oct–mid-May.

Greenville Inn
Norris Street
Tel: 207-695 2206
greenvilleinn.com $$–$$$
Critically-acclaimed New American cuisine in the elegant dining room of an opulent mansion overlooking Moosehead Lake. B and D daily.

Dysart's
Exit 180 off I-95
Tel: 207-942 4878
dysarts.com $
A 24-hour truck stop with a widespread reputation for great homemade food such as macaroni and cheese, pot roast, and baked beans. Breakfast served 24 hours.

Cape Arundel Inn
Ocean Avenue
Tel: 207-967 2125
capearundelinn.com
$$$–$$$$
The innovative chef creates dishes such as lobster stew with truffle oil, and pan-seared leg of

LEFT: lobster roll and fries, the classic Maine fast food.
RIGHT: Cappy's Chowder House in Camden.

lamb piccata in an elegant dining room overlooking the ocean. Reservations essential. D nightly in season.

Federal Jack's Restaurant and Brew Pub
8 Western Avenue
Tel: 207-967 4322
federaljacks.com **$–$$**
A waterfront location, craft-brewed beers, a creative menu, outdoor dining, and entertainment. L and D daily.

Grissini Italian Bistro
27 Western Avenue (Route 9)
Tel: 207-967 2211
restaurantgrissini.com
$$–$$$
Fine contemporary northern Italian fare – such as grilled lamb with Tuscan white beans, and grilled salmon served on sweet potato polenta. D nightly.

Kennebunkport Inn
Dock Square
Tel: 207-967 2621
kennebunkportinn.com
$$–$$$$
This steak house and

seafood grill in the center of town offers indoor and outdoor patio dining, a piano bar, and a pub menu. D nightly.

Mabel's Lobster Claw
124 Ocean Avenue
Tel: 207-967 2562 **$–$$**
Terrific chowders, classic shore dinners, great lobster rolls. L and D April–early Nov.

White Barn Inn
37 Beach Avenue
Tel: 207-967 2321
whitebarninn.com **$$$$**
Housed in the beautifully appointed barn of a Relais et Châteaux inn. The four-course, *prix-fixe* menu ($93 per person) emphasizes nouvelle cuisine. Service is formal. D nightly.

Kingfield
Longfellow's
Main Street
Tel: 207-265 4394 **$**
A casual riverside café with solid, American fare and good prices, across from The Herbert.

Kittery
Bob's Clam Hut
315 Route 1
Tel: 207-439 4233
bobsclamhut.com **$**
This 50+-year-old local institution, next to the Kittery Trading Post, knows how to fry fish. L and D daily.

Warren's Lobster House
Route 1
Tel: 207-439 1630
lobsterhouse.com **$$**
The sprawling waterfront restaurant has been a destination for fresh seafood since 1940. There's also a terrific salad bar. L and D daily.

Lincolnville Beach
Lobster Pound Restaurant
Route 1
Tel: 207-789 5550
midcoast.com/~lobstrlb **$$**
Popular shorefront spot. Vast dining room or outdoor picnic tables. L and D daily.

Little Deer Isle
Eaton's Lobster Pool
Blastow Cove
Tel: 207-348 2383 **$–$$**
Water views, fresh-off-the-boat seafood. Seating on a screened porch. D nightly in summer; Sat–Sun spring and fall.

Northeasy Harbor
Asticou Inn
Tel: 207-276 3344
asticou.com **$$$–$$$$**
Yankee standards in a grand old dining room overlooking the sea. Must book; jackets recommended at dinner. B, L, D daily; Sun brunch.

Ogunquit
Arrows Restaurant
Berwick Road (off Route 1)
Tel: 207-361 1100
arrowsrestaurant.com **$$$$**
Acclaimed spot in 18th-century farmhouse, with gourmet menu. Much of

Prices for a three-course dinner per person with a half-bottle of house wine:
$ = under $20
$$ = $20–45
$$$ = $45–60
$$$$ = over $60

the produce comes from its own garden. Six-course ($95) and 10-course ($135) tasting menus. D nightly.

Portland
Back Bay Grill
65 Portland Street
Tel: 207-772 8833
backbaygrill.com **$$$**
Sophisticated fare with an international flare, creating dishes such as lobster tortellini with lobster foam. D Mon–Sat.

Bintliff's American Grill
98 Portland Street
Tel: 207-774 0005
bintliffsamericancafe.com **$**
Open daily for brunch 7am–2pm, serving internationally-influenced American cuisine as well as classic favorites such as eggs benedict.

Fore Street and Company
33 Wharf Street
Tel: 207-775 0887
forestreetbiz.com **$$–$$$**
Wood-grilled meats and seafoods, fire-roasted mussels. D nightly.

Walter's
15 Exchange Street
Tel: 207-871 9258
walterscafe.com **$$**
Dishes such as oxtail and scamorza egg rolls, and pomegranate wild salmon. Brick walls, high ceilings, bay windows. L Mon–Sat, D nightly.

Rangeley
Country Club Inn
Mingo Loop Road
Tel: 207-864 3831
countryclubinnrangeley.com
$$$–$$$$
White-tablecloth fare in a

a glassed-in dining room with lake and mountain views. Must book. D Wed–Sun summer and fall.

Rockland

Primo Restaurant
2 South Main Street
Tel: 207-596 0770
primorestaurant.com **$$–$$$**
Menu changes daily to incorporate whatever's fresh or in season. D nightly in season; Wed–Mon off-season.

The Water Works
Lindsey Street
Tel: 207-596 2753 **$–$$$**
Two options: an upscale dining room with dishes such as lobster stew and broiled seafood; and a pub serving comfort food and microbrews.

Rockport

Marcel's at the Samoset Resort
220 Warrenton Street
Tel: 207-594 0774
samosetresort.com **$$$$**
Million-dollar views, a formal atmosphere, and eclectic cuisine. B, D and Sun brunch buffet.

Rockwood

The Birches
(Off Route 15)
Tel: 207-534 7305
thebirches.com **$$–$$$**
Hearty fare in a stone-hearthed dining room by Moosehead Lake at this North Woods resort. B, L and D daily in season.

Southwest Harbor

The Claremont Hotel
Clark Point Road
Tel: 207-244 5036
theclaremonthotel.com **$$$**
This 1884 inn has a modernist menu, with dishes such as bourbon roasted lobster. B and D daily late-May–mid-Oct; L July–Aug.

Beal's Lobster Pier
182 Clark Point Road
Tel: 207-244 7178
bealslobster.com **$**
Classic wharfside lobster shack. L and D in season; D off-season.

Wiscasset

Le Garage Restaurant
Water Street
Tel: 207-882 5409
legaragerestaurant.com
$$–$$$
Regional American food in a converted, 1920s garage overlooking the Sheepscot River; porch tables have the best view. L and D Tues–Sun.

Red's Eats
Water Street (Route 1)
Tel: 207-882 6128 **$**
This tiny take-out booth just south of the bridge serves what some say is the state's best lobster roll. No credit cards. L and D April–Sept.

Squire Tarbox Restaurant
1181 Main Road, Route 144
Tel: 207-882 7693
squiretarboxinn.com **$$$**
The Swiss chef at this 18th-century farmhouse inn prepares specialties such as onion soup and rack of lamb. One seating; reservations essential. D nightly late May–late Oct; April, May, Nov–Dec Thur–Sat.

York

The Restaurant at Dockside Guest Quarters
Harris Island Road
Tel: 207-363 2868
docksidegq.com **$$–$$$**
From fried clams and steamed lobsters to "swordfish Pacific Rim" and pesto chicken – all with a water view. L Sun–Fri, D nightly in season.

York Harbor Inn
Route 1A, York Harbor
Tel: 207-363 5119
yorkharborinn.com **$$$**
Well-considered continental and regional fare with a strong seafood focus in a "big night out" room, or in the pub. L in pub; D nightly.

Bars

Asylum Complex, 121 Center Street, Portland. Tel: 207-772 8374. Non-stop TV action in Sports Bar; music downstairs; nightclub with state-of-the-art sound system and room for 700 revelers.

Brian Boru Public House, 57 Center Street, Portland. Tel: 207-780 1506. Small, sometimes noisy, this Irish pub serves up Guinness, microbrews, and a large selection of whiskeys and bourbons.

Carmen Verandah, 119 Main Street, Bar Harbor. Tel: 207-288 2766. Pool, darts, and live music on weekends draw throngs to this lively spot overlooking the village green.

Dog & Pony Tavern, 4 Rodick Place, Bar Harbor. Tel: 207-288 0900. Laid-back watering hole with indoor and outdoor bars and an excellent menu of pub grub/comfort foods.

The Great Lost Bear, 540 Forest Street, Portland. Tel: 207-772 0300. One of Maine's great "beer bars" serves more than 60 labels, including 15 Maine microbrews. Menu includes over 20 hamburgers.

Ship's Cellar Pub, York Harbor Inn, Route 1A, York Harbor. Tel: 207-363-5119. This multi-roomed bar/restaurant with portholes and leather-cushioned settees will make you feel like you're aboard a sailing yacht.

Sunday River Brew Pub, US Route 2, Bethel. Tel: 207-824 4253. The outdoor patio at this airy bar/restaurant near Sunday River ski area is a fine spot to down a pint of Black Bear Porter or one of the other local brews.

LEFT: an alternative to seafood in Portland.
RIGHT: outdoor eating by Casco Bay, Portland.

✵ INSIGHT GUIDES
TRAVEL TIPS
NEW ENGLAND

T RANSPORTATION

GETTING THERE AND GETTING AROUND

GETTING THERE

Flying is by far the easiest way to get to New England from abroad. If you come overland from elsewhere in the US, cars are the preferred mode of travel. Trains are less frequent than flights, and although buses connect most cities and several major towns, they are not much cheaper than a discount airfare, take substantially longer, and are less comfortable.

By Air

Most major US carriers service the New England states. A variety of discount fares and special deals are offered, and many of the lowest are available on their own websites.

Boston's Logan International Airport is one of the busiest in the United States; smaller airports – many served by major carriers including Delta, Jet Blue, and US Air – are scattered throughout New England, near cities including Hartford, Connecticut; Portland and Bangor, Maine; Manchester, New Hampshire; Burlington, Vermont; and Providence, Rhode Island.

Alternatively, you can fly into New York and catch one of the many connecting flights to the New England area, or an hourly shuttle to Boston aboard airlines including Delta and Jet Blue. Although reservations are not required and there is open seating, you may get a lower fare by booking in advance: check airline and discount travel sites. Most airports have hotel reservation desks (which charge no commission), plus car rental outlets.

During holidays it may be difficult to find a flight, especially at Thanksgiving, when most of the US seems to be on the move and discount tickets are virtually non-existent.

Getting to downtown Boston

Boston's Logan Airport is 3 miles (5 km) from downtown, which is easily accessible by public transportation. A free shuttle marked "Massport" transports passengers from all airline terminals to the MBTA Airport station (Blue Line), and the water shuttle dock, where the Harbor Express water shuttle (tel: 617-222 6999; www.harborexpress.com) runs to Long Wharf and Quincy; City Water Taxi (tel: 617-422 0392; www.city watertaxi.com) stops at 20 locations in Boston Harbor. The 1.6-mile (2.6-km) Ted Williams Tunnel (toll payable) starts close to the car rental area and connects the airport easily with downtown and the Massachusetts Turnpike (also toll).

By Train

Amtrak (tel: 800-872 7245; www. amtrak.com) provides rail services to New England from Washington, DC, Philadelphia, and New York, routing through coastal Connecticut and Rhode Island and terminating in Boston. The Acela Express, which travels at speeds of up to 150 mph (240 kmh), costs more than regular trains but is much quicker. Another route extends from Washington and New York to New Haven, Connecticut, Springfield, Massachusetts, and St Albans, Vermont. Amtrak's Down-easter runs between Boston and Portland, Maine. Various commuter trains link Boston with smaller towns in Massachusetts, and Rhode island.

International travellers (but not Canadians) planning to travel extensively on Amtrak can purchase a USA Rail Pass, good for 15 or 30 days. Rates are reduced, and children ages 2–15 are half price (under 2, free), but pass holders cannot use the Acela, and advance tickets and reservations are needed.

GETTING AROUND

By Air

Internal flights are expensive, but if you want to hop from place to place by air, airlines serve the following New England towns and cities:
Massachusetts Boston, Hyannis, Martha's Vineyard, Nantucket, New Bedford, Worcester
Maine Bangor, Portland, Bar Harbor
Connecticut Bradley Airport (near Hartford), Bridgeport, Groton, New Haven
Vermont Burlington, Rutland
New Hampshire Lebanon-Hanover, Manchester
Rhode Island Providence

Airlines

Major domestic airlines include:
American Airlines tel: 800 433-7300
Continental tel: 800-525 0280
Cape Air tel: 800-352 0714
Delta tel: 800-221 1212
Jet Blue tel: 800-538 2583
Northwest Airlines tel: 800-225 2525
USAir tel: 800-428 4322
A leading discount airline, **AirTran Airways,** founded in 1993, (tel: 800 247 8726) has flights from Boston to half a dozen destinations.

Airports

Logan International Airport East Boston, Mass, tel: 617-561 1800/800 235 6426
Bradley International Airport Windsor Locks, CT, tel: 860-292 2000

T.F. Green Airport
Warwick, Rhode Island, tel: 401-737 8222/888-268 7222
Burlington International Airport
Vermont, tel: 802-863 2874
Manchester, New Hampshire Airport
Tel: 603-624 6556
Portland International Jetport
Maine, tel: 207-874 8877
Bangor International Airport
Maine, tel: 207-992 4600/866-359 2264

By Bus

Greyhound has the most comprehensive coverage of the US, and Peter Pan operates extensively throughout New England. Many bus services coordinate connections with Amtrak rail schedules. These companies operate in the region:
C&J Trailways, tel: 800 258 7111; www.ridecj.com. Services northeastern Massachusetts, New Hampshire, and southern Maine; service to Boston's South Station and Logan Airport.
Concord Trailways, tel: 800-639 3317; www.concordcoachlines.com. Services Maine, New Hampshire, Newburyport, Massachusetts, and transports to Boston's South Station and Logan Airport.
Greyhound, tel: 800-231 2222; www.greyhound.com.
Peter Pan, tel: 800-343 9999; www.peterpanbus.com.
Plymouth & Brockton, tel: 508-746 0378; www.p-bo.com. Cape Cod and Massachusetts' South Shore to Boston and Logan Airport.

By Train

The most extensive train service throughout New England is offered by **Amtrak**, tel: 800-872 7245; www.amtrak.com.
Connecticut is served by **Metro-North** (tel: 800-638 7646/212-532 490 in New York; www.mta.info/mnr/index.html) with trains between New York City's Grand Central Station and New Haven, New Canaan, Danbury, and Waterbury.
Boston has numerous commuter lines (MBTA), tel: 617-222 3200/800-392 6100, www.mbta.com, from Boston to outlying towns.

By Car

Although the network of airplanes, buses, trains, ferries, and taxis is reliable, having your own car is the easiest way to get around (except in the congested heart of Boston), and it also offers the greatest opportunity for getting off the beaten path.

Highways

A number of well-maintained interstate highways (ranging from four to eight or more lanes) make covering New England's distances easy. To get an idea of the range, picture a radius from Boston to Burlington, in northwestern Vermont – a trip which, on Routes 93 and 89, would take only about five hours. That radius, extended across New England, would cover all but the northernmost regions of Maine (beyond Bangor).

Secondary roads

Travel on secondary roads is time-consuming, but much more scenic. However, beware of dirt roads – usually represented by a broken line – in mud season (typically, March into late April), when melting snow turns them into rutted and slippery quagmires. Note that mountain roads may be closed in winter.

Car rental

Visitors wishing to lease a car on arrival will find offices of all the major US firms at airports (usually more expensive than elsewhere) and convenient city locations. Toll-free arrangements can be made in advance. Established firms include:
Alamo tel: 800 327 9633 www.alamo.com
Avis, tel: 800-331 1212; www.avis.com
Budget, tel: 800-527 0700; www.budget.com
Enterprise, tel: 800-261 7331; www.enterprise.com, rents cars to those 21 years of age and older.
Hertz, tel: 800-654 3131; www.hertz.com
Thrifty, tel: 800-367 2277; www.thrifty.com
It's also worth calling around, referring to the *Yellow Pages* (under "Automobile Renting and Leasing"), for the best rates. Sometimes local rental firms may offer low rates, especially for lower-quality cars. But be sure to check insurance coverage

provisions. The cheapest rates tend to be available on weekends.

Legal requirements

Most car-rental agencies require drivers to be at least 25, to hold a major credit card, and a driver's license that is current and has been valid for at least a year; some will accept a cash deposit, sometimes as high as $500, in lieu of a credit card.
Foreign travellers will need to show an international driver's license or a license from their own country.

Insurance

Liability is not included in the terms of your lease, so advertised rates usually do not include additional fees for insurance. Collision Damage Waiver (CDW) is recommended, as it covers you if someone else damages your car. Some credit cards offer coverage on rental cars, but conditions vary: be sure to understand your rights before you sign the rental document.

Rules of the Road

States and municipalities have specific laws and regulations regarding parking, speed limits and the like; most are clearly posted. Speed limits on some country roads may not be well posted, and can range from 20 mph to 50 mph (32–80 kmh): be sure to find out what the local regulations are.
The speed limit on interstate highways is mostly 65 mph (104 kmh), although portions in built-up areas may be limited to 55 mph (89 kmh) or lower. Enforcement, if sporadic, can be strict, with high penalties. Drink-driving penalties are very severe in all states.
Roads with solid lines down the middle are "no passing" zones. But in Vermont passing is legal at any time except where explicitly posted as "no passing" (this is a nod to the state's rural character, where tractors and farm vehicles often travel at slow speeds).

BELOW: parking regulations are clearly posted and are enforced.

Moose and deer are particularly active at dawn and dusk, and are a hazard to drivers on country roads, particularly in northern New England. If a deer runs in front of your car, slow down or stop – they often travel in groups and a second or third one may not be far behind. Moose, however, don't usually run. Generally weighing between 800 and 1,200lbs, they don't need to. Give them the right of way, too.

Seatbelts
These are obligatory for all occupants. In some states the police may stop vehicles and ticket unbelted passengers. Children under six must be buckled into safety seats or a proper child restraint, and in some states children must sit in the back seat. Many rental firms supply child seats for a small extra cost.

Fuel
Fuel is lead-free and stations are plentiful, and often open 24 hours a day near major highways (otherwise, usually 5 or 6am until 10 or 11pm). Many pumps can be activated by credit cards. British travelers should note that the US gallon is 17 percent smaller than the English equivalent. Metric users note that 1 gallon equals 3.8 litres.

Special considerations
Unless otherwise posted, a right-hand turn at a red light is permitted throughout New England. On sighting a school bus that has stopped to load or unload children, drivers in both directions must stop completely before reaching the bus and may not proceed until the flashing red warning signals on the school bus have been switched off, or until they are directed to do so.

Ambulances, fire engines, and police cars with emergency lights on always have right of way. Pull over, and wait until they've passed.

Rotaries (roundabouts), especially in Boston, require caution. The official rule is that the cars already in the circle have the right of way in exiting, but this rule is often ignored in practice. It's best to proceed carefully, whether entering or exiting.

Hitching and car-jacking
Hitchhiking is discouraged; so is picking up hitchhikers. Car-jackings are rare, but not unheard of, particularly in Greater Metropolitan Boston and in some larger cities. When you pick up your rental vehicle, ask the clerk which areas to avoid.

Breakdown
Some highways have emergency phones every few miles. You can call 911 on your cell phone for help. Otherwise, park with the hood raised and a police patrol will stop. The **American Automobile Association** (tel: 800-222 4357; www.aaa.com) offers reciprocal breakdown services for some affiliated firms in other countries, and provides members with excellent information on road conditions.

Parking
You must park in the direction of traffic, and never by a fire hydrant. A yellow line or yellow curb means no parking is allowed. In some towns a white line along the curb shows where you can park.

Traffic/Road Conditions
For all New England States, visit www.usroadconditions.com.

Boston, Massachusetts: For up-to-the-minute traffic information, tel: 617-374 1234; www.mass.gov/eot. WBZ Radio provides traffic updates on 1030AM and www.wbztv.com.

By Water
Ferries can save travelers hours of driving time, and, in Massachusetts and Maine, provide transportation to many of the islands. Some ferries service both passengers and vehicles; others are passenger-only. Reservations are highly recommended at all times, and mandatory during peak tourist season, when planning to transport a vehicle. During off-season, ferries may have limited schedules or may suspend operation.

Popular ferry routes include: Boston's Logan Airport to downtown Boston, including stops along Boston Harbor, and at Long Wharf: MBTA, tel: 800-392 6100/617-222 3200; www.mbta.com. A free bus shuttle (Route 66 bus) runs between all airport terminals and the airport dock. Other MBTA ferry routes include: Long Wharf to Charlestown Navy Yard; Hull to Long Wharf and Logan Airport.

Boston to Provincetown (Cape Cod). Ferries include: the passenger-only **Provincetown Fast Ferry** from Long Wharf, tel: 877-733 9425; www.provincetown.com; and **Bay State Cruise Ferry** (accessed by the MBTA's Silver Line), tel: 877-783 3779; www.baystatecruisecompany.com.

Woods Hole (Falmouth, Cape Cod) to Martha's Vineyard: **Steamship Authority**, tel: 508-477 8600; www.steamshipauthority.com.

Hyannis (Cape Cod) to Nantucket: **Steamship Authority**, tel: 508-495 3278; www.steamshipauthority.com.

Hyannis to Martha's Vineyard: passenger only **Hy-Line Fast Ferry**, tel: 508-778 2600; www.hy-line cruises.com.

New Bedford, Massachusetts to Martha's Vineyard: **New England Fast Ferry**, tel: 866-683 3779; www.nefastferry.com; the company also offers a less expensive, slower ferry.

Orient Point, Long Island, New York to New London, Connecticut: **Cross Sound Ferry**, tel: 860-443 5281; www.longislandferry.com.

Montauk, Long Island, New York to Block Island, Rhode Island (passengers only): **Viking Fleet**, tel: 631-668 5700; www.vikingfleet.com.

Quonset Point, Rhode Island to Martha's Vineyard (shuttle from Amtrak and Providence Airport): **Vineyard Fast Ferry**, tel: 401-295 4040; www.vineyardfastferry.com.

Port Jefferson, Long Island to Bridgeport, Connecticut: **Bridgeport & Port Jefferson Ferry Company**, tel: 888-443 3779; www.bpjferry.com.

Maine Ferries, tel: 207-596 2202; www.state.me.us/mdot/opt/ferry/maine-ferry-service.php.

Lake Champlain Ferries from Charlotte, Burlington, and Grand Isle, Vermont to Essex, Port Kent, and Plattsburg, New York, tel: 802-864 9804; www.lakechamplainferries.com.

BELOW: ferry boats line up at Portland, Maine.

ACCOMMODATIONS

HOTELS, YOUTH HOSTELS, BED & BREAKFAST

Many lodgings – particularly those in resort areas – close for at least part of the winter, unless they're in ski territory. Some – particularly in Vermont, Maine and New Hampshire – close for "mud season", generally mid-March through April, and in November between autumn foliage and ski seasons. And a few in particularly buggy areas will delay opening until July, when black flies and mosquitoes taper off.

Rates quoted are the range from low to high season. In general, the least expensive time to travel is Nov–Apr, although Dec–early March is a peak time for lodgings at or near ski areas. High seasons are during summer months and during foliage season, generally late Sept–mid- to late Oct. During these times many lodgings add a premium to their rates and may require a minimum stay of two or three nights.

Here Come the Add-Ons

Each state has a lodging tax ranging from 6 percent to 12 percent; and some cities, including Boston and Cambridge, tack on an additional tax. Most city hotels charge $25–35 a night for parking. Usually, guests can choose to have valet parking or park the car themselves either in the hotel's lot, or a less expensive lot close by. If you opt for valet parking, be sure to ask if there's an additional fee each time you want to take your car out of the garage.

Smoking

Many lodgings ban smoking on the premises, or reserve just a few rooms for smokers. Some make guests sign a paper saying they will

pay for cleaning the room if the no-smoking rule is violated. This surcharge can be significant.

Business services

Many lodgings throughout New England now offer either internet service or wi-fi, and have cell phone service. But some rural areas do not. Check in advance if it's important.

Country Inns and B&Bs

If you are tired of motels and hotels and, at some, willing to forego certain conveniences (such as an in-room phone, TV, or private bath) for more simple pleasures, these lodgings are a wonderful option. They range from weathered farmhouses, with huge fireplaces and homemade muffins, to grand elegance. Most are warm and welcoming, though a few can seem slightly pretentious. If traveling with children, be sure to check minimum age requirements.

Inns and Resorts of New England (www.innsandresortsofnewengland.com) has a site specially designed for visitors from the UK and Germany.

Other resources include: **Bed & Breakfast Agency of Boston** (www.boston-bnbagency.com), tel: 800-248 9262, in UK: 0800-895 128; fax: 617-523 5761. **Host Homes of Boston** (www.hosthomesofboston.com) tel: 800-600 1308/617-244 1308; **Bed & Breakfast Reservations** (www.bbreserve.com) tel: 617-964 1606, 800-832 2632 outside MA; fax: 978-281 9426, for reservations in Massachusetts on the North Shore, Greater Boston, and Cape Cod; **Bed and Breakfast Associates Bay Colony** (www.bnbboston.com) tel: 888-486 6018 in US and Canada; 01-781-449-5302 outside US, for

reservations in Boston, Eastern Massachusetts, and Cape Cod.

Helpful websites include: www.visitnewengland.com, www.discovernewengland.org, and www.vamoose.com.

Holiday Homes

If you're planning to stay a week or longer in one it may be far more affordable to rent a private home or condominium. Popular websites for this service include: www.craigslist.org; www.vrbo.com; and www.homeaway.com.

UK firms specializing in renting homes and helping with inn and B&B accommodations include:
Four Seasons in New England
2 Higher Street, Hatherleigh
EX20 03JD
Tel: 01837 8111278
Fax: 01837 811160
www.nelodgings.com

Hostels and Other Budget Lodgings

Although most prevalent in the Boston area, several cities and towns throughout New England also offer budget accommodations at hostels, YMCAs and YWCAs. Facilities might include shared common spaces and baths and/or dormitory-style rooms, but are generally clean and relatively inexpensive. Resources include:
www.hostelworld.com
Make reservations for YMCAs, budget lodgings, and hostels throughout New England.
Boston International Youth Hostel
12 Hemenway Street,
Boston, MA 02115
Tel: 617-536 9455
www.bostonhostel.org
Hostelling International
8401 Colesville Road, Suite 600,
Silver Spring, MD 20910

Tel: 6301-495 1240/800-909 4776
www.hiusa.org
Facilities throughout New England
YMCA
316 Huntington Avenue,
Boston 02115
Tel: 617-266 4047
www.ymcaboston.org
For reservations: hostelworld.com
YWCA-Berkeley Residence
40 Berkeley Street,
Boston, MA 02116
Tel: 617-375 2524
www.ywcaboston.org

Budget Lodgings in the Mountains
The **Appalachian Mountain Club** operates six roadside lodges with a variety of sleeping and meal options

in Maine and New Hampshire. They also have eight huts a day's hike apart along the Appalachian Trail in the White Mountains.
Appalachian Mountain Club
5 Joy Street, Boston, MA 02108
Tel: 617-523 0655
www.outdoors.org

Hotel Chains

Best Western Tel: 800-528 1234;
www.bestwestern.com
Comfort Inn/Choice Hotels
Tel: 800-424 6423;
www.comfortinn.com
Days Inn Tel: 800-325 2525;
www.daysinn.com
Hilton Tel: 800-445 8667;
www.hilton.com

Holiday Inn Tel: 800-465 4329;
www.basshotels.com
Howard Johnson Tel: 800-654 2000
www.hojo.com
Hyatt Tel: 800-233 1234;
www.hyatt.com
Marriott Tel: 800-872 9563;
www.marriott.com
Quality Inn Tel: 800-228 5151;
www.qualityinn.com
Radisson Tel: 800-333 3333;
www.radisson.com
Ramada Tel: 800-272 6232;
www.ramada.com
Red Roof Inn Tel: 800-843 7663;
www.redroof.com
Sheraton Tel: 800-325 3535;
www.sheraton.com
Super 8 Tel: 800-800 8000;
www.super8.com

ACCOMMODATION LISTINGS

BOSTON

Boston

Boston Harbor Hotel
70 Rowes Wharf, 02110
Tel: 617-439 7000/800-752 7077
Fax: 617-330 9450
www.bhh.com
This 16-story modern beauty with old-world charm stands as a harbour gateway to the city. There are 230 standard rooms and one- and two-bedroom suites. The public spaces exhibit some fine artworks and nautical charts. $$$$
Boston Omni Parker House
60 School Street, 02108
Tel: 617-227 8600/800-843 6664
Fax: 617-742 5729
www.omnihotels.com
After a $30 million renovation, this 1855 landmark hotel sparkles. The 551 rooms range from economy singles to spacious, grandly-furnished one-bedroom suites. Parker House rolls and Boston cream pie were first introduced in the restaurant. $$$–$$$$
Boston Park Plaza Hotel and Towers
50 Park Plaza at Arlington Street, 02102
Tel: 617-426 2000/800-225 2008
Fax: 617-423 1708
www.bostonparkplaza.com
A huge, 15-story hotel with 950 standard units and

one- and two-bedroom suites near the Boston Common and downtown.
$$$–$$$$
Bulfinch Hotel
107 Merrimac Street, 02114
Tel: 617-624 0202/877-267 1776
Fax: 617-624 0211
www.bulfinchhotel.com
80 rooms and suites in a nine-story hotel in an historic flatiron building in the West End. $$$$
Constitution Inn
150 Third Avenue, 02129
Tel: 617-241 8400/800-495 9622
www.constitutioninn.org
Under the auspices of the YMCA, this eight-story, recently-refurbished hotel in the Charlestown Navy Yard has 147 pleasant rooms with refrigerators, microwaves, and A/C. Facilities include a large fitness centre with indoor pool, and free internet access. $$$
Copley Square Hotel
47 Huntington Avenue, 02116
Tel: 617-536 9000/800-225 7062
Fax: 617-267 3547
www.copleysquarehotel.com
This older, centrally located, European-style hotel with 143 rooms is often more affordable than its fancier neighbours.
$$$–$$$$
Courtyard Boston Tremont
275 Tremont Street, 02116

Tel: 617-426 1400/800-331 9998
Fax: 617-482 6730
www.marriott.com
Marriott's handsomely-restored, 15-story historic hotel in the middle of the theatre district offers 322 nicely refurbished rooms.
$$$–$$$$
82 Chandler Street
82 Chandler Street, 02116
Tel: 617-482 0408
Fax: 617-482 0659
www.82chandler.com
A five-room B&B in a 19th-century brownstone with bay windows and fireplaces in the revitalized South End neighbourhood. Credit cards not accepted.
$$–$$$
Eliot Suite Hotel
370 Commonwealth Avenue, 02215
Tel: 617-267 1607/800-443 5468
Fax: 617-536 9114
www.eliothotel.com
Well-appointed European-style hotel built in 1925 has 95 comfortable one-bedroom suites and a popular restaurant. Convenient for both Back Bay and the Fenway. $$$$
Fairmont Copley Plaza
138 Saint James Avenue, 02116
Tel: 617-267 5300/800-527 4727
Fax: 617-267 7668
www.fairmont.com/copleyplaza
A 1912 grand hotel in the heart of Back Bay, with 379

rooms, 54 suites, and plenty of romance.
$$$–$$$$
Four Seasons Hotel
200 Boylston Street, 02116
Tel: 617-338 4400/
800-819 5053
Fax: 617-423 0154
www.fourseasons.com/boston
The standard-setter for luxury and service has 274 rooms and overlooks the Public Garden. $$$$
Gryphon House
9 Bay State Road, 02215
Tel: 617-375 9003/877-375 9003
Fax: 617-425 0716
www.innboston.com
Near Kenmore Square and Boston University, this bowfront brownstone

PRICE CATEGORIES

An approximate guide to rates for a standard double room per night:
$$$$ = more than $200
$$$ = $150–200
$$ = $100–150
$ = under $100

converted to an eight-room luxury hotel offers a variety of high-tech amenities. **$$$–$$$**

Harborside Inn
185 State Street, 02109
Tel: 617-723 7500/888-723 7565
Fax: 617-670 6015
www.harborsideinnboston.com
Near Faneuil Hall, the financial district, and the waterfront, all 54 modern rooms in this renovated, 8-story mercantile warehouse have queen-size beds and Victorian-style furnishings. **$$$–$$$$**

Hyatt Regency Boston
1 Avenue de Lafayette, 02111
Tel: 617-912 1234/800-621 9200
Fax: 617-451 2198
www.regencyboston.hyatt.com
500 rooms on 22 stories offer modern luxury in a convenient location for the financial and theatre districts. **$$$–$$$$**

John Jeffries House
14 David G. Mugar Way, 02114
Tel: 617-367 1866
Fax: 617-742 0313
www.johnjeffrieshouse.com
Many of the 46 small, simply appointed rooms in this red brick inn at the foot of Beacon Hill have kitchens or sitting areas. **$$–$$$**

Langham Boston Hotel
250 Franklin Street, 02110
Tel: 617-451 1900/800-543 4300
Fax: 617-423 2844
www.langhamhotel.com
A modern hotel with old-world ambiance; 314 rooms built atop a Renaissance Revival 1922 bank. The popular Café Fleuri is here. **$$$$**

The Lenox
61 Exeter Street, 02116
Tel: 617-536 5300/800-225 7676
Fax: 617-236 0351
www.lenoxhotel.com
An historic, recently-remodeled 212-room hotel well situated for shopping, with Copley Place and Newbury Street just steps away. Some of the elegant suites have fireplaces. **$$$$**

The Liberty Hotel
215 Charles Street, 02114
Tel: 866-705 5245
Fax: 617-224 4001
www.libertyhotel.com
This 300-room pet-friendly hotel on the site of an old jail retains many of the

former landmark's architectural hallmarks. Some rooms in the 16-story adjoining tower and main building have river views. **$$$$**

Mid-Town Hotel
220 Huntington Avenue, 02115
Tel: 617-369 6240/800-343 1177
Fax: 617-262 8739
www.midtownhotel.com
One of the better deals, a traditional motel with 159 rooms and an outdoor pool, near the Prudential Center and Christian Science HQ. Parking included in rate. **$–$$$$**

The Millennium Bostonian Hotel
Faneuil Hall Marketplace, 02109
Tel: 617-523 3600/800-343 0922
Fax: 617-523 2454
www.millennium-hotels.com
A multi-million dollar renovation has given a new look to this historic hotel overlooking Quincy Market. All 201 rooms have 42-inch LCD TVs; many have fireplaces and balconies. Fitness centre, salon, and day spa. **$$$$**

Newbury Guest House
261 Newbury Street, 02116
Tel: 617-437 7666/800-437 7668
Fax: 617-670 6100
www.newburyguesthouse.com
A trio of 1882 townhouses converted into a Victorian-style inn with 32 guest rooms offers excellent value for the location, so book well in advance. **$–$$$**

The Ritz-Carlton Boston Common
10 Avery Street, 02111
Tel: 617-574 7100
Fax: 617-374 7200
www.ritzcarlton.com
The modern sister of the former Ritz-Carlton (now the

Taj Boston) offers 193 luxury rooms and suites, and a fitness centre. **$$$$**

Taj Boston
15 Arlington Street, 02116
Tel: 800-748 8883
www.tajhotels.com
In 2007, on its 80th birthday, the Ritz-Carlton became a part of the Taj Hotel Resorts and Palaces chain, so there's lots of Indian cuisine. Many of the 273 rooms (including 45 suites, some with wood-burning fireplaces) overlook the Public Gardens. Fitness Centre. **$$$$**

Westin Boston Waterfront
425 Summer Street, 02110
Tel: 617-532 4600
Fax: 617-532 4630
www.westin.com/Boston
One of the city's newest hotels, connected to the Boston Convention and Exhibition Center, has 793 plush rooms and suites. **$$$$**

Brookline

The Bertram Inn B&B
92 Sewall Avenue, 02446
Tel: 617-566 2234/800-295 3822
www.bertraminn.com
Comfortably elegant 1907 Victorian B&B situated on a quiet street and convenient to the Green Line MBTA trolleys to downtown Boston. **$$–$$$**

The Samuel Sewall Inn B&B
143 Saint Paul Street
Tel: 617-713 0123
www.samuelsewallinn.com
The sister property of The Bertram, also convenient to the MBTA, has 14 rooms (five with fireplaces) in a restored 1886 Queen Anne. **$$–$$$**

Cambridge

A Cambridge House B&B
2218 Massachusetts Ave, 02140
Tel: 617-491 6300/800-232 9989
www.acambridgehouse.com
B&B with 15 rooms in a quiet, lavishly-restored 1892 Victorian. Located about one mile north of Harvard Square, but only four blocks from a subway stop. **$$–$$$$**

The Charles Hotel
1 Bennett Street, 02138
Tel: 617-864 1200/800-882 1818
www.charleshotel.com
This Harvard Square hotel overlooking the Charles River has 293 traditional-style rooms. Home to the popular Regattabar, which draws nationally known jazz performers. **$$$$**

The Hotel at MIT
20 Sidney Street (off Massachusetts Avenue), 02139
Tel: 617-577 0200/800-222 8733
www.hotelatmit.com
Business-class hotel be-tween Central and Kendall Squares. Occasional quirky decorating touches in the 210 rooms, such as armoires with circuit-board inlays, play up the hotel's location near the MIT campus. **$$$$**

The Inn at Harvard
1201 Massachusetts Avenue, 02138
Tel: 617-491 2222/800-458 5886
www.theinnatharvard.com
Graham Gund designed this intimate four-story, recently-renovated 111-room inn encircling a peaceful atrium. Fitness centre. **$$$$**

Irving House
24 Irving Street (off Cambridge Street), 02138
Tel: 617-547 4600/877-547 4600
www.cambridgeinns.com/Irving
Basic but comfortable 44-room B&B with some shared baths. Just a short walk from Harvard Square. **$–$$$$**

Mary Prentiss Inn
6 Prentiss Street, 02140
Tel: 617-661 2929
www.maryprentissinn.com
Tastefully appointed three-floor, 20-room Greek Revival B&B with a spacious deck. Situated between Harvard and Porter Squares. Free parking. **$$–$$$$**

BELOW: the colorful entrance to the Boston Harbor Hotel.

CAPE COD AND THE ISLANDS

Barnstable

Beechwood Inn
2839 Main Street (Route 6A)
Tel: 508-362 6618/800-609 6618
Fax: 508-326 0298
www.beechwoodinn.com
Six charming rooms in an
1853 Queen Anne
Victorian; some with
fireplaces and/or water
views. Three-course
candlelight breakfasts. The
owners breed and raise
AKC golden retrievers.
$$–$$$

Charles Hinckley House
8 Scudder Lane, 02630
Tel: 508-362 9924
Fax: 508-362 8861
A B&B with four period
rooms in an 1809 Federal
house. Lavish breakfasts.
$$

**Crocker Tavern Bed and
Breakfast**
3095 Main Street (Route 6A),
02630
Tel: 508-362 5115
Fax: 508-362 5562
The five rooms in this
tastefully renovated 1754
B&B are furnished with
canopy or four-poster beds,
and have claw-foot tubs
and antique sinks. **$–$$**

Brewster

**Bramble Inn and
Restaurant**
2019 Route 6A, 02631
Tel: 508-896 7644
Fax: 508-896 9332
www.brambleinn.com
Historic country inn in two
buildings (1792–1861)
offers eight rooms with
queen canopy or sleigh
beds, and a fine
restaurant. **$$$**

Captain Freeman Inn
15 Breakwater Road, 02631
Tel: 508-896 7481/800-843 4664
Fax: 508-896 5618
www.captainfreemaninn.com
14 antiques-filled spacious
rooms (some with whirlpool
tubs) in a luxurious 1860
shipbuilder's home with a
heated, outdoor pool.
Bicycles available.
$$–$$$$

Old Sea Pines Inn
Route 6A, 2553 Main Street, 02631
Tel: 508-896 6114
Fax: 508-632 0084
www.oldseapinesinn.com

A 1907 shingle-style
mansion that once served
as a girls' boarding school.
There are 24 rooms (some
with shared baths), and the
modern annex is
wheelchair accessible.
Family suites sleep four.
$–$$

Chatham

**Captain's House Inn of
Chatham**
371 Old Harbor Road, 02633
Tel: 508-945 0127/800-315 0728
Fax: 508-945 0866
www.captainshouseinn.com
The 18 rooms at this
elegant 1839 B&B and
outbuildings have luxurious
traditional decor; silver-
service tea is served in the
garden room, as are full
breakfasts. **$$$$**

Chatham Bars Inn
297 Shore Road, 02633
Tel: 508-945 0096/800-332 1577
Fax: 508-945 5491
www.chathambarsinn.com
This 1914 oceanfront
private hunting lodge-
turned- grand hotel/resort
has rooms in the inn,
private cottages, homes
perched on a bluff, and in
the newly-completed spa
building. **$$$$**

Wequassett Inn
Pleasant Bay, Route 28, 02663
Tel: 508-432 5400/800-225 7125
Fax: 508-432 1915
www.wequassett.com
104 rooms – some
oceanfront – in a country
club-style setting. There are
facilities for tennis, a pool
and a bay beach. **$$$$**

**Pleasant Bay Village
Resort**
1191 Route 28, 02633
Tel: 508-945 1133/800-547 1011
Fax: 508-945 9701
www.pleasantbayvillage.com
A complex of 58 rooms,
suites and efficiencies with
contemporary furnishings
on six manicured acres
close to Pleasant Bay.
$$$–$$$$

Dennis area

Beach House Inn
61 Uncle Stephen's Way,
West Dennis, 02670
Tel: 508-398 4575
This gray-shingled,

beachfront house with 7
bright and airy rooms is
simply furnished with
practical oak and wicker
pieces. No credit cards.
$$–$$$

Isaiah Hall B&B Inn
152 Whig Street, Dennis, 02638
Tel: 508-385 9928/800-736 0160
Tax: 508-385 5879
www.isaiahhallinn.com
Performers from the Cape
Playhouse favour this lovely
1857 farmhouse, with its
10 rooms and two suites
furnished with country
antiques, on a residential
street. Open all year.
$$–$$$$

Lighthouse Inn
1 Lighthouse Road
West Dennis, 02670
Tel: 508-398 2244
Fax: 508-398 5658
www.lighthouseinn.com
An old-fashioned, nine-
acre seaside resort B&B
with 61 rooms in cottages
and a 1855 lighthouse-
turned-inn. Supervised
activities for children in
July and August.
$$$–$$$$

Eastham

Inn at the Oaks B&B
3085 Route 6, 02642
Tel: 508-225 1886/877-255 1886
www.innattheoaks.com
Scottish, family-friendly
hospitality in a colourful
1869 Victorian 11-room
B&B near the Salt Pond
Visitors Center. **$$–$$$$**

Whalewalk Inn
220 Bridge Road, 02642
Tel: 508-255 0617/800-440 1281
www.whalewalkinn.com
This elegant 1830s Greek
Revival B&B built as a
whaling master's house
has 16 luxurious rooms in
the main house and five
buildings in spacious
grounds. Spa. **$$$–$$$$**

East Orleans

Nauset House Inn
143 Beach Road, 02643
Tel: 508-255 2195/800-771 5508
Fax: 508-240 6276
www.nausethouseinn.com
A convivial 1810
farmhouse B&B with 14
rooms (some with shared
baths) and a cottage;

stylish 1900s
conservatory. Good
situation near the
magnificent Nauset Beach.
Open Apr–Oct. **$-$$$**

Falmouth Area

Inn on the Sound
313 Grand Avenue South,
Falmouth Heights, 02540
Tel: 508-457 9666/800-564 9668
Fax: 508-457 9631
www.innonthesound.com
A B&B in an 1880 shingled
cottage on a bluff
overlooking Vineyard
Sound. A large porch offers
great water views, as do
four of the 10 rooms that
have private decks.
$$$–$$$$

Mostly Hall
27 Main Street, Falmouth, 02540
Tel: 508-548 3786
Fax: 508-457 1572
www.mostlyhall.com
1849 National Register
Italianate villa built by a
seafarer to please a
homesick wife has six
large, handsome, high-
ceilinged rooms with queen
canopy beds, and friendly,
knowledgeable hosts.
$$–$$$$

Harwich Port Area

Commodore Inn
30 Earle Road, West Harwich,
02671
Tel: 508-432 1180/800-368 1180
Fax: 508-432 3263
www.commodoreinn.com
A seaside motel just yards
from the sandy beaches
and warm waters of

PRICE CATEGORIES

An approximate guide to
rates for a standard double
room per night:
$$$$ = more than $200
$$$ = $150–200
$$ = $100–150
$ = under $100

Nantucket Sound has 27 rooms furnished in pleasing country decor. **$$–$$$$**

Winstead Inn and Beach Resort
4 Braddock Lane, 02646
Tel: 508-432 4444/800-870 4405
Fax: 508-432 9152
www.winsteadinn.com
Fourteen rooms with all the comforts of home including A/C and colour TV. Great location, right on the beach. Also, rooms at inn in the village. **$$$$**

Hyannis

Anchor In Cape Cod Hotel
One South Street, 02601
Tel: 508-775 0357
Fax: 508-775 1313
www.anchorin.com
Some of the 43 luxurious rooms at this hotel overlooking Lewis Bay have private decks and jacuzzis. Close to downtown and ferries. Heated outdoor pool. **$$–$$$**

Four Points by Sheraton Hyannis Resort
35 Scudder Avenue, 02601
Tel: 508-775 7775
www.starwoodhotels.com/fourpoints
This full-service resort on 52 landscaped acres has 224 guest rooms, an 18-hole golf course, fitness centre, spa, indoor and outdoor pools, and restaurants. **$$$–$$$$**

Hyannis Inn Motel
473 Main Street, 02601
Tel: 508-775 0255/800-922 8993
Fax: 508-771 0456
www.hyannisinn.com
A family-run inn in the centre of town, with 77 rooms ranging from standard to deluxe, and a heated indoor pool and saunas. Open April-Oct. **$–$$$**

North Truro

Beachfront White Sands Resort Motel
North Truro 02652
Tel: 508-487 0244
www.provincetownlodging.com
Just minutes from Provincetown, the resort has 51 beachfront and poolside rooms with kitchen units, private beach, heated indoor and outdoor pool, spa, and sauna. **$$$**

Provincetown

Cape Inn Resorts
698 Commercial Street, 02657
Tel: 508-487 1711/800-422 4224
www.capeinn.com
Motel in the East End a mile from town centre with 78 comfortable rooms and ample parking. Some rooms have harbour views. **$$–$$$**

Captain Lysander Inn (B&B)
96 Commercial Street, 02657
Tel: 508-487 2253
Fax: 508-487 7579
An 1850s captain's house in the sedate West End has six rooms with private baths, six with shared baths, and a cottage. Some have decks and views. **$–$$$$**

White Horse Inn
500 Commercial Street, 02657
Tel: 508-487 1790
Twelve rooms and six apartments in an 18th-century East End captain's house inn shaped by Provincetown's 20th-century artistic history. **$–$$**

Sandwich

Belfry Inn and Bistro
8 Jarves Street, 02563
Tel: 508-888-8550/
800-844-4542
www.belfryinn.com
A complex of three restored, period buildings: The Painted Lady, The Abbey, and The Village House. All rooms are unique, and many have fireplaces and whirlpool tubs. **$$–$$$$**

Dan'l Webster Inn and Spa
149 Main Street, 02563
Tel: 508-888 3622/800-444 3566
Fax: 508-888 5156
www.danlwebsterinn.com
Some rooms at this 48-room luxury hotel in the centre of Sandwich village have fireplaces, balconies, and whirlpool tubs. Restaurant and spa. **$$–$$$**

Inn at Sandwich Center
118 Tupper Road, 02563
Tel: 508-888 6958/800-249 6949
Fax: 508-888 2746
www.innatsandwich.com
Five bright bedrooms in a 1750s saltbox across from

the Sandwich Glass Museum. **$$–$$$**

Wingscorton Farm
11 Wing Boulevard, East Sandwich, 02537
Tel: 508-888 0534
Fax: 508-888 0545
A working farm/B&B, once a stop along the Underground Railroad, has rooms in the 1763 main house, a carriage house, and a cottage five minute's walk from the beach. Pets welcome. **$$–$$$$**

Woods Hole

Nautilus Motor Inn
539 Woods Hole Road, 02543
Tel: 508-548 1525
www.nautilusinn.com
Two-story waterfront motel has 54 one-bedroom units, and a swimming pool surrounded by gardens. Seasonal. **$–$$$$**

Woods Hole Passage
186 Woods Hole Road, 02540
Tel: 508-548 9575/800-790 8976
Fax: 508-540 4771
www.woodsholepassage.com
An 1890s carriage house and barn converted into a romantic, five-room B&B. **$$**

Yarmouth Port

Liberty Hall Inn B&B
77 Main Street (Route 6A), 02675
Tel: 508-362 3976/800-821 3977
Fax: 508-362 6485
www.libertyhillinn.com
Handsomely-preserved 1825 Greek Revival shipwright's house has five rooms with A/C, and TV in the main house, and four luxury rooms with gas fireplaces in the carriage house. **$$–$$$$**

One Centre Street Inn
One Centre Street, 02675
Tel: 508-362 9951/866-362 9951
www.onecentrestreetinn.com
Restored, three-story 1824 Colonial inn has five guest rooms and a one-bedroom suite. **$$–$$$**

Martha's Vineyard

Edgartown

Charlotte Inn
27 S Summer Street, 02539
Tel: 508-627 4151
Fax: 508-627 4652
www.elegantsmallhotel.com
An exquisite Relais &

Chateaux country inn encompassing five buildings (from 18th century to new) and a total of 25 rooms and suites, all romantically decorated in various styles. L'Etoile Restaurant. **$$$$**

Colonial Inn
38 N Water Street, 02539
Tel: 508-627 4711/800-627 4701
Fax: 508-627 5904
www.colonialinnmvy.com
Nicely updated and centrally located, this shingled 1911 hotel has 28 rooms and suites. Day spa open Apr–Nov. **$$$–$$$$**

Harbor View Hotel and Resort
131 N Water Street, 02539
Tel: 508-627 7000/800-225 6005
www.harbor-view.com
A lavishly renovated waterfront 1891 shingled grand hotel with 124 rooms and a heated pool near Lighthouse Beach. Seasonal. Home to The Newes in America restaurant. **$$$$**

Menemsha

Menemsha Inn and Cottages
Off North Rd, 02552
Tel: 508-645 2521
Fax: 508-645 9500
www.menemshainn.com
Peaceful simplicity in a 1923 inn with 27 rooms and cottages on 14 acres with water views. Tennis court, gym, ping pong room. **$$$–$$$$**

Oak Bluffs

The Oak House
Seaview Avenue, 02557
Tel: 508-693 4187/866-693 5805
Fax: 508-696 6293
www.vineyardinns.com
A lavish, oak-filled Queen Anne Victorian B&B with 10 rooms (some with balconies) overlooking Nantucket Sound. **$$$–$$$$**

Vineyard Haven

Martha's Place
114 Main Street, 02568
Tel: 508-693 0258
Fax: 508-693 1646
Handsome 1840 Greek Revival B&B with six immaculately designed and spacious bedrooms (some with jacuzzis). **$$$–$$$$**

West Tisbury

Lambert's Cove Inn and Restaurant
Lambert's Cove Road, 02575
Tel: 508-693 2298
Fax: 508-693 7890
www.lambertscoveinn.com
A 1790s farmhouse with 15 rooms in three buildings on seven pastoral acres with an English garden. Gourmet fare. $$$–$$$$

Nantucket

Jared Coffin House
29 Broad Street, 02554
Tel: 508-228 2400/
800-248 2405
Fax: 508-325 7752
www.jaredcoffinhouse.com
Sixty period rooms in a grand 1845 mansion and several adjoining buildings. $–$$$$

Martin House Inn
61 Centre Street, 02554
Tel: 508-228 0678
www.martinhouseinn.net
Reasonably priced, this year-round 13-room 1803 mariner's home is one of the prettiest and most congenial in town. Some rooms have shared bath; some with fireplaces. $–$$$$

The Wauwinet Inn
120 Wauwinet Road, Wauwinet, 02584
Tel: 508-228 0145/800-426 8718
www.wauwinet.com
A fabulously refurbished 1850 waterfront Relais & Chateaux hotel with 35 rooms. Luxurious, secluded, and expensive. Spa. Cruises on 26-seat launch. Seasonal. $$$$

THE REST OF MASSACHUSETTS

Amherst

The Lord Jeffery Inn
30 Boltwood Avenue, 01002
Tel: 413-253 2576/800-742 0358
Fax: 413-256 6152
www.lordjefferyinn.com
A traditional Colonial Revival-style inn with 48 rooms and several restaurants situated on the town green near Amherst College. $–$$$$

The Allen House Victorian Inn
599 Main Street, 01002
Tel: 413-253 5000
www.allenhouse.com
Meticulously restored, seven-room inn/B&B of the Aesthetic period, blending Victoriana with Japanese influences. $–$$$

Blackinton

Blackinton Manor
1391 Massachusetts Avenue, 01247, Blackinton Village
Tel: 413-663 5795/800-795 8613
Fax: 413-663 3121
www.blackinton-manor.com
Between North Adams and Williamstown, this 1832 Federal-style mansion is owned by classical musicians, and all of the antiques-filled guest rooms, and the common rooms, are finished with musical accents. $$

Concord

Concord's Colonial Inn
48 Monument Square, 01742
Tel: 978-369 9200/800-370 9200
Fax: 978-371 1533
www.concordscolonialinn.com
A 1716 inn with 56 rooms on Concord's town common. Music nightly in the tavern. $$–$$$$

Hawthorne Inn
462 Lexington Road, 01742
Tel: 978-369 5610
Fax: 978-287 4949
www.concordmass.com
B&B with seven rooms (some with gas fireplaces) in the historic district, opposite Hawthorne's Wayside. $$–$$$$

Longfellow's Wayside Inn
Wayside Inn Road
South Sudbury, 01776
Tel: 978-443 1776/800-339 1776
Fax: 978-443 8041
www.wayside.org
Ten updated rooms in a mid-18th-century tavern close to Lexington and Concord. The restaurant serves Yankee fare. $$–$$$

Deerfield

Deerfield Inn
81 Old Main Street, 01342
Tel: 413-774 5587/800-926 3865
Fax: 413-775 7221
www.deerfieldinn.com
Impeccably-preserved 1884 inn on the historic main street has 23 large rooms furnished with antiques and period reproductions, a fine restaurant, and lighter fare plus local beer on tap in its tavern. $$–$$$$

Great Barrington

Windflower Inn
684 S Egremont Road, 01230
Tel: 413-528 2720/800-992 1993
Fax: 413-528 5147
www.windflowerinn.com
A B&B in an early 20th-century country estate with gardens and a pool. The 13 rooms have four-poster beds and are decorated with antiques; some have fireplaces. $$–$$$$

Fall River

Lizzie Borden Bed and Breakfast
92 2nd Street, 02720
Tel: 508-675 7333
Fax: 508-673 1545
www.lizzie-borden.com
This is the house where Lizzie allegedly hacked her father and stepmother to death in 1892. The eight small rooms in the 1845 Greek Revival-style home feature Borden family memorabilia. $$$–$$$$

Gloucester

Bass Rocks Ocean Inn
107 Atlantic Road, 01930
Tel: 978-283 7600/888-802 7666
Fax: 978-281 6489
www.bassrocksoceaninn.com
Units at this complex overlooking the ocean are in three buildings: the 48-unit Georgian colonial-style motel, the 1899 Stacy House, and the summer cottage. Breakfast is served on the sun porch. Outdoor pool. Closed Nov–April. $$–$$$

Harborview Inn
71 Western Avenue, 01930
Tel: 978-283 2277/
800-299 6696
Fax: 978-282 7397
www.harborviewinn.com
A comfortable house-turned-B&B near the Fishermen Memorial statue. Six rooms, some with ocean views. $$–$$$

Greenfield

Brandt House Country Inn
29 Highland Avenue, 01301
Tel: 413-774 3329/800-235 3329
Fax:413 772 2908
www.brandthouse.com

An 1890s Victorian B&B with nine comfortable rooms and huge porches. Facilities include a tennis court. Pets welcome. $$–$$$

Hadley

Ivory Creek B&B
31 Chmura Road, 01035
Tel: 413-587 3115/866-331 3115
www.ivorycreek.com
A large, comfortable family-friendly house with antiques-filled guest rooms, decks, balconies, and porches. $$–$$$$

Lenox

Apple Tree Inn
10 Richmond Mountain Road, 01240
Tel: 413-637 1477
Fax: 413-637 2528
www.appletree-inn.com
A 22-acre hilltop estate within earshot of Tanglewood has 15 rooms in the 1885 main house and 24 in the newer lodge. There's an outdoor pool. $$$–$$$$

PRICE CATEGORIES

An approximate guide to rates for a standard double room per night:
$$$$ = more than $200
$$$ = $150–200
$$ = $100–150
$ = under $100

Blantyre

16 Blantyre Road (off Route 20), 01240
Tel: 413-637 3556
Fax: 413-637 4282
www.blantyre.com
An opulent mock-Tudor castle on 100 manicured acres with a heated pool, sauna, tennis courts, croquet lawns, and gourmet dining. Many rooms in the main house have fireplaces; also units in carriage house, and very private cottages. Open year round. $$$$

Canyon Ranch

165 Kemble Street, 01240
Tel: 413-637 4100/800-742 9000
Fax: 413-637 0057
www.canyonranch.com
New England's most elaborate spa occupies an 1890s building modelled on Versailles's Petit Trianon. FAP. 126 rooms. $$$–$$$$

Cliffwood Inn

25 Cliffwood Street, 01240
Tel: 413-637 3330/800-789 3331
Fax: 413-637 0221
www.cliffwood.com
An antiques-filled 1890 colonial mansion with seven bedrooms and an outdoor swimming pool on a quiet residential street. $$–$$$$

Garden Gables

135 Main Street, 01240
Tel: 413-637 0193
www.lenoxinn.com
Country charm in this B&B/winery close to Tanglewood. Rooms in the 1780 house and cottages. Spa. $–$$$$

Rookwood Inn

11 Old Stockbridge Road, 01240
Tel: 413-637 9750/800-223 9750
Fax: 413-637 1352
www.rookwoodinn.com
Twenty rooms in a comfortably-elegant 19th-century "painted lady" B&B at the centre of town. $$$–$$$$

The Summer White House

17 Main Street, 01240
Tel: 413-637 4489/800-382 9401
Fax: 413-637 4489
www.thesummerwhitehouse.com
An original Berkshire Cottage built in 1885 in the heart of town and just one mile from Tanglewood has lavishly decorated rooms, many with canopy beds and air conditioning. $$$–$$$$

The Village Inn

16 Church Street, 01240
Tel: 413-637 0020/800-253 0917
Fax: 413-637 2196
www.villageinn-lenox.com
A 1771 in-town inn, with 31 comfortably furnished rooms with private baths; some fireplaces. Rumplestiltzkin's Restaurant. $$–$$$$

Walker House

64 Walker Street, 01240
Tel: 413-637 1271/800-235 3098
Fax: 413-637 2387
www.walkerhouse.com
The hosts of this 1804 Federal-style, 8-room B&B provide nightly entertainment on a 12-ft (3.5-meter) screen, as well as recitals on the grand piano. $$–$$$$

Marblehead

Harbor Light Inn

58 Washington Street, 01945
Tel: 781-631 2186
Fax: 781-631 2216
www.harborlightinn.com
Some of the 21 rooms in this formally decorated 18th-century inn with a 19th-century addition have jacuzzis, fireplaces, and/or sundecks. $$–$$$$

Marblehead Inn

264 Pleasant Street, 01945
Tel: 781-639 9999/800-399 5843
Fax: 781-639 9996
www.marbleheadinn.com
A stately 1872 Victorian with 10 cozy two-bedroom suites. $$–$$$$

New Bedford

Days Inn

500 Hathaway Road, 02740
Tel: 509-997 1231/800-329 7466
Fax: 508-991 5095
www.daysinn.com
A full-service chain hotel with 153 rooms. $$–$$$

New Marlborough

Old Inn on the Green

Village Green (Route 57), 01230
Tel: 413-229 7924
www.oldinn.com
Chef/owner Peter Platt and his wife, Meredith Kennard, have created a lodging/dining destination. There are five comfortable rooms above the restaurant and six second-floor rooms in the restored Thayer House. $$$$

Newburyport

Clark Currier Inn

45 Green Street, 01950
Tel: 978-465 8363
www.clarkcurrierinn.com
A dignified, three-story 1803 shipbuilder's home in the Federal mode. Many of the eight rooms feature wide-board floors, pencil-post beds and other antique furnishings. $$–$$$$

Garrison Inn

11 Brown Square, 01950
Tel: 978-499 8500
Fax: 978-499 8555
www.garrisoninn.com
1809 former residence-turned-inn has 24 rooms with reproduction antiques, and 6 suites with lofts; some fireplaces. $$$–$$$$

North Adams

The Porches Inn at MASS MOCA

231 River Street, 01247
Tel: 413-664 0400
Fax: 413-664 0401
www.porches.com
This lodging, in a renovated building that once housed mill workers, bills itself as "ultra savvy": all of the 46 rooms are furnished in contemporary-retro décor and fully wired for computer use; some two-room suites have spiral staircases to loft sleeping areas. $$–$$$$

Northampton

Clarion Hotel & Conference Center

One Atwood Drive, 01060
Tel: 413-586 1211/800-582 2929
Fax: 413-586 0630
www.choicehotels.com
On the edge of town, this chain motel has 122 well-appointed rooms, indoor and outdoor pools, tennis courts, a restaurant, and a whirlpool spa. $$–$$$

Hotel Northampton

36 King Street, 01060
Tel: 413-584 3100
Fax: 413-584 9544
www.hotelnorthampton.com
Handsomely-appointed historic inn in the centre of town has 106 rooms, and suites with whirlpool baths. There's an exercise room, and a restaurant serving New England fare. $$$

Northfield

Centennial House

94 Main Street, 01360
Tel: 413-498 5921/877-977 5950
Fax: 413-498 2525
www.thecentennialhouse.com
Handsome in-town 1811 Colonial with four antiques-filled guest rooms (some share baths) and a third floor suite that sleeps four. Landscaped grounds. $$

Plymouth

John Carver Inn and Spa

25 Summer Street, 02360
Tel: 508-746 7100/800-274 1620
Fax: 508-746 8299
www.johncarverinn.com
Near major attractions, this immaculate modern hotel, with 85 rooms and suites (some with fireplaces) has an indoor theme pool with water slide. Restaurant. $$–$$$

Governor Bradford Motor Inn

98 Water Street, 02360
Tel: 508-746 6200/800-332 1620
Fax: 508-747 3032
www.governorbradford.com
A motel with 94 rooms right on the historic (and heavily trafficked) harbour. $–$$$

Pilgrim Sands Motel

150 Warren Avenue, 02360
Tel: 508-747 0900/800-729 7263
Fax: 508-746 8066
www.pilgrimsands.com
Oceanfront motel with standard units and oceanfront housekeeping apartments directly across from Plimoth Plantation. Private beach; indoor and outdoor pools. $–$$$

Rockport

Addison Choate Inn

49 Broadway, 01966
Tel: 978-546 7543
Fax: 978-546 7638
www.addisonchoate.com
Lovely summery decor and a quiet in-town setting for this Greek Revival inn with six rooms and two apartments; breakfast in the fireplaced dining room. $$–$$$

Eden Pines Inn

48 Eden Road, 01966
Tel: 978-546 2505

www.edenpinesinn.com
A cliffside mansion with dramatic ocean views. Seven large bedrooms, many with private balconies. Continental breakfast. Open April–Dec. **$$–$$$$**

Seaward Inn and Cottages
44 Marmion Way, 01966
Tel: 978-546 3471/877-473 9273
Fax: 978-546 7661
www.seawardinn.com
A welcoming summer house-turned-B&B on a beautifully landscaped seaside ledge. Rooms in the main inn, two nearby houses, and adjacent cottages. **$$$–$$$$**

Seacrest Manor
99 Marmion Way, 01966
Tel: 978-546 2211
www.seacrestmanor.com
This 1911 clapboard mansion has eight comfortable rooms (some with shared baths), well-tended gardens, sea views, and some private decks. **$–$$$$**

Linden Tree Inn
26 King Street, 01966
Tel: 978-546 2494/800-865 2122
www.lindentreeinn.com
A one-time captain's home close to the beach, with 12 well-priced B&B rooms, a carriage house with efficiency units, and an innkeeper who bakes marvellous scones. **$$–$$$$**

Sally Webster Inn
34 Mount Pleasant Street, 01966
Tel: 978-546 9251/877-546 9251
www.sallywebster.com
Small antiques-filled in-town lodging. Several of the seven rooms have wide-board pine floors and/or canopy beds. **$$**

The Tuck Inn B&B
17 High Street, 01966
Tel: 978-546 7260/800-789 7260
www.tuckinn.com
Comfortable in-town 1790 Colonial home. Some of the nine rooms have separate entrances and/or decks; all have A/C and Cable TV. There's also an apartment with full kitchen. Outdoor pool. **$$–$$$**

Yankee Clipper Inn
127 Granite Street, 01966
Tel: 978-546 3407/800-545 3699
Fax: 978-546 9730
www.yankeeclipperinn.com

ABOVE: Rockport keeps its maritime heritage on display.

The main building at this 16-room complex on an ocean promontory is an 1840 neoclassical-style house designed by Charles Bulfinch. Facilities include a heated saltwater pool. **$$$–$$$$**

Salem

Amelia Payson Guest House
16 Winter Street, 01970
Tel: 978-744 8304
www.ameliapaysonhouse.com
1845 Greek Revival B&B with four bright, airy rooms; convenient for museums and historic sites. Closed Nov–March. **$$–$$$**

Hawthorne Hotel
18 Washington Square West, 01970
Tel: 978-744 4080/800-729 7829
Fax: 978-745 9842
www.hawthornehotel.com
A 1920s hotel with 89 rooms and six suites, and harbour views from the top floors. The restaurant serves a popular Sunday jazz brunch buffet. **$$–$$$$**

Sheffield

Birch Hill B&B
254 S Undermountain Road, (Route 41), 01257
Tel: 413-229 2143/800-359 3969
www.birchhillbb.com
Casual, sprawling, simply furnished 1780 country inn with pool, set in 20 acres. Some of the seven rooms have fireplaces. **$$$**

Staveleigh House
59 Main Street, 01257
Tel: 413-229 2129/800-980 2129
A B&B with seven rooms in an 1817 parson's home

beside the Housatonic River. **$$**

Stockbridge

Merrell Tavern Inn
1565 Pleasant Street (Route 102), South Lee/Stockbridge, 01260
Tel: 413-243 1794/800-243 1794
Fax: 413-243 2669
www.merrell-Inn.com
An 11 –room (four with fireplaces) B&B in an authentically restored 1794 stagecoach tavern in a rural riverside setting. **$$–$$$$**

Red Lion Inn
30 Main Street, Stockbridge, 01262
Tel: 413-298 5545
Fax: 413-298 5130
www.redlioninn.com
A classic old inn (est. 1773) at the centre of a Norman Rockwell town. Some rooms in the main inn are quite small and share baths; those in the adjacent buildings are a bit larger. 111 rooms. **$$–$$$$**

Williamsville Inn
Route 41, West Stockbridge, 01266
Tel: 413-274 6118
Fax: 413-274 3539
www.williamsvilleinn.com
Sixteen rooms in a restored 1790s farmhouse, barn, and cottages on landscaped grounds. Summer sculpture garden. Taste of Germany Restaurant. **$$–$$$$**

Sturbridge

Publick House Historic Resort
Route 131, The Common, 01566
Tel: 508-347 3313/800-782 5425

Fax: 508-347 5073
www.publickhouse.com
A cluster of historic houses, plus a modern motel-style annex, offering 125 rooms in all. Good situation near Old Sturbridge Village. **$–$$$**

Williamstown

Field Farm Guest House
554 Sloan Road (off Route 43), 01267
Tel: 413-458 3135
Fax: 413-412 2556
www.thetrustees.org
This 1948 American Modern mansion B&B set on over 250 acres of conservation land has five large rooms with modern furnishings. Amenities include a pool, tennis courts, pond (fishing rods available), and hiking trails. **$$$–$$$$**

The Orchards
222 Adams Road (Route 2), 01267
Tel: 413-458 9611/800-225 1517
Fax: 413-458 3273
www.orchardshotel.com
A peaceful, elegant oasis despite its location on an unappealing commercial strip of Route 2. The 49 modern rooms have antique furnishings. **$$$–$$$$**

River Bend Farm
643 Simonds Road, 01267
Tel: 413-458 3121
A painstakingly restored 1770 colonial house. Furnishings are simple, even rustic, as befits the colonial period in this four-room B&B. No credit cards **$–$$$**

Worcester

The Beechwood Hotel
363 Plantation Street, 01605
Tel: 508-754 5789/800-344 2589
Fax:508-752 2060
www.beechwoodhotel.com
A handsome, modern 73-room luxury boutique hotel overlooking the lake. **$$–$$$**

PRICE CATEGORIES

An approximate guide to rates for a standard double room per night:
$$$$ = more than $200
$$$ = $150–200
$$ = $100–150
$ = under $100

RHODE ISLAND

Block Island

Atlantic Inn
High Street, Old Harbor, 02807
Tel: 401-466 5883/800-224 7422
Fax: 401-466 5678
www.atlanticinn.com
Block Island's grande dame, An 1879 white-clapboard hotel with a spacious porch on a hill overlooking the sea. 21 pleasant Victorian-style rooms and two tennis courts. $$$–$$$$

Block island inns
Tel: 800-992 7290
www.blockislandinns.com
A consortium of Inns, cottages and houses throughout the island, including the romantic, award-winning, 11-room Blue Dorey Inn. $–$$$$

Hotel Manisses and The 1661 Inn
Spring Street, Old Harbor, 02807
Tel: 401-466 2421/800-626 4773
Fax: 401-466 3162
www.blockislandresorts.com
Victorian inns with ocean views; there are 53 old-fashioned rooms in the main inns and cottages. A farm on the property is home to llamas and emus. $$$–$$$$

Spring House Hotel
Spring Street, Old Harbor, 02807
Tel: 401-466 5844/800-234 9263
Fax: 401-466 2633
www.springhousehotel.com
A classic 49-room hotel (built in 1852) with Victorian furnishings, a cupola-topped mansard roof and a wraparound porch. Set on 15 acres above the ocean. $$$–$$$$

Bristol

Bradford Dimond Norris House
474 Hope Street, 02809
Tel: 401-253 6338/888-329 6338
Fax: 401-253 4023
www.bdnhouse.com
Handsomely-restored downtown Federal-style B&B, built in 1792, has four air-conditioned guest rooms with four-poster or canopy beds. $$–$$$

Bristol Harbor Inn
259 Thames Street, 02809
Tel: 401-254 1444/866-254 1444

Fax: 401-254 1333
www.bristolharborinn.com
The East Bay's only waterfront lodging, in downtown Bristol, has 40 well-appointed rooms, many with views of Narragansett Bay. $$–$$$

Jamestown

Bay Voyage Inn
150 Conanicus Avenue, 02835
Tel: 401-423 2100
Fax: 401-423 3209
www.bayvoyageinn.com
Formerly a country house in Newport, this 32-room inn was transported across the bay in 1899. It's now an all-suite inn overlooking the harbor. $$–$$$$

Little Compton

Stone House Club
122 Sakonnet Point Road, 02837
Tel: 401-635 2222
www.stonehouseclub.com
This National Register of Historic Places 1854 oceanfront mansion has been completely renovated and now offers 12 handsomely-furnished rooms and a fine restaurant. $$$–$$$$

Narragansett

The Anchor Motel
825 Ocean Road, 02882
Tel: 401-792 8550
www.theanchormotel.com
Thirteen basic but clean rooms just across from Scarborough State Beach and close to the Block Island Ferry. $–$$$

The Richards
144 Gibson Avenue, 02882
Tel: 401-789 7746
Fax: 401-783 7168
An 1884 stone English manor B&B surrounded by gardens. All four antique-furnished rooms have working fireplaces. Private access to the rocky coast. No credit cards. $$–$$$

Newport

Castle Hill Inn
590 Ocean Drive, 02840
Tel: 401-849 3800/888-466 1355
www.castlehillinn.com

Scientist and explorer Alexander Agassiz's 1874 estate is now a first-rate resort which encompasses his mansion along with several other lodgings. The 40-acre property has one of the area's most magnificent views. $$$$

Cliffside Inn
2 Seaview Avenue, 02840
Tel: 401-847 1811/800-845 1811
Fax: 401-848 5850
www.cliffsideinn.com
Near the Cliff Walk, an 1880 Victorian villa, carved into grand, dramatic quarters. The 15 rooms in this B&B are light and airy, and some have working fireplaces and whirlpool tubs. $$$$

Francis Malbone House
392 Thames Street, 02840
Tel: 401-846 0392/800-846 0392
Fax: 401-848 5956
www.malbone.com
A 1760 Colonial brick mansion B&B on the harbour. Twenty lavishly appointed rooms with period reproduction furnishings. $$–$$$$

The Hotel Viking
1 BellevueAvenue, 02840
Tel: 401-847 3300/800-556 7126
www.hotelviking.com
The original wing of the 1926, five-story hotel in the Historic Hill neighbourhood recently received a $6 million renovation. But all 209 rooms and 20 suites are well-appointed and comfortable. Indoor pool, fitness centre, spa, and restaurant. $$$–$$$$

The Inns of Newport
Tel: 401-848 5300/800-524 1386
www.innsofnewport.com
A group of four historic downtown inns, including The Clarkeston & Admiral Farragut, The Wynstone, The Elm Street Inn, and The Cleveland House. All try for a colonial "feel." $$–$$$$

Ivy Lodge
12 Clay Street, 02840
Tel: 401-849 6865/800-834 6865
www.ivylodge.com
Eight-room B&B in a Stanford White-designed Victorian home in the mansion district features a dramatic, old-English entryway, wraparound porch, and 11 fireplaces. $$–$$$$

Lighthouse
Newport
Tel: 401-847 4242
www.roseisland.org
Stay for a night or a week in an operating lighthouse a mile offshore. Open year round.

Melville House
39 Clarke Street, 02840
Tel: 401-847 0640/800-711 7184
Fax: 401-847 0956
www.melvillehouse.com
A 1750 Colonial B&B on a gas lamp-lit street on Historic Hill. Seven small but comfortably appointed guest rooms (some with shared bath), plus a fireplace suite. $–$$$$

Newport Beach Hotel and Suites
Memorial Boulevard and Wave Avenue, 02840
Tel: 888-522 1780
www.newportbeachhotelandsuites.com
Newport's only beachfront hotel has 50 renovated rooms and suites in the original hotel, and 26 one- and two-bedroom suites in a new building. All have refrigerators and microwaves. $$$$

Victorian Ladies Inn
63 Memorial Boulevard, 02840
Tel: 888-849 9960
www.victorianladies.com
A pair of c.1850s vintage lovelies, in period style, offering 11 B&B rooms and elaborate gardens. Near First Beach and the Cliff Walk. Pets welcome. $$$–$$$$

Providence

Hotel Providence
311 Westminster Street, 02903
Tel: 401-861 8000/800-861 8990
www.thehotelprovidence.com
80 elegantly-appointed rooms and suites with European decor in a restored turn-of-the-19th-century building in downtown's Historic

TRANSPORTATION   ACCOMMODATIONS   ACTIVITIES   SHOPPING   A – Z

District. L'Epicureo Restaurant receives accolades. **$$$$**

The Old Court B&B
144 Benefit Street, 02903
Tel: 401-751 2002
Fax: 401-272 4830
www.oldcourt.com
Near the Rhode Island School of Design, an 1863 rectory retrofitted as an elegant Victorian-style inn. Ten spacious rooms with high ceilings, chandeliers, phones, and cable TV. **$$–$$$$**

Providence Biltmore Hotel
Kennedy Plaza, 02903
Tel: 401-421 0700/800-294 7709
Fax: 401-455 3040
www.providencebiltmore.com
A downtown, 1922 Art Deco-style grand hotel with 292 nicely-restored and spacious rooms and suites. Dull-service salon and spa. **$$–$$$$**

State House Inns
43 Jewett Street, 02908
Tel: 401-351 6111
Fax: 401-351 4261
www.providence-inn.com
Two historic downtown B&Bs: the 1858 Christopher Dodge House at 11 West Park Street (**$$–$$$**), and the Mowry-Nicholson House at 57 Brownell Street (**$$–$$$$**). Both offer free parking.

Weekapaug

Weekapaug Inn
25 Spray Rock Road, 02891
Tel: 401-322 0301
Fax: 401-322 1016
www.weekapauginn.com
A classic FAP inn (65 rooms) with a wraparound porch sheltering well-heeled families since 1938 (the original inn was built in 1899). On a peninsula in a coastal village 6 miles (9.6 km) from Westerly. Summer programs for ages 3–10. No credit cards. **$$$$**

Westerly

Andrea Hotel
89 Atlantic Avenue, Misquamicut
Tel: 401-348 8788
www.andreahotel.com
Old-fashioned hotel directly on the beach offers 24 very basic rooms, but some have private balconies and fabulous water views. In-season nightly entertainment and restaurant. **$$–$$$$**

Grandview Bed and Breakfast
212 Shore Road, 02891
Tel: 401-596 6384/800-447 6384
Fax: 401-596 3036
www.grandviewbandb.com
A comfortable turn-of-the-20th-century house with 9 cozy guest rooms (some with ocean views), gardens, and a stone wraparound porch. **$–$$**

Shelter Harbor Inn
10 Wagner Road (Route 1), 02891
Tel: 401-322 8883/800-468 8883
Fax: 401-322 7907
www.shelterharborinn.com
Once a working farm, now a luxury 24-room getaway for B&B in a rural setting near the beach. The roof deck has a barbecue grill and a hot tub. **$$–$$$$**

CONNECTICUT

Avon

Avon Old Farms Hotel
279 Avon Mountain Road, Routes 44 and 10, 06001
Tel: 860-677 1651/800-836 4000
Fax: 860-677 0364
www.avonoldfarmshotel.com
160 modern rooms with traditional furnishings in several red brick buildings spread across 20 acres. Swimming pool. **$$–$$$$**

Bristol

Chimney Crest Manor
5 Founders Drive, 06010
Tel: 860-582 4219
Fax: 860-584 5903
Five-room B&B in an elegantly appointed 1930s National Historic Register Tudor-style mansion overlooking the Farmington Valley, just 20 minutes west of Hartford. **$$–$$$**

Chester

Inn and Vineyard at Chester
318 West Main Street, 06412
Tel: 860-526 9541
Fax: 860-526 1607
www.innatchester.com
Modern amenities in a 42-room inn built around an original 1776 farmhouse. Located between Essex

and East Haddam. Tennis courts, tavern. **$$$–$$$$**

East Haddam

Bishopsgate Inn
7 Norwich Road, 06423
Tel: 860-873 1677
Fax: 860-873 3898
www.bishopsgate.com
Six-room B&B in an 1818 shipwright's home with six fireplaces. **$$–$$$**

Essex

Griswold Inn
36 Main Street, 06426
Tel: 860-767 1776
Fax: 860-767 0481
www.griswoldinn.com
In operation since 1776, historical appointments in the 31 room inn include ancient firearms, antiques, and Currier & Ives prints. Eight of the 14 suites have fireplaces. There's a fine art collection in the Tap Room. **$$–$$$$**

Farmington

Centennial Inn Suites
5 Spring Lane, 06032
Tel: 860-677 4647/
800-852 2052 outside CT
Fax: 860-676 0685
112 one and two-bedroom suites with kitchen, living room, fireplace and TV on 12 wooded acres. Whirlpool, exercise room. Pets welcome. **$$**

Farmington Inn
827 Farmington Avenue, 06032
Tel: 860-677 2821
Fax: 860-677 8332
www.farmingtoninn.com
A handsomely renovated lodging in the Historic District has 72 traditionally decorated rooms furnished with fresh flowers, antiques, and local art work. **$$–$$$**

Glastonbury

Butternut Farm
1654 Main Street, 06033
Tel: 860-633 7197
Fax: 860-659 1758
www.butternutfarmbandb.com
A working farm/B&B with four rooms in a 1720 colonial house with eight fireplaces, period antiques, and herb gardens. **$–$$**

Hartford

Crowne Plaza Hartford Downtown
50 Morgan Street, 06120
Tel: 860-549 2400
Intown hotel with 350 rooms and suites, a restaurant, fitness centre,

and outdoor pool. **$$$–$$$$**

Goodwin Hotel
1 Haynes Street, 06103
Tel: 860-246 7500/800-922 5006
www.goodwinhotel.com
A historic inn with 124 rooms and suites in the heart of town. Fitness centre; good discounts on weekends. Valet parking. **$$$–$$$$**

Hilton Hartford
315 Trumbull Street, 06103
Tel: 860-728 5151
Fax: 860-240 7247
The renovated, 22-floor, downtown hotel connected to the Hartford Civic Center has 390 rooms, a

PRICE CATEGORIES

An approximate guide to rates for a standard double room per night:
$$$$ = more than $200
$$$ = $150–200
$$ = $100–150
$ = under $100

restaurant, a workout room, and an indoor pool. **$$$–$$$$**

Ivorytown

Copper Beech Inn
46 Main Street, 06442
Tel: 860-767 0330/888-809 2056
www.copperbeachinn.com
Luxuriously appointed 1890 Victorian home and carriage house on 7 acres (3 hectares). Nine of the 13 rooms have whirlpool tubs. **$$$–$$$$**

Lakeville

Interlaken Inn
74 Interlaken Road, Route 112, 06039
Tel: 860-435 9878/800-222 2909
Fax: 860-435 2980
www.interlakeninn.com
A romantic country retreat for more than 100 years. There are rooms in the main inn – an English Tudor house – as well as the Townhouse and a private lakefront cottage. Pets welcome in some rooms. Spa. **$$$–$$$$**
Wake Robin Inn
Sharon Road (Route 41), 06039
Tel: 860-435 2000
Fax: 860-435 6523
www.wakerobininn.com
A Georgian, colonial-style inn and motel with 38 rooms set on 15 acres (6 hectares). **$$$**

Ledyard

Stonecroft
515 Pumpkin Hill Road, 06339
Tel: 860-572 0771/800-772 0774
Fax: 860-572 9161
www.stonecroft.com
Close to the casinos but a world away, this 1807 Georgian colonial, a National Register of Historic Places property on six-and-a-half acres, has 10 rooms with private baths; three have fireplaces.
$$$–$$$$
Foxwoods
Tel: 800-369 9663
www.foxwoods.com
The opening of the MGM Grand in May, 2008 added an additional 825 rooms to the 1,400-room casino complex, which includes the 24-floor Pequot Tower, the Great Cedar Hotel, and

– a short drive away by the 24-hour courtesy van – Two Trees Inn. **$$$–$$$$**

Litchfield

Abel Darling B&B
102 West Street, 06759
Tel: 860-567 0384
1782 Colonial overlooking the Green in the historic district has two antiques-filled guest rooms. **$$–$$$**
Litchfield Inn
432 Bantam Road (Route 202), 06759
Tel: 860-567 4503/800-499 3444
Fax: 860-567 5358
www.litchfieldinnct.com
Central location is a plus at this reproduction inn, with its 32 rooms traditionally decorated in the Colonial style. The parlour has a baby grand piano and fireplace. **$$$–$$$$**
Tollgate Hill Inn and Restaurant
Tollgate Road and Route 202, 06759
Tel: 860-567 4545
www.tollgatehill.com
A romantically appointed 1745 Federal inn supplemented by a renovated schoolhouse. Many of the 20 rooms have canopy beds. **$$$–$$$$**

Madison

Tidewater Inn B&B
949 Boston Post Road (Route 1) 06443
Tel: 203-245 8457
Fax: 203-318 0265
www.thetidewater.com
A former, shorefront stage coach stop turned cozy, antiques-filled B&B with nine rooms (some with fireplaces). Walking distance to Madison village. **$$$–$$$$**
Madison Beach Hotel
94 West Wharf Road, 06443
Tel: 203-245 1404
Fax: 203-245 0410
www.madisonbeachhotel.com
An old-fashioned, Victorian wooden hotel with 31 rooms, four suites, and a wraparound porch over-looking the Sound. **$$–$$$**

Mystic Area

Harbour Inne and Cottage
15 Edgemont Street, Mystic, 06355
Tel: 860-572 9253

www.harbourinne-cottage.com
A family-friendly pine-panelled 1950s bungalow with six nautical-themed rooms and a three-room cottage on the Mystic River. Walking distance to the seaport and boat dock.
$$–$$$
House of 1833 B&B
72 N Stonington Road, Mystic, 06355
Tel: 860-536 6325/800-367 1833
www.houseof1833.com
Elegant, 1833 Greek-revival mansion has five antiques-filled guest rooms, some with canopy beds and private porch or balcony and wood burning fireplaces. Pool and tennis court. **$$–$$$$**
Inn at Mystic
Routes 1 and 27, Mystic, 06355
Tel: 860-536 9604/800-237 2415
www.innatmystic.com
Choose from motel units, guest houses, or the National Historic Register Colonial Revival mansion at this 15-acre (6-hectare) property overlooking Mystic Harbor. Outdoor pool, tennis, boating, and kayaking. **$$$–$$$$**
Steamboat Inn
73 Steamboat Wharf, Mystic, 06355
Tel: 860-536 8300
Fax: 860-536 9528
www.steamboatinnmystic.com
Ten waterfront rooms, some with fireplaces and whirlpools, in an elegant inn in the Historic District.
$$–$$$$
Whaler's Inn
20 E Main Street (Route 1), Mystic, 06355
Tel: 860-536 1506/
800-243 2588 outside CT
Fax: 860-572 1250
www.whalersinnmystic.com
Several 19th-century homes clustered near the docks have been transformed into a homey inn with 41 rooms. **$$–$$$**

New Haven

Colony Inn
1157 Chapel Street, 06511
Tel: 203-776 1234/800-458 8810
Fax: 203-772 3929
www.colonyatyale.com
Located near the Yale campus, this European-style inn features a lobby with a grand chandelier and

86 comfortable guest rooms furnished with Colonial reproductions. **$$–$$$**
New Haven Hotel
229 George Street, 06510
Tel: 203-498 3100/800-644 6835
Fax: 203-498 0911
www.newhavenhotel.com
A seven-story, 92-room downtown hotel with the feel of an exclusive inn. Amenities include an indoor swimming pool, in-room data ports, and a health club. **$$–$$$$**
Omni New Haven Hotel at Yale
155 Temple Street, 06510
Tel: 203-772 6664
Fax: 203-974 6777
www.omnihotels.com
This upscale, 19-floor chain hotel on the edge of the campus offers 305 rooms (some with portable treadmills), a spa, and restaurant. **$$$–$$$$**
Touch of Ireland Guest House
670 Whitney Avenue, 06511
Tel: 203-787 7997/866-787 7990
Fax: 203-787 7999
www.touchofirelandguesthouse.com
Four comfortable rooms and a family suite in a nicely-situated 1920s Colonial B&B less than a mile from the Yale campus. Free parking and wi-fi. **$$**

New London

Lighthouse Inn
6 Guthrie Place, 06320
Tel: 860-443 8411/888-443 8411
Fax: 860-437 7027
www.lighthouseinn-ct.com
This restored 1902 mansion just a few blocks from Ocean Beach Park has 51 nicely-furnished rooms; some with water views. There's a private beach and lovely grounds. **$$$–$$$$**

New Preston

Boulders Inn
East Shore Road, Route 45, 06777
Tel: 860-868 0541/800-552 6853
Fax: 860-868 1925
www.bouldersinn.com
17 rooms in an elegant 1895 stone mansion and carriage house overlooking Lake Waramaug. Also, eight fireplaced guesthouses. B&B or MAP. **$$$$**

TRANSPORTATION
ACCOMMODATIONS
ACTIVITIES
SHOPPING
A – Z

Hopkins Inn
22 Hopkins Road, 06777
Tel: 860-868 7295
www.thehopkinsinn.com
1847 Federal-style country
inn perched high above
Lake Waramaug has 11
comfortable, simply-
furnished rooms and two
apartments. **$$–$$$$**

Norfolk

Blackberry River Inn
538 Greenwoods Road, Route 44W,
06058
Tel: 860-542 5100/800-414- 3636
www.blackberryriverinn.com
National Register of
Historic Places 1763
Colonial mansion on 27
acres in the Berkshire
foothills has 24 rooms and
suites with Victorian decor
in the inn and Carriage
House. **$$$–$$$$**

Manor House
69 Maple Avenue, Route 44, 06058
Tel/fax: 860-542 5690
manorhouse-norfolk.com
An opulent 1898 Tudor
summer home B&B with 20
Tiffany stained-glass
windows. Some of the nine
rooms have whirlpool tubs,
fireplaces and balconies.
$$–$$$$

Norwalk

Silvermine Tavern
194 Perry Avenue, 06850
Tel: 203-847 4558
Fax: 203-847 9171
www.silverminetavern.com
A 1785 country inn set by a
waterfall has 11 antiques-
filled bedrooms; some have

fireplaces. There's a popular restaurant with live
entertainment. **$–$$$$**

Old Lyme

Bee & Thistle Inn
100 Lyme Street, 06371
Tel: 860-434 1667/800-622 4946
Fax: 860-434 3402
www.beeandthistleinn.com
A 1756 Colonial home with
11 rooms and a cottage,
set peacefully beside a
river. The elegant dining
room serves prix-fixe
dinners by advance
reservation. **$$$–$$$$**

Old Saybrook

Saybrook Point Inn and Spa
2 Bridge Street, Route 154, 05475
Tel: 860-395 2000/800-243 0212
Fax: 860-388 1504
www.saybrook.com
Well-appointed 81-room
luxury hotel, with water
views, indoor and outdoor
pools, and a spa. The
lighthouse suite has a
kitchenette. **$$$–$$$$**

Salisbury

White Hart Inn
Village Green (Routes 44 and 41),
06068
Tel: 860-435 0030/800-832 0041
Fax: 860-435 0040
www.whitehartinn.com
First opened as an inn in
1867, this landmark
building offers 26 rooms
and suites at the centre of
a timeless town. Restau-
rant has "country dining"
atmosphere. **$$$–$$$$**

Stonington

Inn at Stonington
60 Water Street, 06378
Tel: 860-535 2000/860-535 2000
Fax: 860-535 8193
www.innatstonington.com
Overlooking Stonington
Borough harbor, this
contemporary inn has 18
rooms and suites with
fireplaces; 10 have jacuzzis.
Exercise room, a 400-ft
(120-meter) pier. **$$$–$$$$**

Washington

Mayflower Inn and Spa
118 Woodbury Road (Route 47),
06793
Tel: 860-868 9466
Fax: 860-868 1497
www.mayflowerinn.com
Romantic country luxury:
25 rooms on 58 secluded
acres with gardens, woods,
and ponds. Facilities
include a pool, tennis
courts, a spa, and a highly
regarded restaurant. **$$$$**

Westport

Inn at Longshore
260 Compo Road South, 06880
Tel: 203-226 3316
Fax: 203-227 5344
www.innatlongshore.com

The handsome 12-room inn
on 52 acres, a former
country club, overlooks
Long Island Sound and has
an 18-hole golf course and
a popular restaurant.
$$$–$$$$

Inn at National Hall
2 Post Road West, 06880
Tel: 203-221 1351/800-628 4255
www.innatnationalhall.com
This elegant inn on the
banks of the Saugatuck
was fashioned from a 19th-
century building and styled
like an English manor
house. There are 16
lavishly decorated rooms
and suites and a first-class
restaurant. **$$$$**

Wethersfield

Chester Bulkley House
B&B
184 Main Street, 06109
Tel: 860-563 4236
Five-room B&B (three with
private bath) in an elegant
1830 Greek Revival home
located in an historic town
5 miles (8 km) from
Hartford. **$–$$**

Woodbury

Longwood Country Inn
1204 Main Street South, 06798
Tel: 203-266 0800
Fax: 203-263 3474
www.longwoodcountryinn.com
This rambling 1789
National Historic Register
B&B on 4 wooded acres is
decorated in an English
country style and has four
guest rooms, including a
spacious suite. **$$–$$$$**

VERMONT

Many Vermont inns take a
break between foliage and
the Christmas holidays,
and again during "mud
season" (Mar–Apr).

Arlington

Arlington Inn
Route 7a, 05250
Tel: 802-375 6532/800-443 9442
Fax: 802-375 6534
www.arlingtoninn.com
Nineteen guest rooms with
Victorian-style furnishings
in an elegant Greek Revival
mansion and three

annexes. There's a fine
restaurant here, too.
$$$–$$$$

West Mountain Inn
River Road (off Route 313), 05250
Tel: 802-375 6516
Fax: 802-375 6553
www.westmountaininn.com
Originally built as a
farmhouse in 1849 and
now an 18-room inn with
mountain views on 150
country acres (60
hectares). Miles of
snowshoeing and hiking
trails, children's games
room, and a resident llama

ranch. MAP available.
$$$–$$$$

Bennington

Alexandra Inn B&B
916 Orchard Road, 05201
Tel: 802-442 5619/888-207 9386
Fax: 802-442 4423
A lovingly-restored and
comfortable 1859
farmhouse on two acres
has six rooms in the main
house and six in a recent
addition. All have TV, queen
or king beds, wi-fi, and A/C.
$$–$$$

Four Chimneys Inn and
Restaurant
21 West Road (Route 9),
05201
Tel: 802-447 3500
Fax: 802-447 3692
www.fourchimneys.com

French Provincial decor in a grand Georgian Revival 11-room B&B. **$$–$$$$**

Bolton Valley

The Black Bear
Bolton Access Road, 05477
Tel: 802-434 2126/800-395 6335
Fax: 802-434 5161
www.blkbearinn.com
Cozy countrified decor in a lodge located near the resort. Some of the 24 rooms have balconies, hot tubs, and fire stoves. The owner/chef's restaurant is a popular dinner spot. On-site kennel/pet friendly rooms. **$$–$$$**

Bolton Valley Resort
Bolton Access Road, 05477
Tel: 802-434 3444/877-926 5866
Fax: 802-434 2131
www.boltonvalley.com
This small, four-seasons ski resort has a complex of plain but serviceable hotel rooms, studios, and 1-2 bedroom suites at the base of the mountain. Sports centre near by. **$$–$$$**

Brattleboro

Forty Putney Road B&B
192 Putney Road, Route 5, 05301
Tel: 802-254 6268/800-941 2413
Fax: 802-258 2673
www.fortyputneyroad.com
French chateaux-style, 1930s home on the West River has six pleasant rooms with A/C and TV, and lovely grounds down to the riverfront. **$$$–$$$$**

Latchis Hotel
50 Main Street, 05301
Tel: 802-254 6300/800-798 6301
Fax: 802-254 6304
www.latchis.com
A 1938 Art Deco hotel, right in the heart of downtown. Some of the 30 rooms have refrigerators, some have views of Main Street or the Connecticut River, and some are quite small; but the family suites are a bargain. **$$–$$$**

Bridgewater Corners

October Country Inn
362 Upper Road, 05035
Tel: 802-672 3412/800-648 8421
Fax: 802-672 1163
www.octobercountryinn.com
A cozy, 19th-century

ABOVE: Vermont lodges are popular with leaf-peepers in the fall.

farmhouse with 10 rooms on a back road, about 5 miles (8 km) from the Killington ski area. MAP available, and dinners feature ethnic menus. **$$**

Brookfield

Green Trails Inn
Main Street, 05036
Tel: 802-276 3412
www.greentrailsinn.com
A sprawling 13-room B&B, built around 1790 and 1830 farmhouses. The owners maintain 19 miles (30 km) of trails for cross-country skiing and hiking. **$–$$**

Burlington

Courtyard by Marriott
25 Cherry Street, 05401
Tel: 802-864 4700
Fax: 802-862 1179
www.marriott.com
Burlington's newest hotel, overlooking the waterfront, has 116 nicely-appointed rooms and 11 suites on eight floors. Indoor pool, fitness centre, and restaurant. **$$$–$$$$**

Lang House on Main Street
360 Main Street, 05401
Tel: 877 919 9799
www.langhouse.com
A lovingly- and precisely-restored 11-room, 1881 Victorian is close to the UVM campus and downtown. **$$$–$$$$**

Willard Street Inn
349 S Willard Street, 05401
Tel: 802-651 8710/800-577 8712
Fax: 802-651 8714
www.willardstreetinn.com
Built in the 1880s, this stately, formally appointed house in the historic Hill area and close to downtown has views of Lake Champlain. The 14 rooms are furnished with antiques and down comforters. **$$–$$$$**

Chittenden

Mountain Top Inn
Mountain Top Road, 05737
Tel: 802-483 2311/800-445 2100
Fax: 802-483 6373
www.mountaintopinn.com
A large, comfortable, fully-contained year-round family resort deep in the

countryside north of Rutland. The 52 rooms are in the inn and outlying cottages. Outstanding Nordic skiing. MAP available. **$$$–$$$$**

Fox Creek Inn
Chittenden Dam Road, 05737
Tel: 802-483 6213/800-707 0017
www.foxcreekinn.com
A 1920s retreat 10 miles (16 km) north of Rutland. Five of the eight rooms have whirlpool tubs. The highly-regarded restaurant serves four-course candlelit dinners; MAP available. **$$–$$$$**

Craftsbury Common and environs

Craftsbury Inn
Main Street (Route 14), Craftsbury, 05826
Tel: 802-586 2848/800-336 2848
Fax: 802-586 8060
www.craftsburyinn.com
Country comfort in an 1850 Greek Revival inn. Ten rooms with wraparound verandas overlooking lavish gardens. MAP available. **$–$$**

Craftsbury Outdoor Center
Craftsbury Common, 05827
Tel: 802-586 7767
Fax: 802-586 7768
www.craftsbury.com
The 47-room FAP facility offers dormitory-style rooms, with skilled training available in various outdoor sports. There are more than 100 miles (160 km) of cross-country ski trails, plus sculling, running camps, mountain biking, and canoeing. **$–$$$**

Inn on the Common
Main Street (Route 14)
Craftsbury Common, 05827
Tel: 802-586 9619/800-521 2233
Fax: 802-586 2249
www.innonthecommon.com
A 17-room MAP with luxurious décor as well as a swimming pool, tennis court, and mountain views. Pets welcome (cleaning fee). **$$$–$$$$**

Dorset

Barrows House
Route 30, 05251
Tel: 802-867 4455/800-639 1620
Fax: 802-867 0132
www.barrowshouse.com

Twenty-eight rooms and suites in an 18th-century Federal-style inn and several outbuildings on 7 acres (3 hectares) 6 miles (10 km) north of Manchester. Well-regarded restaurant, pool and tennis courts. MAP available. **$$$–$$$$**

Dorset Inn
Church and Main streets, 05251
Tel: 802-867 5500
Fax: 802-867 5542
www.dorsetinn.com
One of the state's oldest – and reliably commendable – inn with 31 rooms, opened in 1796. The restaurant has a fine reputation, and MAP is available. Pets welcome. **$$$–$$$$**

Marble West Inn
Dorset West Road, 05251
Tel: 802-867 4155/800-453 7629
www.marblewestinn.com
An elegant, eight-room B&B in a marble-columned 1840s Greek Revival manse. The rate includes a candlelit, gourmet breakfast. **$$–$$$**

East Burke

Inn at Mountain View Farm
Darling Hill Road, 05832
Tel: 802-626 9924/800-572 4509
www.innmtnview.com
Fourteen lovely guest rooms with private baths and antiques in an 1890 Georgian inn on the grounds of a one-time creamery. With 440 acres, there are miles of cross-country, hiking, and mountain biking trails. **$$$–$$$$**

Village Inn
606 Route 114, 05832
Tel: 802-626 3161
www.villageinnofeastburke.com
Six cozy rooms with private baths in a homey B&B close to several ski areas and Kingdom Trails mountain biking. Also, three bedrooms in The Annex. **$**

Essex Junction

Inn at Essex
70 Essex Way (off Route 15), 05452
Tel: 802-878 1100/800-727 4295
Fax: 802-878 0063
www.vtculinaryresort.com
A Colonial-style, modern inn with 120 rooms and suites

ABOVE: Lodges at Killington, New England's largest ski resort.

(30 with fireplaces), a swimming pool, and several fine restaurants operated by the New England Culinary Institute. **$$$–$$$$**

Fair Haven

Maplewood Inn
1108 Route 22a South, 05473
Tel: 802-265 8039/800-253 7729
Fax: 802-265 8210
www.maplewoodinn.net
A five-room B&B with fanciful decor and hearty breakfasts in an 1843 Greek Revival home/former dairy farm. **$–$$**

Grafton

Old Tavern at Grafton
Route 121, 05146
Tel: 802-843 2231/800-843 1801
Fax: 802-843 2245
www.old-tavern.com
One of New England's oldest inns, built in 1801 as a stagecoach stop, has 11 rooms in the inn plus 11 additional properties scattered around the grounds. Swimming pond, tennis courts, ice skating, and cross-country ski trails. Many famous former guests. **$$–$$$$**

Highgate Springs

Tyler Place Family Resort
Route 7, 05460
Tel: 802-868 4000
Fax: 802-868 5621
www.tylerplace.com
A popular family destination since the 1930s, accommodations include cottages, an 1820 farmhouse, a Victorian guest house, and a 60-room inn. The 165 acres (67 hectares) includes a private beach and boating. Special children's programs. FAP. **$$$$**

Jay

Jay Peak Ski and Summer Resort
Route 242, 05859
Tel: 802-988 2611/800-451 4449
Fax: 802-988 4049
www.jaypeakresort.com
48 simple, ski lodge-style hotel rooms and 140 modern one- to three-bedroom condos, most slope side. **$–$$$**

Jericho

Sinclair Inn B&B
389 Route 15, 05465
Tel: 802-899 2334/800-433 4658

www.sinclairinnbb.com
An elegant 1890s "painted lady" just 25 minutes from Burlington has six spacious, air conditioned guest rooms and elaborate perennial gardens. Breakfast is served in the Victorian dining room. **$$–$$$**

Killington

Cascades Lodge
58 Old Mill Road 05751
Tel: 800-345 0113
www.cascadeslodge.com
This modern lodge with 45 rooms and suites stands at the base of Killington Mountain, steps from golf and ski lifts. Amenities include an indoor pool and sauna, and theres a restaurant and pub on the premises. Breakfast included. **$$–$$$**

Inn of the Six Mountains
Killington Road, 05751
Tel: 802-422 4302/800-228 4676
Fax: 802-422 4898
www.sixmountains.com
Just a few minutes from the lifts, this 103-room modern hotel has a Rockies feel. Everything, including the central fieldstone hearth, is lavishly overscale. Facilities include indoor and outdoor seasonal pools, a fitness room, outdoor hot tubs, and tennis courts. **$$–$$$**

Inn at Long Trail
Route 4, 05751
Tel: 802-775 7181/800-325 2540
Fax: 802-777 7034
www.innatlongtrail.com
A 1938 rustic 19-room ski inn/B&B constructed around an enormous boulder, which intrudes picturesquely into the dining room and Irish pub, where there's often Irish music. **$–$$$**

Mountain Meadows Lodge
Thundering Brook Road, 05751
Tel: 802-775 1010/800-370 4567

PRICE CATEGORIES

An approximate guide to rates for a standard double room per night:
$$$$ = more than $200
$$$ = $150–200
$$ = $100–150
$ = under $100

Fax: 802-773 4459
www.mtmeadowslodge.com
This large, family-oriented lakeside farmhouse with 18 guest rooms has an extensive network of hiking/cross-country trails. There's a child care centre, and farm animals. **$$**

Lake Champlain Islands

Henry's Sportsman's Cottages Inc.
218 Poor Farm Road, Alburg 05440
Tel: 802-796 3616
Fourteen lakefront, one- two- and three-bedroom housekeeping cottages with screened porches. Private beach; boat and motor rentals. **$–$$**
Terry Lodge
54 West Shore Road
Isle LaMotte 05463
Tel: 802-928 3264
www.geocities.com/terry_lodge
Old-fashioned lakeshore lodge has seven rooms (two with private bath) and four motel units. MAP available. **$$**
North Hero House Inn and Restaurant
Route 2, North Hero 05474
Tel: 802-372 4732/888-525 3644
Fax: 802-372 3218
www.northherohouse.com
This historic lakefront inn complex with three annexes offers a variety of well-furnished rooms, many with jacuzzi tubs and fireplaces. Rate includes an excellent breakfast buffet. Small private beach, and boat rental. **$$–$$$$**
Shore Acres Inn and Restaurant
237 Shoreacres Drive
North Hero 05474
Tel: 802-372 8722
www.shoreacres.com
A comfortable 23-room lakeside motel with a vast veranda affording splendid views. Clay tennis courts. Apr–Nov; B&B year-round. Restaurant. **$$–$$$**

Lower Waterford

Rabbit Hill Inn
Route 18, 05848
Tel: 802-748 5168/800-762 8669
Fax: 802-748 8342
www.rabbithillinn.com
Twenty elegant rooms in a romantic, Greek Revival inn

on 15 wooded acres. There's a superb restaurant, and lots of pampering personal touches. Trails for walking or cross-country skiing; canoes can also be arranged. MAP available. **$$$$**

Ludlow

Governor's Inn
86 Main Street, 05149
Tel: 802-228 8830/800-468 3766
www.thegovernorsinn.com
Just 10 minutes from Okemo Mountain ski area, this nine-rooms inn has formal Victorian decor, a romantic ambiance, and solicitous hospitality. **$$–$$$$**

Lyndonville

Wildflower Inn
Darling Hill Road, 05851
Tel: 802-626 8310/800-627 8310
Fax: 802-626 3039
www.wildflowerinn.com
This 21-room 1796 B&B farmhouse (with modern carriage house annex) is great for families. There's a petting zoo, pool, and panoramic views. **$$–$$$$**

Manchester

1811 House
Route 7A, 05254
Tel: 802-362 1811/800-432 1811
Fax: 802-362 2443
www.1811house.com
At the north end of the village, this Federal manse has 13 spacious, antiques-filled guest rooms, plus rooms in separate cottage. Scottish pub. **$$–$$$$**
The Equinox and the Charles Orvis Inn
Route 7a, 05254
Tel: 802-362 4700/800-362 4747
Fax: 802-362 1595
www.equinoxresort.com
One of Vermont's premier historic hotels has 183 rooms and suites in the main inn, nine suites in the Charles Orvis Inn, and fireplaced rooms in the 1811 House. Spa, three restaurants, indoor and outdoor pools, trout pond, tennis courts, and an 18-hole golf course. **$$$$**
Village Country Inn
3834 Main Street, Route 7A, 05254

Tel: 802-362 1792/800-370 0300
Fax: 802-362 7238
www.villagecountryinn.com
A rambling 32-room inn with romantic French country decor. Suites have fireplaces and canopy beds. MAP available. **$$–$$$$**
Wilburton Inn
River Road (off Route 7a), 05254
Tel: 802-362 2500/800-648 4944
Fax: 802-362 1107
www.wilburton.com
A railroad baron's 100+-year-old brick mansion set on 20 acres (8 hectares). Many of the 30 elegantly appointed guest rooms have canopy beds, fire-places, and/or whirlpool tubs. Cottages are also available. **$$–$$$$**

Marlboro

Whetstone Inn
550 South Road, 05344
Tel: 802-254 2500
www.whetstoneinn.com
A 220-year-old farmhouse with 12 bedrooms (four with shared bath) decorated with a mix of Colonial appointments and contemporary Scandinavian furnishings. Pond for swimming/skating. **$**

Middlebury

Inn on the Green
71 Pleasant Street
Tel: 802-388 7512/888-244 7512
www.innonthegreen.com
Continental breakfast is served in bed at this 1803 National Register of Historic Places Victorian home built in the sold Federal style. Many of the 11 rooms/suites sleep up to four. All have internet hook-up, cable TV, phones, and A/C. **$$$–$$$$**
Middlebury Inn
14 Court House Square, 05753
Tel: 802-388 4961/800-842 4666
Fax: 802-388 4563
middleburyinn.com
An 1827 inn (plus 1827 annex and modern motel extension, offering a total of 80 rooms) overlooking the village green. Dining room serves traditional New England fare. An adjacent 1825 mansion has nine Victorian-style rooms. **$–$$$$**

Middletown Springs

Twin Mountain Farms B&B
549 Coy Hill Road, 05757
Tel: 802-235 3700
Fax: 802-235 3701
www.twinmountainsfarmbb.com
Three comfortable rooms with private baths in a home nestled on 150 acres; on-site spa services are available. Pets by prior arrangement. **$–$$**

Montgomery

English Rose Inn
Route 242, Montgomery Center, 05471
Tel: 802-326 3232
Fax: 802-326 2001
www.theenglishroseinn.com
1850s farmhouse just 3½ miles (6 km) from Jay Peak has 14 guestrooms and suites with Victorian furnishings. **$–$$$**
Inn on Trout River
Main Street, 05471
Tel: 802-326 4391/800-338 7049
Fax: 802-326 3194
www.troutinn.com
A late 1800s inn with 10 B&B rooms furnished in English and Victorian country styles with down quilts and flannel sheets (in winter). The living/dining room has a large wood-burning stove; recreation room has a pool table. **$$**

Montgomery Center

Phineas Swann Country Inn
195 Main Street, 05471
Tel: 802-326 4306
www.phineasswann.com
Dogs rule at this charming, c.1880 "downtown" inn which charges no extra fees for pets, and, indeed, offers dog spa packages. Standards are high: all rooms have internet ports, TVs with DVDs, and A/C. **$–$$$$**

Montpelier

Betsy's Bed & Breakfast
74 East State Street, 05602
Tel: 802-229 0466
Twelve rooms and suites in two adjacent homes and a carriage house near town. Five suites have full kitchens. **$–$$**

Capitol Plaza Hotel and Conference Center
100 State Street, 05602
Tel: 802-223 5252/800-274 5252
Fax: 802-229 5427
www.capitolplaza.com
Full-service hotel adjacent to the State House has 56 nicely-furnished motel-type rooms and a restaurant on the premises. **$–$$$**

Inn at Montpelier
147 Main Street, 05602
Tel: 802-223 2727
Fax: 802-223 0722
www.innatmontpelier.com
A pair of adjoining Federal mansions with 19 rooms make a convenient in-town retreat. The main inn has a wraparound porch and a formal sitting room. Both buildings have small guest pantries. **$$–$$$**

Newfane Area

Four Columns Inn
21 West Street, Newfane, 05345
Tel: 802-365 7713/800-787 6633
Fax: 802-365 0022
www.fourcolumnsinn.com
A majestic white-columned Greek Revival inn on one of New England's most photographed greens. The 16 Colonial-style guest rooms have been updated, and there's a pool and trout pond. **$$$–$$$$**

River Bend Lodge
Route 30, 05345
Tel: 802-365 7952
Fax: 802-365 5004
www.riverbendlodgevt.com
20 recently redecorated rooms with A/C and cable TV in a sprawling lodge on 30 acres with mountain views and private trails. **$**

Putney

Hickory Ridge House
Hickory Ridge Road, 05346
Tel: 802-387 5709/800-380 9218
Fax: 802-387 5387
www.hickoryridgehouse.com
An 1808 National Register of Historic Places brick Federal manor with six country-style rooms and two cottages on 12 pastoral acres. Vegetarian breakfasts are a specialty. **$$–$$$**

The Putney Inn
Depot Road, 05346
Tel: 802-387 5517/800-653 5517
www.putneyinn.com

Great care has been take to preserve the charm and integrity of this 1790s farmhouse. There are rooms in the inn as well as a new, motel-type building. **$$–$$$**

Quechee

Quality Inn at Quechee Gorge
US Route 4, 05059
Tel: 802-295 7600/800-732 4376
Fax: 802-295 1492
www.qualityinnquechee.com
Pleasant chain motel with 63 rooms just a minute from the highway. Facilities include an indoor pool, and a fitness centre. **$$–$$$**

Quechee Inn at Marshland Farm
Clubhouse Road, 05059
Tel: 802-295 3133/800-235 3133
Fax: 802-295 6587
www.quecheeinn.com
An historic, 1793 farmstead with 24 rooms in a bucolic riverside setting. Cross-country skiing, hiking, canoeing. MAP available. **$$$–$$$$**

Rutland

Inn at Rutland
70 N Main Street, 05701
Tel: 802-773 0575/800-808 0575
Fax: 802-775 3506
www.innatrutland.com
An eight-room B&B in a renovated, 1889 Victorian mansion with views of the surrounding mountains and valleys. Traditional appointments include an ornate oak staircase and carved ceiling mouldings. **$$–$$$**

Shelburne

Inn at Shelburne Farms
Harbor Road, 05482
Tel: 802-985 8498
Fax: 802-985 1233
www.shelburnefarms.org
Lila Vanderbilt's turn-of-the-20th-century lakefront Tudor-style mansion, set amid a grandiose working farm, offers 24 guest rooms (some with shared bath), and four cottages, including the three-bedroom Glass House. Superb restaurant. Tennis, boating, and fishing. Open mid-May–mid-Oct. **$$$–$$$$**

Shoreham

Shoreham Inn
51 Inn Street, 05770
Tel: 802-897 5861/800-255 5081
www.shorehaminn.com
Ten antiques-filled B&B rooms with private baths in an historic 18th-century inn on the southern end of Lake Champlain. **$$–$$$**

Stowe

Alpenrose Motel
2619 Mountain Road, 05672
Tel: 802-253 7277/800-962 7002
Fax: 802-253 4707
www.gostowe.com/alpenrose
Small motel halfway between the village and Mount Mansfield offers standard rooms and efficiencies with all the amenities, plus an outdoor pool. **$–$$**

Green Mountain Inn
Route 100, 05672
Tel: 802-253 7301/800-455 6629
www.greenmountaininn.com
A total of 104 units in an 1833 in-town inn, suites, and adjacent townhouses. Facilities include two restaurants, a year-round outdoor heated pool, and a health club. **$$–$$$**

Stone Hill Inn
89 Houston Farm Road, 05672
Tel: 802-253 6282
www.stonehillinn.com
The emphasis is on romance, with fireside jacuzzis for two, king-size beds, and lovely landscaped grounds. **$$$$**

Topnotch at Stowe Resort and Spa
Mountain Road, 05672
Tel: 802-253 8585/800-451 8686
Fax: 802-253 9263
www.topnotch-resort.com
A luxury 105-room establishment with inn rooms and chalets, a world-class spa, plus tennis and stables. **$$$–$$$$**

Trapp Family Lodge
700 Trapp Hill Road, 05672
Tel: 802-253 8511/800-826 7000
Fax: 802-253 5740
www.trappfamily.com
On 2,800 acres (1,100 hectares), this modern, European-style lodge is a replacement for the original lodge, lost to fire. Also rooms in adjacent townhouses. There's a first-rate cross-country ski area,

fitness centre, indoor pool, and tennis courts. **$$$–$$$$**

Vergennes

Basin Harbor Club
Basin Harbor Road, 05491
Tel: 802-475 2311/800-622 4000
Fax: 802-475 6545
www.basinharbor.com
A classic, 700-acre (300-hectare) lakeside summer colony built around an old farmhouse, and full of timeless pleasures. Most of the 138 accommodations are in newer cottages, many with fireplaces and refrigerators. Amenities include a beach, swimming pool, golf course, tennis courts, and a playground. Extensive children's activities. FAP July and August; B&B available other times. **$$$$**

Waitsfield

The Inn at Lareau Farms
Route 100, 05673
Tel: 802-496 4949/800-833 0766
Fax: 802-496 7979
www.lareaufarminn.com
This 13-room B&B on 67 acres of woods and pastures near the Mad River has an authentic farmhouse atmosphere, with country-style rooms. American Flatbread makes pizza here Friday and Saturday nights. **$$–$$$**

Inn at Mad River Barn
Route 17, 05673
Tel: 802-496 3310/800-631 0466
www.madriverbarn.com
A 1948 ski lodge with 15 rooms and vintage game room. Extensive grounds include a pool and trails. MAP available. **$–$$**

Round Barn Farm
1161 E Warren Road, 05673
Tel: 802-496 2276/800-721 8029
Fax: 802-496 8832
www.theroundbarn.com
Luxuriously retrofitted farmhouse B&B on 245

PRICE CATEGORIES

An approximate guide to rates for a standard double room per night:
$$$$ = more than $200
$$$ = $150–200
$$ = $100–150
$ = under $100

acres with 12 plush guest rooms with canopy beds, some with whirlpool baths. The unusual 12-sided Shaker-style barn is used for summer concerts and parties. **$$–$$$$**

Warren Village

Pitcher Inn
275 Main Street, 05674
Tel: 802-496 6350/888-867 4824
Fax: 802-496 6354
www.pitcherinn.com
Each of the 11 elegant rooms and suites at this white clapboard Relais & Chateaux property has been designed by a different architect. All have jacuzzis, and many have steam showers and fireplaces. Restaurant. **$$$$**

Waterbury

The Old Stagecoach Inn
18 North Main Street, 05676
Tel: 802-244 5056/800-262 2206
www.oldstagecoach.com
Beautifully-restored 19th-century stagecoach stop has eight comfortable guest rooms and three efficiency suites. Several rooms have fireplaces and sitting areas; some share bath. **$–$$$**

Weatersfield

Inn at Weathersfield
1342 Route 106, 05151
Tel: 802-263 9217
Fax: 802-263 9219
www.innatweathersfield.com
Twelve guest rooms in an 18th-century country inn where Early American style blends with modern amenities: all rooms have cable TV, private baths, phones, and feather beds. Some have fireplaces. MAP available. **$$$–$$$$**

West Dover

Inn at Sawmill Farm
7 Crosstown Road, Route 100, 05356
Tel: 802-464 8131/800-493 1133
Fax: 802-464 1130
www.theinnatsawmillfarm.com
Twenty guest rooms and a first-rate restaurant in an old farmstead jazzed up with bold decorative

ABOVE: Some inns are classy or overrefined, according to taste.

touches. This is country elegance at its best, plus superb regional cuisine. Convenient to Mount Snow and Haystack Mountain ski areas. **$$$$**

West Townsend

Windham Hill Inn
311 Lawrence Drive, 05359
Tel: 802-874 4080/800-944 4080
Fax: 802-874 4702
www.windhamhill.com
An elegantly appointed 1825 farmhouse-cum-cross-country-ski-centre with 21 rooms. Facilities include a pool, tennis courts, skating pond. Located 10 miles (16 km) north of Newfane and 10 miles (16 km) east of Stratton Mountain ski area. MAP available. **$$$–$$$$**

Wilmington

Trail's End, A Country Inn
Smith Road, 05363
Tel: 802-464 2727/800-859 2585
Fax: 802-464 5532
www.trailsendvt.com
The 15 lovely rooms and suites at this B&B on 10

acres (4 hectares) branch off from a cathedral-ceiling living room with fieldstone hearth. Convenient for Mount Snow and Haystack Mountain ski areas. **$$–$$$**

Windsor

Juniper Hill Inn
153 Pembroke Road, 05089
Tel: 802-674 5273/800-359 2541
Fax: 802-674 2041
www.juniperhillinn.com
An 100-year-old Greek Revival-style, hilltop mansion set on a broad lawn near Ascutney Mountain. The 16 elegant rooms are furnished with Queen Anne and Edwardian pieces; some have working fireplaces. Extensive grounds include beautiful gardens and a pool. **$$–$$$$**

Woodstock Area

Jackson House Inn and Restaurant
37 Route 4 West, Woodstock, 05091
Tel: 802-457 2065/800-448 1890
www.jacksonhouse.com

Refined elegance is the hallmark of this lovingly restored 1890s clapboard house, now a 15-room B&B. The restaurant, with an outstanding wine list, also serves five-course breakfasts. **$$$–$$$$**

Woodstock Inn and Resort
14 The Green (Route 4)
Woodstock, 05091
Tel: 802-457 1100/800-448 7900
Fax: 802-457 6699
www.woodstockinn.com
The Rockefellers' homage to country inns. The decor is corporate/country with modern furniture and patchwork quilts. The impressive facilities include 144 rooms, indoor and outdoor pools, tennis courts, golf, a health club, and racquet ball and squash courts. **$$$–$$$$**

Applebutter Inn
Happy Valley Road, Woodstock, 05091
Tel: 802-457 4158
Fax: 802-457 4158
www.applebutterinn.com
Six-room B&B in an 1854 Federal house full of fluffy comforters; three fireplaced sitting rooms. **$$–$$$**

Kedron Valley Inn
Route 106, South Woodstock 05071
Tel: 802-457 1473/800-836 1193
Fax: 802-457 4469
www.kedronvalleyinn.com
Heirloom quilts dress up the 28 tastefully-decorated rooms of this B&B. Some have fireplaces, jacuzzis, and decks. The ski lodge-style building situated just behind the main inn attracts families, with a swimming pool as an extra attraction. The restaurant is first-rate. **$$–$$$$**

Quechee Inn at Marshland Farm
Main St, Quechee 05059
Tel: 802-295 3133/800-235 3133
www.quecheeinn.com
The original portion of this 25-room inn dates to 1793, and it's furnished with antiques. A wood fire crackles in the common room, where there's always complimentary coffee, tea, and fresh-baked cookies. Acclaimed restaurant features local ingredients; bar. Miles of cross-country ski trails adjacent. **$$–$$$**

NEW HAMPSHIRE

Bedford

Bedford Village Inn
2 Village Inn Lane, 03110
Tel: 603-472 2001/800-852 1166
Fax: 603-472 2379
www.bedfordvillageinn.com
14 luxury suites with four-poster beds and marble bathrooms at an inn carved out of a three-story barn south of Manchester.
$$$–$$$$

Bethlehem

Adair Inn
80 Guider Ln (at Route 302), 03574
Tel: 603-444 2600/888-444 2600
Fax: 603-444 4823
www.adairinn.com
Set on 200 acres, this 1927 Georgian Colonial mansion is now a nine-room B&B with a tap room and vintage pool table. Rooms have either garden or mountain views.
$$$–$$$$

Mulburn Inn
2370 Main Street, 03574
Tel: 603-869 3389/800-457 9440
Fax: 603-869 5633
www.mulburninn.com
The Tudor mansion of the retail magnate Woolworths, built in 1908, has seven spacious and individually decorated guest rooms; architectural touches include stained glass windows, ornately carved mantles, and imported fireplace tiles. **$$–$$$**

Bretton Woods

Mount Washington Hotel and Resort
Route 302, 03575
Tel: 603-278 1000/800-314 1752
www.mountwashingtonresort.com
Built in 1902, this National Historic Landmark grand hotel (195 rooms, MAP) overlooking the Presidential Range has a multitude of family-oriented activities, as well as an indoor pool, tennis courts, horseback riding, movies, and a fitness centre. There's xc skiing on the grounds or alpine skiing at nearby Bretton Woods. **$$$–$$$$**

Bretton Arms Country Inn
Route 302, 03575
Tel: 603-278 1000

Fax: 603-278 8868
www.mountwashingtonresort.com
A small, handsome, 1896 country inn with 34 elegantly furnished guest rooms, on the grounds of the Mount Washington Resort. **$$–$$$$**

Center Harbor

Kona Mansion
50 Jacobs Road, P.O. Box 458, 03226
Tel: 603-253 4900
Ten guest rooms, four one-and two-bedroom housekeeping cottages, and two three-bedroom chalets in a Tudor-style, 1900s mansion on 100 acres. Breakfast and dinner are served in the ornate, Victorian dining room. Nine-hole golf course, tennis courts, private beach. MAP available. **$$–$$$**

Concord

Centennial Hotel
96 Pleasant Street, 03301
Tel: 603-227 9000/800-360 4839
Fax: 603-225 5031
www.thecentennialhotel.com
Restored, 1892 Victorian mansion has 32 individually-appointed guest rooms and suites with all the modern conveniences. **$$–$$$**

Comfort Inn
71 Hall Street, 03301
Tel: 603-226 4100/866-463 5201
www.comfortinn.com
Just off I-93 at exit 13, the 100-room hotel has clean, well-sized rooms and suites with refrigerators, microwaves, and free high-speed internet access. Also, an indoor pool. **$$–$$$**

Dixville Notch

Balsams Grand Resort Hotel
Route 26, 03576
Tel: 603-255 3400/877-225 7267
Fax: 603-255 4221
www.thebalsams.com
A sprawling, 19th-century, 215-room resort hotel, set in its own natural preserve. Activities include dancing and entertainment nightly, pool, tennis courts, skiing,

fishing, and children's programs. FAP. **$$$–$$$$**

Eaton Center

Inn at Crystal Lake
Route 153, 03832
Tel: 603-447 2120/800-343 7336
Fax: 603-447 3599
www.innatcrystallake.com
A comfortable 1884 Victorian B&B in a sleepy lakeside village just minutes from Conway. Walk to the beach. Restaurant. **$–$$$**

Franconia

Franconia Inn
1300 Easton Valley Road, 03583
Tel: 603-823 5542/800-473 5299
Fax: 603-823 8078
www.franconiainn.com
This rambling, 19th-century resort with 29 rooms and three suites has 107 acres to explore. Other amusements include a pool, hot tub, tennis courts, and ice skating. Restaurant and lounge. MAP, B&B, or EP available. **$$–$$$$**

Glen

The Bernerhof
Route 302, 03838
Tel: 603-383 9132/800-548 8007
www.bernerhofinn.com
A Victorian, European-style inn with nine antiques-filled B&B rooms. Modern additions include double whirlpools. The popular restaurant serves Middle European fare. **$$–$$$$**

Covered Bridge House B&B
Route 302, 03838
Tel: 603-383 9109/800-232 9109
www.coveredbridgehouse.com
Six simple B&B rooms in a Colonial home on the banks of the Saco River, near North Conway. Rooms are country-style with quilts, braided rugs, and rocking chairs. **$**

Hampton Beach

Ashworth by the Sea
295 Ocean Boulevard, 03842
Tel: 603-926 6762/800-345 6736
(outside NH)
www.ashworthhotel.com

Built in 1912, this landmark oceanfront hotel with 105 rooms recently underwent a major renovation. Amenities include an indoor heated pool with retractable roof, wireless internet, and three restaurants. **$–$$$$**

Hanover

Hanover Inn at Dartmouth College
Main Street, 03755
Tel: 603-643 4300/800-443 7024
Fax: 603-646 3744/643 4433
www.hanoverinn.com
An integral part of the Dartmouth campus, this four-story, traditionally decorated Georgian brick building with 92 rooms began as a tavern and became a hotel in 1813. It has a gracious porch with rockers overlooking the common. Restaurant. **$$$–$$$$**

Henniker

Colby Hill Inn
3 The Oaks, 03242
Tel: 603-428 3281/800-531 0330
Fax: 603-428 9218
www.colbyhillinn.com
A rambling late 18th-century B&B with a perennial garden and swimming pool. The 14 rooms are furnished with antiques and Colonial reproductions; four rooms have fireplaces. Located west of Concord, near Pat's Peak ski area.
$–$$$

PRICE CATEGORIES

An approximate guide to rates for a standard double room per night:

$$$$ = more than $200
$$$ = $150–200
$$ = $100–150
$ = under $100

Holderness

The Manor on Golden Pond
Route 3 and Shepard Hill Road, 03245
Tel: 603-968 3348/800-545 2141
Fax: 603-968 2116
www.manorongoldenpond.com
A 1903 English manor-style stone mansion and annex with 19 rooms (some with fireplaces) overlooking Squam Lake. Facilities include a clay tennis court, swimming pool, private beach, and canoes. MAP available. **$$$$**

Jackson

Inn at Thorn Hill
Thorn Hill Road, 03846
Tel: 603-383 4242/800-289 8990
Fax: 603-383 8062
www.innatthornhill.com
This estate designed by Stanford White overlooks Mount Washington and has 25 romantically decorated rooms, suites and cottages. Restaurants and spa. MAP available. **$$$-$$$$**

The Wentworth
Route 16A, 03846
Tel: 603-383 9700/800-637 0013
Fax: 603-383 4265
www.thewentworth.com
An 1869 grand hotel in the centre of the village adjoining an 18-hole golf course and xc ski centre. 54 rooms. MAP available. **$$$-$$$$**

Whitney Inn at Jackson
Route 16B, 03846
Tel: 603-383 8916/800-677 5737
Fax: 603-383 6886
www.whitneysinn.com
Rooms in this 1840 inn which was renovated in 2007 include 16 in the main building, eight two-bedroom suites in the lodge, and two two-bedroom cottages. Situated on nine acres at the base of Black Mountain Ski Area. Restaurant and pub. **$$-$$$$**

Wildcat Inn and Tavern
Route 16A, 03846
Tel: 603-383 4245/800-228 4245
A 12-room B&B in the social centre of town with delightful, albeit tiny, suites and an extremely popular restaurant. Includes a Tues evening "Dinner With Your Dog" in the gardens. **$-$$$**

Jaffrey

Benjamin Prescott Inn
Route 124, 03452
Tel/fax: 603 532 6637
This sprawling 150+-year-old farm house/B&B near Mount Monadnock has 10 cozy rooms and suites with country furnishings and decorated with handmade quilts. Wi-fi. **$-$$$**

Keene

Carriage Barn
358 Main Street, 03431
Tel: 603-357 3812
www.carriagebarn.com
A thoroughly renovated Civil War-era barn with four rooms simply furnished with antiques and handmade quilts. Across from Keene State College. **$-$$**

E. F. Lane Hotel
30 Main Street, Central Square 03431
Tel: 603-357 7070/888-300 5056
Fax: 603-357 7075
www.eflane.com
Part of an historic, c.1890s complex, this full-service hotel has 40 rooms and suites (some with whirlpools) with original exposed brick walls and oversize windows. **$$-$$$**

Lincoln

Innseason Resorts Pollard Brook
33 Brookline Street, 03251
Tel: 603-745 9900
Fax: 603-745 8233
www.innseason.com
Modern condominium resort across from Loon Mountain has 133 one- to three-bedroom, fully equipped units with whirlpool baths, and balcony or patio. Indoor and outdoor pools, tennis courts, and fitness centre. **$$$-$$$**

Profile Motel and Cottages
391 Route 3, 03251
Tel: 603-745 2759/800-282 0092
Fax: 603-745 3518
www.profilemotel.com
Clean, homey motel units with microwaves, fridges, TV, and free wireless internet, as well as one- to five-bedroom cottages. Heated outdoor pool and family games. **$-$$**

Littleton

Beal House Inn
2 West Main Street, 03561
Tel: 603-444 2661/888-616 2325
Fax: 603-444 6224
Restored 1833 Federal-style inn close to town has eight cozy, antiques-filled rooms and suites with four-poster beds; some fireplaces. Restaurant and pub. Summer only. **$$-$$$**

Thayer's Inn
111 Main Street, 03561
Tel/fax: 603-444 6469
This white-columned Greek Revival inn in the centre of town is one of New Hampshire's oldest hostelries. The 36 rooms range from small and simple to quite plush, but are all comfortable and reasonably priced. **$-$$$**

Manchester

Ash Street Inn
118 Ash Street 03104
Tel: 603-668 9908
Fax: 603-629 9532
www.ashstreetinn.com
The Queen City's premier in-town B&B, a three-story 1885 Victorian, has many of its original 19th-century accents, including magnificent stained-glass windows. The antiques-filled guest rooms have thick quilts, Egyptian cotton sheets, and down pillows. **$$-$$$**

Radisson Hotel Manchester
700 Elm Street, 03101
Tel: 603-625 1000
www.radisson.com
Downtown, just across from the Verizon Wireless Arena (which seats more than 10,000 people for hockey and basketball games and concerts), this full-service hotel has 250 spacious rooms; a heated, indoor pool; fitness centre; and a restaurant. **$$$**

New Castle

Wentworth by the Sea Hotel and Spa
Wentworth Road, 03854
Tel: 603-422 7322
www.wentworth.com
One of the seacoast's premier destination inns, a Victorian confection owned by Marriott, offers first-class accommodations. Most of the 161 rooms and suites have water views; there's a full-service spa and a fine restaurant. Golf course adjacent. **$$$-$$$$**

New London

The New London Inn
140 Main Street, 03257
Tel: 603-526 2791/800-526 2791
www.newlondoninn.us
An in-town, 24-room 1792 inn with lots of antiques, an eclectic decor, and a well regarded restaurant with an inventive chef/innkeeper. **$$-$$$$**

Inn at Pleasant Lake
Pleasant Street, 03257
Tel: 603-526 6271/800-626 4907
Fax: 603-526 4111
www.innatpleasantlake.com
Overlooking the lake and Mount Kearsarge, this 1790 inn with 10 guest rooms on five acres serves fixed-priced gourmet meals in the candlelit dining room. Canoes and rowboats for guests. **$$-$$$**

Maple Hill Farm
1200 Newport Road, 03257
Tel: 603-526 2248/800-231 8637
www.maplehillfarm.com
A family-friendly, comfortably furnished 1824 farmhouse/B&B near Little Lake Sunapee has 10 basic guest rooms (four with shared baths) with antiques and handmade quilts. **$-$$**

North Conway

Farm By The River B&B
2555 West Side Road, 03860
Tel/fax: 603-356 2694/888 414 8353
www.farmbytheriver.com
Nestled on 70 acres, this 1785 classic country farmhouse with nine guest rooms has a beach on the Saco River. Horses are available for hire. Off Route 16/302, 1 mile (1.6 km) from Echo Lake State Park. **$$-$$$**

The 1785 Inn
Route 16, 03860
Tel: 603-356 9025/800-421 1785
Fax: 603-356 6081
www.the1785inn.com
This colonial inn with spectacular mountain views

is comfortably furnished with colonial, Victorian, and country-style pieces. 17 rooms with some shared baths. Outdoor pool. MAP available. **$–$$**

Stonehurst Manor
Route 16, 03860
Tel: 603-356 3113/800-525 9100
Fax: 603-356 3217
www.stonehurstmanor.com
Once part of the summer estate of carpet baron Erastus Bigelow, this 100-year-old mansion amidst 33 acres of pine forest has 25 rooms (seven with fireplaces), an outdoor pool, hot tub, and tennis court. MAP available. **$–$$**

North Sutton

Follansbee Inn on Kezar Lake
Route 114, 03260
Tel: 603-927 4221/800-626 4221
Fax: 603-927 6307
www.follansbeeinn.com
A cozy, 1840s lakeside inn on the beach. There are 20 rooms for B&B, including two one-bedroom suites. **$–$$$**

North Woodstock

Woodstock Inn
Main Street (Route 3), 03262
Tel: 603-745 3951/800-321 3985
Fax: 603-745 3701
www.woodstockinnnh.com
Three Victorian inns in a bustling tourist town. The 21 rooms vary from romantic to family-friendly. Outdoor hot tub, beer garden brewery, and restaurants. **$–$$**

Pittsburg

The Glen
First Connecticut Lake, 03592
Tel: 603-538 6500/800-445 4536
www.theglen.org
The Connecticut lakes region's premier (and state's northernmost) resort, a mile down a private road, offers six rooms in the main lodge, two one-bedroom hillside cottages, and seven lakefront cottages that sleep up to eight. Hiking, boats, motors, and guides. Open May–Oct. FAP. **$$$$**

Tall Timber
609 Beach Road, 03592
Tel: 800-835 6343
www.talltimber.com
Since 1946 the sporting lodge has been a destination for anglers and nature lovers. Accommodations range from simple rooms with shared or private bath in the main lodge to private, luxury cottages. Restaurant. **$–$$$$**

Portsmouth

Inn at Strawbery Banke
314 Court Street, 03801
Tel: 603-436 7242/800-428 3933
www.innatstrawberybanke.com
1800 sea captain's house adjoining the historic preserve has seven handsome guest rooms and elegant gardens. B&B. **$$–$$$**

Inn at Christian Shore
335 Maplewood Avenue, 03801
Tel: 603-431 6770
Five antiques-filled rooms in an 1800s Federal house near the historic district. B&B. **$$**

Martin Hill Inn
404 Islington Street, 03801
Tel: 603-436 2287
www.martinhillinn.com
An 1812 Colonial main house and a country-style 1850 guest house set amid perennial gardens. Solicitous hosts and lavish breakfasts. Seven rooms. B&B. **$$–$$$$**

Sise Inn
40 Court Street, 03801
Tel: 603-433 1200/877-747 3466
Fax: 603-431 1200
www.siseinn.com
Some of the 34 rooms in this elegant, 1881 Queen Anne Victorian inn in the centre of town have fireplaces, whirlpool baths, and stereos. **$$$–$$$$**

Snowville

Snowvillage Inn
92 Stuart Road, Off Route 153, 03832
Tel: 603-447 2818/800-447 4345
Fax: 603-447 5268
www.snowvillageinn.com
Austrian motifs pervade this high-perched eyrie. The 18 rooms are in the farmhouse-style main house, an old carriage

barn, and a lodge. Tennis courts, hiking trails, sauna, cross-country skiing (including lessons), snowshoeing. MAP available. **$$–$$$$**

Sugar Hill

Sugar Hill Inn
Route 117, 03580
Tel: 603-823 5621/800-548 4748
Fax: 603-823 5639
www.sugarhillinn.com
Classic lodging at this 18th-century farmhouse inn with 13 guest rooms include the Bette Davis Luxury Suite, where the actress often stayed, and a plush and very private cottage. Some rooms/suites have fireplaces and whirlpool tubs. **$–$$$$**

Sunset Hill House
Sunset Hill Road, 03586
Tel: 603-823 5522/800-786 4455
Fax: 603-823 5738
www.sunsethillhouse.com
This sprawling, 28-room inn is perched on a 1,700-ft (520-meter) ridge overlooking the Presidential Range. Accommodations range from small rooms with twin beds to two-room suites, but all have mountain views. Facilities include a restaurant, tavern, pool, golf course, and hiking trails. **$–$$$$**

Hilltop Inn
Route 117, 03585
Tel: 603-823 5695/800-770 5695
Fax: 603-823 5518
www.hilltopinn.com
This homey 1895 Victorian inn in the village is a classic B&B, with six cozy rooms (all with private baths), a crackling hearth, and terrific country-style breakfasts. Pets welcome (fee). **$$–$$$**

Sunapee

Dexter's Inn and Tennis Club
258 Stage Coach Road, 03782
Tel: 603-763 5571/800-232 5571
A secluded yellow clapboard 1801 house with 17 rooms, three all-weather courts and an outdoor pool. Pets welcome (fee). MAP available. **$$–$$$**

Burkehaven Lodge
179 Burkehaven Road, 03782
Tel: 800-567 2788

Fax: 603-763 9065
www.burkehaven.com
Eleven pleasant units and a two-bedroom penthouse suite, all with electric fireplaces, overlooking Sunapee Harbor. Pool; continental breakfast. **$–$$**

Temple

Birchwood Inn
Route 45, 03084
Tel: 603-878 3285
Fax: 603-878 2159
www.thebirchwoodinn.com
British hospitality New Hampshire style in a c. 1800 B&B with seven guest rooms (two with shared bath). The London Tavern, open Wednesday-Sunday, serves English fare and ale. **$–$$**

Troy

The Inn at East Hill Farm
460 Monadnock Street, 03465
Tel: 603-242 6495/800-242 6495
www.east-hill-farm.com
This 150-acre resort/working farm has cottages and inn rooms with mountain views, indoor and outdoor pools, a sauna, and facilities for tennis and horse-riding. Special programs for children. **$–$$**

Waterville Valley

Waterville Valley Resort
Waterville Valley, 03223
Tel: 800-468 2553
Fax: 603-236 4344
www.waterville.com
A resort complex with more than 700 rooms. cupped in a high valley, with skiing in winter, hiking, tennis, and other sports the rest of the year. **$–$$$$**

West Chesterfield

Chesterfield Inn
20 Cross Road, 03466
Tel: 603-256 3211/800-365 5515

PRICE CATEGORIES

An approximate guide to rates for a standard double room per night:

$$$$ = more than $200
$$$ = $150–200
$$ = $100–150
$ = under $100

Fax: 603-256 6131
www.chesterfieldinn.com
Originally a tavern, this 1798 building has been converted into a luxurious 15-room inn. Amenities include wet bars, refrigerators, whirlpool tubs, and antique fireplaces. **$$$–$$$$**

Whitfield

Mountain View Grand
Mountain View Road, 03598
Tel: 603-837 2100/8866-484 3843

www.mountainviewgrand.com
The "grand" mountain view hotel is a faithfully-restored, 1865 hostelry with 146 modern guest-rooms, a European-style spa, restaurant, and a fully-renovated Ralph Barton-designed 18 hole golf course. **$$$–$$$$**

Spalding Inn
199 Mountain View Road, 03598
Tel: 603-837 2572/800-368 8439
Fax: 603-837 3062
www.spaldinginn.com

A quiet but full-scale family resort on 200 acres, operating since 1926, with golf course, tennis courts, and heated pool. Accommodations in the main inn, a lodge, and separate cottages. 45 rooms. B&B or MAP. **$$–$$$**

Wolfeboro

Wolfeboro Inn
90 North Main Street, 03894
Tel: 603-569 3016/800-451 2389

Fax: 603-569 5375
www.wolfeboroinn.com
The village inn, with spectacular views of Lake Winnipesaukee, has been a hostelry since 1812. It has 44 rooms and suites (some modern, some in the historic section), a private beach, and fishing. Its upscale Wolfe's Tavern as several dining rooms, some with fireplaces. A 70-ft replica paddle boat offers lake cruises. **$$–$$$$**

MAINE

Note that many of Maine's hotels and inns are open only in summer.

Acadia National Park Area

Bar Harbor Tides
119 West Street, 04609
Tel: 207-288 4968
www.barharbortides.com
An 1887 Greek Revival manor B&B with views of Frenchman's Bay. Four elegant suites with working fireplaces and ocean vistas. **$$$$**

Bar Harbor Inn and Spa
Newport Drive, 04609
Tel: 207-288 3351/800-248 3351
Fax: 207-288 5296
www.barharborinn.com
For more than 125 years, a vacation destination; 153 rooms in three buildings in town. Most rooms have fireplaces and views; some have private decks. **$$–$$$$**

Manor House Inn
106 West Street, 04609
Tel: 207-288 3759/800-437 0088
Fax: 207-288 2974
www.barharbormanorhouse.com
An 1887 Victorian inn with 14 one- and two-bedroom units and a carriage house both surrounded by gardens. **$$–$$$**

Edgewater Motel and Cottages
Salisbury Cove
Tel: 207-288 3491/888-310 9920
www.edgewaterbarharbor.com
Economical oceanfront lodging, with an eight-unit two story motel (four with fully equipped kitchens and fireplaces), 11 cottages,

and four suites. All face Frenchman's Bay; private pebble beach. **$–$$**

Ellsworth

Twilite Motel
147 Bucksport Road
(Routes 1 and 3), 04605
Clean rooms and friendly service are hallmarks of this small, 22-room motel on six acres and 18 miles from Acadia National Park. Complimentary breakfast in season. **$–$$**

White Birches Country Club
20 Thorsen Road, 04605
Tel: 207-667 3621/800-435 1287
www.whitebirchescountryclub.com
Don't be put off by the name: this well-situated motel offers 67 basic but comfortable motel rooms, along with its nine-hole, par 34 golf course and inexpensive restaurant. **$–$$**

Trenton

Open Hearth Inn
1147 Bar Harbor Road, 04605
Tel: 207-667 2930/800-655 0234
www.openhearthinn.com
Just eight miles from Acadia National Park, this inn offers numerous affordable options, including non-housekeeping cottages, B&B suites, a motel, and apartments. Wi-fi available. **$–$$**

Addison

Pleasant Bay B&B
386 West Side Road,
P.O. Box 222, 04606

Tel: 207-483 4490
Fax: 207-483 4653
www.pleasantbay.com
On the shores of Pleasant River, this 110-acre working llama farm has four guest rooms with shared or private baths, and splendid views. Room four, a two-room suite, has a TV, microwave, and fridge. **$**

Bailey Island

Log Cabin, An Island Inn
P.O. Box 410, 04003
Tel: 207-833 5546
Fax: 207-833 7858
www.logcabin-maine.com
Although the island is attached to the mainland by a bridge, guests will feel they're at sea in this handsome log B&B with nine elegant, waterfront guest rooms. The restaurant ($$–$$$) serves dinner nightly. **$$$–$$$$**

Bath

Inn at Bath
969 Washington Street, 04530
Tel: 207-443 4294/800-423 0964
Fax: 207-443 4295
www.innatbath.com
An elegant, comfortable antiques-filled mid-1800s B&B in the Historic District. Eight guest rooms include two with wood-burning fireplaces and whirlpool baths. **$$–$$$**

Fairhaven Inn
North Bath Road, 04530
Tel: 207-443 4391/888-443 4391
www.mainecoast.com/fairhaveninn
A 1790 Colonial inn B&B set in 20 acres overlooking

the Kennebec river. The eight guest rooms are furnished with four-poster beds and handmade quilts. Trails for hiking and xc skiing. **$–$$**

The Galen C. Moses House
1009 Washington Street, 04530
Tel: 207-442 8771
Fax: 207-442 0808
www.galenmoses.com
National Register of Historic Houses 1874 pink Victorian mansion has five antiques-filled guest rooms; one has a marble fireplace and bay windows. **$$–$$$$**

Belfast

Harbor View House of 1807
213 High Street, 04915
Tel: 207-338 3811/877-393 3811
www.harborviewhouse.com
This vintage Federal mansion offers views of Penobscot Bay and six well-furnished rooms with work-ing fireplaces (five have water views) and TV. **$$**

Bethel

The Ames Place
46 Broad Street, 04217
Tel: 207-824 3170
Fax: 207-824 0276

Two-room B&B in a lovely 1850 home with personable hosts; bookstore attached. **$**

Austin's Holidae House B&B
85 Main Street, 04217
Tel: 207-824 3400
www.holidae-house.com
Seven charming rooms in an intown Victorian all have queen beds, A/C, private baths, cable TV, and wi-fi. German spoken. **$$**

Bethel Inn and Resort
Village Common, 04217
Tel: 207-824 2175/800-654 0125
Fax: 207-824 2233
www.bethelinn.com
A rambling yellow clapboard 1913 country inn and townhouses, with tennis, golf, and a lake for water sports. MAP available. **$$$–$$$$**

Sunday River Inn and Cross Country Ski Center
23 Skiway Road, 04261
Tel: 207-824 2410
Fax: 207-824 3181
www.sundayriverinn.com
Options include rooms with private or shared baths, and bring-your-own-sleeping-bag dorm rooms. Breakfast is included; dinner is available ($20). The year-round inn also has several cabins, including rustic Camp Ella on 30 acres. **$–$$**

Telemark Inn
RFD 2, Box 800, 04217
Tel: 207 836 2703
www.telemarkinn.com
Six B&B rooms in a secluded 1900 Adirondack-style 10 miles (16 km) west of Bethel. Activities include llama treks and "skijoring", cross-country skiing pulled by dogs. **$$**

Blue Hill

Blue Hill Farm Country Inn
Route 15, 04614
Tel: 207-374 5126
Fax: 207-374 5126
www.bluehillfarminn.com
A 14-room B&B (seven rooms in the farmhouse, seven in a renovated barn) in a rural retreat on 48 acres 5 miles (8 km) from Blue Hill village. **$–$$**

Blue Hill Inn
Union Street, 04614
Tel: 207-374 2844/800-826 7415
Fax: 207-374 2829

ABOVE: Boothbay Harbor, a former fishing village, attracts thousands of visitors in summer.

www.bluehillinn.com
Twelve guest rooms (six with fireplaces) in a village 1830s Federal-style inn just one block from Blue Hill bay. Cocktails are served in the garden during clement weather. MAP available. **$$–$$$**

Boothbay Harbor Area

Fisherman's Wharf Inn
22 Commercial Street, Pier 6, 04538
Tel: 207-633 5090/800-628 6872
Fax: 207-633 5092
www.fishermanswharfinn.com
Rooms and suites in a downtown complex overlooking the harbour. The restaurant has outside dining. **$–$$$$**

Five Gables Inn
Murray Hill Road
East Boothbay, 04544
Tel: 207-633 4551/800-451 5048
www.fivegablesinn.com
This 16-room B&B in a spiffed-up 1865 summer hotel has views of Lineken Bay and the ocean from the broad veranda (complete with hammock). **$$–$$$**

Linekin Bay Resort
Wall Point Road
Boothbay Harbor, 04538
Tel: 207-633 2494/866-847 2103
Fax: 207-633 0580
www.linekinbayresort.com
An old-fashioned seaside resort with complimentary sailing instruction. 70 rooms FAP. **$$$$**

Spruce Point Inn Resort and Spa
Grandview Avenue, Boothbay Harbor, 04538
Tel: 207-633 4152/800-553 0289
Fax: 207-433 7138
www.sprucepointinn.com
An historic inn on a 57-acre peninsula has rooms in the main house, luxury lodges, and cottages. Facilities include a swimming pool, tennis court, fitness room, croquet, badminton, and a putting green; and both a formal restaurant and a bistro. **$$$–$$$$**

Brooksville

Oakland House
Herrick Road, 0461
Tel: 207-359 8521/800-359 7352
Fax: 207-359 9865
www.oaklandhouse.com
A casual 1889 complex with waterside cottages offering 33 MAP rooms set on 50 acres near Blue Hill. **$$–$$$$**

Brunswick

Brunswick Inn
165 Park Row, 04011
Tel: 207-729 4914/800-299 4914
Fax: 207-725 1759
www.brunswickbnb.com
This historic house within walking distance to the Bowdoin College campus has five simply furnished guest rooms decorated with handsome handmade quilts. **$–$$**

Captain Daniel Stone Inn
10 Water Street, 04011
Tel/fax: 207-725 9898/877-573 5151
www.captaindanielstoneinn.com
Many of the 34 rooms at this upscale Federal inn overlooking the Adroscoggin River have whirlpool baths. **$$$–$$$$**

Camden

Camden Harbor Inn
83 Bayview Street, 04843
Tel: 207-236 4200/800-236 4266
Fax: 207-236 7063
www.camdenharborinn.com
A broad porch circles this 1874 B&B with 18 rooms. All are furnished with period antiques; some have fireplaces and decks, balconies, or patios. **$$$–$$$$**

Lodge at Camden Hills
P.O. Box 794, Camden, 04843, (Route 1)
Tel: 207-236 8478/800-832 7058
Fax: 207-236 7163
www.thelodgeatcamdenhills.com
Twenty units, including suites and jacuzzi cottages, in a park-like setting with views of woods. **$$–$$$$**

PRICE CATEGORIES

An approximate guide to rates for a standard double room per night:

$$$$ = more than $200
$$$ = $150–200
$$ = $100–150
$ = under $100

Lord Camden Inn
24 Main Street, 04843
Tel: 207-236 4325
www.lordcamdeninn.com
Four-story boutique hotel in
a restored 1893 Masonic
Hall right in town has 36
luxury rooms and suites
with balconies overlooking
the harbour. **$$–$$$**

Maine Stay Inn
22 High Street (Route 1), 04853
Tel: 207-236 9636
Fax: 207-236 0621
www.camdenmainestay.com
An 1802 house with period
furnishings, a five-minute
walk from the town centre.
Two parlours have wood-
burning fireplaces; a glass-
enclosed porch overlooks
the gardens. 8 rooms.
B&B. **$$–$$$$**

Norumbega
63 High Street (Route 1), 04843
Tel: 207-236 4646/877-363 4646
Fax: 207-236 0824
www.norumegainn.com
13 rooms and suites in a
grand c.1886 Victorian
stone castle close to town
and overlooking the bay.
Furnished like an English
country house, the inn has
a three-story turret and
seven fireplaces.
$$$–$$$$

Whitehall Inn
52 High Street (Route 1), 04843
Tel: 207-236 3391/800-789 6565
Fax: 207-236 4427
www.whitehall-inn.com
A venerable 1834 home,
converted into an inn/B&B
in 1901. The 39 rooms are
small and simple and some
share baths, but are all
quite charming. **$$–$$$**

Windward House
6 High Street, 04843
Tel: 207-236 9656
Antiques, an English
garden and all-out
breakfasts in this eight-
room B&B. **$$–$$$**

Cape Elizabeth

Inn by the Sea
40 Bowery Beach Road,
(Route 77), 04107
Tel: 207-799 3134/866-619 2128
Fax: 207-799 4779
www.innbythesea.com
An elegant resort and spa
with 57 rooms, suites and
cottages all connected by a
boardwalk to Crescent
Beach. Pool, tennis courts,
and restaurant. Pets

welcome by advance
reservation. **$$$$**

Cape Newagen

Newagen Seaside Inn
Route 27, 04552
Tel: 207-633 5242/800-654 5242
Fax: 207-633 5340
www.newagenseasideinn.com
Old-fashioned full-service
resort, with saltwater and
freshwater pools, tennis,
and rowboats at the tip of
Southport Island, 6 miles
(10 km) from Boothbay
Harbor. Thirty rooms and
shorefront cottages. MAP
available. **$$–$$$**

Castine

Castine Inn
33 Main Street, 04421
Tel: 207-326 4365
Fax: 207-326 4570
www.castineinn.com
A distinguished 1898
clapboard inn just out of
the town's centre with 17
second- and third-floor
rooms and suites for B&B.
The comfortable living room
has a fireplace. **$$–$$$$**

Pentagoet Inn
Main Street at Perkins Street,
04421
Tel: 207-326 8616/800-845 1701
www.pentagoet.com
Castine's oldest, original
"summer hotel", a turreted,
1894 Queen Anne Victorian
B&B beauty close to the
harbour, has 16 rooms, a
fine restaurant, and a
memorable pub. **$$–$$$$**

Chebeague Island

Chebeague Island Inn
Box 492, 04017
Tel: 207-846 5155
Fax: 207-846 4265
www.chebeagueinn.com
Constructed in 1925 after
the original structure was
destroyed in a fire, this
classic, three-story
clapboard inn/B&B with 21
rooms is accessible only by
ferry. **$$**

Chesuncook

Chesuncook Lake House
Box 656, Route 76, 04441
www.chesuncooklakehouse.com
Accessible only by boat, air
or snowmobile, this 1864
farmhouse in the middle of

an abandoned lumbering
camp 50 miles north of the
Moosehead Lake Region is
on the Federal Historical
Register and has four guest
rooms with shared bath.
Three new housekeeping
cabins are heated by wood
stoves and have
outhouses. Farmhouse is
FAP. **$$–$$$$**

Deer Isle

Pilgrim's Inn
20 Main Street (Route 15A), 04622
Tel: 207-348 6615/888-778 7505
www.pilgrimsinn.com
Four-story, National
Register of Historic Places
1793 inn overlooking
Northwest Harbor has 12
rooms and three seaside
cottages. The restaurant
($$) serves American fare.
$$–$$$

Durham

**Royalsborough Inn at the
Bagley House**
1290 Royalsborough Road,
(Route 136), 04222
Tel: 207-865 6566/800-765 1772
Fax: 207-353 5878
www.royalsboroughinn.com
Just a few minutes from
Freeport, this antiques-
filled 1772 Colonial B&B
has four cozy rooms with
private baths in the inn,
and three spacious suites
with gas log fireplaces and
cable TV in the carriage
house. **$–$$$**

Eastport

The Milliken House
29 Washington Street, 04631
Tel: 207-853 2955/888-507 9370
www.eastport-inn.com
An 1846, antiques-filled
Victorian near the town's
Historic District has five
second- and third-floor
guest rooms with private
baths. Well-behaved
children and pets welcome.
$

Weston House
26 Boynton Street, 04631
Tel: 207-853 2907/800-853 2907
Fax: 207-853 0981
www.westonhouse-maine.com
This 1810 Federal manse
(former minister's house is
now a three-room B&B, with
two baths. One room has a
fireplace and TV. **$**

Freeport

Harraseeket Inn
162 Main Street, 04032
Tel: 207-865 9377/800-342 6423
Fax: 207-865 1684
www.harraseeketinn.com
Luxury in a town of
bargains. An 1850 Greek
Revival home with modern
appointments, an indoor
pool, and elegant gardens.
Many of the 84 rooms have
fireplaces. **$$$–$$$$**

Kendall Tavern Inn B&B
213 Main Street, 04032
Tel: 207-865 1338/800-341 9572
Fax: 207-865 3544
www.kendalltavern.com
This centrally located early
1800s farmhouse has
seven cozy, air conditioned
rooms with private baths on
the second and third floors.
$$–$$$

Georgetown Island

The Grey Havens Inn
Seguinland Road, 04548
Tel: 207-371 2616/800-431 2316
Fax: 207-371 2613
www.greyhavens.com
One of the last of the East
Coast's classic shingle-
style inns is a grand,
oceanfront hillside 1904
building whose 14 guest
accommodations include
four turret rooms. B&B.
$$$–$$$$

Greenville

**Chalet Moosehead
Lakefront Motel**
Route 15, Greenville Junction,
04442
Tel: 207-695 2950/800-290 3645
www.mooseheadlodging.com
The deluxe units at this
modern, intown motel have
private balconies; some of
the standard units and
efficiencies permit pets
($10/nightly). The Indian
Hill Motel in town ($) is
under the Chalet's
auspices. **$–$$**

Lodge at Moosehead Lake
Lily Bay Road, 04441
Tel: 207-695 4400
Fax: 207-695 2281
www.lodgeatmooseheadlake.com
An eminently civilized
wilderness retreat built in
1917 with five bedrooms in
the main lodge and four
suites in the carriage
house. Rooms have four-

poster beds and whirlpool baths, some have private decks and spectacular lake views. Restaurant and bistro. B&B. **$$$$**

Greenville Inn
Norris Street, 04441
Tel: 207-695 2206/888-695 6000
Fax: 207-695 0335
www.greenvilleinn.com
A lumber baron's opulent 1895 mansion, plus six simpler cottages, on a hill in town overlooking Moosehead Lake. Ornate woodwork and stained glass set a formal tone in the inn's common rooms. Superb restaurant. **$$$–$$$$**

Isle au Haut

The Inn at Isle au Haut
P.O. Box 78, 04645
www.innatisleauhaut.com
Four simple rooms in a gracious home overlooking the water on an island six miles out to sea. The first floor room has its own bath and ocean views; three on the second floor share a bath. All meals, including a picnic lunch, included in rate. No TV or phone. **$$$$**

Kennebunk

The Lodge at Kennebunk
95 Alewive Road, Route 35N, 04043
Tel/fax: 207-985 9010/877-918 3701
www.lodgeatkennebunk.com
Family- and pet-friendly resort on eight wooded acres; one, two- and three-room suites, heated pool, game room, BBQ grills. **$–$$**

Kennebunkport

Bufflehead Cove
Bufflehead Cove Road, 04046
Tel/fax: 207-967 3879
www.buffleheadcove.com
A rambling, early 20th-century Victorian B&B on six acres overlooking the Kennebunk River offers five beautifully-furnished and updated rooms, and a sumptuous cottage. Private dock with rowboats. **$$$–$$$$**

Captain Jefferds Inn
Pearl Street, 04046
Tel: 207-967 2311

Fax: 207-967 0721
www.captainjefferdsinn.com
An antique-filled 1804 Federal mansion, with 10 rooms; the five carriage-house suites allow dogs ($30/night), and a pet-sitting service ($10/hr) is available. B&B. **$$–$$$$**

Captain Lord Mansion
Pleasant and Green Streets, 04046
Tel: 207-967 3141
Fax: 207-967 3172
www.captainlord.com
In the historic district, an elegant, formally decorated 1812 B&B topped by an octagonal cupola. 16 opulent rooms in the main inn; four in the 1807 Garden House. **$$$$**

The Colony Hotel
140 Ocean Avenue, 04046
Tel: 207-967 3331/800-552 2363
Fax: 207-967 8738
www.thecolonyhotel.com
Many of the 123 antiques-filled rooms at this coastal grand hotel built in 1914 have splendid ocean views. Private beach and heated saltwater pool. Breakfast buffet included. Dining room ($$$) serves New England fare. FAP available. Pets ($25/night). Open mid-May–October. **$$–$$$$**

Green Heron Inn
Ocean Avenue, 04046
Tel: 207-967 3315
www.greenheroninn.com
Ten basic rooms with private baths and some fireplaces in the main inn; one cove-side two-bedroom cottage. Gourmet, three-course breakfast. Pets ($15/night). **$$–$$$$**

Old Fort Inn and Resort
Old Fort Avenue, 04046
Tel: 207-967 5353/800-828 3678
www.oldfortinn.com
Elegance, service, and seclusion are hallmarks of this 15-acre inn with 16 rooms in the main lodge and brick carriage houses. Heated outdoor pool. **$$$–$$$$**

White Barn Inn
37 Beach Avenue, 04046
Tel: 207-967 2321
www.whitebarninn.com
Relais & Château-level luxury in 1820 farmhouse and adjoining complex between town and beach. Some of the 25 rooms have fireplaces: all are elegantly furnished. **$$$$**

Kingfield

Sugarloaf/USA
RR 1, Box 5000, 04947
Tel: 207-237 2000/800-843 5623
www.sugarloaf.com
Accommodations include a full-service, 120-room slopeside hotel; a 42-room country inn; and studio to five- bedroom condos. **$$–$$$$**

The Herbert Grand Hotel
246 Main Street, P.O. Box 67, 04947
Tel: 207-265 2000/888-656 9922
Fax: 207-265 4594
www.herbertgrandhotel.com
"The Ritz of Carrabassett Valley", an eccentric but charming downtown hotel heralded upon its 1918 debut as "A Palace in the Wilderness", offers 27 rooms ranging from basic to the unique honeymoon suite. Rates include tax. Pets welcome ($25/night). **$$–$$$**

Inn on Winter's Hill
33 Winterhill Street, 04947
Tel: 207-265 5421/800-233 9687
Fax: 207-265 5424
www.wintershill.com
An 1895 Georgian Revival mansion with a total of 20 rooms in the main house and the simply furnished former barn. Indoor and outdoor pool, tennis, and hot tub. A la carte and prix fixe classic French cuisine with a Maine twist. **$$–$$$$**

Three Stanley Avenue
3 Stanley Avenue, 04947
Tel: 207-265 5541
Six comfy rooms (three with private bath) in a Victorian home designed by one of the Stanley brothers. There's fine restaurant next door. B&B. **$**

Kittery

Coachman Inn
380 US Route 1, 03904
Tel: 207-439 4434/800-824 6183
www.coachmaninn.net
Forty-three clean, spacious, and well-appointed rooms located directly across from Kittery's outlet malls. Breakfast buffet; heated outdoor pool. **$$**

Portsmouth Harbor Inn and Spa
6 Water Street, 03904
Tel: 207-439 4040

Fax: 207-438 9286
www.innatportsmouth.com
An 1889 brick Victorian B&B close to the town green and overlooking the harbour and the Piscataqua River has five nicely-furnished rooms with cable TV and data ports; some claw foot tubs. **$$–$$$**

Lubec

Home Port Inn and Restaurant
45 Main Street, P.O. Box 50, 04652
Tel: 207-733 2077/800-457 2077 (outside Maine)
www.homeportinn.com
An 1880s home in the village, with seven guest rooms with private baths, and a spacious and cheery living room for TV watching. The restaurant's ($$–$$$) specialty is seafood. **$–$$**

Milbridge

Guagus River Inn
376 Kansas Road, 04658
Tel: 207-546 9737
www.guagusriverinn.com
A contemporary home on 14 acres overlooking the Narraguagus River with six themed guest rooms (and five baths). Indoor lap pool. **$–$$**

Monhegan Island

The Island Inn
Ocean View Terrace, 04852
Tel: 207-596 0371
Fax: 207-594 5517
www.islandinnmonhegan.com
Hundred-year-old simplicity in a B&B with rooms and suites (some with shared baths) in the main inn and cottage. Some overlook the ocean. Restaurant serves lunch and dinner. **$$–$$$$**

The Monhegan House
1 Main Street, 04852
Tel: 207-594 7983
Fax: 207-596 6472
www.monheganhouse.com

PRICE CATEGORIES

An approximate guide to rates for a standard double room per night:

$$$$ = more than $200
$$$ = $150–200
$$ = $100–150
$ = under $100

Four-story, 1870s B&B with 29 small, basic, but cheerful single and double rooms with shared baths (two on ground floor have private baths). Lunch and dinner (high season only) available. **$–$$$$**

New Harbor

Gosnold Arms
146 State Route 32, 04554
Tel: 207-677 3727
Fax: 207-677 2662
www.gosnold.com
Shoreside rusticity at Pemaquid Point since 1925. The B&B's glassed-in dining room and many rooms overlook the water. Rooms are available in the main inn and in 14 cottages. 26 rooms. **$–$$**

Northeast Harbor

Asticou Inn
Route 3, 04662
Tel: 207-276 3344/800-258 3373
Fax: 207-276 3373
www.asticou.com
A cultured carryover from Bar Harbor's heyday as Society's summer playground. Elegant, 1885 Victorian-style inn and three annexes overlooking Great Harbor. 47 rooms. MAP. **$$$–$$$$**

Harbourside Inn
Northeast Harbor 04662
Tel: 207-276 3272
www.harboursideinn.com
This classic, three-story shingle-style 1889 inn on a wooded hillside has 22 light and airy rooms and suites; some have kitchenettes and working fireplaces. **$$–$$$$**

Ogunquit

Anchorage by the Sea
125 Shore Road, 03907
Tel: 207-646 9384
Fax: 207-646 6256
www.anchoragebythesea.com
A modern oceanfront resort on the Marginal Way foot path offering 245 rooms (some with jacuzzis). Indoor and outdoor pools, hot tubs, a poolside cafe, and gazebos. **$–$$$$**

Cliff House Resort and Spa
Shore Road (off Route 1), 03907
Tel: 207-361 1000
Fax: 207-361 2122

www.cliffhousemaine.com
Many of the rooms at this multi-building resort overlook the ocean. Amenities include wi-fi, swimming pools, tennis courts, a full service spa, and a fitness centre. MAP available; pets permitted ($25/day) in Lower Ledges. **$$–$$$$**

The Dunes on the Waterfront
518 Main Street, Route 1, 03907
Tel: 207-646 2612
www.dunesonthewaterfront.com
A 1930s cottage complex on 12 acres with 19 cottages and 17 guest rooms on the tidal Ogunquit River, 200 yards from Ogunquit Beach. Swimming dock, with rowboats; outdoor pool. **$–$$$$**

Gorges Grant Hotel
449 Main Street, Route 1, 03907
Tel: 207-646 7003/800-646 5001
www.ogunquit.com/gorgesgrant
A sleek contemporary hotel with traditional furnishings, just north of the town centre. 81 rooms, indoor and outdoor pools, a jacuzzi, and fitness centre. **$–$$$$**

Morning Dove
13 Bourne Lane, 03907
Tel: 207-646 3891
www.themorningdove.com
1860s Victorian farmhouse on a quiet street close to town. Five of the seven comfortable rooms have private baths; all have small refrigerators and air conditioning. One has a private deck. B&B. **$$–$$$**

Sparhawk Oceanfront Resort
85 Shore Road, 03907
Tel: 207-646 5562
Fax: 207-646 9143
www.thesparhawk.com
A variety of options in four buildings, including a 51-unit oceanfront motel; suites; and apartments within walking distance of town. The five-acre complex abuts the Marginal Way foot path. Pool, croquet, tennis. **$$–$$$$**

Portland

Eastland Park Hotel
157 High Street, 04101
Tel: 207-775 5411/888-671 8008
Fax: 207-775 2872
www.eastlandparkhotel.com

Landmark, 12-story, 1927 hotel has 204 rooms with all of the modern amenities (including wi-fi), old-fashioned service, and harbour views. The rooftop lounge is a fine spot to watch the sunset. Pets ($25/night). **$$–$$$**

Pomegranate Inn
49 Neal Street, 04102
Tel: 207-772 1006/800-356 0408
Fax: 207-773 4426
www.pomegranateinn.com
One of the city's most elegant inns is an art- and antiques-filled home with eight bedrooms for B&B in the upscale West End. All rooms have phones and TV; five have gas fireplaces. **$$–$$$$**

Portland Regency Hotel
20 Milk Street, 04101
Tel: 207-774 4200/800-727 3436
Fax: 207-775 2150
ww.theregency.com
A snazzily refurbished, five-floor, 19th-century armory in the Old Port. Amenities in the 95 rooms include cable TV, high-speed internet, and an honour bars. Restaurant. **$$$–$$$$**

Prouts Neck

Black Point Inn Resort
510 Black Point Road, 04074
Tel: 207-883 2500
Fax: 207-883 9976
www.blackpointinn.com
An 1870s resort, on a peninsula favoured by Winslow Homer. Facilities include an 18-hole golf course, 14 tennis courts, two beaches, indoor/outdoor pools, boating, nature trails, health club. 84 rooms. FAP. **$$$$**

Rangeley

Country Club Inn
56 Country Club Road, 04970
Tel/fax: 207-864 3831
www.countryclubinnrangeley.com
An all-season 1920s inn, plus 1950s-era motel units. The inn's grand living room has two fireplaces, a cathedral ceiling, and lovely views of the lake. Amenities include a swimming pool, restaurant, and a golf course. B&B. **$$**

Grant's Kennebago Camps
Kennebago Lake Road, 04970

Tel: 207-864 3608/800-633 4815
www.grantscamps.com
Nine miles from Rangeley behind a controlled gate, this classic Maine camp has 18 waterfront rustic cabins with woodstoves and porches for fly fishermen and outdoor enthusiasts. Boat, sailboat and canoe rentals; floatplane rides. FAP. Pets ($15/night). **$$$**

Rangeley Inn
2443 Main Street, 04970
Tel: 207-864 3341
Fax: 207-864 3634
www.rangeleyinn.com
An old-fashioned, c.1907 three-story inn and a modern motel lakeside motor lodge in the center of town. Some rooms have water views, kitchenettes whirlpool baths, and woodstoves. Tavern; seasonal weekend restaurant. Pets in motel ($15/night). **$–$$**

Rockland

Captain Lindsey House Inn
5 Lindsey Street, 04841
Tel: 207-596 7950/800-523 2145
Fax: 207-596 2758
www.lindseyhouse.com
Former windjammer schooner owners run this tight, tidy and well-appointed three-story, 1835 antiques-filled inn with nine spacious guest rooms with air conditioning, phones, and television. **$$–$$$$**

LimeRock Inn
96 Limerock Avenue, 04841
Tel: 207-594 2257/800-546 3762
Fax: 207-594 1846
www.limerockinn.com
Elegantly decorated nine-room Queen Anne Victorian B&B on a residential street near the Farnsworth Museums. Some of the rooms have whirlpool tubs and private decks. B&B. **$$–$$$$**

Rockport

Samoset Resort
220 Warrenton Street, 04856
Tel: 207-594 2511/800-341 1650
Fax: 207-594 0722
www.samosetresort.com
A full-scale, 230-acre golf resort overlooking Penobscot Bay, with 178

rooms and an elegant restaurant. Sports facilities include two swimming pools, a fitness centre, and four tennis courts. **$$$$**

Rockwood (Moosehead Lake)

The Birches
Off Route 15, 04478
Tel: 207-534 7588
Fax: 207-538 8835
www.birches.com
This rustic 1940s all-season lakeside lodge has a large variety of accommodations, including waterfront cabins, private homes, cabin tents, and wilderness yurts. Amenities include boating, saunas, and hot tubs. **$–$$$**
Maynards-in-Maine
Rockwood 04478
Tel: 207-534 7703/866-699 0857
www.maynardsinmaine.com
A classic year-round hunting camp, founded in 1919. Rooms in the main lodge, one- to three-bedroom cabins; and four efficiencies. Pets ($20/night). FAP. **$**
Rockwood Cottages
Route 15, 04478
Tel/fax: 207-534 7725
www.mooseheadlakelodging.com
Eight lakeside two-bedroom cottages with screened porches and fully equipped kitchens. Sauna and boating facilities; guide service. Open May–Nov. **$**

Searsport

Carriage House Inn
120 East Main Street, 04974
Tel; 207-548 2167/800-576 2167
carriagehouseinmaine.com
Lovingly-maintained 1874 Second Empire Victorian on two acres overlooking Penobscot Bay. Three spacious, antiques-filled rooms with queen beds, floor to ceiling windows, and free wi-fi. **B&B. $–$$**

South Casco

Migis Lodge on Sebago Lake
P. O. Box 40, 04077
Tel: 207-655 4524
Fax: 207-655 2054
www.migis.com

An elegant, old-fashioned 100-acre (40-hectare) resort with six lodge rooms and 31 luxurious "cottages" for FAP. Facilities include sailing, canoeing, waterskiing, and tennis courts. The dining room serves traditional New England fare. **$$$$**

Southwest Harbor

The Claremont Hotel
P. O. Box 137,04679
Tel: 207-244 5036/800-244 5036
Fax: 207-244 3512
www.theclaremonthotel.com
Mount Desert Island's 1884 grand hotel. Rooms in the main inn, two guest houses, and 14 cottages. Waterfront location for swimming, boating. Also tennis and croquet. MAP available. **$$$–$$$$**
Inn at Southwest
371 Main Street, 04679
Tel: 207-244 3835
Fax: 207-244 9879
www.innatsouthwest.com
Seven second- and third-floor elegant, romantic rooms and suites with antique furnishings in an 1884 Victorian home overlooking the harbour. B&B. **$$–$$$**

Spruce Head

Craignair Inn at Clark Island
St George, 04859
Tel: 207-594 7644/800-320 9997
Fax: 207-596 7124
www.craignair.com
A basic, cheerful shorefront B&B inn near a nature preserve between Rockland and Tenant's Harbor originally built in 1928 to house workers from the nearby quarries. Six of the 13 rooms in the main inn have private baths; six in the annex have private baths and A/C. **$–$$**

Stonington

Inn on the Harbor
Main Street, 04681
Tel: 207-367 2420/800-942 2420
Fax: 207-367 5165
www.innontheharbor.com
Thirteen comfortable rooms (10 face the water) with phones and cable TV. Some have fireplaces, full

kitchens, and private decks. Open year round. **$–$$$**

Tenants Harbor

East Wind Inn
Mechanic Street (Route 131), 04860
Tel: 207-372 6366/800-241 8439
Fax: 207-372 6320
www.eastwindinn.com
Sixteen of the 22 rooms, suites and apartments at this historic waterfront complex/B&B have private baths; suites and apartments also have TVs. Dining room open nightly in season. **$$–$$$**

Vinalhaven

Tidewater Motel and Gathering Place
Main Street, 04863
Tel: 207-863 4618
www.tidewatermotel.com
The island's only waterfront lodging is on a bridge, and has 11 rooms with private decks; some have full kitchens. Open year round. **$–$$**

Wiscasset

Squire Tarbox Inn
1181 Westport Island Road, Route 144, 04578
Tel: 207-882 7693/800-818 0626
Fax: 207-882 7107
www.squiretarboxinn.com
National Register of Historic Places lodging has 11 rooms in the main inn and carriage barn. Chef/owner Mario shows a deft hand in the restaurant, which serves dinner nightly in season; Thur–Sat off-season. B&B. **$$–$$$**
Marston House
Main Street, 04578
Tel: 207-882 6010
Fax: 207-882 6965
www.marstonhouse.com
A small private carriage house/antique shop with just two spacious, second-floor rooms with fireplaces and wi-fi. Continental breakfast is delivered to your room. **$$**

York Area

Dockside Guest Quarters
Harris Island Road (Off Route 103),

York, 03909
Tel: 207-363 2868/888-860 7428
Fax: 207-363 1977
www.docksidegq.com
Classic 19th-century seacoast home flanked by cottages. 27 rooms. **$$$–$$$$**
Stage Neck Inn
8 Stage Neck Road off Route 1 A, York Harbor, 03911
Tel: 207-363 3850/800-340 2243
Fax: 207-363 2221
www.stageneck.com
A contemporary seaside resort known for its low-key luxury. 60 Queen Anne-style rooms with refrigerators; many with ocean views. Restaurant ($$$); indoor pool with whirlpool spa. **$$$–$$$$**
The Union Bluff Hotel
8 Beach Street
York Beach, 03910
Tel: 207-363 1333
www.unionbluff.com
Five, story oceanfront hotel has 63 guest rooms, some with whirlpools, decks, and ocean views. Popular restaurant and pub. **$–$$$**
View Point Hotel
229 Nubble Road, York Beach, 03910
Tel: 207-363 2661
Fax: 207-363 6788
www.viewpointhotel.com
Nine luxury one- to three-bedroom suites with gas fireplaces and full kitchens at this inn with 300 ft (90 meters) of frontage on the rocky shore. Views of Nubble Light. **$$$$**
York Harbor Inn
Route 1A, York Harbor, 03911
Tel: 207-363 5119/800-596 4926
Fax: 207-363 7151
www.yorkharborinn.com
A seaside inn, which accrued around a 1637 sail loft. Some of the 55 Colonial-style rooms have fireplaces, jacuzzi spa tubs, and ocean views with decks. Restaurant. **$$–$$$$**

PRICE CATEGORIES

An approximate guide to rates for a standard double room per night:
$$$$ = more than $200
$$$ = $150–200
$$ = $100–150
$ = under $100

ACTIVITIES

THE ARTS, MUSIC AND NIGHTLIFE, SPECTATOR SPORTS AND OUTDOOR ACTIVITIES

THE ARTS

Cinema

Massachusetts

In Cambridge, the **Brattle Theater** 40 Brattle Street, tel: 617-876 6837 and the **Harvard Film Archive**, 24 Quincy Street, tel: 617-495 4700, show classic, foreign, nostalgia, and art films. The Art Deco **Kendall Square Cinema** in Kendall Square, tel: 617-499 1996, offers frothy cappuccino with its foreign and art movies.

Pleasant Street Theater, 27 Pleasant Street, Northampton, tel: 413-586 0935, runs independent, foreign, and art films.

Cape Cinema, off Route 6A, Dennis, tel: 508-385 2503, was built in 1930 as a movie theatre and is still true to its mission.

A trip to the **Wellfleet Drive-In,** Route 6, Wellfleet, tel: 508-349 7176, is still a pleasure.

Connecticut

Cinestudio (300 Summit Street, Trinity College, Hartford; tel: 860-297 2463) shows first-run and art films.

There are IMAX theaters at **Showcase Cinemas**, Buckland Hills, 99 Red Stone Road, Manchester, tel: 860-646 9800; and at the **Maritime Aquarium**, 10 North Water Street, Norwalk, tel: 203-952 0700.

Rhode Island

Cable Car Cinema (204 S Main Street, Providence; tel: 401-272 3970) has seen better days, but perhaps that's the point.

The six-story-high screen at **Feinstein IMAX Theatre** (Providence Place; tel: 401-453 4446) shows the latest high-tech films.

Vermont

Catamount Arts (60 Eastern Avenue, St Johnsbury; tel: 802-748 2600) offers a little bit of everything: art films, dance, classical music.

Have dinner and then catch a flick at the **Big Picture Theater and Café**, 48 Carroll Road, Waitsfield, tel: 802-496 8994.

Downtown Montpelier's historic **Savoy Theatre** (26 Main Street, tel: 802-229 0509) offers an old-fashioned theater experience.

Brattleboro's historic, downtown **Latchis Theater** (tel: 800-798 6301) contains three screens, including a 750-seat old-time movie palace.

New Hampshire

In Hanover **Hopkins Center for the Arts** (Dartmouth College, Hanover; tel: 603-646 2422) shows classic and experimental films, while **Nugget Theater** (S Main Street; tel: 603-643 2769) shows current films.

The **Colonial Theatre** (2050 Main Street, Bethlehem; tel: 603-869 3422) is the longest continuously running movie theater in the US.

Maine

There are multiplexes in or near all the major cities, but to experience the old-time theaters, catch a movie or concert at the newly restored **Strand Theater**, built in 1923 at 345 Main Street, Rockland, tel: 207-594 0070. There's even a balcony.

Classical Music

Massachusetts

Boston Symphony Orchestra and **Boston Pops** are heard at the acoustic and aesthetic **Symphony Hall** (301 Massachusetts Avenue; tel: 617-266 1492/888-266 1200).

New England Conservatory's Jordan Hall (30 Gainsborough Street; tel: 617-536 2412) hosts its own classical concerts.

Berklee College of Music Performance Center (136 Massachusetts Avenue, Boston; tel: 617-864 1200/617-876 7777 for tickets) excels in jazz performances by faculty and students, many international.

The **Great House** at Ipswich's Castle Hill (290 Argilla Road; tel: 978-356 4351) presents a season of classical, pop and folk music.

The **Springfield Symphony Orchestra** performs both classical and pops concerts, including a popular Friday lunchtime series, in Symphony Hall, 34 Court Street, tel: 413-733 0636.

Rhode Island

Rhode Island Philharmonic (222 Richmond Street, Providence; tel: 401-831 3123) performs all year.

The 1928 **Providence Performing Arts Center** (220 Weybosset Street; tel: 401-421 2787) has concerts, Broadway shows, and other events.

Theatre-by-the-Sea (Cards Pond Road off Route 1, South Kingston; tel: 401-782 8587) hosts musicals and plays in a National Register of Historic Places building.

Connecticut

Hartford Symphony performs at The Bushnell (166 Capitol Avenue; tel: 860-246 6807).

New Haven Symphony Orchestra, the fourth oldest in the States, holds a concert series at Yale University's Woolsey Hall (33 Whitney Avenue; tel: 203-865 0831).

The renowned **Norfolk Chamber Music Festival** (Route 44 and 272, Norfolk; tel: 860-542 3000) includes chamber music and choral concert.

Vermont

Marlboro Music Festival (Marlboro Music Center; tel: 802-254 2394) has one of the most renowned summer line-ups in New England.

The **Vermont Symphony Orchestra** (tel: 802-864 5741), under the musical direction of Jaime Laredo, performs concerts in more than 20 communities throughout the state. **Vermont Mozart Festival** (tel: 802-862 7352) presents classical music indoors and outdoors July–Aug; winter series in and around Burlington.

New Hampshire

In Portsmouth, **The Music Hall** (28 Chestnut Street; tel: 603-436 2400) features international classical musicians, while **Music in Market Square** is a classical summer series (North Church; tel: 603-436 9109).

North Country Chamber Players (tel: 603-444 0309) performs world-class chamber music throughout the area from mid-July to mid-August.

Maine

Portland Symphony Orchestra (20 Myrtle Street, Portland; tel: 207-773 6128) performs year-round except during September.

Maine Center for the Arts (tel: 207-581 1755) at the University of Maine in Orono hosts classical concerts, dance,children's theater.

The Pierre Monteux School for Conductors and Orchestra Musicians (tel: 207-546 4495) in Hancock presents faculty and student concerts in their concert hall in June and July.

Bowdoin Summer Music Festival (Brunswick; tel: 207-725 3895) hosts renowned six-week concert series.

Kneisel Hall Chamber Music Festival (Route 15, Blue Hill; tel: 207-374 2811), dating back to 1902, has a developed a fine reputation for its summer concerts.

Buying Tickets

Boston

BosTix (tel: 617-262 8632; www.bostix.org), with booths in Copley Square and Faneuil Hall Marketplace, is a major entertainment information centre. Half-price tickets go on sale at 11am on the day of the event. Cash and travelers' checks only.

TickCo (tel: 800-279 4444; www.tickco.com) dispense tickets for sporting events (including the Red Sox), theaters and nightclubs.

At most other venues throughout New England, tickets can be purchased by calling the theater in advance.

Dance

Massachusetts

The world-renowned **Boston Ballet** (tel: 617-695 6950/800-447 7400) performs regularly at the Wang Theatre, 270 Tremont Street.

The volunteer-based **Dance Complex** (536 Massachusetts Avenue, Central Square, Cambridge; tel: 617-547 9363) hosts workshops and performances.

Connecticut

The **Connecticut Ballet** (tel: 203-964 1211) stages performances all over the state. Their cutting edge **Zig Zag Ballet** troupe is headquartered at the Stamford Center for the Arts.

The **Hartford City Ballet** (166 Capitol Avenue; tel: 860-525 9396) stages both classical and modern dance productions.

Free Concerts

Summer and fall in New England are times for festivals and county fairs, and many include free musical performances. On the Fourth of July many towns and cities celebrate with free fireworks and music. College campuses are lively spots for free entertainment. And many small towns offer free band concerts on their town greens in summer. Local papers are good sources of information.

Massachusetts

In summer Boston offers many free outdoor concert series – including a huge July 4th fireworks celebration at the **Hatch Shell** on the Charles River Esplanade. Also check for performances at the waterfront **Bank of America Pavilion** (290 Northern Avenue; tel: 617 728 1600; www.bankofamericapavilion.com) and the **New England Conservatory of Music** (290 Huntington Avenue; tel: 617-585 1260; www.newenglandconservatory.edu); lunchtime concerts at Copley Plaza and City Hall Plaza; and Free Shakespeare on Boston Common – and in Springfield – presented by the **Citi Performing Arts Center** (tel: 617-532 1252; www.citicenter.org).

Springfield also hosts **Concerts in the Park** (www.springfieldcityhall.com) Tuesdays at 7pm at Blunt Park off Roosevelt Avenue.

The city of Worcester's **Music Alive** (www.wesleychurchworcester.org) program at Wesley United Methodist Church includes master organists.

Rhode Island

Every June on Block island the Annual Music Festival features a week-long "battle of the bands".

Westerly's downtown and park are popular venues for free concerts.

Connecticut

Both Foxwoods and Mohegan Sun casinos offer free concerts. Check their websites or local newspapers.

The town of Trumbell hosts outdoors concerts at the Town Hall Gazebo Tuesday evenings from mid-June through mid-September (tel: 203-452 5060).

There are free concerts throughout the summer at Westport's riverfront Levitt Pavilion for the Performing Arts (tel: 203-221 2153).

New Hampshire

In July and August there are free concerts in Portsmouth's Prescott Park and at Hampton Beach.

Maine

Free concert series include LL Bean's Summer Concert Series in Freeport; Alive at Five, and Tuesday nights, in Portland; and at Old Orchard Beach.

Opera

Massachusetts

Boston Lyric Opera Company (114 State Street; tel: 617-542 4912/800-447 7400) produces three operas each season at the Shubert Theater.

Connecticut

The **Connecticut Opera Guild** (tel: 860-527 0713) mounts full-scale performances in Hartford's Bushnell Performing Arts Center. **Goodspeed Opera House** (Goodspeed Landing, East Haddam; tel: 860-873 8668) showcases operas, musicals and revivals from April to December.

Vermont

The Green Mountain Opera Festival (tel: 802-496 7722) mounts full-scale productions at the Barre Opera House in June, and offers free open rehearsals and master classes.

New Hampshire

Each August **Opera North** (Hanover; tel: 603-643 1946) mounts fully-staged productions at the Lebanon Opera House, and offers informal concerts throughout the area.

Theater

Many theaters present special children's productions throughout the season.

Massachusetts

Boston's theater district, at the intersection of Tremont and Stuart streets, has many first-rate and

ABOVE: Boston offers a surprising variety of street performances.

historic theaters, including the **Wang Center, Schubert, Colonial**, and **Wilbur**. High-quality drama is found across the city, however, with performances on show at the **Boston Center for the Arts,** 539 Tremont Street, tel: 617-426 5000; and Boston University's **Huntington Theater,** 264 Huntington Avenue, tel: 617-266 0800, with the city's largest professional company in residence.

American Repertory Theater Company 64 Brattle Street, Harvard Square, Cambridge, tel: 617-495 2668, a highly acclaimed award winner, has two stages at the Loeb Drama Center.

On the north shore, the **Firehouse Center for the Performing Arts,** Market Square, Newburyport, tel: 617-495 2668, produces year-round plays, and specializes in children's theater. **Merrimack Repertory Theater** 50 East Merrimack St, Lowell, tel: 978-454 3926, stages professional productions.

Cape Playhouse, off Route 6A, Dennis, tel: 508-385 3838, offers some of the best summer stock on the Cape; check local listings for other current shows.

The **Center for Arts in Northampton,** 17 New South Street, tel: 413-584 7327, presents theater, dance, music and art.

Rhode Island

Providence's Tony-award-winning group at **Trinity Square Repertory Company** (201 Washington Street, Providence; tel: 401-351 4242) puts on innovative productions. **Brown University** (Leeds Theater, 77 Waterman Street; tel: 401-863 2838) stages contemporary to classical and everything In between. **Sandra**

Feinstein-Gamm Theatre (31 Elbow Street; tel: 401-831 2919) presents classic and contemporary plays in its 75-seat hall.

Astors' Beechwood (580 Bellevue Avenue, Newport; tel: 401-846 3772) stages murder-mystery plays once a week in-season.

Connecticut

In Hartford, the **Hartford Stage Company** (50 Church Street; tel: 860-527 5151), an award-winning ensemble, produces new plays, as well as classics. **Theaterworks** (233 Pearl Street; tel: 860-527 7838) features more experimental theater. The **Bushnell Center for the Performing Arts** (166 Capitol Avenue; tel: 860-987 5900) is one of the city's premier performing arts centers, presenting Broadway and off-Broadway shows, films, and music.

The Little Theater (177 Hartford Road, Manchester; tel: 860-645 6743), Connecticut's oldest theater, presents local talent.

Two Tony-award-winning theater companies reside in New Haven: The **Long Wharf Theater** (222 Sargent Dr; tel: 203-787 4282) premiered Arthur Miller's *The Crucible* and still produces many prize-winning shows. **Yale Repertory Theater** (222 York Street; tel: 203-432 1234) shows experimental work by Yale students.

Westport Country Playhouse (25 Powers Court; tel: 203-227 4177) launches six productions every summer in a renovated barn.

Vermont

In Burlington **St Michael's Playhouse** (tel: 802-654 2281) is Vermont's oldest equity playhouse. **Flynn Theater for the Performing Arts** (153

Main Street; tel: 802-863 8778) is the venue for big-name and big-audience productions.

Weston Playhouse Theater Company (tel: 802-824 5288) is home to Vermont's oldest summer theater.

Dorset Playhouse (Dorset; tel: 802-867 5777) stages professional performances in the summer, but in the winter a fine consortium of community folks takes to the stage.

The new 150-seat **Waterbury Festival Playhouse** (2933 Waterbury-Stowe Road, Waterbury Center; tel: 802-498 3755) launches plays for both adults and children.

New Hamsphire

Seacoast Repertory Theater (125 Bow Street, Portsmouth; tel: 603-433 4472/800-639 7650) features both adult and children's productions year-round.

Colonial Theater (95 Main Street, Keene; tel: 603-352 2033) show-cases live performances and films.

Palace Theater (80 Hanover Street, Manchester; tel: 603-668 5588) puts on six productions a year, including dinner theater by its resident company **Stage One Productions**.

Hopkins Center for the Arts (Dartmouth College, Hanover; tel: 603-646 2422) stages multiple musicals and various other theater productions.

New London Barn Playhouse (290 Main Street; tel: 603-526 4631/800-633 2276), the state's oldest consecutively-operated theater, presents plays and musicians in a renovated barn in the summer.

Hampton Playhouse (Route 101E, Hampton; tel: 603-926 3073) pre-sents theater in a 200-year old barn.

Maine

Portland Performing Arts Center (25a Forest Avenue, Portland; tel: 207-761 0591) is a multi-purpose venue offering space for music, dance, and theater. Also in Portland, check the local newspapers for anything mounted by the **Portland Stage Company** (tel: 207-774 0465).

Ogunquit Playhouse (Route 1, Ogunquit; tel: 207-646 5511) stages musicals, theater, and plays during the summer at one of the oldest playhouses in the US.

Arundel Barn Playhouse (53 Old Post Road; tel: 207-985 5552) in Arundel presents professional classic summer theater June–late Aug.

Hackmatack Playhouse (Route 9, Beaver Dam, Berwick; tel: 207-698 1807) launches plays with local performers.

MUSIC AND NIGHTLIFE

Cabaret

Massachusetts
Zeiterion Performing Arts Center (684 Purchase Street, New Bedford; tel: 508-997 5664) a handsomely-restored all-vaudeville theater, stages theme performances.

Connecticut
The elegantly restored Renaissance Revival **Palace Theater** (100 East Main Street; tel: 203-755 4700) in Waterbury includes cabaret in its entertainment roster.

Casinos

Rhode Island
Twin River (1600 Louisquisset Pike, Lincoln; tel: 401-723 3200; www.twin river.com) has 4,700 video slot machines, and simulcasts throughbred and greyhound racing. There are more than 1,000 machines at Newport's **Grand Slots** (150 Admiral Kalbfus Road; tel: 401-849 5000; www.newportgrand.com). Both casinos stay open around the clock on weekends and holidays.

Connecticut
Foxwoods Resort (Route 2 in Ledyard between I-395 and I-95; tel: 800-363 9663; www.foxwoods.com), which is housed on what was formerly a small Native American reservation, is now the largest gambling casino in the US. *For background, see page 261.*

The massive 115,000-sq-ft (10,700-sq-meter) casino at **Mohegan Sun Resort Casino** (Route 2A, Montville; tel: 888-226 7711; www.mohegansun.com), 10 miles (16 km) south of Foxwoods, rivals Foxwoods. Both casinos offer a full roster of nightly entertainment (some of it free) and present big-name entertainers in their vast theaters.

Comedy

Massachusetts
Boston's Faneuil Hall Market Place has several comedy clubs, including **Comedy Connection** (tel: 617-248 9700). Also of note is **Nick's Comedy Stop** 100 Warrenton Street, tel: 617-482 0930, in the theater area, and **ImprovAsylum** (216 Hanover Street; tel: 617-263 6887), which offers half-price admission to Red Sox ticket holders who have been rained out of that day's game.

In Cambridge, at the **Comedy Studio** (1236 Massachusetts Avenue;

ABOVE: college towns attract buskers.

tel: 617-661 6507) above the Hong Kong Restaurant, tickets to see up-and-coming comedians perform are just $8–10.

Rhode Island
Catch a Rising Star at the Twin River Casino, 100 Twin River Road, tel: 401-331 1221 Thur–Sat evening.

Connecticut
In Hartford, the brew pub **City Steam** (942 Main Street; tel: 860-525 1600) is home to the Brew Ha Ha Club, where comedians perform Thur–Sat. Reserve in advance.

Maine
Thur–Sun evenings some of the region's funniest comedians perform at the **Comedy Connection**, 16 Custom House Wharf, Portland, tel: 207-774 5554.

Dancing

Massachusetts
In Boston's Theatre District, **Venu,** 100 Warrenton Street, tel: 617-388 8061, is one of the hot spots to dance the wee hours away. The fashionable **Gypsy Bar,** 116 Boylston Street, tel: 617-482 7799, attracts Boston's chic dance set. **Aria** (246 Tremont Street; tel: 617-338 7080) beneath the Wilbur Theater, rocks after the theater ends.

Maine
Zootz Nightclub (31 Forest Avenue; tel: 207-773 8187), for the college set, and **Granny Killam's** (55 Market Street; tel: 207-761 5865), for post-college crowd, are two of Portland's better dance clubs.

Folk Music

From small, intimate clubs to large halls, the New England region is studded superb venues for folk music. At the forefront is the legendary **Club Passim** (47 Palmer Street, Cambridge; tel: 617-492 7679), where such famous names as Joan Baez and Bob Dylan have performed over the years. Other Massachusetts spots include **The Narrows Center for the Arts**, 16 Anavan Street, Fall River, tel: 508-324 1926, with Thursday night open mic, and bluegrass jams the first and third Fridays of each month. **Johnny D's** (17 Holland Street, Somerville; tel: 617-776 2004) has folk music on some evenings.

Rhode Island's **Brooklyn Coffee and Tea House**, Douglas Avenue, Providence, tel: 401-575 2284; and **Stone Soup**, 50 Park Place, Pawtucket, tel: 401-921 5115 are well known venues.

In Connecticut, **Wintonbury Coffeehouse** (54 maple Street, Bloomfield; www.wintonburycoffee house.com) offers entertainment the second Saturday of each month.

In tiny Morrisville, Vermont the **Bees Knees** at 188 Main Street (tel: 802-888 7889) is quickly becoming a leading venue for live entertainment. In Burlington, **Radio Bean Coffeehouse**, 8 North Winooski Avenue, tel: 802-660-9346 offers occasional folk music; and **Parima Thai Restaurant**, 185 Pearl Street (tel: 802-864 7917) has Thursday night folk entertainment.

Portsmouth, New Hampshire's **Press Room** (77 Daniel Street; tel: 603-431 5186) offers seven nights of live shows, including folk performers.

Jazz

Massachusetts
In Boston the **Bank of Boston Celebrity Series** (tel: 617-482 2595) hosts jazz performances throughout the area. The landmark **Sculler's Jazz Club**, 400 Soldiers Field Road, Guest Quarters Suites Hotel, tel: 617-783 0811, is one of the best in the city for blues, Latin, and jazz. Students and faculty at the nearby Berklee School of Music perform at **Wally's Café**, 427 Massachusetts Avenue, tel: 617-424 1408.

In Cambridge, the **Regattabar** Bennett and Eliot Streets, Charles

Hotel, Harvard Square, tel: 617-864 1200/617-876 7777 for tickets, presents traditional, big-name jazz personalities; and **Ryles Jazz Club** (212 Hampshire Street, Inman Square, Cambridge; tel: 617-876 9330) features local talent and a weekend jazz brunch. Water Music (www.concertix.com) presents jazz at venues throughout the area, as well as cabaret-style at the **Real Deal Jazz Club and Café** in the Cambridge Multicultural Arts Center, 41 Second Street, tel: 617 876 7777.

Connecticut

Jazz venues in Connecticut include: **Wooster Jazz Society** (Ridgebury Road, Danbury; tel: 203-431 8975); the **Silvermine Tavern** (194 Perry Avenue, Norwalk; tel: 203-847 9171), with music Friday and Saturday evenings; and **The Red Door** (675 Main Street, Watertown; tel: 860-945 6688), with jazz and sushi Wednesday nights.

Vermont

Burlington venues include **Halverson's Upstreet Café**, 16 Church Street, tel: 802-658 0278; and **Leunig's**, 115 Church Street, tel: 802-863 3759.

Rock and Pop
Massachusetts

Although Boston is notorious for shutting down early, its large student population usually keeps things rolling, at least on Friday and Saturday. Most nightclubs on Lansdowne Street are open until 2.30am, but don't forget: most "T" stops running at 12.30am. **Axis**, 13 Lansdowne Street, tel: 617-262 2437, one of the city's largest clubs with a capacity of 1,000 people, has music on several floors. Big-name national rock and alternative talent can be heard at **Mama Kin**, 36 Lansdowne Street, tel: 617-864 1200/617-876 7777, which books a variety of rock bands on three stages. Crowds flock to the **Avalon Ballroom**, 15 Lansdowne Street; tel: 617-262 2424 for performances by both up-and-coming and headline bands. Twenty- and 30-somethings dance and party to alternative and well-known bands at **Paradise Rock Club**, 967 Commonwealth Avenue (tel: 617-562 8800). The **Orpheum Theater** (1 Hamilton Place) and **TD BankNorth Garden** (1 Causeway Street) are also popular venues.

In Allston, local bands perform **at Great Scott**, 1222 Commonwealth Avenue (tel: 617-566 9014).

In Cambridge, try the incomparable **Johnny D's** 17 Holland Street near Davis Square, tel: 617-776 2004) for everything from blues jams to Cajun music. There's live music every night at **T.T. the Bears Place** (10 Brookline Street, Central Square; tel: 617-492 2327), and most nights at the **Middle East** (472 Massachusetts Avenue; tel: 617-354 8238).

Northampton's **Iron Horse Entertainment Group** (www.iheg.com) presents nationally-known groups at several venues throughout the city.

Theodore's at 201 Worthington Street, Springfield, tel: 413-584 0610, offers "booze, blues and BBQ".

Both the **Cape Cod Melody Tent** (tel: 508-775 9100) in Hyannis and the **North Shore Music Theater** (tel: 978 922 8500) in Beverly host acts from April through December.

Rhode Island

The free *Providence Phoenix* (www.the phoenix.com/providence) can be found around town in shops and restaurants, and is slanted towards a younger, hip crowd. The **Providence Civic Center** (1 LaSalle Square; tel: 401-331 6700) hosts big-name touring rock bands.

On Block Island, **Captain Nick's Rock and Roll Bar** (tel: 401-466 5670) on Ocean Avenue rocks nightly in season with live bands. **The National Hotel** (Water Street; tel: 401-466 2901) and **Govern's Yellow Kittens Tavern** (Corn Neck Road; tel: 401-466 5855) have music every night in summer. Govern's agenda is the more diverse of the two, with reggae and R&B included.

Thames Street is where it's happening in Newport. **Thames Street Station (and Great American Pub)** (337 America's Cup Avenue, Newport; tel: 401-849 9480) puts on regular dance-music nights.

Chan's Fine Oriental Dining (267 Main Street, Woonsocket; tel: 401-765 1900) hosts blues, jazz and folk groups. Reservations required.

Connecticut

Concerts are held year-round at the huge **Hartford Civic Center** (1 Civic Center Plaza; tel: 860-727 8010). Hartford clubs **Voodoo** (191 Ann Street; tel: 860-525 3003) and **Arch Street Tavern** (tel: 860-246 7610) both feature live acts.

Toads Place (300 York Street, New Haven; tel: 203-624 8623) is a popular club that books major acts. Hartford's popular **Bourbon Street North** (70 Union Place; tel: 860-525 1014) features a large dance floor and a variety of music styles.

The **"SoNo"** area of downtown South Norfolk has a variety of nightclubs.

Vermont

All of the big ski mountains have a phalanx of nightly live music from which to choose. You're bound to find something to your liking.

Nectar's (tel: 802-658 4771), where the legendary group Phish got its start, and **The Club Metronome** (tel: 802-658 0278), both at 188 Main Street, are two of Burlington's leading venue for live music.

Information Sources
Massachusetts
Boston

The Phoenix (weekly; club line, tel: 617-859 3300; www.thephoenix.com) contains a large Arts and Entertainment section, as does The *Boston Globe*'s (www.boston.com) Thursday Calendar.

Western Massachusetts

For cultural events, consult the *Five College Calendar of Events*, published monthly, *The Valley Advocate* (www.valleyadvocate.com), a free weekly paper; or the Springfield Republican's Week-end section, published in the paper on Thursdays, or their website: www.masslive.com/entertainment.

Rhode Island

Rhode Island Monthly is a good source for what's happening throughout the state, as is their website: www.rimonthly.com.

Connecticut

Pick up a copy of *Connecticut Magazine* at the newsstand, or check www.connecticutmag.com. The state's website, ctvisit.com, lists current information. The free *Hartford Advocate* and *New Haven Advocate*, found in many restaurants, have sharp listings.

Vermont

The free weekly publication *Seven Days* (www.7dvt.com) lists events throughout the state. The weekly Calendar in *Burlington Free Press*'s (www.burlingtonfreepress.com) Thursday edition covers events throughout northern Vermont.

New Hampshire

Each month the magazine *To Do* (www.nhtodo.com) lists events throughout the state.

Maine

The monthly *Down East* (www.down east.com) magazine is an excellent resource.

Up on Route 2, **Higher Ground** (1214 Williston Road; tel: 802-652 0777) hosts nationally-known groups.
Mulligan's (tel: 802-297 9293) on Stratton has music all year-round.
Purple Moon Pub (Route 100; tel: 802-496 3422) in Waitsfield presents a full roster of performers.

New Hampshire

The **Hampton Beach Casino** (tel: 603-926 4541) is a great place to catch big-name acts. Also check out the **Paradise Beach Club** at both Weirs Beach (tel: 603-366 2665) and Laconia (tel: 603-366 2665).
Woodstock Inn, Station and Brewery on Main Street in North Woodstock (tel: 800-321 3985) presents classic rock and reggae throughout the season.

Maine

Sunday River in Bethel is a hopping kind of place (both slopeside and in town) during ski season. Check out the **Sunday River Brewery** (Route 2; tel: 207-824 4253) and **Bumps Pub** (on the mountain; tel: 207-824 3000), which both have rock bands.
In Portland, the **State Theater** (609 Congress Street; tel: 207-780 8265) books headline entertainment and **The Alehouse** (30 Market Street; tel: 207-253 5100) hosts live music.

ABOVE: a baseball game at Boston's Fenway Park.

David's (28 Prospect Hill Street, Newport), mainly a men's bar with DJ.

Connecticut

The country's oldest gay bar is **Cedar Brook Café**, 919 Post Road East, Westport (tel: 203-221 7429).
The all-gay **Triangle**s (66 Sugar Hollow Road, Danbury; tel: 203-798 6995) hosts special nights for men, women, and transgenders.

Maine

Ogunquit has a growing number of gay-friendly establishments; look for the rainbow flags.
In Portland, **Underground** (3 Spring Street; tel: 207-773 3315) is a gay club, as is **Blackstones**, (6 Pine Street; tel: 775-2885).

SPECTATOR SPORTS

Generally, the New England states are represented by Boston's teams: basketball's **Boston Celtics** (Fleet Center, Sept–May; tel: 617-624 1000), baseball's Boston **Red Sox** (Fenway Park, Apr–Oct; tel: 617-267 1700) and hockey's **Boston Bruins** (Fleet Center, Oct–Mar; tel: 617-624 1000/617-931 2222 for tickets).
The **New England Patriots** (Aug–Dec; tel: 508-543 1776/800-543 1776 for tickets), and the city's professional soccer team, **New England Revolution** (www.revolution soccer.net), play at Gillette Stadium in the southern suburb of Foxboro.
Minor league baseball is a New England tradition, and admission is inexpensive (in comparison to major league contests). The games are family-oriented, and most teams go to great lengths to keep the children amused. Among the teams: The AA affiliate of the Boston Red Sox, the

Portland Sea Dogs play in downtown Portland (Hadlock Field; tel: 800-936 3647). In Rhode Island the Red Sox's AAA affiliate, the **Pawtucket Red Sox**, plays 72 home baseball games each season at the McCoy Stadium (1 Ben Mondor Way, Pawtucket; tel: 401-724 7300).
Vermont's **Lake Monsters**, a Class A affiliate of The Washington Nationals, plays home games at Centennial Field in downtown Burlington (tel: 802-655 4200).
For up-to-date information on schedules and locations, check the sports section of any local daily.

OUTDOOR ACTIVITIES

Biking

Massachusetts

In Eastern Massachusetts, mountain bikers can explore the trails of **Blue Hills Reservation** (tel: 617-698 1802) in Milton, just south of Boston, or in **Maudslay State Park** in Newburyport on the North Shore. In the western part of the state, **Mount Greylock State Reservation** (tel: 413-499 4262) near Williamstown has a number of mountain biking trails.
Bikers also flock to the **Cape Cod Rail Trail**, a scenic 30-mile (48-km) paved path along the former Penn Central Railway route from South Dennis to South Wellfleet (see page 164). In Provincetown, the paved **Province Lands Trail** winds for 7¼ miles (11.5 km) through the dunes.
A classic urban bike path is Boston's **Dr Paul Dudley White Bikeway**, an 18-mile (29-km) loop that follows both sides of the Charles River.
The Norwattuck Rail Trail (tel: 413-586 8706) extends 10 miles (16 km) from Northampton to Belchertown.

GAY VENUES

For up-to-the minute entertainment listings throughout New England, log onto www.edgenewengland.com. Also check: www.baywindows.com.

Massachusetts

The website www.edgeboston.com lists activities at clubs in Boston.
At **Avalon**, 15 Lansdowne Street, Boston, tel: 617-262 2424; Sunday is gay night. **Club Café and Lounge** (209 Columbus Avenue; tel: 617-536 0966) is a chic venue for gays.
Provincetown is the East Coast's most popular gathering place for gays. It's best to ask around for the current "in" club, but you can count on tea dances at **The Boatslip** (Commercial Street; tel: 508-487 1669), every summer afternoon on the waterfront deck.
Northampton's clubs include **Grotto**, at 25 West Street, tel: 413-526 6900, which also has dancing.

Rhode Island

Gerardo's (Atwells Avenue at Franklin Square, Providence; tel: 401-274 5560) is a popular gay dance place.

Rhode Island

The 14½-mile (23-km) **East Bay Bicycle Path** follows Narragansett Bay and winds through several towns between East Providence and Bristol.

On Block Island and in Tiverton and Little Compton, the relatively quiet roads are popular with bikers.

Bikers can also follow Newport's **Bellevue Avenue** and **Ocean Drive** for about 15 miles (24 km) past the mansions and along the shore.

For a free *Guide to Cycling in the Ocean State*, call 401-222 4203, extension 4042.

Connecticut

Winding Trails Recreation Area off Route 4 in Farmington (tel: 860-677 8458) and **Woodbury Ski Area** (tel: 203-263 2203) are big with Connecticut mountain bikers.

For a free Connecticut Bicycle Map, write to the Connecticut Department of Transportation, 2800-Berlin Turnpike, P.O. Box 317546, Newington, CT 06131-7546.

Vermont

Several downhill ski areas are converted into mountain-biking centers after the winter season ends.

Mount Snow (tel: 802-464 3333), home to the first American mountain bike school, has 45 miles (72 km) of bike terrain and runs one-day coaching programs, leads mountain tours, and hosts family bike weekends.

At **Killington** (tel: 802-422 6232), mountain bikers can cruise 50 miles (80 km) of trails. Vermont is popular for upscale inn-to-inn tours.

Bike Vermont (tel: 800-257 2226) puts together tours in all six states. Stowe's 5½-mile (9-km) paved bike path winds from downtown to the base of Mount Mansfield.

The Northeast Kingdom's **Kingdom Trails** (tel: 802-626 0737) network which begins in East Burke offers a diverse mountain biking terrain.

New Hampshire

Several ski areas offer summer and fall mountain biking. **Loon Mountain** attracts novice through advanced riders to 21 miles (34 km) of trails, where lifts serve the steepest biking routes. Nearby, the self-guided **Franconia Notch Bike Tour** starts at Echo Lake, passes the Old Man of the Mountain site, and ends at the Loon Mountain ski area.

Near Mount Washington, **Great Glen Trails** (tel: 603-466 2333) offers learn-to-mountain-bike courses, ranging from a short introductory class to more in-depth skill-building.

New England Hiking Holidays

(tel: 800-869 0949) packages inn-to-inn and biking tours in New Hampshire.

Maine

When the snow melts, the Sunday River Ski area turns into the **Sunday River Mountain Bike Park** (tel: 207-824 3000), where bikers can ride the lifts up and then bike down 60 miles (100 km) of trails.

Boston-based **Bike Riders' Tours** (tel: 800-473 7040) is one of several companies offering bicycle tours in the state of Maine. Their week-long Penobscot Bay trip stops off in Camden, Islesboro and Castine.

Canoeing, Kayaking and Rafting

Massachusetts

In Boston and the nearby suburb of Newton, **Charles River Canoe and Kayak Center** (tel: 617-965 5110) rents canoes and kayaks on the Charles River for an hour or more. **Community Boating** (21 David Mugar Way; tel: 617-523 1038) also rents kayaks (a two-day membership fee is required) and gives lessons.

South Bridge Boat House in Concord (tel: 978-369 9438) has canoes for rent on the lazy Sudbury and Concord Rivers.

At Nickerson State Park on Cape Cod, **Jack's Boat Rentals** (tel: 508-896 8556) rents canoes, kayaks, sunfish, pedal boats, sailboards and seacycles.

Sportsmen's Marina Boat Rental Company in Hadley (Route 9; tel: 413-586 2426) rents canoes and kayaks, as does the **Northfield Mountain Recreation and Environmental Center** (tel: 800-859 2960). In western Massachusetts, **Zoar Outdoor** (tel: 800-532 7483), based along the Mohawk Trail in Charlemont, runs whitewater rafting expeditions for all levels on the Deerfield River. Also two- or three-day learn-to-kayak or canoe clinics.

Rhode Island

Coastal sea kayaking is popular and the **Kayak Centre** (tel: 401-295 4400 in Wickford leads a variety of excursions, including a Newport tour with ocean glimpses of mansions; the company also runs a multi-day trip to Block Island. At their Charlestown location Pond (tel: 401-364 8000) they offer kayaking on Ninigret Pond. **Ocean State Adventures** (99 Poppasquash Road, Bristol; tel: 401-254 4000) also offers tours.

Telephone **Blackstone Valley Tourism Council** (800-454 2882) for free information about canoeing the 45-mile (72-km) long Blackstone River. **New Harbor Kayak** (tel: 401-466 2890) rents craft on on Block Island. **Sakonnet Boathouse** in Tiverton (tel: 401-624 1440) has kayak rentals and lessons on Narragansett Bay.

Kayak Today (2428 Kingston Road, South Kingston; tel: 401-207 6511) runs river trips in South County.

Connecticut

For whitewater rafting or canoeing, head for the Housatonic River. **North American Whitewater Expeditions** (tel: 800-727 4379) organizes Housatonic rafting trips.

At 170 Main Street in New Hartford, **Main Stream Canoe and Kayaks** (tel: 860-693 6791) rents canoes and kayaks and conducts day trips on the Farmington River.

Canoes can be rented at several state parks, including Burr Pond in Torrington and Lake Waramaug State Park in New Preston. Rentals are on a first-come, first-served basis. For information, call Clarke Outdoors (tel: 860-672 6365). For general information check: www.ct.gov.com.

Vermont

Vermont Canoe Touring Center (451 Putney Road, Brattleboro; tel: 802-257 5008) organizes trips and rents canoes and kayaks.

Burlington-based **Paddleways** (tel: 802-660 8606) teaches kayaking basics and runs kayaking trips on Lake Champlain, as does **True North Kayak Tours** (tel: 802-860 1910).

In Stowe, **Umiak Outdoor Outfitters** (849 S. Main Street; tel: 802-253 2317) offers tours and rentals.

New Hampshire

Saco Bound River Outfitters (tel: 603-447 2177) runs a river kayaking school and leads canoeing expeditions, guided kayak trips, and white-water rafting trips at several New Hampshire and Maine locations.

North Star Canoe Livery (tel: 603-542 5802), based in Cornish, conducts canoe trips on the Connecticut River.

Appalachian Mountain Club's New Hampshire chapter (tel: 603-466 2725; www.amc-nh.org) offers organized trips, courses and instruction on waterways throughout New England. **Seacoast Kayak** (210 Ocean Boulevard, Route 1A, Seabrook Beach; tel: 603-474 1025) rents kayaks for flatwater and ocean access.

Maine

With more than 2,000 coastal islands and their protected waters,

Maine has become a center for sea kayaking. The **Maine Island Kayak Company** (tel: 800-796 2373), based at Peaks Island near Portland, runs a range of sea-kayaking trips and instructional courses. **Old Quarry Ocean Adventures** (Oceanville Road; tel: 207-367 8977) in Stonington rents kayaks, canoes, and sailboats and organizes boat trips.

H2Outfitters (tel: 207-833 5257), on Orr's Island near Brunswick, offers one-day sea kayaking classes, as well as multi-day trips.

The Kennebec, Dead, and Penobscot Rivers offer challenging whitewater rafting. **North American Whitewater Expeditions** (tel: 800-727 4379) runs Maine river rafting trips for novices through experts.

The **Allagash Wilderness Waterway**, a 92-mile (150-km) corridor of lakes and rivers from Baxter State Park to the Canadian border, is a well-known canoeing and rafting destination. Outfitters in this area include **Allagash Canoe Trips** in Greenville (tel: 207-695 3668) and **Mahoosuc Guide Service**, based in Newry (tel: 207-824 2073).

For more sedate paddling, the **Maine Audubon Society** (tel: 207-781 2330) offers guided canoe trips and rentals in Scarborough Marsh, the state's largest salt marsh.

On Mount Desert Island, **National Park Canoe and Kayak Rentals** (tel: 207-244 5854) has canoes for hire on Long Pond.

Fishing

Fly fishing, ice fishing, kayak fishing, shark fishing, deep-sea angling… there's a remarkable choice of ways to catch your supper, all year round.

Massachusetts

Numerous charters go out of Boston Harbor or nearby Winthrop Harbor. Among them are: **C.J. Victoria** (tel: 617-283 5801); **Good Time Charters** (tel; 617-435 4126); and **Flying Fish Charters** (tel: 617-846 4876), which highlights fly and light spin fishing.

For salt-water fly-fishing, check with **Orvis Saltwater School** (Chatham; tel: 800-235 9763) on Cape Cod. They run a course that teaches basic saltwater techniques. Also on the Cape, **Patriot Party Boats** (tel: 508-548 2626), operating out of Falmouth Harbor, offers deep-sea fishing trips.

The Orleans-based **Rock Harbor Charter Fleet** (tel: 508-255 9757) also run fishing excursions.

On Cape Ann, **Yankee Deep Sea Fishing** (75 Essex Avenue, Gloucester; tel: 978 283 0313/800-942 5464)

journeys out to Stellwagen Bank and Jeffrey's Ledge.

Rhode Island

Saltwater Edge (Newport; tel: 401-842 0062) offers fly-fishing lessons as well as guided saltwater fishing outings. Several charter fishing boats are based in Narragansett, including **Persuader** (tel: 401-783 5644).

Numerous fishing charter boats line the harbor near the ferry terminal on Block Island.

Connecticut

All along the Connecticut coast, charter boats run half-day or full-day fishing expeditions. The best thing to do is get a list of operators from the **Connecticut State Tourism** Office (tel: 800-282 6863) or head to the harbor where you want to go out and talk to the captains directly. There's lots of info at www.ctfisherman.com.

Catch-and-release fly fishing is popular on the Housantanic River.

Vermont

With 7,000 miles (11,000 km) of river and more than 800 lakes and ponds, Vermont is a fishing paradise. Vermont Fish and Wildlife has a good website: www.vtfishandwildlife.com.

Anglers flock to the trout-laded Battenkill River near Manchester, where **Orvis** (tel: 802-362 3622/800-235 9763) runs a program of fly-fishing classes for all levels of skill.

Battenkill Anglers (6204 Main Street, Manchester; tel: 802-379 1444) provides a fly fishing guide service in both Vermont and the Catskills (New York).

Fishing guides at **Strictly Trout** (5607 Westminster West Road, Putney; tel: 802-869 3116) work all Vermont rivers but specialize in the Connecticut River.

The **Fly Rod Shop and Fly Fish Vermont** (2703 Waterbury Road, Route 100, Stowe; tel: 803-253 7346) is an outfitter and provides a guide service.

New Hampshire

Great Glen Trails (tel: 603-466 2333) offers introductory fishing classes and arranges guided fly fishing trips. **North Country Angler** (tel: 603-356 6000), also in the White Mountains, runs guided fly-fishing weekends.

For ocean fishing, several charter companies operate on the seacoast, including **Atlantic Fishing Fleet** (Rye; tel: 603-964 5220) and **Al Gauron Deep Sea Fishing** (Hampton Beach; tel: 603-926 2469).

Maine

The Rangeley area is a popular destination for those who fly-fish.

For ocean fishing excursions, **Devils Den** (tel: 207-761 4466) runs half- and full-day trips from DiMillo's Marina in Portland.

In Kennebunkport, **Tidewater Fishing Charters** (tel: 207-229 0201) operates fly fising and light tackle charters from the Nonatum Resort, 95 Ocean Avenue.

Four-hour fishing trips on Frenchman's Bay depart from the **Bar Harbor Inn Pier** at 8am and 1pm.

In the Boothbay region, **Sweet Action Charters** sails daily from June–September from Kaler's Crab and Lobster House (tel: 207-633 4741).

Hiking

Massachusetts

Close to Boston, hikers can explore the 150 miles (240 km) of trails at **Blue Hills Reservation** (see *Biking* above). More ambitious hikers head west to **Mount Tom State**

BELOW: fly fishing on the Contoocoock River, New Hampshire.

Reservation in Holyoke or **Mount Greylock State Reservation** (see *Biking* above), which includes a stretch of the Appalachian Trail.

Rhode Island

Rhode Island Audubon Society (tel: 401-949 5454) leads nature hikes. On Block Island, contact the **Nature Conservancy** (Ocean Avenue; tel: 401-466 2129) for the best hikes.

Connecticut

The **Appalachian Trail**, a 2,000-mile (3,200-km) trail linking Maine and Georgia, traverses about 50 miles (80 km) of western Connecticut and the Appalachian Mountain Club (Boston; tel: 617-523 0636) provides detailed trail information.

At **Talcott Mountain State Park** in Simsbury, hikers who reach the peak of the 1½-mile (2.5-km) walk get panoramic vistas of the Farmington River Valley. On clear days, visibility can be up to 50 miles (80 km).

Macedonia Brook State Park in Kent and **Sleeping Giant State Park** in Hamden run scenic day hikes. Contact **The Connecticut State Bureau of Parks and Recreation** (tel: 860-424 3200) for details.

Vermont

Vermont's topography offers everything from easy day hikes to multi-day mountain jaunts. Long-distance hikers gravitate to the **Appalachian Trail**, which cuts across southern Vermont, and to the **Long Trail**, a 270-mile (435-km) traverse across Vermont's highest peaks between the Massachusetts state line and the Canadian border.

Green Mountain Club (4711 Waterbury-Stowe Road, Waterbury Center; tel: 802-244 7037) has specific trail information and publishes *Day Hiker's Guide to Vermont*.

To mix serious hiking with country-inn comforts, contact **Country Inns Along the Trail** (tel: 802-247 3300), which organizes inn-to-inn tours. **New England Hiking Holidays** (tel: 800-869 0949) also packages inn-to-inn hiking (and biking) tours in Vermont, New Hampshire and Maine.

New Hampshire

The 86 major peaks of the White Mountains provide plenty of hiking challenges. The **US Forest Service** (719 N Main Street, Laconia; tel: 603-528 8721) provides specific trail info.

The **Appalachian Mountain Club** (tel: 603-466 2725) has detailed trail information; this group maintains a network of huts in the White Mountains providing overnight accommodations. For hut

reservations, tel: 603-466 2727.

For inn-to-inn hiking tours, contact **New England Hiking Holidays** (tel: 800-869 0949) in North Conway.

Maine

The website www.maineoutdoors.com/hiking has reliable information.

Baxter State Park (tel: 207-723 5140) in Maine's North Woods draws thousands of hikers who tackle the day-long climb to the summit of **Mount Katahdin**, the state's highest peak (5,267 ft/1,755 meters). Eighteen mountains in the park are taller than 3,000 ft (900 meters).

Sailing

Massachusetts

Boston's **Community Boating** (tel: 617-523 1038), America's oldest public sailing program, sells two-day (and longer) memberships for Charles River sailing. Experience is required.

In Marblehead, **Atlantic Charters** (tel: 978-590 4318) offers lessons and charters.

Rhode Island

Newport, "the Sailing Capital of the World", is a good base for short harbor excursions and learn-to-sail vacations. **Sightsailing of Newport** (tel: 401-849 3333) offers harbor sails, rentals and instruction. **Newport Sailing School** (tel: 401-848 2266) runs narrated one- and two-hour sailing tours plus classes. **Sail Newport** (tel: 401-846 1983) in Newport's Fort Adams State Park rents sailboats by the hour.

Block Island Club (tel: 401-466 5939) offers full sailing instruction and one-week family memberships.

Connecticut

Mystic is a center for sailing activity. The **Offshore Sailing School** (tel: 800-221 4326) conducts five-day learn-to-sail courses in the town. **Mystic Seaport** (tel: 888-973 2767) rents sailboats to ticket holders.

Vermont

Lake Champlain and **Lake Memphre-magog** are the principal sailing lakes. **Burlington Community Boathouse** (tel: 802-865 3377) rents sailboats and runs charters and "bareboats" on Lake Champlain. **Winds of Ireland** (Burlington Boathouse; tel: 802-863 5090) runs day and sunset sailing cruises. On Lake Memphremagog, you can rent pontoon boats at **Newport Marine** (tel: 802-334 5911).

New Hampshire

Marinas abound on Lake Winnipesaukee, the state's largest lake.

Although it's a popular power boating spot, some marinas rent sailboats, including **Fay's Boat Yard** (Guilford; tel: 603-293 8000), whose fleet has 16-ft daysailers and 26-ft sloops.

Maine

The Rockport-Camden area is Maine's center for windjammer cruising. The **Maine Windjammer Association** (tel: 800-807 9463), headquartered in Blue Hill, represents a number of windjammers that offer multi-day excursions. **Maine Classic Schooners** (tel: 888-807 6921/207-549 3908) and **Maine Windjammer Cruises** (tel: 888-692 7245) are also good bets.

Do-it-yourself sailors can contact **Manset Yacht Service** (tel: 207-244 4040), near Acadia National Park, to arrange sailboat rentals. **Sebago Sailing** on Sebago Lake rents sailboats by the week and offers lessons (tel: 207-647 4400).

Sightseeing Cruises

Massachusetts

Numerous tour boats cruise Boston Harbor, including the **Spirit of Boston** (tel: 866-856 3463), which offers lunch and dinner sailings; and **Harbor Cruises** (tel: 617-227 4321), which also runs whale watches.

The schooner **Bay Lady II** (tel: 508-487 9308) makes two-hour sails from Provincetown into Cape Cod Bay. **Cape Ann Whale Watch** (415 Main Street, Gloucester; tel: 800-877 5110) guarantees sightings.

Rhode Island

In Newport, **America's Cup Charters**, with a fleet of Cup winners, (tel: 401-846 9886) runs evening sails and half- or full-day sailboat charters. Other charters include *Flyer* (tel: 401-848 2100), a 57-ft catamaran; *Spirit of Newport* (tel: 401-849 3575); the 72-ft schooner *Madeline*, and the 58-ft classic speedboat *Rum Runner II* (tel: 401-847 0298).

Connecticut

Deep River Navigation Company (Saybrook Point; tel: 860-526 4954) offers narrated cruises along the Connecticut River shoreline. Among companies that offer cruises along the Thimble Islands are **Volsunga IV** (tel: 203-481 3345) and **Sea Mist II** (tel: 203-488 8905), which also operates dinnner cruises and seal watches. **Captain John's Sports Fishing Center** (tel: 860-443 7259) in Waterford gives lighthouse, seal and bald eagle cruises.

At **Voyager Cruises** (tel: 860-536 0416) in Mystic sail aboard the tall ships *Argia* or *Mystic*; there are also

TRANSPORTATION

ACCOMMODATIONS

ACTIVITIES

SHOPPING

A – Z

two- to six-day cruising adventures. The tall ship *Mystic Whaler* (tel: 800-697 8420) hosts day, overnight,and lobster dinner cruises. **Mystic Seaport** (tel: 888-973 2767) offers cruises aboard a variety of craft, including the 1908 coal-fired steamboat *Sabrino*, and the 20-ft Crosby cat boat *Breck Marshall*.

Maine

Beal & Bunker (tel: 207-244 3575) and **Islesford Ferry** (tel: 207-276 3717) set sail from Northeast Harbor to Little Cranberry Island. **Island Cruises** (tel: 207-244 5785) in Bass Harbor cruises to nearby islands.

Near the Bar Harbor Town Pier hop aboard the *Acadian* for two-hour narrated tours of Frenchman Bay (tel: 888-533 9253). Nearby, **The Katherine** (tel: 207-288 3322) runs lobstering and seal-watching cruises.

Songo River Queen II, a replica of a Mississippi sternpaddle wheeler, sails from Naples (tel: 207-935 2369).

Skiing

Massachusetts

Massachusetts' best downhill skiing is in the Berkshires. Two of the major areas are **Jiminy Peak** in Hancock (tel: 413-738 5500) and **Brodie Mountain** in New Ashford (Route 7; tel: 413-443 4752).

In the eastern part of the state, the largest area is **Wachusett Mountain** in Princeton, about an hour west of Boston (tel: 978-464 2300/800-754 1234).

The Berkshires are the most reliable for cross-country skiing. **Northfield Mountain Recreation and Environmental Center** (99 Miller's Falls Road; tel: 800-859 2960) has 26 miles (42 km) of trails.

Closer to Boston, two smaller areas are **Weston Ski Track** (tel: 781-891 6575) and in Carlisle, **Great Brook Farm** (tel: 978-369 7486).

Connecticut

There are several small downhill areas in the Litchfield Hills region: **White Memorial Foundation** (tel: 860-678 9582) in Litchfield, **Mohawk Mountain** in Cornwall (tel: 860-672 6100), and **Mount Southington** in Southington (tel: 860-628 0954).

For cross-country skiing, try the **Woodbury Ski and Racquet Area** (tel: 203-263 2203) or Farmington's **Winding Trails Cross Country Ski Center** (tel: 860-678 9582).

Vermont

For many, Vermont is synonymous with New England skiing. In the south, the largest downhill mountains are: **Stratton** (Jamaica; tel: 802-297

4000/800-787 2886), **Okemo** (Ludlow; tel: 802-228 4041/800-786 5366), and **Mount Snow** (tel: 800-245 7669). **Killington** (Rutland; tel: 802-422 3261/800-621 6867) – the Beast of the East – is monumental.

In the north, check out: **Stowe** (tel: 802-253 3600), **Sugarbush** (Warren; tel: 802-583 2381/800-537 8427), **Jay Peak** (Jay; tel: 802-988 2611/800-451 4449), and **Smugglers' Notch** (tel: 800-419 4615).

One of Vermont's largest cross-country skiing areas is **Craftsbury Nordic Center** (tel: 800-729 7751), but Stowe also has several excellent centers, including **Edson Hill** (tel: 802-253 8954), **Topnotch** (tel: 802-253 8585), and **Trapp Family Lodge** (tel: 802-253 8511).

Serious Nordic skiers ski the 300-mile (480-km) **Catamount Trail**, which runs nearly the length of the state; contact the Catamount Trail Association (Burlington; tel: 802-864 5794).

New Hampshire

Major areas include: **Waterville Valley** (tel: 603-236 8311), **Loon Mountain** (Lincoln; tel: 603-745 8111), and **Cannon Mountain** (Franconia; tel: 603-823 5563).

Smaller areas include: **Attitash Bear Peak** (Bartlett; tel: 603-374 2368/800-223 7669), **Bretton Woods** (tel: 603-278 5000) and **Wildcat** (tel: 603-466 3326/800-255 6439), both in Jackson.

The state's largest cross-country ski centers are **Jackson Ski Touring Foundation** (tel: 800-927 6697) and **Mt Washington Valley Ski Touring** (off Route 16, Intervale; tel: 603-356 9920).

South of the White Mountains you'll find the **Nordic Center** (Waterville Valley; tel: 603-236 4666) and **Franconia Village Cross Country Center** at the Franconia Inn (tel: 603-823 5542/800-473 5299).

Maine

Largest areas for downhill skiing are: **Sunday River** in Bethel (tel: 207-824 3000/800-543 2754), **Sugarloaf/USA** in Kingfield (tel: 207-237 2000/800-843 5623), and **Saddleback** in Rangley (tel: 207-864 5671). Bethel is also home to several cross-country ski centers including: **The Bethel Inn Ski Center** (tel: 207-824 6276), **Carter's Cross Country Ski Centers** in Bethel and Oxford (tel: 207-539 4848), and **Sunday River Inn Ski Touring Center** (tel: 207-824 2410).

Other Nordic skiing spots include the **Harris Farm Cross Country Ski Center** in Dayton (tel: 207-499 2678).

FOR CHILDREN

Carousels

Massachusetts

Downtown Holyoke's **Heritage State Park** (tel: 413-538 9838) carousel dates back to 1929; rides still $1.

Rhode Island

The **Flying Horse Carousel** (Bay Street, Watch Hill; tel: 401-348 6007), with beautiful hand-carved horses, lays claim as the oldest merry-go-round in the country.

Connecticut

The Carousel (Bushnell Park, Hartford; tel: 860-246 7739) is a 1914 merry-go-round with hand-carved horses.

Museums

Massachusetts

In Boston, the **Children's Museum**, Museum Wharf, 300 Congress Street, Boston, tel: 617-426 8855 provides hours of hands-on fun for kids of all ages. There are hundreds of hands-on exhibits to spark the excitement of children aged three and up; and an Omni Theater, at The **Museum of Science** (Science Park at the Charles River Dam; tel: 617-723 2500). The **New England Aquarium** (Central Wharf, tel: 617-973 5200) is a world-class facility that supports serious marine research.

In Sandwich, on Cape Cod, the **Thornton W Burgess Museum** (4 Water Street; tel: 508-888 6870) is dedicated to the creator of Peter Rabbit and other children's books.

Connecticut

Children 10 and under will delight in the hands-on exhibits at **Stepping Stones Museum for Children** (303 West Avenue, Mathews Park, Norwalk; tel: 203-899 0606).

Children of all ages will enjoy the live animals and digital space and science show at the **Children's Museum** in West Hartford (950 Trout Brook Drive; tel: 860-231 2824)

Vermont

ECHO Lake Aquarium and Science Center (One College Street, Burlington, tel: 802-864 1848) teaches youngsters and "oldsters" about the lake's history and ecology.

New Hampshire

Montshire Museum of Science (Montshire Road, Norwich; tel: 802-649 2200) is small in scale, but

ABOVE: Boston's Franklin Park Zoo has more than 220 species of animals.

there's a lot to explore and discover in the natural and man-made worlds.

Maine

The highly interactive **Children's Museum of Maine** (142 Free Street, Portland; tel: 207-828 1234) will keep even the most boisterous youngsters occupied for hours – hauling in traps on a lobster boat, broadcasting the news, making stained glass, and more.

Bangor's new **Maine Discovery Museum** (74 Main Street; tel: 207-262 7200) has three floors of interactive, fun exhibits for kids.

Theme Parks

Massachusetts

Six Flags (1623 Main Street, Agawam; tel: 413-786 9300) is New England's largest theme park with more than 35 rides just for kids. **Whalom Park** (Route 13, Lunenburg; tel: 978-342 3707) has a waterslide, 50 carnival-style rides and a beach on Whalom Lake. Closed Mon.

Connecticut

Lake Compounce (822 Lake Avenue, Bristol; tel: 860-583 3631) is America's oldest amusement park.

New Hampshire

Children can explore caves carved by the Ice Age at **Lost River Gorge and Boulder Caves** (Route 112; tel: 603-745 8031) in North Woodstock. **Clark's Trading Post and the White Mountain Central Railroad** (Route 3, Lincoln; tel: 603-745 8913) has live bear shows, a family circus, and train excursions.

Christmas is alive all summer at **Santa's Village** (Route 2, Jefferson; tel: 603-586 4445), with rides and live reindeer. Next door, bumper boats, waterslides, and go karts are just part of the fun at **Six Gun City**

and **Fort Splash Water Park** (tel: 603-586 4592). Theme rides, shows, and storybook characters are all part of the fun at **Story Land** (tel: 603-383 4186), on Route 16 in Glen.

Maine

Palace Playland (Old Orchard Street, Old Orchard Beach; tel: 207-934 2001) features an old carousel and Ferris wheel and lots of other rides.

Seacoast Fun Park (tel: 207-892 5952) in Windham has a 100-ft (30-meter) free-fall ride, driving range, bumper boats, go karts, mini-golf.

A wooden roller coaster is one of the main attractions at **Funtown/Splashtown** (tel: 800-878 2900) on Route 1 in Saco. There's also a water park with slides, a tube river run and play area.

Train Journeys

Massachusetts

Berkshire Scenic Railway Museum, 10 Willow Creek Road, Lenox, tel: 413-637 2210, has train rides from May through October.

Connecticut

Naugatuck Railroad of New England (83 Bank Street, Waterbury; tel: 203-575 1931) offers a historic ride through Black Rock State Park.

Essex Steam Train (Railroad Avenue, Essex; tel: 860-767 0103) runs an old-fashioned service that can be combined with a riverboat ride.

In East Haven, ride vintage streetcars at the **Shore Line Trolley Museum** (17 River Street; tel: 203-467 6927).

New Hampshire

Winnipesaukee Railroad (S. Main Street, Weirs Beach; tel: 603-279 5253) runs historic coaches around the lake.

Conway Scenic Railroad (North

Conway; tel: 603-356 5251/800-232 5251) offers excursions from the 1874 station.

Mount Washington Cog Railway (tel: 603-278 5404) has the second-steepest railway track in the world.

Maine

Belfast & Moosehead Lake Railroad (Unity; tel: 207-338 2330/800-392 5500) operates two scenic trains: one passes along a river, another by villages. Children will particularly like the open-air cars.

Seashore Trolley Museum (Log Cabin Road, Kennebunkport; tel: 207-967 2800) offers a 4-mile (6-km) trolley tips aboard restored antiques.

Maine Eastern Railroad (tel: 866-637 2457) tours the mid-Coast with restored vintage cars.

Boothbay Railway Village (Route 27, Boothbay; tel: 207-633 4727) offers a short train ride through a re-created New England village; its museum houses an excellent collection of antique vehicles.

Dozens of antique steam locomotives, coaches and cars are housed in an historic waterfront building at **Maine Narrow Gauge Railroad** in Portland (58 Fore Street; tel: 207-828 0814); there's also a 3-mile (5-km) ride on a 2-ft narrow gauge train along Casco Bay.

Zoos

Massachusetts

In Boston, **Franklin Park Zoo**, Blue Hill Ave at Columbia Road, tel: 617-541 5466, has a free-flight aviary and African Tropical Rain Forest exhibit, along with animals including giraffes, gorillas, kangaroos and zebras.

Rhode Island

Roger Williams Park Zoo (Elmwood Avenue, Providence; tel: 401-785 3510), a 400-plus-acre (160-hectare) park with an antique carousel, tiny train, and lots of animals to keep the children entertained.

Connecticut

Beardsley Zoo (1875 Noble Avenue, Beardsley Park, Bridgeport; tel: 203-394 6565). North and South American animals, a carousel, and a New England farmyard petting zoo.

Maine

In Gray, rescue and rehabilitation are the focus at **Maine Wildlife Park**, with more than 25 Maine species (tel: 207-657 4977).

Acadia Zoological Park (Route 3, Trenton; tel: 207-667 3244) is small (just 15 acres/6 hectares) but it will occupy the kids.

S HOPPING

BEST BUYS

While shopping isn't usually the prime reason people visit New England, the region offers a large and diverse number of options ranging from giant malls to tiny shops selling homemade specialty foods including chocolates, maple syrup, salsas, and artisanal cheeses. Some retail giants, such as Maine's L.L. Bean, and the Vermont Country Store, have become tourist destinations in their own right. Several states, including Connecticut with its Wine Trail (www.ctwine.com), and Vermont with its Cheese Trail (www.vtcheese.com) have developed touring routes for visitors.

Boston, home to Pilgrims and, later, Boston's upper-crust Brahmins, has never been famous for high fashion. Legend has it that one day a woman strolling along Newbury Street passed by one of the local aristocracy and complimented her on her lovely hat. She asked where the lady had purchased it. The other woman haughtily replied, "we don't buy our hats, we have them." But fashions – and faces – have changed over the years, and retailers such as Saks Fifth Avenue, Neiman Marcus, Barney's New York, and Lord & Taylor have established outposts in the city, offering shoppers a wide range of upscale merchandise. The store that first became synonymous with bargains – Filene's Basement – closed its Washington Street location and resurfaced at 497 Boylston Street, but the colorful days of frantic shoppers shoving others aside to get at the fabulous bargains are past.

Today, New England's factory outlets are well known to bargain hunters. Once places where manufacturers sold discounted wares to employees, the modern concept of the outlets was born in the mid-1970s in Fall River, Massachusetts, when a local clothing maker opened the first retail outlet.

The concept – and business – mushroomed, and today the towns of Kittery and Freeport in Maine, and Manchester Center, Vermont, have converted themselves into giant outlet centers, vying to offer shoppers discounts on big names such as Reebok, Armani, Anne Klein, and Crate & Barrel.

Other sprawling outlet complexes have opened up throughout the region, including in Manchester and North Conway, New Hampshire, where the absence of a state sales tax makes the deals even sweeter.

In general, retail stores open Monday through Saturday between 9am and 10am and close between 5 and 6pm. Sundays, stores in malls and outlet centers open between 11am and noon. Although some close at 5pm, others, particularly those in malls, stay open Thursdays until 9pm, and, in many cases, also remain open later on other evenings.

All states except New Hampshire have a sales tax of 5–6 percent, but generally do not charge a tax on "small" clothing and footwear purchases. The amount in each state varies. Also, some cities such as Vermont's Burlington and Williston, add an additional 1 percent on top of the state tax.

Arts and Crafts Galleries

Painters, sculptors, potters, weavers, woodworkers – New England is home to many fine artists, some with studios tucked into renovated factory complexes, some working out of their basements, and others displaying their works in collectives. Crafts fairs such as the League of New Hampshire Craftsmen's (nhcrafts.org) show each August at Mount Sunapee, Vermont's Stowe Foliage Art and Craft Festival (craftproducers.com) in August, and Hildene Foliage Art and Craft Festival (hildene.org) in October, are a fine way to see the wares of local craftspeople.

Massachusetts

Many of Boston's largest galleries are on Newbury Street and in the Fort Point Channel area near South Station. Also try Tremont Street in the South End. The non-profit **Society of Arts and Crafts** at 175 Newbury Street (tel: 617-266 1810) sells high-quality crafts.

In the Berkshires are the **Berkshire Center for Contemporary Glass**, 6 Harris Street, West Stockbridge, tel: 413-232 4666; and **Great Barrington Pottery**, Route 41, tel: 413-274 6259, which sells pieces glazed in Japanese wood burning kilns.

The **Worcester Center for Crafts**, 25 Sagamore Road, Worcester, tel: 508-753 8183 houses one of America's oldest crafts complexes.

The north shore town of Rockport has more than two dozen art galleries, as does Northampton in western Massachusetts.

In Lowell, **Brush Art Gallery and Studios,** 256 Market Street, tel: 978-

459 7819, houses the studios of a dozen working artists.

On Cape Cod, head to Wellfleet and Provincetown and simply wander from gallery to gallery. Visitors can follow the **Arts & Artisans Trails** of Cape Cod, Martha's Vineyard and Nantucket (capeandislandsartsguide.com).

Rhode Island

Providence's Wickenden Street has numerous galleries, including **Alaimao Gallery** (301 Wickenden Street; tel: 401-421 5360) which specializes in prints, playbills, and posters. **OOP!** (339 Ives Street, and 220 Westminster Street) features a whimsical collection of crafts and jewelry.

Newport, too, has many fine galleries. **MacDowell Pottery** (220 Spring Street; tel: 401-846 6313) displays New England potters' work; and **Newport Scrimshanders** (14 Bowen's Wharf; tel: 800-635 5234) sells Nantucket lightship baskets.

Connecticut

"**SoNo**" (short for South Norwalk) has revitalized itself with art galleries, chichi cafés, and shops. Kent also has more than a dozen galleries.

In Hartford, The **Artists' Collective** (1200 Albany Avenue; tel: 860-527 3205) exhibits the arts and culture of the African Diaspora.

In Kent, the **Bachelier-Cardonsky Gallery** (10 Main Street; tel: 860-927 3129) exhibits works by some of the country's finest contemporary artists.

Dozens of pottery and crafts shops are located in the Litchfield Hills. On Route 128 in West Cornwall, visit **Cornwall Bridge Pottery and Store** (tel: 860-672 6545) and **Ingersoll Cabinetmakers** (tel: 860-672 6334). **O'Reilly's Irish Gifts** (248 Main Street, Farmington; tel: 860-677 6958) is the largest purveyor of Irish goods in the US.

Also worth a stop: **Brookfield Craft Center**, 286 Whisconier Road (Route 25), tel: 203-775 4526;

Woodbury Pewter Factory Seconds Outlet, 860 Main Street South, Woodbury. Route 6, tel: 800-648 2014; and **Wesleyan Potters**, 350 South Main Street (Route 17), Middletown, tel: 860-347 5925.

Vermont

Many artists exhibit their works in collectives and communal galleries, including: Montpelier's **Artisans Hand**, 89 Main Street, tel: 802-229 942; and **Bryan Memorial Gallery**, 180 Main Street, Jeffersonville, tel: 802-644 5100. **Frog Hollow State Craft Centers** (4716 Main Street, Manchester; Church Street Marketplace, Burlington, One Mill Street, Middlebury) show works by leading artists and craftspeople.

Bennington Potters (324 County Street, Bennington and 127 College Street, Burlington; tel: 802-447 7531) sells both first and-quality and bargain-priced seconds.

North Wind Artisans' Gallery (81 Central Street, Woodstock; tel: 802-457 4587) exhibits a variety of excellent work.

Luminosity Studios (Route 100, Waitsfield; tel: 802-496 2231) sells stained glass from a former church.

Other spots worth visiting include: **Danforth Pewter**, 52 Seymour Street, Middlebury, tel: 802-388 0098, and in Burlington, Manchester, and Quechee; Artist **Stephen Huneck's Dog Mountain Gallery & Dog Chapel**, 143 Parks Road, St Johnsbury, tel: 802-748 2700; **Vermont Artisan Designs**, 106 Main Street, Brattleboro, tel: 802-257 7044; and **Vermont Teddy Bear Company** (2236 Shelburne Road, Shelburne; tel: 802-985 3001), which sells rather expensive furry handmade creatures; kids can make their own bears.

New Hampshire

In Portsmouth: **New Hampshire Art Association-Robert Lincoln Levy Gallery** (136 State Street; tel: 603-

431 4230) exhibits paintings, photographs, and prints, while **Pierce Gallery** (105 Market Street; tel: 603-436 1988) offers New Hampshire and Maine coastal scenics.

The non-profit, state-wide **League of NH Craftsmen**; 32 Main Street, Center Sandwich, tel: 603-224 3375; nhcrafts.org, open mid-May–mid-Oct, represents some of the state's finest artists. There are also year-round locations in Concord, Hanover, Littleton, Meredith, North Conway, and Wolfeboro.

The **Sharon Arts Center**, 20-40 Depot Street, Peterborough; 603-924 2787 exhibits both a rotating show of regional and national artists and a juried gallery of 130 member artists. **Village Arts & Gallery**, 51 Main Street, Ashland, tel. 603-968 4445 represents more than 40 artists.

The **Artisan's Workshop** (in Sunapee Harbor and at 186 Main Street in New London; tel: 603-763 5226) sells local crafts.

Hampshire Pewter (43 Mill Street, Wolfeboro; tel: 603-569 4944) hand crafts pewter items and offers weekday tours.

The **Dorr Mill Store** (Hale Street; tel: 800-846 3677) in Guild is a national craft center for hand hooking, braiding, and wool quilting.

Maine

Students and teachers at the nearby **Haystack Mountain School for Crafts** show their work at 22 Church Street, Deer Isle, tel: 207-348 2306.

The **Maine State Prison Industries Store**, 358 Main Street, Route 1, Thomaston, tel: 207-354 9237, sells handicrafts made by prisoners. **Bayview Gallery** (75 Market Street, Portland; tel: 207-773 3007/ 800-244 3007) represents pre-eminent Maine artists. **Eclipse Gallery** (12 Mount Desert Street; tel: 207-288 9048) in Bar Harbor exhibits contemporary hand-blown glass, ceramics, and furniture.

There are galleries along Northeast Harbor's Main Street; clustered around the Farnsworth Museum in Rockland; and in downtown Ogunquit. Tiny Blue Hill has a thriving arts and crafts community. The **Leighton Gallery** (Parker Point Road; tel: 207-374 5001) houses three floors of contemporary art. On Main Street, **Handworks Gallery** (tel: 207-374 5613) and **North Country Textiles** (tel: 207-374 2715) carry excellent hand-made crafts. Don't miss **Rackliffe Pottery** (Route 172; tel: 207-374 2297) and **Rowantrees Pottery** (Union Street; tel: 207-374 5535).

Edgecomb Potters (Route 27; tel: 207-882 6802) and **Sheepscot River**

BELOW: shop while you stroll at Boston's popular Faneuil Hall Marketplace.

Pottery (Route 1; tel: 207-882 9410), both in Edgecomb, sell distinctive pottery.

China and Glass

Massachusetts

In the Berkshires, **Fellerman & Raabe Glassworks**, Main Street, Sheffield; tel; 413-229 8533, sells handmade glass. **The Berkshire Center for Contemporary Glass**, 6 Harris Street, West Stockbridge, tel: 413-232 4666, has glassblowers at work during the summer months.

At **Pairpoint Crystal**, Route 6 A, Sagamore; tel: 508-888 2344/800-899 0953, glassmakers use a variety of techniques developed in nearby Sandwich, world-renowned in the 1800s for innovative glassmaking.

Rhode Island

Watch glassblowers at work at **Thames Glass** (688 Thames Street, Newport; tel: 401-846 0576); make your own paperweight or Christmas ornament.

Vermont

The renowned **Simon Pearce** (Main Street, Quechee and Industrial Park, Windsor; tel: 802-295 2711) makes and sells first- and second-quality glassware and other fragile items; there is a fine restaurant in the Quechee complex.

Maine

Stained glass artist **Richard MacDonald** welcomes visitors to his studio at 7 Wall Point Road in Bar Harbor (tel: 207-633 4815.)

Stein Gallery Contemporary Glass (195 Middle Street, Portland; tel: 207-772 9072) make modern functional and decorative glassware.

The work of 100 of the country's finest glass artists is at **Prism Glass Studio & Gallery** (297 Commercial Street, Rockport; tel: 207-230 0061; Wed–Sun), where Patti Kissinger demonstrates glass blowing.

Destination Retailers

Massachusetts

Yankee Candle Flagship Store, 25 Greenfield Road, South Deerfield, tel: 877-636 7707, it's always Christmas at one of the region's most imaginative stores. Great for children.

Vermont

Vermont Country Store, flagship store at 657 Main Street, Weston, tel: 802-824 3184; also 1292 Rockingham Road, Rockingham, tel: 802-463-2224. Sells everything you ever needed, thought you needed, or didn't know you needed until you saw it.

The huge **Orvis** superstore (4200 Route 7A, Manchester; tel: 802-362 3750) has everything necessary to take to the great outdoors.

Maine

Kittery Trading Post, 301 US Route 1, Kittery; tel: 888-587-6246; outdoor outfitters since 1938.

The legendary **L.L. Bean Flagship Store** (95 Main Street, Freeport; tel: 800-441 5713), open 24 hours, is a paradise for outdoors enthusiasts. (Also stores in West Lebanon, NH, Burlington and Mansfield, Mass, and South Windsor, CT.)

Malls/Retail Stores

Massachusetts

In Boston, **Copley Place**, 100 Huntington Avenue, tel: 617 369-5000, has almost 100 upscale stores and restaurants. **Macy's**, 450 Washington Street, tel: 617-357 3000 anchors the pedestrian-only Downtown Crossing. **Faneuil Hall Marketplace**, North End, tel: 617 523 1300, one of the city's major tourist attractions, has more than 150 small shops and food stands, and sells everything from funky sportswear to Red Sox souvenirs.

Chic Newbury Street is the place for high fashions, with stores such as Brooks Brothers at no. 46 (tel: 617-267 2600) and Alan Bilzerian at no. 34 (tel: 617-536 1001).

The **Cambridgeside Galleria** (100 Cambridgeside Place, Cambridge; tel: 617-621 8666), is a three-story mall with over 100 shops. There's a free shuttle from Kendall Square MBTA Mon–Sat 9am–7pm, Sun noon–7pm.

Elsewhere in the state, the **Holyoke Mall**, just off I-91 in Holyoke, is one of the biggest in western Massachusetts. **Cape Cod Mall**, (Routes 132 and 28, Hyannis; tel: 508-771 0200) is a sprawling indoor complex.

Major retailers in the downtown Boston area include: **Barney's New York**, 5 Copley Place, tel: 617-385 3300; **Lord & Taylor**, 760 Boylston Street, tel: 617-262 6000; **Macy's**, 450 Washington Street, tel: 617-357 3000; **Neiman Marcus**, 5 Copley Place, tel: 617-536 3660; **Saks Fifth Avenue**, Prudential Center, tel: 617-262 6000; and **Louis Boston** (234 Berkeley Street; tel: 617-262 6100), one of Boston's oldest men's stores.

Rhode Island

In Providence, **The Arcade** (65 Weybosset Street; tel: 401-861 9150), the country's first indoor mall, built in 1828, is still a bastion of consumerism, although styles have

changed quite a bit over the years.

The **Warwick Mall,** 400 Bald Hill Road, Warwick, tel: 401-739 7500, houses many national chains.

Connecticut

Hartford Civic Center (1 Civic Center Plaza; tel: 860-275 6100) has more than 60 shops.

The **Danbury Fair Mall** (Backus Ave, off I-84, Danbury; tel: 203-743 3247) has 240 shops, including five department stores.

Olde Mistick Village (Exit 90 off I-95, Mystic; tel: 860-536 4941) has 60 Colonial-style shops.

West Farms Mall (tel: 860-561 3024) in Farmington has many upscale department stores.

Vermont

The state's largest malls are in Burlington. Macy's is the primary anchor in **Burlington Town Center** at 49 Church Street, tel: 802-658 2545, on the pedestrian-only Church Street Marketplace. Just off Route 2, Penney's, Kohl's and Bon Ton are at **University Mall,** 155 Dorset Street, South Burlington, tel: 802-863 1066.

New Hampshire

Shops fill Portsmouth's revitalized waterfront area near Market, Bow and Ceres streets.

The 19th-century **Colony Mill Marketplace** (222 West Street, Keene; tel: 603-357 1240) encompasses 33 stores.

The **Mall of New Hampshire** (1500 S Willow Street, Manchester; tel: 603-669 0433) has 88 shops and three department stores.

Steeplegate Mall, 270 Loudon Road, Concord, tel: 603-224 1523; and **Fox Run Mall**, 50 Fox Run Road, Newington, tel: 603-431 5911 are two of the state's largest.

Maine

Maine Mall (tel: 207-774 0303), 5 miles (8 km) south of Portland, has almost 150 stores, including large anchor department stores. The **Bangor Mall**, exit 49 off I-91, is the area's pre-eminent shopping area.

The Dock Square area in Kennebunkport is lined with upscale shops.

Portland's Old Port, a dense few blocks along Fore and Exchange Streets, is great place for browsing and buying.

Outlet Shopping

Discount men's, women's and children's clothing chains with branches throughout New England include **Marshall's, T.J. Maxx,** and **Filene's Basement**.

Massachusetts

Filene's Basement closed its doors on Washington Street in Boston and reopened at 497 Boylston Street, Boston (other locations in Watertown and Newton), tel: 617-424 5520.

There are major outlet complexes in Lee at **Prime Outlets**, 50 Water Street, Route 20, Lee; tel: 413-243 8186; and at **Wrentham Premium Outlets**, One Premium Outlets Boulevard, Wrentham, tel: 508-384 0600.

Connecticut

Clinton Crossing Premium Outlets, Route 81, Clinton, tel: 860-664 0700, and **Tanger Factory Outlet Center**, 314 Flat Rock Place, Westbrook; tel: 860-399 8656, are both multi-store complexes.

Vermont

The chic **Outlets of Manchester**, including stores such as Armani, Gap, and Bose are together, close to town.

Stock up on java at the **Green Mountain Coffee Factory Outlet**, 40 Foundry Street, Waterbury; tel: 802-882 2134 (closed Sunday).

The **Essex Outlet Mall** just off Route 15 in Essex is a densely concentrated collection of outlets which include Orvis and Brooks Brothers.

New Hampshire

Route 16 in North Conway, with more than 200 outlet stores (and no sales tax), is one of the region's premier shopping destinations.

There is also a complex in Tilton at **Tanger Outlet Center**, 120 Laconia Road, tel: 866-665 8683.

Seventy **State of New Hampshire Liquor Outlets** sell tax-free wines and liquors, many at bargain prices.

Maine

Major outlet shopping destinations include **Freeport** (Freeport Merchants Association, Freeport; tel: 800-865 1994) and **Kittery** (tel: 888-548 8370), anchored by the megalithic **L.L. Bean**, 95 Main Street, tel: 207-552 7772; llbean.com (also in: Bangor, Ellsworth and Portland, Maine; Orange, Connecticut).

Speciality Foods

Massachusetts

Vendors at Boston's historic **Haymarket**, near Faneuil Hall Marketplace, sell inexpensive , vegetables, fruit, meat and seafood Fri/Sat.

Organic meats and produce are sold at **Whole Foods Market**, 15 Westland Avenue, Boston, tel: 617-375 1010.

Cardullo's, 8 Brattle Street, Cambridge, tel: 617-491-8888

ABOVE: the Cambridgeshire Galleria.

displays New England's largest selection of chocolates and teas.

Verrill Farm, 11 Wheeler Road, Concord, tel: 978-369 4494 carries local cheeses, honey, cider, pasta, and ice cream.

Rhode Island

Del's Frozen Lemonade, the frozen treat first served in Cranston in 1948, is now available throughout New England.

Gray's Ice Cream, 16 East Road, Tiverton, tel: 401-624 4500 has been a popular stop for homemade ice cream for more than 80 years.

Close by, **Milk and Honey Bazaar**, 3838 Main Road, Tiverton, tel: 401-624 1974, sells more than 100 artisanal cheeses.

In Providence, homemade almond and hazelnut biscotti are specialties at **Scialo Brothers**, 257 Atwells Avenue, tel: 401-421-0986. **Gasbarro's** (361 Atwells Avenue; tel: 401-421 4170) sells one of – if not the – largest wine selections in the state. **Costantino's Venda Ravioli** (275 Atwells Avenue; tel: 401-421 9105) sells more than 50 varieties of fresh made pasta, as well as fresh baked bread and Italian cold cuts, and serve lunch Monday–Saturday.

Connecticut

Pick your own fruit and purchase fresh baked pies at **Lyman Orchards** (routes 147 and 157, Middlefield; tel: 203-869-349 1793) and at **Silverman's Farm**, 451 Sport Hill Road, in Easton, tel: 203-261 3306.

Romeo & Cesare Gourmet Shoppe, 771 Orange Street, New Haven, tel: 203-776 1614, is a great

place for Italian prepared foods, baked goods, cheeses, and deli fare.

Vermont

Although **Ben & Jerry's Ice Cream Factory**, Route 100, Waterbury, is now owned by the multinational Unilever, it still remains a big tourist attraction. For a schedule of daily tours daily; tel. 866-258 6877; charge for tour). To see ice cream being made, come on a weekday.

One of Vermont's premier cooperative cheese companies lets visitors sample their fine wares at the **Cabot Annex Store**, 2653 Waterbury-Stowe Road, Waterbury Center, tel: 802-244 6334.

Cider is made all year at **Cold Hollow Cider Mill**, 3600 Waterbury-Stowe Road, Waterbury Center, tel: 802-244 7212, where there's also a huge retail store.

Dakin Farm sells smoked meats, maple syrup, cheeses, and jams at 5797 Route 7 in Ferrisburgh, tel: 800-993 2546.

Samples are plentiful at the **Grafton Village Cheese Company** (tel: 800-472 3866), a part of the historic Grafton Village complex. Vermont's own **Green Mountain Coffee** has opened a **Visitors Center and Café** in the Train Station, Waterbury Village, tel: 877-879 2326.

Sugarbush Farm, 591 Sugarbush Farm Road, Woodstock, tel: 800-281 1757, is one of the state's many fine sugarhouses open for tours. They also make cheeses and homemade mustards. Call for directions.

New Hampshire

Granite State Candy Shoppe LLC, 13 Warren Street, Concord 03301; tel: 888-225 2531, has been making chocolates and confections since 1927.

Littleton Grist Mill (18 Mill Street; tel: 603-444 8489/999-284 8489), in a restored, waterwheel-powered 1798 working grist mill, sells fine crafts, gifts, and organically-grown whole grains and stone-ground flour.

Maine

Pick your own apples, wander through the corn maze, and watch cider being pressed at **Ricker Hill Orchards** (11 Ricker Hill Road, Turner; tel: 207-225 5552).

Rooster Brothers (29 Main Street, Ellsworth; tel: 800-866 0054) sells specialty foods, wine, cheeses, and fresh roasted coffee (closed Sun).

There are free samples at **Stonewall Kitchens**, (Stonewall Lane, York; tel: 207-351 2712), makers of sauces, preserves, condiments, toppings. Also in Portland and Camden.

A–Z

A HANDY SUMMARY OF PRACTICAL INFORMATION, ARRANGED ALPHABETICALLY

A Accidents, Emergencies 414

Alcohol 414

B Budgeting for a trip 414

C Childcare 414

Climate 415

Clothing 415

Credit Cards 415

Customs Regulations 415

D Disabled Access 416

Discounts 416

E Electricity 416

Embassies/Consulates 416

F Foliage 416

G Gasoline 416

Gays and lesbians 416

H Health and medical care 416

I Internet access 417

M Money matters 417

N Newspapers, magazines 417

O Opening hours 417

P Passports and Immigration 418

Pets 418

Postal services 418

Public holidays 418

R Radio stations 418

S Smoking 418

T Telephones 418

Television stations 419

Tipping 419

Tourist Information 419

W Websites 419

Weights and measures 419

What to read 420

A ccidents, Emergencies

For all emergencies, dial 911.
New England Poison Center (all states): tel: 800-222-1222.
Alcoholics Anonymous (to find a local meeting); tel: 212-870 3400; alcoholics-anonymous.org.
National Sex Assault 24/7 online hotline: rainn.org, or tel: 800-656-4673
Depression Hotline (suicide and depression in children and teens), tel: 800-448 3000.
Teen Crisis Hotline for Gay, lesbian, bisexual, transgender and questioning teens: tel: 866-488 7386.
National Suicide and Crisis 24/7 hotline: tel: 800-784 2433/800-273 8255.

Alcohol

The legal age for both the purchase and consumption of alcoholic drinks is 21. Liquor stores are state-owned or franchised in Vermont, New Hampshire and Maine; privately owned in southern New England. Laws on Sunday purchase vary between states.
Some restaurants have a license restricting them to serve only beer and wine. Restaurants without a liquor license usually permit customers to bring their own beer or wine (BYOB); some may charge a "corkage" or "set-up" fee. When driving, keep bottles of alcohol unopened and out of sight in the car.

B udgeting for a trip

Double room per night in a three-star hotel in high season: $160–$260; in a city, parking may be an additional $30–$40 per night.
Simple lunch for two (without alcohol, with tax and 15 percent gratuity: $30–$35.
Three-course dinner for two (without alcohol, with tax and 20 percent gratuity): $80–$120.
Car hire per week (excluding taxes and fees) $200.
Admission charges for two: about $50 per day.
Miscellaneous (drinks, taxis, etc): $75–$100 per day.

C hildcare

It's quite easy to travel in New England with children. There are hands-on museums, state and theme parks, and toy and book stores throughout the region; and, with proper planning, driving distances between destinations can be kept quite short.
Many restaurants offer children's menus, but some – particularly the more expensive – may not welcome young children at dinner. Lodgings generally welcome children and do not charge for those under 18, although may add on $10 or $15 for a cot or crib. It is quite common for country inns and B&Bs to have age restrictions, so be sure to check in advance.
Many hotel concierges will provide lists of local agencies which provide sitters; this can be quite costly, as the agencies charge a referral fee plus an hourly fee, but the sitters are carefully screened. Two agencies in Boston include: **Parents in a Pinch**, 45 Bartlett Crescent, Brookline, MA, tel: 617-739 5437; parentsinapinch.com; and **Boston's Best Baby Sitters**, 513 East Broadway, Boston, tel: 617-268 7148; bbbabysitters.com.
Laws in each state are quite specific about driving with children in

a car. If you are renting, be sure to tell the agency in advance how old your children are so that they will have the proper size car seats available, and check with them about state requirements.

● **STORES:** There are many excellent children's stores throughout the area. Standouts in the Boston area include **The Red Wagon** (69 Charles Street, Boston, tel: 617-523 9402), featuring classy clothes for kids under 10 and a large selection of shoes, toys, and books: **Calliope** (33 Brattle Street, Cambridge, tel: 617-876 4149), with an excellent selection of stuffed animals, toys, designer kids' clothing, and bibs designed by local artists; and **Curious George Goes to Wordsworth** (1 JFK Street, Cambridge, tel: 617-498 0062), one of the area's best book stores for both young children and teens, and a fun place for all ages.

Climate

New England's climate is as varied as its landscape, with large variations from state to state and from season to season:
Massachusetts Pittsfield in the west has an average annual temperature of around 7.2°C (about 45°F), while Boston in the east is about 10.8°C (about 51.5°C) and Nantucket about 9.7°C (49.5°F).
Rhode Island Summer temperatures are moderated by proximity to the ocean, but winters are quite cold. Providence has an average January temperature of about –2°C (about 28°F) and an average July temperature of about 22°C (about 72°F); Block Island has a mean January temperature of about –1°C (about 31°F) and a mean July temperature of about 21°C (about 70°F).
Connecticut Winters average just below freezing, and summers are warm and humid. Average yearly temperature along the coast is 10.6°F (51°F), while in the northwest it is 7.2°C (45°F); for most of the rest of the state the yearly mean is 8.3–9.4°C (47–49°F).
Vermont There are considerable variations in temperature depending on proximity to the mountains (which have heavy snows). St Johnsbury, in the northeast, has an average January temperature of about –8.1°C (about 17.5°F) and an average July temperature of about 20.8°C (about 69.5°F); Rutland, in the central part of the state, has a mean January temperature of around –5.8°C (about 21.5°F) and a mean July temperature of around 20.8°C (about 69.5°F).

CLIMATE CHART

Boston

▢ Maximum temperature
▢ Minimum temperature
— Rainfall

New Hampshire Concord has an average July temperature of about 21°C (around 70°F) and a mean January temperature of about –6°C (about 21°F); atop Mount Washington, on the other hand, the average July temperature is around 10°C (about 50°F) and the mean January temperature about –14°C (about 6°F). In April 1934, winds of 231 mph (372 kph) were recorded on the summit of Mount Washington.
Maine The coastal part of the state has a maritime climate. Winter temperatures are much milder than those inland; summer temperatures are cooler. Northern Maine, however, it is extremely cold with a high snowfall. In 1925, Maine's lowest recorded temperature of –44.4°C (–48°F) was observed. The south is the warmest part of the state.

Clothing

Clothing styles in New England vary from state to state, as well as from region to region. In New Hampshire, Maine, Vermont and the Berkshires in Massachusetts people tend to dress in casual clothes geared towards outdoor life, whereas attire in cities in Massachusetts, Connecticut and Rhode Island is more traditional.

To cover all occasions, bring a variety of clothing. For men, a jacket and tie, although not necessarily a suit, is standard dress for more formal restaurants and, at a few, may in fact be required; women have more latitude, in terms of pants versus dresses, but be warned that some urban or resort bars and nightclubs may ban jeans and T-shirts.

Some warm clothing, such as sweaters, jackets, and windbreakers, should be packed even during the summer, when evening temperatures tend to dip, especially in the

mountains and on the coast. Winters generally necessitate heavy outer-wear, including hats, scarves, gloves, and boots.

Credit cards

If your credit card is lost or stolen, report it to the company immediately. Visa's US emergency number: tel. 800-847-2911. For American Express cardholders, tel: 800-992 3404. American Express traveler's check holders: tel. 800-221-7282. For MasterCard: tel. 800-307 7309. To find phone numbers of other credit cards, call the toll-free directory at tel. 800-555 1212.

Customs regulations

Visitors aged 21 or over may bring the following to the US, providing they are staying in the country for at least 72 hours, and have not declared the same amounts within the past six months:
● 1 liter of duty-free alcohol
● 1,200 duty-free cigarettes, or 2 kg tobacco or 100 cigars (non-Cuban)
● Gifts worth $100 if non-US citizens or $800 if US citizens up to $10,000 in US or foreign cash, travelers' checks or so on; any more must be declared.
● Import of meat, seeds, plants, and fruit is forbidden.
For more information, contact US Customs: tel. 202/927-1770; customs.ustreas.gov.
When returning to your country from · the US:
Australian citizens: Australian Customs Service, tel: 1300/363-263; outside Australia, tel: 61 2 6275 6666; customs.gov.au.
Canadian citizens: the Canada Border Services Agency, tel: 800-461-9999 in Canada (24-hour computer information; live operators Mon–Fri 8am–6pm), or outside Canada, tel: 204-983-3500 or check their website: cbsa-asfc.gc.ca.
New Zealand citizens: New Zealand Customs Service, tel: 0800/428-786 or 04/473-6099; outside New Zealand, tel: 0064 9300 5399; customs.govt.nz.
UK citizens: HM Revenue & Customs, tel. 0845/010-9000 in the UK (8am–8pm Mon–Fri), or, outside the UK, tel: 44/2920-501-261; hmce.gov.uk.

D isabled access

Federal regulations have promoted handicapped accessibility, but the work is by no means complete. Many attractions, restaurants, and lodgings in New England have ramps and

TRANSPORTATION · ACCOMMODATIONS · ACTIVITIES · SHOPPING · A – Z facilities, but it's a good idea to check in advance.

Resources include: **Society for Accessible Travel and Hospitality**, 347 Fifth Avenue, Suite 610, New York, NY 10016; tel; 212-447 7284; sath.org; **Access-Able Travel Source**, tel: 303-232 2979; accessable.com, which provides information for disabled and mature travelers, and recommends travel agents who specialize in bookings for the disabled; and the comprehensive information website at **MossRehab**, mossresourcenet.org.

For access on public transportation throughout Boston, contact the **Massachusetts Bay Transportation Authority's Office for Transportation Access**, tel: 617-222 5976 or 800-543 8287 Mon–Fri or check their website: mbta.com.

Discounts

Apart from family passes, discounts are often available for disabled people, students, and senior citizens.
● **PASSES:** In Boston, **CityPass** ($44 adults; $24 children ages 3-11), good for nine consecutive days, saves 50 percent at six popular attractions: the Museum of Science, New England Aquarium, Skywalk Observatory, Museum of Fine Arts, Harvard Museum of Natural History, and John F. Kennedy Library & Museum. Passes are sold at all six venues. Call 888-330 5008 (8am–5pm Mon–Fri Mountain Time), or check citypass.com for details. The **GoBoston Card**, tel: 800-887 9103, gobostoncard.com, available for 1, 2, 3, 5 or 7 days, gives visitors unlimited access to more than 60 attractions as well as restaurant and shopping discounts, and excursions outside the city.

Many other cities with multiple attractions also offer combination rates: be sure to ask in advance of ticket purchase.
Entertainment.com publishes a thick book full of discounts of up to 50 percent, and two-for-one coupons at restaurants, lodgings, and attractions. If you're going to be in one area for any length of time, the book, sold on their website and in many bookstores, can be a good investment.
● **DISABLED PERSONS:** US citizens and permanent residents with disabilities can apply for a free lifetime pass (documentation required) to all US National Parks (nps.gov).
● **ACCOMMODATIONS:** Discounted lodgings and airfare are available on numerous websites including: hotwire.com; travelocity.com; sidestep.com;

priceline.com; and roomsaver.com. Discount hotel and motel coupons for last-minute hotel reservations are distributed free of charge at most interstate rest stops.
Information resources include:
American Automobile Association (AAA), aaa.org; **American Association for Retired Persons** (AARP), aarp.org; and **Student Advantage**, studentadvantage.com.
● **SENIORS:** Many businesses and attractions offer discounts of 10–15 percent to senior citizens; the qualifying age can range from 60 to 65, although ID is seldom requested. The **American Association for Retired Persons** (AARP), aarp.org, is an excellent resource. **Elderhostel** (tel: 877-426 7788; elderhostel.org) offers educational travel for seniors throughout New England (as well as in all 50 states and 90 countries. US and permanent citizens ages 62 and over can purchase a lifetime pass to all US National Parks (nps.org) for $10.
● **STUDENTS:** Both the **Student Advantage Card** (tel: 800-333 2920; studentadvantage.com) and the **STA Travel Discount Card** (tel: 800-781 4040; statravel.com) provides students with substantial discounts while traveling in the US.

E lectricity

Most wall outlets have 110-volt, 60-cycle, alternating current. If using European-made appliances, step down the voltage with a transformer and bring a plug adaptor as sockets are two-prong.

Embassies

For a listing of embassies in the US, log onto: embassy.org/embassies. For addresses of US embassies around the world, log onto: travel.state.gov.

F oliage

Fall in New England, when leaves turn color from green to brilliant shades of reds and yellows, is a glorious time of year. But varying weather conditions from year to year means that "peak foliage" time also varies, and even experts have difficulty predicting when the season will begin, peak, and end. The leaves begin to change earlier in the season in the north, and then move south. Because of the brilliance of nature's display, however, Fall is the busiest tourist time, particularly in Vermont and New Hampshire, and lodgings are often reserved a year in advance.

Foliage Hotlines:
Massachusetts: tel: 800-227 6277
Rhode Island: tel: 800-556 2484
Connecticut: tel: 888-288 4748
Vermont: tel: 800-837 6668
New Hampshire: tel:800-258 3608
Maine: tel: 800-777-0317
USDA Forest Service: tel: 800-354 4595

G asoline

One US gallon equals 3.8 liters or 0.85 Imperial gallons. Most cars accept "unleaded regular." Fuel remains relatively cheap by European standards. You can use credit cards to activate pumps at many stations.

Gays and lesbians

Boston has a vibrant gay community, as do, to a lesser extent, other cities and college towns. Northampton, Massachusetts, for instance, emerged as a lively enclave for lesbians in the late 20th century, and Provincetown on Cape Cod has long been one of the country's best known gay summer vacation spots. The Provincetown Business Guild (tel: 508-487 2313, 800-637 8696; ptown.org) is an excellent source of information.

Information concerning gay-oriented activities and businesses can be found in alternative weeklies such as northern Vermont's *Seven Days*; western Massachusetts' and Connecticut's *The Advocate*; and Boston's *Bay Windows*. and in the Boston and regional editions of *The Phoenix*. "One in Ten", broadcast Sundays 8–10pm on Boston's WFNX Radio (92.1 FM), is also a worthwhile source of information for the gay and lesbian communities.

A good in-town networking source, for those visiting Boston, is Calamus Books, 92B South Street, tel: 617-338 1931, calamusbooks.com.

H ealth and medical care

Most visitors to New England have no health problems during their stay: sunburn is the main nuisance for the majority. Even so, non-Americans should never leave home without travel insurance to cover themselves and their belongings. It's not cheap to get sick in the United States. Your own insurance company or travel agent can advise you on policies, but shop around, as rates vary. Make sure you are covered for accidental death, emergency medical care, cancellation of trip, and baggage or document loss.

Pharmacies stock most standard medication (though some painkillers that are available over the counter in other countries may be prescription-only in the US), and staff are trained to help with most minor ailments.

Hospitals are signposted on highways with a white H on a blue background. Major hospitals have 24-hour emergency rooms – you may have a long wait before you get to see the doctor, but the care and treatment are thorough and professional.

Walk-in clinics are commonplace in cities, where you can consult a nurse or doctor for a minor ailment without an appointment. If cost is a concern, turn first to clinics offering free or pro-rated care (look under "Clinics" in the Yellow Pages).

A couple of serious – and easily contracted – health hazards exist in the region:

● Lyme disease (borne by deer ticks hiding in high grass) is a potentially dangerous chronic condition. Starting with a rash, it develops into flu-like symptoms and joint inflammation, and possible long-term complications such as meningitis and heart failure. Precautions are in order, particularly along the coast (so far, it is not as common in the northern interior). When hiking in grass or brush, wear light-colored pants tucked into socks, and spray the clothing with an insecticide. Inspect your skin afterwards: if a tick has attached itself, it should be removed very carefully, using a tweezers or a special tick remover, sold at outdoor specialty shops. Place the tweezers as low on the tick's body as possible, and remove slowly and deliberately; tick mouth parts left in the skin can still deliver the infection. Disinfect the area with alcohol, and visit a doctor or clinic if a red rash begins to appear. A prompt course of antibiotics will halt the progress of the disease.

● Poison ivy causes only temporary discomfort, but this can be avoided by keeping an eye out for the shiny three-leaf clusters and washing immediately upon accidental contact. Camomile lotion is good for soothing the skin.

Tap water is safe to drink, but avoid stream water as it can cause giardia, an intestinal disorder spread by wild animal wastes. Use a filter or purification tablets, or boil water, when hiking or camping.

Internet access

Internet cafés, where you can retrieve email from your account, are increasingly popular. Most lodgings have service and will let you check for messages; larger

hotels often have business centers. Many public libraries have access, and will let you use their computers for free or a small fee. However, don't count on finding access in small towns. It's sometimes best to plan on faxing messages unless you are in a big city.

Money matters

Paper money is issued in $1, $2 (not commonly used), $5, $10, $20, $50 and $100 denominations.

Coins come in seven denominations: 1¢; 5¢ (a nickel); 10¢ (a dime); 25¢ (a quarter); 50¢ (a half dollar); gold-colored coins worth $1; and the silver dollar.

International visitors can exchange funds at exchange booths at Logan Airport: Sovereign Bank BCE Travelex Foreign Exchange (tel: 800-287 7362; travelex.com) booths are open daily at terminals B and E, and they have an office open daily at 745 Boylston Street in downtown Boston. There is a Bank of America Exchange at terminal C. All exchanges charge a processing, service, and/or administration fee.

Up-to-the-minute exchange rates are posted on x-rates.com and finance.yahoo.com/currency.

Banks are generally open Monday through Friday from 9am until 5pm. Some may remain open later on Thursdays and Fridays, and others may open Saturday mornings (but don't count on it).

ATMs are ubiquitous in all but the smallest of towns throughout New England, and although they charge a fee, are an extremely convenient way to get cash as you need it. Most merchants also accept credit cards; the most common are MasterCard and Visa. Be aware that most cards charge a fee of 3 percent for international transactions and don't convert at a favourable rate. The use of ATM debit cards is becoming increasingly widespread, which allows users to get cash back without paying a transaction or cash advance fee.

Traveler's checks are accepted by most businesses, although smaller establishments may be hesitant to accept, and make change, for larger denominations. When exchanging checks for cash, you will get the best rate at banks: hotels generally give a poor rate. Most financial establishments will charge a commission fee when cashing traveler's checks.

All states levy taxes on meals and accommodation, and all but

New Hampshire on all sales. When restaurants and hotels quote prices, these taxes are not normally included – so ask, as they can bump up the cost by up to 12 percent. Ticket prices for transport have the tax included.

Newspapers and magazines

As well as the US nationals such as *USA Today* and the financial *Wall Street Journal*, New England has many local newspapers, including the *Boston Globe* and the *Boston Herald*. Boston's free, weekly *Phoenix* has coverage throughout New England and includes the largest entertainment listings (also available on its website, thephoenix.com).

The *New York Times* is widely distributed in New England, and larger cities have their own dailies such as the *Hartford Courant* (Connecticut), the *Portland Press Herald* (Maine), and the *Burlington Free Press* (Vermont). Alternative papers, often with excellent events and entertainment listings, thrive in college towns. Foreign magazines and papers are sold on newsstands in the larger cities.

In western Massachusetts the *Springfield Republican* (repub.com) is the area's largest newspaper; the free, weekly *Valley Advocate* (valleyadvocate.com) is also an excellent resource for the Pioneer Valley.

Opening hours

Government, and most business, offices are open weekdays from 9am to 5pm. Most large retail stores open at 9am and stay open at least until 5pm; many stay open until 6pm, and often later on Thursday and Friday nights. Stores in malls generally open at 10am and close at 6pm Monday through Saturday, although many stay open later in the evening; on Sundays malls generally open at noon and close at 6pm.

Smaller shops throughout New England, particularly in tourist areas, are usually open in the summer from 10am until at least 5 or 6pm. But these hours vary tremendously with location and season, so be sure to call in advance.

Many museums are open daily from 10am to 5pm in the summer, but others are closed on Monday or Tuesday. Off-season hours will vary a great deal, particularly at attractions in smaller towns.

In larger cities many gas stations and convenience stores remain open 24 hours, as do those close to interstate exits.

P assports and visas

To enter the United States, most foreign visitors need a passport and many also need a visa. You may be asked to provide evidence that you intend to leave the United States after your visit is over (usually in the form of a return or onward ticket).

You may not need a visa if you are a resident of one of 27 countries that participate in the Visa Waiver Program (VWP) and are planning to stay in the US for less than 90 days. You must, however, log onto the Electronic System for Travel Authorization's unmemorably named website, esta.cbp.dhs.gov, at least 48 hours before traveling and provide personal information and travel details; either your application will be accepted (and will be valid for multiple visits over two years) or you will be told to apply for a visa. If you don't have internet access, you'll need to find someone who does.

Anyone wishing to stay longer than 90 days must apply for a visa in any case. This can be done by mail to the nearest US Embassy or Consulate. Visa extensions can be obtained in the US from the United States Immigration and Naturalization Service offices. Applications can be downloaded at travel.state.gov.

Canadian citizens traveling to the US by air or across the land border need a passport to enter the country.

The US Department of Homeland Security maintains a website at: dhs.gov/xtrvlsec.

● **HIV**: Travelers who are HIV-positive may not enter the US under the Visa Waiver Program. They must file for a visa. For information, log onto: travel.state.gov.

● **IMMUNIZATION REQUIREMENTS** Log onto travel.state.gov for a complete list of immunization requirements by country.

Pets

In recent years, travel with pets has become increasingly popular in New England, and some lodgings are now setting aside "pet-friendly" units. Many will charge a cleaning fee ranging from $25 to $35 a night; and some will request a damage deposit, returnable at the end of a stay provided the pet did no permanent harm. Pets are not permitted in restaurants, but are generally welcome at establishments with outdoor seating, providing the pet does not have to go through the restaurant to get in.

Some stores will permit pets. Burlington, Vermont, is particularly

ABOVE: Rural mailboxes: a classic design.

pet-friendly, and stores welcoming them have signs posted in their windows.

New Englanders are a pet-loving group in general, and know how quickly a car interior can heat up in summer. Do not leave your pet unattended in a car on a warm day, even with windows ajar. The heat can quickly cause brain damage or death, and at the least may cause a concerned passer-by to break your window to rescue your pet.

Postal services

There are post offices in most New England villages and towns. Opening hours vary between central big city branches and those in smaller places, but are generally open daily Monday through Friday, and Saturday mornings; hotel personnel can tell you when the nearest post office is open.

If you do not know where you will be staying in a particular town, you can receive mail simply by having it addressed to you, care of General Delivery, at the main office in that town – but you must pick up such mail personally (within 30 days). Check with postal officials about charges and the variety of mail-delivery services available.

Stamps may be purchased from vending machines installed in hotel lobbies, in shops and airports, and at bus and train stations. For domestic and international rates, log onto usps.com and click on "calculate postage."

To facilitate quick delivery within the US, include the five-digit zip code when addressing communications. Zip code information may be obtained from any post office or on: usps.com.

Public holidays

During the holidays listed below, some or all state, local and federal agencies may be closed. Local banks and businesses may also close on the following days:
● New Year's Day
● Third Monday in January: Martin Luther King's Birthday
● Third Monday in February: Presidents Day, marking Lincoln's and Washington's birthdays
● Third Monday in April: Patriots' Day (Massachusetts only)
● Last Monday in May: Memorial Day
● July 4: Independence Day
● First Monday in Sept: Labor Day
● Second Monday in October: Columbus Day
● November 11: Veterans Day
● Fourth Thursday in November: Thanksgiving
● December 25: Christmas Day

R adio stations

AM radio is geared toward talk, news and information programming. FM stations tend to offer specific music formats, such as country or classic rock. Red Sox games are broadcast on 68 stations throughout New England, anchored in Boston by WRKO-680 AM and WEEI-850 AM. New England Patriot games are aired on WBCN-104.1 FM.

National Public Radio, known for in-depth news coverage, classical music, and special programming, has affiliates throughout New England. Among them: 88.5 FM in western Massachusetts, 89.5 FM in southern Vermont, 89.7 FM in the Boston area, and 89.1 FM in Concord, New Hampshire. WBUR-90.9 FM is NPR's news source in Boston.

Other New England stations include:
Boston: WICN-90.5 FM, jazz and folk; WBZ-1030 AM, news radio (including traffic reports).
Rhode Island: WWLI-105.1 FM, light rock.
Connecticut: WWYZ-92.5 FM, country; WPLR-99.1, classic rock; WHCN-105.9, classic hits.
Vermont: WEZE-92.9 FM, rock and top 40; WIZN-106.7 FM, rock.
New Hampshire: WUNH-91.3 FM, University of New Hampshire's eclectic mix; WMWV, 93.5 FM, rock, blues, jazz, and swing; and WOKQ-97.5 FM, country.
Maine: WCLZ-98.9, classic rock, blues, and jazz; WBZN-107.3 FM, top 40.

S moking

The legal age in New England to buy tobacco is 18. Smoking is banned in most indoor public places and on transport. Some states ban smoking in restaurants; others specify non-smoking areas. Hotels have non-smoking rooms; many inns and B&Bs ban smoking.

T elephones

Although not as numerous as a few years ago, public telephones can still be found in hotel lobbies, restaurants, drugstores, street corners, garages, convenience stores, and other general locations. Local calls require a deposit of 50¢–$1 (change of quarters or less) before you dial the number. If your call lasts longer than three minutes, the operator will require an additional deposit to continue the call.

● For **emergencies**, dial 911; coins are not needed.

Long-distance call rates decrease after 5pm, going down still further after 11pm, and are lowest on weekends. Many countries can be dialed directly from New England, without operator assistance. For all specific information concerning telephone rates and conveniences, simply call the operator (0) and inquire. The charge for using a phone in your hotel room can vary greatly from one lodging to another: some will charge an access and per-minute fee even if you use a calling card; some may charge for local calls; and others will offer the service at no charge. This information is usually posted in your room.

If you are visiting from outside the US and your mobile phone plan does not cover international calls, consider renting one when you arrive. The cost is generally under $50 a week for unlimited incoming and outgoing calls. Providers in the US include: **All Cell Rental** (tel: 877-724 2355; allcellrentals.com); and **Travel Cell** (tel: 877-235 5746; travelcell.com).

● All 800, 877, 866, and 888 numbers are toll-free.

● To find if a business has a **toll-free number**, dial 1-800-555 1212 (this is a free call). For information dial: (1)-area code-555-1212. There is a charge for this service.

● Dial the following **area codes**, preceded by 1, when phoning from a different state or area:
Connecticut (Fairfield County, including New Haven) 203
Connecticut (New Haven, Greenwich, Southwestern region) 475
Connecticut (Fairfield County, outside New Haven) 860
Connecticut (Hartford, New London) 959

Maine 207
Massachusetts (Boston area) 617
Massachusetts (western) 413
Massachusetts (other areas) 508, 978, 351, 774, 857, 781, 339, 351
New Hampshire 603
Rhode Island 401
Vermont 802

Television stations

Flick through the channels on both TV and radio, and you'll experience the gamut of American life, from game shows to in-depth news. Most hotels receive the three major national networks (ABC, CBS and NBC), many cable networks including CNN, Fox, and ESPN (sports), and several premium movie channels including HBO. The Public Broadcasting System (PBS) has some of the better-quality programs.

Tipping

Tip appropriately (unless the service is poor) or it will be interpreted as an insult. For meals, hairdressers, bartenders, and taxi drivers, around 15 percent is the norm (20 percent for exceptional waiter service or if the bill is $100 or more). Don't tip on the tax portion of the bill.

Give a few dollars to the doorman if he performs a service such as hailing a cab, $1 per bag to the bellhop, and $1 to the parking attendant each time you use valet parking; housekeepers should get $2 per day.

Tourist information

The following state tourist agencies provide information on attractions, restaurants, lodgings, recreational options, and events. They can also refer you to local chambers of commerce, if required.

Connecticut
One Financial Plaza
775 Main Street
Hartford, CT 0610 3
Tel: 888-288 4748
ctvisit.com

Maine
State House Station 59
Augusta, ME 04333
Tel: 207-287 5711/888-624 6345
visitmaine.com

Massachusetts
10 Park Plaza, Suite 4510
Boston, MA 02116
Tel: 800-227 6277
massvacation.com

New Hampshire
Box 1856
Concord, NH 03302

Tel: 603-271 2665/800-386 4664
www.visitnh.gov
Rhode Island
315 Iron Horse Way, Suite 101
Providence, RI 02908
Tel: 800-556 2484
visitrhodeisland.com
Vermont
National Life Building
Montpelier, VT 05620
Tel: 802-828 3237/800-837 6668
www.travel-vermont.com
Information overseas: There is no American Tourist Office as such in the UK, US or Australia. Each state runs its own publicity campaigns.
Discover New England supplies telephone numbers and accommodation, plus maps of each state:
P.O. Box 3809,
Stowe, Vermont 05672, US
Tel: 802-253 2500
Fax: 802-253 9064
discovernewengland.org
There is a Massachusetts Office of Travel and Tourism in the UK at: c/o First Public Relations, Molasses House, Clove Hitch Quay, Plantation Wharf, York Place, London SW11 3TN. Tel: 020 7978 7429.

W ebsites

visitingnewengland.com
gonewengland.about.com
discovernewengland.org
visitnewengland.com
The above sites provide general information on visiting the region.
visitingnewengland.com Hotel, B&B, inns, motels, and resort reservations throughout the region.
roomsaver.com Print out discount coupons for same-day lodgings throughout the region.
511maine.com Road conditions (including travel advisories) in Maine, Vermont, and New Hampshire.
traffic.com Free, real-time information on road conditions and travel times.
newenglandweather.com Real-time weather reports.
highfield.com Southern New England weather report.
smartraveler.com Traffic reports (including up-to-the-minute camera coverage) of the Boston area.

Weights and measures

32°F = 0°C; 60°F = 15.5°C;
80°F = 26.7°C; 100°F = 37.8°C
1 US gallon = 0.83 Imperial gallon or
3.79 liters
1 mile = 1.6 km
1 inch = 2.54 cm
1 ft = 0.3048 meter
65 mph = 105 kmh
1 acre = 0.4 hectares
1 US pound = 0.45kg

TRANSPORTATION

ACCOMMODATIONS

ACTIVITIES

SHOPPING

A–Z

FURTHER READING

Not all the books cited are currently in print, but most can be easily tracked down on the web or, more adventurously, in New England's hundreds of second-hand bookshops. Publication data refers to the most recent editions, with year of original publication given in parentheses.

History and culture

● *Builders of the Bay Colony*, by Samuel Eliot Morison. Kessinger, 2004 (1930). New England's most celebrated historian tells the story of the men – and one woman –who gave New England its intellectual underpinnings.
● *A Week on the Concord and Merrimack Rivers, Walden, The Maine Woods, your Cape Cod*, by Henry David Thoreau. The Library of America, 1985. Thoreau's four greatest works describe his travels on foot and by canoe – and his sojourn at Walden Pond; detailed

Send Us Your Thoughts

We do our best to ensure the information in our books is as accurate and up-to-date as possible. The books are updated on a regular basis using local contacts, who painstakingly add, amend and correct as required. However, some details (such as telephone numbers and opening times) are liable to change, and we are ultimately reliant on our readers to put us in the picture.

We welcome your feedback, especially your experience of using the book "on the road". Maybe we recommended a hotel that you liked (or another that you didn't), or you came across a great bar or new attraction we missed.

We will acknowledge all contributions, and we'll offer an Insight Guide to the best letters received.

Please write to us at:
Insight Guides
PO Box 7910
London SE1 1WE
Or email us at:
insight@apaguide.co.uk

descriptions of mid-19th century landscape and people combine with the blunt, often ornery musings of an archetypal New England intellect.
● *Paul Revere and the World He Lived*, by Esther Forbes. Mariner, 1999 (1942). Biography at its best, not only humanizing the "Midnight Ride" icon, but bringing his era and surroundings vividly to life.
● *The Encyclopedia of New England*, Edited by Burt Feintuch and David H. Watters, Yale University Press, 2005. A magisterial compendium of New England persons, places, and accomplishments (in the same vein, look for the New England University Press's The Vermont Encyclopedia (2003, ed. by Duffy, Hand, and Orth, a very readable Green Mountain gather-all).
● *The Proper Bostonians*, by Cleveland Amory. Parnassus, 1984 (1947). Not satire or skewering, but a lighthearted yet near-anthropological study of a Brahmin elite with "grandfather on the brain."
● *Boston: A Topographical History*, by Walter Muir Whitehill; 3rd ed. revised by Lawrence R. Kennedy. Belknap Press, 2000 (1956). Whitehill, a former Boston Athenaeum director, chronicles the astounding physical expansion – mostly the work of pick and shovel – of a once-scrawny peninsula.
● *The Enduring Shore: A History of Cape Cod, Martha's Vineyard, and Nantucket* by Paul Schneider. Holt, 2001. Natural and social history, with an emphasis on human impact on a fragile, ultimately ephemeral environment.
● *The Outermost House: A Year of Life on the Great Beach of Cape Cod* by Henry Beston. Holt, 2003 (1928). Beston's classic rivals Thoreau's Walden as an account of a year of blissful solitude in the loveliest of natural surroundings.
● *String Too Short to Be Saved: Recollections of Summers on a New England Farm* by Donald Hall. Nonpareil, 2001 (1961). A poet's warm, elegiac recollections of life on his grandfather's small New England farm in the 1940s.
● *The Survival of the Bark Canoe*, by John McPhee. Farrar, Straus and

Giroux, 1982 (1975). An account of a Maine river trip in a modern bark canoe, interwoven with the story of an uncompromising New Englander who builds the timeless craft.
● *The Lobster Chronicles: Life on a Very Small Island*, by Linda Greenlaw. Hyperion, 2002. New England's iconic fishery, seen from the inside by one of the first women captains to break a famously rigid gender barrier.

Landscape, natural history

● *A Guide to New England's Landscape* by Neil Jorgensen. Clarkson Potter, 1988 (1971). Written in layperson's English, a comprehensive look at how today's mountains, lakes, farmland, and coastline evolved in deep and recent geological time.
● *These Fragile Outposts: A Geological Look at Cape Cod, Martha's Vineyard and Nantucket* by Barbara B. Chamberlain. Parnassus, 1982 (1964). The quite recent phenomenon of the creation of the Cape and Islands, and their likely geological future.
● *Hands on the Land: A History of the Vermont Landscape* by Jan Albers. MIT Press, 2000. The story of human interaction with the land the glaciers left – a never-easy process that yielded a remarkably beautiful balance between the natural and built environments.
● *In Season: A Natural History of the New England Year*, by Nona Bell Estrin. University Press of New England, 2002. In a region with some of the world's sharpest seasonal divisions, the drama of life's winter ebb and summer flow.

Architecture

● *Cityscapes of Boston: An American City through Time* by Robert Campbell and Peter Vanderwarker. Mariner, 1994. Paired photographs show the same Boston locations past and present; accompanying text describes the city's transition.
● *Houses of Boston's Back Bay: An Architectural History, 1840–1917*, by Bainbridge Bunting. Belknap, 1999

(1967). A social as well as an architectural history, this amply illustrated book describes the evolution – and living style – of Boston's fist planned neighborhood.
● New England's Architecture, by Wallace Nutting, Tina Skinner and Tammy Ward, eds. Schiffer, 2007. A fine collection of sketches and photographs drawn from books on the architecture of individual New England states by the late antiquarian Nutting, who pioneered the preservation of the region's vintage homes and furnishings.

Fiction

● Writing New England: An Anthology from the Puritans to the Present, Andrew Delbanco, ed. Belknap, 2001. This carefully chosen collection of New England authors represents nearly four centuries of the region's intellectual development.
● Boston, by Upton Sinclair. Classic, 1999 (1928). The great muckraker's fictionalization of the Sacco-Vanzetti case, Boston's 1920s cause celebre involving foreign anarchists and the Brahmin-led establishment.

● The Last Puritan: A Memoir in the Form of a Novel, by George Santayana. MIT Press, 1995 (1935). The renowned philosopher's only novel, a case study of Puritanical high-mindedness as it weighs down oppressively on the life of its 20th-century protagonist.
● The Late George Apley by John P. Marquand., Bck Bay Books, 2004 (1936). A deft and wry portrayal of a Brahmin trapped within his class, as its grip on Boston weakens.
● The Last Hurrah by Edwin O'Connor., Amareon Limited, 2001 (1956). The ethnic-based machine politics of 20th-century Boston shape the career of a protagonist based on Boston's roguish Mayor James Michael Curley.
● Northern Borders, by Howard Frank Mosher. Mariner, 2002 (1995). A coming-of-age tale, set among Mosher's vanishing breed of back-country Vermonters equally at home with sawmills and Shakespeare.
● The Beans of Egypt, Maine by Carolyn Chute. Grove Press, 2008 (1984). The L.L. variety, these Beans inhabit a poor, hardscrabble inland Maine that few outsiders ever encounter.

Other Insight Guides

Companion **Insight Guide** titles cover every major travel destination in North America, from Alaska to Arizona. City titles include Boston, New York, Philadelphia, Chicago, Orlando, Miami, San Francisco, and Washington DC. Regional titles include New England, USA: On the Road, and The New South.
These are complemented by a comprehensive range of easy-fold **Insight FlexiMaps**, laminated to make them durable and waterproof, and containing useful travel details. Local titles include Boston.
Two compact series cover a range of US destinations:
● **Insight Step by Step Guides** provide precise itineraries and recommendations from a local, expert writer for dining, lodgings and sightseeing; titles include Las Vegas, New York and Orlando.
● **Insight Smart Guides** are packed with information, arranged in a unique and easy accessible A–Z format. Titles include Boston, Hawaii, Las Vegas, New York, Orlando, and San Francisco.

WHAT TO SEE: MOVIES SET IN NEW ENGLAND

● Revolutionary Road (2008), based on the Richard Yates novel, depicts the disaffections of striving Connecticut suburbanites in the 1950s.
● The Departed (2006) is Martin Scorsese's Oscar-winning take on the Boston underworld. Jack Nicholson's character was allegedly based on fugitive gangster Whitey Bulger.
● Mystic River (2003), director Clint Eastwood's retelling of the Dennis Lehane novel, examines lives tightly intertwined in an working-class Irish Boston neighborhood.
● The Perfect Storm (2000), starring George Clooney and based on the real-life Andrea Gail tragedy, is a paean to the 10,000 Gloucester men who have lost their lives in the North Atlantic fishery.
● A Stranger in the Kingdom (1998), a retelling of an early Howard Frank Mosher novel, examines a racial incident in a small Vermont town.
● Where the Rivers Flow North (1994) features Rip Torn in a Howard Frank Mosher tale of fierce Yankee independence run to ground in 1920s Vermont.
● Dead Poets Society (1989), set in a New England prep school, centers on Robin Williams' performance as an inspiring English teacher.

ABOVE: Mark Walberg and George Clooney greet The Perfect Storm.

● The Bostonians (1984), an elegant Merchant-Ivory production, screens Henry James's tale of propriety's clash with social activism in the 19th-century Hub.
● On Golden Pond (1981), filmed at New Hampshire's Squam Lake, was Henry Fonda's final role, as crusty Yankee professor Norman Thayer.
● Jaws (1975), the Spielberg shark-shocker, is set in a fictional resort but was filmed on Martha's Vineyard.
● The Last Hurrah (1958), a political drama based on the career of Boston Mayor James M. Curley, features Spencer Tracy as a master of machine politics.
● Peyton Place (1958), perhaps tame today, shocked midcentury America by "taking the lid" off a prim New Hampshire town; novel author Grace Metalious did live in the Granite State so people suspected there was truth to the scandals.
● Northwest Passage (1940) features Spencer Tracy as French-and-Indian War hero Major Robert Rogers, in one of cinema's better New England historical dramas; they even got the geography right.

ART & PHOTO CREDITS

INDEX

Numbers in italics refer to photographs

A

Abenaki tribe 32, 340
Acadia National Park 355–8
accommodations 373–98
activities 226, 299, 399–409
Adams, John 78, 111, 152, 153
Adams, John Quincy 152, 218
Adams, Samuel 42, 44, 105, *111*, 113, 149
African-Americans 24–5, 101, 116–17, 173, 177, 286
Agawam, MA 194
agriculture, 45–6, 53, *see also* farms
Alcott, Louisa May 116, 149–150, 186
Algonquin tribes 22, 32–3, 34, 36, 37, 178
Allagash Wilderness Waterway 360
Allen, Ethan 238, 272, *290*, 291
America's Cup Hall of Fame 220
America's Stonehenge 313
Amesbury, MA *136*, 137
Amherst, MA 74, 196–7
amusement parks *see* theme and amusement parks
Ando, Tadao 87, 207
antiques 19, 138, *197*, 244, *251*, 252, 274, 312, 317
Appalachian Gap 282
Appalachian Trail 9, 226, 243, 245, 323, 407
aquariums 108–9, 171, 253, 259, 290, 350
architecture 82–7
Arlington, VT 297–8
armories 188, 192–3
art museums and collections
  Aldrich Contemporary Art Museum 251
  Art Complex Museum 154
  Arthur M. Sackler Museum 87, 126
  Bennington Museum 74, **298**
  Berkshire Museum 205–6
  Bowdoin Museum of Art 347
  Brattleboro Museum & Art Center, 273
  Busch-Reisinger Museum 126
  Cahoon Museum of American Art 170
  Cape Ann Museum 139
  Cape Cod Museum of Art 163
  Carpenter Center for the Visual Arts 87, 125
  Center for Maine Contemporary Art 353
  Cornish Colony Museum 276
  Currier Museum of Art 314
  DeCordova Sculpture Park 147
  Eric Carle Museum of Picture Art 197
  Farnsworth Art Museum & Wyeth Center 352
  Florence Griswold Museum 257
  Fogg Museum (Harvard) 125–6
  Hood Museum of Art 319
  Institute of Contemporary Art 87, 109–110
  Isabella Stewart Gardner Museum 121–2
  Lyman Allyn Art Museum 258
  Massachusetts Museum of Contemporary Art 207
  Mead Art Museum 197
  Michele and Donald D'Amour Museum of Fine Arts 193
  Middlebury College Museum of Art 293
  Museum of African Culture 345
  Museum of Fine Arts *14–15*, 46, **121**
  National Museum of American Illustration 223
  New Britain Museum of American Art 250–51
  Norman Rockwell Exhibition 297
  Norman Rockwell Museum 203
  Ogunquit Museum of American Art 342
  Portland Museum of Art 345
  Provincetown Art Association & Museum 166
  Rhode Island School of Design Museum 217
  Robert Hull Fleming Museum 290
  St Johnsbury Athaeneum 285
  Shelburne Museum 9, **291**
  Sloane-Stanley Museum 245
  Smith College Museum of Art 195
  Sterling and Francine Clark Art Institute 9, 87, **206–7**
  Thorne-Sagendorph Art Gallery 317
  University of Maine Museum of Art 360
  Wadsworth Atheneum of Art 46, 239
  Wendell Gilley Museum 358
  Whistler House Museum of Art 146
  William Benton Museum of Art 247
  Williams College Museum of Art 206
  Worcester Art Museum *188*, 189
  Works Progress Administration murals 253
  Yale Center for British Art 255
  Yale University Art Gallery 255
artists' colonies 138, 167, 203, 252, 276, 311, 316
artists' studios and galleries, 118, 166, 174, 179, 284, 316, **410–12**, *see also* crafts
Ascutney Mountain Resort, VT 276
Ashintully Gardens 203–4
Ashley Falls, MA 200
Augusta, ME 363

B

Bangor, ME 71, 359–60
Bar Harbor, ME 357
Barnstable, MA 163
Barre, VT 280
Bartholomew's Cobble 201
Bartlett Arboretum 252
baseball 75, 122
Bash Bish Falls State Park 202
basketball 75, 122, 192
Bath, ME 50, 348
Battle of Bennington 298, 314
Battle of Bunker Hill *29*, *43*, 105, 108
Battle of Concord 43, 149, 150, 317
Battle of Lexington *42*, 148–9, 317
Battle Road 148
Battleship Cove 156
Baxter State Park 335, **360**, *361*
beaches
  Cape Cod *11*, *20*, 164–5, *166*, 167, 168, 169
  Connecticut 11, 254, *255*, 257, 258
  Crane's Beach, MA *4*, 11, 137
  Maine 341, 342, 343, 348, 349, 361
  Martha's Vineyard 171, 174
  Nantucket 176, 180
  New Hampshire 309, 312, 321
  Plum Island, MA 11, **136–7**
  Rhode Island 11, *213*, 215, 225, 228, 229
Bean, L.L. (Freeport, ME) 346, *347*
Bear Swamp Reservation 208
Beardsley Zoo 254
Beavertail State Park 225
Becket, MA 204
beer 78, 247, 276
Belfast, ME 354
Bellows Falls diner, VT *81*
Ben & Jerry's Homemade Ice Cream Factory, VT 9, **282**
Benjamin, Asher 85–6
Bennington, VT 74, 298
Berkshires 200–208, *226*
Bethel, VT 299, 362
biking 164, 219, **226**, 228, 275, 404–5
birds 136–7, 163, 168, 190, 229, 288, *316*, 335
Blackstone River Valley 187, *189*, 219
Block Island, RI 60, *210–211*, 225, 228–9
Blue Hill, ME 355
Boothbay Harbor & Railway Village, ME 349–50
Boston & Maine Railroad 299
Boston, MA *30*, *34*, 44, 45, *49*, 50, 51, 72, *92–3*, **101–133**, 181
  architecture 84–5, 86–7
  Athenaeum 46, *113*

Back Bay *23*, 50, 117–18
Bay Village 113
Beacon Hill 50, 85, *101*, 115
Black Heritage Trail 101
Boston Center for the Arts 120
Boston Common 114, *203*
Boston National Historical Park Visitors Center 108
Bunker Hill Monument *105*, *108*
Charles River 122–3, 226
Charles Street & Meeting House 117
Charlestown & Navy Yard 72, 107
Cheers Bar 78
Chestnut Street 116
Children's Museum 109
Chinatown 101, 112
Christian Science Center 87, 119
City Hall *51*, 111
Commonwealth Avenue 117–18
Copley Place & Square 118, 119–20
Copp's Hill Burying Ground 107
Custom House Tower *110*
Downtown Crossing 112
Faneuil Hall 86, *103*, 110, *111*
Fenway Park 122
Freedom Trail 101, *102–5*
Gibson House Museum 118
Government Center 111
Harbor & Islands 57, **108**, 153
Harrison Gray Otis Houses *19*, 85, 116, 117
Hatch Memorial Shell 123
Haymarket Square 111
Institute of Contemporary Art (ICA) 87, 109–110
Irish Famine Memorial *112*
Isabella Stewart Gardner Museum 9, **121–2**
John F. Kennedy Presidential Library & Museum 123
John Hancock Tower 87, *120*
King's Chapel 113
Louisburg Square 116
Mapparium 119
Museum of African-American History 116–17
Museum of Fine Arts *14–15*, 46, 121, **132–3**
Museum of Science 9, **122–3**
New England Aquarium 108–9
New England Holocaust Memorial *111*
Newbury Street 118
Nichols House Museum 116
North End 101, 106
Old City Hall 113
Old Corner Bookstore *103*, 111
Old Granary Burying Ground *105*, 113
Old North Church *105*, 106–7
Old South Meetinghouse *105*, 111–12
Old State House *45*, *103*, 111
Opera House 112
Park Street Church 114
Paul Revere House *104*, 106
Prudential Tower *92–3*, 118
Public Garden 114–15, *114*

Public Library 46, *73*, 87, 107, **119–20**
Quincy Marketplace 86, 110
shopping 110, 111, 118
South End 120–21
State House *85*, *115*
Symphony Hall 121
Theater District 112
Trinity Church *87*, 120, *121*
University 107
USS *Constitution* *44*, *104*, 107
Wang Center for the Performing Arts 112–13
Waterfront *53*, 108–110
Boston Brahmins 24, 46, 70, 106
Boston Celtics 75, 122
Boston College 74, 75
Boston Landmarks Orchestra 123
Boston Marathon 75
Boston Marine Society 107
Boston Massacre *41*, 42, 103, 105, 106, 111, 113
Boston Pops Orchestra 11, 46, 121, 123, 204
Boston Red Sox *31*, 75, 122
Boston Symphony Orchestra 11, 46, 107, 121, 204
Boston Tea Party 42, 105, 106, 109
Bourne, MA 161
Bowdoin College, ME 74, 347
Brandon, VT 293
Branford, CT 256
Brattleboro, VT 272–3
Bread Loaf Mountain 293
Brenton Point State Park 225
Bretton Woods, NH 328–9, *331*
Brewster, MA 163–4
Bridgeport, CT 254
bridges, 150, 159, 207, 208, *225*, 279, 354, *see also* **covered bridges**
Bristol, CT 243
Bristol, RI 220
Broad Meadows Brook Wildlife Sanctuary 189
Brodie Mountain ski area, MA 206
Bromley Mountain ski area, VT 297
Brookfield, VT 279
Brown University 46, *73*, 217–18, *218*
Brownington, VT 286
Brownsville, VT 276
Brunswick, ME 347–8
Bucksport, ME 354
Bulfinch, Charles 84–5, *103*, 115–16, 125, 238, 363
Bulls Bridge Scenic Area 245
Burgess, Thornton 162
Burke Mountain ski area, VT 285, *286*
Burlington, VT 10, **289–90**
butterflies 189, 197
Buzzards Bay 161, 164

C

Cabot, John 33
Cabot, VT 284
Cabot Annex Store, VT 282

Cadillac Mountain 357, 358
Calendar Islands 344
Cambridge, MA, 10, 72, **124–7**
Camden, ME *88–89*, 353, *365*
Camden Hills State Park 353
candle-making 197, *198*
Cannon Mountain ski area, NH 326
canoeing **226**, 245, 360, 405–6
Canterbury, CT 247
Canterbury Shaker Village, NH 47, 315
Cape Ann, MA 138
Cape Cod 20, 23, 34, *54–5*, 59, 76, **158–71**
Cape Cod Canal 158–9
Cape Cod Central Railroad 164, 169
Cape Cod Melody Tent 168
Cape Cod National Seashore 60, 158, **164–5**
Cape Cod Rail Trail 164
Cape Cod School of Art 166, 167
Cape Elizabeth, ME *132–3*, 343
Cape Poge Wildlife Refuge 174
Cape Porpoise 343
Captain's Cove Seaport 254
Carle, Eric 197
Carnegie, Andrew 205
carousels 153, 156, 162, *173*, *194*, *218*, 229, 243, 408
Carrabassett Valley, ME 299
Carson, Rachel 343
casinos 23, 219, 252, **261**, 402
Cassatt, Mary 133, 243
Castine, ME 354
Cathedral of the Pines (Rindge, NH) 316
Center Sandwich, NH 321
Chapel Brook Reservation 208
Chappaquiddick Island 174
Charlemont, MA 207
Charles W. Morgan **(ship)** *7*, *12–13*, 39, 58, *259*
Charlestown, NH 318
Charlestown, RI 229
Charlotte, VT 32, 292
Chatham, MA 168
cheesemaking *79*, 275, 284–5, 292
Chester, CT 248–9
Chester, VT 275
Chesterfield Gorge 318
Chesuncook, ME *340*, 360
Chichester, NH 312
children 408–9, 414–15
Chilmark Center 174–5
Choate Island 137
Christiantown, MA 175
churches and meetinghouses 83
    African American Meeting House (Nantucket, MA) 177
    Cathedral of the Pines (Rindge, NH) 316
    Charles Street Meeting House (Boston, MA) 117
    Christian Science Center (Boston, MA) 87, 119
    Community Church (Dublin, NH) *317*

Dog Mountain chapel (St Johnsbury, VT) *285*
First Congregational Church (Litchfield, CT) *243*
First Congregational Church (Nantucket, MA) 177
First Unitarian Universalist Society Church (Burlington, VT) *290*
King's Chapel (Boston, MA) 113
Mary Keane Chapel (Enfield, NH) 318
Meeting House of the First Baptist Church in America (Providence, RI) 216
Memorial Church (Harvard) 125
Methodist Meetinghouse (Sandwich, NH) 321
MIT Chapel (Cambridge, MA) 87, 124
Old First Church (Bennington, VT) 74, 298
Old Indian Meetinghouse (Mashpee, MA) 170
Old Narragansett Church, RI 227
Old North Church (Boston, MA) *105*, 106–7
Old Ship Meetinghouse (Hingham, MA) 83, 152
Old South Meeting House (Boston, MA) *105*, 111–12
Old Whaling Church (Edgartown, MA) 173
Our Lady of Good Voyage Church (Gloucester, MA) 139
Park Street Church (Boston, MA) 114
Quaker Meetinghouse (Nantucket, MA) 177
Rockingham Meetinghouse, VT 275
St James Episcopal Church (Great Barrington, MA) 202, 204
Seamen's Bethel (New Bedford, MA) 156
Shrine of Our Lady of Grace (Colebrook, NH) 329–30
Touro Synagogue (Newport, RI) 221
Town House (Strafford, VT) 279
Trinity Church (Boston, MA) 87, 120, *121*
Trinity Episcopal Church (Newport, RI) 222
Union Chapel (Oak Bluffs, MA) 173
United Church of Christ (Keene, NH) 317
Weathersfield Meetinghouse, VT *268–9*
West Parish Meetinghouse (Barnstable, MA) 163
cider 78, 283
cinema 399
Civil Rights 25, 53
Civil War 26, 46, 288–9
clams 61, 76, 79, 138
Cliff House Resort & Spa (York, ME) 343
climate 415
Coatue-Coskata Wildlife Refuge 180

codfish 44, 52, 57, 58, 61, 76–7, 106, 115
Colebrook, NH 329–30
colleges 10, 46, 51, 63, 64, **72–4**, 75
Columbia Falls 358
Comstock, Ferre & Co. 250
Conanicut Island, RI 225–7
Concord, MA *19*, 43, 148, **149–50**
Concord, NH 314–15
Connecticut Firefighters Memorial 246
Connecticut River 192–8, 238, 247–8, 308
Connecticut River Valley 272–6, 318–19
Connecticut Wine Trail 243–4
Conway, NH 323, 325
Conway Scenic Railroad, NH 323
Coolidge, Calvin 8, 195, **278**
Copley, John Singleton 133, 189
Cornish, NH 318
Cos Cob's Bush-Holley Historic Site 252
Cotuit, MA 170
Coventry, CT 247
covered bridges 201, *245*, 274, 278, 279, **294**, *317*, 362
  Windsor-Cornish bridge 276, *294*, *306*, 318
crabs 61, 79
crafts 118, 120, 195, 197, 315, 320, 321, 355
  Vermont 272, 276, 278, 293
The Craftsburys, VT 286, *300*
cranberries 77, 165, *178*, 180
Cranberry Isles, ME 357, 358
Crane Wildlife Refuge 137
Crawford Notch State Park 323, 328
cruises 407–8
Cummington, MA 208
Cushing, ME 352
customs regulations 415

D

Danbury, CT 251
dance *11*, 204
Dartmouth College 46, 73–4, 319
Dawes, William 42, 105
Deep River, CT 248–9
Deer Isle, ME 354–5
Deerfield, MA 83, 197–8
Deerfield River 198, *200*, *207*, *208*, 226
Dennis, MA 163
Depression years 50
Desert of Maine 346–7
Dickinson, Emily 68, 196, *197*
diners *80–81*, 189
Dinosaur State Park *250*
disabled access 415–16
Dixville Notch State Park 330
Dorset, VT 297
Dover, MA 311–12
Dresden, ME 349
Dublin, NH 317
dune shacks 167
Duxbury, MA 153–4

E

Eagle Island, ME 344
East Bay, RI 220
East Burke, VT 285
East Granby, CT 247
East Haddam, CT 249
East Haven, CT 256
East Providence, RI 218
Eastern States Exposition 9, **194**
Eastham, MA 164
eating out 79, *80–81*
Echo Lake Beach 358
Edgartown, MA 171, 173–4
Edgecomb, ME 349
education 51, 53, 64, **72–4**
Emerson, Ralph Waldo 64, *67*, *103*, 150, 283
Enfield, NH 318
Equinox Resort & Spa, VT 295–6
Essex, CT 248, *263*
Essex, MA 138
Essex, VT 291
ethnic groups 22–7, 79
Exeter, NH 312–13
Exhibition Whydah 167

F

fairs *see* **festivals and fairs**
fall foliage *201*, 202, 322, **324**, 325, 416
Fall River, MA 156
Falls Village Heritage State Park 245
Falmouth, MA 170, *171*
Farmington, CT 242–3, *263*
farms 64, 79, *270*
  Billings Farm & Museum (Woodstock, VT) 38, 277
  Casey Farm (Saunderstown, RI) 227
  Choate Island, MA 137
  Drumlin Farm (Lowell, MA) 148
  Dudley Farm (Guilford, CT) 257
  Manisses Farm (Block Island, RI) 229
  National Estuarine Research Reserve (Laudholm Farm, ME) 342
  Pliny Freeman Farm (Old Sturbridge Village, MA) 190
  Remick Country Doctor Museum & Farm (Tamworth, NH) 322
  River Bend Farm (Uxbridge, MA) 189
  Shelburne Farms, VT 291–2
  South Hero farms, VT 78, 287–8
  UVM Morgan Horse Farm (Weybridge, VT) 293
  Vermont Icelandic Horse Farm (Fayston, VT) 282
  Vermont Wildflower Farm (Charlotte, VT) 292
  Watson Farm (Jamestown, RI) 225–7
  White Flower Farm, CT 244
Fayston, VT) 282
Ferrisburg, VT 292

festivals and fairs *18*, 23, *26*, 105, *106*, 140, 147, 194, 279, 283, 295, 320
culinary *25*, 77, 164, *178*, *231*, 352, *359*
music and arts 11, 147, 166, 204, 224, 245, 246, 273, 289, 321, 347
financial services industry 51
First Encounter Beach 164
Fishermen's Memorial 138–9, *139*
fishing (sport) 190, *208*, **226**, 255, 296, 314, 406
fishing industry, 52, *54–5*, 57–8, 61, *see also* codfish; shellfish; whaling
food and drink 76–81, 413
football 75
Fort Adams, RI 225
Fort Constitution State Historic Site 311
Fort Edgecomb State Historic Site 349
Fort Griswold Battlefield State Park 259
Fort Knox State Park 354
Fort McClary State Historic Site 341
Fort Popham State Historic Park 348–9
Fort Revere Park 153
Fort St George (Parker's Island, ME) 34
Fort Saybrook Monument Park 257
Fort William Henry, ME 350
Foxwoods Resort Casino, CT 23, 252, 260, **261**
Franconia, NH 299, 326–7
Franconia Notch State Park 226, 325–6
Franklin, Benjamin *103*
Franklin, NH 315–16
Freedom Trail (Boston, MA) 7, 101, **102–5**
Freeport, ME 346
French, Daniel Chester 119, 125, 203
Frost, Robert 70, 293, 298, 326
Fruitlands Museums (Harvard, MA) 64, 186
Fuller Gardens (North Hampton) 312

G

Gage, Thomas 42, 43, 149
Galilee, RI 228
gardens, 126, *127*, 170, 197, 201, 203–4, 220, 240, 312, 316, 356, *see also* farms; historic houses; parks
Garrison, William Lloyd 64, 68, 114, 117
Gay Head cliffs *175*
gay and lesbian travellers 404, 416
geology 20, 159, 171, 175, 288, 340, 363
Georgetown, ME 349
Gillette Castle State Park 249
Glen, NH 325

Gloucester, MA 61, **138–9**, 181
Glover, VT 286
golf 278, 287, 296, *328*, 362
Goodspeed Opera House (East Haddam, CT) 11, 249
Gorges, Fernandino 36, 308, 340
Grafton, VT 274–5, *301*
Grafton Notch State Park, ME 362
granite 138, 280, 340
Graniteville, VT 280
Great Barrington, MA 202, 204
Great Depression 50
Great Wass Island 358
Green Animals Topiary Gardens 220
Green Mountain Flyer 275
Green Mountains 272, 281, 282, 293, 295, 324
Greenbriar Nature Center 162
Greensboro, VT 285–6
Greenville, ME 361
Greenwich, CT 252
Greylock State Reservation 206
grist (corn) mills *155*, 163, *168*, 177, 227, 275
Gropius, Walter 87, 147–8
Groton, CT 258
Guilford, CT 237, 256–7
Guthrie, Arlo 202

H

Hadley, MA 195–6
Haight-Brown Vineyard, CT 243–4
Hale, Nathan 238, 247
Halibut Point State Park 138
Hammonasset Beach State Park 257
Hammond Castle, MA 140
Hancock, John 42, 44, 105, 113, 149, 341
Hancock Shaker Village, MA 38, *39*, 47, *205*
Hanover, NH 10, 46, 73–4, **319**
Harrisville, NH 86, 317
Hartford, CT 46, 50, 51, 70, **237–42**
Hart's Location, NH *90–91*, *304–5*
Harvard, Rev. John 72, *125*
Harvard, MA 64, 186, *187*
Harvard University *24*, 35, 46, 63, *72*, *74*, 87, **125–6**
Harwichport, MA 168
Hawthorne, Charles 166, 167
Hawthorne, Nathaniel *67*, 68–9, *103*, 141, 150, 204–5, 206
Haystack Mountain School of Crafts, ME 355
Haystack Mountain State Park, CT 246
Haystack/Mount Snow ski area & resort, VT 274
health 416–17
Herring Cove, MA 167
hiking 9, 226, 406–7
Hillsborough, NH 318
Hingham, MA 83, 152
historic houses 82–7, *232–3* see also museums and art collections
Abigail Adams Birthplace 153

Adams National Historical Park (Quincy, MA) 152
Admiral Robert Peary summer home (Eagle Island, ME) 344
Alden House (Duxbury, MA) 154
Arrowhead (Pittsfield, MA) 205
Asa Stebbins House (Old Deerfield, MA) 198
Ashley House (Old Deerfield, MA) 83, 198
Austin House (Hartford, CT) 239
Beauport – Sleeper-McCann House (Gloucester, MA) 139
Beechwood Mansion & Victorian Living History Museum (Newport, RI) *10*, 223, 232
Belcourt Castle (Newport, RI) 224
Blithewold Mansion, Gardens & Arboretum (Bristol, RI) 220
The Breakers (Newport, RI) 87, 232, *233*
Briggs-McDermott House (Bourne, MA) 161
Butler-McCook House & Garden (Hartford, CT) 240
Buttolph-Williams House (Wethersfield, CT) 250
Calvin Coolidge State Historic Site (Plymouth, VT) 8, **278**
Capen House (Topsfield, MA) *82*
Captain Bangs Hallett House (Cape Cod) 163
Captain Francis Pease House (Edgartown, MA) 173–4
Captain Nathaniel B. Palmer House (Stonington) 260
Castle in the Clouds (Moultonborough, NH) 321
Castle Tucker (Wiscasset, ME) 349
Château-sur-Mer (Newport, RI) 87, 223
Chesterwood (Stockbridge, MA) 203
Codman House (Lowell, MA) 147
Coffin House Museum (Newbury) 137
Colonel John Ashley House (Berkshires) 200–201
Colony House (Kennebunkport) 343
Cushing House (Newburyport, MA) 136
Daggett House (Slater Park, RI) 219
Daniel Webster Birthplace (Franklin, NH) 315–16
Deacon John Grave House (Madison, CT) 257
Dr Daniel Fisher residence (Edgartown, MA) 173
Ebenezer Fiske House Site (Lexington) 149
Edward Gorey House (Yarmouth Port) 163
Elizabeth Perkins House (York, ME) 341
The Elms (Newport, RI) *212*, 222, 223, *232*
Emily Dickinson Homestead (Amherst, MA) 196

Ethan Allen Homestead (Burlington, VT) 290
Farnsworth Homestead (Rockland, ME) 352
Florence Higginbotham House (Nantucket) 177
Forest Hall – the Barrett House (New Ipswich, NH) 316
Franklin Pierce Homestead (Hillsborough, NH) 318
Gardner-Pingree House (Salem, MA) 84
Gibson House Museum (Boston) 118
Gilbert Stuart Birthplace (Saunderstown, RI) 227
Gillette Castle (Hadlyme) 249
Glass House (New Canaan, CT) 252–3
Governor John Langdon House (Portsmouth, NH) 310
Gray Gables Railroad Station (Bourne, MA) 161
Great House at Castle Hill (Ipswich, MA) *137*
Griswold Inn (Essex, CT) 248, *263*
Gropius House (Lowell, MA) 147–8
Hadwen House (Nantucket) 177
Hall Tavern (Old Deerfield, MA) 198
Hammersmith Farm (Newport, RI) 87, 225
Hammond Castle (Gloucester, MA) 140
Hancock-Clarke House (Lexington) 149
Harriet Beecher Stowe Center (Hartford, CT) 241
Harrison Gray Otis Houses (Boston, MA) *19*, 85, 116, 117
Hawks House (Old Deerfield, MA) 83
Hempstead Houses (New London, CT) 258
Henry Whitfield State Museum (Guilford, CT) 256
Hildene (Manchester, VT) 297
Hill-Stead Museum (Farmington, CT) 242–3
Horatio Colony House Museum & Nature Preserve (Keene, NH) 317
House of the Seven Gables (Salem, MA) *141*
Hoxie House (Sandwich) 162
Hunter House (Newport, RI) 222
Hyde Cabin (Grand Isle, VT) 288
Hyland House (Guilford, CT) 257
Jabez Howland House (Plymouth, MA) 155
Jackson House (Portsmouth, NH) 310
Jared Coffin House (Nantucket) 177
Jefferds Tavern (York, ME) 341
Jeremiah Lee Mansion (Marblehead, MA) 142
Jethro Coffin House (Nantucket) 177

John Brown House Museum (Providence, RI) 218
John F. Kennedy birthplace (Cambridge, MA) 127
John Paul Jones House (Portsmouth, NH) 310
John Whipple House (Ipswich, MA) 82, 137
Justin Morrill Homestead (Strafford, VT) *279*
King Caesar House (Duxbury, MA) 154
Kingscote (Newport, RI) 222–3
Ladd-Gilman House (Exeter, NH) 313
Latchis Building & Hotel (Brattleboro, VT) 273
Litchfield Law School, CT 243
Lockwood-Mathews Mansion Museum (Norwalk, CT) 253
Longfellow House (Cambridge, MA) 127
Marble House (Newport, RI) 87, *224*, 232, *233*
Mark Twain House (Hartford, CT) 70, 240, *241*
Marsh-Billings-Rockefeller National Historical Park 277–8
Mayflower Society House (Plymouth, MA) 155
Mission House (Stockbridge, MA) 202, *202*
Moffatt-Ladd House & Garden (Portsmouth, NH) 84, 309–310
Monte Cristo Cottage (New London, CT) 258
Moses Mason House (Bethel, VT) 299, 362
The Mount (Lenox, MA) 204
Mount Hope Farm & Governor Bradford House Country Inn (Bristol, RI) 220
Nathan Hale Homestead (Coventry, CT) 247
Naulahka (Brattleboro, VT) 273
Naumkeag (Stockbridge, MA) *202*, 203
Nichols House Museum (Boston) 116
Nickels-Sortwell House (Wiscasset, ME) *349*
No.99 Main Street (Nantucket) 177–9
Noah Webster House (West Hartford, CT) 242
Nott House (Kennebunkport) 343
Ochre Court (Newport, RI) *232*
Old Constitution House (Windsor) 275–6
Old Manse (Concord, MA) 150
Oliver Ellsworth Homestead (Windsor) 246
Olson House (Cushing, ME) 352
Orchard House (Concord, MA) 150
Paper House (Rockport, MA) 138
Park-McCullough House (North Bennington, VT) 298
Paul Revere House (Boston) *104*, 106

Pejepscot Historical Society Museum (Brunswick, ME) 347
Porter-Phelps-Huntington Historic House Museum (Hadley, MA) 195–6
Ralph Waldo Emerson House (Concord, MA) 150
Richard Sparrow House (Plymouth, MA) 155
Robert Frost log cabin (Ripton, VT) 293
Robert Frost Place (Franconia, NH) 326
Robert Frost Stone House Museum (Shaftsbury, VT) 298
Roosevelt House (Campobello Island) 359
Ropes Mansion (Marblehead, MA) 143
Rosecliff (Newport, RI) 223
Rotch-Jones-Duff House & Garden (New Bedford, MA) 156
Rough Point (Newport, RI) 223
Ruggles House (Columbia Falls) 359
Rundlet-May House (Portsmouth, NH) 310
Saint-Gaudens National Historic Site *318*
Santarella (Tyringham, MA) 204
Skolfield-Whittier House (Brunswick, ME) 347
Smith's Castle (Wickford, RI) 227
Spencer-Peirce-Little Farm (Newbury) 137
Stanley-Whitman House (Farmington, CT) 243
Stark House (Manchester, NH) 314
Stephen Phillips Memorial Trust House (Salem, MA) 142
Strong-Porter House Museum (Coventry, CT) 247
Summit House (J.A. Skinner State Park, Hadley, MA) 196
Swift-Daley House (Eastham, MA) 164
Tapping Reeve House (Litchfield, CT) 243
Tate House Museum (Portland, ME) 346
Thomas A. Hill house (Bangor, ME) 360
Thomas Griswold House (Guilford, CT) 257
Three Bricks (Nantucket) 177
Two Greeks (Nantucket) 177
Victoria Mansion (Portland, ME) 345
Wadsworth Mansion at Long Hill Estate, (Middletown, CT) 251
Wadsworth-Longfellow House (Portland, ME) 345
Warner House (Portsmouth, NH) 310
Webb-Deane-Stevens Museum (Wethersfield, CT) 250
Wedding Cake House (Kennebunk) *343*
Wentworth-Coolidge Mansion (Portsmouth, NH) 84, 311

Wentworth-Gardner House
(Portsmouth, NH) 310
White Horse Tavern (Newport, RI)
221
Whittier Home (Amesbury, MA) 137
Wilbur Kelly House Museum
(Lincoln, RI) 219
William Cullen Bryant Homestead
(Cummington, MA) 208
Wilson Castle (Vermont) 295
Wing Fort House (East Sandwich)
82
Winslow Crocker House
(Yarmouth Port) 163
Wisteriahurst Museum (Holyoake)
95, 194
Wyman Tavern (Keene, NH) 317
Zimmerman House (Manchester,
NH) 314
hockey 74, 122
Holderness, NH 322, 324
Holyoake, MA 194
Homer, Winslow 189, 222, 290,
319, 345, 347, 352
Hopper, Edward *132–3*, 165, 342,
345
horseback riding 282, 356
Housatonic River 200, 201, 243–5
Hull Peninsula, MA 153
Hulls Cove, ME 356
Hunt, Richard Morris 223, 232,
233, 244
Hyannis, MA 164, 168–9

I

ice cream 76, 77, 78, 282
immigration 23–7, 33–7, 48, 147,
214, 220
Indian tribes *see* **Native Americans**
industry 48–53, 239
information sources 403–4, 419
Ipswich, MA 82, 137
Irish-Americans 25–6, 48–9, 107,
112, 214
Island Pond, VT 50
Isle au Haut, ME 355
Isleford, ME 358
Isles of Shoals, NH 311
Italian-Americans 26, 79, 107,
139, 214, 280
Ivoryton, CT 248

J

Jamaica State Park 274
Jamestown, RI 225–7
Jay Peak ski area, VT 11, 287
Jefferson, NH 329
Jesuits 74
Jewish community 26–7, *111*,
126, 197, 214, 221
Jiminy Peak ski area, MA 206
Johnson, Philip 119, 252
Johnson, VT 284

K

Kancamagus Highway 324, 325
kayaking 226, 245, 405–6

Keene, NH 317
Kennebunkport, ME *79*, 343
Kennedy, Joe 26
Kennedy, John F. *31*, 52, 53, 123,
127, 168–9
Kent Falls State Park 245
Kent, Rockwell 163, 342
Kerouac, Jack 70, 146
Kerry, John F. 52
Killington ski area, VT 11, **279**, 299
King, Stephen 71, 360
Kingfield, ME 362
Kipling, Rudyard 273
Kittery, ME 340
Kripalu, MA 205

L

Lake Champlain Islands, VT 287–92
Lake Compounce Theme Park, CT
243
Lake Memphremagog, VT 286
Lake Sunapee, NH 319–20
**Lake Umbagog National Wildlife
Refuge** 330
Lake Waramaug State Park 244
Lake Winnipesaukee, NH 320, *321*
**Laudholm Farm National Estuarine
Research Reserve** 342
Lawrence, MA 45, 147
Le Corbusier 87, 125
Lenox, MA 204
Lexington 42, 148–9
libraries 46
Adams National Historical Park
(Quincy, MA) 152
American Antiquarian Society
(Worcester, MA) 188
Baker-Barry Library (Hanover, NH)
319
Beinecke Rare Book &
Manuscript Library (New Haven,
CT) 255
Boston Athenaeum 46, *113*
Boston Public Library 46, *73*, 87,
107, **119–20**
Dr G.A. Russell Collection of
Vermontiana (Arlington, VT)
297–846
Forbes Library (Northampton, MA)
195
Goddard Library (Worcester, MA)
187–8
John F. Kennedy Presidential
Library & Museum (Boston) 123
Nantucket Atheneum 177
National Yiddish Book Center
(Amherst, MA) 197
Old Library (West Tisbury, MA) 174
Providence Atheneum, RI 46, 217
Redwood Library & Atheneum
(Newport, RI) 222
St Johnsbury Athaeneum, VT 285
Tuck Library (Concord) 314
Widener Library (Harvard) 125
lighthouses
Boston Light *94*, *108*, 153
Cape Cod lights 164–5, 166, 168
Chappaquiddick Island, MA 174
Connecticut lights 253, 260

East Chop (Oak Bluffs, MA) 173
Maine lights *132–3*, *336–7*, 342,
343, 350, 353, **357**, 358, 359
Martha's Vineyard, MA 174, 175
Nantucket, MA *176*, 179, 180
Portsmouth, NH *20*
Rhode Island lights *210–211*,
214, *214*, 225, 229, *229*
Lily Bay State Park 361
Lincoln, Abraham 293, 296
Lincoln Gap, ME 282
Lincoln, MA 147–8
Lincoln, NH 325
Lincoln, RI 219
liquor laws 65, 307, 341, 414
Litchfield, CT 84, *234–5*, 243–4
literature 66–71
Little Compton, RI 78
lobsters 52, 61, 76, 79, *345*, *348*,
352
logging 52, 360
Long Island Sound 61, 237,
251–2, 253
Long Point Wildlife Refuge 174
Long Trail 9, 226, 282, 407
Longfellow, Henry Wadsworth 10,
67, 68, **127**, *345*
Loon Mountain ski area, NH 299,
325
Lowell, Francis Cabot 23–4, 45, *86*
Lowell, MA *50*, 70, 86, 87, **146–7**
**Lowell's Boat Shop (Amesbury,
MA)** *136*, 137
Lubec, ME 359

M

Machias, ME 358–9
McIntire, Samuel 84, 142
McKim, Mead & White 87, 215
Mad River Glen ski area, VT 281
Madison, CT 257
**Magic Wings Butterfly
Conservatory & Gardens** 197
Maine Maritime Academy 354
Manchester, NH 45, 50, 309,
313–14
Manchester, VT 295–7
Manuel F. Correllus State Forest
172
maple products 77–8, *272*, 281,
285, 293
marble 293–5
Marblehead, MA 142
Marconi Beach 165
Marlboro, VT 273–4
Marsh, George Perkins 277
Marsh, Reginald 342
Martha's Vineyard 60, 78, 87,
171–5
**Mashantucket Pequot Museum &
Research Center** *260*, 261
Mashpee, MA 23, 170
Massachusett tribe 32, 34
Massachusetts Bay Colony 35–6,
63, 66
**Massachusetts Institute of
Technology (MIT)** 74, 87, 107,
124, *125*
Mather, Cotton 63–4, *66*, 143

Mather, Increase 63, *64*, 65, 66
Mayflower 34, 35, 104, **153–4,**
  159, 166–7
Mayflower II (replica) 38, *154*
Mayhew, Thomas 171
meetinghouses see churches and
  meetinghouses
Melville, Herman 69, 156, 179, 205
Mendon, MA 190
Menemsha, MA 175
Meredith, NH 320
Merrimack, MA 81
Merrimack River 45, 309, 313, 314
Middleborough, MA 261
Middlebury, VT 74, 293
Middletown, CT 251
Mill River, MA 201
mills, 316–17, 227, 340, 363, *see
  also* **grist mills**; **textile industry**
Minutemen 8, 42–43, **148–149,**
  204, 317
Misquamicut State Beach 229
Mitchell, Maria 179
Mohawk Trail 207, 324
Mohegan Bluffs, RI 229
Mohegan Sun Resort 260, 261
Mohegan tribe 22, 34, 202, 261
Monadnock State Park 316
money matters 415, 416
Monhegan Island, ME 350–51
Monomoy (Nantucket) 180
Monomoy National Wildlife Refuge
  168
Montgomery, VT 294
Montpelier, VT 280–81
Monument Mountain 202
Moosehead Lake 361
Mormons 279
Moses, Grandma 74, 298
Mosher, Howard Frank 71, 284,
  421
Moultonborough, NH 321
Mount Ascutney 206
Mount Battie 353
Mount Chocorua 322
Mount Desert Island 355–8
Mount Greylock 206
Mount Holyoake College 64, 196
Mount Holyoake Range State Park
  197
Mount Independence 293
Mount Katahdin 335, 360, *361,*
  362
Mount Mansfield 283, 299
Mount Monadnock 316
Mount Snow/Haystack ski area &
  resort, VT 274, 299
Mount Sunapee Resort 319–20
Mount Washington 202, 299, 322,
  326, **327–8,** *334, 335*
Mount Washington Auto Road 327
Mount Washington Cog Railway 9,
  329
Mount Willard *323*
movies set in New England 421
museums 9, 408–9
  see also **art museums and**
    collections; **historic houses**
  Abbe Museum 356, 357
  Albacore Museum 311

American Clock & Watch Museum
  243
American Independence Museum
  313
American Museum of Fly Fishing
  296
American Precision Museum 275
American Textile History Museum
  146
America's Stonehenge 313
Aptucxet Trading Post & Museum
  161
Ballard Museum of Puppetry 247
Barnum Museum 254
Bennington Museum 74, 298
Berkshire Museum 205–6
Big Black Bear Shop & Museum
  274
Billings Farm & Museum 38, 277
Boott Cotton Mills Museum 146
Boston Tea Party Ships &
  Museum 109
Botanical Museum 126, *127*
Brattleboro Museum 273
Bread & Puppet Theater Museum
  286
Brick Store Museum 343
Bruce Museum 252
Cape Ann Museum 139
Cape Cod Museum of Natural
  History 164
Chatham Railroad Museum 168
Children's Discovery Museum 363
Children's Museum (Boston) 109
Children's Museum (Holyoake) 195
Children's Museum of Maine 345
Children's Museum of New
  Hampshire 311–12
Children's Museum (West
  Hartford, CT) 242
Colonial Pemaquid State Historic
  Site 350
Concord Museum 150
Connecticut Eastern Railroad
  Museum 247
Connecticut Fire Museum 246
Connecticut Historical Society
  Museum 241
Connecticut Museum of Natural
  History 247
Connecticut River Museum 248
Connecticut Trolley Museum 246
Connecticut Valley Historical
  Museum 193
Cornish Colony Museum 276
Cos Cob's Bush-Holley Historic
  Site 252
Cottage Museum 172–3
Custom House Maritime Museum
  136
Danbury Museum & Historical
  Society 251
Danbury Railway Museum 251
Enfield Shaker Museum 318
Essex Shipbuilding Museum 138
Fairbanks Museum and
  Planetarium 285
Falmouth Museums on the Green
  170
Fishermen's Museum 350

Florence Griswold Museum 257
Fort at Number 4 Living History
  Museum 318
Francis Foster Maritime Gallery
  173
French Cable Station Museum 167
Fruitlands Museums 64, 186
General Henry Knox Museum 350
George W.V. Smith Art Museum
  193
Grafton Historical Society
  Museum 275
Hadley Farm Museum 195
Haffenreffer Museum 220
Hart Nautical Gallery 124
Harvard Museum of Natural
  History 126
Henry Sheldon Museum of
  Vermont History 293
Heritage Museum & Gardens 162
Herreshoff Marine & America's
  Cup Hall of Fame Museum 220
Higgins Armory Museum 188
Highland House Museum 166
Hull Lifesaving Museum 153
John F. Kennedy Hyannis Museum
  168–9
John F. Kennedy Presidential
  Library & Museum 123
Joseph Smith Memorial &
  Birthplace 279
Joshua L. Chamberlain Museum
  347–8
Kendall Whaling Museum 181
Kittery Historical & Naval
  Museum 340–41
Lake Champlain Maritime
  Museum 292
Libby Museum 321
Litchfield History Museum 243
Luddy/Taylor Connecticut Valley
  Tobacco Museum 246
Lumberman's Museum 360
Maine Discovery Center 352
Maine Discovery Museum 360
Maine Maritime Museum 348
Maine State Museum 363
Marblehead Museum & Historical
  Society 142
Maria Mitchell Science Center 179
Marine Museum & Battleship
  Cove 156
Marine Narrow Gauge Railroad &
  Museum 346
Martha's Vineyard Museum 173
Mashantucket Pequot Museum &
  Research Center 260, 261
Mattatuck Museum (251
Memorial Hall Museum 198
Millyard Museum & See Science
  Center 313
Mineralogical & Geological
  Museum (Harvard) 126
MIT Museum 124
Montshire Museum of Science 319
Mooseheard Marine Museum 361
Mount Washington Summit
  Museum 328
Museum of African American
  History (Nantucket, MA) 177

Museum of African-American History (Boston, MA) 116–17
Museum of Childhood 322
Museum of Comparative Zoology (Harvard) 126
Museum of Connecticut History 240
Museum of Fife & Drum 248
Museum of Fire History 243
Museum of Natural History & Planetarium 219
Museum of Natural History 197
Museum of New Hampshire History 314
Museum of Newport History 221
Museum at Portland Head Light 343
Museum of Science 122–3
Museum of Work & Culture 220
Museum of Yachting 224
Musical Wonder House 349
Nantucket Life-saving Museum 180
Nantucket Lightship Basket Museum 179
Nantucket Whaling Museum 58, 177
National Heritage Museum 148
National Streetcar Museum 147
New Bedford Whaling Museum 58, 156
New England Air Museum 246
New England Carousel Museum 243
New England Maple Museum 293
New England Quilt Museum 146
New England Ski Museum 299, 327
New Hampshire Antique and Classic Boat Museum 321
Newport Art Museum 221
Old Lincoln County Jail & Museum 349
Old Schoolhouse Museum 172
Old Stone House Museum 286
Old Sturbridge Village 7, 39, 190
Owl's Head Transportation Museum 353
Peabody Essex Museum 46, 141
Peabody Museum of Archaeology & Ethnology (Harvard) 126, 127
Peabody Museum of Natural History (New Haven, CT) 255
Peary-Macmillan Arctic Museum 347
Penobscot Marine Museum 354
Pilgrim Hall Museum 155
Provincetown Museum 167
Prudence Crandall Museum 247
Rokeby Museum 292
Ross Fresnel Lens Building 173
St Albans Historical Museum 289
Salem witches museums 140–42
Sandwich Glass Museum 161
Science Museum 193
Seashore Trolley Museum 343
Semitic Museum (Harvard) 127
Shelburne Falls Trolley Museum 208
Shelburne Museum 9, **291**
Shore Line Trolley Museum 256

Springfield Museums at the Quadrangle 193
Stanley Museum 362
Stepping Stones Museum for Children 253
Storrowton Village Museum 194
Strawbery Banke 308–9
Sugar Hill Historical Museum 326–7
Swanzey Historical Museum 317
Thornton Burgess Museum 162
Trayser Memorial Museum 163
US Naval Submarine Force Museum 258
USS *Constitution* Museum *44, 104,* 107
Vermont Historical Society & Museum 281
Vermont Marble Museum 293–5
Vermont Ski Museum 282, 299
Vincent House Museum 173
Wells Auto Museum, ME 343
White Memorial Conservation Center Museum 244
Wilhelm Reich Museum 362
Willowbrook at Newfield 346
Windham Textile & History Museum 247
Woodman Institute Museum 312
Worcester Historical Museum 188
Wright Museum of American Enterprise 321
Yale Collection of Musical Instruments 255–6
music venues 399–400, 402–3
mussels 77, 79
Myles Standish Monument State Reservation 153–4
Mystery Hill, NH 313
Mystic, CT 258–9
Mystic Seaport, CT *12–13, 39,* 58, *59, 259,* **259–60**

N

Nantasket, MA 153
Nantucket 58, 60, 69, **176–80**
Narragansett Bay, RI 215, 225, 227–8
Narragansett tribe 22, 23, 32, 34, 37
National Estuarine Research Reserve (Laudholm Farm) 342
National Marine Life Center (Buzzards Bay) 161
National Yiddish Book Center (Amherst, MA) 197
Native Americans, 22–3, 32–3, 34, *36,* 170, 202, *207,* 244, 261, 356, 361, *see also* names *of tribes*
Natural Bridge State Park 207
New Bedford, MA 58, 61, 69, **155–6**
New Britain, CT 250–51
New Brunswick, ME 359
New Canaan, CT 252–3
New Castle, NH 311
New England Culinary Institute (Montpelier, VT) 281

New Haven, CT, 72, **254–6,** *see also* **Yale University**
New Ipswich, NH 316
New London, CT 257–8
New Marlborough, MA 201–2
New Preston, CT 244
Newbury, MA 137
Newbury, NH 319–20
Newburyport, MA *84,* 135–6
Newfane, VT 274
Newport, RI 10, *80,* 87, *212,* 214, **220–25,** 226, 261
Newport, VT 286–7
Newry, ME 362
newspapers 49, 64, 68, 188, 208, 307, 417
Nickerson State Park 164
nightlife 402
Ninigret National Wildlife Refuge 229
Nipmuck tribe 34, 37
Norfolk, CT 245–6
North Adams, MA 207
North Bennington, VT 298
North Conway, NH 323, 325
North Hampton, NH 312
North Hero, VT 288
North Salem, NH 313
North Woods, ME *340,* 360–61
Northampton, MA 10, **195**
Northeast Kingdom 284, 334
Northwood, NH 312
Norwalk, CT 253
Norwich, NH 319

O

Oak Bluffs, MA 171, 172–3
Obama, Barack 52, *80*
Ocean Beach Park, CT 258
Ocean Drive, RI 225
Odiorne Point State Park 312
Ogunquit 342
Old Deerfield, MA *83,* 197–8
Old Fort Western, ME 363
Old Lyme, CT 257
Old Man of the Mountains 326
Old Orchard Beach, ME 343
Old Saybrook, CT 257
Old Sturbridge Village, MA 7, *39,* 190
Olmsted, Frederick Law 152, 196, 251, 291
O'Neill, Eugene 70, *258*
opening hours 417–18
Orford, NH 319
Orleans, MA 167
Orvis, VT 296
Ossipee Lake 322
Otis, Harrison Gray *19,* 85, 116, 117
Otis, James 105, 111
oysters 76, *130,* 165

P

Pairpoint Glass Works 161
Parker, John *148,* 149
Parker River National Wildlife Refuge 136–7

parks, 114–15, 193, 218–19, 239, 241, 30, see also gardens; theme and amusement parks
Parris, Alexander 86
Parrish, Maxfield 223, 276
Passamaquoddy tribe 34
passports and visas 418
Patten, ME 360
Pawtucket, RI 45, 81, 215, 219
Peary, Robert 344, 347
Pei, I.M. 87, 120, 121, 123, 345
Pemaquid Point 336–7, 350
Pennacook tribe 32, 34
Penobscot Bay 34, 52, 351–8
Pequot tribes 22, 23, 34, 37, 260, 261
Peterborough, NH 316–17
pets, importing 418
Pilgrims 22, 23, 34–7, 38–9, 40, 78, 153–5, 166–7
Pioneer Valley, MA 192–8
Pioneers 38–9, 45–6, 83, 190, 197–8
Pittsburg, NH 330, 334
Pittsfield, MA 204, 205–6
Pittsford, VT 293
planetariums 123, 219, 285, 315
Plimoth Plantation, MA 22, 35, 38, 82, 154, 155
Plymouth, MA 35, 38, 154–5
Plymouth, VT 278
Plymouth Rock, MA 34, 154
Pocumtuck tribe 198
Poe, Edgar Allan 46, 217
poetry 66, 67, 68, 70
Point Judith, RI 228
politics 52, 65
polo 276, 277, 281
Popham Beach State Park 348
Port Clyde, ME 351
Portland, ME 50, 344–6, 367
Portsmouth, NH 10, 20, 38, 308–311, 332, 333
Portsmouth, RI 220
Portuguese-Americans 27, 79, 139, 159, 217, 218
postal services 418
Prescott, Col. William 43, 104–5
Princeton, MA 186–7
Proctor, VT 293–5
Profile Lake, NH 326
Providence, RI 46, 73, 80, 86, 187, 214–18
Providence River, RI 216, 217
Provincetown, MA 15, 61, 166–7, 181
public holidays 418
puppetry 247, 273, 286
Puritans 22, 23, 34–7, 40–41, 62–5, 66, 82–3
Putney, VT 273

Q

Quabbin Reservoir 190
Quakers 36, 68, 214, 292
Quechee Gorge & State Park 276, 294
Quincy, MA 50, 153
Quoddy Head State Park 359

R

Race Point, MA 167
Rachel Carson National Wildlife Refuge 343
Radcliffe College 64, 127
radio and TV stations 418, 419
rafting 207, 226, 360, 361, 405–6
railroads 9, 164, 169, 299, 320, 323, 329, 409
museums 161, 168, 247, 251, 346, 349–50, 409
Rangeley 362–3
Reid State Park 349
Revere, Paul 40, 42, 104, 105, 113, 149
Revolutionary War 40–44
Connecticut 238, 248, 258
Maine 341, 349, 358–9
Massachusetts 101, 102–5, 106, 142, 148–50
New Hampshire 309, 310, 313
Vermont 90, 272, 292, 293
Rhode Island Public Sailing Center 224–5
Rhode Island Red 219
Rhododendron State Park 316
Richardson, Henry Hobson 87, 120, 125, 127
Ridgefield, CT 251
Rindge, NH 316
Ripton, VT 293
Rock of Ages Quarry 280
Rockingham, VT 275
Rockland, ME 351–3
Rockport, MA 21, 61, 138
Rockport, ME 353
Rockwell, Norman 203, 206, 223, 297, 316
Rocky Hill, CT 250
Rodman's Hollow, RI 229
Roosevelt Campobello International Park 359
Roque Bluffs State Park 358
Rose Island, RI 225
rowing 75
Rutland, VT 81, 295
Rye, NH 312

S

Saarinen, Eero 87, 124, 204
Sabbathday Lake, ME 47
sailing, 60–61, 142, 224–5, 226, 290, 407, see also yacht racing
St Albans, VT 288–9
St Anne's Shrine (Isle La Motte, VT) 288
St Johnsbury, VT 284, 285
Salem, MA 44, 46, 63–4, 68, 81, 84, 85, 140–43
Salmon Falls Glacial Potholes 208
Sandwich, MA 161–2
Sandwich, NH 321–2
Sandy Neck Beach, MA 162–3
Sargent, John Singer 133, 154, 189, 239, 290
Saugus Ironworks National Historic Site 135

Saunderstown, RI 215, 227
scallops 61, 77, 79, 164
seafood 61, 76–7
Searsport, ME 354
Sebago Lake State Park 346
Seuss, Dr. 193
Shaftsbury, VT 298
Shakers 38, 39, 47, 205, 315, 318
Sharon, MA 181
Shawville, VT 32
Sheffield, MA 200, 201–2
Sheffield Island, CT 253
Shelburne, VT 291–2
Shelburne Falls, MA 208
shellfish, 61, 76–7, 79, 130, 138, 164, see also lobsters
Sherwood Island State Park 254, 255
shipbuilding 39, 44, 57, 135, 137, 138, 258–9, 309, 339, 343, 348
shipping trade 44, 58–60, 339
shopping 410–413
outlets 156, 161, 291, 296, 325, 340, 412–13
Siasconset, MA 178
Six Flags New England 194
skiing 275, 299, 408
Maine 361–2
Massachusetts 186–7, 206, 207
New Hampshire 319–20, 325, 326, 327, 328, 329
Vermont 274, 275, 276, 278, 279, 281–4, 285, 287, 297
Skyline Drive, VT 295–6
Slater Mill Historic Site 219
Smith, Captain John 34, 340
Smith College 64, 195
Smuggler's Notch Resort, VT 283–4, 299
snowboarding 11, 299
Snug Harbor, RI 210–211
Somes Sound 357
South Deerfield, MA 197
South Dennis, MA 168
South Hadley, MA 196
South Hero, VT 25, 78, 287–8, 302
South Kingston, RI 229
South Norwalk, CT 253, 265
South Royalton, VT 279
Southwick's Zoo 190
Spohr's Gardens 170
sports, 75, 404, see also individual sports
Springfield, MA 50, 192–194
Squam Lakes Natural Science Center (Holderness, NH) 322
Stamford, CT 252
Standish, Myles 34, 153
Stark, NH 307
Stellwagen Bank 181
Sterling Diners 81
Stewart B. McKinney National Wildlife Refuge 253
Stirling, James 87
Stockbridge, MA 202–3, 204
Stonington, CT 56, 78, 260
Stonington, ME 355

Stony Brook Mill (Brewster, MA) 163
Storrs, CT 247
Story Land (Glen, NH) 325
Stowe, Harriet Beecher 41, 64, 68, 241
Stowe, VT 11, *271*, **282–3**, 299
Strafford, VT 279
Stratton, VT 299
Stuart, Gilbert 27, 133, 215, 222, 310, 347
Sugar Hill, NH 299, 326–7
Sugarbush ski area, VT 281–2, 299
Sugarloaf/USA ski area, ME 11, 299, **361–2**
Suicide Six ski area, VT 278
Sunapee State Park 320
Sunday River Ski Resort, ME *11*, 299, **362**
surfing **226**, 229
Swanton, VT 288
Swanzey, NH 317
swimming, **226**, 255, 274, *see also* beaches

T

Tamworth, NH 322
Tanglewood, MA 204
telephones 418–19
tennis 223
textile industry **44–5**, 50, 86, 145–6, 147, 156, 219, 309, 313–14, 316, 317
Thanksgiving (origin) *63*
theater 11, 70, 112, 163, 193, 204, 254, 297, 342, **400–401**
theaters, historic 112–13, 224, 248, 249, 251, 314, 322
theme and amusement parks 193, 194, 243, 325, 329, 409
Thimble Islands *256*
Thomaston, ME 350
Thoreau, Henry David 64, 67–8, *103, 150*
Ticonderoga (sidewheeler) *291*
tipping 419
Tisbury, MA 172
Titanic (steamship) **156**
Topnotch Resort & Spa, VT 283
Topsfield, MA *82*
tourist information 403–4, 419
Townshend, VT 274
Transcendentalism 64, 67, 69, 186
transportation 370–72
Trapp Family Lodge 283
Truro, MA 165
Trustom Pond National Wildlife Refuge 229
Tunbridge, VT *16–17*, 279
Twain, Mark *70*, 240–41, *241*
Twin River Casino, RI 219, 261
Tyringham, MA 203–4

U

Uncasville, CT 260, 261
Unitarianism 64, *290*
United House Wrecking Co. 252

Upjohn, Richard 156, 360
US Coastguard Academy 258
US Navy 258, 340–41, 348
USS *Cassin Young* 108
USS *Constitution* 44, *104, 107*
USS *Lionfish* 156
USS *Massachusetts* 156
USS *Nautilus* 258
Uxbridge, MA 189

V

Vergennes, VT 292
Vermont Country Store (Weston, VT) *297*
Veterans' Memorial Tower 206
Vikings *28*, 32
Vineyard Haven, MA 171, 172
vineyards **78**, 243, 287, 291
Volleyball Hall of Fame 194

W

Wachusett State Reservation & Ski Area 186–7
Wadsworth, Daniel 46, 239
Waitsfield, VT 281
Wakefield Corner National Historical Area 322
Walden Pond, MA 64, *150*
Wampanoag tribes 22, 23, 34, 37, 159, 261
Wapunucket, MA 33
War of Independence 42–4
Ward, Nathaniel 66
Warren, VT 281
Washington, George 10, 43, 106, 126, 215
Washington, CT 244
Wasque Reservation 174
Watch Hill, RI 229
Waterbury, CT 251
Waterbury, VT 282
watersports 226
Waterville Valley, VT 299
Wauwinet, MA 180
websites 419
Webster, Noah 242
Weirs Beach, NH 320
Wellesley College 64
Wellfleet, MA 76, 165
Wellfleet Bay Wildlife Sanctuary 165
Wells, ME 342
Wentworth, John 308, 311, 320–21, 328
West Barnstable, MA 163
West Boothbay Harbor, ME 350
West Brattleboro, VT *80–81*
West Cornwall, CT 245
West Dover, VT 274
West Forks, ME 361
West Hartford, CT 241–2
West Paris, ME 363
West Quoddy Point, ME 359
West Springfield, MA 193–4
West Tisbury, MA 174
Westerly, RI 229
Western Gateway Heritage State Park 207

Weston, VT 297
Westport, CT 254
Wethersfield, CT 238, 250
Weybridge, VT 293
whale-watching 60, 139, 163, 178, **181**, 228
whaling *30*, 44, **57–8**, 69, 173, *178, 181*, 257
   museums 58, 156, 177, 260
   ship, *Charles W. Morgan 7, 12–13*, 39, 58, *259*
Wharton, Edith 204
Whistler, James Abbott 146, 243
White, Stanford 203, 222, 223, 232, 242
White Memorial Foundation 244
White Mountains 226, 308, 309, 322–9
White River Junction, VT 276
Whittier, John Greenleaf 67, 68, 137
Whydah (pirate ship) **167**
Wickford, RI 227
Wild Gardens of Acadia 356
Wildcat Mountain ski area, NH 327
wildlife, 165, 174, 180, 189, 244, 322, 330, **334–5**, 342, 360–61
Willard, Archibald, *Yankee Doodle* 142
Williams, Roger *36*, 213, *216*, 217, 218
Williams College 74, 206
Williamstown, MA 87, 204, 206
Willimantic, CT 247
Wilton, NH 316–17
Windsor, CT 238, 246
Windsor, VT 275–6
wine, *78, see also* vineyards
Winnipesaukee Railroad 320
Winooski, VT 291
Winter Harbor, ME 358
Winthrop, John 40, *62*, 63, 104, 106, 114
Wiscasset, ME 349
witches 63–4, *65*, 140, 142, **143**
Wolfeboro, NH 320–21
Woods Hole, MA 170–71
Woodstock, VT 38, 276–8, 299
Woolwich, ME 349
Woonsocket, RI 220
Worcester, MA 81, 187–9
Wright, Frank Lloyd 314
writers 66–71
Wyeth family 223, 345, 347, 352

Y–Z

yacht racing, 60, 220, 224, *see also* sailing
Yale University 10, 46, 72–73, **255–6**
Yankee Doodle 142
Yankees 23–4
Yarmouth, ME 346
Yarmouth, Nova Scotia 344
Yarmouth Port, MA 163
York, ME 341–2
zoos 190, 219, 254, 4

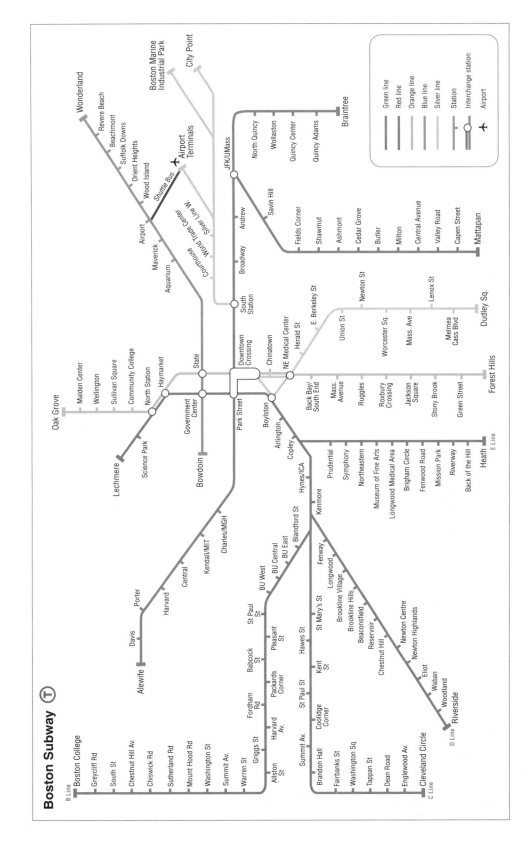

Boston Subway Ⓣ

Boston

0   500 yds
0   500 m

Cambridge Street

Monsignor O'Brien Highway

Winter Street
Gore Street
Cambridge Street

Elm Street
Columbia St
Lincoln Street
Palermo St
Willow
Webster
York
Berkshire Street
H. Cardinal Medeiros Av

Otis St
Sacred Heart
Thorndike Street
Lechmere
Middlesex Registry
Lechmere Square

DONNELLY FIELD

Broadway
Tremont Street
Norfolk Street
Elm Street
Union
Market St
Plymouth
Windsor
Hampshire Street
Bristol St
Binney Street

Spring Street
Holy Cross Polish Church
Otis St
Bulfinch Place
Middlesex County Courthouse

EDWARD J SENNOTT PARK

Harvard
Prospect
Essex
Street
Street
Columbia St

Worcester St
Norfolk St
Suffolk St
Washington St

AHERN FIELD

Hurley Street
Charles Street

EAST CAMBRIDGE

Cambr Ga

Central
Massachusetts Avenue
Green St
Brookline
Franklin
Pacific
Blanche St
Pine
Cherry
Windsor
Washington Street
Harvard Street
Broadway
Landsdowne
Street

CAMBRIDGE

Main Street
State Street
Albany Street
Osborn St
Smart St
Vassar Street
Bent
Charles St
6th Street
5th Street
Rogers
Binney
Street
Street
Street
2nd
Munroe

Potter St
Broadway
Main Street
Kendall/MIT
Athenaeum St
Cambridg Land

CAMBRIDGEPORT

Purlington
Albany Street
Street
Vassar

Ray and Maria Stata Center
List Visual Arts Center
Carleton St
Wadsworth St
Amherst St
Main Street
Longfello

MIT Museum
Massachusetts Institute of Technology (MIT)
Great Court
MIT Chapel
Hart Nautical Gallery
Harvard Boat Club

Steinbrenner Stadium
Kresge Auditorium
Memorial Drive
Memorial Drive

Charles   **River**

Harvard Bridge

Esplanade
Lagoon
Storrow

Storrow   **Drive**

Beacon Street
Fairfield
Marlborough
Ames-Webster Mansion
Hunnew Mansio

Dartmouth
Clare

Back Street
Storrow Drive
Boston University
Bay
State
Road
Sherborn St
John F. Andrews House
Gloucester
Hereford Street
Exeter
BACK BAY
Fir
Bapt Chur
Old South Church
Cop

Commonwealth Avenue
Kenmore Square
Commonwealth
Kenmore
Commonwealth
Newbury
Avenue
Commonwealth
Newbury
Street
Boylston
Street
Boston Public Library
Lord & Taylor
Exeter St

Cummington St
John F. Kennedy NHS
Beacon
Street
Massachusetts Av
Burrage House
Institute of Contemporary Art
Sak's
Copley Place

Turnpike
Ipswich Street
Hynes/ICA
Berklee Performance Center
Dalton St
Prudential Center
Prudential Tower

Landsdowne Street
Fenway Park
Belvidere
St Germain St
Prudential
St Botolph Street
CARLETON COURT

Fenway
Brookline Avenue
Van Ness
Yawkey Way
Street
FENWAY
Park Dr.
Norway St
Edgerly St
Hemenway
Massachusetts
Huntington
Newton St

Boylston
Street
Publishing Co. Bldg
Christian Science Center
Street
HARRIET TUBMAN PARK
West
Newton St

BACK BAY FENS
Peterborough Street
Burbank St
Westland
Mother Church
Horticultural Hall
Symphony Hall
Symphony

Park Dr.
Museum of Fine Arts, Isabella Stewart Gardner Museum